BARRON'S

THE TRUSTED NAME IN TEST PREP

7 ACT®

Practice Tests

PREMIUM

2023

Patsy J. Prince, M.Ed.,
and James D. Giovannini

About the Author

Jim Giovannini, an educator for more than thirty years, is the owner and founder of Academic Tutoring, LLC. Nationally recognized as a leading expert in both ACT and SAT test preparation, Mr. Giovannini's company partners with hundreds of school districts across the country and serves tens of thousands of students each year. Mr. Giovannini's passion is to help students achieve their Personal A+ on both the ACT and SAT exams by raising both skills and scores.

Published by Kaplan North America, LLC d/b/a Barron's Educational Series
1515 West Cypress Creek Road
Fort Lauderdale, Florida 33309
www.barronseduc.com

ISBN: 978-1-5062-8635-8

10 9 8 7 6 5 4 3 2 1

Kaplan North America, LLC, d/b/a Barron's Educational Series print books are available at special quantity discounts to use for sales promotions, employee premiums, or educational purposes. For more information or to purchase books, please call the Simon & Schuster special sales department at 866-506-1949.

Contents

PRACTICE TESTS

Introductory Words

This must be a stressful time in your life: balancing schoolwork, family, friends, extracurriculars, jobs, AND college admissions! Whew . . . that's a lot! Not to worry, this ACT prep program has been created with your busy life in mind.

The ACT is a five-section test: English, math, reading, science, and an optional essay (writing). Our prep program covers all of these areas. We made a point of reviewing and teaching only material that is presented on this high-stakes test.

The ACT is unlike any test you have ever taken. It requires a new way of thinking. Look at it this way: in your math class or English courses, 70% is typically the lowest percentage to earn a grade of C. However, on the ACT, 70% correct would equate to a score of about a 25, and while a 25 might or might not be a good score for you, it is far above the national average (typically about a 21). This means that you can actually get a lot of questions wrong on the ACT and still earn a good score! The key is to learn the correct strategies for each section and to never give up while taking the test.

The rules and strategies that follow have been used successfully by thousands of students. They are the perfect tool to help you reach your maximum score.

COMPUTER BASED TESTING (CBT), SECTION RETESTING, AND SUPERSCORING

Students who have previously taken a full-length, paper and pencil ACT will be allowed to register for additional ACT section tests that are administered via computer.

As the push for Computer Based Testing (CBT) grows, we fully expect the ACT to eventually offer students the option of taking the entire exam via computer. For now, students should prepare using a combination of pencil and paper along with at least a familiarity with CBT and how it works. Either way, the strategies and skills required to earn your top score are the same.

ACT will superscore your multiple test administrations. In other words, if you take the ACT more than once, they will automatically submit your best section scores from each administration to the colleges and universities where you apply, thus giving you the highest possible composite score.

STUDENTS WITH ACCOMMODATIONS

If you have been pre-approved by ACT for extended time testing or for any other accommodation, please utilize those same accommodations while practicing. For the majority of students with learning differences, the most common accommodation is called extended time, but there are many others. Again, no matter your official, pre-approved accommodation, please practice accordingly.

About the ACT

FORMAT

The ACT test consists of four multiple-choice sections plus an optional writing exercise. Here's the breakdown:

Section	Time	No. of Questions
English	45 minutes	75
Math	60 minutes	60
Reading	35 minutes	40
Science	35 minutes	40
Writing (optional)	40 minutes	1 essay

SCORING

The four multiple-choice sections (English, Mathematics, Reading, and Science) are scored on a scale from 1 to 36; the more questions you answer correctly, the higher your score will be. You will receive an individual score for each subject test, as well as a *composite* score. Your composite score is found by averaging your four subject test scores—that is, adding them all together and dividing the sum by 4—rounding up at .5 or above.

For example, let's say you took a practice test and received the following scores:

English: 26

Mathematics: 21

Reading: 24

Science: 24

Your composite score would be 24. (Added together, these scores total 95. Divide that value by 4, and you get 23.75. Because 23.75 has a decimal value greater than or equal to .5, you round up to 24.)

When colleges speak of ACT scores or list the median ACT score of their student bodies, they are referring to composite scores.

The only aspect of the ACT not scored from 1 to 36 is the Writing section. Every essay is read by two essay graders, who each give the writing sample a score ranging from 1 to 6. These scores are added together, resulting in a Writing score ranging from 2 to 12. Students will also receive a combined English/Writing score (on a scale of 1–36), drawing one-third from your Writing score and two-thirds from your English score.

PRACTICE TESTS

The best way to prepare for the ACT is to take several full-length practice tests. Once you have reviewed all of the skills presented in this book and learned our proven strategies, you can truly begin to measure your progress as a test taker. Do not expect to reach your score goals on the first practice test. **It takes time to familiarize yourself with the ACT**. As you move through the various practice tests, always keep one goal in mind—**steady progress**.

Although scale scores (explained earlier) are certainly important, the most helpful tool to measure your progress is actually your raw score on each subject test. In other words, on each successive practice test, your goal should always be to answer more questions correctly than you did on the previous test. Always think of how many questions you answer correctly, because in most cases, for every one question you get right on the Reading and Science sections, your scale scores go up by a full point; on the English and Mathematics sections, you get 1 scale point for every two questions you answer correctly. Keep track of your scores on the sheets provided after each practice test, and push yourself to answer at least one more question correctly per section as you move through the tests. If you can reach this very modest goal, **by the time you finish working through this book, you will have raised your composite score by 3 points!**

You might think that one little question doesn't matter, but nothing could be further from the truth. Getting one or two more questions right might just help you get into the college of your dreams! Since there is no penalty for incorrect answers, be sure you answer every question. Do not leave blanks.

MONITORING TIME

We will discuss pacing for each section in the strategies for that particular section. To succeed on this test, both during practice and on the actual test, you need to be responsible for keeping track of time. Practice pacing yourself so that you are not surprised during the actual ACT.

Suggestion for timekeeping: Use a digital watch on both the practice tests and on the actual test. Be sure it has a stopwatch feature and does not beep. If you must use a watch with a sweeping second hand, set it to noon before you begin each test. It is far easier to gauge your time from this setting.

Regardless of which type of watch you choose, **the most important thing is that you use the same watch for the practice tests and for the actual ACT**.

BUILDING ENDURANCE

The ACT is nearly 4 hours long. Your ultimate goal should be to complete at least one full practice test in one sitting before the actual test. Begin to build endurance by doing at least two sections together (e.g., English, then Mathematics or Reading, then Science). Additionally, the ACT is always given in the morning, so it is a good idea to do at least some of your practicing in the morning (especially if you are not a "morning person!").

English Rules

The ACT English test is possibly the easiest section for you to make vast skill and score improvements.

HIGHLIGHTS

- 5 passages, each with 15 questions
- 75 questions total
- 45 minutes
- Answer *every* question

DO'S AND DON'TS

- **DO** know the difference between a sentence and a fragment. A sentence has a subject and a verb and expresses a complete thought.

  Fragment: *She, acting like an infant, crying and whining.*
  Sentence: *I swim.*

- **DO** pick the clearest, most concise way of stating something. SHORTEST IS BEST, as long as you have a complete sentence.
- **DO** read to the very end of a sentence before answering a question. This way you will be sure that you pick an answer that creates a complete sentence.
- **DO** test the "DELETE the underlined portion" choice first: it is the correct answer about 50 percent of the time. Remember, though, that means it is a wrong answer 50 percent of the time as well, so choose DELETE when the underlined portion is repetitive or does not fit the main idea of the passage.
- **DO** be cautious when considering any answer with the word *being* in it, as it is seldom correct.
- **DO** look for wrong answers. Wrong answers are often much easier to find than right ones. Unless the right answer comes to you immediately, **ELIMINATE WRONG ANSWERS!**
- **DON'T** jump from question to question.
- **DON'T** be afraid to pick NO CHANGE. It is typically correct as often as any other answer.

PACING AND PRACTICING

- You have 45 minutes to complete the five English passages—that's 9 minutes per passage.
- Here's a tip for practicing your pacing: Draw a box at the end of each section. Under each box write in multiples of 9 (9, 18, 27, 36, and 45). Don't forget, you only have 45 minutes. As you take the exam, time yourself and write in the actual time it took you to finish each passage. This will help you know whether you need to speed up or slow down.
- The sections do not get more difficult as you go, so it is better to finish even if you have to make a few guesses along the way.

- It takes practice to get used to the English section. If you apply the rules and strategies while taking the practice tests, you will be fully prepared for the actual test.

PUNCTUATION

COMMAS

There are six comma rules to learn for the ACT.

1. Commas are used to mark the end of an introductory clause and are followed by a complete sentence. Introductory clauses often begin with words such as *although, when, while, since, if,* and *because.* (Yes. The word *because* can start a sentence!)

   EXAMPLE: *When it stops raining, Mark is going to wash his car.*

   EXAMPLE: *Although I'd love to go to the movie with you, I need to study for the ACT.*

   Please notice that each clause is followed by a comma and then a complete sentence. Also, the subject of the sentence must be mentioned immediately after the comma in order for it to make sense.

   EXAMPLE: *Feeling very sad, she felt a tear run down her cheek.*

   This is correct because it is clear that "she" was feeling very sad. If the sentence were written, "Feeling very sad, a tear ran down her cheek" it would be incorrect. A tear cannot feel sad!

2. Commas are used to set off nonrestrictive clauses/appositives (phrases that interrupt the flow of the sentence).

   EXAMPLE: *Jim, a champion swimmer, hoped to make the Olympic team.*

   To check for interruptions, remove the words between the commas. If the remaining portion is a complete sentence and the meaning is not changed, then the commas are correct. If not, then test another answer. <u>Be sure to read the whole sentence!</u> Words such as *however, for example, for instance,* and *although* are usually surrounded by commas.

3. Commas are used to separate two or more coordinate adjectives preceding a noun.

   EXAMPLE: *The ACT is not a stressful, difficult test.*

   However, do not use a comma if the adjectives are cumulative.

4. Commas separate more than two words in a series.

   EXAMPLE: *I bought eggs, cheese, milk, and butter at the store.*

   (The last comma after "milk" is optional, although the ACT tends to leave it in.)

5. A comma <u>before a conjunction</u> can be used to separate two complete sentences. (Conjunction words are *and, but, or, so.*)

   EXAMPLE: *The palm trees blew softly in the wind, and the hot sun beat down from the sky.*

   Do not use a comma without the conjunction to separate two complete sentences!

   EXAMPLE: *The palm trees blew softly in the wind, the hot sun beat down from the sky.*

6. A comma can be used at the end of a sentence followed by an afterthought.

   EXAMPLE: *The football game was a massacre, 49 to 0.*

OTHER COMMA TIPS

- When in doubt, leave the comma out!
- Just because you pause when reading a sentence does not mean the sentence requires a comma.
- If all four answer choices are identically worded and three of the four answer choices contain commas in various places, the correct answer is likely to be the one that omits the commas.

DASH

There are two dash rules used on the ACT.

1. The dash, like the comma, is used to mark an interruption.

   EXAMPLE: *The Chicago Marathon—a race of endurance, strength, and skill—is difficult to complete.*

   Two dashes or two commas can be used interchangeably; however, never use one of each.

2. The dash can also be used just like a colon.

   EXAMPLE: *Roxann's hair is unlike anyone else's in the family—thick and dark.*

COLON

There are three colon rules for the ACT.

1. The colon is used **after a complete sentence** followed by a summary list.

   EXAMPLE: *I have many hobbies: golfing, rock climbing, sailing, and windsurfing.*

   Complete sentence + COLON + list

2. The colon is also used at the end of a complete sentence followed by an afterthought.

   EXAMPLE: *Japan has a high literacy rate: 99 percent.*

   Complete sentence + COLON + afterthought

3. The colon is also used to separate two complete sentences when the second sentence explains or restates an idea in the first.

   EXAMPLE: *These seat covers are the most durable kind: they are reinforced with double stitching and covered with a heavy plastic coating.*

   Complete sentence + COLON + explanation

SEMICOLON

There are two semicolon rules to know for the ACT.

1. The semicolon is used to separate complete sentences.

    EXAMPLE: *Harris practiced diligently for the ACT; he wanted to maximize his score.*

2. The semicolon is also used before a coordinating adverb (*however, therefore, since*) to separate two sentences.

    EXAMPLE: *I enjoy living in a small community; however, the neighbors are often too nosy.*

APOSTROPHE

An apostrophe is used to show ownership.

1. If there is one owner, use '*s*.

    EXAMPLE: *Patsy's car is brand new.*

2. If there is more than one owner, use *s*'.

    EXAMPLE: *Ten boys' bikes were stolen.*

3. Words that are plural without adding the *s* form the possessive by adding '*s*.

    EXAMPLE: *Women's, men's, people's, children's*

GRAMMAR

POSSESSIVES

One owner = '*s*
More than one owner = *s*'
Words that are plural without adding *s* like *women, men,* or *people*: use '*s*.

    EXAMPLE: *I went into the men's locker room to change into my bathing suit.*

It's = it is
Its = one owner
Its' = **THIS IS NOT A WORD**, but ACT gives it as an answer choice—**NEVER** choose it!

Their = more than one owner
They're = they are
There = location

SUBJECT-VERB AGREEMENT

Always check for agreement. Within a sentence, a singular subject must be followed by a singular verb and a plural subject must be followed by a plural verb.

    EXAMPLE: *The stack of books is on the floor.*

    The subject here is "stack," which is singular, so the verb *is* is correct.

BE CAREFUL!

Verbs are not made plural just by putting an *s* on the end. If you want a singular verb, put the word *he* or *she* in front of it and make sure it works. If you want a plural verb, put the word *they* in front of it and make sure it works.

EXAMPLE: *He sits*

They sit.

One of the ACT's most common questions begins with a singular subject and is followed by several prepositional phrases with plural nouns and then a verb. This verb MUST be singular so as to agree with the sentence's singular subject.

EXAMPLE: *The color of the glass in the panes of glass in the windows of the nearby house is actually a reflection of the sun's rays.*

Although there are multiple nouns in the prepositional phrase above, the subject in this sentence is in fact *color*. You must, therefore, use the singular verb *is*.

SUBJECT-PRONOUN AGREEMENT

Within a sentence a singular subject must be followed by a singular pronoun, and a plural subject must be followed by a plural pronoun.

EXAMPLE: *Each of the boys took his seat on the bus.*

Since the subject is "each of the boys" it is singular. *His* is a singular pronoun.

PARALLEL PHRASING

Express ideas in a consistent, grammatical way. Phrases or words in a series must be in the same form.

DO THIS: *I like to run, bike, and swim.*

NOT THIS: I like to run, biking, and swimming.

TRANSITIONS

If all answers except one have a transition, read the sentence before to see whether you really need a transition.

A. Consequently, the dog
B. Therefore, the dog
C. *The dog*
D. For example, the dog

If all answers contain transitions …

1. Look for two transitions that have similar meanings.
2. Eliminate the two with similar meanings.
3. Look at the sentence before and after the transition to determine how the sentences should be linked. One of the two remaining answers should clearly be the better choice.

Math Rules

The ACT Math test covers most areas of high school mathematics. Regardless of your math level or proficiency, you will achieve your maximum potential score by completing the practice tests in this book.

HIGHLIGHTS

- 60 multiple-choice questions
- 60 minutes
- No penalty for guessing; answer *every* question
- Questions increase in difficulty throughout the test
- The TI-83 and TI-84 calculators are allowed on the test. The TI-89 is **not** allowed.

The Math test is the only section of the ACT arranged in order of difficulty; generally speaking, you will find significantly easier questions toward the beginning of the test and more difficult questions toward the end. (This is not to say, of course, that you will never find a "tough" question on the first half or an "easy" question at the end.) Knowing that the test is laid out in this way can help you tremendously as you work through the section on test day. For instance, if one of the first questions seems extremely complicated, you are probably overthinking it; if the answer to one of the last 10 questions appears extremely obvious and straightforward, it likely is not the correct answer.

While there is no precise point where the Math section jumps from easy to difficult questions, a good rule of thumb is that typically the first 30 questions cover the more basic skill sets, and the last 30 questions test more advanced topics. You might find that you are entirely unfamiliar with some of the advanced topics, and that's okay! If you have never taken an advanced algebra or a trigonometry class, you are not expected to know the answers to these questions. **Remember: You can still receive an excellent score on the ACT Math section without any knowledge of these advanced skills!**

DO'S AND DON'TS

- **DO** use your test booklet! Often a quick sketch will help you solve the problem. If a diagram is already provided, begin by marking all known information.
- **DO** work backwards. This is especially true when there are variables in the question and numbers in the answer choices. For these questions, use the "**Plug and Chug**" strategy: Plug answer choices back into the problem to find the correct solution to the problem.
- **DO** use the "**Plug in C Strategy**" when working backwards: all ACT math answers are listed in numerical order, either smallest to largest or vice versa. Therefore, when possible, plug in choice C (or H). If it is not the right answer, it will be immediately clear whether a larger or smaller answer choice would have led you to the correct answer. If you need a larger number, you can immediately eliminate choices A and B; if you need a smaller one, you can eliminate D and E. By using this method, you can eliminate three choices by checking only one!
- **DO** read the question first on long word problems. Previewing the actual question helps you eliminate unnecessary words and information.

- **DO** assign the variable(s) a number and evaluate the problem accordingly if a question has variables in the answer choices. Plug in an easy number to work with, like 2 or 3. (Beware of using zero or 1—they are more trouble than they are worth!)
- **DO** be sure to **answer the question being asked!** One of the most commonly made mistakes on the ACT is also one of the most avoidable. A good way to avoid this scenario is to underline the part of the question that directly poses the question (e.g., "What is the value of x?"). That way, after you finish solving the problem, you can quickly glance back at the part of the question that you have underlined and double check that you are answering the right question (i.e., circling the answer that corresponds to the value of x, rather than the value of y).
- **DO** assume that diagrams are drawn to scale if you don't know where to start on a problem or cannot find the answer mathematically and estimate lengths and angle measures from the diagram.
- **DO** look for wrong answers in addition to correct ones, and use **process of elimination**. Even if you do not find the answer, guessing after eliminating three answer choices will increase your probability of guessing correctly from 20 percent to 50 percent!
- **DO** start the test with your calculator in degree mode. To put a TI-83 or TI-84 in degree mode, first press the "MODE" button, located directly to the right of the yellow "2nd" button. Once in the "MODE" screen, look to the third line down. It will say "Radian" and "Degree." Make sure "Degree" is highlighted. If it is not, place the cursor on "Degree" and press the "ENTER" button. "Degree" should now be highlighted, and your calculator will be in degree mode.
- **DO** be alert for charts/graphs that apply to more than one question.
- **DON'T** spend too much time on any one question.

PACING AND PRACTICING

Sixty minutes to answer 60 questions corresponds to 1 minute per question. However, you should limit yourself to 25 minutes for the first 30 questions, and save the extra time to work through the more difficult questions on the second half of the test.

Remember, DO NOT leave any answers blank! However, on the practice tests, it is helpful to mark which questions you guessed on, so you can see which math concepts you might need to review again.

Reading Rules

To be successful on the Reading test, you must be an **active reader**. This means being able to determine main ideas, evaluate supporting details, and arrive at appropriate conclusions. Don't let your mind wander; stay focused on what the passage is saying.

Completing the practice tests in this book will enable you to improve your reading proficiency. The reading tests/passages in this book reflect the word count of actual ACT test passages.

HIGHLIGHTS

- 35 minutes
- 4 reading passages, each with 10 questions

PASSAGE 1: PROSE FICTION/LITERARY NARRATIVE

- This passage is a story.
- The first paragraph will indicate who (the character or characters) and what about that person.
- Use the **CAPS** strategy by identifying: **C**haracters, **A**ttitudes, **P**roblems (or issues), and **S**olutions (or ending). Know each character's personality traits and to whom they are related in the passage.

PASSAGE 2: SOCIAL SCIENCE

- This passage is informative.
- Read the first paragraph carefully for the author's purpose. To determine the author's purpose, ask yourself, "Why did the author write this?" or "What is the one main thing the author wants me to know after reading this passage?"
- Pay close attention to the first sentence or two of each paragraph and to the last paragraph, particularly the last sentence, because it often restates the main idea.
- If often helps to write down a key word for each paragraph.

PASSAGE 3: HUMANITIES

- This passage is often a narrative but sometimes resembles a social science passage.
- While reading, focus on the author/narrator's attitudes toward the subject of the passage.
- If it's a narrative, use the **CAPS** strategy.
- If it's informative, use the **T**hesis and **D**etails (**TD**) strategy.

PASSAGE 4: NATURAL SCIENCE

- This passage is also informative, so use the **TD** strategy.
- Read the passage for the big picture, focusing on the first and last paragraphs for the thesis.
- Don't spend too much time learning details; read for location of information.

TEST-TAKING STRATEGIES

1. Questions about a passage usually follow one main idea. The author wrote the passage for a reason; once you figure out the point that the author is trying to make, you will be well on your way to answering questions correctly.

Placing a star (*) next to the main points helps you to focus and locate important information as you read. Main points are key ideas in the passage.

2. On the prose fiction and (sometimes) the humanities passages, use the **CAPS** strategy: look for **C**haracters, **A**ttitudes, **P**roblems, and **S**olutions. There is always an issue (the problem) in the passage, so identify it! Every prose fiction passage will also have a conclusion or resolution, even if it's not a final one.

3. On the nonfiction passages—social science, natural science, and (sometimes) humanities— focus on the **TD: T**hesis and **D**etails. Be sure to read the first two paragraphs carefully, as they generally contain the author's purpose, thesis, or main idea. The rest of the passage contains details that support the author's main idea. You do not need to memorize them all on your initial read. If you can simply pick out the author's important supporting details (each paragraph generally corresponds to one major detail), you will be in great shape as you move on to the questions.

4. Each student will approach the ACT Reading test slightly differently. No two brains are identical; therefore, no two strategies are identical. However, for most students there is a definitive reading strategy that produces the highest possible ACT reading score, and it's very simple.

   Step 1: <u>Read the entire passage quickly but actively, seeking out the most important information</u>. Place a star in the margin next to significant information. When you finish reading the passage, you should be able to mentally answer the **CAPS** or **TD** questions! If you cannot do this easily, you were not actively reading! (Reading the passage should take between 4 and 5 minutes.)

   Step 2: <u>Answer the questions</u>. Be sure to read ALL FOUR answer choices, using the process of elimination, BEFORE looking back to the passage. (Answering questions should take about 4–5 minutes.) Do not keep looking back. Keep moving.

No matter what, you must complete each passage in LESS THAN 9 MINUTES! In order to reach your maximum reading score, it is imperative that you get to all four passages. Remember, it is possible to get some answers wrong on the ACT and still achieve a great score.

An alternative strategy that works for some students is to actively read only the first and last paragraphs while skimming the body of the passage and then answering the questions as described above.

You waste precious time by reading the questions first. On a rare occasion, this strategy will work, but for 99 percent of students it does not help with comprehension or with earning a high reading score.

5. Although the content of the passages changes from test to test, the types of questions do not. If you know how to answer each type of question, you will be in good shape.

   ■ **Main Idea or Author's Purpose**
   Look for a general, vague, or broad answer.

   ■ **Inferences**
   Make an assumption based on what you read; don't bother looking back.

   ■ **Tone**
   Usually positive; look for a "nice" answer.

   ■ **Detail**
   If the question includes "the passage states" or "the passage indicates," the answer is in the passage. When referring to line numbers, read before and after the lines given.

However, be sure to still read all the answer choices before looking back in order to save valuable time.

- **Vocabulary Words**
  You must look back for context: read the lines before and after for clues as to meaning and then plug in words.

- **"Except" or "Not" Questions**
  Answer as if they are true/false questions.

DO'S AND DON'TS

- **DO** read all choices and try to eliminate some before looking back. It is acceptable to look back as long as you first use the process of elimination. If you do look back, you must do so very quickly!
- **DO** be consistent with theme; questions often repeat themselves.
- **DO** be careful on questions with specific line references. When looking back in the passage, make sure to read a few lines before and after the given line reference for context.
- **DO** look at the title of the passage for social science, humanities, and natural science. It can often give you a clear hint as to what the passage is primarily about.
- **DO** match ideas from the passage to the questions.
- **DO** choose moderate words such as *sometimes*, *tend to be*, and *likely*.
- **DON'T** look back for the answer without reading all choices and eliminating wrong answers first.
- **DON'T** just match words, match ideas. Be sure your selection answers the question.
- **DON'T** choose answers containing definitive words such as *always*, *never*, *only*, and *alone*.

PACING AND PRACTICING

- You have approximately 9 minutes per passage. Always spend more time answering questions (e.g., 5 minutes) than reading the passage (e.g., 4 minutes).
- You can speed up your reading by using an index card or pencil to help you focus. Be sure to place a star next to key ideas.
- It is better to make educated guesses throughout the test than to guess on an entire passage. Remember, each passage contains easy, medium, and difficult questions. If you spend too much time on the truly difficult questions early on, you might run out of time and end up missing some easy questions because you never got to them. You want to get to all questions if possible.
- Try the following to practice your pacing: Draw a box at the end of each reading passage. Under the first box, write in 8–9. Under the second, write in 17–18. Under the third, write in 26–27, and under the fourth, write in 35. With 35 minutes to complete four passages, you actually get 8 minutes and 45 seconds per passage, so try your best to complete each passage in less than 9 minutes! You MUST be finished in 35 minutes. As you take the practice exams, time yourself and write in the actual time you take to finish. This will give you a strong idea of where you need to speed up or slow down.

REMEMBER

To get a good score on the Reading test, you must finish it—even if you have to guess along the way!

Science Rules

For most students, the ACT Science Reasoning test appears to be the most difficult of the four, but with a little practice, it becomes fairly straightforward. This is the point in the test where many students lose focus. *Do not let this happen!*

HIGHLIGHTS

- The Science section is not arranged in order of difficulty. Each passage contains a difficult question or two, so it is important not to spend too much time on challenging questions. If necessary, make an educated guess and move on.
- The Science section is really a reasoning or logic test. You may need to have prior knowledge of the subject matter, although usually it is a basic concept.
- Think of the Science section as a puzzle or riddle that you have to figure out.
- The focus is on interpreting data and information and making logical conclusions.
- It is important to be FLEXIBLE and to be able to SHIFT GEARS in the Science section. In other words, if one method doesn't work, try another. If looking at one piece of information doesn't help you, look in a different place.
- With all of the information put in front of you and only 35 minutes to answer all of the questions, the Science section can seem overwhelming. The most important thing you can do to conserve time is orient yourself. Use the headings on charts and graphs the same way you would at the grocery store, and the ACT Science Reasoning test can be as straightforward as buying a loaf of bread.
- The Science section contains three distinct types of passages.

    1. **Data representation**
    2. **Research summaries**
    3. **Conflicting viewpoints**

The conflicting viewpoints passage is unique and is not usually accompanied by charts and graphs. Instead, it involves interpreting data. It can fall anywhere in the test, but you will easily recognize it because it will consist of a brief introduction to the topic followed by two to four sections (e.g., Scientist 1, Scientist 2 … or The Dust Theory, The Dirt Theory, The Rock Theory) written in paragraph form. It may look like you need to read everything but you do not!

In many ways, the conflicting viewpoints passage is similar to the passages in the Reading section: It is essential that you determine the MAIN IDEA of each view.

REMEMBER

"Conflicting viewpoints" is called that for a reason. Although they will discuss the same general topic, the views must oppose each other in some fundamental way. Once you have figured out each view's main idea and where the views disagree, you will be in great shape on the questions.

Follow these steps on the conflicting viewpoints passage:

1. Skim the introductory paragraph.
2. Then read enough of each viewpoint to determine the main idea of each one. (The main idea can usually be found in the first two sentences of each viewpoint.)

3. Then go straight to the questions. Look back when you need to, using as much logic as possible.

4. There are two basic types of questions. The first is a simple word match—just look for the words in the passages. The second asks you to define the viewpoint. These may seem more difficult, but they should revolve around the first two sentences of each viewpoint that you read.

5. Questions often ask about one of the viewpoints but list answer choices that correspond to the other(s). Look to eliminate these extraneous answer choices first.

In general, there are three types of questions on the Science section:

1. **PATTERNS AND TRENDS**: For this type of question, you need to find the answer based on the data. Focus on investigating the information *directionally* (e.g., Does the pressure increase or decrease when velocity increases? When exposed to more sunlight, do the plants flower more frequently, less frequently, or is there no relationship?).

2. **HYPOTHESIS**: This question involves yes/no or true/false answers. These questions can be best tackled by a **"Plug and Chug"** method. Try out each answer as you go through them.

3. **LOGIC**: These questions are designed to challenge your thinking. You should focus on connecting the information. If the question talks about the *design* of the experiment, you may need to read a little bit.

ACT science questions can also be thought of as either <u>navigation</u> or <u>manipulation</u> questions.

Navigation. Within each passage there are typically three questions that you can answer simply by locating (navigating) the necessary information in a chart or graph.

Manipulation. There are approximately two per passage. These questions involve three steps: first you must locate the appropriate information, then you must use the data in some way to find the correct answer, and finally you must decide if you need additional information from the reading.

TEST-TAKING STRATEGIES

1. For most of the passages, your first step should be to skim the introduction. Look at the data, reading the labels and headings quickly. Your goal is to just get a general idea of where everything is. DO NOT WORRY IF YOU DON'T UNDERSTAND WHAT'S GOING ON. It may be confusing, but there isn't enough time to try to completely comprehend each experiment.

2. Your focus then becomes the questions. Read through the first question and underline key words. DO NOT go straight to the data yet.

3. Next, match the information in the question to the appropriate chart/graph(s). BE SURE THAT YOU ARE LOOKING AT THE CORRECT GRAPH OR CHART! **Then, work backward from the answers.** Use the process of elimination to help you determine the true answer. Almost every question refers to a data table even though the question might not specifically mention that table. *Use the answers as a guide to locate the correct table.*

4. Think simply and linearly! Try not to overthink—the answers are usually simpler than you realize.

5. If you are not able to find the answer using just the charts and graphs, then you may have to go to the text. Sometimes italicized words can be helpful. If the question states "based on the information," you should look at the text. The introductory passage may have some information to help you.

DO'S AND DON'TS

- **DO** focus on the charts and graphs. You may have to use data from two sources to answer the question.
- **DO** pretend that you are shopping at an unfamiliar grocery store. Use the headings on the tables, charts, and graphs to help you!
- **DO** look for patterns, trends, and directions. If there is an obvious pattern, such as a column of numbers increasing or decreasing, it might be helpful to draw an arrow showing that trend.
- **DO** write in the test booklet. Circling and underlining both help prevent careless errors.
- **DO** work backward from each answer—using the process of elimination. (Check each answer to see if it is true. There should only be one true answer.)
- **DON'T** let the wording of the questions confuse you. Break them down; underline key words. There is often more information in the questions than you actually need to answer.

PACING AND PRACTICING

- Over the last several years, ACT Science has presented students with 6 passages. However, ACT still states that the Science section could have either 6 or 7 passages. With 6 or 7 passages and 35 minutes, you have essentially 5 or 6 minutes per passage; however, some will take a minute less while others may take a minute more. Try to use pacing boxes during practice.
- Don't rush; just be conscious of your time from the beginning.
- If you can't figure out a question, **make your best guess and move on.** You will not have enough time to dwell on questions, and it is better to guess on one or two than to not even make it to an entire passage.
- If you find yourself struggling with finishing, complete the conflicting views passage last. (Be careful on your answer sheet!)
- Don't panic as you begin to practice. It may take you longer at first! You *will* get the hang of it!

Writing Rules

The ACT Writing will be administered about five minutes after the end of the ACT Science test. During the Writing test, you will have 40 minutes to plan and write an analytical essay in response to a prompt. Although there is no length requirement, the higher-scoring essays tend to be at least 1.5 pages long (more like 2 pages if you have very big handwriting), and although you should *definitely* spend more time writing than you should spend on planning, making outlines or whatever your personal pre-writing process is important.

You will be provided with three hypothetical people's opinions—i.e., "some quotes"—at least one of which you are required to address in your response. Overall, your essay response represents the "fourth perspective." Think of your essay as "joining a conversation" in which you are the fourth person, rather than as "judging" any or all of the other perspectives in turn as "right" or "wrong"—although you may of course say so, if that is your real opinion. You will *always* write a better essay by saying what you *really* think than you will if you worry about guessing what the graders "want to hear."

After the specific issue that your essay must concern is explained, and the three hypothetical perspectives are given, the instructions at the bottom will state:

- clearly state your own perspective on the issue and analyze the relationship between your perspective and at least one other perspective
- develop and support your ideas with reasoning and examples
- organize your ideas clearly and logically
- communicate your ideas effectively in standard written English

Regarding these instructions, here are some things to notice and keep in mind:

- Although you are only *required* to discuss *one* of the three provided perspectives, you can discuss more than one of them.
- Although no one way of structuring your essay is "the right way," be advised that it is NOT the best idea to use a "first half/second half" structure, where "first" you discuss the perspectives and "then" you give your own opinion. You'll note that the directions specifically tell you to "analyze the *relationship between*" your own opinion and the provided perspective(s) that you choose to discuss—not just to talk about both things separately. Yes, by the "home stretch" of your essay you should have dispensed with the provided perspectives and just be discussing your own views, but you certainly shouldn't "wait" until you are "done" discussing the other perspectives to introduce it. Instead, let the other perspectives "help" you introduce your own views bit-by-bit, adding a "this makes me think of …" or an "I think that's interesting because …" to your assessments of the perspectives you pick. Think of the provided perspectives as being like the "boosters" that help a space shuttle take off: their assistance is needed in order for the shuttle (i.e., your own opinion) to get off the ground, and they do most of the work at first, but then, as the shuttle gains altitude and momentum, they fall away one by one as their fuel is spent, until finally the shuttle is soaring under its own power!
- You are asked to "develop and support your ideas with reasoning and examples." Be careful not to be repetitive. You may use examples from your own experiences, but remember, your examples are your evidence. Make sure to have a clear thesis (it need not be complex), strong topic sentences, and transitions between paragraphs.

OVERALL APPROACH: THE "BOW" STRATEGY

BRAINSTORM

Think about the issue in general as described in the prompt, and also about the three provided perspectives. What popped into your head when you were thinking about *just* the issue? And did any or all of the three perspectives make you want to *modify* those initial ideas? If so, then you've already gotten some ideas on how to "pay respect to" the three perspectives (e.g., "I was inclined to think this way until Perspective Two reminded me of how …").

ORGANIZE

While it *is* important that you *use paragraphs* (when a reader sees that an essay is just one long paragraph, she or he will expect it to be bad—because, frankly, most essays written as one long paragraph really *are* bad), it is by no means required that you use the traditional five-paragraph "Introduction, Three Points, Conclusion" essay. Nor do you have to open with a rhetorical question, or make the second sentence the "topic sentence," or any other rule you may have learned in school. If you like some or all of those rules, and feel more comfortable using them, then go right ahead—but using them is not mandatory, or even necessarily the best idea. All that the first paragraph has to do is get the reader interested and make you seem like you understand the issue and have interesting things that you're eager to start saying about it (be advised that quoting word-for-word from the opening paragraph of the prompt is NOT the way to make this impression—that's what students do when they can't think of anything to say!); all that the last paragraph has to do is provide a satisfying "sense of an ending" (i.e., it seems like you meant for that to be the end, rather than seeming like you ran out of time); and all that the paragraphs in the middle have to do is demonstrate understanding of one or more perspectives, provide original ideas that are somehow connected to them, and back up these original ideas with effective persuasion . . . in *whatever order you're comfortable with!* After all, the *most* important thing is NOT to worry so much about organization that you end up not writing enough! As long as everything you need is in there *somewhere*, the graders aren't going to lose their minds over whether everything is in the "right" place!

WRITE

As the saying goes, "you never get a second chance to make a first impression," and your first paragraph is the first impression you make on the graders. This doesn't mean you should be terrified that it's going to "make or break" your essay—but it does mean that you should try to make it interesting! If you think of a great quotation or an interesting fact that is relevant to the issue, for example, don't "save it for later"—put it right at the beginning and open with a bang! The graders, of course, *have to* read your essay (just like you *have to* write it), but you should be thinking about what might make people *want to* read it: If somebody just came across your essay somewhere and read the beginning, would he or she be "hooked" and want to keep going?

While the opening paragraph should be "motivating," the keyword for the rest of the essay is "memorable." Are your ideas and examples you use to support them going to "stick with" a reader? Are they insightful? Moving? Amusing? Whatever sort of rhetoric you use to get the reader interested, the idea is that you want *your* essay to be the one that the readers remember at the end of the day! So, ask yourself: What sort of ideas make *you* remember a piece of writing?

As far as conclusions go, keep in mind that the oft-repeated advice of "tell them what you told them" is NOT the best strategy for the ACT Writing. While you do want to provide a sense of "summing up" your big ideas (i.e., the end should *feel like the end*), it makes for dull writing to simply repeat them, "ticking them off" one-by-one as though the conclusion were a checklist. You want to end "with a bang," just like you started with one in the introduction! (And whatever you do, DON'T begin the last paragraph with the words "In conclusion …"— after all, "real" essays in magazines never do that, but you can still tell when it's the end!)

It is better to have a longer essay that may involve some "twists and turns" than to have a meticulously organized essay that is too short. The best strategy is to do a "good enough" amount of pre-planning and then just "jump in," as opposed to wasting precious writing time making sure that you will have exactly five paragraphs of precisely equal length.

SCORING

Two readers will read your essay, and each will assign it a score from 1 to 6. If, by chance, these two scorers disagree by more than one point, then the scoring supervisor will step in to resolve the discrepancy. The Writing Score is based on Ideas and Analysis, Development and Support, and Organization—Language Use and Conventions. Performance on the Writing test will not affect the English, Math, Reading, Science, or composite scores. You will receive two additional scores on your score sheet—a combined English/Writing score (1–36) and a Writing test sub-score (2–12). Neither of these scores will affect your composite score.

EXERCISES TO IMPROVE YOUR ESSAY-WRITING SKILLS, AND TIPS TO IMPROVE YOUR ACT WRITING SCORE

- Just as you use every muscle during a game but build up your strength by working out one muscle group at a time in the gym, you can build up your writing skills by practicing one part of an essay at a time: Using the prompts and skill-builders in this book, try practicing writing only topic sentences, or only introductions or conclusions, or only listing quotes, examples, and interesting facts, rather than feeling as though you need to only practice writing an entire essay at a time (although you should *certainly* practice writing entire essays, too).

- A stirring (or insightful, or amusing) quotation can enhance an essay, especially if it appears in the introduction. The "Big Four" people to Google when it comes to great quotations are Abraham Lincoln, Mark Twain, Albert Einstein, and Oscar Wilde!

- You don't always need to say "In my opinion …" before stating an opinion. After all, it's your essay, so the reader already knows it's your opinion! However, doing this *once or twice* can be a good idea, especially when the opinion you're about to state might be controversial, because it makes you seem humble.

- It's important to vary your sentence structure. So, try to write as few sentences as possible that begin with the word "The." And you *definitely* want to avoid beginning sentences with the word "Also," especially consecutive sentences!

- Vocabulary is important but using words correctly is even more important. (If you are not used to using a particular word, then there's a good chance you'll end up using it *incorrectly*, which will make your score go *down*.)

- Although the prompt provides you with "three perspectives" representing other people's opinions, these people are not named or identified in any way, so you do not know whether they are male or female (the quotes aren't real, so there is no right answer). Feel free to use what ever pronouns make you most comfortable.

How to Practice Effectively for the ACT

A SUGGESTED LESSON PLAN

Preparing for the ACT is one of the most important steps a high school student can take. Your ACT score helps determine where you will go to college and whether or not schools will offer you scholarship money.

When taking the practice exams in this book, please simulate actual test conditions:

- Find a quiet location that is free from distractions.
- Leave your phone in a separate room!
- Be sure to wear the same wrist watch during practice that you will wear during the actual exam.
- Be sure to use the same calculator, as well.
- Try to do an entire test in one sitting, whenever possible.
- Do not "read out loud" as this is not allowed during the ACT.

After completing a practice test, it is imperative that you carefully review your errors. Each test is accompanied by a set of explanations. When you miss a question, carefully review the explanation for the correct answer. It is virtually impossible to improve your ACT score without this corrective input.

All students should carefully read, review, and learn the strategies listed at the beginning of this book, found in the "About the ACT" section. These "Rules" will help you score to your maximum potential.

We suggest the following lesson plans:

Full Prep: (12 week plan)

Ideally, students will begin their prep twelve weeks (about 3 months) prior to their test date. There are seven full exams in this book. Be sure to review the "Rules" found in the "About the ACT" section at the beginning of the book. We then suggest taking and reviewing one practice exam every two weeks or so.

Fast Prep: (4–8 week plan)

When time is a bit short, students should attempt to complete and review at least 3–4 of the practice exams found in this book. Be sure to first review the "Rules" found in the "About the ACT" section at the beginning of the book.

Lightning Prep: (1–4 week plan)

We understand that sometimes time is limited and that some prep is better than no prep. In this case, be sure to review the "Rules" found in the "About the ACT" section at the beginning of the book. Then, try to take and review at least 2 of the practice exams found in the book.

Practice Tests

ANSWER SHEET
Practice Test 1

Directions: Mark one answer only for each question. Make the mark dark. Erase completely any mark made in error. (Additional or stray marks will be counted as mistakes.)

English

1. Ⓐ Ⓑ Ⓒ Ⓓ
2. Ⓕ Ⓖ Ⓗ Ⓙ
3. Ⓐ Ⓑ Ⓒ Ⓓ
4. Ⓕ Ⓖ Ⓗ Ⓙ
5. Ⓐ Ⓑ Ⓒ Ⓓ
6. Ⓕ Ⓖ Ⓗ Ⓙ
7. Ⓐ Ⓑ Ⓒ Ⓓ
8. Ⓕ Ⓖ Ⓗ Ⓙ
9. Ⓐ Ⓑ Ⓒ Ⓓ
10. Ⓕ Ⓖ Ⓗ Ⓙ
11. Ⓐ Ⓑ Ⓒ Ⓓ
12. Ⓕ Ⓖ Ⓗ Ⓙ
13. Ⓐ Ⓑ Ⓒ Ⓓ
14. Ⓕ Ⓖ Ⓗ Ⓙ
15. Ⓐ Ⓑ Ⓒ Ⓓ

16. Ⓕ Ⓖ Ⓗ Ⓙ
17. Ⓐ Ⓑ Ⓒ Ⓓ
18. Ⓕ Ⓖ Ⓗ Ⓙ
19. Ⓐ Ⓑ Ⓒ Ⓓ
20. Ⓕ Ⓖ Ⓗ Ⓙ
21. Ⓐ Ⓑ Ⓒ Ⓓ
22. Ⓕ Ⓖ Ⓗ Ⓙ
23. Ⓐ Ⓑ Ⓒ Ⓓ
24. Ⓕ Ⓖ Ⓗ Ⓙ
25. Ⓐ Ⓑ Ⓒ Ⓓ
26. Ⓕ Ⓖ Ⓗ Ⓙ
27. Ⓐ Ⓑ Ⓒ Ⓓ
28. Ⓕ Ⓖ Ⓗ Ⓙ
29. Ⓐ Ⓑ Ⓒ Ⓓ
30. Ⓕ Ⓖ Ⓗ Ⓙ

31. Ⓐ Ⓑ Ⓒ Ⓓ
32. Ⓕ Ⓖ Ⓗ Ⓙ
33. Ⓐ Ⓑ Ⓒ Ⓓ
34. Ⓕ Ⓖ Ⓗ Ⓙ
35. Ⓐ Ⓑ Ⓒ Ⓓ
36. Ⓕ Ⓖ Ⓗ Ⓙ
37. Ⓐ Ⓑ Ⓒ Ⓓ
38. Ⓕ Ⓖ Ⓗ Ⓙ
39. Ⓐ Ⓑ Ⓒ Ⓓ
40. Ⓕ Ⓖ Ⓗ Ⓙ
41. Ⓐ Ⓑ Ⓒ Ⓓ
42. Ⓕ Ⓖ Ⓗ Ⓙ
43. Ⓐ Ⓑ Ⓒ Ⓓ
44. Ⓕ Ⓖ Ⓗ Ⓙ
45. Ⓐ Ⓑ Ⓒ Ⓓ

46. Ⓕ Ⓖ Ⓗ Ⓙ
47. Ⓐ Ⓑ Ⓒ Ⓓ
48. Ⓕ Ⓖ Ⓗ Ⓙ
49. Ⓐ Ⓑ Ⓒ Ⓓ
50. Ⓕ Ⓖ Ⓗ Ⓙ
51. Ⓐ Ⓑ Ⓒ Ⓓ
52. Ⓕ Ⓖ Ⓗ Ⓙ
53. Ⓐ Ⓑ Ⓒ Ⓓ
54. Ⓕ Ⓖ Ⓗ Ⓙ
55. Ⓐ Ⓑ Ⓒ Ⓓ
56. Ⓕ Ⓖ Ⓗ Ⓙ
57. Ⓐ Ⓑ Ⓒ Ⓓ
58. Ⓕ Ⓖ Ⓗ Ⓙ
59. Ⓐ Ⓑ Ⓒ Ⓓ
60. Ⓕ Ⓖ Ⓗ Ⓙ

61. Ⓐ Ⓑ Ⓒ Ⓓ
62. Ⓕ Ⓖ Ⓗ Ⓙ
63. Ⓐ Ⓑ Ⓒ Ⓓ
64. Ⓕ Ⓖ Ⓗ Ⓙ
65. Ⓐ Ⓑ Ⓒ Ⓓ
66. Ⓕ Ⓖ Ⓗ Ⓙ
67. Ⓐ Ⓑ Ⓒ Ⓓ
68. Ⓕ Ⓖ Ⓗ Ⓙ
69. Ⓐ Ⓑ Ⓒ Ⓓ
70. Ⓕ Ⓖ Ⓗ Ⓙ
71. Ⓐ Ⓑ Ⓒ Ⓓ
72. Ⓕ Ⓖ Ⓗ Ⓙ
73. Ⓐ Ⓑ Ⓒ Ⓓ
74. Ⓕ Ⓖ Ⓗ Ⓙ
75. Ⓐ Ⓑ Ⓒ Ⓓ

Mathematics

1. Ⓐ Ⓑ Ⓒ Ⓓ Ⓔ
2. Ⓕ Ⓖ Ⓗ Ⓙ Ⓚ
3. Ⓐ Ⓑ Ⓒ Ⓓ Ⓔ
4. Ⓕ Ⓖ Ⓗ Ⓙ Ⓚ
5. Ⓐ Ⓑ Ⓒ Ⓓ Ⓔ
6. Ⓕ Ⓖ Ⓗ Ⓙ Ⓚ
7. Ⓐ Ⓑ Ⓒ Ⓓ Ⓔ
8. Ⓕ Ⓖ Ⓗ Ⓙ Ⓚ
9. Ⓐ Ⓑ Ⓒ Ⓓ Ⓔ
10. Ⓕ Ⓖ Ⓗ Ⓙ Ⓚ
11. Ⓐ Ⓑ Ⓒ Ⓓ Ⓔ
12. Ⓕ Ⓖ Ⓗ Ⓙ Ⓚ
13. Ⓐ Ⓑ Ⓒ Ⓓ Ⓔ
14. Ⓕ Ⓖ Ⓗ Ⓙ Ⓚ
15. Ⓐ Ⓑ Ⓒ Ⓓ Ⓔ

16. Ⓕ Ⓖ Ⓗ Ⓙ Ⓚ
17. Ⓐ Ⓑ Ⓒ Ⓓ Ⓔ
18. Ⓕ Ⓖ Ⓗ Ⓙ Ⓚ
19. Ⓐ Ⓑ Ⓒ Ⓓ Ⓔ
20. Ⓕ Ⓖ Ⓗ Ⓙ Ⓚ
21. Ⓐ Ⓑ Ⓒ Ⓓ Ⓔ
22. Ⓕ Ⓖ Ⓗ Ⓙ Ⓚ
23. Ⓐ Ⓑ Ⓒ Ⓓ Ⓔ
24. Ⓕ Ⓖ Ⓗ Ⓙ Ⓚ
25. Ⓐ Ⓑ Ⓒ Ⓓ Ⓔ
26. Ⓕ Ⓖ Ⓗ Ⓙ Ⓚ
27. Ⓐ Ⓑ Ⓒ Ⓓ Ⓔ
28. Ⓕ Ⓖ Ⓗ Ⓙ Ⓚ
29. Ⓐ Ⓑ Ⓒ Ⓓ Ⓔ
30. Ⓕ Ⓖ Ⓗ Ⓙ Ⓚ

31. Ⓐ Ⓑ Ⓒ Ⓓ Ⓔ
32. Ⓕ Ⓖ Ⓗ Ⓙ Ⓚ
33. Ⓐ Ⓑ Ⓒ Ⓓ Ⓔ
34. Ⓕ Ⓖ Ⓗ Ⓙ Ⓚ
35. Ⓐ Ⓑ Ⓒ Ⓓ Ⓔ
36. Ⓕ Ⓖ Ⓗ Ⓙ Ⓚ
37. Ⓐ Ⓑ Ⓒ Ⓓ Ⓔ
38. Ⓕ Ⓖ Ⓗ Ⓙ Ⓚ
39. Ⓐ Ⓑ Ⓒ Ⓓ Ⓔ
40. Ⓕ Ⓖ Ⓗ Ⓙ Ⓚ
41. Ⓐ Ⓑ Ⓒ Ⓓ Ⓔ
42. Ⓕ Ⓖ Ⓗ Ⓙ Ⓚ
43. Ⓐ Ⓑ Ⓒ Ⓓ Ⓔ
44. Ⓕ Ⓖ Ⓗ Ⓙ Ⓚ
45. Ⓐ Ⓑ Ⓒ Ⓓ Ⓔ

46. Ⓕ Ⓖ Ⓗ Ⓙ Ⓚ
47. Ⓐ Ⓑ Ⓒ Ⓓ Ⓔ
48. Ⓕ Ⓖ Ⓗ Ⓙ Ⓚ
49. Ⓐ Ⓑ Ⓒ Ⓓ Ⓔ
50. Ⓕ Ⓖ Ⓗ Ⓙ Ⓚ
51. Ⓐ Ⓑ Ⓒ Ⓓ Ⓔ
52. Ⓕ Ⓖ Ⓗ Ⓙ Ⓚ
53. Ⓐ Ⓑ Ⓒ Ⓓ Ⓔ
54. Ⓕ Ⓖ Ⓗ Ⓙ Ⓚ
55. Ⓐ Ⓑ Ⓒ Ⓓ Ⓔ
56. Ⓕ Ⓖ Ⓗ Ⓙ Ⓚ
57. Ⓐ Ⓑ Ⓒ Ⓓ Ⓔ
58. Ⓕ Ⓖ Ⓗ Ⓙ Ⓚ
59. Ⓐ Ⓑ Ⓒ Ⓓ Ⓔ
60. Ⓕ Ⓖ Ⓗ Ⓙ Ⓚ

ANSWER SHEET
Practice Test 1

Reading

1. Ⓐ Ⓑ Ⓒ Ⓓ	9. Ⓐ Ⓑ Ⓒ Ⓓ	17. Ⓐ Ⓑ Ⓒ Ⓓ	25. Ⓐ Ⓑ Ⓒ Ⓓ	33. Ⓐ Ⓑ Ⓒ Ⓓ
2. Ⓕ Ⓖ Ⓗ Ⓙ	10. Ⓕ Ⓖ Ⓗ Ⓙ	18. Ⓕ Ⓖ Ⓗ Ⓙ	26. Ⓕ Ⓖ Ⓗ Ⓙ	34. Ⓕ Ⓖ Ⓗ Ⓙ
3. Ⓐ Ⓑ Ⓒ Ⓓ	11. Ⓐ Ⓑ Ⓒ Ⓓ	19. Ⓐ Ⓑ Ⓒ Ⓓ	27. Ⓐ Ⓑ Ⓒ Ⓓ	35. Ⓐ Ⓑ Ⓒ Ⓓ
4. Ⓕ Ⓖ Ⓗ Ⓙ	12. Ⓕ Ⓖ Ⓗ Ⓙ	20. Ⓕ Ⓖ Ⓗ Ⓙ	28. Ⓕ Ⓖ Ⓗ Ⓙ	36. Ⓕ Ⓖ Ⓗ Ⓙ
5. Ⓐ Ⓑ Ⓒ Ⓓ	13. Ⓐ Ⓑ Ⓒ Ⓓ	21. Ⓐ Ⓑ Ⓒ Ⓓ	29. Ⓐ Ⓑ Ⓒ Ⓓ	37. Ⓐ Ⓑ Ⓒ Ⓓ
6. Ⓕ Ⓖ Ⓗ Ⓙ	14. Ⓕ Ⓖ Ⓗ Ⓙ	22. Ⓕ Ⓖ Ⓗ Ⓙ	30. Ⓕ Ⓖ Ⓗ Ⓙ	38. Ⓕ Ⓖ Ⓗ Ⓙ
7. Ⓐ Ⓑ Ⓒ Ⓓ	15. Ⓐ Ⓑ Ⓒ Ⓓ	23. Ⓐ Ⓑ Ⓒ Ⓓ	31. Ⓐ Ⓑ Ⓒ Ⓓ	39. Ⓐ Ⓑ Ⓒ Ⓓ
8. Ⓕ Ⓖ Ⓗ Ⓙ	16. Ⓕ Ⓖ Ⓗ Ⓙ	24. Ⓕ Ⓖ Ⓗ Ⓙ	32. Ⓕ Ⓖ Ⓗ Ⓙ	40. Ⓕ Ⓖ Ⓗ Ⓙ

Science

1. Ⓐ Ⓑ Ⓒ Ⓓ	9. Ⓐ Ⓑ Ⓒ Ⓓ	17. Ⓐ Ⓑ Ⓒ Ⓓ	25. Ⓐ Ⓑ Ⓒ Ⓓ	33. Ⓐ Ⓑ Ⓒ Ⓓ
2. Ⓕ Ⓖ Ⓗ Ⓙ	10. Ⓕ Ⓖ Ⓗ Ⓙ	18. Ⓕ Ⓖ Ⓗ Ⓙ	26. Ⓕ Ⓖ Ⓗ Ⓙ	34. Ⓕ Ⓖ Ⓗ Ⓙ
3. Ⓐ Ⓑ Ⓒ Ⓓ	11. Ⓐ Ⓑ Ⓒ Ⓓ	19. Ⓐ Ⓑ Ⓒ Ⓓ	27. Ⓐ Ⓑ Ⓒ Ⓓ	35. Ⓐ Ⓑ Ⓒ Ⓓ
4. Ⓕ Ⓖ Ⓗ Ⓙ	12. Ⓕ Ⓖ Ⓗ Ⓙ	20. Ⓕ Ⓖ Ⓗ Ⓙ	28. Ⓕ Ⓖ Ⓗ Ⓙ	36. Ⓕ Ⓖ Ⓗ Ⓙ
5. Ⓐ Ⓑ Ⓒ Ⓓ	13. Ⓐ Ⓑ Ⓒ Ⓓ	21. Ⓐ Ⓑ Ⓒ Ⓓ	29. Ⓐ Ⓑ Ⓒ Ⓓ	37. Ⓐ Ⓑ Ⓒ Ⓓ
6. Ⓕ Ⓖ Ⓗ Ⓙ	14. Ⓕ Ⓖ Ⓗ Ⓙ	22. Ⓕ Ⓖ Ⓗ Ⓙ	30. Ⓕ Ⓖ Ⓗ Ⓙ	38. Ⓕ Ⓖ Ⓗ Ⓙ
7. Ⓐ Ⓑ Ⓒ Ⓓ	15. Ⓐ Ⓑ Ⓒ Ⓓ	23. Ⓐ Ⓑ Ⓒ Ⓓ	31. Ⓐ Ⓑ Ⓒ Ⓓ	39. Ⓐ Ⓑ Ⓒ Ⓓ
8. Ⓕ Ⓖ Ⓗ Ⓙ	16. Ⓕ Ⓖ Ⓗ Ⓙ	24. Ⓕ Ⓖ Ⓗ Ⓙ	32. Ⓕ Ⓖ Ⓗ Ⓙ	40. Ⓕ Ⓖ Ⓗ Ⓙ

ENGLISH TEST

Time: 45 Minutes—75 Questions

> **Directions:** In the five passages that follow, certain words and phrases are underlined and numbered. In the right-hand column, you will find alternatives for the underlined part. In most cases, you are to choose the one that best expresses the idea, makes the statement appropriate for standard written English, or is worded most consistently with the style and tone of the passage as a whole. If you think the original version is best, choose "NO CHANGE." In some cases, you will find in the right-hand column a question about the underlined part. You are to choose the best answer to the question.
>
> You will also find questions about a section of the passage, or about the passage as a whole. These questions do not refer to an underlined portion of the passage, but rather are identified by a number or numbers in a box.
>
> For each question, choose the alternative you consider best and fill in the corresponding oval on your answer sheet. Read each passage through once before you begin to answer the questions that accompany it. For many of the questions, you must read several sentences beyond the question to determine the answer. Be sure that you have read far enough ahead each time you choose an alternative.

PASSAGE I

No Place I'd Rather Be

[1]

I started taking group skating lessons when I was four. I progressed through various levels rapidly and gave my first ice performance at age seven, soon I started winning local and regional competitions. I began seriously training when I was nine years old.

Mom and I would wake up at four o'clock in the morning, six days a week. I'd skate for five hours. Then I'd go to school.

1. **A.** NO CHANGE
   B. seven. Soon I started
   C. seven, soon I was
   D. seven. Soon I had

[2]

Saying good-bye to my <u>family, and friends</u> made me
                              2

homesick before I <u>even left, but I knew</u> deep down
                        3
that I had to leave and train full-time in Canada

to give my dreams a chance at reality. I went to

compete in the Olympic Games in 1992. No one,

not my coach or even my family, ever talked to

me about <u>giving up.</u> In fact, I wouldn't even allow
          4
myself to think about it. I thought my thoughts

would jinx me. <u>Yet, I</u> went with the attitude that I
                5

wanted to enjoy the Olympic spirit. ⑥

2. **F.** NO CHANGE
   G. family, and, friends
   H. family and friends,
   J. family and friends

3. Which of the following alternatives to the underlined portion would NOT be acceptable?
   A. even left yet I knew
   B. even left. I knew
   C. even left; I knew
   D. even left; however, I knew

4. Given that all of the choices are true, which one provides information that is most relevant at this point in the essay?
   F. NO CHANGE
   G. all the hard work required
   H. the joy of competing in the Olympics
   J. winning a gold medal

5. **A.** NO CHANGE
   B. Nevertheless, I
   C. However, I
   D. I

6. Which of the following statements, if added at the beginning of Paragraph 2, would most effectively introduce readers to the information presented in the paragraph?
   F. I had always wanted to move away from home, so when the opportunity presented itself, I jumped.
   G. Knowing that it was time to leave my childhood behind, I followed my coach's advice and randomly moved to Canada.
   H. Twenty-four hours after graduating from high school, I moved to Canada to train with other Olympic candidates.
   J. There was only one road to success, and hanging around my hometown waiting to be discovered wasn't it.

[3]

My practice sessions felt great leading up to the

competition. Finally, the day arrived. I remember

stepping onto the ice and thinking, *I can't do this.*

How am I going to keep myself from freaking out?

I took a deep breath and begun a solid performance
                                7

that placed me first going into the finals.

7. **A.** NO CHANGE
   B. begin
   C. began
   D. had begun

[4]

When medals were awarded, I found myself on

the top step, the gold hanging around my neck and
        8

8. **F.** NO CHANGE
   G. top step the gold, hanging
   H. top, step the gold hanging
   J. top step the gold hanging

Americas national anthem playing. Words can't
              9

describe the overwhelming mixture of emotions

I felt.

9. **A.** NO CHANGE
   B. Americas national anthem's
   C. Americas' national anthem
   D. America's national anthem

[5]

[1] Two days later, I was the first of the final six

skaters on the cold, but shimmering ice. [2] My
                10

long performance started well, but I slipped while

completing one of my easiest triple jumps, and my

hand touched the ice. [3] I didn't want to make two

mistakes in a row, so next I did a jump with just two

spins to play it safe. [4] Usually jumps have three

10. **F.** NO CHANGE
    G. cold yet shimmering, ice
    H. cold, shimmering, ice
    J. cold, shimmering ice

spins. [5] As I neared the end, I had one more jump,

the triple Lutz. [6] Okay, this is it. [7] You have to do

this, I told myself. [8] I landed perfectly. 11

[6]

Why is ice so popular? Frozen water can be
12

so painfully hard and oh so cold—just as life can be.

Ice doesn't care who skates across its surface.

It doesn't care who loses balance and falls on its
13

slippery back. Still, when the lights go on and

the crowd roars its welcome, there's no place I'd

rather be.

11. Which of the following sentences in this paragraph is LEAST relevant to the purpose of describing the narrator's actions, and therefore, could be deleted?
A. Sentence 3
B. Sentence 4
C. Sentence 5
D. Sentence 7

12. Which of the following choices best introduces this paragraph?
F. NO CHANGE
G. There are so many reasons to love ice.
H. How can anyone love ice?
J. Ice has been around forever.

13. A. NO CHANGE
B. it's
C. their
D. there

Questions 14 and 15 ask about the preceding passage as a whole.

14. For the sake of the logic and coherence of this essay, Paragraph 5 should be placed:
F. where it is now.
G. after Paragraph 3.
H. before Paragraph 1.
J. after Paragraph 6.

15. Suppose the writer's goal had been to write a brief essay about a significant event in her life. Would this essay successfully accomplish that goal?

   A. Yes, because it focuses on a specific time in the narrator's life and goes into detail about winning an Olympic gold medal.

   B. Yes, because it details every event that indirectly led to an important achievement in the narrator's life.

   C. No, because it is more of a persuasive essay motivating the readers to pursue their dreams, even if it means personal sacrifice.

   D. No, because the narrator mentions several events and doesn't go into much detail about any one event.

PASSAGE II

A Journey on Cane River

   Growing up, I knew for an absolute fact that no one on the planet was stronger than my mother. So when she told me stories of people she admired growing up, I paid attention. She was clearly in awe of her grandmother, Emily. She described her 16 grandmother as iron-willed and devilish, physically beautiful and demanding of beauty from others, determined to make her farmhouse in central Louisiana a fun place to be on Sundays when family gathered, and fanatical and unforgiving about the

16. **F.** NO CHANGE
   G. She describes
   H. Describing
   J. Because she described

responsibilities generated from family ties. On one

hand, Emily was refined, graceful, elegant,
                    17
soft-spoken, and classy. On the other, she was a

woman from the backwoods of Louisiana, possibly

born a slave, unapologetic about dipping snuff,

who buzzed on her homemade muscadine wine

each and every day.

Emily intrigued me, and the puzzle of this
                18
woman simmered on the back burner of my

conscious mind for decades, undoubtedly

activating questions about who I was as well.
  19
Hooked, I traced my mother's line to a place in

Louisiana called Cane River,

a unique area that before the Civil War housed one
                            20
of the largest and wealthiest collections of free
                            20
people of color in the United States.
                20

17. **A.** NO CHANGE
  B. Emily was, refined, graceful, elegant,
  C. Emily was refined, and graceful and
     elegant
  D. Emily was; refined, graceful, elegant,

18. **F.** NO CHANGE
  G. intrigued me, and, the puzzle
  H. intrigued me and, the puzzle
  J. intrigued me and the puzzle,

19. Which of the following alternatives to
  the underlined portion would be LEAST
  acceptable?
  A. prompting
  B. halting
  C. stirring
  D. triggering

20. If the writer were to delete the underlined
  portion from the sentence, the paragraph
  would primarily lose:
  F. details that emphasize the historical
     importance of the geographical location.
  G. a comparison of this location with the rest
     of the state of Louisiana.
  H. information that explains the narrator's
     reasons for wanting to explore the Cane River.
  J. nothing at all, since these geographical
     details are irrelevant to the paragraph.

I decided to hire a specialist on Cane River culture;
21
a genealogist to find my great-grandmother Emily's
21
grandmother.

In a collection of ten thousand unindexed local

records written in poor preserved Creole French,
22
she found the bill of sale for my great-great-great-

great-grandmother Elisabeth, whom was sold in
23
1850 in Cane River, Louisiana, for eight hundred

dollars.

One day, I had no choice. I had to write their story
24

and document their lives—my history. They were,
25
after all, real flesh-and-blood people. I pieced their

21. A. NO CHANGE
B. culture a genealogist, to
C. culture—a genealogist—to
D. culture a genealogist

22. F. NO CHANGE
G. poorly preserved
H. preserved poorly
J. preserved poor

23. A. NO CHANGE
B. whom
C. who have
D. who was

24. Given that all choices are true, which one provides the best transition between paragraphs?
F. NO CHANGE
G. Sooner or later,
H. At this point,
J. However,

25. A. NO CHANGE
B. They are,
C. I am,
D. We could be,

lives together as best I could, re-creating what life

must have been like for them during the 1800s and

1900s. 26

26. The writer is considering adding the following phrase to the preceding sentence, after the word *could*:

> from over a thousand documents uncovered in my years of research.

Should the writer make this addition?

- **F.** Yes, because it emphasizes how much work the writer had to do in order to complete the book.
- **G.** Yes, because it provides details that prove that *Cane River* is a fictional novel.
- **H.** No, because the information is unnecessary and detracts from the main idea of the sentence.
- **J.** No, because the phrase fails to specify the precise number of documents examined.

Resulting with *Cane River*, a novelized account
27
covering one hundred years in America's history and

following four generations of Creole slave women

in Cane River, Louisiana. As they struggled to keep
28
their families intact through the dark days of slavery,

the Civil War, Reconstruction, and the pre-civil rights

era of Jim Crow South. The book ended up on
29
Oprah's book list and made the *New York Times*
29
Bestseller list.
29

27.
- **A.** NO CHANGE
- **B.** The result was
- **C.** Having the result of
- **D.** Results were

28.
- **F.** NO CHANGE
- **G.** Louisiana when they
- **H.** Louisiana, they
- **J.** Louisiana, who

29. Given that all of the choices are true, which one best concludes this essay by tying this paragraph to the essay's introduction?
- **A.** NO CHANGE
- **B.** I had always wanted to write a book, and was proud of my accomplishment.
- **C.** Finally I, along with the rest of the world, had an idea of who Emily really was.
- **D.** This was the first book published about Creole slave women.

Question 30 asks about the preceding passage as a whole.

30. Suppose the writer's goal had been to describe the personal benefits of writing a book. Does this essay successfully accomplish that goal?
F. Yes, the author explains how writing *Cane River* made her a better person.
G. Yes, the author discusses why she wanted to write a book and then details the many steps involved.
H. No, because it focuses instead on biographical information about the author's family.
J. No, the essay fails to provide enough information about what the author gained from the experience of writing the book.

PASSAGE III

Illinois Prairies

There are different kinds of prairies in Illinois

depending on the moisture gradient and soil type.

The different kinds of prairie <u>wildflowers, are often</u>
                                        31

associated with these different moisture gradients

and soil types. As an ecological habitat, grasses

and herbaceous wildflowers, rather than trees and

shrubs, or areas with more or less permanent water,

<u>dominated</u> prairies.
    32

31. A. NO CHANGE
    B. wildflowers are often
    C. wildflowers often
    D. wildflowers: often

32. F. NO CHANGE
    G. dominates
    H. dominating
    J. dominate

33 High-quality prairies are interesting and

colorful places to visit during the growing season

because they demonstrate high biodiversity.
                        34

Black soil prairie was the dominant type of

prairie in central and northern Illinois, until it was
                                        35
almost totally destroyed by agricultural development

during the 19th century. The landscape of such

prairies is rather flat. A high-quality black soil prairie

has lots of wildflowers in bloom from late spring until

33. At this point in the opening paragraph, the
writer is considering adding the following
true statement:

    In Iowa, six different types of coneflowers
sway in summer breezes.

Should the writer make this addition here?

A. Yes, because it helps establish that the
essay is set in the Midwest.

B. Yes, because it helps reinforce the main
idea of the paragraph.

C. No, because it does not make clear
whether coneflowers grow in every state.

D. No, because it distracts from the main
focus of the paragraph.

34. The writer is considering deleting the
underlined portion from the sentence.
Should the phrase be kept or deleted?

F. Kept, because it provides supporting
details that reinforce the main idea of the
sentence.

G. Kept, because it establishes that prairies
contain more biodiversity than any other
habitat.

H. Deleted, because it has already been
established earlier in the paragraph that
prairies have low biodiversity.

J. Deleted, because it draws attention away
from the different types of prairies.

35. A. NO CHANGE
B. Illinois,
C. Illinois: until
D. Illinois. Until

the middle of fall. Today, small remnants of original

black soil prairie can be found in pioneer <u>cemeteries</u>
                                              36

<u>or at construction sites.</u>
      36

    [1] Gravel and dolomite prairies were never very

common in Illinois, and can be found primarily in

northern Illinois. [2] Gravel and dolomite prairies can

be rather flat, or slightly hilly. [3] <u>Yet,</u> the original
                                        37

gravel and dolomite prairies have been largely

destroyed by modern development. [4] They tend

to be rather dry and well drained. [5] More recently,

such prairies have been found along the gravelly

ballast of railroads, where they probably did not

formerly exist. 38

36. Given that all choices are grammatically correct, which one best establishes that black soil prairies are difficult to find today?
  F. NO CHANGE
  G. cemeteries or along old railroads.
  H. cemeteries, state parks, and surrounding farmland.
  J. cemeteries and in many neighborhoods.

37. A. NO CHANGE
  B. However,
  C. Unfortunately,
  D. Accordingly,

38. The writer is considering deleting the phrase "where they probably did not formerly exist" from the preceding sentence (and placing a period after the word *railroads*). Should the phrase be kept or deleted?
  F. Kept, because the information helps to establish the rampant proliferation of gravel and dolomite prairies in Illinois.
  G. Kept, because it strengthens the paragraph's focus on the unchanging landscape of prairies.
  H. Deleted, because it is not relevant to the description of gravel and dolomite prairies found in Illinois.
  J. Deleted, because the speculation is inconsistent with the claim made earlier in the paragraph that the prairies have been largely destroyed.

[6] In this case, they are degraded <u>and often contain</u>
39

<u>flora</u> from Western states. [40]
39

Hill prairies occur primarily along the Illinois

and Mississippi <u>Rivers, hill</u> prairies are very dry
41

and exposed to prevailing winds from the south or

west. The wildflowers of hill prairies are similar to

those <u>who are found</u> in the drier areas of gravel and
42

dolomite prairies.

Some species that are found in hill prairies <u>is typical</u>
43

of western areas.

Sand prairies can be <u>moist mesic or dry and</u> their
44

landscape is either flat or slightly hilly. They usually

39. A. NO CHANGE
B. and many bird species migrate to them
C. consisting of a mix of native grasses and flowers and flora
D. and are of particular interest to tourists

40. For the sake of the logic and coherence of this paragraph, Sentence 4 should be placed:
F. where it is now.
G. before Sentence 1.
H. before Sentence 3.
J. before Sentence 6.

41. A. NO CHANGE
B. rivers. Hill
C. rivers hill
D. rivers; hill,

42. F. NO CHANGE
G. which are finding
H. if found
J. that can be found

43. A. NO CHANGE
B. are more typical
C. typify
D. are more usual

44. F. NO CHANGE
G. moist mesic, or dry; and
H. moist: mesic or dry, and
J. moist, mesic, or dry, and

occur near current or former bodies of water. Their
45

vegetation is sparser than that of black soil prairies.
45

45. Given that all of the choices are true, which best
concludes the paragraph with a colorful image
that relates to the description of a sand prairie?
   A. NO CHANGE
   B. Vegetation includes woody shrubs,
   wildflowers, and native prairie grasses.
   C. The spectacular vegetation includes the
   vibrant hues of purple spiderwort, orange
   butterfly weed, and yellow goldenrod.
   D. More than sixty colorful species of
   wildflowers have been identified as being
   native to sand prairies.

PASSAGE IV

Money Monkeys

The mountainous regions of northern Japan

renowned not only for their beauty but also
46

for their hot springs, known as *onsen*. Created

naturally by the same volcanic activity that formed

the Japanese islands initially, the springs are not
47

only relaxing but believed to be therapeutic, due to

the high mineral content of their waters.

   [1] At many onsen, native populations of

Japanese Macaques, a gray, pink-faced monkey

species famed for the intelligence, make a habit
48

of dipping in them as well. [2] For the most part,

the monkeys are well mannered and cause no

problems for humans. [3] Tourists are always

especially entertained by them, and so the monkeys

46. **F.** NO CHANGE
   G. renown
   H. are renowned
   J. have been renown

47. Which of the following alternatives to
the underlined portion would NOT be
acceptable?
   A. later,
   B. themselves,
   C. on which they sit,
   D. DELETE the underlined portion (but
   preserve the comma).

48. **F.** NO CHANGE
   G. it's
   H. its
   J. they're

are gladly tolerated by the operators of the various

springs. [4] Humans are not the only creatures who

enjoy bathing in the springs. 49

At one onsen however, the clever apes are
                50
causing an amusing problem. Visitors to this

particular location encourage strongly to keep their
                      51
cars locked and their wallets and purses hidden,

because the monkeys are focused on getting their
                       52
money! After years of observing humans in line at

the gift and snack shops, the macaques at this

onsen have deduced that certain special objects
                                         53
namely paper money and coins can be exchanged
                    53
for food. In short order, the hungry simians were

sneaking into unlocked cars, grabbing money, and

trotting over to the shops to purchase themselves a

snack.

49. For the sake of the logic and coherence of this
    paragraph, Sentence 4 should be placed:
    A. where it is now.
    B. before Sentence 1.
    C. before Sentence 2.
    D. before Sentence 3.

50. F. NO CHANGE
    G. onsen, however the
    H. onsen, however, the
    J. onsen—however, the

51. A. NO CHANGE
    B. are strong with encouragement
    C. being strongly encouraged
    D. are strongly encouraged

52. Which of the following alternatives to
    the underlined portion would be LEAST
    acceptable?
    F. fixated on getting
    G. intent on getting
    H. centered on getting
    J. seeking on getting

53. A. NO CHANGE
    B. objects—namely, paper money and
       coins—can be exchanged
    C. objects, namely, paper money—and
       coins—can be exchanged
    D. objects, namely paper money and coins—
       can be exchanged

At first, <u>the flabbergasted employees didn't know</u>
    54

<u>what to do.</u> After all, the monkeys were waiting
    54

politely in line and paying for their purchases, just

like the human customers, so there was no real

reason not to accept their business.

        <u>Meanwhile,</u> however, someone pointed out that
        55

there was no possible way a monkey could get

money <u>other than</u> stealing it from a human. So
       56

now, when a cash-carrying macaque steps into

line, special monkey-specific security guards are

on hand to chase him <u>out in the hopes that</u> this will
                        57

eliminate the monkey's motive for theft.

        I suppose that makes sense, but <u>I'm disappointedly</u>
                                        58

<u>personable.</u> I'm not much of a traveler, but if there
    58

was one thing that could <u>have motivated me to fly</u>
                            59

54. If the writer were to delete the underlined
portion, the paragraph would primarily lose:
- **F.** an explanation of the fact that the
employees at this onsen were particularly
inexperienced.
- **G.** further detail about the cleverness of this
species of monkey.
- **H.** emphasis on the extremely bizarre nature
of the situation.
- **J.** foreshadowing of the fact that things
are not going to turn out well for the
monkeys.

55.
- **A.** NO CHANGE
- **B.** Additionally,
- **C.** Eventually,
- **D.** Although

56. Which of the following alternatives to
the underlined portion would be LEAST
acceptable?
- **F.** would be
- **G.** except for
- **H.** besides
- **J.** outside of

57.
- **A.** NO CHANGE
- **B.** out, in the hopes that
- **C.** out in the hopes, that
- **D.** out, in the hopes, that

58.
- **F.** NO CHANGE
- **G.** I disappoint people.
- **H.** personally I'm disappointed.
- **J.** I'm personally disappointed.

59.
- **A.** NO CHANGE
- **B.** motivate me flying
- **C.** be motivating me flying
- **D.** be motivating me to fly

halfway around the world, it's the possibility of

seeing a monkey with a wad of bills in his paw

waiting in line to buy a bag of chips. 60

60. At this point, the writer is considering adding the following true statement:

> Although I'm not even sure monkeys like chips, so I suppose I shouldn't buy my ticket just yet.

Should the writer make this addition here?

F. Yes, because it provides the necessary information that the author is a cautious person.
G. Yes, because this is a question about monkeys that is important for the reader to consider.
H. No, because the previous sentence already effectively and humorously ended the passage.
J. No, because the tone of the sentence is inconsistent with that of the rest of the passage.

PASSAGE V

The Birth of Surrealism

Joan Miró was a Catalan painter, sculptor, and

ceramicist born in Barcelona, Spain, in 1893. His work
                                                    61
has been interpreted with international acclaim,
                      61
earning a reputation as Surrealism, a sandbox
        61
for the subconscious mind, a re-creation of

the childlike, and a manifestation of Catalan

pride. In numerous interviews dating from the

1930s onwards, Miró expressing contempt for
                          62
conventional painting methods as a way of

61. A. NO CHANGE
B. He has earned international acclaim, his work
C. Interpreted as having earned international acclaim, his work is seen
D. Earning international acclaim, his work has been interpreted

62. F. NO CHANGE
G. expressed
H. had express
J. were to express

supporting bourgeois society, and famously

declared an "assassination of painting" in favor

of <u>utilizing common traditional methods of</u>
                                    63

<u>blending colors.</u>
        63

Born to the family of a goldsmith and
                        64

<u>watchmaker, the young Miró was drawn toward</u>
                            64

<u>the arts community</u> that was gathering in
        64

Montparnasse and in 1920 moved to Paris. There,

under the influence of the poets and

<u>writers, developing</u> his unique style: organic forms
            65

and flattened picture planes drawn with a sharp line.

Generally thought of as a Surrealist because of his

interest in automatism and the use of sexual symbols,

Miró was influenced in <u>varying</u> degrees by Surrealism
                            66

and Dada, yet he rejected membership in any artistic

movement in the interwar European years.

63. Which choice best illustrates Miró's contempt for conventional painting and helps explain the "assassination of painting" mentioned earlier in the sentence?
A. NO CHANGE
B. applying works of art by famous Renaissance painters.
C. boycotting painting as an art form and turning to sculpting instead.
D. rejecting the visual elements of established painting.

64. F. NO CHANGE
G. Miró was drawn to the arts community, born to the family of a goldsmith and watchmaker
H. The arts community, born to the family of a goldsmith and watchmaker, the young Miró was drawn to
J. The young Miró was drawn to the family of a goldsmith and watchmaker, born to the arts community

65. A. NO CHANGE
B. writers. He developed
C. writers, he developed
D. writers develops

66. F. NO CHANGE
G. variety
H. different and varying
J. various, multiple

Andre Breton, the founder of Surrealism described
                                            67

him as "the most Surrealist of us all."

67. **A.** NO CHANGE
    B. Breton the founder of Surrealism, described
    C. Breton: the founder of Surrealism, describe
    D. Breton, the founder of Surrealism, described

Miró often received inspiration for his paintings
                                            68

in visions, and thus, with Andre Masson, represented
  68

the beginning of Surrealism as an art movement.

68. At this point in the essay, the writer wants to highlight the influence that Miró had on painting as an art form. Given that all of the choices are true, which one would best accomplish that purpose?
    F. NO CHANGE
    G. Miró greatly disliked all bourgeois art, especially Cubism,
    H. Miró was the first artist to develop automatic drawing as a way to undo previous established techniques in painting,
    J. Miró worked heavily in ceramics in the last phase of his career,

However, Miró chose not to become an official
  69

member of the Surrealists in order to be free to

experiment with other artistic styles without

compromising his position within the group.

69. **A.** NO CHANGE
    B. Consequently,
    C. Furthermore,
    D. Thus,

He pursued his own interests in the art world,
                                            70

ranges from automatic drawing and Surrealism to
  70

Expressionism and Color Field painting.

70. **F.** NO CHANGE
    G. world, ranging
    H. world which ranges
    J. world and range

In his final decades, Miró were to accelerate his
                           71

work in different media and produced hundreds

of ceramics, including the *Wall of the Moon* and

71. **A.** NO CHANGE
    B. is accelerating
    C. accelerates
    D. accelerated

Wall of the Sun. He also made temporary window

paintings (on glass) for an exhibit. In the last years

of his life Miró wrote his most radical and least

known ideas: explored the possibilities of gas
         72

sculpture and four-dimensional painting.

He died bedridden, at his home in Palma,

Mallorca, on December 25, 1983. He suffered from

heart disease, and visits a clinic for respiratory
                      73

problems two weeks before his death. Many of his

pieces are exhibited today in the Fundació Joan

Miró in Barcelona and the U.S. National Gallery

in Washington, D.C. he is buried in Barcelona at
        74

the Montjuïc cemetery. Today, his paintings sell

for between $250,000 and $17 million, that was
                            75

the auction price for the *La Caresse des Etoiles* on

May 6, 2008, and is the highest amount paid for one

of Miró's works to date.

72. **F.** NO CHANGE
    G. known ideas exploring—
    H. known ideas. He explored
    J. known ideas, he explored

73. **A.** NO CHANGE
    B. had visited
    C. visiting
    D. were to visit

74. **F.** NO CHANGE
    G. Washington D.C. he is buried in Barcelona,
    H. Washington, D.C., he is buried, in Barcelona
    J. Washington, D.C.; he is buried in Barcelona

75. **A.** NO CHANGE
    B. million and that
    C. million, which
    D. million which

STOP

If there is still time remaining, you may review your answers.

MATHEMATICS TEST

Time: 60 Minutes—60 Questions

Directions: Solve each problem, choose the correct answer, and then fill in the corresponding oval on your answer sheet.

Do not linger over problems that take too much time. Solve as many as you can; then return to the others in the time you have left for this test.

You are permitted to use a calculator on this test. You may use your calculator for any problems you choose, but some of the problems may best be done without using a calculator.

Note: Unless otherwise stated, all of the following should be assumed.

1. Illustrative figures are NOT necessarily drawn to scale.
2. Geometric figures lie in a plane.
3. The word *line* indicates a straight line.
4. The word *average* indicates arithmetic mean.

DO YOUR FIGURING HERE

1. If $x = 3$, then $x^2 + 2x - 12 = ?$
   A. -3
   B. 0
   C. 3
   D. 6
   E. 21

2. If $3(2x - 1) = 11x + 27$, then $x = ?$
   F. -6
   G. -2
   H. 2
   J. 6
   K. 7

3. To make space for new merchandise, a clothing store offered a 15% discount on all current stock. What is the sale price of a jacket that regularly sells for $42?
   A. $6.30
   B. $8.40
   C. $35.70
   D. $37.80
   E. $41.85

4. In the figure below, line *m* is parallel to line *n*. One angle formed with transversal line *t* measures 60°, as shown. What is the measure of $\angle a$?

DO YOUR FIGURING HERE

    F. 30°
    G. 60°
    H. 90°
    J. 120°
    K. Cannot be determined

5. If $x = 3$, $y = 5$, and $w = 4$, what is the value of $xw^3 + \dfrac{3w}{2} - x^2y$?

    A.   9.0
    B.   12.0
    C.   79.5
    D. 153.0
    E. 1,689.0

6. For all x, $(3x - 5)(4x + 3) = ?$
    F. $12x^2 - 15$
    G. $12x^2 + 11x - 15$
    H. $12x^2 - 11x - 15$
    J. $12x^2 + 29x - 15$
    K. $12x^2 - 29x - 15$

7. $|5 - 8| - |9 - 3| = ?$
    A. −9
    B. −3
    C. 1
    D. 3
    E. 9

8. $(5\sqrt{3})^2 = ?$
    F. 15
    G. $10\sqrt{6}$
    H. 45
    J. $34 + 10\sqrt{3}$
    K. 75

DO YOUR FIGURING HERE

9. An urn contains 7 blue balls, 5 white balls, and 3 red balls. What is the probability that the first ball drawn at random from the urn will NOT be red?

   A. $\dfrac{7}{45}$

   B. $\dfrac{1}{5}$

   C. $\dfrac{1}{3}$

   D. $\dfrac{7}{15}$

   E. $\dfrac{4}{5}$

10. A certain watch costs $100 and a certain pearl necklace costs $300. If the cost of the watch increases by 5% and the cost of the pearl necklace decreases by 10%, what will be the sum of their new costs?

    F. $375
    G. $385
    H. $395
    J. $405
    K. $415

11. In the figure below, $\overline{CA}$ is tangent to circle O at point T. If $\overline{AT}$ = 6 units, $\overline{CT}$ = 8 units, and $\overline{CO}$ = 10 units, how many units long is the radius of the circle?

    A. 2
    B. 5
    C. 6
    D. 8
    E. 10

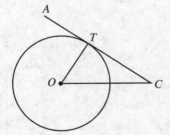

12. If $A = BC$, $B = x$, and $C = yz$, then $AB = ?$

    F. $xyzx$
    G. $yzxy$
    H. $zxyz$
    J. $xyyz$
    K. xyz

13. Which of the following inequalities specifies precisely the real values of x that are solutions to the inequality $-5 < -3x - 7$?

A. $x < 4$

B. $x < -\dfrac{2}{3}$

C. $x > -\dfrac{2}{3}$

D. $x < \dfrac{2}{3}$

E. $x > 4$

14. Which of the following expresses the equation $4x - 2y = 12$ in slope-intercept form?

F. $x = \dfrac{1}{2}y + 3$

G. $x = -\dfrac{1}{2}y + 3$

H. $y = 2x - 6$

J. $y = -2x + 6$

K. $y = -2x - 6$

15. Which of the following values for a in the equation $3x + 3a - 5 = 5x - a$ causes the solution for x to be 6?

A. -8.5

B. -4.25

C. 4.25

D. 8.5

E. 13.25

16. The centers of 3 identically sized circles lie on the diameter of a larger circle, as shown in the figure below. Each of the 4 circles is tangent to 2 other circles, as shown. If the circumference of each small circle is 8π inches, what is the circumference of the largest circle, in inches?

F. 16π

G. 24π

H. 48π

J. 64π

K. 144π

17. A recipe calls for cooking a turkey 1 hour for every 3 pounds it weighs. How long should a 19-pound turkey cook?

   A. 6 hours and 15 minutes

   B. 6 hours and 20 minutes

   C. 6 hours and 30 minutes

   D. 6 hours and $33\frac{1}{3}$ minutes

   E. 6 hours and 40 minutes

18. Dee and 4 of her friends went to a Chicago Cubs game. Their 5 seats were consecutive in the same row. The 5 people were seated randomly in those 5 seats. What is the probability that Dee would be in the middle seat?

   F. $\dfrac{1}{625}$

   G. $\dfrac{5}{625}$

   H. $\dfrac{1}{120}$

   J. $\dfrac{1}{5}$

   K. $\dfrac{4}{5}$

19. A photocopy machine enlarges a small triangle to produce a larger, similar triangle, as shown below. If the lengths of the sides, in inches, are as marked on the figure, and the triangles are similarly oriented, what is the value of x in inches?

   A. $7\frac{1}{5}$

   B. 9

   C. $9\frac{1}{2}$

   D. $9\frac{3}{5}$

   E. 11

DO YOUR FIGURING HERE

20. If the lengths of adjacent sides of a rectangular playground have measures of $4x - 3$ and $2x^2 + 7$ units, respectively, then which of the following expressions represents the area, in square units, of the playground?

    F. $2x^2 + 4x + 4$

    G. $4x^2 + 8x + 8$

    H. $8x^3 - 21$

    J. $8x^3 - 6x^2 + 28x - 21$

    K. $8x^3 + 6x^2 + 28x + 21$

DO YOUR FIGURING HERE

21. Which of the following is a prime factorization of 2,100?

    A. $2 \cdot 3 \cdot 5 \cdot 7$

    B. $2^2 \cdot 3 \cdot 5^2 \cdot 7$

    C. $2^2 \cdot 3 \cdot 5 \cdot 35$

    D. $2^2 \cdot 5^2 \cdot 21$

    E. $2^2 \cdot 550$

22. After Jean spent 90% of her vacation money, $100 remained. How much vacation money did she originally have?

    F. $111

    G. $191

    H. $900

    J. $1,000

    K. $1,111

23. Which of the following is a simplified version of $\dfrac{2x+1}{x} - \dfrac{x-3}{5x}$ whenever $x \neq 0$?

    A. $9x + 2$

    B. $9x^2 + 2x$

    C. $\dfrac{-(x-4)}{4x}$

    D. $\dfrac{9x+8}{5x}$

    E. $\dfrac{9x^2+8x}{5x^2}$

PRACTICE TEST 1

DO YOUR FIGURING HERE

24. If $2x^2 - x - 15 = 0$, what are the 2 possible values for x?

F. -5 and $\frac{3}{2}$

G. -3 and $\frac{2}{5}$

H. -3 and $\frac{5}{2}$

J. 3 and $-\frac{5}{2}$

K. 5 and $-\frac{3}{2}$

25. All angles in the figure shown below are right angles. If each side has a length of 4 centimeters, what is the area of the figure in square centimeters?

A. 32
B. 40
C. 44
D. 48
E. 80

26. In the figure below, lengths in units and angle measures in degrees are as marked. How many units long is $\overline{BC}$?

F. 3

G. $3\sqrt{2}$

H. $3\sqrt{3}$

J. 6

K. $3\sqrt{5}$

27. To increase the mean of 5 numbers by 3, by how much would the sum of the 5 numbers need to increase?

A. 3

B. 6

C. 9

D. 15

E. 18

DO YOUR FIGURING HERE

28. Josh pounded a stake into the ground. When he attached a leash to both the stake and his dog's collar, the dog could walk 12 feet from the stake in any direction. Using 3.14 for π, what is the approximate area of the lawn, in square feet, that the dog could roam while tied to the stake?

F. 38

G. 75

H. 151

J. 377

K. 452

29. Television screen sizes are determined by the diagonal length of the rectangular screen. Chad recently changed from watching a television with a 19-inch screen to a television with a similarly shaped 32-inch screen. If a car on the 19-inch screen appeared 12 inches long, how long, to the nearest inch, would the same car appear on the 32-inch screen?

A. 16

B. 18

C. 20

D. 22

E. 24

Use the following information to answer questions 30–32.

The figure below shows the top view of the Wright family's house and yard. The Wrights' rectangular house is 48 feet wide and 36 feet long, and their rectangular yard is 90 feet wide and 120 feet long. The Wrights have a rectangular garden in the back corner of their yard that is 36 feet wide and 30 feet long. The garden currently contains 60 flower bulbs: 14 hyacinth bulbs, 20 daffodil bulbs, and 26 tulip bulbs.

30. The yard will be enclosed by a fence and the back side of the house. The fence will begin at one back corner of the house and will end at the other. What is the minimum number of feet of fencing needed to enclose the yard?

F. 330
G. 360
H. 372
J. 378
K. 420

31. The area of the garden is what percent of the area of the yard (rounded to the nearest percent)?

A. 10%
B. 16%
C. 30%
D. 33%
E. 63%

32. Beginning next year, Mr. Wright will increase the number of bulbs in the garden each year so that the numbers form a geometric sequence. In 3 years, there will be 480 bulbs in the garden. By what factor will the number of bulbs be multiplied by each year?

F. 1.5

G. 2

H. 8

J. 140

K. Cannot be determined from the given information

DO YOUR FIGURING HERE

33. In the figure below, *ABCD* is a square. Points are connected on each pair of adjacent sides of *ABCD* to form 4 congruent right triangles, as shown below. Each of these triangles has one leg that is twice as long as the other leg. If the area of the shaded region is 25 square feet, what is the area of square *ABCD* in square feet?

A. 225

B. 112.5

C. 56.25

D. 45

E. 27

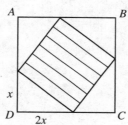

34. Which of the following is the graph of the equation $y = \dfrac{4x - 2x^2}{x}$ in the standard (x, y) coordinate plane?

F.

G.

H.

J.

K.

35. A line in a plane separates the plane into how many regions of points that do not contain the line?

A. 0

B. 1

C. 2

D. 3

E. Cannot be determined

36. What is the maximum number of distinct diagonals that can be drawn in the hexagon shown below?

    F. 12
    G. 9
    H. 6
    J. 5
    K. 4

DO YOUR FIGURING HERE

37. In the standard (x, y) coordinate plane, the center of a circle lies in quadrant III. If the circle is tangent to the x-axis and the y-axis and its radius is 4, which of the following is an equation for the circle?

    A. $(x + 4)^2 + (y + 4)^2 = 4$
    B. $(x - 4)^2 + (y - 4)^2 = 4$
    C. $x^2 + (y - 4)^2 = 16$
    D. $(x + 4)^2 + (y + 4)^2 = 16$
    E. $(x + 4)^2 + (y - 4)^2 = 16$

38. How must $-\dfrac{3}{5}, -\dfrac{4}{7}, -\dfrac{5}{6},$ and $-\dfrac{8}{9}$ be arranged so that they are listed in increasing order?

    F. $-\dfrac{8}{9} < -\dfrac{5}{6} < -\dfrac{3}{5} < -\dfrac{4}{7}$
    G. $-\dfrac{8}{9} < -\dfrac{5}{6} < -\dfrac{4}{7} < -\dfrac{3}{5}$
    H. $-\dfrac{4}{7} < -\dfrac{3}{5} < -\dfrac{5}{6} < -\dfrac{8}{9}$
    J. $-\dfrac{3}{5} < -\dfrac{4}{7} < -\dfrac{5}{6} < -\dfrac{8}{9}$
    K. $-\dfrac{5}{6} < -\dfrac{8}{9} < -\dfrac{3}{5} < -\dfrac{4}{7}$

PRACTICE TEST 1

Use the following information to answer
questions 39–42.

In the standard (x, y) coordinate plane below,
P is located at $(0, 2)$, Q is located at $(4, 2)$, and
R is located at $(0, 5)$ to form right triangle
$\triangle PQR$. The given lengths are in coordinate
units.

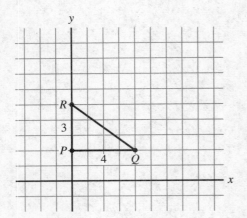

39. What is the slope of $\overline{QR}$?

A. $-\dfrac{4}{3}$

B. $-\dfrac{3}{4}$

C. 0

D. $\dfrac{3}{4}$

E. $\dfrac{4}{3}$

40. What is the midpoint of $\overline{QR}$?

F. $\left(2, \dfrac{3}{2}\right)$

G. $\left(2, \dfrac{7}{2}\right)$

H. $\left(\dfrac{7}{2}, 2\right)$

J. $4, 2$

K. $\left(4, \dfrac{3}{2}\right)$

41. Which of the following expressions gives the measure of $\angle PRQ$?

   A. $\cos^{-1}\left(\frac{4}{3}\right)$

   B. $\cos^{-1}\left(\frac{3}{4}\right)$

   C. $\sin^{-1}\left(\frac{4}{3}\right)$

   D. $\tan^{-1}\left(\frac{4}{3}\right)$

   E. $\tan^{-1}\left(\frac{3}{4}\right)$

42. Right triangle $\triangle PQR$ will be rotated about the y-axis to form a right circular cone. How long, in coordinate units, is the diameter of the cone's base?

   F. 3

   G. 4

   H. 6

   J. 8

   K. 16

43. The perimeter of an elliptical billiard table is to be covered with red velvet. The perimeter of an ellipse is given by the formula $p = \frac{\pi}{2}\sqrt{2(l^2 + w^2)}$, where l is the length and w is the width, as shown in the diagram below.

If the length is 4 feet and the width is 3 feet, what is the outside perimeter of the ellipse in feet?

   A. $\frac{5}{2}\pi\sqrt{2}$

   B. $\frac{\pi}{2}(4\sqrt{2}+3)$

   C. $\frac{7}{2}\pi\sqrt{2}$

   D. $(4\pi+3)\sqrt{2}$

   E. $5\pi\sqrt{2}$

DO YOUR FIGURING HERE

PRACTICE TEST 1

44. If $\dfrac{A}{28} + \dfrac{B}{126} = \dfrac{9A + 2B}{x}$, and A, B, and x are integers greater than 1, what must x equal?

DO YOUR FIGURING HERE

   F.   11

   G.   154

   H.   252

   J. 1,134

   K. 3,528

45. Which one of the following expresses the number of meters that a contestant must travel in a 5-lap race around a circular track with a radius of R meters?

   A. $5R$

   B. $5\pi R$

   C. $5\pi R^2$

   D. $6R$

   E. $10\pi R$

46 In $\triangle ABC$, shown below, the measure of $\angle B$ is 40°, the measure of $\angle C$ is 35°, and $\overline{AB}$ is 27 units long. Which one of the following is an expression of the length, in units, of $\overline{BC}$?

(Note: The law of sines states that for any triangle, the ratio between the sine of an angle and the length of the side opposite that angle is the same for all of the interior angles in the triangle.)

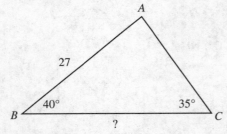

   F. $\dfrac{27(\sin 105°)}{\sin 40°}$

   G. $\dfrac{27(\sin 105°)}{\sin 35°}$

   H. $\dfrac{27(\sin 75°)}{\sin 40°}$

   J. $\dfrac{27(\sin 40°)}{\sin 105°}$

   K. $\dfrac{27(\sin 35°)}{\sin 75°}$

47. For $i^2 = -1$, $(5 - i)^2 = ?$

    A. 24

    B. 26

    C. $24 - 5i$

    D. $24 - 10i$

    E. $26 + 10i$

48. If x and y are integers such that $y > 12$ and $2x + y = 19$, which of the following is the solution set for x?

    F. $x \geq 4$

    G. $x \geq 3$

    H. $x \leq 4$

    J. $x \leq 3$

    K. $x \leq 0$

49. If $pq^3t^4 > 0$, which of the following products must be positive?

    A. pq

    B. pt

    C. qt

    D. pqt

    E. pq^2

50. If $\log_3 81 = x + 1$, then $x = ?$

    F. 3

    G. 4

    H. 5

    J. 6

    K. 243

51. A flight instructor charges $75 per lesson, plus an additional fee for the use of his plane. The charge for the use of his plane varies directly with the cube root of the time the plane is used. If a lesson plus 27 minutes of plane usage costs $120, what is the total amount charged for a lesson involving 64 minutes of plane usage?

    A. $195

    B. $180

    C. $157

    D. $135

    E. $60

DO YOUR FIGURING HERE

52. In △ABD shown below, C is on $\overline{BD}$, $\overline{AC} \perp \overline{BD}$, the length of $\overline{AD}$ is 6 inches, the length of $\overline{BD}$ is 10 inches, and sin d = 0.8. What is the area of △ABD in square inches?

DO YOUR FIGURING HERE

F. 6
G. 12
H. 24
J. 30
K. 60

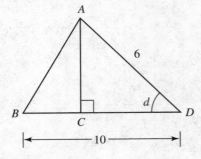

53. For real numbers x and y, when is the equation |2x + 3y| = |2x − 3y| true?

A. Never
B. Always
C. Only when 2x = 3y
D. Only when x = 0 and y = 0
E. Only when x = 0 or y = 0

54. Bronwyn has $4.23 in quarters ($0.25), dimes ($0.10), nickels ($0.05), and pennies ($0.01). She arranges these coins in rows and notices that there are 6 more dimes than quarters, 3 more nickels than quarters, and 20 more pennies than quarters. How many pennies does Bronwyn have?

F. 8
G. 13
H. 20
J. 27
K. 28

55. For some real number A, the graph of y = (A + 3)x + 5 in the standard (x, y) coordinate plane passes through the point (3, 11). What is the slope of this line?

A. −5
B. −2
C. −1
D. 2
E. $5\frac{1}{3}$

56. In the figure below, $\overline{BF}$ is a line segment with point C between B and F; all distances are given in inches. What is the ratio of the area of quadrilateral *RBCS* to the area of quadrilateral *SCFT*?

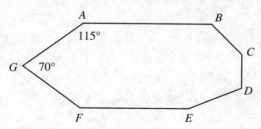

F. 9:7

G. 7:9

H. 11:13

J. 11:39

K. 11:50

57. When graphed in the standard (x, y) coordinate plane, the graphs of $y = x^2 - 5$ and $y = x + 1$ intersect at which of the following points?

A. $(-3, 2)$ and $(2, 3)$

B. $(-3, 4)$ and $(2, -1)$

C. $(3, -4)$ and $(-2, 1)$

D. $(3, 4)$ and $(-2, -1)$

E. The graphs do not intersect.

58. In septagon *ABCDEFG* shown below, $\angle A = 115°$ and $\angle G = 70°$. What is the sum of the measures of the other 5 interior angles?

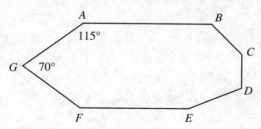

F. 585°

G. 595°

H. 655°

J. 690°

K. 715°

59. For all real numbers x and y such that the product of y and 4 is x, which of the following expressions represents the sum of y and 4 in terms of x?

A. $x + 4$

B. $4x + 4$

C. $4(x + 4)$

D. $\dfrac{x + 4}{4}$

E. $\dfrac{x + 16}{4}$

60. What is $\cos \dfrac{7\pi}{12}$ given that $\dfrac{7\pi}{12} = \dfrac{\pi}{3} + \dfrac{\pi}{4}$ and that $\cos (A + B) = \cos A\,(\cos B) - \sin A\,(\sin B)$?

(Note: You may use the following table of values.)

θ	$\sin \theta$	$\cos \theta$
$\dfrac{\pi}{6}$	$\dfrac{1}{2}$	$\dfrac{\sqrt{3}}{2}$
$\dfrac{\pi}{4}$	$\dfrac{\sqrt{2}}{2}$	$\dfrac{\sqrt{2}}{2}$
$\dfrac{\pi}{3}$	$\dfrac{\sqrt{3}}{2}$	$\dfrac{1}{2}$

F. $\dfrac{\sqrt{2} - \sqrt{6}}{4}$

G. $-\dfrac{1}{4}$

H. $\dfrac{\sqrt{2} - \sqrt{3}}{4}$

J. 0.999

K. $\dfrac{1 + \sqrt{2}}{2}$

If there is still time remaining, you may review your answers.

READING TEST

Time: 35 Minutes—40 Questions

Directions: There are four passages in this test. Each passage is followed by several questions. After reading a passage, choose the best answer to each question and fill in the corresponding oval on your answer sheet. You may refer to the passages as often as necessary.

PASSAGE I—LITERARY NARRATIVE

This passage is adapted from the short story *The First Sense* by Nadine Gordimer (© 2006).

She has never felt any resentment that he became a musician and she didn't. Could hardly call her amateur flute playing a vocation. She sits at a computer in a city-government office earn-
(5) ing a salary that has at least provided regularly for their basic needs.

She found when she was still an adolescent that her father, with his sports shop and the beguiling heartiness that is a qualification for
(10) that business, and her mother, with her group-ies exchanging talk of female maladies, did not have in their comprehension what it was that she wanted to do.

A school outing at sixteen had taken her to a
(15) concert where she heard, coming out of a slim tube held to human lips, the call of the flute. The teacher who had arranged the cultural event was understanding enough to put the girl in touch with a musical youth group in the city. She ba-
(20) bysat on weekends to pay for the hire of a flute, and began to attempt to learn how to produce with her own breath and fingers something of what she had heard.

He was among the Youth Players. His instrument
(25) was the very antithesis of the flute. The sounds he drew from the overgrown violin between his knees: the complaining moo of a sick cow, the rasp of a blunt saw. "Excuse me!" he would say, with a clownish lift of the eyebrows and a down-
(30) twisted mouth. Within a year, his exceptional talent had been recognized by the professional musicians who coached these young people.

They played together when alone, to amuse themselves and secretly imagine that they were
(35) already in concert performance, the low, powerful cadence coming from the golden-brown body of the cello making her flute voice sound, by contrast, more like that of a squeaking mouse. In time, she reached a certain level of minor
(40) accomplishment. He couldn't deceive her and let her suffer the disillusions of persisting with a career that was not open to her level of perfor-mance. "You'll still have the pleasure of playing the instrument you love best." She would always
(45) remember what she said: "The cello is the instru-ment I love best."

Sometimes she fell asleep to the low tender tones of what had become his voice, the voice of that big curved instrument, sharing the intimacy
(50) that was hers. At concerts, when his solo part came, she did not realize that she was smiling in recognition, that his was a voice she would have recognized anywhere. She was aware that, without a particular ability of her own, she was
(55) privileged enough to have an interesting life, and a remarkably talented man whose milieu was also hers.

He began to absent himself from her at un-explained times or for obligations that he must
(60) have known she knew didn't exist. She had sug-gestions for relaxation: a film or a dinner. He was not enthusiastic. "Next week, next week." He took the revered cello out of its solitude in the case and played, to himself, to her—well,
(65) she was in the room those evenings. It was his voice, that glorious voice of his cello, saying something different, speaking not to her but to some other. The voice of the cello doesn't lie.

She waited for him to speak. About what had
(70) happened. To trust the long confidence between
them. He never did. And she did not ask, because
she was also afraid that what had happened, once
admitted, would be irrevocably real.

One night, he got up in the dark, took the
(75) cello out of its bed, and played. She woke to the
voice, saying something passionately angry in
its deepest bass. She knew that the affair was
over. She felt a pull of sadness—for him. For
herself, nothing. By never confronting him she
(80) had stunned herself.

1. If the fourth paragraph (lines 24–32) were
    omitted from the passage, the reader would
    not know:
    A. that he played the violin.
    B. how the couple met.
    C. that he became a famous musician.
    D. that he was an angry person.

2. Which of the following best describes
    what the first paragraph reveals about
    her character?
    F. She has a rewarding and high-paying
        career.
    G. She earns money playing a flute.
    H. She is generous and pragmatic.
    J. She regrets not becoming a musician.

3. Which of the following can most reasonably
    be inferred from the passage about her
    parents' feelings about music?
    A. They are accomplished musicians.
    B. They do not have a capacity for music
        themselves, but support her interest.
    C. They are opposed to her becoming a
        musician.
    D. They didn't understand why she would
        want to pursue a career in music.

4. In lines 45–46 the statement "The cello is
    the instrument I love best" most nearly
    communicates what?
    F. She would rather play the cello than play
        the flute.
    G. She will stop playing the flute so that she
        can play the cello.
    H. She never really loved playing the flute.
    J. She loves him more than she loves playing
        the flute.

5. The main conflict in this passage can best be
    described as:
    A. both he and she want to become famous
        musicians, but only one of them is able.
    B. challenges she faces as the girlfriend of a
        famous musician.
    C. tension created when he starts distancing
        himself from her.
    D. her need to choose between the flute and
        the cello.

6. It can reasonably be inferred from the
    passage that she views him as:
    F. a competent competitor.
    G. a teacher and a mentor.
    H. someone whose responsibility it is to
        entertain her.
    J. a talented musician whose opinion she
        respects.

7. In line 68 the statement "The voice of the
    cello doesn't lie" mostly means:
    A. that she can tell something is wrong
        because of the music he plays.
    B. the cello is telling her what is bothering him.
    C. he is using music to communicate his
        love for her.
    D. he is playing the cello in order to
        demonstrate its power to deliver a
        message to her.

8. Which of the following statements describing how she feels about his musical ability is most clearly supported by the passage?

F. She respects him, but gets annoyed at how often he is out of town playing concerts.

G. She is jealous that he is so much better than she is.

H. She loves listening to him play, and enjoys the life of a musician's partner.

J. She is proud of his success and takes advantage of the opportunities that brings for her to play the flute.

9. The main purpose of the sixth paragraph (lines 47–57) is to:

A. illustrate his success.

B. show how intimate their relationship is.

C. explain why she gets upset when he leaves her.

D. tell the reader more about his voice.

10. Why didn't he encourage her to pursue a career as a musician?

F. He didn't want the competition.

G. He was jealous of her abilities.

H. He wanted her to earn steady money for them.

J. He didn't think she was talented enough.

PASSAGE II—SOCIAL SCIENCE

This passage is adapted from "The Disappearing Computer" by Bill Gates, which appeared in *The World in 2003* (*The Economist*) (© 2002 by The Economist).

A few years from now, the average home entertainment system might not look much different than it does today. But it will probably have an Internet connection that enables it to
(5) download and play digital music and video, display album artwork and song titles on the television, and even interrupt your listening if an important message arrives. It will have a central processor, disk storage, graphics hardware
(10) and some kind of intuitive user interface. Add a wireless mouse and keyboard, and this home entertainment system will start looking a lot like a personal computer. Will people buy and use these systems in large numbers? Absolutely. Will
(15) they think of them as computers? Probably not.

According to Gartner Dataquest, an American research firm, the world computer industry shipped its one billionth PC in 2002, and another billion more are expected to be built in the next
(20) six years. Add to this the exploding number of embedded computers—the kind found in mobile phones, gas pumps and retail point-of-sale systems—which are fast approaching the power and complexity of desktop PCs. On one
(25) estimate, people in the United States already interact with about 150 embedded systems every day, whether they know it or not. These systems, which use up to 90 percent of the microprocessors produced today, will inevitably
(30) take on more PC-like characteristics, and will be able to communicate seamlessly with their traditional PC counterparts. They will also become amazingly ubiquitous. In 2001, according to the Semiconductor Industry Association, the
(35) world microchip industry produced around 60 million transistors for every man, woman and child on earth. That number will rise to one billion by 2010.

At the same time, the general-purpose PC as we
(40) know it today will continue to play an important, and increasingly central, role in most people's lives, but it will be at the center of a wide range of intelligent devices that most people wouldn't think of as "computers" today. This scenario is
(45) in sharp contrast to the computers of just a few years ago—back in the pre-Internet age—which were still mostly passive appliances that sat in the corner of the den or living room. Back then, people used their PCs for little more than writ-
(50) ing letters and documents, playing games or managing their family finances.

But today we are truly in a digital decade, in which the intelligence of the PC is finding its way into all kinds of devices, transforming them from
(55) passive appliances into far more significant and indispensable tools for everyday life. Many of the core technologies of computing-processing power, storage capacity, graphics capabilities and network connectivity are all continuing to
(60) advance at a pace that matches or even exceeds Moore's Law (which famously, and correctly, predicted that the number of transistors on a computer chip would double every two years).

As people find more ways to incorporate these
(65) inexpensive, flexible and infinitely customizable devices into their lives, the computers themselves will gradually "disappear" into the fabric of our lives. We are still a long way from a world full of disembodied intelligent machines, but the
(70) computing experience of the coming decade will be so seamless and intuitive that, increasingly, we will barely notice it. At the same time, computing will become widespread enough that we will take it for granted—just as most
(75) people in the developed world today trust the telephone service.

The pervasiveness and near-invisibility of computing will be helped along by new technologies such as cheap, flexible displays, fingernail-
(80) sized chips capable of storing terabytes of data, or inductively powered computers that rely on heat and motion from their environment to run without batteries.

The economics of computing will also bring
(85) change. Decreasing costs will make it easy for electronics manufacturers to include PC-like intelligence and connectivity in even the most mundane devices.

All this will lead to a fundamental change in
(90) the way we perceive computers. Using one will become like using electricity when you turn on a light. Computers, like electricity, will play a role in almost everything you do, but computing itself will no longer be a discrete experience. We will
(95) be focused on what we can do with computers,

not on the devices themselves. They will be all around us, essential to almost every part of our lives, but they will effectively have "disappeared."

11. This passage is best described as being:
   A. an analysis of how computers are vanishing from everyday use in society.
   B. an argument in support of introducing more computer-friendly products.
   C. an examination of the changing roles computers have in people's lives.
   D. a thorough evaluation of the benefits and drawbacks of using computers.

12. The author uses all of the following sources of evidence to support his claims EXCEPT:
   F. research data gathered by professionals.
   G. the opinion of a scientist.
   H. statistics provided by industry experts.
   J. reference to a famous mathematical prediction.

13. The word *ubiquitous*, as used in line 33, most likely means:
   A. small.
   B. difficult to find.
   C. inexpensive.
   D. ever-present.

14. According to the passage, new technologies and decreasing costs of electronics will lead directly to an increase in all of the following EXCEPT:
   F. interconnectivity among objects.
   G. the presence of computer intelligence in everyday objects.
   H. the amount of power and batteries that will be required to run computers.
   J. computers being involved in most aspects of life.

15. Which of the following best describes how the author predicts people will perceive computers in the future?
    A. Computers will be so much a part of everyday life that people will hardly notice them.
    B. Computers will have disappeared from people's lives.
    C. People will be afraid of how invasive computers have become and will use them less.
    D. Computers will be everywhere and people will be very aware of using them constantly and will become dependent on them.

16. The word *disappeared* used in line 98 most likely refers to the idea that:
    F. people will no longer use computers.
    G. computers will be so embedded in people's everyday lives that they won't even notice them anymore.
    H. computers will become invisible.
    J. computers will become so small and will be inside so many other objects that people will not be able to see them anymore.

17. All of the following are identified in the passage as parts of a future entertainment system EXCEPT:
    A. a satellite.
    B. graphics hardware.
    C. a wireless keyboard.
    D. an Internet connection.

18. The author refers to computers of the past as "passive appliances" (line 55) because:
    F. they were indispensable tools for everyday life.
    G. they were incapable of complex tasks.
    H. they remained in one location.
    J. people only used them occasionally for specific tasks.

19. The main point of the second paragraph (lines 16–38) can best be summarized as:
    A. there are more microchips than people.
    B. microprocessors are being produced more quickly than we can use them.
    C. both the number of and uses for microprocessors is rapidly increasing.
    D. there is more need for microprocessors than for personal computers.

20. In the first paragraph, the author suggests that all of the following are core technologies EXCEPT:
    F. storage capacity.
    G. power profiles.
    H. graphics capabilities.
    J. network connectivity.

PASSAGE III—HUMANITIES

Passage A is adapted from "A Defence of Poetry" by Percy Bysshe Shelley (1821). Passage B is adapted from "The Poetics of Disobedience" by Alice Notley (1998).

Passage A by Percy Bysshe Shelley

A poem is the very image of life expressed in its eternal truth. There is this difference between a story and a poem, that a story is a catalogue of detached facts, which have no other connection
(5) than time, place, circumstance, cause and effect; the other is the creation of actions according to the unchangeable forms of human nature, which is itself the image of all other minds. Time, which destroys the beauty and the use of the story of
(10) particular facts, stripped of the poetry which should invest them, augments that of poetry, and forever develops new and wonderful applications of the eternal truth which it contains.

The functions of the poetical faculty are two-
(15) fold: by one it creates new materials of knowledge, and power, and pleasure; by the other it engenders in the mind a desire to reproduce and arrange them according to a certain rhythm and order which may be called the beautiful and the

(20) good. The cultivation of poetry is never more to be desired than at periods when, from an excess of the selfish and calculating principle, the accumulation of the materials of external life exceed the quantity of the power of assimilating them (25) to the internal laws of human nature. Poetry is the record of the best and happiest moments of the happiest and best minds.

The most unfailing herald, companion, and follower of the awakening of a great people to (30) work a beneficial change in opinion or institution, is poetry. At such periods there is an accumulation of the power of communicating and receiving intense and impassioned conceptions respecting man and nature. The person (35) in whom this power resides, may often, as far as regards many portions of their nature, have little apparent correspondence with that spirit of good of which they are the ministers. But even whilst they deny, they are yet compelled to (40) serve that power which is seated on the throne of their own soul.

It is impossible to read the compositions of the most celebrated writers without being startled with the electric life which burns within (45) their words. They measure the circumference and sound the depths of human nature with a comprehensive and all-penetrating spirit, and they are themselves perhaps the most sincerely astonished at its manifestations; for it is less their (50) spirit than the spirit of the age. Poets are the hierophants of an unapprehended inspiration; the mirrors of the gigantic shadows which futurity casts upon the present; the words which express what they understand not; the trumpets which (55) sing to battle, and feel not what they inspire; the influence which is moved not, but moves. Poets are the unacknowledged legislators of the world.

Passage B by Alice Notley

For a long time I've seen my job as bound up with the necessity of noncompliance with (60) pressures, dictates, atmospheres of society at large, my own past practices as well. For a long time—well in fact since the beginning, since I learned how to be a poet inside the more rebellious wing of poetry. Learning itself meant (65) a kind of disobedience, so like most words the Dis word, the Dis form, cannot be worshipped either—that would be an obedience anyway. I've spoken in other places of the problems, too, of subjects that hadn't been broached much in (70) poetry and of how it seemed one had to disobey the past and the practices of literary males in order to talk about what was going on most literarily around one.

It seems as if one must disobey everyone else (75) in order to see at all. This is a persistent feeling in a poet, but staying alert to all the ways one is coerced into denying experience, sense, and reason is a huge task. I recently completed a very long poem called *Disobedience* but I didn't (80) realize that disobeying was what I was doing, what perhaps I'd always been doing until the beginning of the end of it, though the tone throughout was one of rejection of everything I was supposed to be or to affirm.

(85) It's possible that my biggest act of disobedience has consistently, since I was an adolescent, been against the idea that all truth comes from books, really other people's books. I hate the fact that whatever I say or write, someone reading or (90) listening will try to find something out of their reading I "sound like." 'You sound just like ...,' 'you remind me of ...,' 'have you read ...?' I've been trying to train myself for thirty or forty years not to believe anything anyone tells me. (95) It's necessary to maintain a state of disobedience against ... everything.

Questions 21–24 ask about Passage A.

21. The passage characterizes poetry as being all of the following EXCEPT:
   A. produced by special and advanced people.
   B. an accurate source of scientific information.
   C. true for all time.
   D. a valuable corrective to society.

22. As it is used in line 14, the word *faculty* most nearly means:
   F. easiness.
   G. staff.
   H. goal.
   J. ability.

23. The passage cites "the selfish and calculating principle" (line 22) as an example of:
   A. something that keeps the work of inferior poets from being truly great and immortal.
   B. a character flaw that even the greatest poets seek to cover up in themselves.
   C. a socially influenced human tendency that makes poetry immediately necessary.
   D. a reason why certain politically powerful individuals pretend to dislike poetry.

24. The passage closes by suggesting that poets:
   F. have a much greater influence on the course of human civilization than most people realize.
   G. are on rare occasions even imbued with the ability to predict the future.
   H. are generally less emotionally affected by their own work than other people are.
   J. may have had a hand in starting wars from time to time in history.

Questions 25–27 ask about Passage B.

25. The author characterizes disobedience as being all of the following EXCEPT:
   A. a healthy way of taking people's opinions.
   B. an attitude that she even applies to poetry.
   C. the title of her own most famous work.
   D. something that must itself be disobeyed.

26. In the context of the passage, the phrases that appear in quotation marks in the final paragraph function as examples of:
   F. "pressures, dictates, atmospheres of society" (line 60).
   G. "subjects that hadn't been broached much in poetry" (lines 69–70).
   H. "all the ways one is coerced into denying experience" (lines 76–77).
   J. "my biggest act of disobedience" (lines 85–86).

27. Based on the passage, the author seems to regard her duty as a poet as involving:
   A. protest against traditional concept of ethics and justice.
   B. preventing her mode of expression from becoming contaminated.
   C. questioning whether writing poetry is a morally acceptable way of making a living.
   D. preventing male poets of the past from being taught so frequently in schools.

Questions 28–30 ask about both passages.

28. One of the most obvious differences between the two passages is that:
   F. Passage B regards society with skepticism, whereas Passage A is in agreement with most of society's opinions.
   G. Only Passage A makes reference to any of the author's own poetical works.
   H. Only Passage B attempts to explain the essential difference between poetry and fiction.
   J. Passage A sees poetry as serving something objective, whereas Passage B sees it as a totally subjective matter.

29. Which of the following does *neither* of the two passages contain?

A. An opinion about whether poetry should be read in books or heard aloud

B. A characterization of what poets themselves are like as people

C. An assertion that poets speak for someone or something other than themselves

D. A reference to the types of poetical subjects the author favors in his or her work

30. Despite their many differences, which of the following is something about which the two passages *agree*?

F. The idea that only a certain rare type of person is able to write poetry well

G. The fact that poetry ideally performs a necessary moral duty for society

H. The suggestion that writing poetry the right way will make one a happier person

J. The assertion that the poetry of the past is less valuable than the poetry of the present

PASSAGE IV—NATURAL SCIENCE

This passage is adapted from "The Truth Behind Lightsaber Technology" by Matt Gluesenkamp (© 2010 General Electric).

There are a lot of myths and legends about lasers that Hollywood has generated or perpetu-ated over the years, but perhaps the most well-known instance of "lasers" in cinema are the
(5) lightsabers from the *Star Wars* saga. I put quotes around "lasers" because the way lightsabers behave in these movies is quite a bit different from the way lasers behave in real life.

In the *Star Wars* universe, lightsabers are typi-
(10) cally custom-built by Jedi and Sith warriors, and all have several common elements. Each has a power source, a lightsaber crystal, one or more focusing crystals, and a stabilizing emitter system.

The power source is typically a diatium power cell,
(15) often with a capacity of several megawatt-hours. The lightsaber crystal converts the power cell's energy into a plasma that is then passed through and directed by the focusing crystals. Finally, the emitter system stabilizes the plasma into a
(20) blade shape using a mix of power modulation and magnetic field containment.

Did that make sense to anyone? No? Good, then I'm not alone. Science fiction is typically a blend of materials or physical laws that exist
(25) and some that don't. Although real-life battery technology is coming along great, we are a long way off from creating handheld batteries with capacities like the ones found in the lightsaber's diatium power cell. Perhaps the key lies in dis-
(30) covering this fictional "diatium" material? And although crystals do have many useful optical and piezoelectric properties, I don't know of one that could magically create plasma from electricity. (However, I read that the crystals must
(35) be "attuned to the Force" by a Jedi or Sith in a meditation ritual that can take days, so maybe we should start there.)

Where the explanations of lightsaber technology get really convoluted is when they start talking
(40) about how the blade is shaped and contained. Magnetic fields are currently used to contain plasmas, but they are generated by machinery that must also surround it—generating such a magnetic envelope from a single, unidirectional
(45) source would likely require some new laws of physics. There are no crystals that can "direct" a plasma.

In fact, a plasma being "directed" by a crystal lens doesn't even make any physical sense. A
(50) plasma is really just an ionized gas—a gas in which the electrons have been stripped from their atomic nuclei. We see plasmas all the time. They make up and are emitted from every star, like our solar wind and solar flares. The inter-
(55) action of the solar wind with Earth's magnetic field produces the *aurora borealis*, or northern

lights—another form of plasma. Plasmas are also the stuff of every spark and lightning bolt.

(60) Plasmas can be created by bringing gases up to a high energy level. The higher the energy, the more atoms will be stripped of their electrons, and the better quality plasma we will have. It's completely possible that one could create a plasma by producing a large enough voltage difference—as (65) with lightning—or a powerful enough laser focus. However, enormous amounts of energy are required with either of these approaches, and it would be extremely difficult to control the plasma's shape. An electrical arc can have wild shifts in direction, (70) and it can hardly be controlled without being surrounded by magnets. A laser will go in a straight line … but, of course, it doesn't stop. A laser-based lightsaber would require a block or a couple of mirrors floating in midair, moving in sync with (75) the hilt, which is largely impossible. On top of that, they would certainly melt in the presence of such a plasma anyway. Furthermore, all of this says nothing about what the actual quality of the plasma would be and how reliably or quickly it (80) would cut through objects.

So it seems quite impossible to create a lightsaber, as seen in the *Star Wars* films, using existing technologies, materials, and physical laws. But given the enthusiasm of *Star Wars* (85) superfans out there, I wouldn't be surprised if people are trying.

31. The author of this passage would most likely agree with which of the following statements?
   A. The authors who invented science fiction never intended for it to depict things like lightsabers.
   B. Science-fiction films can give people inaccurate ideas about the world that really surrounds them.
   C. One should "never say never," because anything might be possible someday.
   D. The content of science-fiction films should be more carefully regulated by the government.

32. The main point of the fifth paragraph (lines 48–58) is that:
   F. Real-life crystals are not nearly powerful enough to direct plasma at high temperatures.
   G. Studying lightning would be the logical first step in the construction of a lightsaber.
   H. The commonness of plasmas in the real world is a good sign for lightsaber technology.
   J. The idea of plasma having a predetermined "shape" is inherently absurd.

33. According to the passage, which of the following is an example of a plasma, either real or fictional?
   A. The *aurora borealis*
   B. A wild electrical arc
   C. Earth's magnetic field
   D. Diatium crystals

34. As it is used in line 39, the word *convoluted* most nearly means:
   F. possible.
   G. precise.
   H. interesting.
   J. confusing.

35. If a new crystal were discovered that might make plasma-lightsaber technology possible, how would the author most likely feel about this discovery?
   A. Embarrassed and angry at having been proven wrong
   B. Excited that his lifelong dream of owning a lightsaber might be about to come true
   C. Interested in the new opportunities promised by such a discovery
   D. Concerned that such a discovery will detract from the seriousness of the scientific profession

36. The main purpose of the third paragraph (lines 22–37) is to:
    F. establish that the author is not in fact an expert in the type of science being discussed.
    G. explain in a humorous fashion that the official explanation of lightsabers borders on nonsense.
    H. remind the reader of the important difference between science fiction and fantasy.
    J. express disdain for the silliness of the *Star Wars* film series.

37. According to the passage, which of the following would be LEAST likely to be involved in a real-life lightsaber?
    A. Crystals
    B. Batteries
    C. Magnetic fields
    D. An ionized gas

38. Which of the following statements about plasmas is accurate, according to information in the passage?
    F. They can be directed by magnetic fields.
    G. They are rarely visible to the naked eye.
    H. They are typically slow moving.
    J. They nearly always take up large amounts of space.

39. Which of the following is true about the author's attitude toward the *Star Wars* films?
    A. Even by Hollywood standards, they are exceptionally inaccurate in their presentation of science.
    B. They have an adoring fan base that retains hope in fanciful scientific ideas despite the odds.
    C. They insult their audience by depicting wildly unfeasible technology with little explanation.
    D. They have indirectly helped society by making generations of people more enthusiastic about science.

40. Which of the following is NOT mentioned in the passage as an obstacle to the creation of a real lightsaber?
    F. The difficulty of developing a sufficiently compact power source
    G. The practical impossibility of containing a plasma field in a way that renders it small and portable
    H. The likelihood that such "blades" would just pass through each other, making dueling impossible
    J. The difficulty of controlling a plasma's shape

STOP

If there is still time remaining, you may review your answers.

SCIENCE TEST

Time: 35 Minutes—40 Questions

Directions: There are six passages in this test. Each passage is followed by several questions. After reading a passage, choose the best answer to each question and fill in the corresponding oval on your answer sheet. You may refer to the passages as often as necessary.

You are NOT permitted to use a calculator on this test.

PASSAGE I

Astronomers have found over 400 planets orbiting stars. The discovered planets have a variety of compositions, masses, and orbits. Despite the variety, the universal rules of physics and chemistry allow scientists to broadly categorize these planets into just a few types: Gas Giant, Carbon Orb, Water World, and Rocky Earth. Table 1 shows the composition of the various planet types and typical mass ranges relative to Earth.

Table 1

Planet Classification	Composition	Stars Orbited by Planet Type	Mass Range (Earth = 1)
Gas Giant	Hydrogen/helium Rock	OGLE TR 132 Gliese 777	250–1000
Carbon Orb	Iron/nickel/carbon Diamond Carbon monoxide Silicon carbide	PSR 1257	.5–25
Water World	Silicates Iron Water	Gliese 581	.5–25
Rocky Earth	Silicate Nickel (molten and solid) Rock	Kepler 11 HD 69830	.5–25

Table 2 shows a sampling of planets orbiting various stars described in Table 1. These planets are merely numbered 1–7. Table 2 details the masses and orbital radii of the planets.

Table 2

Planet	Star That the Planet Orbits	Planet Mass (Earth Mass = 1)	Orbital Radius (Earth Orbit = 1)
1	Gliese 777	500	4.0
2	Gliese 581	20	2.0
3	Gliese 581	10	4.0
4	Kepler 11	15	3.5
5	OGLE TR 132	315	.35
6	HD 69830	15	.5
7	PSR 1257	4	.25

1. The data in Table 1 and Table 2 support which of the following statements?
   A. Gas Giant planets have the largest orbital radii.
   B. Orbital radius is directly related to mass.
   C. Orbital radius is inversely related to mass.
   D. The data does not support a correlation between mass and orbital radius.

2. According to Table 1 and Table 2, which of the following stars has the most massive Gas Giant planet orbiting it?
   F. Gliese 777
   G. OGLE TR 132
   H. PSR 1257
   J. Gliese 581

3. If a new planet were discovered, with a mass of 325, an orbital radius of 1.5, and a composition of mostly hydrogen, what would be its most likely classification?
   A. Carbon Orb
   B. Water World
   C. Rocky Earth
   D. Gas Giant

4. All of the following are true about the star Gliese 581 EXCEPT:
   F. Gliese 581 has multiple planets orbiting it.
   G. Gliese 581 has the most massive planet orbiting it.
   H. Gliese 581 has planets orbiting it that are classified as water.
   J. Gliese 581 has only planets with masses less than 50 Earth masses orbiting it.

5. The Rocky Earth planets in Table 2 have what in common?
   A. Their masses are less than 20 Earth masses.
   B. They are only found in deep space.
   C. Hydrogen is a major component of the crust.
   D. Their orbits are all less than 1 Earth radius.

6. Based on the information in Tables 1 and 2, a planet with a mass of 20 and silicate found in its composition, with an orbiting star of Gliese 581, would belong to which planet classification?
   F. Gas Giant
   G. Carbon Orb
   H. Water World
   J. Rocky Earth

PASSAGE II

A group of researchers studied the greenhouse gas (GHG) and energy savings associated with rigid plastic foam sheathing used to insulate single-family housing. The results show the typical annual energy savings for a single house in the United States. Table 1 displays energy savings for various temperature zones, whereas Table 2 shows GHGs avoided.

Table 1

Energy Savings (in million BTUs)	Zone 1 (colder)	Zone 3	Zone 5 (warmer)	U.S. Average
Natural gas	4.2	2.7	0.9	2.37
Petroleum	0.04	0.02	0.22	0.04
Coal	0.81	0.98	0.93	0.76
Hydropower	0.06	0.02	0.03	0.06
Nuclear	0.26	0.26	0.19	0.25
Other	0.03	0.02	0.23	0.03
Total annual	5.41	4.01	2.50	3.51

Table 2

GHGs (in pounds)	Zone 1 (colder)	Zone 3	Zone 5 (warmer)	U.S. Average
Carbon dioxide	609	608	606	599
Methane	101	101	101	101
Nitrous oxide	4.5	4.5	4.5	4.5
HCFC-141b	588	588	588	588
HCFC-142b	1511	1511	1511	1511
Total	2813	2812	2811	2803

There is an initial use of energy and GHG released when the insulation is installed, but large savings result from the use of the product over time. After the "payback" time expires, there is a net savings in energy and GHG emissions for as long as the insulation is in place. Figure 1 displays the payback time in years for energy savings and GHGs avoided.

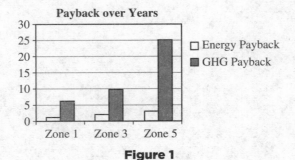

Payback over Years

☐ Energy Payback
■ GHG Payback

Figure 1

7. Foam sheathing proved to create the highest energy savings in Zone 5 for what type of energy?
   A. Coal
   B. Nuclear
   C. Natural gas
   D. Petroleum

8. According to the data presented in Table 1 and Table 2, which of the following is true?
   F. Foam sheathing prevents more HCFC-141b than HCFC-142b from entering the atmosphere.
   G. The yearly energy savings vary more by zone than the yearly GHGs avoided.
   H. The warmer the zone, the less the energy savings from petroleum.
   J. The U.S. average for GHGs avoided is greatest for carbon dioxide.

9. According to Figure 1, the GHG payback for Zone 3 is approximately:
   A. 12 years.
   B. 2 years.
   C. 13 years.
   D. 9 years.

10. According to Table 1, what zone and fuel combination yield the greatest energy savings after 1 year?
    F. Nuclear in Zone 1
    G. HCFC-142b in Zone 3
    H. Coal in Zone 5
    J. Natural gas in Zone 1

11. Ten years after installing rigid plastic foam sheathing in Zone 3, which of the following is true?
    A. The customer will have produced fewer GHGs, but will not yet have saved money on energy.
    B. The customer will have saved money on energy, but will not yet have produced fewer GHGs.
    C. The customer will have neither saved money on energy nor produced fewer GHGs.
    D. The customer will have both saved money on energy and produced fewer GHGs.

12. Based on the data in Table 1, which of the following lists the fuels that yielded the highest average energy savings, in decreasing order?
    F. Natural gas, coal, and nuclear
    G. Hydropower, nuclear, and other
    H. Coal, natural gas, and nuclear
    J. Nuclear, petroleum, and coal

13. Which of the following statements is FALSE concerning the typical annual energy savings associated with rigid plastic foam sheathing insulation?
    A. Petroleum energy saves the most energy in a warmer zone.
    B. Natural gas energy is most efficient in Zone 1.
    C. Hydropower is the most efficient energy overall.
    D. The U.S. average for natural gas is the highest average savings of all energy types.

PASSAGE III

Ohm's law states that $V = I \times R$ and WRC/L, where V = voltage, I = current, R = resistance, C = cross-sectional area of the wire, W = resistivity of the wire, and L = length of the wire. Using the circuit pictured in Figure 1, a student performed two experiments.

Figure 1

Experiment 1

A 5 V battery was used and the resistance was varied. Table 1 displays the results.

Table 1

Trial	Resistance (ohms)	Current (amperes)
1	2	2.5
2	4	1.25
3	10	0.5
4	20	0.25

Experiment 2

A battery of 1 volt was used and three different wires, each with the same resistivity and length, were used to complete the circuit. Table 2 shows the results and Figure 2 shows the relationship between the diameter of the wire and the measured resistance of each wire.

Table 2

Trial	Diameter (mm)	Resistance (ohms)	Current (amperes)
1	0.22	5.11	0.21
2	0.41	1.51	0.70
3	0.68	0.56	1.84
4	1.04	0.20	4.91

Figure 2

14. In Table 1, what is true about the relationship between current and resistance?
F. As resistance increased, current increased.
G. As resistance increased, current was unchanged.
H. As resistance increased, current decreased.
J. There is no relationship between current and resistance.

15. Based on Table 2 or Figure 2, it could be determined that a wire with a diameter of 0.5 mm would have a resistance close to
A. 2.6 ohms.
B. 1.0 ohms.
C. 0.5 ohms.
D. 0.25 ohms.

16. In Experiment 2, which of the following factors was varied?
F. Voltage of the battery
G. Diameter of the wire
H. Length of the wire
J. The material of the wire

17. The following hypothesis was put forth prior to the experiments: Current is inversely related to resistance. An inverse relationship implies that when one quantity increases, the other decreases. Do Tables 1 and 2 support this hypothesis?
A. No. Experiment 1 contradicts the hypothesis and shows a direct relationship between current and resistance. The current increases with the resistance.
B. No. Experiment 2 contradicts the hypothesis and shows a direct relationship between current and resistance. The current increases with resistance.
C. Yes. The results of both experiments show an inverse relationship between current and resistance. When the resistance increases, current decreases.
D. No. Neither experiment shows any relationship between current and resistance.

18. Using the circuit in Figure 1 and the results of both experiments, which of the following conditions would result in the largest current?

   F. 5-volt battery, 0.5-mm wire
   G. 5-volt battery, 0.25-mm wire
   H. 2.5-volt battery, 0.5-mm wire
   J. 2-volt battery, 0.25-mm wire

19. Consider a circuit like that in Figure 1. Based on Experiment 2, which of the following will produce a current of about 5 amperes (assume the wire used is the same wire in Experiment 2)?

   A. 0.22 mm; 5.11 ohms
   B. 0.41 mm; 1.51 ohms
   C. 1.04 mm; 0.20 ohms
   D. 1.04 mm; 0.56 ohms

20. There is a known relationship between the length of wires and the measured resistance of a wire. Which of the following changes to Experiment 2 would permit a test of this relationship?

   F. Use varying wire diameter and one common wire length
   G. Choose one wire diameter and vary wire length
   H. Choose one wire diameter and change the type of wire to copper
   J. Change to a battery of 2 volts

PASSAGE IV

Scientists tested a new method of titration, called atomic absorption inhibition titration (AAIT). They ran a series of experiments to determine if AAIT could be used successfully to determine the presence of phosphate, silicate, and sulfate in river and waste water. AAIT involves continually adding magnesium to a stirred sample solution while monitoring the solution for magnesium absorption.

Experiment 1

The scientists conducted an experiment to determine the effect of sulfate on titration of phosphate. Four trials were conducted, varying the concentration of both the sulfate and the magnesium used for the titration. Table 1 displays the results of the AAIT for solutions containing phosphate and sulfate and varying concentrations of magnesium.

Table 1

Trial	PO_4 ppm	SO_4 ppm	Mg		
			2.5 ppm	4.0 ppm	4.5 ppm
1	10	0	0.556	0	0
2	10	5	0.527	0.297	0.244
3	10	10	0.551	0.321	0.263
4	10	15	0.538	0.366	0.289

Experiment 2

Analysis of water from the Milwaukee River was performed. Solutions containing phosphate and sulfate were analyzed using AAIT. Titrations were performed on river water, river water plus the addition of phosphate, and standardized phosphate solution. The endpoint was noted for each trial when the titration reached the conditions under which only silicate would be detected. Table 2 shows the data collected, in ml.

Table 2

Trial	PO_4	River Water	River Water + PO_4
1	0.73	1.50	2.24
2	0.59	1.23	1.80
3	0.50	1.08	1.60
4	0.51	1.05	1.61
5	0.57	1.29	1.84

Experiment 3

Scientists created artificial waste water by adding phosphate, silicate, and sulfate to water and then conducting AAIT to simultaneously determine how much of each substance was in the water. Four titrations were conducted. Table 3 displays the results.

Table 3

Trial	Added μ/ml			Found μ/ml		
	PO_4	SO_4	SiO_2	PO_4	SO_4	SiO_2
1	3.00	20.00	1.50	3.04	20.50	1.44
2	2.00	20.00	1.50	1.56	20.30	1.60
3	2.00	20.00	4.00	2.38	20.30	3.48
4	5.00	20.00	10.00	9.56	20.00	7.30

21. According to the data in Table 2, which trial resulted in the most silicate being detected in river water?
   A. Trial 1
   B. Trial 2
   C. Trial 3
   D. Trial 4

22. Based on the information presented in Table 3, which trial resulted in less PO_4 being found than was initially added?
   F. Trial 1
   G. Trial 2
   H. Trial 3
   J. Trial 4

23. Before conducting Experiment 1, the scientists hypothesized that the higher the concentration of Mg used, the more Mg that would be absorbed. Do the results of the experiment support the hypothesis?
   A. Yes. For each trial as the concentration of Mg used increased from 2.5 to 4.5 ppm, more Mg was absorbed.
   B. Yes. Table 1 shows that the most Mg absorbed was during Trial 1 and with an Mg concentration of 2.5 ppm.
   C. No. The opposite has been shown to be the case. For each trial as the Mg concentration increased, the amount of Mg absorbed decreased.
   D. No. There is not a clear relationship between the Mg concentration and the amount of Mg absorbed.

24. Based on the results of Experiment 2, what type of solution was found to reach the endpoint with the least amount of solution?
   F. Phosphate and sulfate
   G. Standardized phosphate solution
   H. River water
   J. River water plus phosphate

25. The data in Table 1 supports which of the following statements?
   A. The titrations done using Mg with a concentration of 4.0 ppm resulted in the most Mg being absorbed.
   B. The titrations done using Mg with a concentration of 2.5 ppm resulted in the least Mg being absorbed.
   C. With a Mg concentration of 4.5 ppm, as the titrations included more concentrated SO_4, less Mg was absorbed.
   D. With a Mg concentration of 4.5 ppm, as the titrations included more concentrated SO_4, more Mg was absorbed.

26. In Experiment 3 scientists conducted atomic absorption inhibition titration (AAIT) in four separate trials. Which of the following conclusions is FALSE based on the results of those four trials?
   F. All four trials found amounts of sulfate right at or above the amount added.
   G. In all four trials the AAIT method underestimated the amount of silicate in the water.
   H. The same amount of sulfate was added to water in all four trials.
   J. In the fourth trial the amount of phosphate found in the water was almost double the amount initially added.

PASSAGE V

More than 5 percent of Americans have asthma, a chronic disease that affects the airways and lungs, causing shortness of breath, wheezing, and sometimes death. In the United States, rates for asthma have steadily increased, nearly doubling during the past 20 years. There is no cure for asthma. Two researchers discuss factors that cause individuals to develop asthma.

Researcher 1

There has long been an association between the allergen *Dermatophagoides pteronyssinus* (dust mites) and asthma. Evidence for a causal relationship has been supported by bronchial challenge studies and avoidance experiments. Studies have shown that exposure in the child's own house was the primary determinant of sensitization. Research from around the world has provided evidence about other indoor allergens, specifically cats, dogs, and the German cockroach. These studies showed that perennial exposure to allergens was an important cause of inflammation in the lungs and associated nonspecific bronchial hyperreactivity. Children are being exposed to more perennial allergens now than ever before. Houses are built more tightly and are better insulated and have more furnishings and fitted carpets. In addition, children are spending more time indoors. This increased exposure to allergens, including dust mites, has led to increased sensitization, and more cases of asthma.

Since assays for total serum IgE (immunoglobulin E) became available, it has been clear that patients with asthma have, on average, higher total IgE than patients with hay fever or no allergy. Recent work on patients hospitalized for asthma has suggested that the interaction between rhinovirus and allergy occurs predominantly among patients with total IgE > 200 IU/ml. Thus, the different properties of allergens could influence both the prevalence and severity of asthma.

Researcher 2

It is widely accepted that air pollution exacerbates asthma. For example, when traffic controls were put in place during the 1996 Summer Olympic Games in Atlanta, Georgia, morning peak traffic counts declined by 23 percent. This in turn lowered ozone (O_3) concentrations by 13 percent, carbon monoxide (CO) by 19 percent, and nitrogen dioxide (NO_2) by 7 percent. Associated with these declines in ambient air pollution were drops in Medicaid-related emergency room visits and hospitalizations for asthma (down 42 percent), asthma-related care for health maintenance organizations (down 44 percent), and citywide hospitalizations for asthma (down 19 percent). Despite such striking relationships between exposure to air pollution and asthma aggravation, air pollution has not been regarded as a cause of the disease. Increasingly, however, recent studies have been suggesting that air pollution may, indeed, be a cause of asthma.

The Children's Health Study (CHS) followed 3,535 children with no lifetime history of asthma for five years. During that period 265 reported a new physician diagnosis of asthma. Analysis of CHS data has shown that children living in communities with high ozone levels developed asthma more often than those in less polluted areas. The hypothesis that ozone might cause asthma is reinforced by a study of 3,091 nonsmoking adults aged 27 to 87 years who were followed for 15 years. The results of this study showed that 3.2 percent of the men and 4.3 percent of the women reported new doctor-diagnosed asthma. The researchers concluded that there was a connection between ozone concentration and development of asthma.

27. If ozone levels decrease nationwide, Researcher 2 would expect to see what change in asthma rates?

   A. An increase in the prevalence of asthma

   B. A decrease in the prevalence of asthma

   C. No change in the prevalence of asthma

   D. First a decrease and then an increase in the prevalence of asthma

28. Researcher 1 would agree with which of the following statements:

   F. Asthma rates are lower in rural areas.

   G. Men are more likely to have asthma than women.

   H. People who have pets are more likely to have asthma.

   J. Asthma rates are related to the quality of air.

29. Researcher 1 would most likely agree with which of the following statements about IgE?

   A. People who have IgE levels of 400 IU/ml have a high chance of having severe asthma.

   B. People who have IgE levels of 100 IU/ml have a high chance of having severe asthma.

   C. Most people who have asthma have low levels of IgE: less than 200 IU/ml.

   D. There has been no connection made between IgE levels and the prevalence of asthma.

30. If the prevalence of asthma in the United States continues to increase, Researcher 1 would likely cite which of the following as a solution to the problem?

   F. People need to spend less time outside.

   G. Houses need to be better insulated.

   H. People need to be given supplements to increase their IgE levels.

   J. Fans need to be added to houses to allow more circulation and to bring more outside air into the house.

31. Researchers 1 and 2 would both agree with which of the following statements?

   A. Asthma rates are likely to decline over the next 20 years.

   B. Air pollution and high IgE levels are the two leading causes of asthma.

   C. Women are more likely to develop asthma than men.

   D. Measures can be taken to lower a person's risk of developing asthma.

32. If Researcher 2 is correct, which of the following graphs would best represent the relationship between CO concentrations and cases of asthma?

   F.

   G.

   H.

   J.

33. Researcher 2 would most likely agree with which of the following statements regarding the prevalence of asthma 20 years ago?
   A. There was a higher prevalence of asthma 20 years ago because there was less pollution.
   B. There was a lower prevalence of asthma 20 years ago because there were higher ozone levels and less pollution.
   C. There was a lower prevalence of asthma 20 years ago because there was less pollution and lower ozone levels.
   D. There was a lower prevalence of asthma 20 years ago because people spent more time outside.

PASSAGE VI

Pertussis, commonly known as whooping cough, is a highly infectious disease of the respiratory tract caused by bacteria. The disease spreads by direct contact with secretions from the nose or throat of an infected person, or by breathing in the air when an infected person coughs. Pertussis most easily passes between people in the initial stage of illness, but it can be spread at any time during the course of the illness. Figure 1 depicts the course of pertussis from exposure to recovery.

Incubation Period 5–21 days			Catarrhal Stage 1–2 weeks	
Weeks: –3	–2	–1	0 + 1 (onset)	2
Maximum incubation period 21 days	Average incubation period 7–10 days		*Communicability* Cold symptoms: rhinorrhea, anorexia, conjunctivitis, lacrimation, malaise, sneezing, and low-grade fever	
Paroxysmal Stage 1–6 weeks						Convalescent Stage 2–3 weeks			
3	4	5	6	7	8	9	10	11	12
Paroxysmal cough, vomiting, cyanosis									
Communicability ends after 5 days of antibiotics	Communicability ends 3 weeks after onset of cough if no antibiotics taken		Coughing				

Figure 1

The number of reported cases of pertussis from 1974 through 2004 is depicted in Figure 2.

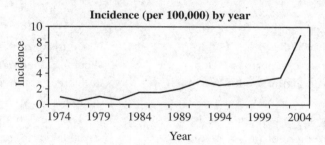

Incidence (per 100,000) by year

Figure 2

The number of reported cases of pertussis in 2004 by age group is shown in Figure 3.

Number of reported cases in 2004

Figure 3

34. A new vaccine for pertussis was introduced in 1991, which claimed to be more effective than the previous vaccine. Do the data in Figure 2 support this claim?

F. No. Rates of pertussis increased after 1991.

G. No. Rates of pertussis remained the same after 1991.

H. Yes. Rates of pertussis decreased after 1991.

J. Yes. Rates of pertussis increased after 1991.

35. If a person was experiencing a cough, was medicated, and was still contagious, he or she would be in what stage of the disease?

A. Incubation

B. Catarrhal

C. Paroxysmal

D. Convalescent

36. What is the maximum number of weeks that pertussis can be transmitted?

F. 1

G. 3

H. 8

J. 12

37. Doctors hypothesized that because of their immature immune systems, young children are the most susceptible to pertussis. Do the data from 2004, in Figure 3, support this theory?

A. No. Pertussis mostly affects the elderly.

B. No. Ten- to fourteen-year-olds were the most likely to contract pertussis.

C. Yes. Infants had the highest rate of pertussis.

D. Yes. Seven thousand young children contracted pertussis.

38. Which of the following statements could be a plausible explanation for increased incidence of pertussis?

F. Fewer infants are being vaccinated for pertussis, and are therefore contracting the disease.

G. Regulations on reporting pertussis are more lax now, so the numbers are inaccurate.

H. There are more blood transfusions performed now, increasing people's risks of contracting pertussis.

J. Vaccine immunity wanes after 5–10 years, so more young adults are succumbing to pertussis.

39. Which of the following statements about pertussis is NOT true?

A. The disease has an incubation period ranging from 1 to 3 weeks.

B. Symptoms are similar to those of a common cold.

C. The disease is a virus that cannot be treated with antibiotics.

D. Pertussis can be communicated via particles left in the air after a person coughs.

40. If scientists were in the testing phase of a new vaccine, which of the following results might indicate that the new vaccine was helping to decrease the spread of pertussis?

F. The incidence of pertussis in 2007 was 600,000 cases.

G. Children 5–9 years of age developed more cases of the disease.

H. The incubation period of the disease was reduced by 4 days.

J. Antibiotics were more effective in reducing the length of pertussis.

If there is still time remaining, you may review your answers.

WRITING TEST

Time: 40 Minutes

Zoos

The 2013 documentary *Blackfish*, which exposed poor treatment of orcas in captivity, added more fuel to a growing movement arguing that zoos, aquariums, and other venues that keep wild animals in captivity should become a thing of the past. No matter how expensive and modern a facility may be, it is always going to pale in comparison to an animal's natural environment. Even when we treat them well, perhaps we humans don't have the right to keep innocent animals in what is essentially a prison merely for our own amusement.

Read and carefully consider these perspectives. Each suggests a particular way of thinking about the controversy surrounding zoos.

Perspective One	Perspective Two	Perspective Three
We have to look at the big picture. If humans are going to conserve nature and respect animals, we have to learn to love them first, and zoos are the places where most children learn to do so. Additionally, research done on animals in captivity often helps preserve them in the wild, and there are also the species-saving breeding programs for endangered animals to consider.	In this day and age, zoos are hardly the only way for young people to learn to love and respect animals. Kids can watch videos of animals in their natural environments all day long on their computers if they wish. Live video feeds from nature preserves are far more educational than a depressed animal in a cage.	We can't make sweeping statements about "wild animals" as if they're all the same. Large predators like orcas or great white sharks can't thrive in captivity, and imprisoning extremely intelligent animals like the great apes is simply inhuman. But the vast majority of animals—especially prey animals who might end up getting eaten in the wild—are probably happier in well-maintained zoos.

ESSAY TASK

Write a unified, coherent essay concerning the pros and cons of zoos. In your essay, be sure to:

- clearly state your own perspective on the issue and analyze the relationship between your perspective and at least one other perspective
- develop and support your ideas with reasoning and examples
- organize your ideas clearly and logically
- communicate your ideas effectively in standard written English

Your perspective may be in full agreement with any of those given, in partial agreement, or completely different.

Planning Your Response

Your prewriting notes on this page will not be considered in your score.

Use the following space to brainstorm ideas and map out your response. You may want to think about the following as you analyze the given prompt:

Strengths and weaknesses of the three viewpoints

- What good points do they make, and what potential objections do they ignore?
- Why might they be convincing to readers, and why might their perspectives fall short?

Your previous experience, background knowledge, and personal values

- What is your viewpoint on this topic, and what are the pros and cons of this viewpoint?
- How will you craft an argument in support of your point of view?

_____

_____

_____

_____

_____

_____

_____

_____

_____

_____

_____

_____

_____

_____

_____

_____

If there is still time remaining, you may review your answers.

ANSWER KEY
Practice Test 1

English

1. **B**	16. **F**	31. **B**	46. **H**	61. **D**
2. **J**	17. **A**	32. **J**	47. **A**	62. **G**
3. **A**	18. **F**	33. **D**	48. **H**	63. **D**
4. **J**	19. **B**	34. **F**	49. **B**	64. **F**
5. **D**	20. **F**	35. **A**	50. **H**	65. **C**
6. **H**	21. **C**	36. **G**	51. **D**	66. **F**
7. **C**	22. **G**	37. **C**	52. **J**	67. **D**
8. **F**	23. **D**	38. **J**	53. **B**	68. **H**
9. **D**	24. **H**	39. **A**	54. **H**	69. **A**
10. **J**	25. **A**	40. **H**	55. **C**	70. **G**
11. **B**	26. **F**	41. **B**	56. **F**	71. **D**
12. **H**	27. **B**	42. **J**	57. **B**	72. **H**
13. **A**	28. **J**	43. **B**	58. **H**	73. **B**
14. **G**	29. **C**	44. **J**	59. **A**	74. **J**
15. **A**	30. **J**	45. **C**	60. **H**	75. **C**

Mathematics

1. **C**	13. **B**	25. **E**	37. **D**	49. **A**
2. **F**	14. **H**	26. **H**	38. **F**	50. **F**
3. **C**	15. **C**	27. **D**	39. **B**	51. **D**
4. **J**	16. **G**	28. **K**	40. **G**	52. **H**
5. **D**	17. **B**	29. **C**	41. **D**	53. **E**
6. **H**	18. **J**	30. **H**	42. **J**	54. **K**
7. **B**	19. **D**	31. **A**	43. **A**	55. **D**
8. **K**	20. **J**	32. **G**	44. **H**	56. **J**
9. **E**	21. **B**	33. **D**	45. **E**	57. **D**
10. **F**	22. **J**	34. **H**	46. **G**	58. **K**
11. **C**	23. **D**	35. **C**	47. **D**	59. **E**
12. **F**	24. **J**	36. **G**	48. **J**	60. **F**

ANSWER KEY
Practice Test 1

Reading

1.	**B**	9.	**B**	17.	**A**	25.	**C**	33.	**A**
2.	**H**	10.	**J**	18.	**J**	26.	**F**	34.	**J**
3.	**D**	11.	**C**	19.	**C**	27.	**B**	35.	**C**
4.	**J**	12.	**G**	20.	**G**	28.	**J**	36.	**G**
5.	**C**	13.	**D**	21.	**B**	29.	**A**	37.	**A**
6.	**J**	14.	**H**	22.	**J**	30.	**G**	38.	**F**
7.	**A**	15.	**A**	23.	**C**	31.	**B**	39.	**B**
8.	**H**	16.	**G**	24.	**F**	32.	**J**	40.	**H**

Science

1.	**D**	9.	**D**	17.	**C**	25.	**D**	33.	**C**
2.	**F**	10.	**J**	18.	**F**	26.	**G**	34.	**F**
3.	**D**	11.	**D**	19.	**C**	27.	**B**	35.	**C**
4.	**G**	12.	**F**	20.	**G**	28.	**H**	36.	**H**
5.	**A**	13.	**C**	21.	**A**	29.	**A**	37.	**B**
6.	**H**	14.	**H**	22.	**G**	30.	**J**	38.	**J**
7.	**A**	15.	**B**	23.	**C**	31.	**D**	39.	**C**
8.	**G**	16.	**G**	24.	**G**	32.	**G**	40.	**F**

HOW TO SCORE YOUR PRACTICE TEST

Step 1: Add up the number correct for each section and write that number in the blank under the Raw Score column on the Score Conversion Table. (Your goal is to get more questions correct on each subsequent practice test.)

Step 2: Using the Score Conversion Chart, find your scale score for each section and write it down. Then add up all four sections and divide by 4 to find your overall composite score. (Composite scores are rounded up at .5 or higher.)

SCORE CONVERSION TABLE

Section	Raw Score	Scaled Score
English	(out of 75)	____ / 36
Math	(out of 60)	____ / 36
Reading	(out of 40)	____ / 36
Science	(out of 40)	____ / 36
		Add and divide by 4
Overall Composite =		____ / 36

SCORE CONVERSION CHART

	Number Correct				
ACT Score*	English Section	Mathematics Section	Reading Section	Science Section	ACT Score*
36	75	60	40	40	36
35	74	59	39	39	35
34	73	58	38	38	34
33	72	57	37	—	33
32	71	56	36	37	32
31	70	54–55	35	36	31
30	69	53	34	35	30
29	67–68	51–52	33	34	29
28	65–66	49–50	32	33	28
27	64	46–48	31	31–32	27
26	62–63	44–45	30	30	26
25	60–61	41–43	29	28–29	25
24	58–59	39–40	27–28	25–27	24
23	55–57	37–38	25–26	24	23

(continued)

SCORE CONVERSION CHART (*Continued*)

| | Number Correct | | | | |
ACT Score*	English Section	Mathematics Section	Reading Section	Science Section	ACT Score*
22	53–54	35–36	23–24	22–23	22
21	50–52	33–34	22	20–21	21
20	47–49	31–32	21	18–19	20
19	44–46	28–30	19–20	17	19
18	42–43	25–27	18	15–16	18
17	40–41	22–24	17	14	17
16	37–39	19–21	16	13	16
15	34–36	15–17	15	12	15
14	31–33	11–14	13–14	11	14
13	29–30	09–10	12	10	13
12	27–28	07–08	10–11	09	12
11	25–26	06	08–09	08	11
10	23–24	05	07	07	10
9	21–22	04	06	05–06	9
8	18–20	03	05	—	8
7	15–17	—	—	04	7
6	12–14	02	04	03	6
5	09–11	—	03	02	5
4	07–08	01	02	—	4
3	05–06	—	—	01	3
2	03–04	—	01	—	2
1	00–02	00	00	00	1

*These scores are based on student trials rather than national norms.

SCORING YOUR ESSAY

As mentioned earlier in this text, two readers will evaluate your essay and each person will then assign it a score from 1 to 6. If, by chance, these two scorers disagree by more than 1 point, a third reader will step in and resolve the discrepancy. Performance on the essay will not affect your English, math, reading, science, or composite scores. You will receive two additional scores on your score sheet—a combined English/writing score (1–36) and a writing test subscore (1–12). Neither of these scores will affect your composite score!

The sample essay that follows reflects higher-level writing. It meets the criteria that ACT has put forth for essays that demonstrate effective writing skills.

- It takes a definite position.
- It addresses and expands on the counterargument.
- It has details that support the topic sentences and is well organized.
- It is not repetitive, and while there may be errors, they do not interfere with the competence of the essay.
- It is consistent and well balanced.
- The essay has a clear introduction and a conclusion that is not just a summary but ends with a significant thought.
- The vocabulary demonstrates good use of language and the sentence structure is varied.

ANSWER EXPLANATIONS

English

1. **(B)** This choice correctly separates two grammatically correct independent clauses into two sentences with a period.

2. **(J)** No comma is necessary. The narrator is saying goodbye to *both* her family and her friends, so the conjunction should not be preceded by a comma—both *family* and *friends* are objects of the preposition *to*. Furthermore, *saying goodbye to my family and friends* acts as one single noun phrase (with *saying* acting as a gerund noun), so no comma is needed between it and the verb *made* (you do not need a comma between the subject and the verb, no matter how long the subject is).

3. **(A)** This is a run-on sentence. Two independent clauses are mashed together with no punctuation. The fact that the conjunction *yet* is present does not make any difference (although the sentence would be correct if there was a comma before *yet*).

4. **(J)** The subsequent sentences mention being afraid to "jinx" something. This implies that the narrator is trying not to think about a desirable outcome, for fear that it will not come true. The idea of winning a gold medal is the only one of the choices that involves a desirable outcome that may or may not happen and is therefore vulnerable to being "jinxed."

5. **(D)** As a general rule, when three of the choices open with a transition word and one does not, the one without a transition word is correct (except in the case of the "*although* trick," where removing *although* would result in a comma splice). Choice D is a correct and comprehensible independent clause, so why mess with it? Besides, none of the proposed transition words makes sense in context.

6. **(H)** This choice explains that the narrator moved to Canada and adds the interesting detail that she did so only 24 hours after graduating, without adding any further details or implications that are unsupported by the text.

7. **(C)** Like the rest of the passage, this sentence is in the past tense (as indicated by the past-tense verb *took*, which appears earlier in the sentence). *I began* is the correct past-tense form.

8. **(F)** This choice correctly presents an independent clause followed by a dependent "afterthought" clause, with the two clauses separated by a comma.

9. **(D)** The national anthem belongs to America, and so the noun *America* needs to be possessive: *America's national anthem*.

10. **(J)** This choice correctly separates multiple adjectives with a comma.

11. **(B)** The phrase *usually jumps have three spins* does not describe the narrator's actions and is not necessary in order to understand the actions mentioned elsewhere in the paragraph, as the fact that jumps usually have three spins is implied by the phrase *a jump with just two spins* in the preceding sentence.

12. **(H)** The cold, unfeeling qualities of ice described in the subsequent sentences render the idea that anyone would love it is unexpected or ironic. Therefore, the rhetorical question, *How can anyone love ice?* is the best introduction.

13. **(A)** *Its* is the possessive form, with no apostrophe.

14. **(G)** Paragraph 3 describes the narrator waiting to perform, and Paragraph 4 describes the medal ceremony. Therefore, Paragraph 5, which describes the narrator's performance, should go in between them.

15. **(A)** The essay centers around the narrator's winning an Olympic gold medal. This certainly qualifies as a "significant event," and none of the details mentioned in choice A are wrong or irrelevant.

16. **(F)** Although the sentence is long, the last several clauses concerning the grandmother's qualities are essentially a list; they are not going to affect the grammar of the beginning of the sentence. We need the first few words here to form an independent clause, and one that is in the past tense, like the rest of the passage: only *She described her grandmother* accomplishes this.

17. **(A)** This choice correctly inserts commas after each item in the list of adjectives, and refrains from inserting any unnecessary commas elsewhere.

18. **(F)** In this choice, two independent clauses are correctly joined with a comma + conjunction (*and*). The fact that the first clause is short and the second is long does not matter; they are both independent clauses.

19. **(B)** The idea we need here is a synonym for *activating*, something like *starting* or *spurring*. The other choices are all synonymous with that idea, but *halting* (which means *stopping*) is the opposite and so the LEAST acceptable.

20. **(F)** The only information contained in the underlined portion deals with who lived in that area before the Civil War. Therefore, the underlined portion contains *details that emphasize the historical importance* of the area.

21. **(C)** The phrase *a genealogist* is a "lift-out" appositive clause containing extra information, inserted in the middle of a single independent clause. It needs to be set off with something, and the only choice that works is a pair of dashes (a pair of commas would also be correct, but is not one of the choices).

22. **(G)** What we are supposed to have here is an adverb modifying an adjective that is modifying a noun: *poorly* (adverb) *preserved* (adjective) *Creole French* (noun phrase).

23. **(D)** The pronoun *who* is used here to introduce a clause containing further information, and *was* is used as part of a passive-voice phrase: *Elisabeth, who was sold.*

24. **(H)** The narrator means to say that *immediately* after finding out this new information, she felt uncontrollably compelled to write her family's history. Of the choices, only *At this point* refers to the *specific moment* in question.

25. **(A)** Both the preceding sentence ("their lives") and the rest of this sentence ("people") demonstrate that we are talking about more than one person. As the people we are talking about have long since passed away, we need the past-tense plural form *They were.*

26. **(F)** The fact that over a thousand documents were used is valuable information, as it demonstrates how hard the author worked and how thorough the resulting account must be.

27. **(B)** Although the sentence is long, everything after the comma is an "afterthought" clause containing extra information, so the part before the comma needs to be an independent clause. Of the choices, only *The result was Cane River* is a grammatically correct independent clause.

28. **(J)** Although some may be made nervous by the fact that this choice results in a very long sentence, it is the only correct one. It combines an independent clause (ending at *Louisiana*) with a dependent clause containing extra information, and separates the two with a comma.

29. **(C)** The beginning of the essay was about the author's great-grandmother Emily. Since this is the only one of the choices that is about her, it is the only one that "ties in" to the beginning.

30. **(J)** Although it may safely be assumed that the experience of writing *Cane River* was personally enriching for the author, the essay is not primarily about the author's feelings or why writing a book is personally beneficial in general. Nothing specific to this effect is said.

31. **(B)** Assuming that they are right next to each other, as they are here, no punctuation is necessary between the subject of a sentence and the main verb. *The different kinds of prairie wildflowers* is our noun phrase (technically, the subject is *kinds*, and *of prairie wildflowers* is a prepositional phrase, but this doesn't make a difference here), and the main verb is *are*.

32. **(J)** This section of the passage is in the present tense, and the subject phrase is *grasses and herbaceous wildflowers*, so the correct form for the main verb is *dominate* (present-tense plural).

33. **(D)** Coneflowers, and how many types there are, are not mentioned anywhere else in this paragraph or the entire passage. The passage is about prairies, not specific types of flowers. Therefore, this sentence would distract from the main idea.

34. **(F)** The entire passage so far has been about the diverse flora found on prairies. The reader would expect that the assertion that prairies are "interesting and colorful" would have something to do with biodiversity.

35. **(A)** This choice correctly results in an independent clause followed by a dependent clause, with the two clauses separated by a comma.

36. **(G)** Old railroads are the rarest of the four environments offered as choices, and so this choice best establishes that black soil prairies are difficult to find today.

37. **(C)** The implication of the sentence in the context of the paragraph is that it is regrettable that the original prairies have been destroyed. Therefore, *Unfortunately* is the appropriate introductory word.

38. **(J)** The main idea of the paragraph concerns the depletion of gravel prairies, and so a guess that some of these prairies are probably new seems out of place.

39. **(A)** Since the noun *they* performs both the verb *are* and the verb *contain*, no comma is necessary after *degraded*. Furthermore, the information presented in this choice is the most relevant to the paragraph. (In this question, the right and wrong answers are determined by a combination of grammatical and stylistic factors—the test does not do this often, but it does happen, so watch out for it!)

40. **(H)** The antecedent of the pronoun *they* is the noun phrase *gravel and dolomite prairies*. Therefore, Sentence 4 should come right after a sentence that makes this apparent. It should also not come between Sentences 3 and 5, as Sentence 5 is clearly supposed to immediately follow Sentence 3. And it makes sense that Sentence 4 should be next to Sentence 2, as both concern the physical characteristics of gravel and dolomite prairies. Of the choices, only H (which places Sentence 4 between Sentences 2 and 3) resolves all of these issues.

41. **(B)** This choice correctly separates two independent clauses into two separate sentences by use of a period.

42. **(J)** This choice correctly uses *that* (with no comma) to attach a grammatically correct essential/limiting clause to the pronoun *those*.

43. **(B)** The subject noun *species* is plural here (although the singular form is identical), and so the plural verb *are* is necessary.

44. **(J)** The adjectives *moist, mesic,* and *dry* constitute a list of three different things that sand prairies can be. Therefore, commas are necessary after *moist* and *mesic*. (Although the comma before the conjunction that separates the final two items in a list is optional when the conjunction is *and*, it is mandatory when the conjunction is *or*!) The word *dry* ends one independent clause, which then needs to be joined to the subsequent one via a comma + conjunction, and so a comma is also necessary after *dry*.

45. **(C)** The question asks for a "colorful image," and choice C offers us the most vivid and specific image: *purple spiderwort, orange butterfly weed, and yellow goldenrod.*

46. **(H)** *Renowned* means "widely known" (by others). The correct construction would be to say that the regions *are renowned* for their beauty. Also, the subject, "regions," is plural, so you need the plural verb "are."

47. **(A)** If the springs are on the islands, then the springs couldn't have been formed before the islands were. So, *later* makes no sense in context.

48. **(H)** Species is singular, and so we need the singular (gender-neutral) possessive pronoun *its* here.

49. **(B)** The sentence in question foreshadows the presence of monkeys, and so could only be used *before* the monkeys are specifically introduced. After that, we would already know about the monkeys.

50. **(H)** *However* is set off with a pair of commas when it is inserted into the middle of a single independent clause.

51. **(D)** The visitors *are encouraged* by others; other people are doing the encouraging to the visitors. The addition of the adverb *strongly* provides additional information.

52. **(J)** *"Are seeking on getting" their money* is an extremely awkward construction in English. It is simply not something we would say.

53. **(B)** The pair of dashes should set off the portion of the sentence that "interrupts" the main independent clause. If that phrase were taken out, the words around it would form a complete correct independent clause. (Parentheses would also be correct, but are not one of the choices.)

54. **(H)** This sentence merely serves to emphasize how weird the situation is, and does not do too much more than that. (Sometimes the least ambitious answer choice is the safe bet.)

55. **(C)** Someone pointed this out *later*, or *after a while*, or *in due time*—in other words, *eventually*.

56. **(F)** *There was no possible way a monkey could get money would be stealing it* does not make sense. (Remember, read the *whole* sentence, not just the part around the underline!)

57. **(B)** This choice correctly precedes an afterthought clause with a single comma.

58. **(H)** *Personally I'm disappointed* is the preferred construction, with *personally* coming before the first-person contraction *I'm*.

59. **(A)** This choice correctly presents the hypothetical *could have motivated me* with the infinitive *to fly*.

60. **(H)** The previous sentence already eloquently ends the passage. The additional aside about whether monkeys like chips is less funny, and also doesn't make much sense, since the author has already established that the monkey problem has been taken care of.

61. **(D)** This choice correctly presents an independent clause (the end of which is a list) preceded by a dependent modifying clause. Because the modifying clause refers to Miró's work, the independent clause correctly begins with "his work" (otherwise it would be a misplaced modifier).

62. **(G)** The sentence, like the rest of the passage, is in the past tense, and the regular past-tense form *expressed* is all that is needed here.

63. **(D)** Even if you don't know what "visual elements" traditional painting involved, this choice clearly refers to Miró *rejecting* something about *established painting*, and so demonstrates his contempt for conventional painting, as the question requests.

64. **(F)** This is the only grammatically correct choice that says what you mean to say: that Miró was *born* to a goldsmith and watchmaker, and that he was *drawn* to the arts community.

65. **(C)** This choice correctly presents an independent clause (*He developed his unique style*) preceded by a dependent clause containing extra information, and followed by a colon and description.

66. **(F)** *Varying* here is correctly used as an adjective to modify *degrees* (*varying degrees* basically means "many ways").

67. **(D)** *The founder of surrealism* is a "lift-out" appositive clause that gives extra information about Andre Breton, and as such, it is set off with a pair of commas.

68. **(H)** Only this choice makes reference to a specific influential technique that Miró developed, thereby demonstrating his importance in the history of painting.

69. **(A)** The fact that Miró chose not to become an official Surrealist is surprising in light of the fact that he helped start the movement, and so the appropriate transition word is *However*, which is used to introduce contrasting information. (It also helps to notice that the other three choices are basically interchangeable.)

70. **(G)** This choice correctly results in an independent clause followed by a dependent participial modifier clause containing extra information.

71. **(D)** The passage is in the past tense, and the regular past-tense form *accelerated* is all we need here.

72. **(H)** This choice correctly makes two independent clauses into two separate sentences, separated by a period.

73. **(B)** The past perfect (the "past of the past") form *had visited* is correct here (the normal past tense would also work, but is not one of the choices).

74. **(J)** This choice correctly presents two independent clauses separated with a semicolon.

75. **(C)** This choice correctly presents a nonessential *which* clause preceded by a comma.

Mathematics

1. **(C)** Substituting $x = 3$ into the equation $x^2 + 2x - 12$ gives $(3)^2 + 2(3) - 12 = 9 + 6 - 12 = 3$.

2. **(F)** $3(2x - 1) = 11x + 27 \rightarrow 6x - 3 = 11x + 27 \rightarrow -5x = 30 \rightarrow x = -6$.

3. **(C)** 15% of \$42 is $0.15 \cdot 42 = \$6.30$. This answer is the amount the \$42 jacket is discounted, so to find the discounted price take $\$42 - \$6.30 = \$35.70$.

4. **(J)** $\angle a$ is a same-side exterior angle to the given angle, which is supplementary to $60°$. Therefore, $m\angle a = 180 - 60 = 120°$.

5. **(D)** Substituting $x = 3$, $y = 5$, and $w = 4$ into the given expression yields
   $(3)(4)^3 + \dfrac{3(4)}{2} - (3)^2(5) = (3)(64) + 6 - 45 = 192 + 6 - 45 = 153$.

6. **(H)** Distributing the given expression gives $(3x - 5)(4x + 3) = 12x^2 + 9x - 20x - 15$. Combining like terms gives $12x^2 - 11x - 15$.

7. **(B)** $|5 - 8| - |9 - 3| = |-3| - |6| = 3 - 6 = -3$. Remember when evaluating absolute values to simplify inside the absolute value bars first, then evaluate the absolute value of the resulting number.

8. **(K)** $\left(5\sqrt{3}\right)^2 = 5\sqrt{3} \cdot 5\sqrt{3} = 25\sqrt{9}$. Evaluating the square root gives $25 \cdot 3 = 75$.

9. **(E)** To calculate probability use the formula $P = \dfrac{\text{number of successful outcomes}}{\text{total number of outcomes}} = \dfrac{7 + 5}{15} = \dfrac{12}{15}$. Simplifying the fraction gives $\dfrac{4}{5}$.

10. **(F)** The watch increases by 5%, which is an increase of $100 \cdot 0.05 = \$5$, making the new price of the watch $100 + 5 = \$105$. The necklace decreases by 10%, which is a decrease of $300 \cdot 0.10 = \$30$, making the new price $300 - 30 = \$270$. Adding these two prices together gives the sum of costs as $\$105 + \$270 = \$375$.

11. **(C)** The triangle in the figure is a right triangle given that $\overline{CA}$ is tangent to the circle and $\overline{OT}$ is a radius (all tangents to circles are perpendicular to the radius of the circle at the point of tangency). Using this along with the facts $\overline{TC} = 8$ and $\overline{OC} = 10$ we can set up the Pythagorean Theorem to calculate the leg $\overline{OT}$ as $a^2 + b^2 = c^2 \rightarrow 8^2 + x^2 = 10^2 \rightarrow 64 + x^2 = 100$. Solving for x gives $x^2 = 36 \rightarrow x = 6$. It is also a Pythagorean triple: 6, 8, 10 (3, 4, 5 doubled).

12. **(F)** We are asked to find AB and by looking at the answer choices, we want our answer in terms of x, y, and z. First substituting BC in for A we get $AB = (BC)B$. Now substituting x in for B and yz in for C we get $(BC)B = (xyz)x$, which equals $xyzx$.

13. **(B)** Solving an inequality is almost identical to solving an equation except if you multiply or divide by a negative number you have to switch the direction of the inequality. Solving this inequality for x we get $-5 < -3x - 7 \rightarrow 2 < -3x \rightarrow -\frac{2}{3} > x$, which is equivalent to $x < -\frac{2}{3}$.

14. **(H)** The slope-intercept form is $y = mx + b$. Solving the given equation for y gives $4x - 2y = 12 \rightarrow -2y = -4x + 12$. Dividing both sides by -2 gives $y = 2x - 6$.

15. **(C)** If the solution for x is 6, then we can substitute 6 into the equation for x and solve for a. Plugging 6 in for x gives $3(6) + 3a - 5 = 5(6) - a$. Solving the equation for a gives $18 + 3a - 5 = 30 - a \rightarrow 13 + 3a = 30 - a \rightarrow 4a = 17$. Dividing both sides by 4 gives $a = 4.25$.

16. **(G)** The formula for the circumference of a circle is $C = \pi d$, where d is the diameter of the circle. Using the formula, we can find the diameter of each of the smaller circles by substituting 8π for C and solving for d: $8\pi = \pi d \rightarrow 8 = d$. Therefore, the diameter of each of the small circles is 8 inches. The large circle's diameter is equivalent to all 3 of the smaller circles' diameters combined, which is $8 + 8 + 8 = 24$ inches. Now, using the formula again to find the circumference of a circle with $d = 24$, we get $C = \pi(24) = 24\pi$.

17. **(B)** The length of time needed to cook the turkey is proportional to the weight of the turkey. In other words, $\frac{\text{time}}{\text{weight}} = \frac{\text{time}}{\text{weight}}$. Plugging in 1 hour for time, 3 pounds for the weight, and 19 pounds for the other weight gives: $\frac{1}{3} = \frac{x}{19}$. Cross multiplying gives $1(19) = 3(x)$. Solving for x gives $x = 6\frac{1}{3}$ hours. One-third of an hour is $\frac{1}{3}(60) = 20$ minutes, so the answer is 6 hours and 20 minutes.

18. **(J)** Since the seating was random, Dee would have the same probability for any position. Therefore, the probability of Dee being in the middle is $\frac{1}{5}$.

19. **(D)** The problem states the triangles are similar, so the corresponding parts are proportional. Setting up the ratio as $\frac{\text{big left side}}{\text{big hypotenuse}} = \frac{\text{little left side}}{\text{little hypotenuse}}$ we get $\frac{x}{12} = \frac{4}{5}$. Cross multiplying and solving for x gives $5x = 4(12) \rightarrow x = 9.6$ or $x = 9\frac{3}{5}$.

20. **(J)** To find the area of a rectangle use the formula $A = L \cdot W$. The problem states the length and width are $4x - 3$ and $2x^2 + 7$. Substituting these expressions in for L and W in the formula gives $A = (4x - 3) \cdot (2x^2 + 7)$. Multiplying the expressions together gives $A = 8x^3 + 28x - 6x^2 - 21$. Rewriting in standard form gives $A = 8x^3 - 6x^2 + 28x - 21$.

21. **(B)** Building a prime factor tree for 2,100 gives the prime factorization as $2 \cdot 2 \cdot 3 \cdot 5 \cdot 5 \cdot 7 = 2^2 \cdot 3 \cdot 5^2 \cdot 7$.

22. **(J)** If Jean spent 90% of her vacation money, the percent that remained equals $100 - 90 = 10\%$. Setting up a proportion we get $\frac{\% \text{ remained}}{\text{total \%}} = \frac{\text{amount remained}}{\text{total amount}} \rightarrow \frac{10}{100} = \frac{100}{x}$. Cross multiplying and solving for x we get $10x = 10{,}000 \rightarrow x = 1{,}000$.

23. **(D)** To subtract two fractions we must first have a common denominator. Multiplying the first fraction by $\frac{5}{5}$ gives $\frac{5}{5} \cdot \frac{2x+1}{x} - \frac{x-3}{5x} = \frac{5(2x+1)}{5x} - \frac{x-3}{5x} = \frac{10x+5}{5x} - \frac{x-3}{5x}$. Combining the numerators together gives $\frac{10x+5-(x-3)}{5x} = \frac{9x+8}{5x}$.

24. **(J)** Factoring the equation gives $(2x+5)(x-3) = 0$. Setting each factor equal to zero and solving gives $2x+5 = 0 \rightarrow x = -\frac{5}{2}$ and $x-3 = 0 \rightarrow x = 3$. Keep in mind there are several ways to solve this problem. You could also use the quadratic formula if factoring is not your strength.

25. **(E)** The figure is made up of 5 congruent squares. Each square has side length 4. To find the area of one square, use the formula $A = s^2$. Substituting in 4 for s gives $A = (4)^2 = 16$. Since there are 5 squares, the total area is $5 \cdot 16 = 80$.

26. **(H)** The given triangle is a 30°–60°–90° right triangle. Using 30°–60°–90° ratios of x, $x\sqrt{3}$, $2x$, we get $x = 3$. The question asks us to find $\overline{BC}$, the side opposite the 60° angle, which has the value $x\sqrt{3}$. Plugging in 3 for x gives $\overline{BC} = 3\sqrt{3}$.

27. **(D)** To increase the mean of 5 numbers by 3, each number could be increased by 3. Increasing each of 5 numbers by 3 gives a total increase of $3 + 3 + 3 + 3 + 3 = 15$.

28. **(K)** The area the dog is able to roam is the shape of a circle with radius equal to the length of the leash, 12 feet. To find the area of a circle use the formula $A = \pi r^2$. Plugging in 12 for the radius gives $A = \pi(12)^2 = 144\pi$. Using 3.14 for π gives $144(3.14) \approx 452.16 \approx 452$.

29. **(C)** Setting up a proportion gives $\frac{\text{original TV size}}{\text{original car size}} = \frac{\text{new TV size}}{\text{new car size}} = \frac{19}{12} = \frac{32}{x}$. Solving for x gives $19x = 12(32) \rightarrow x \approx 20.21 \approx 20$.

30. **(H)** We need 120 twice, 90, and 42 (the other 90, less the 48 from the house).

31. **(A)** We need to take $\frac{\text{area of garden}}{\text{area of yard}} = \frac{30 \cdot 36}{120 \cdot 90} = 0.10 = 10\%$.

32. **(G)** A geometric sequence is a sequence of numbers in which each number is multiplied by some fixed constant r, called a common ratio, to find the next number in the sequence. G is correct because year 1: $60 \cdot 2 = 120$; year 2: $120 \cdot 2 = 240$; year 3: $240 \cdot 2 = 480$.

33. **(D)** The little white triangles in the figure are all right triangles with legs x and $2x$. Since the shaded square has area 25 square feet, each side of the square has measure 5 feet, making the hypotenuse of the right triangles each 5. Setting up the Pythagorean Theorem we get $a^2 + b^2 = c^2 \rightarrow x^2 + (2x)^2 = 5^2$. Solving for x we get $x^2 + 4x^2 = 25 \rightarrow 5x^2 = 25 \rightarrow x = \sqrt{5}$. To find the area of square $ABCD$ we first need to know the length of one side. Each side is made of $x + 2x$, which equals $3x$. Substituting for x gives each side of square $ABCD = 3\sqrt{5}$. Now, to find the area, square the length of the side of $ABCD$ to get $(3\sqrt{5})^2 = 45$. This is quite a lengthy problem, but using your eye to approximate the area could help eliminate 3 of the 5 answers, giving you a 50% chance of guessing and saving several minutes of computations.

34. **(H)** The given equation will simplify by dividing the numerator and the denominator by x giving $y = 4 - 2x$. Graph the linear equation with y-intercept 4 and slope -2 to get choice H as the correct answer. Also, this problem could have been solved using a graphing calculator as long as parentheses are put around the numerator. Remember, since x was divided out, a hole will remain when $x = 0$.

35. **(C)** Dividing a plane using a single line splits the plane into two parts: one part on one side of the plane and another part on the other side of the plane.

36. **(G)** To calculate the number of diagonals in a given polygon, use the formula $D = \frac{n(n-3)}{2}$ where n represents the number of sides of the polygon. Substituting 6 for n gives $D = \frac{6(6-3)}{2} = 9$.

37. **(D)** Using the circle formula $(x-h)^2 + (y-k)^2 = r^2$, the center of circle J is at $(-4, -4)$ putting it in the third quadrant and the radius is $\sqrt{16} = 4$, meaning it just touches the x-axis and y-axis from the center.

38. **(F)** Converting each of the fractions to decimals gives $-\frac{3}{5} = -0.6$, $-\frac{4}{7} \approx -0.57$, $-\frac{5}{6} \approx -0.83$, $-\frac{8}{9} = -0.89$. Order the decimals from least to greatest to get $-0.89 < -0.83 < -0.6 < -0.57$, then substitute the fractions back in to get $-\frac{8}{9} < -\frac{5}{6} < -\frac{3}{5} < -\frac{4}{7}$.

39. **(B)** Slope is the change in y divided by the change in x. Since $\overline{QR}$ goes down 3 units and right 4 units from R to Q, the slope is $-\frac{3}{4}$.

40. **(G)** The midpoint of $(0, 5)$ and $(4, 2)$ is $\left(\frac{0+4}{2}, \frac{5+2}{2}\right) = \left(2, \frac{7}{2}\right)$.

41. **(D)** We divide the opposite side by the adjacent side (relative to $\angle PRQ$), which is the definition of the tangent function.

42. **(J)** When the triangle is rotated about the y-axis, $\overline{PQ}$ becomes the radius and diameter = radius $\times 2$.

43. **(A)** Substituting $L = 4$ and $W = 3$ into the formula gives $p = \frac{\pi}{2}\sqrt{2(4^2 + 3^2)} = \frac{\pi}{2}\sqrt{50}$. Simplifying the square root gives $\frac{\pi}{2} \cdot \sqrt{25} \cdot \sqrt{2} = \frac{\pi}{2} \cdot 5 \cdot \sqrt{2} = \frac{5}{2}\pi\sqrt{2}$.

44. **(H)** x is the common denominator you get when combining the two given fractions. The least common denominator of 28 and 126 is 252 because $28 \cdot 9 = 252$ and $126 \cdot 2 = 252$. Therefore, $x = 252$.

45. **(E)** The circumference of a circle is calculated using the formula $C = 2\pi r$. Substituting R for the radius gives $C = 2\pi R$. Since the runner needs to run 5 laps, multiply the circumference by 5 to get $2\pi R \cdot 5 = 10\pi R$.

46. **(G)** Setting up the law of sines we get $\frac{\sin A}{a} = \frac{\sin C}{c} \rightarrow \frac{\sin(105)}{x} = \frac{\sin(35)}{27}$. Angle A is calculated from $180 - (40 + 35) = 105$. Cross multiplying and solving for x gives $27 \cdot \sin(105) = x \cdot \sin(35) \rightarrow x = \frac{27\sin(105)}{\sin(35)}$.

47. **(D)** $(5-i)^2 = (5-i)(5-i)$. Distributing the expression gives $25 - 5i - 5i + i^2$. Recall that $i^2 = -1$, so the expression becomes $25 - 5i - 5i + (-1)$. Combining like terms gives $24 - 10i$.

48. **(J)** Solving the second equation for y gives $y = 19 - 2x$. Substituting this expression into the inequality for y gives $19 - 2x > 12$. Solve the inequality for x to get $-2x > -7 \rightarrow x < 3.5$. Since the solution for x must be an integer, the inequality becomes $x \leq 3$.

49. **(A)** For the product of pq^3t^4 to be greater than zero it must be positive. The only way the product of three expressions can be positive is if each is positive or if exactly two are negative and the other is positive. Since t^4 is always positive, p and q^3 must either both be positive or both be negative; either way, the product of pq must be positive.

50. **(F)** $3^4 = 81$; therefore, $\log_3 81 = 4$. The equation then becomes $4 = x + 1$. Solve for x to get $x = 3$.

51. **(D)** Setting up an equation for the total charge by the flight instructor gives $C = 75 + k\sqrt[3]{t}$ where C is the cost of the flight, k is the constant of variation, and t is time. Substituting 27 for time and \$120 for cost yields the equation $120 = 75 + k\sqrt[3]{27}$. Solving for k gives $120 = 75 + 3k \rightarrow 45 = 3k \rightarrow k = 15$. Now that we know the constant of variation, use it along with $t = 64$ to find the cost of a 64-minute lesson: $C = 75 + 15\sqrt[3]{64} = 75 + 15(4) = \$135$.

52. **(H)** The ratio for the sine of an angle is $\sin d = \dfrac{\text{opposite}}{\text{hypotenuse}} = \dfrac{\overline{AC}}{6}$. Setting this ratio equal to the ratio given in the problem gives the new equation: $\dfrac{\overline{AC}}{6} = 0.8$. Solve for $\overline{AC}$ to get $\overline{AC} = 4.8$. Now that we know the height of the triangle, calculate the area using the formula $A = \dfrac{1}{2}bh = \dfrac{1}{2}(10)(4.8) = 24$.

53. **(E)** Sometimes the best way to find the correct answer is to plug in values and eliminate incorrect answers. Pick values of x and y such that $2x = 3y$, say $x = 3$ and $y = 2$.

    We get $|2(3) + 3(2)| = |2(3) - 3(2)| \rightarrow |12| = |0| \rightarrow 12 = 0$.

    This is not true, which eliminates choices B and C.

    Then, let $x = 0$ and $y = 1$. We get $|2(0) + 3(1)| = |2(0) - 3(1)| \rightarrow |3| = |-3| \rightarrow 3 = 3$, which is true. This eliminates choices A and D. Therefore, **E** is the correct answer.

54. **(K)** There have to be 20 or more pennies since there are 20 more pennies than quarters. Since the total ends in 3, the number of pennies must end in 3 or 8 because the other coins have 0s or 5s in their ones places and combinations of nickels, dimes, and quarters can only have 0s or 5s in the ones place. Thus, the answer must be K (if the sum of the nickels, dimes, and quarters ended in 0 and there were _5 pennies, the total would end in 8; if the sum of the nickels, dimes, and quarters ended in 5 and there were _3 pennies, the total would end in 8). This problem can also be solved using equations.

55. **(D)** Substituting the given point for x and y into the equation and solving for A gives $11 = (A + 3)(3) + 5 \rightarrow 11 = 3A + 9 + 5 \rightarrow 11 = 3A + 14 \rightarrow A = -1$. Now, to find the slope we need to get the equation into $y = mx + b$ form. Substituting $A = -1$ we get $y = 2x + 5$, so the slope is 2.

56. **(J)** To find the area of a trapezoid we need to know the heights of each of the trapezoids. Draw a strategic line parallel to $\overline{BF}$ to make two special 3-4-5 and 5-12-13 right triangles at the top of the figure. Now that we know the heights of the two trapezoids are 4 and 12, we can use the area of a trapezoid formula: $A = \frac{1}{2}(b_1 + b_2) \cdot h$. The area of the smaller trapezoid is $A = \frac{1}{2}(7+4) \cdot 4 = 22$. The area of the larger trapezoid is $A = \frac{1}{2}(9+4) \cdot 12 = 78$. The ratio of the two trapezoids is now $\frac{22}{78} = \frac{11}{39} \rightarrow 11{:}39$.

57. **(D)** Substituting $x + 1$ for y in the first equation gives $x + 1 = x^2 - 5$. Solving for x gives $x^2 - x - 6 = 0$. Factor to get $(x-3)(x+2) = 0$. Solve for x: $x - 3 = 0 \rightarrow x = 3$ and $x + 2 = 0 \rightarrow x = -2$. Substitute these values back into either equation for x to solve for y. Solving for y we get $y = (3) + 1 \rightarrow y = 4$ and $y = (-2) + 1 \rightarrow y = -1$, so the two points of intersection are $(3, 4)$ and $(-2, -1)$.

58. **(K)** To find the sum of the interior angles of a septagon, use the formula $(n - 2) \cdot 180$. Substituting 7 for n gives $(7 - 2) \cdot 180 = 900$. Since two of the angles have measures 70° and 115° the remaining angles have a sum of $900 - (70 + 115) = 715°$.

59. **(E)** "The product of y and 4 is x" can be represented as the equation $y \cdot 4 = x$. Solving for y gives $y = \frac{x}{4}$. The question asks to find the "sum of y and 4 in terms of x." Writing this as an expression we get $y + 4$. Substitute $\frac{x}{4}$ for y to get $\frac{x}{4} + 4$. Add the two fractions to get $\frac{x}{4} + \frac{16}{4} = \frac{x + 16}{4}$.

60. **(F)** $\cos \frac{7\pi}{12} = \cos\left(\frac{\pi}{3} + \frac{\pi}{4}\right)$. Using the given formula, the expression becomes $\cos\left(\frac{\pi}{3}\right) \cdot \cos\left(\frac{\pi}{4}\right) - \sin\left(\frac{\pi}{3}\right) \cdot \sin\left(\frac{\pi}{4}\right)$. Substituting the values from the chart gives $\frac{1}{2} \cdot \frac{\sqrt{2}}{2} - \frac{\sqrt{3}}{2} \cdot \frac{\sqrt{2}}{2} = \frac{\sqrt{2}}{4} - \frac{\sqrt{6}}{4} = \frac{\sqrt{2} - \sqrt{6}}{4}$. You can also ignore the chart, set your calculator in radian mode, and get the decimal answer, –0.2588. You would then evaluate all the possible answers as decimals and also arrive at choice F as correct.

Reading

1. **(B)** The fourth paragraph reveals that the narrator met her boyfriend when he was one of the Youth Players that she had gone to see on a school outing, and describes her earliest memories of him. Though it does not explicitly depict their meeting, this is still how she first learned of his existence.

2. **(H)** The last sentence of the first paragraph establishes that the narrator works an office job to pay the bills for both herself and her boyfriend, so that her boyfriend can pursue his music. This means she is *generous* (because she supports him) and *pragmatic* (which means that she is a logical person who does what is necessary to achieve specific goals).

3. **(D)** Paragraph 2, which concerns the narrator's parents, states that they "did not have in their comprehension what it was that she wanted to do." Choice D simply paraphrases this without adding anything further, and so cannot possibly be wrong.

4. **(J)** The narrator's boyfriend is a cellist, and so when the narrator says "the cello is the instrument I love best," she means that she loves him and his playing more than her own comparatively meager musical talent. This is the only one of the four choices where what the narrator says works as a metaphor, whereas the other three are very similar literal paraphrases of one another. (As in so many places on the ACT, "which of these things is not like the others" is a very good strategy here!)

5. **(C)** Although it does not become clear until the last three paragraphs, the main conflict concerns the tension and emotional distance between the narrator and her boyfriend. Everything else serves merely as background to underscore this.

6. **(J)** Although saying that the narrator views her boyfriend as a *talented musician whose opinion she respects* does not tell the whole story, there is certainly nothing in it that is incorrect. (Remember, on the ACT Reading, the right answer is just the one with nothing wrong in it!)

7. **(A)** Although all of the answer choices seem very similar, there are important differences between them, and the line in question most nearly means that *she can tell something is wrong because of the music he plays*. The point of the paragraph is that his feelings are revealed through his music despite his efforts to conceal them.

8. **(H)** It is most directly established in Paragraph 6 (lines 47–57) that the narrator loves listening to her boyfriend play the cello and enjoys the life of a musician's partner.

9. **(B)** The descriptions in Paragraph 6 of the narrator falling asleep to the sound of her boyfriend's playing and smiling unconsciously at his solos are evidence of emotional intimacy. This is all that choice B suggests, and so it is the right answer.

10. **(J)** Lines 40–43 establish that the narrator's boyfriend was honest with her about the fact that her talents would not be sufficient for her to make a living by playing the flute.

11. **(C)** The main idea of the passage is that computer technology is steadily being incorporated into more and more things that are not themselves computers. This can be simply paraphrased as "the changing roles computers have in people's lives," and choice C doesn't assert anything beyond this.

12. **(G)** Nowhere in the passage does the *opinion of a scientist* appear (a clue to this would be the fact that the author never incorporates a single proper name or direct quote).

13. **(D)** *Ubiquitous* means "ever-present" (or "all over the place"). The subsequent sentence deals with the sheer number of transistors and embedded systems being produced, and so it should have been possible to intuit this.

14. **(H)** The passage never hints that more *power and batteries* will be required to run computers, and is in fact explicitly contradicted in lines 79–83, so all of the answer choices are correct EXCEPT this one. And regardless of the passage, the suggestion that computers in the future would need "more batteries" probably sounded funny to you. (It is always

a good idea to *remember real life* on the ACT Reading; although outside knowledge is never necessary, it can reliably be used to eliminate wrong answers!)

15. **(A)** The statement "Computers will be so much a part of everyday life that people will hardly notice them" is essentially a paraphrase of the main idea of the passage, which is stated most directly in the final sentence (lines 96–98). Remembering the right answers to questions 11, 13, and 14 would also be a big help here.

16. **(G)** Yet again, the correct answer is a paraphrase of the main idea: that computers will be so omnipresent that people will hardly notice them. (You may have thought that the fact that choice G is nearly identical to the correct answer on question 15 meant it was a trick, but this is not how the ACT Reading typically works: the main idea is the main idea, and several right answers on a given passage will more or less be paraphrases of the main idea!)

17. **(A)** The *future entertainment system* is described in Paragraph 1, and nothing about a satellite is mentioned. All of the other choices are mentioned EXCEPT this one.

18. **(J)** The subsequent sentence describes how people used to use computers *occasionally for specific tasks*. This is what the author means by *passive appliances*, since it stands in sharp contrast to today's interactive devices that are at the center of so many modern activities, as described throughout the passage.

19. **(C)** Lines 20–27 establish that the number of uses for microprocessors is increasing, and lines 33–38 establish that the number of microprocessors themselves is also dramatically increasing. This is overwhelmingly the main focus and "point" of Paragraph 2.

20. **(G)** All of the choices are mentioned (although not always word-for-word) in Paragraph 1 EXCEPT *power profiles*.

21. **(B)** The passage never brings up science, and never discusses poetry as a source of factual information.

22. **(J)** The "poetical *faculty*" is the *ability* to write poetry.

23. **(C)** The passage mentions how poetry is "to be desired" at such times—i.e., that it can ameliorate the bad influence of selfishness.

24. **(F)** Shelley's famous closing phrase "Poets are the unacknowledged legislators of the world" concerns poetry's influence on society—*legislators* means "lawmakers," and *unacknowledged* means "not openly admitted or known."

25. **(C)** The author mentions *Disobedience* merely as a "very long poem" that she "recently completed"—there is no indication that it is her *most famous* work.

26. **(F)** The quoted snippets of conversation in these lines represent poetry fans trying to characterize the author, something that she regards as pressure coming from society.

27. **(B)** Throughout the passage, the author discusses wanting to prevent her own poetic voice (i.e., her "mode of expression") from being influenced (or "contaminated") by tradition and society.

28. **(J)** Passage A sees poets as serving and channeling some ultimate truth that exists outside themselves (in lines 42–45, for example), whereas the author of Passage B talks only about her own "experience."

29. **(A)** Nothing about reading poetry in books versus hearing it read aloud appears in either passage.

30. **(G)** Despite their differences, both Shelley and Notley agree that poetry can change society for the better, at least when it is done well.

31. **(B)** Although he doesn't seem especially angry about it or necessarily want things to be any different, the author would clearly agree with the simple fact that science-fiction films can misinform people about how certain principles work in real life. (Well, don't they?) The last sentence of Paragraph 1 and the first few sentences of Paragraph 3 make this pretty clear.

32. **(J)** The author opens the paragraph by deriding the idea of a plasma's being "directed" (that's why it's in quotation marks), before going on to explain that this is because a plasma is basically a gas.

33. **(A)** Lines 54–57 explicitly state that the *aurora borealis*, or "northern lights," is composed of plasma.

34. **(J)** *Convoluted* means "hard to follow or make sense of," and if one is speaking casually, then *confusing* works as a synonym (remember, the author's point here is that the explanation makes no sense).

35. **(C)** The author doesn't seem especially emotionally invested in this debate one way or the other (he is simply calmly analyzing the issue), and so it is probably best to say that he would simply be "interested" in the new opportunities in the quest for real lightsabers.

36. **(G)** The author opens the paragraph with a joke about how the explanation in the previous paragraph made no sense, and goes on to mock the idea of compact crystal batteries powerful enough to generate plasma, as well as the fact that even the writers of the extended *Star Wars* universe themselves seem to know how ridiculous this is, since they bothered to specify that the crystals must, in effect, be rendered magical by the mystical Jedi and Sith warriors in some sort of meditation ritual.

37. **(A)** The author spends lines 30–37 mocking the idea that crystals could play any role whatsoever in the generation, direction, or containment of plasma.

38. **(F)** The passage establishes repeatedly in lines 41–52 that plasmas can indeed be contained by magnetic fields.

39. **(B)** The author closes the paragraph by stating that enthusiastic *Star Wars* "superfans" will probably never abandon the quest for a real lightsaber.

40. **(H)** Although the idea that laser or plasma "blades" would just pass through each other like the beams of two flashlights has often been suggested as an obstacle to real lightsabers, this particular passage never brings this up.

Science

1. **(D)** If there were a correlation one way or the other between mass and orbital distance, then the planets in Table 2 would be getting either consistently larger or smaller as the orbital distances increase. But they're not: there are large and small planets all over the place. For example, the two largest planets have orbital distances of 4.0 and 0.35, whereas the two smallest planets have orbital distances of 4.0 and 0.25. Therefore, there is no correlation between mass and orbital distance.

2. **(F)** By looking at Table 1, we know that the answer has to be either OGLE TR 132 or Gliese 777, because those are the two stars with Gas Giants orbiting them. Next, we look at Table 2 and see that the planet orbiting Gliese 777 (500 Earth masses) is bigger than the planet orbiting OGLE TR 132 (315 Earth masses).

3. **(D)** Table 1 establishes the only planet type with a mass over 250 Earth masses and composed of hydrogen is a Gas Giant.

4. **(G)** Table 1 shows the planets orbiting Gliese 581 are Water type with a mass range of 0.5–25 Earth masses. Also, Table 2 shows the most massive planet is orbiting Gliese 777. Therefore, the statement is NOT true and must be correct.

5. **(A)** Every planet shown in Table 2 has a mass less than 20 Earth masses. The Kepler 11 planet has a mass of 15 and the HD 6980 planet has a mass of 15.

6. **(H)** Gliese 581 orbits around Gas Giant and Water planets and with a mass of 20 the planet must be a water type. Water classification also has silicates in its composition.

7. **(A)** All you have to do here is go to Figure 1, look at the (vertical) column for Zone 5, and find the biggest number. The biggest number is 0.93, which is in the (horizontal) column for coal.

8. **(G)** The numbers across zones vary more in Table 1 (energy savings) than they do in Table 2 (GHGs avoided). In Table 2, the numbers for all three zones are often identical, and are still very close even when they are not identical.

9. **(D)** In Figure 1, the black bar representing GHG payback for Zone 3 stops just under the line representing 10 years, and so 9 years is clearly the closest of the answer choices.

10. **(J)** All the question is asking is "Which box in Table 1 has the highest number in it, not counting averages and totals?" The highest number is 4.2, representing the savings for natural gas in Zone 1.

11. **(D)** The bars in Figure 1 represent how long it takes to profit from the installation of plastic foam insulation. Since both the white and black bars in Zone 3 have "run out" by the 10-year mark, this means that at that point the customer will have both saved on energy costs and produced fewer pounds of GHGs.

12. **(F)** In Table 1, the three highest numbers in the U.S. Average column, starting with the highest and decreasing, are for natural gas (2.37), coal (0.76), and nuclear (0.25).

13. **(C)** With some of the lowest BTU, hydropower is one of the least efficient on Table 1, second only to the "other" category.

14. **(H)** In Table 1, the numbers in the Resistance column get bigger trial by trial, and the numbers in the Current column get smaller trial by trial. Therefore, as the resistance increased, the current decreased.

15. **(B)** This is a simple "Go Up, Hit Line, Go Over" question. In Figure 2, a diameter of 0.5 mm would be a little less than halfway between 0.41 and 0.68 mm. Moving upward from this point to the black line, we hit it somewhere around the line representing a resistance of 1 ohm. (The answer can also be gotten by looking at Table 2 and doing math, but getting it from Figure 2 is easier.)

16. **(G)** In Experiment 2, the student uses three different wires of varying diameters.

17. **(C)** Both Table 1 and Table 2 show current decreasing as resistance increases, and vice versa. Remembering the answer to question 12 would be a big help here. (It is often the case on the ACT Science that two questions in the same passage will be closely related!)

18. **(F)** $V = IR$ from the opening paragraph and Experiment 2 establishes that the largest diameter will allow the greatest current. Therefore, the largest voltage from the choices and the largest diameter would be 5 volts and a 0.5-mm diameter.

19. **(C)** We know from Table 2 that as diameter increases and resistance decreases the current increases. The current closest to 5 amperes is 4.91 amperes; therefore, we need a diameter of 1.04 mm and a resistance of 0.20 ohms.

20. **(G)** All other factors must remain constant (control variable) except the factor(s) being tested. Therefore, only wire length should be varied.

21. **(A)** This is correct because of the data presented in Table 2. The third column has the heading "River Water." The largest number in that column is the first one, 1.50. The first row represents Trial 1.

22. **(G)** This is correct because of the data presented in Table 3. To find the correct answer, the values for the columns with the headings PO_4 must be compared—the one on the left side of the table under "Added µg/ml" and the one on the right side of the table under "Found µg/ml." For Trial 2 the amount under "Found µg/ml" is 1.56, whereas the number under "Added µg/ml" is 2.00.

23. **(C)** This is correct because of the data presented in Table 1. Compare the values in the three columns under the heading "Mg." For every trial the value under the concentration 2.5 ppm is the highest, whereas the value under the concentration 4.0 ppm is in the middle, and the value under the concentration 4.5 ppm is the lowest.

24. **(G)** This is correct because of the data presented in Table 2. Find the smallest number in the table. It is 0.50, found in the column for PO_4 and the row for Trial 3, making this the correct answer.

25. **(D)** This is correct because of the data presented in Table 1. For Trials 1–4, each subsequent trial used a higher concentration of SO_4. Compare this to the values in the column with the heading "4.5 ppm" to see that as the SO_4 concentration increased, the amount of Mg absorbed also increased.

26. **(G)** In Trials 1, 3 and 4 the amount of silicate found was below the amount added. However, in Trial 2 the scientists added 1.50 µg/ml and the higher amount of 1.60 µg/ml was found. Therefore, results were inconsistent and not under the amount added.

27. **(B)** In the third sentence of her first paragraph, Researcher 2 mentions ozone as one of the air pollutants that had their concentrations lowered by a decrease in traffic, which also led to a decrease in asthma-related emergencies. Therefore, she would expect a decrease in ozone levels to lead to a decrease in the prevalence of asthma.

28. **(H)** Researcher 1 thinks that asthma is caused by allergens, and mentions dogs and cats as being among these allergens in the middle of her first paragraph. Therefore, she would view pet owners as more likely to have asthma.

29. **(A)** In her second paragraph, Researcher 1 states that high IgE levels and asthma are positively correlated, and that a "high" IgE level is considered to be one above 200 IU/ml. Therefore, she would regard someone with an IgE level of 400 IU/ml as being significantly at risk for asthma.

30. **(J)** In her first paragraph, Researcher 1 names indoor allergens as a cause of asthma, and suggests that less exposure to outside air increased the detrimental effects of these allergens (*Houses are built more tightly and are better insulated*). Therefore, she would expect *more circulation* and *more outside air* to lessen the prevalence of asthma.

31. **(D)** Researcher 1 blames asthma on indoor allergens, and Researcher 2 blames asthma on air pollution. Since these are both things that people can do something about, both researchers would agree that *measures can be taken to lower a person's risk of developing asthma*.

32. **(G)** Researcher 2 names CO as one of the air pollutants linked to high rates of asthma-related emergencies. Therefore, she would expect CO concentration and asthma rates to increase concurrently. Only choice G depicts a graph where CO and cases of asthma increase together, as indicated by the line going steadily upward from left to right.

33. **(C)** Researcher 2 regards air pollution (of which high ozone levels are a component) as a cause of asthma. Therefore, she would expect asthma rates to have been lower 20 years ago when there was less air pollution (including lower ozone levels).

34. **(F)** If the new vaccine introduced in 1991 had really been more effective, then rates of pertussis would have dropped thereafter, but instead they increased (the line starts going upward). Therefore, the data in Figure 2 do not support this claim.

35. **(C)** According to Figure 1, the only stage in which someone would have a cough *and* be contagious is the paroxysmal stage. Although Figure 1 establishes that medication can significantly shorten the period of time that one is contagious, the fact that the person in the question is medicated is superfluous information. (Questions on the ACT Science frequently provide more information than is necessary to answer the question!)

36. **(H)** Figure 1 states that the two stages in which a patient is contagious are the catarrhal and the paroxysmal. It also shows that the maximum amount of time the catarrhal stage can last is 2 weeks, and that the maximum amount of time the paroxysmal stage can last is 6 weeks. Therefore, the maximum amount of time a patient can be contagious is 8 weeks.

37. **(B)** The highest bars in Figure 3 are the ones representing the 10–14 and 15–19 age groups, and so Figure 3 does not support the idea that young children are the most susceptible to pertussis.

38. **(J)** The claim that vaccine immunity wanes after 5–10 years is consistent with the data in Figure 3, which indicates the greatest numbers of pertussis cases are in children ages 10–19.

39. **(C)** Figure 1 states that antibiotics make a big difference in how long pertussis communicability lasts. Therefore, the assertion that pertussis cannot be treated with antibiotics is the one that is NOT true.

40. **(F)** A decrease in the number of cases from approximately 800,000 in 2004 to 600,000 in 2007 may show that the new vaccine is protecting people from the spread of the disease.

Writing Sample

ZOOS

I'll admit that I was a little dismayed to see that the essay prompt concerned zoos, and the question of whether they do good work and should continue to exist or are criminally unfair to the animals and should become a thing of the past. To be perfectly honest, I feel no small amount of hesitation when it comes to writing about this issue—not because I don't feel strongly about it, but because I do.

The Bronx Zoo in New York City is probably my favorite place on the face of the earth. I have gone there every single summer with my father ever since I was too young to even remember, and even though I'm now at an age where most people would be embarrassed to go places with their parents, I still look forward to it every year. I feel like many of the animals are family friends that I've grown up with. Even just seeing commercials for the zoo on TV almost brings a tear to my eye. Because of all this, I feel like I am heavily biased and couldn't possibly be impartial with regard to this issue. If I were a legislator and some sort of resolution concerning the fate of zoos were coming to a vote, I feel I would be honor-bound to recuse myself.

Therefore, it brings me some relief to see Perspective #1 arguing that zoos teach young people to love nature, and that this will in turn make future generations more likely to conserve it. I suppose you could say

I'm living proof that a person knows what he or she is talking about. When it's a friend or relative's birthday, I always get them one of those sponsorships of an endangered animal in their name, and last year I even started a club at my school to raise awareness of climate change and inform people of things they can do to help fight it (melting icecaps are especially hard on my favorites, the polar bears!).

So maybe it's not that I'm "biased" so much as that, in my case, exposure to zoos has done exactly what it's supposed to do: fill me with love, respect, and concern for the animals with whom we humans share (or ought to share) the planet. But although it pains me to consider the possibility, I can't just let myself ignore the idea that zoo animals can be miserable. I couldn't very well say that I "love" the animals in the zoo if they're suffering and I don't care, could I?

All my research and reading on animals over the years backs up the fact one can make the distinction that life in a zoo is much more harmful to certain animals than to others. I support Great Ape Project, which argues that the great apes (chimpanzees, bonobos, gorillas, and orangutans) should be afforded human rights, which in turn would mean that keeping one in a zoo is unlawful imprisonment. And I wholeheartedly agree that trying to keep large ocean predators like orcas or great white sharks in aquariums is unconscionable. No matter how much space they give one of these awesome hunting machines that evolution has spent so many millions of years perfecting, it always dies in a matter of days (I would say of a broken heart, but I can't really back that up scientifically).

But although some animals clearly just weren't meant to be kept in captivity, for other animals it may be the best option at this point. For certain large herbivorous mammals like elephants and rhinos that are frequently the targets of poachers and therefore critically endangered in the wild, well-funded zoos that can give them comfortable homes might be their only chance at this point. Endangered carnivores like the tiger are harder to keep happy in a zoo, but I'm sure both humans and tigers would agree that tigers in zoos would be better than no tigers at all. Ideally, of course, humans would be wise enough to leave them in peace and let them thrive in their natural environments – but we animal lovers have no control over what less enlightened people do, so rescuing certain animals into zoos is the best option that lies within our power.

I hope that in the future there will be no need for zoos, because the human race will have reined in its overpopulation and its destruction of the environment to the point where all my beloved animal friends can naturally do the things they were meant to do in the places they were meant to do them, while interested and appreciative humans of all ages watch them over satellite feeds. But don't see that happening anytime soon—so instead, I hope to see you this summer at the zoo!

ANSWER SHEET
Practice Test 2

Directions: Mark one answer only for each question. Make the mark dark. Erase completely any mark made in error. (Additional or stray marks will be counted as mistakes.)

English

1. Ⓐ Ⓑ Ⓒ Ⓓ
2. Ⓕ Ⓖ Ⓗ Ⓙ
3. Ⓐ Ⓑ Ⓒ Ⓓ
4. Ⓕ Ⓖ Ⓗ Ⓙ
5. Ⓐ Ⓑ Ⓒ Ⓓ
6. Ⓕ Ⓖ Ⓗ Ⓙ
7. Ⓐ Ⓑ Ⓒ Ⓓ
8. Ⓕ Ⓖ Ⓗ Ⓙ
9. Ⓐ Ⓑ Ⓒ Ⓓ
10. Ⓕ Ⓖ Ⓗ Ⓙ
11. Ⓐ Ⓑ Ⓒ Ⓓ
12. Ⓕ Ⓖ Ⓗ Ⓙ
13. Ⓐ Ⓑ Ⓒ Ⓓ
14. Ⓕ Ⓖ Ⓗ Ⓙ
15. Ⓐ Ⓑ Ⓒ Ⓓ
16. Ⓕ Ⓖ Ⓗ Ⓙ
17. Ⓐ Ⓑ Ⓒ Ⓓ
18. Ⓕ Ⓖ Ⓗ Ⓙ
19. Ⓐ Ⓑ Ⓒ Ⓓ
20. Ⓕ Ⓖ Ⓗ Ⓙ
21. Ⓐ Ⓑ Ⓒ Ⓓ
22. Ⓕ Ⓖ Ⓗ Ⓙ
23. Ⓐ Ⓑ Ⓒ Ⓓ
24. Ⓕ Ⓖ Ⓗ Ⓙ
25. Ⓐ Ⓑ Ⓒ Ⓓ
26. Ⓕ Ⓖ Ⓗ Ⓙ
27. Ⓐ Ⓑ Ⓒ Ⓓ
28. Ⓕ Ⓖ Ⓗ Ⓙ
29. Ⓐ Ⓑ Ⓒ Ⓓ
30. Ⓕ Ⓖ Ⓗ Ⓙ
31. Ⓐ Ⓑ Ⓒ Ⓓ
32. Ⓕ Ⓖ Ⓗ Ⓙ
33. Ⓐ Ⓑ Ⓒ Ⓓ
34. Ⓕ Ⓖ Ⓗ Ⓙ
35. Ⓐ Ⓑ Ⓒ Ⓓ
36. Ⓕ Ⓖ Ⓗ Ⓙ
37. Ⓐ Ⓑ Ⓒ Ⓓ
38. Ⓕ Ⓖ Ⓗ Ⓙ
39. Ⓐ Ⓑ Ⓒ Ⓓ
40. Ⓕ Ⓖ Ⓗ Ⓙ
41. Ⓐ Ⓑ Ⓒ Ⓓ
42. Ⓕ Ⓖ Ⓗ Ⓙ
43. Ⓐ Ⓑ Ⓒ Ⓓ
44. Ⓕ Ⓖ Ⓗ Ⓙ
45. Ⓐ Ⓑ Ⓒ Ⓓ
46. Ⓕ Ⓖ Ⓗ Ⓙ
47. Ⓐ Ⓑ Ⓒ Ⓓ
48. Ⓕ Ⓖ Ⓗ Ⓙ
49. Ⓐ Ⓑ Ⓒ Ⓓ
50. Ⓕ Ⓖ Ⓗ Ⓙ
51. Ⓐ Ⓑ Ⓒ Ⓓ
52. Ⓕ Ⓖ Ⓗ Ⓙ
53. Ⓐ Ⓑ Ⓒ Ⓓ
54. Ⓕ Ⓖ Ⓗ Ⓙ
55. Ⓐ Ⓑ Ⓒ Ⓓ
56. Ⓕ Ⓖ Ⓗ Ⓙ
57. Ⓐ Ⓑ Ⓒ Ⓓ
58. Ⓕ Ⓖ Ⓗ Ⓙ
59. Ⓐ Ⓑ Ⓒ Ⓓ
60. Ⓕ Ⓖ Ⓗ Ⓙ
61. Ⓐ Ⓑ Ⓒ Ⓓ
62. Ⓕ Ⓖ Ⓗ Ⓙ
63. Ⓐ Ⓑ Ⓒ Ⓓ
64. Ⓕ Ⓖ Ⓗ Ⓙ
65. Ⓐ Ⓑ Ⓒ Ⓓ
66. Ⓕ Ⓖ Ⓗ Ⓙ
67. Ⓐ Ⓑ Ⓒ Ⓓ
68. Ⓕ Ⓖ Ⓗ Ⓙ
69. Ⓐ Ⓑ Ⓒ Ⓓ
70. Ⓕ Ⓖ Ⓗ Ⓙ
71. Ⓐ Ⓑ Ⓒ Ⓓ
72. Ⓕ Ⓖ Ⓗ Ⓙ
73. Ⓐ Ⓑ Ⓒ Ⓓ
74. Ⓕ Ⓖ Ⓗ Ⓙ
75. Ⓐ Ⓑ Ⓒ Ⓓ

Mathematics

1. Ⓐ Ⓑ Ⓒ Ⓓ Ⓔ
2. Ⓕ Ⓖ Ⓗ Ⓙ Ⓚ
3. Ⓐ Ⓑ Ⓒ Ⓓ Ⓔ
4. Ⓕ Ⓖ Ⓗ Ⓙ Ⓚ
5. Ⓐ Ⓑ Ⓒ Ⓓ Ⓔ
6. Ⓕ Ⓖ Ⓗ Ⓙ Ⓚ
7. Ⓐ Ⓑ Ⓒ Ⓓ Ⓔ
8. Ⓕ Ⓖ Ⓗ Ⓙ Ⓚ
9. Ⓐ Ⓑ Ⓒ Ⓓ Ⓔ
10. Ⓕ Ⓖ Ⓗ Ⓙ Ⓚ
11. Ⓐ Ⓑ Ⓒ Ⓓ Ⓔ
12. Ⓕ Ⓖ Ⓗ Ⓙ Ⓚ
13. Ⓐ Ⓑ Ⓒ Ⓓ Ⓔ
14. Ⓕ Ⓖ Ⓗ Ⓙ Ⓚ
15. Ⓐ Ⓑ Ⓒ Ⓓ Ⓔ
16. Ⓕ Ⓖ Ⓗ Ⓙ Ⓚ
17. Ⓐ Ⓑ Ⓒ Ⓓ Ⓔ
18. Ⓕ Ⓖ Ⓗ Ⓙ Ⓚ
19. Ⓐ Ⓑ Ⓒ Ⓓ Ⓔ
20. Ⓕ Ⓖ Ⓗ Ⓙ Ⓚ
21. Ⓐ Ⓑ Ⓒ Ⓓ Ⓔ
22. Ⓕ Ⓖ Ⓗ Ⓙ Ⓚ
23. Ⓐ Ⓑ Ⓒ Ⓓ Ⓔ
24. Ⓕ Ⓖ Ⓗ Ⓙ Ⓚ
25. Ⓐ Ⓑ Ⓒ Ⓓ Ⓔ
26. Ⓕ Ⓖ Ⓗ Ⓙ Ⓚ
27. Ⓐ Ⓑ Ⓒ Ⓓ Ⓔ
28. Ⓕ Ⓖ Ⓗ Ⓙ Ⓚ
29. Ⓐ Ⓑ Ⓒ Ⓓ Ⓔ
30. Ⓕ Ⓖ Ⓗ Ⓙ Ⓚ
31. Ⓐ Ⓑ Ⓒ Ⓓ Ⓔ
32. Ⓕ Ⓖ Ⓗ Ⓙ Ⓚ
33. Ⓐ Ⓑ Ⓒ Ⓓ Ⓔ
34. Ⓕ Ⓖ Ⓗ Ⓙ Ⓚ
35. Ⓐ Ⓑ Ⓒ Ⓓ Ⓔ
36. Ⓕ Ⓖ Ⓗ Ⓙ Ⓚ
37. Ⓐ Ⓑ Ⓒ Ⓓ Ⓔ
38. Ⓕ Ⓖ Ⓗ Ⓙ Ⓚ
39. Ⓐ Ⓑ Ⓒ Ⓓ Ⓔ
40. Ⓕ Ⓖ Ⓗ Ⓙ Ⓚ
41. Ⓐ Ⓑ Ⓒ Ⓓ Ⓔ
42. Ⓕ Ⓖ Ⓗ Ⓙ Ⓚ
43. Ⓐ Ⓑ Ⓒ Ⓓ Ⓔ
44. Ⓕ Ⓖ Ⓗ Ⓙ Ⓚ
45. Ⓐ Ⓑ Ⓒ Ⓓ Ⓔ
46. Ⓕ Ⓖ Ⓗ Ⓙ Ⓚ
47. Ⓐ Ⓑ Ⓒ Ⓓ Ⓔ
48. Ⓕ Ⓖ Ⓗ Ⓙ Ⓚ
49. Ⓐ Ⓑ Ⓒ Ⓓ Ⓔ
50. Ⓕ Ⓖ Ⓗ Ⓙ Ⓚ
51. Ⓐ Ⓑ Ⓒ Ⓓ Ⓔ
52. Ⓕ Ⓖ Ⓗ Ⓙ Ⓚ
53. Ⓐ Ⓑ Ⓒ Ⓓ Ⓔ
54. Ⓕ Ⓖ Ⓗ Ⓙ Ⓚ
55. Ⓐ Ⓑ Ⓒ Ⓓ Ⓔ
56. Ⓕ Ⓖ Ⓗ Ⓙ Ⓚ
57. Ⓐ Ⓑ Ⓒ Ⓓ Ⓔ
58. Ⓕ Ⓖ Ⓗ Ⓙ Ⓚ
59. Ⓐ Ⓑ Ⓒ Ⓓ Ⓔ
60. Ⓕ Ⓖ Ⓗ Ⓙ Ⓚ

ANSWER SHEET
Practice Test 2

Reading

1. Ⓐ Ⓑ Ⓒ Ⓓ
2. Ⓕ Ⓖ Ⓗ Ⓙ
3. Ⓐ Ⓑ Ⓒ Ⓓ
4. Ⓕ Ⓖ Ⓗ Ⓙ
5. Ⓐ Ⓑ Ⓒ Ⓓ
6. Ⓕ Ⓖ Ⓗ Ⓙ
7. Ⓐ Ⓑ Ⓒ Ⓓ
8. Ⓕ Ⓖ Ⓗ Ⓙ

9. Ⓐ Ⓑ Ⓒ Ⓓ
10. Ⓕ Ⓖ Ⓗ Ⓙ
11. Ⓐ Ⓑ Ⓒ Ⓓ
12. Ⓕ Ⓖ Ⓗ Ⓙ
13. Ⓐ Ⓑ Ⓒ Ⓓ
14. Ⓕ Ⓖ Ⓗ Ⓙ
15. Ⓐ Ⓑ Ⓒ Ⓓ
16. Ⓕ Ⓖ Ⓗ Ⓙ

17. Ⓐ Ⓑ Ⓒ Ⓓ
18. Ⓕ Ⓖ Ⓗ Ⓙ
19. Ⓐ Ⓑ Ⓒ Ⓓ
20. Ⓕ Ⓖ Ⓗ Ⓙ
21. Ⓐ Ⓑ Ⓒ Ⓓ
22. Ⓕ Ⓖ Ⓗ Ⓙ
23. Ⓐ Ⓑ Ⓒ Ⓓ
24. Ⓕ Ⓖ Ⓗ Ⓙ

25. Ⓐ Ⓑ Ⓒ Ⓓ
26. Ⓕ Ⓖ Ⓗ Ⓙ
27. Ⓐ Ⓑ Ⓒ Ⓓ
28. Ⓕ Ⓖ Ⓗ Ⓙ
29. Ⓐ Ⓑ Ⓒ Ⓓ
30. Ⓕ Ⓖ Ⓗ Ⓙ
31. Ⓐ Ⓑ Ⓒ Ⓓ
32. Ⓕ Ⓖ Ⓗ Ⓙ

33. Ⓐ Ⓑ Ⓒ Ⓓ
34. Ⓕ Ⓖ Ⓗ Ⓙ
35. Ⓐ Ⓑ Ⓒ Ⓓ
36. Ⓕ Ⓖ Ⓗ Ⓙ
37. Ⓐ Ⓑ Ⓒ Ⓓ
38. Ⓕ Ⓖ Ⓗ Ⓙ
39. Ⓐ Ⓑ Ⓒ Ⓓ
40. Ⓕ Ⓖ Ⓗ Ⓙ

Science

1. Ⓐ Ⓑ Ⓒ Ⓓ
2. Ⓕ Ⓖ Ⓗ Ⓙ
3. Ⓐ Ⓑ Ⓒ Ⓓ
4. Ⓕ Ⓖ Ⓗ Ⓙ
5. Ⓐ Ⓑ Ⓒ Ⓓ
6. Ⓕ Ⓖ Ⓗ Ⓙ
7. Ⓐ Ⓑ Ⓒ Ⓓ
8. Ⓕ Ⓖ Ⓗ Ⓙ

9. Ⓐ Ⓑ Ⓒ Ⓓ
10. Ⓕ Ⓖ Ⓗ Ⓙ
11. Ⓐ Ⓑ Ⓒ Ⓓ
12. Ⓕ Ⓖ Ⓗ Ⓙ
13. Ⓐ Ⓑ Ⓒ Ⓓ
14. Ⓕ Ⓖ Ⓗ Ⓙ
15. Ⓐ Ⓑ Ⓒ Ⓓ
16. Ⓕ Ⓖ Ⓗ Ⓙ

17. Ⓐ Ⓑ Ⓒ Ⓓ
18. Ⓕ Ⓖ Ⓗ Ⓙ
19. Ⓐ Ⓑ Ⓒ Ⓓ
20. Ⓕ Ⓖ Ⓗ Ⓙ
21. Ⓐ Ⓑ Ⓒ Ⓓ
22. Ⓕ Ⓖ Ⓗ Ⓙ
23. Ⓐ Ⓑ Ⓒ Ⓓ
24. Ⓕ Ⓖ Ⓗ Ⓙ

25. Ⓐ Ⓑ Ⓒ Ⓓ
26. Ⓕ Ⓖ Ⓗ Ⓙ
27. Ⓐ Ⓑ Ⓒ Ⓓ
28. Ⓕ Ⓖ Ⓗ Ⓙ
29. Ⓐ Ⓑ Ⓒ Ⓓ
30. Ⓕ Ⓖ Ⓗ Ⓙ
31. Ⓐ Ⓑ Ⓒ Ⓓ
32. Ⓕ Ⓖ Ⓗ Ⓙ

33. Ⓐ Ⓑ Ⓒ Ⓓ
34. Ⓕ Ⓖ Ⓗ Ⓙ
35. Ⓐ Ⓑ Ⓒ Ⓓ
36. Ⓕ Ⓖ Ⓗ Ⓙ
37. Ⓐ Ⓑ Ⓒ Ⓓ
38. Ⓕ Ⓖ Ⓗ Ⓙ
39. Ⓐ Ⓑ Ⓒ Ⓓ
40. Ⓕ Ⓖ Ⓗ Ⓙ

ENGLISH TEST

Time: 45 Minutes—75 Questions

> **Directions:** In the five passages that follow, certain words and phrases are underlined and numbered. In the right-hand column, you will find alternatives for the underlined part. In most cases, you are to choose the one that best expresses the idea, makes the statement appropriate for standard written English, or is worded most consistently with the style and tone of the passage as a whole. If you think the original version is best, choose "NO CHANGE." In some cases, you will find in the right-hand column a question about the underlined part. You are to choose the best answer to the question.
>
> You will also find questions about a section of the passage, or about the passage as a whole. These questions do not refer to an underlined portion of the passage, but rather are identified by a number or numbers in a box.
>
> For each question, choose the alternative you consider best and fill in the corresponding oval on your answer sheet. Read each passage through once before you begin to answer the questions that accompany it. For many of the questions, you must read several sentences beyond the question to determine the answer. Be sure that you have read far enough ahead each time you choose an alternative.

PASSAGE I

Why I Ride a Bicycle

I waited thirty-two years before I rode a bicycle

for the first time, down a tree-lined street in Toronto.

I had barely sat on one before, so there were a few

false starts as my boyfriend Stephen called out
                          _____
                                   1

instructions beside me. But then I found I was

moving. And since I, more than most objects, seem

to obey Newton's first law of motion—an object in

motion will remain in motion until acted upon by

an external force—off I went, whizzing downhill,

1. **A.** NO CHANGE
   B. boyfriend, Stephen called
   C. boyfriend Stephen, called
   D. boyfriend, called

weaving like a drunk, and smiled idiotically. I
                                   __2__

didn't stop until three blocks later; where a car was
                                    __3__

speeding toward the intersection. I'd not yet learned

to brake, so I just dropped both feet to the ground

inelegantly. Then I got back on the bicycle and did

the whole thing again.

   I don't know why I'd never learned to ride before,

a rite of passage that most people understand
                                     __4__

somewhere around age six. Clearly, not all middle-

class parents in India teach they're children to ride
                                  __5__

bicycles. Mine certainly didn't. I had singing lessons

and, briefly, dancing lessons. I had math tutors and

physics tutors. I even had swimming lessons but no

bicycles.

   It's strange to come to this mysterious activity

as an adult. Most people my age are riding for
                                  __6__

so long they give little thought to an act that is

nothing short of miraculous. But getting on a bike

for the first time at thirty-two reveals the triumph

of physics and human will that is cycling. Five

2. F. NO CHANGE
    G. smiling
    H. had been smiling
    J. smiles

3. A. NO CHANGE
    B. later. Where
    C. later, where
    D. later, and—when

4. F. NO CHANGE
    G. experience
    H. practice
    J. need

5. A. NO CHANGE
    B. there
    C. their
    D. one's

6. F. NO CHANGE
    G. rode
    H. had ridden
    J. have been riding

hundred years ago, someone (the tireless Leonardo
da Vinci, it was thought) drew a sketch of what was
meant to be the world's first bicycle, though both
                        7

sketch and artist are now disputed. 8 Since then
we've had the "walking machine" (Baron von Drais
of Sauerbrun's wooden two-wheeled contraption
without pedals, designed to aid walkers—a bicycle
even I could have ridden), velocipedes, ordinaries,

and high-wheel tricycles. They are all results of
                                9
engineering and machine-age design, but also of
something more intangible.

7. **A.** NO CHANGE
   B. worlds first bicycle
   C. world's first bicycle
   D. worlds first bicycle,

8. The writer is considering adding the
   following true statement:

   > The sketch was done in pencil and
   > charcoal.

   Should the writer make this addition here?

   F. Yes, because it helps support the idea
   that bicycles have an important place in
   history.
   G. Yes, because it provides necessary insight
   into the variety of bicycles that exist.
   H. No, because it is not relevant to the
   narrative at this point in the essay.
   J. No, because this information has already
   been presented elsewhere in the essay.

9. Given that all of the choices are true,
   which one most strongly reinforces the
   writer's attitude that bicycles are amazing
   inventions?
   A. Each is a marvel
   B. They are debacles
   C. Each is a creation
   D. Each is a product

The saying that <u>to ride on a bicycle is to balance</u>
10

<u>upon</u> two tubes of rubber and wire, connected by
11

a frame, and to propel them forward with no more

than a little foot power and the conviction that

you can. We think bicycles carry us forward, but

they <u>don't, we carry</u> them. It is largely human will
12

that <u>keep</u> bicycle and rider in motion, as well as
13

<u>that law of Newton's, that it can</u> be adapted into an
14

exhortation: move, because if you are moving, you

will keep moving. 15

10. Which choice provides the most concise and stylistically effective wording here?
   F. NO CHANGE
   G. Operating a bicycle one can say
   H. A person riding a bicycle
   J. To operate a bicycle

11. Which of the following alternatives to the underlined portion would be LEAST acceptable?
   A. NO CHANGE
   B. on top of
   C. atop
   D. on which

12. F. NO CHANGE
   G. don't we must carry
   H. don't: we carry
   J. don't, we are carrying

13. A. NO CHANGE
   B. by keeping
   C. keeps
   D. kept

14. F. NO CHANGE
   G. Newton's Law, which can
   H. Newton's Law which is
   J. Newton's Law and that can

15. The writer is considering concluding the essay with the following statement:

   How much of our lives are lived like this?

   Should the writer end the essay with this statement?

   A. Yes, because it adds to the writer's persuasive goal of convincing the reader to learn to ride a bicycle.
   B. Yes, because it sums up the main points of the essay in a memorable way.
   C. No, because it does not have a meaningful connection to the topic of this essay.
   D. No, because it conflicts with the overall tone and message of this essay.

PASSAGE II

I Give Update

Everyone talks about how social networking

sites like Facebook have brought us together and
16

aloud us to connect with friends 24 hours a day. To
17

some people, however, this "connecting" is more

complicated than it looks. Sometimes I'll stare at

that blank status-update box for half an hour trying

to think of what to type, and usually I just give up

without typing anything. This strikes me as odd,
18

considering that I'm a professional writer. Back in

school, the other kids used to beg me for help with

their English papers, so why am I suddenly the only

one who can't remember most of the grammatical
19

rules?
19

I've always hated computers. After all, other
20

people's status updates aren't especially brilliant

or interesting, and nobody seems to mind.

Sometimes, they don't even make sense. "Sitting in

Starbucks LOL?" What the heck is up with that? Are

16. **F.** NO CHANGE
    G. have brought to us
    H. has brought to us
    J. has brought us

17. **A.** NO CHANGE
    B. aloud us too
    C. allowed us to
    D. allowed us too

18. Which of the following choices would provide the most logical opening to this sentence?
    F. NO CHANGE
    G. My life has always been like this,
    H. I have everybody fooled,
    J. Nobody is very interested in what I have to say anyway,

19. Which of the following choices would provide the most logical conclusion to this sentence?
    A. NO CHANGE
    B. spends most of his time online?
    C. cares about what other people think?
    D. can't think of anything to say?

20. Given that all of the choices are true, which one would make the most logical opening for this paragraph?
    F. NO CHANGE
    G. Maybe I'm overthinking this.
    H. Obviously, there are more productive things I could be doing with my time.
    J. As everyone knows nowadays, Facebook was developed by Mark Zuckerberg at Harvard in 2003.

you really sitting in a Starbucks, laughing out loud?

Doesn't <u>everyone think you're</u> insane?
          21

It feels like I'm the only <u>one has</u> figured out that
                              22

"social networking" is really just a big competition

for attention, with success measured in the number

of comments other people leave on your updates.

<u>Theirs</u> nothing wrong with competition, but some
 23

people have such a big advantage in this one that it's

not even fun to play. A pretty girl can type "Bought

a new swimsuit today!" and get 35 comments in

about six minutes. I'm just as interested in pretty

<u>girls swimsuits</u> as the next guy, but come on. I didn't
   24

get 35 comments when I announced that my first

book was being published. Maybe I should have

announced it from a Starbucks, in which I was

laughing out loud.

   <u>It's all so</u> depressing.
      25

<u>Being depressed</u> would at least give me something to
   26

type, if not for the fact that depressing status updates

are looked down upon. Social networking isn't just

21. A. NO CHANGE
B. everyone thinks you're
C. everyone think your
D. everyone thinks your

22. F. NO CHANGE
G. one had
H. one whose
J. one who's

23. A. NO CHANGE
B. Theres
C. There's
D. Their's

24. F. NO CHANGE
G. girl's swimsuits
H. girls' swimsuits
J. girl's swimsuit's

25. A. NO CHANGE
B. Its' also
C. Its all so
D. Its also

26. F. NO CHANGE
G. It is depressed
H. It is depressing
J. I am depressed

about <u>attention; it's also</u> about making other people
27

<u>think, which you're having more fun there then.</u>
28
I'm starting to wonder how many status updates

are even true. Did that person really just have "the

best day ever" or just get back from "the best party

ever," or does he just want everyone to think he did?

It would certainly be ironic if a program designed

to help us connect with friends has instead forced

us to spend all <u>our</u> time lying to them. I've spent so
29
much time thinking about this, I could probably

write a book. Unfortunately, nobody would care, so

I think instead I'll just go buy a swimsuit.

27. Which of the following alternatives to the underlined portion would NOT be acceptable?
- **A.** attention. It is also
- **B.** attention, you see, it's also
- **C.** attention, you see; it's also
- **D.** attention—it's also

28. **F.** NO CHANGE
- **G.** think that your having more fun than there.
- **H.** think, which your having more fun then theirs.
- **J.** think that you're having more fun than they are.

29. **A.** NO CHANGE
- **B.** is
- **C.** are
- **D.** hour

Question 30 asks about the preceding passage as a whole.

30. Suppose the writer's goal had been to write a brief essay arguing in favor of increased legal regulation of people's online behavior. Would this essay fulfill that goal?
- **F.** Yes, because the author established that other people's online behavior lowers his self-esteem, which constitutes cyberbullying.
- **G.** Yes, because the author clearly doesn't like the way people act on social networking sites, which logically means he must want it to be illegal.
- **H.** No, because the author does not sound angry, and therefore this cannot be an argumentative essay.
- **J.** No, because the essay never mentions legal regulations or implies that the government needs to get involved in the matter.

PASSAGE III

The Rodeo

I could hear their whispers as we begun
                                    31
cantering around the rodeo grounds after our

number was called. "I can't believe she's riding that

horse in this competition. Look at him!" Monte

snorted as if he heard their collective voices in the

wind. Yet his head was up, proud as ever and so was
                          32
mine, hearing a stronger, unwavering voice.

If the truth were told, he wasn't the most
                  33

beautiful horse in the world. 34

31. **A.** NO CHANGE
    B. beginning
    C. begin
    D. began

32. **F.** NO CHANGE
    G. up, proud as ever, and
    H. up proud as ever, and
    J. up proud as ever and

33. **A.** NO CHANGE
    B. were, told he
    C. were told; he
    D. were told he,

34. At this point, the writer is considering adding the following sentence:

    His huge workhorse body and thoroughbred legs made him appear clumsy and out of proportion.

    Would this be a relevant addition to make here?

    F. Yes, because it provides clarity about why Monte is so graceful.
    G. Yes, because it adds details relevant to the focus of the paragraph.
    H. No, because it provides a digression that leads the paragraph away from its primary focus.
    J. No, because the information is already provided elsewhere in the passage.

PRACTICE TEST 2

Naturally, Monte had learned a grace that
     35

could only have come from sheer spirit and

determination.

[1] "No way! No way!" [2] My butt firmly in the

saddle, my back straight, and the reins held just

right, we smoothly turned into the barrels.

[3] Western equitation had been as unfamiliar to
                          36

Monte and me as five forks in a place setting at

an upscale restaurant. [4] The voices in the wind

followed us as Monte galloped faster around the

ring. [5] Far from the bareback rides across the desert

we had cherished over the years, we had learned the
                                              37

rules and were making believers out of the crowd.

[6] Monte, now almost on his side, was racing

around the barrels as gracefully as if he had wings

touched by angels, not grazing even one barrel. [39]
                       38

35. **A.** NO CHANGE
     B. In fact,
     C. Meanwhile,
     D. Yet

36. **F.** NO CHANGE
     G. is
     H. will be
     J. has been

37. Which of the following alternatives to the underlined portion would be LEAST acceptable?
     A. NO CHANGE
     B. beat
     C. mastered
     D. grasped

38. If the writer were to delete the underlined portion, placing a period after the word *angels*, the paragraph would primarily lose:
     F. an emphasis on how quickly Monte raced.
     G. information about how Monte was judged.
     H. an explanation for how Monte raced gracefully.
     J. an unnecessary detail.

39. For the sake of the logic and coherence of this paragraph, Sentence 4 should be placed:
     A. where it is now.
     B. before Sentence 2.
     C. after Sentence 2.
     D. after Sentence 6.

PRACTICE TEST 2

I patted Monte's neck as we cantered out of
      40

the ring and suddenly I didn't see or hear anyone

accepting my family. "No one will hurt your spirit
     41

but you," my grandfather's voice
                    42

echoed in the gentle wind that kissed my cheeks
   43
and my spirit.

Monte looked so proud when he and me won first
                                    44

place.

40. Given that all of the choices are true, which one most effectively introduces the action in this paragraph while suggesting the writer's nervousness?
  F. NO CHANGE
  G. I proudly held up my head
  H. I dropped the reins
  J. I glanced anxiously at the crowd

41. A. NO CHANGE
  B. accept for
  C. except for
  D. excepting

42. F. NO CHANGE
  G. grandfathers
  H. grandfathers'
  J. grandfather

43. A. NO CHANGE
  B. will echo
  C. echoing
  D. echoes

44. F. NO CHANGE
  G. he and I
  H. him and me
  J. him and I

Question 45 asks about the preceding passage as a whole.

45. Suppose that one of the writer's goals had been to illustrate that spirit and determination are just as important as inborn ability. Would this essay fulfill this goal?
  A. Yes, because Monte was a beautiful racehorse who helped the writer overcome her challenges.
  B. Yes, because the writer was able to win the race riding Monte, even though Monte wasn't born with grace.
  C. No, because the essay doesn't address inborn abilities.
  D. No, because neither Monte nor the writer demonstrated spirit and determination.

PASSAGE IV

Not in Our Stars

I guess I can't blame people <u>from</u> thousands
46

of years ago for believing in astrology—there was

simply <u>no way for them to now</u> any better. But it's
47

honestly incredible to me that, after all the knowledge

science has given us about how the universe really

works, there are still millions of people who eagerly

read their horoscopes in the paper every morning

and actually expect <u>them</u> to mean anything. 49
48

46. Which of the following alternatives to the
    underlined portion would be LEAST acceptable?
    F. in which
    G. who lived
    H. all those
    J. DELETE the underlined portion.

47. A. NO CHANGE
    B. know way for them to now
    C. no way for them to know
    D. now way for them to no

48. F. NO CHANGE
    G. it
    H. themselves
    J. DELETE the underlined portion.

49. At this point, the writer is considering adding
    the following sentence:

    > Just imagine if a newspaper ever
    > accidentally printed the horoscopes
    > under the wrong signs—people would be
    > so confused, watching things happen to
    > the wrong people all day!

    Should the writer add this sentence here?

    A. Yes, because it is a humorous way of
       illustrating the fact that horoscopes are
       meaningless.
    B. Yes, because this is something that might
       actually happen, and people deserve to be
       warned.
    C. No, because it is disrespectful to people
       who work in graphic design for newspapers.
    D. No, because it does not offer definitive
       proof that horoscopes do not accurately
       predict the future.

Even when I was little, I didn't believe in
50
horoscopes. We're all familiar with the twelve signs
50

of the zodiac and the traits of people supposedly
51
personally born under different signs: a Pisces is
51
emotional, a Taurus is stubborn, an Aquarius is

clever. The problem, of course, is that these vague

qualities can appear to apply to anyone. Who isn't

emotional or stubborn at times? And all people

think they're clever—even when they aren't! If only

astrology made claims which were a little more
52
specific, we might be rid of it by now. For example,

if "the stars" predicted that all Sagittarians would

be left-handed, or that all Libras would have 20/20

vision, we would be able to test these claims,

and astrology would fail. But since the only "test"

involves people who *want* to believe in it decide
53
whether to apply broad compliments like "brave"

50. Which of the following would make for the most logical opening to this paragraph?
F. NO CHANGE
G. Modern astronomy first became distinct from astrology in the second century.
H. I do have a few friends who believe in astrology, which has led to some amusing arguments.
J. I'm sure I don't need to explain what astrology is.

51. **A.** NO CHANGE
B. personality traits of people supposed to be
C. people's traits supposedly personally
D. supposed personality traits of people

52. **F.** NO CHANGE
G. claims, which were
H. claims that were
J. claims, that were

53. **A.** NO CHANGE
B. deciding
C. to decide
D. and decided

or "insightful" to <u>their friends and them,</u> astrology
54

probably won't be going away anytime soon.

    I can see how people centuries ago <u>would</u>
55

<u>be thinking</u> it was logical for heavenly bodies to
55

"influence" events on Earth, but the funny part

is that the math is all wrong. All of the star charts

on which astrology is based were drawn up when

people still thought that the Earth, rather than the

sun, was at the center of the solar system. Plus, as

Einstein figured out <u>anyway,</u> the stars' apparent
56

positions aren't really where they are, because the

light they emit is bent by gravity before it reaches our

eyes. So even if astrology were true, it would be full

of mistakes! Luckily for <u>astrologers, it's</u> a bunch of
57

nonsense, so nobody ever noticed.

    I'm not ready for astrology to go away just

<u>yet, however, I</u> always enjoy meeting people who
58

believe in it at a party. Once someone brings it up, I

know it's only a matter of time before he or she asks

me what my sign is, and my answer is always the

54. **F.** NO CHANGE
    G. their friends and they,
    H. their friends, and themselves,
    J. themselves and their friends,

55. **A.** NO CHANGE
    B. could've thought
    C. should have thought
    D. might of thought

56. The best placement for the underlined portion would be:
    F. where it is now.
    G. after the word *are* (but before the comma).
    H. after the word *emit.*
    J. after the word *gravity.*

57. **A.** NO CHANGE
    B. astrologers are
    C. astrologers, and
    D. astrologers, and it's

58. **F.** NO CHANGE
    G. yet, however I
    H. yet, however; I
    J. yet—however—I

same. "Well, you've been talking to me all night,"

I replied.
59

"Shouldn't you be able to tell?" 60

59. **A.** NO CHANGE
    B. I'll reply.
    C. and I replied.
    D. and replied:

60. The writer is considering concluding the essay with the following statement:

> At the end of the day, though, I don't think anything annoys me as much as going into a bookstore and seeing all the space they waste with books on astrology.

Should the writer end the essay with this statement?

    F. Yes, because it is logical for a writer to end an essay with a reference to bookstores.
    G. Yes, because unnecessary books are a waste of trees and therefore bad for the environment.
    H. No, because this is an essay about people's superstitions, not how bookstores are arranged.
    J. No, because the previous sentence makes for a much more pointed and memorable ending.

PASSAGE V

Gut Feelings

Intuitions or gut feelings, are sudden, strong
61

judgments whose origin they can't immediately
62

explain. Although they seem to emerge from an

obscure inner force, they actually begin with

a perception of something outside—a facial

61. **A.** NO CHANGE
    B. Intuitions, or gut feelings
    C. Intuitions, or gut feelings,
    D. Intuitions or gut feelings

62. **F.** NO CHANGE
    G. you can't
    H. people won't
    J. one doesn't

expression, a tone of voice, or a visual inconsistency

so fleeting you're not even aware you <u>had noticed it.</u>
63

63. **A.** NO CHANGE
B. notice
C. felt
D. feel

<u>Think of them</u> as rapid cognition or condensed
64

reasoning that takes advantage of the brain's

built-in shortcuts. Or think of intuition as an

unconscious associative process. 65

64. **F.** NO CHANGE
G. Think of intuition
H. Think on it
J. Thinking of them

65. At this point, the writer is considering adding the following sentence:

> Long dismissed as magical or beneath the dignity of science, intuition appears to consist of fast mental operations.

Would this be a relevant addition to make here?

A. Yes, because it provides a needed transition between sentences.
B. Yes, because it finally provides the official definition of *intuition*.
C. No, because it contradicts the idea expressed in the following sentence.
D. No, because it provides a digression that leads the paragraph away from its primary focus.

<u>The best explanation psychologists now offer is</u>
66

that intuition is a mental matching game. The

brain <u>takes in a situation, doing a very quick search</u>
67

of its files, and then finds its best analogy among

the stored sprawl of memories and knowledge.

66. Which phrase best introduces the sentence?
F. NO CHANGE
G. The only thing we know for sure is
H. The only possible explanation is
J. Psychologists now believe

67. **A.** NO CHANGE
B. takes in a situation, does a very quick search
C. took in a situation, doing a very quick search
D. take in a situation, does a very quick search

1 ■ ■ ■ ■ ■ ■ ■ ■ 1

Based on that <u>analogy, you</u> ascribe meaning to the
68

situation in front of you. A doctor might simply

glance at a pallid young woman complaining of

fatigue and shortness of breath and immediately

intuit <u>one</u> suffers from anemia.
69

68. F. NO CHANGE
G. analogy: you
H. analogy—you
J. analogy; you

69. A. NO CHANGE
B. she
C. he
D. her

<u>Experience is encoded In our brains as a web</u>
70

<u>of fact and feeling.</u> When a new experience calls
70

up a similar pattern, it doesn't unleash just stored

knowledge but also an emotional state of mind and

a predisposition to <u>respond by it</u> in a certain way.
71

70. Which choice best illustrates how
information is stored in our brains?
F. NO CHANGE
G. Everything we do is stored in our brain.
H. Experience is processed by our brain.
J. Our brain remembers all of our
experiences.

71. A. NO CHANGE
B. respond
C. have responded
D. be responding

<u>While endless reasoning in the absence of</u>
72
<u>intuitions is unproductive, some people champion</u>
72
<u>the other extreme—"going with the gut" at all times.</u>
72

72. The writer is considering deleting this
sentence. Should the sentence be kept or
deleted?
F. Kept, because it gives an explanation of
the usefulness of intuitions.
G. Kept, because it provides a useful
introduction to the paragraph.
H. Deleted, because it contradicts the idea
that people should pay attention to their
intuitions.
J. Deleted, because it is stylistically
inconsistent with the rest of the essay.

PRACTICE TEST 2

Accordingly, intuition is best used as the first
  73

step in solving a problem or deciding what to do.

The more experience you have in a particular

domain, the more reliable your intuitions, because
  74

they haven't been used many times before. But
  74

even in your area of expertise, it's wisest to test out

your hunches—you could easily have latched on to

the wrong detail and pulled up the wrong web of

associations in your brain. So pay attention to your

intuition, because the information you received is
  75

valid. But it's important to balance this with reason

so that you don't make an error of judgment in an

impulsive moment.

73. **A.** NO CHANGE
    B. Also,
    C. For instance,
    D. But

74. Which phrase best supports the idea
    presented in this sentence?
    F. NO CHANGE
    G. because you haven't formed many
    situational analogies.
    H. because they arise out of the richest array
    of collected patterns of experience.
    J. because you should trust your
    unconscious mind.

75. **A.** NO CHANGE
    B. have received
    C. will be receiving
    D. receive

PRACTICE TEST 2

STOP

If there is still time remaining, you may review your answers.

MATHEMATICS TEST

Time: 60 Minutes—60 Questions

> **Directions:** Solve each problem, choose the correct answer, and then fill in the corresponding oval on your answer sheet.
>
> Do not linger over problems that take too much time. Solve as many as you can; then return to the others in the time you have left for this test.
>
> You are permitted to use a calculator on this test. You may use your calculator for any problems you choose, but some of the problems may best be done without using a calculator.
>
> Note: Unless otherwise stated, all of the following should be assumed.
>
> 1. Illustrative figures are NOT necessarily drawn to scale.
> 2. Geometric figures lie in a plane.
> 3. The word *line* indicates a straight line.
> 4. The word *average* indicates arithmetic mean.

1. What is the value of the expression $(y - x)^3$ when $x = 5$ and $y = 1$?
   A. -64
   B. -4
   C. 4
   D. 16
   E. 64

DO YOUR FIGURING HERE

2. What is the smallest positive integer that is divisible by 3, divisible by 5, and divisible by 6 (with no remainders)?
   F. 15
   G. 30
   H. 60
   J. 90
   K. 180

3. If $[-s + h(t \cdot 3 - w)]r = 1$, then which of the following variables CANNOT equal 0?
   A. h
   B. r
   C. s
   D. t
   E. w

4. In a certain school district, exactly 30% of the students come from families that have only one child. If there are 7,340 students in the district, how many do NOT come from families with only one child?

DO YOUR FIGURING HERE

F. 220

G. 514

H. 2,202

J. 5,138

K. 7,120

5. What is the slope-intercept form of the equation $3y + 2x = 24$?

A. $y = -\dfrac{2x}{3} + 8$

B. $y = -\dfrac{3x}{2} + 12$

C. $3 = 2m + b$

D. $m = 2b + 24$

E. $y = 2x + 24$

6. What is the slope of a line perpendicular to the line $3x + 2y = 19$?

F. $-\dfrac{3}{2}$

G. $-\dfrac{2}{3}$

H. $\dfrac{2}{3}$

J. $\dfrac{3}{2}$

K. 3

DO YOUR FIGURING HERE

7. The volume of a cone is given by the formula $V = \frac{\pi}{3}r^2h$, where r is the radius of the base of the cone and h is the height of the cone. What is the volume, in cubic centimeters, of a cone with a height of 8 cm that has a base with a radius of 3 cm?

A. 72π
B. 48π
C. 24π
D. 12π
E. 8π

8. Given that m and n are parallel lines, t is a transversal crossing both m and n, and $m\angle b = 100°$, what is the measure of $\angle e$?

F. $40°$
G. $50°$
H. $80°$
J. $100°$
K. $120°$

9. In the figure below, 3 lines intersect at the indicated angles.

What is the measure of $\angle x$?

A. 35°

B. 52.5°

C. 65°

D. 70°

E. 75°

10. Find two numbers between 11 and 26 such that the numbers form an arithmetic sequence.

11, _____, _____, 26

F. 14, 18

G. 15, 20

H. 16, 21

J. 17, 23

K. 18, 24

11. For all real numbers x and y, $(2x + 3y)^2 = $?

A. $6x^2y^2$

B. $4x^2 + 6y^2$

C. $4x^2 + 9y^2$

D. $4x^2 + 6xy + 6y^2$

E. $4x^2 + 12xy + 9y^2$

12. In a certain town in New Hampshire, there are 7,695 registered voters, 60% of whom are Democrats. How many of the town's registered voters are Democrats?

F. 513

G. 2,565

H. 3,078

J. 4,617

K. 7,695

13. What is the value of tan *Y* in right triangle △*XYZ* below?

A. $\dfrac{7}{25}$

B. $\dfrac{7}{24}$

C. $\dfrac{24}{25}$

D. $\dfrac{24}{7}$

E. $\dfrac{25}{7}$

14. When $\dfrac{1}{3}w + \dfrac{2}{5}w = 1$, what is the value of *w*?

F. $\dfrac{1}{11}$

G. $\dfrac{3}{8}$

H. $\dfrac{11}{15}$

J. $\dfrac{15}{11}$

K. $\dfrac{8}{3}$

15. In the figure below, $\overline{AB}$ and $\overline{CD}$ bisect each other at *E*. The measure of ∠*CAE* is 80° and the measure of ∠*BDE* is 60°. What is the measure of ∠*CEA*?

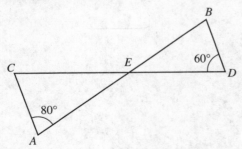

A. 10°

B. 30°

C. 40°

D. 60°

E. Cannot be determined

16. Given that $A = (3, 2)$ and $B = (15, 8)$ in the standard (x, y) coordinate plane, what is the distance from A to B?

F. $5\sqrt{2}$

G. 8

H. $4\sqrt{10}$

J. $6\sqrt{5}$

K. 18

DO YOUR FIGURING HERE

17. For all real numbers a, b, and c such that $a < b$ and $c > 0$, which of the following inequalities, if any, must be true?

A. $a < c$

B. $b < c$

C. $a > c$

D. $b > c$

E. None of the above inequalities must be true.

18. A deli offers 4 types of sandwich meat, 3 kinds of cheese, and 5 bread varieties. When you order a sandwich at the deli, you are allowed to choose 1 meat, 1 cheese, and 1 type of bread. How many different sandwich combinations are possible at the deli?

F. 3

G. 12

H. 15

J. 30

K. 60

19. Alana leaves home to drive to college. She drives 200 miles in 4 hours before stopping for gas. She then drives 10 miles per hour faster than she did on the first part of her trip, and arrives at her dorm in 3 hours. How many miles did she drive in total?

A. 200

B. 300

C. 350

D. 380

E. 430

20. If the monthly payment, M dollars, on a house that costs P dollars is given by the formula $M = \dfrac{P}{200} - 0.0008P + 40$, what is the monthly payment, to the nearest dollar, on a house that costs $200,000?

F. $868

G. $880

H. $960

J. $1,060

K. $1,200

21. What is the sum of the prime factors of the number 330?

A. 6

B. 19

C. 21

D. 22

E. 43

DO YOUR FIGURING HERE

> Use the following information to answer questions 22–24.

Quinn is bowling a series of 3 games. She has bowled 2 of 3 games with scores of 112 and 144. The figure below is a top view of the bowling lane. The *dimensions* for the bowling lane are given in the figure. The *pin deck* is the rectangular region within the bowling lane where the 10 bowling pins are set up.

(Note: The figure is not drawn to scale.)

22. In *duckpin* bowling, different balls and pins are used. The diameter of each duckpin at its widest is 4.125 in. When all of the pins are set up, which of the following values is closest to the area, in square inches, that is covered by the widest part of the pins?

F.   130
G.   134
H.   267
J.   535
K.   1,260

DO YOUR FIGURING HERE

23. What is the ratio of the total area of the bowling lane to the area of the lane that is NOT the pin deck?

A.   12:1
B.   13:1
C.   13:12
D.   10:7
E.   120:7

24. What score will Quinn need to earn in her third game to have an average score of 140 for the 3 games?

F.   128
G.   132
H.   140
J.   164
K.   176

25. In the standard (x, y) coordinate plane, a line passes through the points $(1, -2)$ and $(5, 10)$. At which of the following points does the line cross the y-axis?

A. $(-8, 0)$
B. $(-5, 0)$
C. $(0, 0)$
D. $(0, -5)$
E. $(0, -8)$

26. The scores below were earned by 10 students on a recent history test. What is the median score?

68, 96, 85, 72, 89, 93, 89, 82, 77, 99

- F. 85
- G. 86
- H. 87
- J. 89
- K. 91

DO YOUR FIGURING HERE

27. For all positive a, b, and c, $\dfrac{2^{-1}a^{-3}b^7c^2}{(5a)^2\,b^{-1}c^7} = ?$

- A. $\dfrac{2b^6}{5a^2c^5}$
- B. $\dfrac{2b^8c^9}{2a^5}$
- C. $\dfrac{2b^8c^9}{25a^5}$
- D. $\dfrac{b^8}{10a^5c^5}$
- E. $\dfrac{b^8}{50a^5c^5}$

28. One endpoint of a diameter of a circle with center $(2, -3)$ has coordinates at $(5, -2)$ in the standard (x, y) plane. What are the coordinates of the other endpoint of the diameter?

- F. $(2 - \sqrt{10}, -3 - \sqrt{10})$
- G. $(-1, -4)$
- H. $(0, -4)$
- J. $(2 + \sqrt{10}, -3 + \sqrt{10})$
- K. $(8, -1)$

29. What is the y-coordinate of the point of intersection of the lines $y = 3x - 7$ and $y = 5x + 5$ in the standard (x, y) coordinate plane?

- A. -25
- B. -11
- C. -6
- D. 6
- E. 11

30. What is the area, in square inches, of the figure shown below?

- **F.** 24
- **G.** 32
- **H.** 36
- **J.** 42
- **K.** 72

31. What is the solution set for the inequality $6 - 4(x - 2) > 4x + 5$?

- **A.** $x < -\dfrac{7}{8}$
- **B.** $x < -\dfrac{1}{4}$
- **C.** $x < \dfrac{9}{8}$
- **D.** $x > -\dfrac{7}{8}$
- **E.** $x > \dfrac{9}{8}$

Use the following information to answer questions 32–34.

The circle in the standard (x, y) coordinate plane below has center $(6, -7)$ and radius 4 coordinate units.

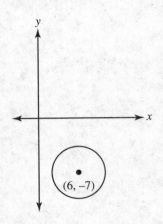

32. Which of the following is an equation for this circle?

F. $(x - 6)^2 + (y + 7)^2 = 8$

G. $(x + 6)^2 + (y - 7)^2 = 8$

H. $(x - 6)^2 + (y + 7)^2 = 16$

J. $(x - 6)^2 + (y - 7)^2 = 16$

K. $(x + 6)^2 + (y + 7)^2 = 16$

33. The circle will be rotated 90° counterclockwise (↺) about the origin. What will be the coordinates of the image of the center of the circle?

A. $(-6, 7)$

B. $(6, 7)$

C. $(7, 6)$

D. $(7, -6)$

E. $(-7, 6)$

34. What is the area, in square coordinate units, of this circle?

F. 2π

G. 4π

H. 8π

J. 16π

K. 32π

35. Parallelogram *RSTU* is shown below, with $\overline{UA}$ = 4 inches, $\overline{AS}$ = 7 inches, and $\overline{ST}$ = 5 inches. What is the area of *RSTU* in square inches?

- **A.** 16
- **B.** 20
- **C.** 28
- **D.** 35
- **E.** 40

36. If the lengths of the sides of the triangle below are shown in inches, how many inches long is side $\overline{AB}$?

- **F.** $2\sqrt{13}$
- **G.** 10
- **H.** $4\sqrt{13}$
- **J.** 26
- **K.** 42

37. Which of the following comprises all of the values of x for which $\frac{2}{3}x - \frac{1}{2} < \frac{1}{2}x + \frac{2}{3}$?

A. $x < 1$

B. $x < \frac{7}{6}$

C. $x < 7$

D. $x > \frac{7}{3}$

E. $x > 7$

DO YOUR FIGURING HERE

38. A guide wire for a telephone tower makes an angle of 50° with the level ground and is 14 meters from the base of the tower. How many meters long is the guide wire?

F. 3.80

G. 13.50

H. 16.68

J. 21.78

K. 22.58

39. For all $x^2 \neq 9$, $\frac{(x-3)^2}{x^2-9}$ is equivalent to:

A. -1

B. $\frac{1}{2}$

C. 1

D. $\frac{1}{x+3}$

E. $\frac{x-3}{x+3}$

PRACTICE TEST 2

40. In the standard (x, y) coordinate plane, the midpoint of $\overline{AB}$ is (5, 7) and A is located at (2, 3). If the coordinates of B are (x, y), what is the value of $(x + y)$?

F. 19
G. 17
H. 11
J. 8.5
K. 8

DO YOUR FIGURING HERE

41. If the solutions to the equation $(x + a)(x + b)$ = 0 are $x = 8$ and $x = -\dfrac{3}{2}$, then $a + b = ?$

A. −13
B. −12
C. −6.5
D. 6.5
E. 12

42. In the figure below, all line segments intersect at right angles, and all measurements are given in inches. What is the perimeter of the figure in inches?

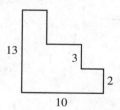

F. 23
G. 28
H. 46
J. 130
K. Cannot be determined

43. A line in the standard (x, y) coordinate plane contains the points (5, 9) and (8, 3). What is the x-intercept of this line?

A. 19
B. $\dfrac{19}{2}$
C. 0
D. −2
E. $-\dfrac{19}{2}$

44. Each side of a given cube is a square with an area of 729 square inches. What is the volume of the cube in cubic inches?

F. 3^3

G. 3^9

H. 3^{12}

J. 3^{18}

K. 3^{64}

45. If p and q are positive integers, and $6pq^4$ and $12p^2q^2$ have a greatest common factor of 1,050, then which of the following is a possible value for the sum of p and q?

A. 6

B. 8

C. 12

D. 35

E. 42

46. In the figure shown below, $\triangle ABC$ is a right triangle, $\overline{AB}$ is 8 inches long, and $\overline{BC}$ is 10 inches long. What is the area, in square inches, of square $ACDE$?

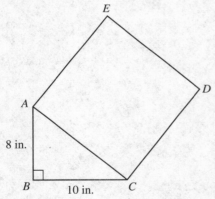

F. $2\sqrt{41}$

G. $\sqrt{164}$

H. 36

J. $8\sqrt{41}$

K. 164

DO YOUR FIGURING HERE

DO YOUR FIGURING HERE

47. The decimal equivalent of $\frac{1}{13}$ is $0.\overline{076923}$.
    What is the digit in the sixty-third place after the decimal point?
    A. 2
    B. 3
    C. 6
    D. 7
    E. 9

48. What value must be added to $9x^2 - 30x$ in order to *complete the square* (that is, make it a perfect square trinomial)?
    F. -5
    G. 5
    H. 9
    J. 25
    K. 45

49. A circle in the standard (x, y) coordinate plane is tangent to the x-axis at $-a$, and tangent to the y-axis at a, with $a > 0$. The radius of the circle is 4 units. What is the equation of the circle?
    A. $x^2 + y^2 = 4$
    B. $x^2 + y^2 = 16$
    C. $(x-4)^2 + (y-4)^2 = 4$
    D. $(x+4)^2 + (y+4)^2 = 16$
    E. $(x+4)^2 + (y-4)^2 = 16$

50. Compared to the graph of $y = \sin x$, the graph of $y = 2\sin(4x)$ has:
    F. 8 times the amplitude and the same period.
    G. 2 times the amplitude and 4 times the period.
    H. 2 times the amplitude and $\frac{1}{4}$ the period.
    J. $\frac{1}{2}$ the amplitude and 4 times the period.
    K. $\frac{1}{2}$ the amplitude and $\frac{1}{4}$ the period.

51. Which of the following is the solution set for x such that $3x - 9 \geq -3(9 - x)$?

   A. The empty set

   B. The set containing only zero

   C. The set of negative numbers

   D. The set of positive numbers

   E. The set of real numbers

DO YOUR FIGURING HERE

52. In the figure below, square $ABCD$ has a side length of 6 inches, and squares $AEFG$ and $CHIJ$ each have a side length of 1 inch. What is the area, in square inches, of the shaded pentagon $DGFIJ$?

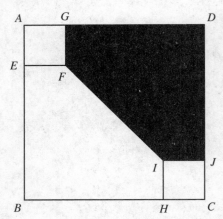

   F. 9

   G. 12.5

   H. 17

   J. 18

   K. 20.5

53. Consider matrices A, B, C, and D with dimensions as follows:

$A = 2 \times 2 \quad B = 2 \times 3 \quad C = 3 \times 2 \quad D = 3 \times 3$

Which of the following matrix products is NOT defined?

   A. AB

   B. BC

   C. CB

   D. CD

   E. DC

54. If $x^2 - 36a^2 = 5ax$, what are the two solutions for x in terms of a?

DO YOUR FIGURING HERE

    F. $-4a$ and $-9a$

    G. $-4a$ and $9a$

    H. $-3a$ and $12a$

    J. $3a$ and $-12a$

    K. $4a$ and $-9a$

55. For all values of θ over which $\sin \theta$ and $\cos \theta$ are positive, $\dfrac{\sqrt{1 - \cos^2 \theta}}{\sin^2 \theta} \cdot \cos \theta = ?$

    A. 1

    B. $\tan \theta$

    C. $\cot \theta$

    D. $\sec \theta$

    E. $\csc \theta$

56. If $\log_a x = p$, $\log_a y = q$, and $\log_a z = t$, then $\log_a\left(\dfrac{x^2 y^3}{\sqrt{z}}\right)$ is equivalent to:

    F. $p^2 q^3 - \sqrt{z}$

    G. $\dfrac{p^2 q^3}{\sqrt{z}}$

    H. $2p + 3q + \dfrac{1}{2}t$

    J. $2p + 3q - \dfrac{1}{2}t$

    K. $2p + 3q - t^{\frac{1}{2}}$

57. What is the solution set for the equation $|-x| = x$?

A. All real numbers

B. $x \geq 0$

C. $x \leq 0$

D. Only $x = 0$

E. Only $x = -1$

58. For which of the following values of a will there be exactly one real solution to the equation $2x^2 - ax + 8 = 0$?

F. $2\sqrt{3}$

G. 4

H. $4\sqrt{3}$

J. 6

K. 8

59. If $x = 3t + 4$ and $y = 5 - t$, then which of the following equations expresses y in terms of x?

A. $y = \dfrac{19 - x}{3}$

B. $y = \dfrac{1 - x}{3}$

C. $y = 9 - x$

D. $y = x + 9$

E. $y = x - 1$

DO YOUR FIGURING HERE

60. In the circle below, radius $\overline{OA}$ has a length of 10 meters, and central angle $\angle AOB$ measures 30°. What is the area, in square meters, of shaded sector *AOB*?

F. $\dfrac{5\pi}{6}$

G. $\dfrac{5\pi}{3}$

H. $\dfrac{10\pi}{3}$

J. $\dfrac{25\pi}{6}$

K. $\dfrac{25\pi}{3}$

STOP

If there is still time remaining, you may review your answers.

READING TEST

Time: 35 Minutes—40 Questions

Directions: There are four passages in this test. Each passage is followed by several questions. After reading a passage, choose the best answer to each question and fill in the corresponding oval on your answer sheet. You may refer to the passages as often as necessary.

PASSAGE I—LITERARY NARRATIVE

This passage is adapted from the short story "A Very Old Man With Enormous Wings" by Gabriel Garcia Márquez (© 1971 by Gabriel Garcia Márquez).

The light was so weak at noon that when Pelayo was coming back to the house, it was hard for him to see what it was that was moving and groaning in the rear of the courtyard. He had
(5) to go very close to see that it was an old man lying face down in the mud, who, in spite of his tremendous efforts, couldn't get up, impeded by his enormous wings.

Pelayo ran to get Elisenda, his wife, who was
(10) putting compresses on the sick child, and he took her to the rear of the courtyard. They both looked at the fallen body with a mute stupor. There were only a few faded hairs left on his bald skull and very few teeth in his mouth, and his
(15) pitiful condition took away any sense of grandeur he might have had. And yet, they called in a neighbor woman who knew everything about life and death to see him, and all she needed was one look.

(20) "He's an angel," she told them. "He must have been coming for the child, but the poor fellow is so old that the rain knocked him down."

On the following day everyone knew that a flesh-and-blood angel was held captive in Pelayo's
(25) house. With the first light of dawn, they found the whole neighborhood in front of the chicken coop having fun with the angel, tossing him things to eat through the openings in the wire.

The news of the captive angel spread with
(30) such rapidity that after a few hours the courtyard had the bustle of a marketplace and they had to call in troops with fixed bayonets to disperse the mob that was about to knock the house down. Elisenda, her spine all twisted from sweeping up
(35) so much marketplace trash, then got the idea of fencing in the yard and charging five cents admission to see the angel.

The curious came from far away. The most unfortunate invalids on earth came in search of
(40) health: a poor woman who since childhood has been counting her heartbeats and had run out of numbers; a Portuguese man who couldn't sleep because the noise of the stars disturbed him; a sleepwalker who got up at night to undo the things
(45) he had done while awake; and many others with less serious ailments. Pelayo and Elisenda were happy with fatigue, for in less than a week they had crammed their rooms with money and the line of pilgrims waiting their turn to enter still
(50) reached beyond the horizon.

The angel was the only one who took no part in his own act. He spent his time trying to get comfortable in his borrowed nest, befuddled by the heat of the oil lamps and sacramen-
(55) tal candles that had been placed along the wire. At first they tried to make him eat some mothballs, which, according to the wisdom of the wise neighbor woman, were the food prescribed for angels. But he turned them
(60) down. His only supernatural virtue seemed to be patience. Especially during the first days, when the hens pecked at him, searching for the stellar parasites that proliferated in his wings, and even the most merciful threw stones
(65) at him, trying to get him to rise so they could see him standing.

It so happened that during those days there arrived in the town the traveling show of the woman who had been changed into a spider for (70) having disobeyed her parents. The admission to see her was not only less than the admission to see the angel, but people were permitted to ask her all manner of questions and to examine her up and down. While still practically a child (75) she had sneaked out of her parents' house to go to a dance, and while she was coming back through the woods after having danced all night without permission, a fearful thunderclap rent the sky in two and through the crack came the (80) lightning bolt of brimstone that changed her into a spider. A spectacle like that, with such a fearful lesson, was bound to defeat that of a haughty angel who scarcely deigned to look at mortals. Pelayo's courtyard went back to being as (85) empty as during the time it had rained for three days and crabs walked through the bedrooms.

With the money they saved they built a two-story mansion with iron bars on the windows so that angels wouldn't get in. Pelayo also set up a (90) rabbit warren close to town and gave up his job as a bailiff for good, and Elisenda bought some satin pumps with high heels and many dresses of iridescent silk, the kind worn on Sunday by the most desirable women in those times.

(95) One morning Elisenda was cutting some bunches of onions for lunch when a wind that seemed to come from the high seas blew into the kitchen. Then she went to the window and caught the angel in his first attempts at flight. He was on (100) the point of knocking the shed down with the ungainly flapping that slipped on the light and couldn't get a grip on the air. But he did manage to gain altitude. Elisenda let out a sigh of relief, for herself and for him, when she watched him pass (105) over the last houses. She kept watching him even when she was through cutting the onions, until it was no longer possible for her to see him, because then he was no longer an annoyance in her life but an imaginary dot on the horizon of the sea.

1. The inhabitants of the town in which the story takes place are depicted as:
   A. proud and stubborn people who are always arguing about religion.
   B. laid-back people who react to odd events with less surprise than one might expect.
   C. wise people who are always constructing elaborate theories about the universe.
   D. devious people who will do anything to make money.

2. The "neighbor woman" believes that the angel is a (an):
   F. angel of death.
   G. angel of good fortune.
   H. warrior angel.
   J. angel who can predict the future.

3. All of the following are described in detail EXCEPT:
   A. the ailments of the invalids.
   B. the girl who disobeyed her parents.
   C. the clothes bought by Elisenda.
   D. the crabs brought by the rainstorm.

4. The character of the angel can best be described as
   F. wise and loving.
   G. powerful but unforgiving.
   H. baffling and mysterious.
   J. pessimistic but determined.

5. Elisenda's idea to start charging people admission to see the angel is a (an):
   A. disrespectful decision motivated by greed.
   B. understandable decision motivated by necessity.
   C. risky decision motivated by poor business sense.
   D. weak decision motivated by her tendency to be influenced by others.

6. When they first encounter him, the townspeople treat the angel as if he is a (an):
   F. animal.
   G. impostor.
   H. impartial judge.
   J. bad omen.

7. All of the following are reasons why people became more interested in the spider girl than they had been in the angel EXCEPT:
   A. it is more obvious what moral they are supposed to learn from her.
   B. she is more willing to interact with her audience.
   C. she has been officially approved by local religious authorities.
   D. it is less expensive to see her.

8. Which of the following phrases indicates that the appearance of the angel is regarded as a somewhat normal occurrence?
   F. "They both looked at the fallen body with a mute stupor." (lines 11–12)
   G. "The most unfortunate invalids on earth came in search of health." (lines 38–40)
   H. "The angel was the only one who took no part in his own act." (lines 51–52)
   J. "they built a two-story mansion with iron bars on the windows so that angels wouldn't get in." (lines 87–89)

9. At the beginning of the story, Pelayo is employed as a (an):
   A. farmer.
   B. fisherman.
   C. bailiff.
   D. architect.

10. The main point of the last paragraph is that after the departure of the angel, Elisenda feels:
    F. remorseful about how poorly the townspeople treated the angel.
    G. frightened about what the angel might do if he ever comes back.
    H. optimistic about the new lifestyle that was made possible for her by the angel.
    J. unburdened now that she doesn't have to worry about the angel anymore.

PASSAGE II—SOCIAL SCIENCE

Passage A is adapted from "Whether Toleration Is Dangerous" by Voltaire. Passage B is adapted from *Civilization and Its Discontents* by Sigmund Freud.

Passage A by Voltaire

There are some who say that, if we treated with paternal indulgence those erring brethren who pray to God in bad French (instead of bad Latin), we should be putting weapons in their
(5) hands, and would once more witness the battles of Jarnac, Moncontour, Coutras, Dreux, and St. Denis. I do not know anything about this, as I am not a prophet; but it seems to me an illogical piece of reasoning to say "These men rebelled
(10) when I treated them ill; therefore, they will rebel when I treat them well."

I would venture to take the liberty to invite those who are at the head of the government, and those who are destined for high positions,
(15) to reflect carefully whether one really has ground to fear that kindness will lead to the same revolts as cruelty; whether what happened in certain circumstances is sure to happen in different circumstances; if the times, public opinion, and
(20) morals are unchanged.

The Huguenots, it is true, have been as inebriated with fanaticism and stained with blood as we. But are this generation as barbaric as their fathers? Have not time, the progress of reason,

(25) good books, and the humanising influence of society had an effect on the leaders of these people? And do we not perceive that the aspect of nearly the whole of Europe has been changed within the last fifty years? Government is stronger (30) everywhere, and morals have improved. Different times have different needs. It would be absurd to decimate the Sorbonne today because it once presented a demand for the burning of the Maid of Orleans, as stupid as to purge all (35) the inhabitants of Marseilles because they had the plague in 1720.

Toleration never led to civil war; intolerance has covered the earth with carnage. I speak here only of the interest of nations. While respecting (40) theology, as I do, I regard in this article only the physical and moral well-being of society. I beg every impartial reader to weigh these truths, verify them, and add to them. Attentive readers, who restrain not their thoughts, always go (45) farther than the author.

Passage B by Sigmund Freud

The clue may be supplied by one of the ideal demands, as we have called them, of civilized society. It runs: "Thou shall love thy neighbour as thyself." Let us adopt a naive attitude towards (50) it, as though we were hearing it for the first time; we shall be unable to suppress a feeling of bewilderment. Why should we do it? What good will it do us? My love is something valuable to me which I ought not to throw away without (55) reflection. It imposes duties on me for whose fulfilment I must be ready to make sacrifices. If I love someone, he must deserve it in some way. He deserves it if he is so like me in important ways that I can love myself in him; and he (60) deserves it if he is so much more perfect than myself that I can love my ideal of my own self in him. I have to love him if he is my friend's son, since the pain my friend would feel if any harm came to him would be my pain too. But if he is

(65) a stranger to me and cannot attract me by any worth of his own, it will be hard for me to love him. Indeed, I should be wrong to do so, for my love is valued by all my own people, and it is an injustice to them if I put a stranger on a par with (70) them. What is the point of a precept enunciated with so much solemnity if its fulfilment cannot be recommended as reasonable?

On closer inspection, I find still further difficulties. Not merely is this stranger in general (75) unworthy of my love; I must honestly confess that he has more claim to my hostility and even my hatred. He seems not to have the least trace of love for me and shows me not the slightest consideration. If it will do him any good he has (80) no hesitation in injuring me, nor does he ask himself whether the amount of advantage he gains bears any proportion to the extent of the harm he does to me. Indeed, he need not even obtain an advantage; if he can satisfy any sort (85) of desire by it, he thinks nothing of jeering at me, insulting me, slandering me and showing his superior power; and the more secure he feels and the more helpless I am, the more certainly I can expect him to behave like this to (90) me. If he behaves differently, I am ready to treat him in the same way. Indeed, if this grandiose commandment had run "Love thy neighbour as thy neighbour loves thee," I should not take exception to it.

(95) The truth behind all this, which people are so ready to disavow, is that men are not gentle creatures who merely defend themselves if attacked; they are, on the contrary, creatures among whose instinctual endowments is a (100) powerful share of aggressiveness. As a result, their neighbour is someone who tempts them to satisfy their aggressiveness on him, to humiliate him, to cause him pain, to torture and to kill him. Who, in the face of all his experience (105) of life and of history, will have the courage to dispute this assertion?

Questions 11–13 ask about Passage A.

11. Which of the following inferences would be most strongly supported by a reading of Passage A?

   A. The Huguenots were a French religious minority that had violently revolted in the past, but not recently as of the time of the passage's composition.

   B. The battles referenced by the author in line 5 were not real historical events, but legendary battles that have great symbolic significance in French culture.

   C. The author believes praying in Latin to be absurd and self-important but praying in French to be an admirable mark of humility.

   D. Marseilles was a French ghost town, all of its former inhabitants having perished in the year 1720.

12. Based on an understanding of the passage as a whole, it is most logical to assume that, in his discussion upon how much Europe has improved in the recent past (lines 24–35), the author of Passage A is:

   F. being sarcastic.

   G. being completely serious.

   H. seeking to prompt discussion of complex questions to which he genuinely does not know the answers.

   J. testing the reader's knowledge.

13. Based on the contexts of the passage as a whole and of the closing paragraph specifically, the concluding sentence of Passage A ("Attentive readers … the author") was most likely intended by Voltaire to be a:

   A. clue to the fact that the essay contains some sort of hidden message that was too controversial for him to state openly.

   B. subtle foreshadowing of the fact that Voltaire was dying, suspected that this might be his final essay, and wished his readers to carry on his work.

   C. genuine compliment to his readers, made in the hopes of enlisting the aid of as many of them as possible in a worthy cause.

   D. biting joke at the expense of readers who would seek to imply that his authorship of this essay implicates Voltaire as a party to some Huguenot conspiracy.

Questions 14–17 ask about Passage B.

14. Which of the following statements best captures how Passage B characterizes the obstacle(s) to "Love thy neighbor as thyself" ever being widely practiced?

   F. Human beings are simply biologically predisposed to regular acts of unprovoked aggression.

   G. The expression has become so familiar by now that it is difficult for people to stop and think about what it truly means, as though hearing it for the first time.

   H. Mankind's long history of violence means that different groups of people have built up too much resentment for each other at this point to ever get over it.

   J. Psychologists and philosophers have historically always failed in their attempts to establish that the advice is reasonable.

15. In lines 52–72, the author of Passage B presents:

  A. his own personal argument for why "Love thy neighbor" is flawed advice.

  B. his approximation of what he deems the average person's true inner reaction to "Love thy neighbor" to be, on an unspoken emotional level.

  C. a deliberately bad argument against "Love thy neighbor," the flaws of which he will explain later in the passage.

  D. a lament for the sad act that "Love thy neighbor" is impossible because humans do not have any control over who they love.

16. As it is used in line 91, the word *grandiose* is most nearly synonymous with which of the following phrases?

  F. "A wolf in sheep's clothing"

  G. "The canary in the coal mine"

  H. "Full of hot air"

  J. "As clear as mud"

17. In light of Sigmund Freud's status as one of the most innovative thinkers in human history, the style and structure of Passage A is unexpected and ironic because:

  A. nearly every claim it makes is presented as something that everybody already knows.

  B. it analyzes a religious proverb as though it were a scientific hypothesis.

  C. Freud concludes it with a pessimistic and overdramatic prophecy about how nobody will believe him.

  D. most of its assertions are supported solely by personal anecdotes from Freud's own life.

Questions 18–20 ask about both passages.

18. The potential rebuttal to Passage A that is implicit in the conclusions of Passage B would most nearly be that:

  F. policies of tolerance will not end violence, as people will find excuses to hate one another no matter what.

  G. tolerance could only ever be proposed by someone who sees his own position as weak—if he were confident of his strength, he would seek to oppress his enemies.

  H. people only preach tolerance as a means of distracting themselves from truths they are unwilling to admit.

  J. the fact that revenge is a moral obligation means that tolerance itself is an injustice.

19. Based on the two passages, the question that the author of Passage A would presumably be most eager to ask the author of Passage B would concern whether:

  A. increasingly fair and just laws are at least capable of significantly decreasing violence, even if the aggressive instinct must forever remain with us.

  B. he is willing to admit the fact that the world has been improved by unreasonable things occasionally.

  C. there is a chance that, rather than human nature being inherently bad, human beings are merely reinforcing the worst parts of it by concentrating on the past.

  D. he believes that human beings' treatment of one another has been getting steadily better throughout history, or whether this assessment is just an illusion.

20. Which of the following is the most accurate and thought-provoking comparison of the two passages' closing paragraphs?

   F. Both authors take it for granted that violence is a bad thing, despite admitting that it has been common at all times in all places.

   G. Though Passage B primarily seeks to rebut a religious concept, it is Passage A that sees theology as being inherently at odds with the interest of nations.

   H. Neither author draws a distinction between humans and the rest of the animal kingdom, despite the fact that both closing paragraphs demand one.

   J. Though the passages' claims contradict each other, both authors expect all readers to assess their points as self-evident and undeniable.

PASSAGE III—HUMANITIES

This passage is adapted from the essay "My Father's Suitcase" by Orhan Pamuk (© 2006 Orhan Pamuk).

Two years before my father died, he gave me a small suitcase filled with his manuscripts and notebooks. Assuming his usual jocular, mock-
(5) ing air, he told me that he wanted me to read them after he was gone, by which he meant after his death.

"Just take a look," he said, slightly embarrassed. "See if there's anything in there that you can use. Maybe after I'm gone you can make a
(10) selection and publish it." We were in my study, surrounded by books. My father was searching for a place to set down the suitcase, wandering around like a man who wished to rid himself of a painful burden. In the end, he deposited it
(15) quietly, unobtrusively, in a corner.

For several days after that, I walked back and forth past the suitcase without ever actually touching it. I knew what was inside some of the notebooks it held. I had seen my father writing

(20) in them. In his youth, he had wanted to be an Istanbul poet, but he had not wanted to live the sort of life that came with writing poetry in a poor country where there were few readers.

The first thing that kept me away from my
(25) father's suitcase was, of course, a fear that I might not like what I read. Because my father understood this, he had taken the precaution of acting as if he did not take the contents of the case seriously. By this time, I had been working as a writer for
(30) twenty-five years, and his failure to take literature seriously pained me. But my real fear—the crucial thing that I did not wish to discover—was that my father might be a good writer. If great literature emerged from my father's suitcase, I would have
(35) to acknowledge that inside my father there existed a man entirely different from the one I knew. This was a frightening possibility. Even at my advanced age, I wanted my father to be my father and my father only—not a writer.

(40) A writer is someone who spends years patiently trying to discover the second being inside him, and the world that makes him who he is. To write is to transform that inward gaze into words, to study the worlds into which we pass
(45) when we retire into ourselves, and to do so with patience, obstinacy, and joy. As I sit at my table, for days, months, years, slowly adding words to empty pages, I feel as if I were bringing into being that other person inside me, in the same
(50) way that one might build a bridge or a dome, stone by stone.

I was afraid of opening my father's suitcase and reading his notebooks because I knew that he would never have tolerated the difficulties that
(55) I had tolerated, that it was not solitude he loved but mixing with friends, crowds, company. I would have to remember that my father enjoyed being alone with his books and his thoughts—and not pay too much attention to the literary quality
(60) of his writing. But as I gazed so anxiously at the suitcase he had bequeathed to me I also felt that this was the very thing I would not be able to do.

In fact, I was angry at my father because he had not led a life like mine—because he had
(65) never quarreled with his life, and had spent it happily laughing with his friends and his loved ones. But part of me also knew that I was not so much "angry" as "jealous," and this, too, made me uneasy. What is happiness? Is happiness
(70) believing that you live a deep life in your lonely room? Or is happiness leading a comfortable life in society, believing in the same things as everyone else, or, at least, acting as if you did? Is it happiness or unhappiness to go through
(75) life writing in secret, while seeming to be in harmony with all that surrounds you?

On some deeper level, I was able to become a writer because my father, in his youth, had also wished to be one. I would have to read him
(80) with tolerance—to seek to understand what he had written in those hotel rooms. It was with these hopeful thoughts that I walked over to the suitcase, which was still sitting where my father had left it. Using all my will power, I read
(85) through a few manuscripts and notebooks. What had my father written about? I recall a few views from the windows of Paris hotels, a few poems, paradoxes, analyses …

A week after he left me his suitcase, my father
(90) paid me another visit; as always, he brought me a bar of chocolate (he had forgotten that I was forty-eight years old). As always, we chatted and laughed about life, politics, and family gossip. A moment arrived when my father's gaze drifted
(95) to the corner where he had left his suitcase, and he saw that I had moved it. We looked each other in the eye. There followed a pressing silence. I did not tell him that I had opened the suitcase and tried to read its contents; instead, I looked
(100) away. But he understood. Just as I understood that he had understood. Because my father was a happy, easygoing man who had faith in himself, he smiled at me the way he always did. And, as he left the house, he repeated all the
(105) lovely and encouraging things he always said to me, like a father.

As always, I watched him leave, envying his happiness, his carefree and unflappable temperament. But I remember that on that day
(110) there was also a flash of joy inside me that made me ashamed. It was prompted by the thought that maybe I wasn't as comfortable in life as he was, maybe I had not led as happy or footloose a life as he had, but at least I had devoted mine
(115) to writing. I was ashamed to be thinking such things at my father's expense—of all people, my father, who had never been a source of pain to me, who had left me free. All this should remind us that writing and literature are intimately
(120) linked to a void at the center of our lives, to our feelings of happiness and guilt.

21. The author of the passage would most strongly agree with which of the following statements?
   A. Happiness can only be found through others.
   B. The paths that children take can be predicted by anyone who knows their parents well.
   C. Good writing is actually the opposite of what has traditionally been viewed as "great literature."
   D. Writing is largely a solitary endeavor.

22. All of the following are reasons why the author is afraid to open the suitcase and read its contents EXCEPT:
   F. he fears that he will come to see his father as a writer, rather than as just his father.
   G. he suspects that the notebooks might contain painful secrets about his parents' relationship.
   H. he suspects that his father's writing will force him to examine his own ideas about happiness.
   J. he is afraid that his father's writing will be very good.

23. In the context of the passage, the statement "he had forgotten that I was forty-eight years old" (lines 91–92) suggests that the:
    A. author's father is becoming absent-minded in his old age.
    B. author's father was absent for most of his childhood.
    C. author's father still treats him like a child in some small ways.
    D. author may have been adopted.

24. When the author says that his father "would never have tolerated the difficulties that I had tolerated" (lines 54–55), he means that his father:
    F. prioritized making money when he was a younger man.
    G. could not have endured the solitude that real writing demands.
    H. tended toward orthodoxy in his political and religious opinions.
    J. fled their native country rather than trying to improve it from within.

25. As it is used in line 15, *unobtrusively* most nearly means:
    A. inconspicuously.
    B. rudely.
    C. painfully.
    D. ashamedly.

26. The author mentions feeling all of the following emotions concerning his father EXCEPT:
    F. anger.
    G. joy.
    H. jealousy.
    J. suspicion.

27. The main point of paragraph 7 (lines 63–76) is that:
    A. the author is jealous of his father for being able to make friends so easily wherever he goes.
    B. happiness means being in harmony with all that surrounds you.
    C. it is unclear whether the author's approach to life or his father's is ultimately more satisfying.
    D. there is really no such thing as true happiness.

28. Writing, according to the author, is a lifelong process of discovering:
    F. an alternate version of oneself.
    G. one's relationship to one's native country.
    H. one's true feelings about one's family.
    J. the true nature of happiness.

29. When the author's father was young, he aspired to write:
    A. novels.
    B. poetry.
    C. plays.
    D. comedy.

30. The point of the last paragraph (lines 107–121) is that:
    F. the author did not realize until that day that his father truly loved him.
    G. the author is ashamed of his father.
    H. writing draws on negative emotions as well as positive ones.
    J. the author has finally decided to have children of his own.

PASSAGE IV—NATURAL SCIENCE

This passage is adapted from *The Selfish Gene* by Richard Dawkins (© 1976 Oxford University Press).

Most of what is unusual about man can be summed up in one word: "culture." I use the word not in its snobbish sense, but as a scientist uses it. Cultural transmission is analogous to genetic
(5) transmission in that, although basically conservative, it can give rise to a form of evolution. Geoffrey Chaucer could not hold a conversation with a modern Englishman, even though they are linked to each other by an unbroken chain of
(10) some twenty generations of Englishmen, each of whom could speak to his immediate neighbors in the chain as a son speaks to his father. Language seems to "evolve" by non-genetic means, and at a rate which is orders of magnitude faster than
(15) genetic evolution.

As an enthusiastic Darwinian, I have been dissatisfied with explanations that my fellow-enthusiasts have offered for human behavior. They have tried to look for "biological advan-
(20) tages" in various attributes of human civilization. These ideas are plausible as far as they go, but I find that they do not begin to square up to the formidable challenge of explaining culture, cultural evolution, and the immense
(25) differences between human cultures around the world. I think we have got to start again and go right back to first principles. The argument I shall advance is that, for an understanding of the evolution of modern man, we must begin
(30) by throwing out the gene as the sole basis of our ideas on evolution.

What, after all, is so special about genes? The answer is that they are replicators. But do we have to go to distant worlds to find other kinds
(35) of replicators and other kinds of evolution? I think that a new kind of replicator has recently emerged on this very planet. It is staring us in the face. It is still in its infancy, still drifting clumsily about in its primeval soup, but already

(40) it is achieving evolutionary change at a rate that leaves the old gene panting far behind.

The new soup is the soup of human culture. We need a name for the new replicator, a noun that conveys the idea of a unit of cultural
(45) transmission, or a unit of *imitation*. "Mimeme" comes from a suitable Greek root, but I want a monosyllable that sounds a bit like "gene." I hope my classicist friends will forgive me if I abbreviate "mimeme" to *meme*. Examples of
(50) memes are tunes, ideas, catch-phrases, clothes fashions, ways of making pots or of building arches. Just as genes propagate themselves in the gene pool by leaping from body to body, so memes propagate themselves in the meme pool
(55) by leaping from brain to brain. If a scientist hears, or reads about, a good idea, he passes it on to his colleagues and students. He mentions it in his articles and his lectures. If the idea catches on, it can be said to propagate itself, spreading
(60) from brain to brain.

Imitation, in the broad sense, is how memes *can* replicate. But just as not all genes that can replicate do so successfully, so some memes are more successful in the meme-pool than others.
(65) The longevity of any one copy of a meme is probably relatively unimportant, as it is for any one copy of a gene. The copy of the tune "Auld Lang Syne" that exists in my brain will last only for the rest of my life. But I expect there will be copies of
(70) the same tune on paper and in people's brains for centuries to come. If the meme is a scientific idea, its spread will depend on how acceptable it is to the population of individual scientists; a rough measure of its survival value could be obtained
(75) by counting the number of times it is referred to in successive years in scientific journals. If it is a popular tune, its spread through the meme pool may be gauged by the number of people heard whistling it in the streets. If it is a style of
(80) women's shoe, the population memeticist may use sales statistics from shoe shops.

Some memes, like some genes, achieve brilliant short-term success in spreading rapidly,

but do not last long in the meme pool. Popular
(85) songs and stiletto heels are examples. Others may
continue to propagate themselves for thousands
of years, usually because of the great potential
permanence of written records.

When we die there are two things we can leave
(90) behind us: genes and memes. We were built as
gene machines, created to pass on our genes.
But that aspect of us will be forgotten in three
generations. Your child, even your grandchild,
may bear a resemblance to you, perhaps in fa-
(95) cial features, in a talent for music, in the color
of her hair. But as each generation passes, the
contribution of your genes is halved. It does not
take long to reach negligible proportions. We
should not seek immortality in reproduction.
(100) But if you contribute to the world's culture, if
you have a good idea, compose a tune, invent a
sparking plug, write a poem, it may live on, intact,
long after your genes have dissolved in the common pool. Socrates may or may not have a gene
(105) or two alive in the world today, but who cares?
The meme-complexes of Socrates, Leonardo,
Copernicus and Marconi are still going strong.

31. The author's motivation in writing the
passage is his belief that:
A. genes actually have nothing to do with
human evolution.
B. genetics does not sufficiently explain
human culture.
C. culture is too obsessed with trivial things
like fashion and pop songs.
D. humans are too concerned with seeking
immortality.

32. When the author says that he uses the word
culture "not in its snobbish sense, but as a
scientist uses it" (lines 3–4), he means that
he:
F. plans to honestly admit what aspects
of culture he really likes, rather than
pretending he only likes the critically
respected things.
G. does not believe that there is really such a
thing as culture at all.
H. thinks that culture can be completely
explained by Darwinian evolution.
J. does not distinguish between "good" and
"bad" culture, but refers merely to the
facts of human civilization.

33. The author argues that all of the following
would constitute examples of *memes*
EXCEPT:
A. a word.
B. a piece of music.
C. a particular hair color.
D. a fashion item.

34. According to the author, one thing that genes
and memes have in common is that they are
both:
F. examples of replicators.
G. still only unproven theories rather than
facts.
H. ideas that people in the future will only
know about because of written records.
J. capable of inspiring great art.

35. The author mentions Geoffrey Chaucer in the first paragraph as an example of:
  A. a pioneer in the field of mimetics.
  B. one of the first major poets to write in English.
  C. someone who would not have understood modern science, even though he was a genius for his time.
  D. a speaker of English as it existed twenty generations ago.

36. As it is used in lines 52, 54, 59, and 86, the word *propagate* most nearly means:
  F. multiply.
  G. change.
  H. prove.
  J. conceal.

37. According to the passage, the word *memes* was invented by:
  A. the ancient Greeks.
  B. friends of the author.
  C. the author's former teacher.
  D. the author himself.

38. The author states that "[t]he copy of the tune 'Auld Lang Syne' that exists in my brain will last only for the rest of my life" (lines 67–69) in order to demonstrate that:
  F. no two people's brains are alike.
  G. memories do not survive death.
  H. no one copy of an idea is vital, as long as the idea survives.
  J. he is older than he imagines most of his readers will be, and accordingly has memories of older songs.

39. According to the author, the "survival value" of a meme is expressed by:
  A. how widespread the meme itself becomes.
  B. how it contributes to the survival of the people who have memories of it.
  C. whether it makes the people who have memories of it into better people or worse people.
  D. whether scientists believe that it is true or false.

40. The author mentions "Socrates, Leonardo, Copernicus and Marconi" in the closing paragraph because they are:
  F. people whose genes have become extremely widespread.
  G. people whose ideas have become extremely influential.
  H. the four most complex thinkers in the history of science.
  J. the people who made the biggest contributions to the field of memetics.

If there is still time remaining, you may review your answers.

SCIENCE TEST

Time: 35 Minutes—40 Questions

> **Directions:** There are six passages in this test. Each passage is followed by several questions. After reading a passage, choose the best answer to each question and fill in the corresponding oval on your answer sheet. You may refer to the passages as often as necessary.
>
> You are NOT permitted to use a calculator on this test.

PASSAGE I

Scientists examined several ingredients commonly used as active agents in sunscreen. The goal of the study was to determine which ingredients are most effective at blocking harmful UV rays.

Scientists used PABA, oxybenzone, octyl salicylate, and a broad-spectrum commercial sunscreen (SPF 45). The samples were exposed to sunlight with wavelengths ranging from 240 to 440 nm. The percent transmittance of UV rays at each wavelength was recorded. The data was collected manually using a spectrophotometer. The results, in 20-nm increments, are shown in Table 1.

Table 1

nm	PABA	Oxybenzone	Octyl Salicylate	Commercial Sunscreen
240	38.2	15.7	12.7	15.2
260	2.9	19.2	83.5	24.5
280	1.7	3.2	33.1	4.2
300	9	4.2	3	1.5
320	82.9	6	10.8	2.5
340	99.2	9.7	93.5	25.5
360	100	45.3	100	67.6
380	100	92.6	100	96.8
400	100	100	100	99.8
420	100	100	100	100
440	100	100	100	100

Figure 1 displays the intensity of sunlight across the spectrum.

Figure 1

In 1975, Thomas B. Fitzpatrick, MD, Ph.D., of Harvard Medical School, developed a classification system for skin type. This system was based on a person's complexion and responses to sun exposure. Table 2 lists the skin types and their characteristics.

Table 2

Skin Type	Color	Reaction to UVA	Reaction to Sun
Type I	Very fair skin tone	Very sensitive	Always burns easily, never tans
Type II	Fair skin tone	Very sensitive	Usually burns easily, tans with difficulty
Type III	Fair to medium skin tone	Sensitive	Burns moderately, tans gradually
Type IV	Medium skin tone	Moderately sensitive	Rarely burns, always tans well
Type V	Olive or dark skin tone	Minimally sensitive	Very rarely burns, tans very easily
Type VI	Very dark skin tone	Least sensitive	Never burns, deeply pigmented

1. According to Table 1, which substance had the highest percent transmittance of UV rays for sunlight with a wavelength of 260 nm?
   A. Octyl salicylate
   B. PABA
   C. Oxybenzone
   D. Commercial sunscreen

2. Based on the information in Figure 1, sunlight is most intense at which of the following wavelengths?
   F. 290 nm
   G. 300 nm
   H. 320 nm
   J. 340 nm

3. A person with fair skin tone, whose skin burns but also tans slowly, likely has which of the following skin types?
   A. Type I
   B. Type II
   C. Type III
   D. Type IV

4. Experts state that anyone whose skin is sensitive or very sensitive to UVA should always wear sunscreen. According to Table 2, people with which skin types should always wear sunscreen?
   F. Types I and II
   G. Types I, II, and III
   H. Types II, III, and IV
   J. Types V and VI

5. In sunlight with an irradiance of 0.01 W/m²/nm, oxybenzone would be expected to have a UV ray percent transmittance of:
   A. 3.8
   B. 5
   C. 9.7
   D. 100

6. If an individual with Type II skin type was exposed to the sun at a wavelength of 320 nm immediately after applying commercial sunscreen SPF 45, how would their skin most likely be affected?
   F. Their skin would burn because Type II skin is sensitive and sunscreen SPF 45 does not block most of the sun's harmful rays at 320 nm wavelength.
   G. Their skin would burn because 320 nm wavelength is very damaging and would burn any skin type.
   H. Their skin would not burn because though they have sensitive skin, sunscreen SPF 45 blocks most of the sun's rays at 320 nm.
   J. Their skin would not burn because Type II skin is not sensitive enough to cause a burn at 320 nm.

PRACTICE TEST 2

PASSAGE II

The most common type of red-green color perception defect is caused by a mutation on the X chromosome. X-linked red color blindness is a recessive trait. The eggs of the mother will contain either a normal X chromosome (X^R) or an X chromosome with the mutation (X^r) causing red-green color blindness. The sperm of the father will contain the normal X chromosome, the X chromosome with the mutation, or the Y chromosome. Females *heterozygous* (one normal gene, one mutated gene) for this trait have normal vision. The color perception defect manifests itself in females only when it is inherited from both parents. By contrast, males inherit their sole X chromosome from their mothers, and become red-green color blind when this one X chromosome has the color perception defect.

Genotype refers to the combination of alleles that an individual has for a gene. Table 1 lists the possible genotypes for red-green color perception and their corresponding effects on vision.

Table 1

Female Genotype	Vision
$X^R X^R$	normal
$X^R X^r$	normal, carrier
$X^r X^r$	red-green color blind
Male Genotype	Vision
$X^R Y$	normal
$X^r Y$	red-green color blind

Students interviewed members of the Allen family to investigate the inheritance of red-green color blindness. Figure 1 displays the family tree of the Allen family.

Figure 1

Study 1

Students interviewed Barbara and John and learned that Barbara is red-green color blind, while John is not. Based on this information, the students deduced that their four children have the following genotypes:

Females:	$X^R X^r$
Males:	$X^r Y$

Figure 2

Study 2

Students assumed that Liz would have children with a man who has normal vision, and using a Punnett square calculated all of the possible genotypes for their children:

$X^R X^R$	$X^R X^r$
$X^R X^r$	$X^r Y$

Figure 3

Study 3

Students assumed that David would have children with a woman who has red-green color blindness, and using a Punnett square calculated all of the possible genotypes for their children:

$X^r X^r$	$X^r Y$

Figure 4

4 ⬭ ⬭ ⬭ ⬭ ⬭ ⬭ ⬭ ⬭ **4**

7. A female who has normal vision but is a carrier of red-green color blindness must have which of the following genotypes?
   A. $X^R X^R$
   B. $X^R X^r$
   C. $X^r X^r$
   D. $X^R Y$

8. For a couple to produce only red-green color-blind children, regardless of the child's sex, they would need to have which of the following pairs of genotypes?
   F. $X^R X^R$ and $X^r Y$
   G. $X^r X^r$ and $X^R Y$
   H. $X^R X^r$ and $X^r Y$
   J. $X^r X^r$ and $X^r Y$

9. All of the male offspring exhibited red-green color blindness in Studies:
   A. 1 and 3.
   B. 1, 2, and 3.
   C. 2 and 3.
   D. 1 and 2.

10. Suppose that Barbara and John have 4 daughters. According to the information in Study 1 and the passage, how many of their daughters will manifest the color blind defect?
    F. 0
    G. 1
    H. 2
    J. 4

11. The ratio of Barbara and John's offspring with normal vision to offspring with red-green color blindness is:
    A. 1:2
    B. 2:1
    C. 1:1
    D. 3:1

12. Barbara's parents could have had which of the following pairs of genotypes?
    F. $X^r X^r$ and $X^R Y$
    G. $X^R X^r$ and $X^r Y$
    H. $X^R X^R$ and $X^r Y$
    J. $X^R X^R$ and $X^R Y$

13. Using the information in Study 1, if Barbara and John had a daughter who married a man with a genotype of $X^r Y$, what is the chance that the two would produce an offspring that is a carrier for red-green color blindness, but has normal vision?
    A. 25%
    B. 50%
    C. 75%
    D. 100%

PASSAGE III

Crude oil contains many different types of carbons. Different carbon chain lengths have different boiling points, so they can be separated using *distillation*—the process of boiling and then condensing a liquid in order to separate and purify its components (see Figure 1).

Figure 1

Crude oil is put into a boiler. The boiler is connected to a distillation column filled with collection trays. As the heated oil boils, the vapors released enter the distillation column and rise to the top. When a substance in the vapor reaches a height where the temperature of the column is equal to that substance's boiling point, it will condense to form a liquid. The liquid is gathered on the collection trays.

Experiment 1
Students determined the boiling points of various components of crude oil by recording the temperature of the vapor at various heights in the distillation column, then determining which component was collected in each of the eight collection trays. See Table 1 and Table 2.

Table 1

Boiling Point	Tray #
20°C	1
40°C	2
120°C	3
200°C	4
350°C	5
400°C	6
500°C	7
600°C	8

Table 2

Crude Oil Component	Tray #
Gas	1
Naphtha	2
Gasoline	3
Kerosene	4
Diesel	5
Lubricating oil	6
Heavy gas oil	7
Residual oil	8

The students distilled one barrel of crude oil. Figure 2 shows the breakdown of that barrel, in terms of which components were collected.

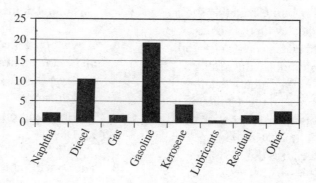

Gallons/barrel of crude oil

Figure 2

Experiment 2

Students determined the number of carbons in each component of crude oil and recorded the data in Table 3.

Table 3

Crude Oil Component	# of Carbons
Diesel	12+
Gas	1–4
Gasoline	5–12
Heavy gas oil	20–70
Kerosene	10–18
Lubricating oil	20–50
Naphtha	5–9
Residual oil	70+

14. Based on the results of Experiment 1, the boiling temperature of naphtha is:
    F. 20°C
    G. 40°C
    H. 120°C
    J. 200°C

15. According to the results of Experiment 1, one barrel of crude oil contains about how many gallons of diesel?
    A. 2
    B. 6
    C. 11
    D. 29

16. One of the students hypothesized that the components of crude oil with the highest boiling points would be collected at the top of the distillation column. Do the results of Experiment 1 support the student's claim?
    F. No. As the vapor rose in the distillation column, the temperature cooled, so the components with the lowest boiling points were collected at the top of the column.
    G. No. There was no correlation between boiling point and location in the distillation column.
    H. Yes. Gasoline and diesel had the highest boiling points, and they were collected in the top two trays.
    J. Yes. The lower the collection tray was in the distillation column, the lower the component's boiling point.

17. A scientist claimed that the more carbons a substance has, the higher its boiling point will be. Do the results of Experiment 1 and Experiment 2 support this claim?
    A. No. There is no relationship between the number of carbons and the boiling point.
    B. No. Diesel has more carbons than gasoline, yet its boiling point is lower.
    C. Yes. Residual oil has the most carbons and the lowest boiling point, whereas gas has the fewest carbons and the highest boiling point.
    D. Yes. Residual oil has the most carbons and the highest boiling point, whereas gas has the fewest carbons and the lowest boiling point.

18. Which of the following components of crude oil has the highest boiling point?
    F. Naphtha
    G. Kerosene
    H. Heavy gas oil
    J. Diesel

19. The data in Table 1 and Figure 2 support which of the following?
    A. Components with the highest boiling points are collected in greatest quantity.
    B. Components with the lowest boiling points are collected in greatest quantity.
    C. Components with medium boiling points are collected in greatest quantity.
    D. Components with higher boiling points are collected in the same quantities as those with medium boiling points.

20. A scientist conducting studies on crude oil discovered another substance contained in the oil with a boiling point of 300 degrees. How many carbons would it likely have in its composition?
    F. 12–18
    G. 5–9
    H. 70+
    J. 20–50

PASSAGE IV

Solubility refers to the ability of one substance, the solute, to dissolve in another (the *solvent*). The balance of molecules between the solvent and the solute determines the solubility of one substance in another. Factors such as temperature and pressure will alter this balance, thus changing the solubility.

Experiments to determine the solubility of methane and carbon dioxide in polyamide (PA-11) were performed in the temperature range 50–90°C, and the pressure range 50–150 atm for methane and 20–40 atm for carbon dioxide. Table 1 displays the solubility (sol) of methane in PA-11. Table 2 shows the solubility (sol) of carbon dioxide in PA-11.

$$\text{Solubility} = (g \text{ gas}/g \text{ PA-11}) \times 10^3$$

Table 1—Methane

T = 50°C		T = 70°C		T = 90°C	
Pressure (atm)	Sol	Pressure (atm)	Sol	Pressure (atm)	Sol
51.2	3.18	55.3	2.61	53.1	2.38
107.2	4.51	104.0	4.97	106.5	5.14
156.6	3.45	158.1	5.33	144.4	6.52

Table 2—Carbon Dioxide

T = 50°C		T = 70°C		T = 90°C	
Pressure (atm)	Sol	Pressure (atm)	Sol	Pressure (atm)	Sol
22.1	12.8	20.3	11.8	20	6.93
31.1	18.9	26.4	14.3	30.4	12.0
39.8	23.1	37.5	18.7	42.4	14.0

Figure 1 shows the pressurization cycle for methane at 100 atm and 50°C. The mass gain divided by the net polyamide mass determines the solubility of the gas.

Figure 1

PRACTICE TEST 2

21. Which of the following substances did NOT become more soluble as pressure increased?
  A. Methane at 70°C
  B. Methane at 50°C
  C. Carbon dioxide at 50°C
  D. Carbon dioxide at 90°C

22. According to Table 2, at which temperature was carbon dioxide the most soluble under pressure of 31.1 atm?
  F. 50°C
  G. 70°C
  H. 90°C
  J. 100°C

23. Figure 1 supports which of the following claims about polyamide mass gain over time?
  A. The polyamide steadily gained mass.
  B. The polyamide lost mass over time.
  C. The polyamide gained mass at first, and then lost mass.
  D. The polyamide quickly gained mass and then leveled off.

24. If the experiment was repeated at a temperature of 90°C and a pressure of 80 atm, the solubility of methane would be closest to:
  F. 2.61 atm.
  G. 3.75 atm.
  H. 5.08 atm.
  J. 14.0 atm.

25. Based on the results shown in Table 2, which of the following conclusions can be drawn regarding the relationship between pressure and solubility?
  A. Solubility increases with pressure only above 70°C.
  B. As pressure increases, solubility decreases.
  C. As pressure increases, so does solubility.
  D. There is no correlation between pressure and solubility.

26. In this experiment, which substance functioned as the *solvent*?
  F. Methane
  G. Carbon dioxide
  H. Mass
  J. Polyamide

27. Scientists wanted to conduct further tests and needed to ensure that experimental conditions were ideal for the solubility of methane. What temperature and pressure would they have to maintain in their experiment?
  A. Temperature of 70 degrees; pressure of 104 atm
  B. Temperature of 90 degrees; pressure of 144.4 atm
  C. Temperature of 50 degrees; pressure of 39.8 atm
  D. Temperature of 70 degrees; pressure of 158.1 atm

PASSAGE V

Ever since Darwin proposed his theory of natural selection in 1859, biologists have regarded the gene as the sole unit of inheritance, and the discovery of DNA in the twentieth century only served to reinforce this view, known as "hard inheritance." The idea that environmental factors could produce heritable changes in an organism without altering the organism's DNA (as occurs in gene mutation due to radiation exposure, for example), known as "soft inheritance," had long been written off as an impossibility. "Inheritance of acquired traits" became a biological fallacy associated with pre-Darwinians like Jean-Baptiste Lamarck and fanatical Soviet scientists like Trofim Lysenko. But the very recent discovery of what has been termed *epigenetics*—biological mechanisms that leave DNA unchanged but can alter the ways in which individual genes express themselves—has opened the door on the possibility of "soft inheritance" once again, although many biologists remain skeptical.

Scientist 1

Although study of the so-called "epigenome" is worthwhile and possesses the potential to answer questions about a host of problems from diabetes to cancer, it would be premature to call true "soft inheritance" a reality, at least in animal species. Isolated situations in which environmental factors could affect an organism's immediate descendants—a mother with a zinc deficiency producing children and grandchildren with weakened immune systems, for example—had already been documented without anyone ever suggesting that there was more to heritability than the gene. Immediate successive generations may exhibit observable effects, but the bloodline always reverts to the true expression of its DNA. A map with dust on it may be hard to read, but the information on the map remains unchanged, and it is simply a matter of how long it takes for a strong wind to blow away the dust.

Scientist 2

Someone who is determined never to see "true soft inheritance" will never see it, but that doesn't change the fact that it occurs, and indeed has been occurring all along without our realizing it. Epigenetic mechanisms may not alter DNA, but they possess the ability to turn genes "on" or "off" for the duration of an organism's bloodline, at least until such time as the genes are affected by another epigenetic mechanism. There is already compelling evidence, for example, that tobacco smoking poses risks not only to the individual smoker, but to all of his or her descendants. Imagine a three-way lightbulb with three possible brightness settings being put into a three-way lamp on which one of the settings is broken. The fact that the bulb still possesses three settings is immaterial if it is permanently set into a broken lamp. It will continue to "express itself" in a limited way. And the same thing can happen to a gene. If environmental factors can permanently alter the way in which an unaltered gene expresses itself down along a bloodline, resulting in observable effects in the members of that bloodline, then what can we possibly call this other than true soft inheritance?

28. According to the information in the passage, which of the following might constitute an example of true soft inheritance?
    F. Inherited gene damage due to a parent's heavy radiation exposure
    G. A susceptibility to diabetes as the result of a malnourished grandparent
    H. A left-handed parent producing predominantly left-handed offspring
    J. A parent who loves books teaching her children to love books

29. Who first proposed the theory of epigenetics?
    A. Charles Darwin
    B. Trofim Lysenko
    C. Scientist 2
    D. The information is not included in the passage.

30. In the offspring of which of the following organisms might Scientist 1 currently be willing to concede the documented existence of true soft inheritance?
    F. A rhinoceros
    G. A radiation-exposed human being
    H. An apple tree
    J. A zinc-deficient human being

31. Scientist 2 would most likely *disagree* with the suggestion that genes:
    A. are the primary units of inheritance.
    B. act in isolation to produce traits.
    C. possess the ability to express themselves.
    D. are made up of stretches of DNA.

32. Scientist 1 would be most likely to predict that any ill effects on the grandchildren of a tobacco smoker:
    F. have nothing to do with the epigenome.
    G. are probably psychological rather than biological in origin.
    H. must be the result of tobacco use having altered the smoker's DNA.
    J. will cease to be expressed in the bloodline given enough time.

33. *Histones* are proteins that attach themselves to sequences of DNA and can alter the expression of genes depending on whether they are *acetylated* or *methylated*. Given this information, it would appear that *histones* are analogous to the:
    A. sole unit of inheritance.
    B. zinc-deficient mother mentioned by Scientist 1.
    C. map mentioned by Scientist 1.
    D. lamp mentioned by Scientist 2.

34. A study of what would be most likely to resolve the disagreement between Scientist 1 and Scientist 2?
    F. the length of time that epigenetic mechanisms tend to remain in a bloodline
    G. the unpublished work of Jean-Baptiste Lamarck
    H. a comparison of cancer rates among identical twins
    J. the inner workings of three-way lightbulbs

PRACTICE TEST 2

PASSAGE VI

Figure 1 shows the average sleep pattern of a child, Figure 2 shows the average sleep pattern of a young adult, and Figure 3 shows the average sleep pattern of an elderly person. At Stage 0, the person is awake. As sleep moves from Stage 1 to Stage 4, it grows progressively deeper. REM sleep, commonly associated with dreaming, is predominant in the final third of a sleep cycle.

Figure 1

Figure 2

Figure 3

35. According to Figure 2, a young adult who has been asleep for 5 hours will most likely be in which sleep stage?
- **A.** Stage 0
- **B.** Stage 1
- **C.** Stage 3
- **D.** Stage 5

36. Based on the information in the passage, a child will wake up how many times during a 7-hour stretch of sleep?
- **F.** 7
- **G.** 2
- **H.** 1
- **J.** 0

37. Based on the data presented in Figures 1, 2, and 3, which of the following conclusions can be properly drawn?
- **A.** As people age, they wake up more frequently during the night.
- **B.** As people age, they wake up less frequently during the night.
- **C.** As people age, they spend more time in deep sleep.
- **D.** As people age, they spend more consecutive time in each sleep stage.

38. Based on the information in the passage and in Figure 2, at which of the following hours into a sleep interval will a young adult be most likely to experience REM sleep?
- **F.** 0
- **G.** 1
- **H.** 2
- **J.** 7

39. At which of the following hours of sleep will a child most likely be in the deepest sleep?
- **A.** 2
- **B.** 3
- **C.** 5
- **D.** 7

40. A scientist decided to do a comparative study between the sleep cycles of a child and an elderly person. From the information given in the figures, which of the following results would he most likely NOT find at the end of the study?
- **F.** The elderly generally wake up more often during the night.
- **G.** The elderly and children generally reach Stage 4 within the first hour of sleep.
- **H.** The elderly wake more often than children in the last two hours of sleep.
- **J.** The elderly and children generally reach Stage 4 at least three times during the night.

If there is still time remaining, you may review your answers.

WRITING TEST

Time: 40 Minutes

Online Culture

The Internet enables people all over the world to express themselves to one another directly, but the nature of this interaction is often antagonistic. Online anonymity, combined with the absence of the emotional recognition that comes with face-to-face communication, has created an Internet culture in which many people will say anything they can think of to hurt someone else's feelings, or even to threaten them with real-life harm, often over the slightest of disagreements. "Diversity," in the form of exposure to viewpoints other than our own, is usually hailed as a desirable goal, but when diverse environments are both anonymous and unpoliced, the result can be insults and hurt feelings, or even threats and fear.

Read and carefully consider these perspectives. Each suggests a particular way of thinking about online culture.

Perspective One	Perspective Two	Perspective Three
When people are able to communicate anonymously, they will behave like jerks. And when most people are communicating anonymously most of the time, most communication will be combative and unnecessarily cruel.	Before the Internet, people were mostly only exposed to the viewpoints of others who were like them. The amazing ability to interact with someone of a completely different background and experience at the click of a button is bound to cause some tensions, but overall it is moving humanity forward.	The Internet hasn't replaced the real world, but only extended it. The groups of people who have privilege and power in real life have merely transferred their bullying and oppression into the virtual world. Their targets aren't just afraid for their online selves, but for their physical selves as well—just like they already were before the web was invented.

ESSAY TASK

Write a unified, coherent essay about online culture. In your essay, be sure to:

- clearly state your own perspective on the issue and analyze the relationship between your perspective and at least one other perspective
- develop and support your ideas with reasoning and examples
- organize your ideas clearly and logically
- communicate your ideas effectively in standard written English

   Your perspective may be in full agreement with any of those given, in partial agreement, or completely different.

Planning Your Response

Your prewriting notes on this page will not be considered in your score.

Use the following space to brainstorm ideas and map out your response. You may want to think about the following as you analyze the given prompt:

Strengths and weaknesses of the three viewpoints

- What good points do they make, and what potential objections do they ignore?
- Why might they be convincing to readers, and why might their perspectives fall short?

Your previous experience, background knowledge, and personal values

- What is your viewpoint on this topic, and what are the pros and cons of this viewpoint?
- How will you craft an argument in support of your point of view?

PRACTICE TEST 2

_____

_____

_____

_____

_____

_____

_____

_____

_____

_____

_____

_____

_____

_____

_____

_____

If there is still time remaining, you may review your answers.

ANSWER KEY
Practice Test 2

English

1. **A**	16. **F**	31. **D**	46. **F**	61. **C**
2. **G**	17. **C**	32. **G**	47. **C**	62. **G**
3. **C**	18. **F**	33. **A**	48. **F**	63. **B**
4. **G**	19. **D**	34. **G**	49. **A**	64. **G**
5. **C**	20. **G**	35. **D**	50. **J**	65. **A**
6. **J**	21. **A**	36. **F**	51. **D**	66. **J**
7. **A**	22. **J**	37. **B**	52. **H**	67. **B**
8. **H**	23. **C**	38. **H**	53. **B**	68. **F**
9. **A**	24. **H**	39. **B**	54. **J**	69. **B**
10. **J**	25. **A**	40. **J**	55. **B**	70. **F**
11. **D**	26. **F**	41. **C**	56. **G**	71. **B**
12. **H**	27. **B**	42. **F**	57. **A**	72. **G**
13. **C**	28. **J**	43. **A**	58. **H**	73. **D**
14. **G**	29. **A**	44. **G**	59. **B**	74. **H**
15. **C**	30. **J**	45. **B**	60. **J**	75. **D**

Mathematics

1. **A**	13. **D**	25. **D**	37. **C**	49. **E**
2. **G**	14. **J**	26. **H**	38. **J**	50. **H**
3. **B**	15. **C**	27. **E**	39. **E**	51. **E**
4. **J**	16. **J**	28. **G**	40. **F**	52. **H**
5. **A**	17. **E**	29. **A**	41. **C**	53. **D**
6. **H**	18. **K**	30. **H**	42. **H**	54. **G**
7. **C**	19. **D**	31. **C**	43. **B**	55. **C**
8. **H**	20. **G**	32. **H**	44. **G**	56. **J**
9. **C**	21. **C**	33. **C**	45. **C**	57. **B**
10. **H**	22. **G**	34. **J**	46. **K**	58. **K**
11. **E**	23. **C**	35. **E**	47. **C**	59. **A**
12. **J**	24. **J**	36. **F**	48. **J**	60. **K**

ANSWER KEY
Practice Test 2

Reading

1.	**B**	9.	**C**	17.	**A**	25.	**A**	33.	**C**
2.	**F**	10.	**J**	18.	**F**	26.	**J**	34.	**F**
3.	**D**	11.	**A**	19.	**A**	27.	**C**	35.	**D**
4.	**H**	12.	**G**	20.	**J**	28.	**F**	36.	**F**
5.	**B**	13.	**C**	21.	**D**	29.	**B**	37.	**D**
6.	**F**	14.	**F**	22.	**G**	30.	**H**	38.	**H**
7.	**C**	15.	**B**	23.	**C**	31.	**B**	39.	**A**
8.	**J**	16.	**H**	24.	**G**	32.	**J**	40.	**G**

Science

1.	**A**	9.	**A**	17.	**D**	25.	**C**	33.	**D**
2.	**J**	10.	**F**	18.	**H**	26.	**J**	34.	**F**
3.	**C**	11.	**C**	19.	**C**	27.	**B**	35.	**B**
4.	**G**	12.	**G**	20.	**F**	28.	**G**	36.	**H**
5.	**B**	13.	**A**	21.	**B**	29.	**D**	37.	**A**
6.	**H**	14.	**G**	22.	**F**	30.	**H**	38.	**J**
7.	**B**	15.	**C**	23.	**D**	31.	**B**	39.	**B**
8.	**J**	16.	**F**	24.	**G**	32.	**J**	40.	**J**

HOW TO SCORE YOUR PRACTICE TEST

Step 1: Add up the number correct for each section and write that number in the blank under the Raw Score column on the Score Conversion Table. (Your goal is to get more questions correct on each subsequent practice test.)

Step 2: Using the Score Conversion Chart, find your scale score for each section and write it down. Then add up all four sections and divide by 4 to find your overall composite score. (Composite scores are rounded up at .5 or higher.)

SCORE CONVERSION TABLE

Section	Raw Score	Scaled Score
English	(out of 75)	_____ / 36
Math	(out of 60)	_____ / 36
Reading	(out of 40)	_____ / 36
Science	(out of 40)	_____ / 36
		Add and divide by 4
Overall Composite =		_____ / 36

SCORE CONVERSION CHART

		Number Correct			
ACT Score*	English Section	Mathematics Section	Reading Section	Science Section	ACT Score*
36	75	60	40	40	36
35	74	59	39	39	35
34	73	58	38	38	34
33	72	57	37	—	33
32	71	56	36	37	32
31	70	54–55	35	36	31
30	69	53	34	35	30
29	67–68	51–52	33	34	29
28	65–66	49–50	32	33	28
27	64	46–48	31	31–32	27
26	62–63	44–45	30	30	26
25	60–61	41–43	29	28–29	25
24	58–59	39–40	27–28	25–27	24
23	55–57	37–38	25–26	24	23

(continued)

SCORE CONVERSION CHART (*Continued*)

		Number Correct			
ACT Score*	English Section	Mathematics Section	Reading Section	Science Section	ACT Score*
22	53–54	35–36	23–24	22–23	22
21	50–52	33–34	22	20–21	21
20	47–49	31–32	21	18–19	20
19	44–46	28–30	19–20	17	19
18	42–43	25–27	18	15–16	18
17	40–41	22–24	17	14	17
16	37–39	19–21	16	13	16
15	34–36	15–17	15	12	15
14	31–33	11–14	13–14	11	14
13	29–30	09–10	12	10	13
12	27–28	07–08	10–11	09	12
11	25–26	06	08–09	08	11
10	23–24	05	07	07	10
9	21–22	04	06	05–06	9
8	18–20	03	05	—	8
7	15–17	—	—	04	7
6	12–14	02	04	03	6
5	09–11	—	03	02	5
4	07–08	01	02	—	4
3	05–06	—	—	01	3
2	03–04	—	01	—	2
1	00–02	00	00	00	1

*These scores are based on student trials rather than national norms.

PRACTICE TEST 2

SCORING YOUR ESSAY

As mentioned earlier in this text, two readers will evaluate your essay and each person will then assign it a score from 1 to 6. If, by chance, these two scorers disagree by more than 1 point, a third reader will step in and resolve the discrepancy. Performance on the essay will not affect your English, math, reading, science, or composite scores. You will receive two additional scores on your score sheet—a combined English/writing score (1–36) and a writing test subscore (1–12). Neither of these scores will affect your composite score!

The sample essay that follows reflects higher-level writing. It meets the criteria that ACT has put forth for essays that demonstrate effective writing skills.

- It takes a definite position.
- It addresses and expands on the counterargument.
- It has details that support the topic sentences and is well organized.
- It is not repetitive, and while there may be errors, they do not interfere with the competence of the essay.
- It is consistent and well balanced.
- The essay has a clear introduction and a conclusion that is not just a summary but ends with a significant thought.
- The vocabulary demonstrates good use of language and the sentence structure is varied.

ANSWER EXPLANATIONS
English

1. **(A)** Although it would also be correct to turn the name *Stephen* into an appositive clause set off with commas on both sides (since you could take out the name and it would still be a complete sentence), when the appositive clause is *just the person's name and nothing else* it is fine to leave out the commas. (For example, you could write *My friend Adam has a car* without having to put commas before and after *Adam*.) But remember, *only one* comma in this situation is wrong; you have to either have two or none.

2. **(G)** This is a <u>parallel phrasing</u> question. The end of the sentence presents a list of three actions, and the previous two verbs (*whizzing* and *weaving*) are in the progressive tense (meaning they end in -*ing*, to signify an ongoing action), so this verb has to be too.

3. **(C)** The first clause is an independent one, and then the clause beginning with the relative pronoun *where* is a dependent descriptive one, and so all we need is a comma. Although the second clause would be an independent one if you got rid of the *where*, with the *where* it is not. (Remember, when you see that two of the choices are a semicolon and a period, it is <u>almost always</u> the case that they cancel each other out and the right answer is a comma!)

4. **(G)** A *rite of passage* is an event or ceremony you go through that changes you in some important way and makes you part of something. So, *experience* would be the right verb here, because you *go through* it.

5. **(C)** The third-person plural possessive pronoun is spelled *their*. You can remember that this is the possessive one because it contains the word *heir* (as in a person who eventually *possesses* something), and distinguish it from the other spellings by memorizing the sentence *They're in there with their bear*.

6. **(J)** What we need here is *have been riding*, which is in the present perfect continuous tense. That sounds complicated, but all it means is that someone is currently in the state of having been doing something for a long time—in other words, the verb needs to include both the present *and* the past, and choice J is the only option that does. (Remember, you don't need to know what tenses are *called* to get tense questions right!)

7. **(A)** *How many* worlds are there here? One. And does it *possess* something? Yes (the first bicycle). So, what we need is the <u>singular possessive</u> *world's*. The sentence is an independent clause up through the word *bicycle*, and the clause beginning with <u>though</u> is an "afterthought clause" that adds extra information, so it needs to be preceded by a comma.

8. **(H)** The essay is about the narrator and her relationship to bicycles, not about da Vinci or the history of bicycles themselves, and so specifics about da Vinci's bicycle sketch are unnecessary and distracting.

9. **(A)** The question asks for the phrase that reinforces the idea that bicycles are *amazing inventions*, and so you want the one that is extremely complimentary. The best choice is A, which refers to bicycles as a *marvel*.

10. **(J)** Since the underlined part is followed by *is*, we know that the right answer has to be a noun phrase, because it will function as the subject of the sentence. The infinitive form of a verb represents a concept, and so can work like a noun (as in *To err is human*). It also

matches the infinitive *to balance* that comes after the *is*, and so obeys the rule of <u>parallel phrasing</u>. That is pretty complicated, but hopefully the wrong answers all "sounded strange," even if you couldn't explain why. (Remember, when in doubt on the ACT English, always go with the <u>shortest</u> answer, as long as it makes a complete sentence and doesn't sound strange!)

11. **(D)** All of the choices are prepositions or prepositional phrases that simply mean "on" and can be used in its place, except for *on which*, which would be used to introduce extra information and would precede the thing that is on something else: *The dog, on which there were fleas, was brown.*

12. **(H)** Every answer choice involves how to separate two independent clauses. A colon can be used to separate two independent clauses, although it does not always have to.

13. **(C)** The earlier *is* establishes that the sentence is in the present tense, and *human will* is singular. So, what we need here is the present third-person singular form of the verb, which is *keeps*.

14. **(G)** This is the only choice that efficiently completes the preceding independent clause and appropriately introduces the subsequent dependent clause with a comma and *which*.

15. **(C)** The proposed sentence doesn't have anything directly to do with the subject of the essay, and the previous sentence conveyed a much more forceful "sense of an ending."

16. **(F)** The plural verb *have* agrees with the plural noun *sites*. *Like* acts as a preposition here, and the prepositional phrase *like Facebook* must be "jumped over." As the pronoun *us* is the object of *have*, there is no reason to add the preposition *to* (no object is being brought *to* us; rather, *we* are being brought together).

17. **(C)** What we need here is the adjective *allowed*, which means "permitted" (rather than the adverb *aloud*, which means "out loud"), and the preposition *to*, which introduces infinitives (rather than the adverb *too*, which means "also").

18. **(F)** The fact that the author is a professional writer means that he would find it odd or ironic that he is having more trouble writing something simple than nonwriters are having.

19. **(D)** The preceding paragraph has been about how the author has difficulty thinking of Facebook status updates. Although being good at writing English papers involves many different skills, the one that is relevant in context is the ability to think of things to say.

20. **(G)** The subsequent sentences joke about how no one cares that other people's status updates are boring, and yet the author is still agonizing over making his perfect. Therefore, *Maybe I'm overthinking this* is a logical opening.

21. **(A)** We need the contraction *you're* here ("you are"), rather than the possessive pronoun *your*. Additionally, although normally *thinks* would be required by the noun *everyone* (which is singular, despite the fact that it refers to many people), the fact that this is a question beginning with *doesn't* changes things. It's "everyone *thinks*," but "everyone does/doesn't *think*." That may sound complicated, but it's easy if you just remain calm and think about what *sounds* right.

22. **(J)** The author is calling himself the only one *who has* figured this out, and *who's* is a contraction for "who has" (or "who is").

23. **(C)** What we need here is the contraction *there's*, for "there is" ("There is nothing wrong with …").

24. **(H)** We are talking about girls in general, and so we need the plural possessive *girls'* (with the apostrophe after the *s*). *Swimsuits* is not possessive, and does not need an apostrophe anywhere.

25. **(A)** The author means to say *It's* ("It is") *all* (meaning the "whole situation") *so* (as in "very") *depressing*. This is the only one of the choices that presents a comprehensible sentence. ("It's also depressing" would also be a comprehensible sentence, but it is not one of the choices.)

26. **(F)** *Being* is a gerund here, and *being depressed* is the subject clause of the sentence. None of the other choices make sense. (Remember, just because the test tries to trick you with *being* a lot, that doesn't mean that it's *never* the right answer!)

27. **(B)** This is a comma splice, albeit a comma splice in disguise. The clauses before and after "you see" are both independent clauses, and putting "you see" between them doesn't change this. Remember, you can't fix a comma splice by just inserting *any* words—the words you add have to render one of the independent clauses dependent! The other choices are all correct, but this one is NOT acceptable.

28. **(J)** The clause is an essential one (it is not "extra") and so we need to begin it with *that*, not with comma + *which*. Furthermore, we need the contraction *you're* ("you are"), not the possessive pronoun *your*. We also need the comparative conjunction *than*, rather than the time-related adverb *then*. Finally, we need the pronoun + verb *they are*, rather than the possessive pronoun *theirs* or adverb/pronoun *there*. That sounds complicated, but the clause we're trying to construct here is perfectly straightforward: "making people think *that you're* having more fun *than they are*." None of the other choices make even a little bit of sense.

29. **(A)** What we need here is the possessive pronoun *our*.

30. **(J)** An argument that something should be legally regulated would have to mention the law or the government at some point, and this passage does not.

31. **(D)** The other verb phrases in the sentence (*could hear, was called*) establish that it is in the past tense. Therefore, the past tense form *we began* is what is needed.

32. **(G)** The descriptive phrase *proud as ever* is an "extra" clause providing additional information that could be lifted out of the sentence. Therefore, it should be set off with commas on both sides.

33. **(A)** *He wasn't the most beautiful horse in the world* is an independent clause, and *If the truth were told* is a dependent introductory clause that needs to be followed by a comma.

34. **(G)** As the preceding and subsequent sentences indicate, the paragraph is about how Monte is a fine horse despite not being beautiful. This sentence offers a physical description of the ways in which he is not beautiful, and so it is relevant and necessary here. Furthermore, without it the paragraph would only have two sentences and seem bizarrely short, further indicating that you are probably supposed to include it.

35. **(D)** The information in this sentence stands in opposition or contrast to the information contained in the previous sentence. Therefore, the appropriate transition phrase is *Yet*, which implies contrast or counterpoint; the other choices do not. (As with so many places on the ACT, "which of these things is not like the others" is a <u>very</u> good strategy here!)

36. **(F)** The idea is that once upon a time Western equitation was unfamiliar to them, but it is not now. Therefore, what is needed is the past perfect tense *had been*. The regular past tense might be acceptable too, but it is not one of the choices; the past perfect is the only type of past tense that is an option.

37. **(B)** All of the answers are synonyms for *learned* or *understood* except for *beat*, which means "overcome." Therefore, *beat* is the LEAST acceptable alternative to the underlined portion. An athlete might say that they beat their competition, but not that they beat the *rules* of the sport themselves. (As with so many places on the ACT, "which of these things is not like the others" is a <u>very</u> good strategy here!)

38. **(H)** The fact that Monte did not touch any of the barrels provides more specific information about the nature of his graceful racing; it explains that he was not just good, but perfect.

39. **(B)** This sentence concerns the portion of the race *before* the narrator and Monte entered the barrels. Therefore, it needs to come before Sentence 2, where they enter the barrels.

40. **(J)** The question asks for a phrase that suggests the narrator's nervousness. Only choice J, which includes the word *anxiously*, does so. The others all make her seem satisfied and confident. (Remember, even when it seems obvious what a question on the ACT English is asking for, <u>always</u> carefully read the little directions in their entirety, because they usually give a fairly big hint!)

41. **(C)** What you need here is a phrase that means *besides*, and *except for* is the only one of the choices that does.

42. **(F)** *How many* grandfathers are we talking about? One. And does he *possess* anything? Yes (his voice). So, what we need is the <u>singular possessive</u>, which is *grandfather's*. It is just that simple.

43. **(A)** The story is in the past tense, and the past tense verb *kissed* in the same sentence reminds us of this. The form we need here is the past tense *echoed*.

44. **(G)** The underlined portion is followed by the verb *won*, which means that the pronouns in the underlined portion are performing a verb. Therefore, they should both be in the subjective case, which means what we need is *he and I* (you wouldn't say *him won* or *me won*; you would say *he won* and *I won*).

45. **(B)** The point of the story is that Monte was able to win the race even though he wasn't a natural-born athlete. This successfully fulfills the question's requirement about spirit and determination being just as important as inborn ability.

46. **(F)** The phrase "people *in which* thousands of years ago" makes no sense. It would mean that "thousands of years ago" is a subject phrase that *did* something *inside* people. All of the other choices make sense.

47. **(C)** This choice correctly uses *no* (i.e., "not any") and *know* (i.e., "to understand").

48. **(F)** This choice correctly uses the plural pronoun *them* to stand in for the plural noun *horoscopes*.

49. **(A)** The phrase is indeed humorous, and does indeed illustrate the fact that horoscopes are meaningless (i.e., they are so vague that there would be no way to know they are wrong, even if they had been misprinted).

50. **(J)** The next sentence continues the idea that the reader already knows what astrology is ("We're all familiar with ….").

51. **(D)** This results in a comprehensible sentence with the clauses in the right order. The *supposed personality traits* are what we're all familiar with, and these traits allegedly belong to *people* (who were) born under certain signs.

52. **(H)** The issue is *essential* versus *nonessential* clauses. We already know that astrology makes claims; the issue is whether it makes sufficiently specific claims. Therefore, the part about whether the claims are specific is not "extra," but essential, and should be introduced with *that* (and no comma).

53. **(B)** The so-called test involves *people* (who are) *deciding*. The test involves *people deciding whether to apply* terms. The present progressive *-ing* form is necessary, as this is an *ongoing* state. This is easy to see if you just "jump over" the extra descriptive clause *who want to believe*.

54. **(J)** The people in question are self-applying the terms, and so the reflexive *themselves* is needed, rather than the nominative *they* or objective *them*. Since the preposition *to* extends to both objects, no comma before the conjunction is necessary. Though it is a polite convention to name oneself after others, it is not a grammatical rule, and so the fact that *themselves* comes before *their friends* is not enough to make this choice wrong, especially in light of the serious errors in the other choices.

55. **(B)** *Could've* is a contraction of *could have*, and so makes perfect sense in context.

56. **(G)** *Anyway* (here acting like "in the first place") makes the most sense after *are*: "the stars' apparent positions aren't really where they are *in the first place*."

57. **(A)** *It's all a bunch of nonsense* is the main independent clause. *Luckily for astrologers* is a dependent introductory clause followed by a comma, and *so nobody ever noticed* is a dependent clause preceded by a comma.

58. **(H)** The semicolon correctly separates two independent clauses. This is a deliberate trick question. Although *however* is typically inserted into the middle of a single independent clause and set off with a pair of commas, it can also appear as the first word of an independent clause (meaning "on the other hand") or the last word of an independent clause (meaning "though" or "despite this"), set off with a single comma. In this sentence, an independent clause that *happens to end* with *however* is followed by a semicolon and a second independent clause. Although this would hardly ever happen in real life because it's so confusing, it is technically grammatically correct, and so the ACT English does it occasionally to trick you. If you see *however* set off with two commas, make sure that a *single* independent clause exists *around* it—not one on each side.

59. **(B)** As the preceding sentence implies ("my answer is always the same"), this describes a *habitual* practice, and so the future tense ("I'll reply") is used.

60. **(J)** In addition to being funny and memorable, the previous sentence sums up what the entire final paragraph was about. Adding the bit about bookstores would be a weaker ending and randomly introduces a new idea.

61. **(C)** The subject of the sentence is *Intuitions* and the verb is *are*. The phrase *or gut feelings* is extra information that can be lifted out of the sentence, and so should be set off with commas.

62. **(G)** Although there has been no indication of this so far, by the end of the subsequent sentence it is established that the passage is written in the second person. Therefore, what we need here is *you can't*. (Remember, person and tense questions on the ACT English <u>frequently</u> necessitate reading ahead, especially when they appear early in a passage!)

63. **(B)** The passage is in the present tense, as indicated in this sentence by the verbs *emerge* and *begin*, and by the contraction *you're* ("you are"). And the antecedent of *it* is *visual inconsistency*, which you would *notice* rather than *feel*. Therefore, what we need is the second-person present tense form *notice*.

64. **(G)** As the first sentence of the first paragraph establishes, what is being referred to here is *intuition*. You must be clear. "It" has no reference.

65. **(A)** The proposed sentence explains that intuition is now acknowledged by science, and therefore provides a needed transition between the previous sentence and the following one, which involves psychologists studying intuition.

66. **(J)** *Psychologists now believe* is the most direct way of saying what you want to say here. (Remember, on the ACT English, when a question presents alternate ways of arranging a phrase, and the question does not ask for something specific such as "the most vivid description," the right answer is <u>almost always</u> the shortest one as long as it results in a complete sentence!)

67. **(B)** The rule of parallel phrasing dictates that the other verbs in the series need to match the third-person singular present tense form *finds* (which is in that form because the sentence is in the present tense and the subject is *brain*). Therefore, the forms we need for the other verbs are *takes* and *does*.

68. **(F)** *You ascribe meaning to the situation in front of you* is the independent clause, and *Based on that analogy* is the introductory dependent clause. They should be separated with a comma.

69. **(B)** The antecedent of the pronoun is the *young woman*, and so the pronoun needed here is *she*.

70. **(F)** The question asks for the best illustration of how information is stored in our brain; only choice A, which includes the phrase *as a web of fact and feeling*, offers an *illustration* of this.

71. **(B)** The sentence is in the present tense, and there is no indication that we need anything other than the simplest form of the infinitive: a new experience unleashes a predisposition *to respond*.

72. **(G)** The sentence provides a useful introduction to the closing paragraph by contextualizing intuition alongside another means of arriving at knowledge. You would also do well to notice that, regardless of how you answer question 73, the subsequent sentence is going to begin with a transition phrase that suggests it is not the first sentence of the paragraph (which means you are supposed to keep this one).

73. **(D)** The sentence suggests a third option different from the two explored in the previous sentence. A simple *But* is the most effective transition phrase. (Remember, although you may have been told in grade school not to begin a sentence with a conjunction such as *and* or *but*, it is actually acceptable to begin a sentence with a conjunction under certain circumstances, and so an answer choice on the ACT English cannot be eliminated solely because it begins a sentence with a conjunction!)

74. **(H)** The question asks for a phrase supporting the idea that intuitions are reliable in an area where one is experienced. Only choice H, which points out that such intuitions *arise out of the richest array of collected patterns of experience*, gets the job done.

75. **(D)** The sentence, along with the rest of the passage, is in the present tense. There is no indication that anything other than the regular present tense *receive* is what is needed here.

Mathematics

1. **(A)** $(1 - 5)^3 = (-4)^3 = -64$.

2. **(G)** 30 is divisible by 3, 5, and 6. It is the lowest common multiple.

3. **(B)** If $r = 0$, $[-s + h(t \cdot 3 - w)](0) = 0$, not 1.

4. **(J)** If 30% come from families that have only one child, then 70% come from families that do not have one child. 70% of 7,340 = 0.70(7,340) = 5,138.

5. **(A)** $3y + 2x = 24$ is $3y = -2x + 24$ when we subtract $2x$ from both sides. Finally, dividing each term by 3 gives $y = \dfrac{-2}{3}x + 8$.

6. **(H)** The equation $3x + 2y = 19$ is equivalent to $y = \dfrac{-3}{2}x + \dfrac{19}{2}$. The slopes of perpendicular lines are opposite reciprocals. Therefore, the slope would be $\dfrac{2}{3}$.

7. **(C)** $V = \dfrac{\pi}{3}(3)^2(8) = \dfrac{\pi}{3}(9)(8) = 24\pi$.

8. **(H)** $\angle b \cong \angle d$ by vertical angles. $\angle d$ and $\angle e$ are supplementary because they are interior angles on the same side of the transversal. Since m$\angle d$ = m$\angle b$ = 100°, m$\angle e$ = 80°.

9. **(C)** In the diagram m∠1 = 40° by vertical angles. Then, m∠2 = 65°, since the angles of a triangle add to 180°. By vertical angles $x = 65$.

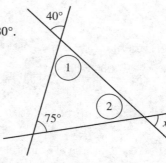

10. **(H)** 11, 16, 21, 26 is an arithmetic sequence with a common difference equal to 5.

11. **(E)** $(2x + 3y)^2$ means $(2x + 3y)(2x + 3y) = 2x(2x) + 2x(3y) + 3y(2x) + (3y)(3y)$. This simplifies to $4x^2 + 6xy + 6xy + 9y^2$ and finally to $4x^2 + 12xy + 9y^2$.

12. **(J)** 60% are Democrats translates to $(0.60)(7,695) = 4,617$. This problem can also be done by using the proportion: $\dfrac{60}{100} = \dfrac{x}{7,695}$.

13. **(D)** The tangent of an angle in a right triangle is defined as the length of the opposite side divided by the length of the adjacent side.

14. **(J)** $\dfrac{1}{3}w + \dfrac{2}{5}w = 1$ equals $\dfrac{5}{15}w + \dfrac{6}{15}w = 1$ when we get a common denominator. (You could also add $\dfrac{1}{3} + \dfrac{2}{5}$ on your calculator.) Combining like terms we have $\dfrac{11}{15}w = 1$. Either multiply by $\dfrac{15}{11}$ or divide by $\dfrac{11}{15} \cdot \dfrac{15}{11} \cdot \dfrac{11}{15}w = \dfrac{15(1)}{11} \cdot w = \dfrac{15}{11}$.

15. **(C)** $\triangle CEA \cong \triangle DEB$. To see this we have $\overline{CE} \cong \overline{DE}$ and $\overline{AE} \cong \overline{BE}$ and $\angle CEA \cong \angle DEB$. The segments are congruent since $\overline{AB}$ and $\overline{CD}$ bisect each other. The angles are vertical angles. So, the triangles are congruent by SAS. By CPCTC, $\angle C \cong \angle D$. That means m∠C = 60°. In $\triangle CEA$ we have a 60° and an 80° angle, so the third angle ($\angle CEA$) must be 40° since the three angles of a triangle must add up to 180°.

16. **(J)** The distance formula is $\sqrt{(x_2 - x_1)^2 + (y_2 - y_1)^2}$. For $A(3, 2)$ and $B(15, 8)$, we have $\sqrt{(15 - 3)^2 + (8 - 2)^2} = \sqrt{144 + 36} = \sqrt{180} = \sqrt{36}\sqrt{5} = 6\sqrt{5}$.

17. **(E)** Although we are not told that a and b are positive, we can use positive values to help us eliminate incorrect choices. Let $a = 2$ and $b = 3$. c can be any number greater than zero. Now we can eliminate answers. We see that A, B, C, and D can be eliminated, which leaves E. So, E must be correct because the others cannot be correct.

18. **(K)** This problem is done by using the fundamental counting principle that if Event 1 can be done in M ways and Event 2 can be done in N ways, then the total number of ways that we can do both events is M(N). Applying this we have $(4)(3)(5) = 60$ ways of choosing meat, cheese, and bread.

19. **(D)** We will use the equation $d = rt$, where d = distance, r = rate, and t = time. $200 = (4)r$, which gives $r = 50$ mph before stopping for gas. She then drives 10 mph faster for 3 hours. $50 + 10 = 60$ mph. $d = 60(3) = 180$ miles. The total number of miles equals $200 + 180 = 380$ miles.

20. **(G)** We are given the formula $M = \dfrac{P}{200} - 0.0008P + 40$, where M is the monthly payment and P is the cost of the house. Since the house costs \$200,000, $P = 200,000$ and $M = \dfrac{200,000}{200} - 0.0008(200,000) + 40$. $M = \$880$.

21. **(C)** The prime factorization of 330 is $2(3)(5)(11)$. The sum is $2 + 3 + 5 + 11 = 21$.

22. **(G)** The area of a circle is πr^2. There are 10 pins and the radius is half of the given diameter of 4.125 in.

23. **(C)** The entire lane is 65 feet long and the part of the lane that is NOT the pin deck is 60 feet long. Since the width is the same, it does not matter. 65:60 reduces to 13:12.

24. **(J)** $3 \times 140 = 420$ points are needed in order to average 140. Quinn has $112 + 144 = 256$ points already, so she needs $420 - 256 = 164$ more points in the third game.

25. **(D)** If you sketch the points and draw the line that contains the two points, it appears that it crosses the y-axis at –5. Mathematically, the slope of the line is $\dfrac{10-(-2)}{5-1} = \dfrac{12}{4} = 3$. Using $y = mx + b$ and the point $(5, 10)$, we have $10 = 3(5) + b$. Thus, $b = -5$. The y-intercept is –5, so the point is $(0, -5)$.

26. **(H)** The median is the middle number of a data set when the numbers are written in order. When there are an even number of data, take the average of the middle two numbers. Since the middle two numbers are 85 and 89, we take the average of those, which is 87.

27. **(E)** $\dfrac{2^{-1}a^{-3}b^7c^2}{(5a)^2 b^{-1}c^7}$ can be rewritten as $\dfrac{2^{-1}a^{-3}b^7c^2}{25a^2b^{-1}c^7}$ by squaring $(5a)$, then as $\dfrac{b \cdot b^7 c^2}{2 \cdot 25a^2a^3c^7}$ by eliminating the negative exponents, and, finally, $\dfrac{b^8}{50a^5c^5}$.

28. **(G)** The center of the circle is the midpoint of any diameter. Thus, if we say the other endpoint is (a, b) and use the midpoint formula we have $\left(\dfrac{a+5}{2}, \dfrac{b+-2}{2} \right) = (2, -3)$. The x-coordinates must be equal. $\dfrac{a+5}{2} = 2 \rightarrow a + 5 = 4$, so $a = -1$. There is only one answer choice with $x = -1$, so we really don't need to find y. But $\dfrac{b-2}{2} = -3 \rightarrow b - 2 = -6$, so $b = -4$.

29. **(A)** This can be solved easily by the substitution method. $5x + 5 = 3x - 7$ is equivalent to $2x = -12$. Therefore, $x = -6$. But we were asked for the y-coordinate. Using the equation $y = 3x - 7$ and substituting (-6) for x we find that $y = 3(-6) - 7 = -25$.

30. **(H)** The figure is a trapezoid. The area formula is $A = \dfrac{h(b_1 + b_2)}{2}$, where h is the height and b_1 and b_2 are the bases. $A = \dfrac{3(10+14)}{2} = \dfrac{72}{2} = 36$.

31. **(C)** $6 - 4(x - 2) > 4x + 5$ is equivalent to $6 - 4x + 8 > 4x + 5$. $14 - 4x > 4x + 5$ is equivalent to $-8x > -9$. Now, we divide by (-8). When dividing an inequality by a negative number, the inequality sign must be switched. The answer then is $x < \dfrac{9}{8}$.

32. **(H)** $(x - h)^2 + (y - k)^2 = r^2$ is the equation for a circle with center (h, k) and radius r.

33. **(C)** When a 90 degree counterclockwise rotation is performed, the point (x, y) becomes $(-y, x)$.

34. **(J)** The area of a circle is πr^2 and the radius was given as 4.

35. **(E)** The area of a parallelogram is base times height. The base is $\overline{RS}$, so we must find $\overline{RA}$. $\overline{UR}$ is 5 since opposite sides of a parallelogram are congruent. Either by the Pythagorean Theorem or by a 3–4–5 right triangle, $\overline{RA} = 3$. So, $\overline{RS} = 3 + 7 = 10$. Height of $\overline{UA} = 4$. $A = 10(4) = 40$.

36. **(F)** We have a right triangle and are given the lengths of two sides. Therefore, we use the Pythagorean Theorem: $a^2 + b^2 = c^2$. $6^2 + 4^2 = c^2 \rightarrow c^2 = 52$. Taking square roots gives us $c = \sqrt{52} = 2\sqrt{13}$.

37. **(C)** If we multiply both sides of the inequality by 6 (the lowest common denominator), we get an inequality with no fractions. $4x - 3 < 3x + 4$, which is equivalent to $x < 7$.

38. **(J)** For this problem we have a right triangle shown with x (the hypotenuse) representing the length of the guide wire and 14 representing the base. Since $\cos 50° = \dfrac{\text{adj}}{\text{hyp}}$, we have $\cos 50° = \dfrac{14}{x}$. So, $x = \dfrac{14}{\cos 50°}$, which is 21.78 (to the nearest hundredth).

39. **(E)** $x^2 - 9 = (x - 3)(x + 3)$. This gives $\dfrac{(x-3)(x-3)}{(x-3)(x+3)} = \dfrac{x-3}{x+3}$. Another method that will work on a problem such as this is to pick a value for x such that $x^2 \neq 9$, say $x = 2$. Then, $\dfrac{(2-3)^2}{2^2 - 9} = \dfrac{1}{-5} = \dfrac{-1}{5}$. Now, put $x = 2$ in for x in the answer choices and see which one equals $\dfrac{-1}{5}$. Only choice E yields this value.

40. **(F)** We know the midpoint is $(5, 7)$ and $A\,(2, 3)$ with $B\,(x, y)$ as endpoints. By the midpoint formula $\left(\dfrac{x+2}{2}, \dfrac{y+3}{2} \right) = (5, 7)$. Thus, $\dfrac{x+2}{2}$ must equal 5 and $\dfrac{y+3}{2}$ must equal 7. Solving these two equations $\dfrac{x+2}{2} = 5$ and $\dfrac{y+3}{2} = 7$, we get $x = 8$ and $y = 11$. Therefore, $x + y = 19$.

41. **(C)** $(x + a)(x + b) = x^2 + (a + b)x + ab$. Since the solutions are $x = 8$ and $x = \dfrac{-3}{2}$, we have $(x - 8)(x - \dfrac{-3}{2}) = 0$. This multiplies to $x^2 - 8x + \dfrac{3}{2}x - 12 = 0$ and simplifies to $x^2 - 6.5x - 12 = 0$. Therefore, $a + b = -6.5$. Or we could use the theorem that says for quadratic equations of the type $x^2 + Bx + C = 0$ that the sum of the solutions equals $(-B)$. Therefore, $8 + \dfrac{-3}{2} = -B \rightarrow 6.5 = -B$ or $B = -6.5$.

42. **(H)** We do not have enough information to find the lengths of the three horizontal segments but we know their sum is 10. The missing vertical segment is 8. So, the perimeter is $10 + 13 + 10 + 8 + 3 + 2 = 46$. If we make a rectangle out of the figure, the perimeter

is the same as the perimeter of the original figure. So, the perimeter of the figure is 13 + 10 + 13 + 10 = 46.

43. **(B)** If you graph the two points, it should be clear that the x-intercept should be greater than 8, leaving two options: 19 and $\frac{19}{2}$. Since 19 is too large, that leaves $\frac{19}{2}$. The slope of the line is $\frac{3-9}{8-5} = \frac{-6}{3} = -2$. From $y = mx + b$ and the point $(5, 9)$, we have $9 = -2(5) + b$. Therefore, $b = 19$. The equation of the line is $y = -2x + 19$. To find the x-intercept, let $y = 0$. $0 = -2x + 19$ and $x = \frac{19}{2}$. For a problem with coordinates, we can often find the answer from a sketch. Clearly, the x-intercept cannot be zero or negative. That leaves only (A) 19 and (B) $\frac{19}{2}$. 19 is not a reasonable answer.

44. **(G)** If a square has an area of 729, the length of a side is $\sqrt{729} = 27 = 3^3$. The volume of a cube is s^3, where s is the length of a side. Thus, in this problem $V = (3^3)^3 = 3^9$.

45. **(C)** The GCF of $6pq^4$ and $12p^2q^2$ is $6pq^2$. Thus, $6pq^2 = 1,050$ or $pq^2 = 175$. It asks for a possible value of p and q. One way of finding p and q is to find the prime factorization of 175. It is $7(5)^2$. Comparing pq^2 to $7(5)^2$, we see that $p = 7$ and $q = 5$. So, $p + q = 7 + 5 = 12$.

46. **(K)** $AC = \sqrt{164}$. We get this value by using the Pythagorean Theorem on $\triangle ABC$. $8^2 + 10^2 = (AC)^2$, $(AC)^2 = 64 + 100 = 164$. Taking square roots leaves $AC = \sqrt{164}$. $\overline{AC}$ is a side of square $ACDE$. Therefore, the area of square $ACDE$ is $(\sqrt{164})^2 = 164$. You could also get this value by taking $\sqrt{164}$ on your calculator and squaring the answer.

47. **(C)** Since there are 6 digits that repeat, we will want to know how many complete cycles of 6 there are that are less than 63. 60 is the largest multiple of 6 that is less than 63. Therefore, the 61st digit will be the start of a new cycle. So, the digit in the sixty-third place will be the third in the cycle, which is C.

48. **(J)** A perfect square trinomial will factor to a binomial squared: $(x + y)^2 = x^2 + 2xy + y^2$. This tells us that the number to be added must be a perfect square. If we add 9, it would have to factor to $(3x - 3)^2$. But this equals $9x^2 - 18x + 9$, and we need $(-30x)$. Adding 25, we have $9x^2 - 30x + 25 = (3x - 5)^2$.

49. **(E)** From the data given in the problem, we can conclude that the center of the circle is $(-a, a)$. Since the radius of the circle is 4, a must equal 4. Therefore, the center is $(-4, 4)$. The formula for a circle with center (h, k) and radius r is $(x - h)^2 + (y - k)^2 = r^2$. Substituting in the formula, we get $(x + 4)^2 + (y - 4)^2 = 16$.

50. **(H)** In the equation $y = A \sin Bx$, the amplitude is $|A|$ and the period is $\frac{2\pi}{|B|}$. From $y = \sin x$ to $y = 2\sin(4x)$, the amplitude increases from 1 to 2 and the period decreases from $\frac{2\pi}{1} = 2\pi$ to $\frac{2\pi}{4} = \frac{1}{2}\pi$.

51. **(E)** Applying the Distributive Property to $3x - 9 \geq -3(9 - x)$ is equivalent to $3x - 9 \geq -27 + 3x$. Subtracting $3x$ from both sides leaves $-9 \geq -27$. This is true and since there is no x in the inequality, it is true for all real numbers.

52. **(H)** Extend $\overline{GF}$ and $\overline{IJ}$ to intersect at a new point P. $GDJP$ is a square with side length of 5. Its area is $5^2 = 25$. The area of the shaded pentagon equals the area of $GDJP$ minus the area of $\triangle FIP$. Area of $\triangle FIP = \frac{1}{2}(4)(4) = 8$. Therefore, the area of pentagon $DGFIJ$ is $25 - 8 = 17$.

53. **(D)** In order for the product of 2 matrices to be defined, the inner dimensions of the matrices must match. Since CD would be a 3×2 matrix and a 3×3 matrix, this will not work because the 2 from matrix C and the first 3 from matrix D are not equal.

54. **(G)** This is a quadratic equation. To solve, we must get one side equal to zero. So, we come up with $x^2 - 5ax - 36a^2 = 0$. This factors to $(x - 9a)(x + 4a) = 0$. Now, we use the zero product property and set each factor equal to zero.

$$x - 9a = 0 \qquad x + 4a = 0$$
$$x = 9a \qquad\qquad x = -4a$$

55. **(C)** To simplify this we will use the identity $\sin^2 \theta + \cos^2 \theta = 1$. From this we have $1 - \cos^2 = \sin^2$. Substituting, we now have $\frac{\sqrt{\sin^2 \theta}}{\sin^2 \theta} \cdot \cos \theta = \frac{\sin \theta}{\sin^2 \theta} \cdot \cos \theta$. This simplifies to $\frac{\cos \theta}{\sin \theta}$, which is equivalent to cot θ.

56. **(J)** By multiplication and division properties of logarithms, $\log_a \left(\frac{x^2 y^3}{\sqrt{z}} \right) = \log_a x^2 + \log_a y^3 - \log_a \sqrt{z}$. By power rule, $\log_a x^2 + \log_a y^3 - \log_a z^{\frac{1}{2}}$ equals $2\log_a x + 3\log_a y - \frac{1}{2}\log_a z = 2p + 3q - \frac{1}{2}t$. So, choice J is the correct answer.

57. **(B)** We know that the absolute value of a number is non-negative. Since $|-x| = x$, x must be non-negative, which means $x \ge 0$. Mathematically, $|x| = x$ if $x \ge 0$ and $|x| = -x$ if $x \le 0$. We could also substitute numbers in for x.

58. **(K)** When a quadratic equation has exactly one real solution, the discriminant "$b^2 - 4ac$" must equal zero. This gives us the equation $(-a)^2 - 4(2)(8) = 0$ OR $a^2 - 64 = 0$ OR $a^2 = 64$. Taking the square root we get $a = \pm 8$. We could also plug 8 (or another number) into the equation. $2x^2 - 8x + 8 = 0 \rightarrow 2(x^2 - 4x + 4) = 0$. $2(x - 2)^2 = 0$.

59. **(A)** Because all the possible answers only contain x and y, we want to eliminate t. Solve $y = 5 - t$ for t and substitute into the other equation. $t = 5 - y$, so $x = 3(5 - y) + 4 \rightarrow x = 15 - 3y + 4$. Solving for y, we first combine the 15 and 4. $x = 19 - 3y \rightarrow x - 19 = -3y$. Multiply both sides by (-1) to get $19 - x = 3y$. Divide by 3 and $y = \frac{19 - x}{3}$. If you had solved the other equation for t, the work would look like this: $t = \frac{x - 4}{3}$ and $y = 5 - \frac{x - 4}{3} \rightarrow y = \frac{15}{3} - \frac{x - 4}{3}$ and $y = \frac{15 - (x - 4)}{3} = \frac{15 - x + 4}{3} = \frac{19 - x}{3}$.

60. **(K)** To find the area of a sector we use this formula: $\frac{\text{central angle}}{360}$ (area of circle). Substituting the given values, we get $\frac{30}{360}(\pi(10)^2)$. Simplify to get $\frac{25\pi}{3}$.

Reading

1. **(B)** The cavalier reaction of the townspeople to the angel in lines 23–28, as well as Elisenda's casual reaction to his departure at the end, establish that the appearance of an angel was not a terribly big deal to these people. In other words, they are *laid-back* and *react with less surprise* than others would to such things.

2. **(F)** In light of the child's illness (line 10), it is safe to assume that when the neighbor woman says the angel was "coming for the child" (line 21), she means that he is an angel of death.

3. **(D)** The crabs from the rainstorm are mentioned in line 86, but only mentioned, and not described.

4. **(H)** This angel never really does much of anything. We know basically nothing about him other than the fact that he has wings. He may not even be an angel, for all anyone knows. Therefore, the only possible answer is that he is *baffling and mysterious.*

5. **(B)** Right before she gets the idea to charge admission, we are told that Elisenda is practically crippled from the hard work she is compelled to do (lines 34–37). We are supposed to feel pity for her, and regard her idea to charge admission as *understandable and motivated by necessity.*

6. **(F)** In lines 27–28, the first reaction of the townspeople to the angel involves *tossing him things to eat through … the wire*. This is clearly supposed to mirror the behavior of humans toward an *animal* at the zoo.

7. **(C)** Nowhere is it stated or implied that the spider girl had the approval of any religious authority of any kind.

8. **(J)** Building a mansion with bars to keep out angels implies that Pelayo and Elisenda considered it likely that more angels would show up someday—that is, that the appearance of angels is *somewhat normal.*

9. **(C)** The question is structured in a tricky way: it refers to *the beginning of the story*, but the fact that Pelayo had been employed as a *bailiff* is not mentioned until line 91.

10. **(J)** Elisenda's sigh of relief (line 103) and the statement that the angel was no longer an annoyance in her life (line 108) both imply that she feels unburdened by not having to deal with him anymore. (Remember, on a question like this, you have to look at the *emotion words!*)

11. **(A)** The first three sentences of Paragraph 3 (lines 21–27) definitely establish all of this information, albeit a bit indirectly.

12. **(G)** It would not support Voltaire's point about the wisdom of tolerance very effectively if he didn't mean it when he says here that Europe has gotten less violent and more civilized in recent decades (the point being that you can trust people not to take advantage of your tolerance now, because things aren't like they were in the past).

13. **(C)** Once again, the answer is that Voltaire is wearing his heart on his sleeve here and saying exactly what he means—his goal in this piece is to rally as many readers as possible to a political cause, rather than to showcase his wit to the sharpest of them.

14. **(F)** Lines 98–100 explicitly state this very theory, albeit in more flowery and challenging language.

15. **(B)** The basic, nonspecific universality of the thoughts narrated here, as well as the fact that Freud employs the plural "we" for the first few questions, all implies that Freud is presenting this as a generic "everyman's" private reaction to the command to love his neighbor as himself, rather than the particular reaction of some specific person or type of person.

16. **(H)** *Grandiose* means "pretentiously self-important," and when we say that someone is "full of hot air," we mean that they speak much, and assign great value to their own words, but that their speech is ultimately of little value. The former word and the latter phrase are not exactly synonymous, but this phrase is by far the closest to *grandiose* of the four choices.

17. **(A)** Freud spends most of the first two paragraphs assuming the voice of the "average" person, and he sums up his assertions in the last paragraph by pointing out that anyone else's life experience would have shown him the same things too. Though his writing was often at odds with, or even offensive to, popular opinion, in this case Freud seems to be trying to make an entire essay out of common knowledge—or at least, what he presents as common knowledge.

18. **(F)** Throughout Passage A, Voltaire argues as though violence is typically a response to injustice—Freud, meanwhile, posits that human beings are just naturally aggressive, and would therefore presumably seek out excuses to hate and to do violence even in a perfectly just society.

19. **(A)** Freud clearly argues that "man's inhumanity to man" is here to stay, but he never addresses the extent to which its prevalence might be lessened, and by what means. Voltaire states a number of facts about European society becoming markedly less violent over the course of the few generations preceding his own time—so presumably something must be capable of at least making people *less* mean, if not altogether altruistic.

20. **(J)** As has already been established in previous questions, these essays are unusual for both Voltaire and Freud in that they aim to present only ideas that the authors figure as self-evident and undeniable. And what's really interesting is that, although both arguments do indeed seem undeniable based on lived experience when one first reads them, they largely present mutually exclusive views of human nature. How can two ideas that contradict each other *both* be self-evidently true?!

21. **(D)** In lines 40–45, the author characterizes a writer as someone who tries to *discover the second being inside him*, who tries to *transform that inward gaze into words*, and who studies *the worlds into which we pass when we retire into ourselves*. These phrases clearly characterize writing as a solitary activity.

22. **(G)** The author never mentions anything at all about his parents' relationship, and certainly doesn't hint that the suitcase might hold painful secrets about it.

23. **(C)** Since the author says this in response to his father's having brought him a candy bar, it is clear in context that he is merely making a joke about how his father still sees him as a child in some ways—that is, his father has not *really* forgotten his age.

24. **(G)** Immediately after this statement, the author goes on to say that his father was a very social man who disliked solitude and loved company—that is, he could not have endured the solitude that is necessary in order to be a real writer.

25. **(A)** The fact that the author's father put the suitcase quietly in a corner implies that he is depositing it shyly and without fanfare: *unobtrusively* means "inconspicuously."

26. **(J)** The author never mentions being *suspicious* of his father about anything, for any reason.

27. **(C)** The series of rhetorical questions that ends the paragraph makes it clear that the point is ultimately about the true source of happiness.

28. **(F)** Lines 40–46 establish that, according to the author, writing is a long process of self-discovery.

29. **(B)** It is mentioned in lines 20–21 that the author's father had wanted to write poetry as a young man.

30. **(H)** The linkage of opposites in the final paragraph (*a flash of joy inside me that made me ashamed … our feelings of happiness and guilt*) establishes that the author sees writing as wrapped up in both positive and negative emotions.

31. **(B)** The first paragraph establishes something to do with "culture" as our topic, and the end of the second and beginning of the third paragraphs (lines 30–35) establish that the author feels that something besides genes is necessary to explain culture.

32. **(J)** The remainder of the first paragraph (as well as the passage itself) establishes that the author's goal is to dispassionately analyze the means by which culture changes—that is, he is using the word *culture* to mean everything about society, rather than to distinguish between the good and bad things about it.

33. **(C)** A hair color is not an *idea* (though a hair*style* is), and thus could not succeed or fail as a meme.

34. **(F)** Lines 33–49 explain that, just as genes are replicators of DNA, memes are replicators of ideas.

35. **(D)** Chaucer is mentioned merely as an example of someone who spoke English as it existed twenty generations ago (lines 7–12).

36. **(F)** It is clear in all four contexts that *propagate* means something like "spread," or *multiply* (in the sense that living beings *multiply* by reproduction).

37. **(D)** Lines 43–49 establish that the author is making up the word *meme* himself ("*if I abbreviate 'mimeme' to meme*").

38. **(H)** In the sentence immediately following, the author explains that other copies of the same tune will continue to exist on paper or in other people's brains—that is, no one copy of an idea is the "real" one, as long as the idea continues to exist somewhere.

39. **(A)** The examples in lines 76–81 (immediately following the term *survival value*) all concern possible ways to measure how widespread a particular concept has become.

40. **(G)** When the author says that their *meme-complexes … are still going strong* (lines 106–107), he means that the ideas these people came up with are continuing to thrive after their deaths.

Science

1. **(A)** All this question is asking you to do is look at Table 1 and find the biggest number in the (horizontal) 260 nm row. The biggest number in that row by a wide margin is 83.5, which falls in the (vertical) Octyl Salicylate column. The fact that the numbers represent *percent transmittance of UV rays* is explained in the text, rather than in Table 1 itself, but this is the only thing Table 1 measures, and the question tells you that the answer is in Table 1.

2. **(J)** This is a simple "Go Up, Hit Line, Go Over" question. The black line in Figure 1 is higher at the point on the *x*-axis (horizontal) representing a wavelength of 340 nm than it is at the points representing any of the other choices. Since the line in Figure 1 only increases (it goes up and up but never down), another reliable method of getting the answer would be to just look at the choices and pick the highest number.

3. **(C)** The question asks about someone whose skin *burns but also tans slowly*. "Gradually" is a synonym for "slowly," and so the question is likely asking about Skin Type III, which Table 2 says *Burns moderately, tans gradually*. Although the person *could possibly* have Skin Type II, the question is clearly indicating Skin Type III as the preferable answer.

4. **(G)** All you have to do here is look at Table 2 and list all the skin types identified as *sensitive* or *very sensitive*. Skin Types I and II are identified as *very sensitive*, and Skin Type III is identified as *sensitive*. You probably also already know from real life that sunscreen should be worn by pale people, and so the answer is going to be the people on the paler half of the table. (Remember, although the ACT Science <u>does not require</u> real-life knowledge, the questions are always accurate, and so any real-life knowledge you <u>happen to have</u> can be useful!)

5. **(B)** This is one of those questions that require looking in two places. Figure 1 establishes that sunlight with an irradiance of 0.01 W/m²/nm would have a wavelength of *a little more than* 300 nm (because the black line at the 0.01 point on the *y*-axis is a little past the 300 point on the *x*-axis). Then you look in Table 1 and see that the percent transmittance for oxybenzone at a wavelength of 300 nm would be 4.2, and so the answer is *a little more than* 4.2, in other words 5%.

6. **(H)** According to Table 1, sunscreen SPF 45 blocks all but 2.5% of UV rays. Even though Type II skin is very sensitive to UV rays, at 320 nm skin Type II would not burn easily using SPF 45 sunblock.

7. **(B)** Table 1 establishes that a female who has normal vision but is a carrier of red-green color blindness would have one normal X chromosome and one mutated X chromosome. (It is also entirely possible to figure this out without Table 1, assuming you knew that women have two X chromosomes and a bit about how heritability works.)

8. **(J)** For a couple to be assured of producing only red-green color-blind children, both parents would have to be red-green color blind. The genotypes in choice J represent a red-green color-blind female and a red-green color-blind male.

9. **(A)** The top right corner of the Punnett square in Figure 3 (Study 2) represents a male with normal vision. All of the males represented in Figures 2 and 4 (in Studies 1 and 3) are red-green color blind.

10. **(F)** The information in the passage states that the defect appears in women only when both parents possess the gene.

11. **(C)** Study 1 establishes that all of Barbara and John's male children are red-green color blind, while none of their female children are (though they all carry the mutated gene). Figure 1 establishes that Barbara and John have two girls and two boys; that is, they have an equal number of red-green color-blind children and children with normal vision, for a ratio of 1:1 (2:2 reduced).

12. **(G)** A red-green color-blind female would have to have had a red-green color-blind father and a mother who was either red-green color-blind herself or a carrier. Only choice G presents one of these options (red-green color-blind father and carrier mother).

13. **(A)** Based on Study 1, the daughter of Barbara and John would have a genotype of $X^R X^r$. Combining the daughter's genotype with a man of genotype $X^r Y$ would produce the following offspring:

	X^R	X^r
X^r	$X^R X^r$	$X^r X^r$
Y	$X^R Y$	$X^r Y$

According to Table 1, only a genotype of $X^R X^r$ is a genotype that is a carrier with normal vision. One of the squares above shows the needed genotype and one out of four is represented as 25%.

14. **(G)** This is one of those questions that requires you to look in two places. Table 2 indicates that naphtha is in Tray 2, and Table 1 indicates that the boiling point of whatever is in Tray 2 is 40°C.

15. **(C)** In Figure 2, the bar representing diesel goes up to 11, indicating 11 gallons of diesel per barrel of crude oil.

16. **(F)** This question involves looking in three places, but still is not really that hard (technically, getting the right answer only requires looking in two places, but eliminating some of the wrong answers requires looking in three). Figure 1 establishes that the trays are arranged from 1 to 8 from the top to the bottom of the Distillation Column, Table 2 indicates which substances are in which trays, and Table 1 indicates their boiling points. All together, these data indicate that the substances with the lowest boiling points are at the top of the column, and so the student's hypothesis is wrong (it is not necessary to understand the explanation in choice F about the rising vapor and all that, only to see that the substances with the lowest boiling points are on top).

17. **(D)** A comparison of Table 3 with Tables 1 and 2 establishes that the greater the number of carbons in a substance, the higher the boiling point, in decreasing order from residual oil to gas.

18. **(H)** Tables 1 and 2 establish that heavy gas oil has a boiling point of 500°C, higher than that of any of the components except residual oil, which is not one of the choices.

19. **(C)** Components with medium boiling points on Table 1 in a range of 120 to 350 degrees correspond to the gasoline, kerosene, and diesel on Figure 2, which are collected in greatest quantity.

20. **(F)** Tables 1 and 2 show you that kerosene has a boiling point of 200 degrees and diesel has a boiling point of 350 degrees, so the new substance would have a number of carbons that fall somewhere in the range of carbons for kerosene and diesel. Diesel has 12+ carbons and kerosene has carbons in a range of 10–18. Therefore, the new substance should have a number of carbons between 12 and 18.

21. **(B)** Table 1 indicates that the solubility of methane at 50°C *increases and then decreases* as pressure is increased. All of the other choices involve substances that steadily increased in solubility as pressure increased, but NOT this one.

22. **(F)** At 50°C, the solubility is 18.9.

23. **(D)** The line in Figure 1 climbs until about the 200-second mark and then levels off. It is not necessary to understand the paragraph above Figure 1 in order to answer the question: all you need to know is that the graph is measuring an increase in the PA-11 mass over time.

24. **(G)** In Table 1, we see that the solubility of methane at 90°C and 53.1 atm is 2.38. At a pressure of 106.5, the solubility is 5.14. Since 3.75 is halfway between 2.38 and 5.14 and 80 is roughly halfway between 53.1 and 106.5, the best answer is 3.75.

25. **(C)** Table 2 establishes that the solubility of carbon dioxide increases as pressure increases, at all three temperatures.

26. **(J)** The first paragraph states that the *solvent* is the substance that another substance is being dissolved in. The second paragraph states that methane and carbon dioxide are being dissolved in polyamide. Therefore, polyamide is the solvent and carbon dioxide and methane are the solutes.

27. **(B)** According to Table 1, methane has the highest solubility reading of 6.52 at a temperature of 90 degrees and pressure of 144.4 atm.

28. **(G)** Nutrition or the lack thereof is an environmental factor, and does not alter an individual's DNA, so if ill effects due to a grandparent's malnutrition are turning up in grandchildren, then this would be an example of "soft inheritance."

29. **(D)** The passage does not say who proposed the theory of epigenetics. It only mentions that the discovery was "very recent."

30. **(H)** Scientist 1 states that it would be premature to acknowledge true soft inheritance *in animal species*. This implies that she might be willing to concede its existence in plant

species (as many otherwise skeptical biologists indeed do). An apple tree is the only one of the choices that is a plant.

31. **(B)** A believer in epigenetic soft inheritance would disagree with the idea than genes *act in isolation* to produce traits. In other words, he or she would believe that an organism's expressed traits are the result partly of genes and partly of other factors.

32. **(J)** Scientist 1 dismisses apparent evidence for epigenetic theory by arguing that the inherited acquired traits would work themselves out of the bloodline in time ("the bloodline always reverts to the true expression of its DNA," and the map and wind analogy).

33. **(D)** If *histones* are the modules through which genes express themselves, and Scientist 2 figures genes (i.e., "sequences of DNA") as lightbulbs, then it follows that histones would be analogous to the lamp.

34. **(F)** Scientist 1's defense against all epigenetic arguments is to imply that all apparently epigenetic effects are only temporary. And Scientist 2 appears to have no proof so far that they are not. Only a conclusive study of how long the "altered expression" of a gene truly lasts (which would take a pretty long time) can settle the matter for good.

35. **(B)** This is a simple "Go Up, Hit Line, Go Over" question. In Figure 2, right above the 5-hour mark on the *x*-axis (horizontal), the line representing sleep stages is at a height of around 1 on the *y*-axis (vertical).

36. **(H)** The line in Figure 1, which represents the sleep pattern of a child, hits the bottom of the graph (Stage 0, or being awake) only once. The 0 at the left of the graph is not included because this represents the beginning of sleep.

37. **(A)** The subjects of the figures get increasingly older, and the line in Figure 3 hits bottom more than the lines in the other figures do. Therefore, the conclusion that people wake up more frequently as they age is supported by the data. Remember, each touch at the bottom is Stage 0 and Stage 0 indicates awake.

38. **(J)** The introductory paragraph states that REM sleep is associated with the final third of a sleep cycle. Of the answer choices, only the 7-hour mark is in the final third of the sleep cycle depicted in Figure 2, which represents a young adult (although since the passage states that REM sleep occurs in the final third of a sleep cycle for everyone, it wouldn't matter which figure you looked at).

39. **(B)** The introduction says sleep gets deeper as it moves from Stage 1 to Stage 4.

40. **(J)** Though the child reached Stage 4 during hours 1, 3, and 6, the elderly chart shows that the sleep cycle reaches Stage 4 only in hour one.

Writing Sample

Online Culture

Are we losing the Internet to the culture of hate? A recent <u>Time</u> magazine cover suggests that, at least in the U.S., the answer to this question is a gloomy "Yes." The very characteristics that make online communication (via Twitter, Snapchat, Reddit, and other media) so appealing also provide fertile ground for everything from harmless pranking to harassment and even violent threats against society's most vulnerable, including women, religious and ethnic minorities, and young people. Although online anonymity can bring out the worst in people, Perspective 3, in arguing for the Internet's "moving humanity forward," correctly sees the plentiful, if less sensational, positives of virtual communication. Despite its considerable drawbacks, the Internet provides young people unparalleled opportunities to connect their important causes to larger audiences, empowering them to use their wide social networks for good on a global scale.

Daily news stories of cyberbullying suggest that the culture of hate just might be winning. Perspective 1 points out that the Internet emboldens people to be "combative and cruel," and such combativeness shows up even among Facebook friends. Perspective 2 mentions the very real threats to "online" and "physical" selves that tormentors pose. At my suburban high school, bullying doesn't stop when the last bell rings. Overweight kids, skinny kids, kids with acne, kids with accents —they all become easy targets in cyberspace. Online discussion board Reddit recently revealed that the group with the largest user base happens to be "fatpeoplehate," just one forum where "trolls" are free to body shame unsuspecting victims, sending images and rude comments through the Web while preserving their own anonymity. Most disturbing of all are instances where already depressed teens are bullied into taking their own lives, clear examples of the "game" of hate taken to extremes.

Such horrific stories of hate and intolerance steal attention away from the myriad ways young people create meaningful, constructive change through their online presence. Many kids my age, either unwilling or unable to confide in parents or relatives, rightly or wrongly turn to Facebook or other social media for solace, advice, or support. But teens are also more outward thinking and philanthropic than adults give them credit for, using the Internet to raise money and awareness and to spread their inspirational stories. GoFundMe and other crowdfunding platforms raise money for teens' charitable projects like my World History class's efforts to aid schools in Ghana and Costa Rica. Everyone knows about YouTube, but how many people are familiar with its nonprofit program that allows charitable organizations to post videos with a "donate now" button? My cousin recently made me aware of Dosomething.org, which integrates with Facebook and is specifically designed to get teens involved in social causes, tapping into young people's large social networks, but for the betterment of society. Finally, teen TedTalks include the stories of kids who have done amazing things, including building nuclear fusion reactors, honestly dealing with depression, or something seemingly simple as "just trying to figure it out." Judging by the popularity of these sites and the reach of their messages, charitable works can be just as contagious as hateful acts.

Touting the unlimited potential of Internet communication to do good does not in any way downplay its sinister side, particularly when it comes to my peers and their brutal online assessments of each other. But the words "online culture" do not have to be oxymoronic. Even as some argue that we have not yet lost the battle against hate, we face the challenge of balancing First Amendment rights against the right of every American to safety and security. With unbridled free speech come abuses of that privilege, but the benefits of harnessing the power of multitudes outweigh the more sensationalized harmful effects.

ANSWER SHEET
Practice Test 3

Directions: Mark one answer only for each question. Make the mark dark. Erase completely any mark made in error. (Additional or stray marks will be counted as mistakes.)

English

1. (A) (B) (C) (D)
2. (F) (G) (H) (J)
3. (A) (B) (C) (D)
4. (F) (G) (H) (J)
5. (A) (B) (C) (D)
6. (F) (G) (H) (J)
7. (A) (B) (C) (D)
8. (F) (G) (H) (J)
9. (A) (B) (C) (D)
10. (F) (G) (H) (J)
11. (A) (B) (C) (D)
12. (F) (G) (H) (J)
13. (A) (B) (C) (D)
14. (F) (G) (H) (J)
15. (A) (B) (C) (D)

16. (F) (G) (H) (J)
17. (A) (B) (C) (D)
18. (F) (G) (H) (J)
19. (A) (B) (C) (D)
20. (F) (G) (H) (J)
21. (A) (B) (C) (D)
22. (F) (G) (H) (J)
23. (A) (B) (C) (D)
24. (F) (G) (H) (J)
25. (A) (B) (C) (D)
26. (F) (G) (H) (J)
27. (A) (B) (C) (D)
28. (F) (G) (H) (J)
29. (A) (B) (C) (D)
30. (F) (G) (H) (J)

31. (A) (B) (C) (D)
32. (F) (G) (H) (J)
33. (A) (B) (C) (D)
34. (F) (G) (H) (J)
35. (A) (B) (C) (D)
36. (F) (G) (H) (J)
37. (A) (B) (C) (D)
38. (F) (G) (H) (J)
39. (A) (B) (C) (D)
40. (F) (G) (H) (J)
41. (A) (B) (C) (D)
42. (F) (G) (H) (J)
43. (A) (B) (C) (D)
44. (F) (G) (H) (J)
45. (A) (B) (C) (D)

46. (F) (G) (H) (J)
47. (A) (B) (C) (D)
48. (F) (G) (H) (J)
49. (A) (B) (C) (D)
50. (F) (G) (H) (J)
51. (A) (B) (C) (D)
52. (F) (G) (H) (J)
53. (A) (B) (C) (D)
54. (F) (G) (H) (J)
55. (A) (B) (C) (D)
56. (F) (G) (H) (J)
57. (A) (B) (C) (D)
58. (F) (G) (H) (J)
59. (A) (B) (C) (D)
60. (F) (G) (H) (J)

61. (A) (B) (C) (D)
62. (F) (G) (H) (J)
63. (A) (B) (C) (D)
64. (F) (G) (H) (J)
65. (A) (B) (C) (D)
66. (F) (G) (H) (J)
67. (A) (B) (C) (D)
68. (F) (G) (H) (J)
69. (A) (B) (C) (D)
70. (F) (G) (H) (J)
71. (A) (B) (C) (D)
72. (F) (G) (H) (J)
73. (A) (B) (C) (D)
74. (F) (G) (H) (J)
75. (A) (B) (C) (D)

Mathematics

1. (A) (B) (C) (D) (E)
2. (F) (G) (H) (J) (K)
3. (A) (B) (C) (D) (E)
4. (F) (G) (H) (J) (K)
5. (A) (B) (C) (D) (E)
6. (F) (G) (H) (J) (K)
7. (A) (B) (C) (D) (E)
8. (F) (G) (H) (J) (K)
9. (A) (B) (C) (D) (E)
10. (F) (G) (H) (J) (K)
11. (A) (B) (C) (D) (E)
12. (F) (G) (H) (J) (K)
13. (A) (B) (C) (D) (E)
14. (F) (G) (H) (J) (K)
15. (A) (B) (C) (D) (E)

16. (F) (G) (H) (J) (K)
17. (A) (B) (C) (D) (E)
18. (F) (G) (H) (J) (K)
19. (A) (B) (C) (D) (E)
20. (F) (G) (H) (J) (K)
21. (A) (B) (C) (D) (E)
22. (F) (G) (H) (J) (K)
23. (A) (B) (C) (D) (E)
24. (F) (G) (H) (J) (K)
25. (A) (B) (C) (D) (E)
26. (F) (G) (H) (J) (K)
27. (A) (B) (C) (D) (E)
28. (F) (G) (H) (J) (K)
29. (A) (B) (C) (D) (E)
30. (F) (G) (H) (J) (K)

31. (A) (B) (C) (D) (E)
32. (F) (G) (H) (J) (K)
33. (A) (B) (C) (D) (E)
34. (F) (G) (H) (J) (K)
35. (A) (B) (C) (D) (E)
36. (F) (G) (H) (J) (K)
37. (A) (B) (C) (D) (E)
38. (F) (G) (H) (J) (K)
39. (A) (B) (C) (D) (E)
40. (F) (G) (H) (J) (K)
41. (A) (B) (C) (D) (E)
42. (F) (G) (H) (J) (K)
43. (A) (B) (C) (D) (E)
44. (F) (G) (H) (J) (K)
45. (A) (B) (C) (D) (E)

46. (F) (G) (H) (J) (K)
47. (A) (B) (C) (D) (E)
48. (F) (G) (H) (J) (K)
49. (A) (B) (C) (D) (E)
50. (F) (G) (H) (J) (K)
51. (A) (B) (C) (D) (E)
52. (F) (G) (H) (J) (K)
53. (A) (B) (C) (D) (E)
54. (F) (G) (H) (J) (K)
55. (A) (B) (C) (D) (E)
56. (F) (G) (H) (J) (K)
57. (A) (B) (C) (D) (E)
58. (F) (G) (H) (J) (K)
59. (A) (B) (C) (D) (E)
60. (F) (G) (H) (J) (K)

ANSWER SHEET
Practice Test 3

Reading

1. Ⓐ Ⓑ Ⓒ Ⓓ
2. Ⓕ Ⓖ Ⓗ Ⓙ
3. Ⓐ Ⓑ Ⓒ Ⓓ
4. Ⓕ Ⓖ Ⓗ Ⓙ
5. Ⓐ Ⓑ Ⓒ Ⓓ
6. Ⓕ Ⓖ Ⓗ Ⓙ
7. Ⓐ Ⓑ Ⓒ Ⓓ
8. Ⓕ Ⓖ Ⓗ Ⓙ

9. Ⓐ Ⓑ Ⓒ Ⓓ
10. Ⓕ Ⓖ Ⓗ Ⓙ
11. Ⓐ Ⓑ Ⓒ Ⓓ
12. Ⓕ Ⓖ Ⓗ Ⓙ
13. Ⓐ Ⓑ Ⓒ Ⓓ
14. Ⓕ Ⓖ Ⓗ Ⓙ
15. Ⓐ Ⓑ Ⓒ Ⓓ
16. Ⓕ Ⓖ Ⓗ Ⓙ

17. Ⓐ Ⓑ Ⓒ Ⓓ
18. Ⓕ Ⓖ Ⓗ Ⓙ
19. Ⓐ Ⓑ Ⓒ Ⓓ
20. Ⓕ Ⓖ Ⓗ Ⓙ
21. Ⓐ Ⓑ Ⓒ Ⓓ
22. Ⓕ Ⓖ Ⓗ Ⓙ
23. Ⓐ Ⓑ Ⓒ Ⓓ
24. Ⓕ Ⓖ Ⓗ Ⓙ

25. Ⓐ Ⓑ Ⓒ Ⓓ
26. Ⓕ Ⓖ Ⓗ Ⓙ
27. Ⓐ Ⓑ Ⓒ Ⓓ
28. Ⓕ Ⓖ Ⓗ Ⓙ
29. Ⓐ Ⓑ Ⓒ Ⓓ
30. Ⓕ Ⓖ Ⓗ Ⓙ
31. Ⓐ Ⓑ Ⓒ Ⓓ
32. Ⓕ Ⓖ Ⓗ Ⓙ

33. Ⓐ Ⓑ Ⓒ Ⓓ
34. Ⓕ Ⓖ Ⓗ Ⓙ
35. Ⓐ Ⓑ Ⓒ Ⓓ
36. Ⓕ Ⓖ Ⓗ Ⓙ
37. Ⓐ Ⓑ Ⓒ Ⓓ
38. Ⓕ Ⓖ Ⓗ Ⓙ
39. Ⓐ Ⓑ Ⓒ Ⓓ
40. Ⓕ Ⓖ Ⓗ Ⓙ

Science

1. Ⓐ Ⓑ Ⓒ Ⓓ
2. Ⓕ Ⓖ Ⓗ Ⓙ
3. Ⓐ Ⓑ Ⓒ Ⓓ
4. Ⓕ Ⓖ Ⓗ Ⓙ
5. Ⓐ Ⓑ Ⓒ Ⓓ
6. Ⓕ Ⓖ Ⓗ Ⓙ
7. Ⓐ Ⓑ Ⓒ Ⓓ
8. Ⓕ Ⓖ Ⓗ Ⓙ

9. Ⓐ Ⓑ Ⓒ Ⓓ
10. Ⓕ Ⓖ Ⓗ Ⓙ
11. Ⓐ Ⓑ Ⓒ Ⓓ
12. Ⓕ Ⓖ Ⓗ Ⓙ
13. Ⓐ Ⓑ Ⓒ Ⓓ
14. Ⓕ Ⓖ Ⓗ Ⓙ
15. Ⓐ Ⓑ Ⓒ Ⓓ
16. Ⓕ Ⓖ Ⓗ Ⓙ

17. Ⓐ Ⓑ Ⓒ Ⓓ
18. Ⓕ Ⓖ Ⓗ Ⓙ
19. Ⓐ Ⓑ Ⓒ Ⓓ
20. Ⓕ Ⓖ Ⓗ Ⓙ
21. Ⓐ Ⓑ Ⓒ Ⓓ
22. Ⓕ Ⓖ Ⓗ Ⓙ
23. Ⓐ Ⓑ Ⓒ Ⓓ
24. Ⓕ Ⓖ Ⓗ Ⓙ

25. Ⓐ Ⓑ Ⓒ Ⓓ
26. Ⓕ Ⓖ Ⓗ Ⓙ
27. Ⓐ Ⓑ Ⓒ Ⓓ
28. Ⓕ Ⓖ Ⓗ Ⓙ
29. Ⓐ Ⓑ Ⓒ Ⓓ
30. Ⓕ Ⓖ Ⓗ Ⓙ
31. Ⓐ Ⓑ Ⓒ Ⓓ
32. Ⓕ Ⓖ Ⓗ Ⓙ

33. Ⓐ Ⓑ Ⓒ Ⓓ
34. Ⓕ Ⓖ Ⓗ Ⓙ
35. Ⓐ Ⓑ Ⓒ Ⓓ
36. Ⓕ Ⓖ Ⓗ Ⓙ
37. Ⓐ Ⓑ Ⓒ Ⓓ
38. Ⓕ Ⓖ Ⓗ Ⓙ
39. Ⓐ Ⓑ Ⓒ Ⓓ
40. Ⓕ Ⓖ Ⓗ Ⓙ

ENGLISH TEST

Time: 45 Minutes—75 Questions

Directions: In the five passages that follow, certain words and phrases are underlined and numbered. In the right-hand column, you will find alternatives for the underlined part. In most cases, you are to choose the one that best expresses the idea, makes the statement appropriate for standard written English, or is worded most consistently with the style and tone of the passage as a whole. If you think the original version is best, choose "NO CHANGE." In some cases, you will find in the right-hand column a question about the underlined part. You are to choose the best answer to the question.

You will also find questions about a section of the passage, or about the passage as a whole. These questions do not refer to an underlined portion of the passage, but rather are identified by a number or numbers in a box.

For each question, choose the alternative you consider best and fill in the corresponding oval on your answer sheet. Read each passage through once before you begin to answer the questions that accompany it. For many of the questions, you must read several sentences beyond the question to determine the answer. Be sure that you have read far enough ahead each time you choose an alternative.

PASSAGE I

The Real Johnny B. Goode?

No one person invented rock and roll single-handedly, but for years both critics, and fans have
agreed that no individual is due more credit than
Chuck Berry. The singer, songwriter, and guitarist

behind such rock classics as "Maybelline" and

"Johnny B. Goode" was a major influence on

everything from the songwriting of the Beatles to

the guitar playing of Jimi Hendrix.

He sold millions of records and in 1986 among
the first class of inductees into the Rock and Roll

Hall of Fame. But in 2000, the music world was

1. **A.** NO CHANGE
   B. critics and fans have agreed, that
   C. critics, and fans have agreed, that
   D. critics and fans have agreed that

2. **F.** NO CHANGE
   G. were a major influence
   H. were major influences
   J. have had a major influence

3. **A.** NO CHANGE
   B. was
   C. was among
   D. would have been among

shocked when Berry was sued by an old piano

player of his, Johnnie <u>Johnson claimed</u> it was really
                              4

he who had composed the music for nearly all of

Berry's hits.

    Could the great Chuck Berry <u>is</u> a fraud, and the
                                              5

virtually unknown Johnson the true force behind

the songs that shaped rock and roll? It seemed

<u>distracting</u> at first, but eventually even the biggest
     6

Berry fans had to admit that certain details seemed

<u>to corroborate</u> Johnson's story. The band that
       7

became the Chuck Berry Trio in 1955 was originally

the Johnnie Johnson Trio, and Berry, a struggling

local musician, had joined as a last-minute addition

<u>when a member fell ill before a St. Louis gig in 1953.</u>
                        8

<u>Although</u> Berry claimed sole responsibility
   9

for the many hits that soon followed, his gift

for composition mysteriously dried up after he

4. **F.** NO CHANGE
   G. Johnson, claimed
   H. Johnson, claiming
   J. Johnson, who claimed

5. **A.** NO CHANGE
   B. be
   C. possibly was
   D. DELETE the underlined portion.

6. Which word or phrase best emphasizes the shocking nature of the allegations?
   F. NO CHANGE
   G. silly
   H. unthinkable
   J. impossible to determine

7. Which of the following alternatives to the underlined portion would be LEAST acceptable?
   A. to prove
   B. to verify
   C. to confirm
   D. to dispute

8. If the writer were to delete the underlined portion, the paragraph would primarily lose:
   F. an instance of foreshadowing.
   G. an explanation of why the type of music Berry played was popular in the South.
   H. a reminder of how cruel the music business can be.
   J. evidence of how close Berry came to not being a rock star at all.

9. **A.** NO CHANGE
   B. Since
   C. On the other hand,
   D. DELETE the underlined portion.

stopped working with Johnson. Berry was jailed in

1959 over shady goings-on at a nightclub he owned,

and his only Top Ten hits after his 1963 release was

10

a silly novelty record called "My Ding-a-Ling" and a

tune called "No Particular Place to Go," which was

clearly just the Berry classic "School Days" with new

lyrics. Even lifelong Berry fan Bruce Springsteen

from remarking years earlier that their songs were

11

written in unusual keys for a guitar player—keys

more commonly found in songs composed on

piano. 12

   Why had Johnnie not spoken up at the time?

Tragically, Johnson was plagued by alcoholism for

most of his life, and took little notice of what went

on outside the studio. He also knew far less about

10. **F.** NO CHANGE
    G. had
    H. were
    J. being

11. **A.** NO CHANGE
    B. had remarked
    C. did remark
    D. would remark

12. At this point, the writer is considering adding the following true statement:

    > Berry had been in trouble with the law many times before, so allegations that he had cheated a former partner were hardly inconsistent with his character.

    Should the writer make this addition?

    F. Yes, as it provides relevant information.
    G. Yes, because it proves Berry is a fraud.
    H. No, because only Berry's talent is the issue, and not his character.
    J. No, because it doesn't specify every crime of which Berry was accused.

things like rights and royalties than did the more

educated and business-savvy Berry. 13

A judge dismissed the suit because too much

time had elapsed until the songs in question were
                     14
written, and Johnnie Johnson passed away in 2005,
  14
so the world will never know exactly who wrote

what in all those immortal songs. Johnson never

claimed he wrote them alone, however, and Chuck

Berry still deserves his legendary status even if all

he did was pen the lyrics and play the guitar—but

maybe the name of Johnnie Johnson should be no

less famous than his.

13. Given that all the following statements are true, which one, if added here, would most effectively conclude the paragraph and support information given in the preceding sentence?
  A. As far as Johnson knew, what he was paid for his time at the end of a session was fair.
  B. Many African-American musicians of that era never received the money they deserved.
  C. Of course, how music publishing works has changed a great deal since the 1950s.
  D. Later rock stars were even more educated, a notable example being Mick Jagger.

14. F. NO CHANGE
  G. between the writing of most of the songs,
  H. since the writing of the songs in question,
  J. before any more songs could be written,

Question 15 asks about the preceding passage as a whole.

15. Suppose the author had intended to write an essay about how celebrities are almost never really the people we think they are. Would this essay fulfill that goal?
  A. Yes, because it makes a strong case that one of the greatest rock stars of all time did not write his own songs.
  B. Yes, because the essay just confirms what most people already suspected anyway.
  C. No, because the essay deals only with Chuck Berry, and not celebrities in general.
  D. No, because the concept of "celebrities" did not exist yet in the 1950s.

PASSAGE II

Stealing *Mona Lisa*

It is the world's most famous painting, and endlessly
                                                    16

admired, analyzed, parodied for over 500 years.
                    17

You'd think that any sane thief would set his sights

on a less ambitious target. But in 1911, Leonardo da

Vinci's masterpiece, the *Mona Lisa*, was stolen, and
                                                    18

it remained missing for two years.
       18

     Vincenzo Perrugia was an Italian immigrant who

had worked at France's famous Louvre museum for

barely a month, but this was enough time for him to
                  19

formulate a daring plan. Knowing that the museum

would be closed for restorations on August 21, he

hid inside at closing the night before. The following

day, Peruggia tried his hardest to keep calm until
         20

he found himself alone in the gallery where the

Mona Lisa hung.

16. **F.** NO CHANGE
    G. endlessly
    H. it was endlessly
    J. that has been endlessly

17. **A.** NO CHANGE
    B. and parodied
    C. and it was parodied
    D. it was parodied

18. **F.** NO CHANGE
    G. went missing and was stolen
    H. had been stolen, remaining missing
    J. was missing

19. Which of the following alternatives to the underlined portion would NOT be acceptable?
    A. this was
    B. which was
    C. evidently
    D. DELETE the underlined portion.

20. Given that all the choices are true, which one provides the most specific information about Perrugia's methods?
    F. NO CHANGE
    G. Perrugia somehow managed to evade detection
    H. just as he would eventually tell his grandchildren, Perrugia remained in the museum
    J. disguised in a smock, Perrugia walked around looking busy

He quickly snatched it off the wall and absconded
                          21

into a stairwell, where he smashed the frame, then

rolled up the painting and hid it in his smock.

He found the door at the bottom of the stairs
22

locked, he smashed the knob and calmly reported

the broken lock to a custodian on his way out of the

building.

    Perrugia wasn't the only one in the Louvre that
                                                23

day who had a plan. Many workers passed the
    23

empty space on the wall where they knew the

Mona Lisa usually hung, but since restorations

were taking place all day, just assumed that the

museum's prized possession was being touched

up or reframed as quickly as possible. When it was
                   24

discovered that the painting was gone, a massive

manhunt began. Theorizing that a radical young

artist might have stolen it as a publicity stunt,
                                 25

police even arrested and questioned such figures

as Pablo Picasso and surrealist poet Guillaume

Apollinaire.

21. Which of the following alternatives to
the underlined portion would be LEAST
acceptable?
A. from
B. off of
C. from of
D. from off

22. F. NO CHANGE
G. Although he would find
H. Just before he found
J. Finding

23. Given that all the choices are true, which one
most effectively introduces the paragraph?
A. NO CHANGE
B. There's no record of how long it took for
the lock to be repaired, if it ever was.
C. The staff of the Louvre did not
immediately realize that a theft had
occurred.
D. The Louvre had seen its share of troubles
since it was first constructed as a fortress
in the twelfth century.

24. F. NO CHANGE
G. in private.
H. by Italian artisans.
J. automatically.

25. Which of the following alternatives to
the underlined portion would be LEAST
acceptable?
A. out of ignorance
B. as a form of protest
C. to make a point
D. as some pretentious prank

Perrugia hid the painting in his apartment and waited. As time passed, the search lost momentum and the feared masterwork was gone forever.
26

Fortunately, Perrugia was motivated for the
27
crime led to its recovery: he felt that the *Mona Lisa* belonged in da Vinci's native Italy, from whence
28
it had been stolen by Napoleon a century earlier. In 1913, he smuggled it there and offered it to the director of the Uffizi Gallery in Florence. Perrugia expected a hero's welcome and a reward for his patriotic crime, but gallery personnel stalled him while police were called, and he was arrested.

Still, a lot of good came out of the business after
29
all: the *Mona Lisa* was exhibited all over Italy for
29
months before being returned to the Louvre, and as for Vincenzo Perrugia himself, the Italian courts took his patriotism (and the popularity of his crime in Italy) into consideration, and for the theft of the most priceless portable object on the face of the earth, he served only a few months in jail!

26. **F.** NO CHANGE
     G. gone masterwork was forever feared.
     H. masterwork was feared gone forever.
     J. masterwork was forever feared gone.

27. **A.** NO CHANGE
     B. the motivation had
     C. Perrugia being motivated
     D. Perrugia's motivation

28. **F.** NO CHANGE
     G. after which
     H. into there
     J. whereas

29. The writer would like to begin the final sentence with a phrase that indicates Perrugia might not have been as crazy as he seems. Given that all the choices are true, which one best accomplishes the writer's goal?
     A. NO CHANGE
     B. Still, his expectations were not entirely off-base:
     C. Curiously, it was the last time he ever felt the need to steal anything:
     D. Curiously, a war between France and Italy was only a few short years away:

Question 30 asks about the preceding passage as a whole.

30. Suppose the writer's goal had been to write a brief essay explaining the background, execution, and aftermath of a famous crime. Would this essay accomplish that goal?

F. Yes, because it establishes that everyone knew about the theft at the time, even though some people don't nowadays.

G. Yes, because it presents a sufficiently complete picture of Perrugia's theft of the *Mona Lisa*.

H. No, because it tells us virtually nothing about why the *Mona Lisa* is so important.

J. No, because it clearly states that Perrugia's punishment was not nearly harsh enough.

PASSAGE III

The following paragraphs may or may not be in the most logical order. Each paragraph is numbered in brackets, and question 45 will ask you to choose where Paragraph 1 should most logically be placed.

Whom Are You Calling a Barbarian?

[1]

His enemies <u>dubbed</u> "The Scourge of God." His
31

name is synonymous <u>to</u> cruelty, mercilessness,
32

and barbarism of all kinds. But has history really

been fair to the fifth-century king and military

31. A. NO CHANGE
B. dubbed him
C. dubbed to him
D. dubbed him for

32. F. NO CHANGE
G. of
H. as
J. with

leader known to us as Attila the Hun? It is modern
                                     33
historians who agree that it has not. Traditional
          33
views of this period in Europe have been based on

Roman sources, which even at their best are still

biased against Attila, and at worst contain outright

lies. 34

[2]

The Huns were not the nomadic tribe of brutes

that popular culture has often portrayed them as

being. At the time of Attila's birth in 406, the Huns
                                      35
were a vast and efficiently run nation stretching all

the way from Asias central seas to the west of what
                36
is now Germany, and this was far larger and less
                37
fragmented than the Western Roman Empire then

was. And unlike aristocratic Roman society, the Hun

world was a meritocracy with little to no separation
                                                 38
because of class division. At least a few sources who
      38

33. **A.** NO CHANGE
     B. It is agreed by modern historians
     C. Modern historians had finally agreed
     D. Modern historians agree

34. If the writer were to delete the preceding
     sentence, the paragraph would primarily lose
     information that:
     F. demonstrates that Roman historians were
          typically less honest than were historians
          from other cultures.
     G. proves that modern Europe is more
          indebted to Rome for its culture than to
          any other ancient society.
     H. explains the reasons behind the long-
          standing negative opinion of Attila.
     J. explains which myths about Attila were
          invented by the Romans.

35. **A.** NO CHANGE
     B. 406, and the
     C. 406; the
     D. 406. The

36. **F.** NO CHANGE
     G. Asia's central seas
     H. Asias central sea's
     J. Asias' central sea's

37. **A.** NO CHANGE
     B. this was
     C. which was
     D. DELETE the underlined portion.

38. **F.** NO CHANGE
     G. class division
     H. people being separated by class division
     J. unfair class division keeping people apart

had lived in both societies said that they preferred

the Hun civilization to the Roman.

Yes, the Huns had beards and wore furs, but this

was only common sense: it was much colder where

they lived than it was in Rome. 39

[3]

Attila became king upon the death of his uncle

in 434 and <u>coexisting peacefully</u> with Western Rome
                    40
for the first part of his reign. Roman armies in what

is now France recruited soldiers from Hun lands

with Attila's permission, and the two empires traded

freely and even extradited criminals to each other.

The trouble started in 450, when Honoria, the sister

of the emperor, offered herself in marriage to Attila

in an attempt to escape an arranged union with a

much older senator. Valentinian, her brother, tried

to deny that the offer was genuine, but Attila was

39. At this point, the writer is considering adding the following true statement:

> The Vikings wore even more furs and had even longer beards, and they sailed to America 500 years before Columbus!

Should the writer make this addition?
A. Yes, because it provides a much-needed additional example for the same point.
B. Yes, because this little-known fact should be provided to people whenever possible.
C. No, because it distracts the reader from the main focus of the essay.
D. No, because the essay does not explain whether the Huns and Vikings got along.

40. F. NO CHANGE
G. coexists in peace
H. coexisted peacefully
J. peaceful coexistence

understandably unwilling to pass up a chance to

unite his royal line <u>with that of Rome</u> and create the
41

greatest empire in history. Rome was so frightened

by this prospect that they aligned themselves with

the Visigoths—formerly the common enemy of

both the <u>Huns, and Rome further insulted Attila.</u>
42

Hun forces entered Italy in 452, and sacked several

cities, but were forced to turn back before reaching

the capital, as a famine prevented the army from

obtaining sufficient food. Attila died in his native

lands a year later, supposedly after partying too hard

at a feast.

[4]

Contrary to popular belief, neither Attila nor any

Hun commander ever sacked Rome (the Visigoths

took the city in 410, and the Vandals in 454, but

neither nation was aligned or even friendly with the

Huns). Although his tactics were brutal by modern

standards, <u>they were</u> no more so than those of
43

any military leader from that time, the "civilized"

Romans included. Attila may be known as a

monster in the West, but is revered as a national

41. A. NO CHANGE
    B. with they're own
    C. with Rome's one
    D. plus the Roman one

42. F. NO CHANGE
    G. Huns and Rome's, who had further
       insulted Attila.
    H. Huns and Rome—further insulting Attila.
    J. Huns everywhere. Rome thus insulted
       Attila further.

43. A. NO CHANGE
    B. but they were
    C. since they were
    D. it was

hero in much of Eastern Europe to this day. Should
44

you visit that part of the world, you will be amazed
44

at how often you see his name! 45
44

44. Given that all of the following statements are true, which one provides the most relevant and specific information?
F. NO CHANGE
G. There is almost certainly at least one giant statue of him there!
H. In Budapest, there are more than ten "Attila Streets!"
J. Of course, the map of Eastern Europe is now very different from the one most Americans remember from school!

Question 45 asks about the preceding passage as a whole.

---

45. For the sake of logic and coherence, Paragraph 1 should be placed:
A. where it is now.
B. after Paragraph 2.
C. after Paragraph 3.
D. after Paragraph 4.

PASSAGE IV

The Christmas Truce

When it started with the assassination of an
46

Austrian nobleman in the summer of 1914, and

by the end of that year all Europe was scarred by

trenches full of soldiers and pits full of poison gas.

Tanks and warplanes made their first
47

appearances. Old-fashioned commanders
47

accustomed to valiant charges on horseback sent

countless waves of young men to instant death in

the face of another new invention, the machine

gun. The Great War, or World War I as it would come

46. F. NO CHANGE
G. Since it started
H. Although it started
J. It started

47. Which of the following alternatives to the underlined portion would be LEAST acceptable?
A. were first put into use.
B. were first introduced.
C. were used in combat for the first time.
D. reared their ugly heads.

to be called, <u>was the deadliest conflict the Western</u>
48

<u>World had ever seen.</u> But out of its horror came one
48

of the most reassuring accounts of the essential

goodness of the human spirit.

     On Christmas Eve of 1914, near the town of

<u>Ypres, Belgium, German</u>, and English forces had
49

fought to a standstill from their opposed trenches.

Both sides had sent miners to dig tunnels toward

the enemy <u>line. Underground</u>, each unit could hear
50

the sounds of the <u>other's</u> digging getting closer,
51

and knew that the tunnels would soon meet and a

firefight would erupt in the darkness at point-blank

range.

     At that moment, <u>every soldier must have thought</u>
52

<u>that he was about to die.</u> Recognizing the melodies,
52

the men in the other tunnel responded, singing

along in their own language. The singing picked up

above ground, where the armies lit candles visible

48. The writer wishes to finish this sentence with a phrase that emphasizes the human cost of the war. Which of the following true statements best achieves that goal?
  F. NO CHANGE
  G. was the first modern war, involving horrors beyond description.
  H. led directly to the deadly Spanish Flu epidemic.
  J. is the only major war where the inhuman weapon of mustard gas was used.

49. **A.** NO CHANGE
  B. Ypres, Belgium, German
  C. Ypres, Belgium German
  D. Ypres, Belgium, and German

50. Which of the following alternatives to the underlined portion would NOT be acceptable?
  F. NO CHANGE
  G. line, underground,
  H. line; underground
  J. line: underground

51. **A.** NO CHANGE
  B. others
  C. others'
  D. other is

52. Given that all the choices are true, which one would be the best transition between the first and last parts of the paragraph?
  F. NO CHANGE
  G. you could have cut the tension with a knife.
  H. soldiers from one side began singing Christmas carols.
  J. no soldier in the tunnels had ever been more scared in his life.

to the enemy at the edges of their trenches. The

fighting ceased, and slowly, some individuals even

dared to cross No Man's Land and meet enemy

soldiers in the middle, where they exchanged food
                         53
and drink from their respective homelands.

When word of the Christmas Truce got out, the

high command on both sides were furious and
                     54
ordered the fighting to resume. When Christmas

1915 approached again, they took steps to ensure
               55
that such things would not happen, ordering artillery

bombardments on Christmas Eve and Christmas

Day to make No Man's Land uncrossable. The

commanders in the trenches had to follow orders,

on pain of court martial. But as the generals had
                          56
never specified coordinates for the mandatory

bombardments, entrenched officers in several

locations came up with the idea of ordering wildly

inaccurate shelling, allowing gift-giving between

enemy combatants once again. For example, in one
                              57
location English and German soldiers even organized

a soccer game in the middle of the battlefield.

53. Which of the following alternatives to
the underlined portion would NOT be
acceptable?
- **A.** middle. There, they exchanged
- **B.** middle to exchange
- **C.** middle they exchanged
- **D.** middle, exchanging

54. **F.** NO CHANGE
- **G.** both sides, they were furious
- **H.** both sides furiously
- **J.** both sides was furious

55. The best placement for the underlined
portion would be:
- **A.** where it is now.
- **B.** after the word *they*.
- **C.** after the word *happen*.
- **D.** after the word *bombardments*.

56. **F.** NO CHANGE
- **G.** when the generals
- **H.** that the generals
- **J.** the generals

57. **A.** NO CHANGE
- **B.** In addition,
- **C.** Meanwhile,
- **D.** On the other hand,

By the time World War I ended in 1918, 16

million people had been killed in battle, three

world powers had ceased to exist altogether, and

nothing discernible had been accomplished.

The devastation ended up leading directly to
                    58
the existence of both the Soviet Union and Nazi
                    58
Germany. Just about the only good thing that came
    58
out of it was the story of a few young men who

couldn't understand or comprehend each other's
                    59
languages but still decided that they would rather

play soccer than fight.

58. If the writer were to delete the underlined sentence, the paragraph would primarily lose:
- **F.** an example of how World War I shaped the major conflicts of the twentieth century.
- **G.** the answer to a question posed at the beginning of the essay.
- **H.** an example of pure speculation on the part of the writer.
- **J.** some minor details unrelated to the main point.

59. **A.** NO CHANGE
- **B.** understand nor comprehend
- **C.** understandably comprehend
- **D.** understand

Question 60 asks about the preceding passage as a whole.

60. Suppose the writer had intended to write a brief essay focusing on acts of protest within the armed forces during wars. Would this essay fulfill that goal?
- **F.** Yes, because the Christmas Truce is the most famous battlefield protest of all time.
- **G.** Yes, because the Christmas Truce was spontaneous in origin, rather than being planned in advance.
- **H.** No, because it only discusses examples of soldiers acting in protest from one war.
- **J.** No, because American troops had not yet entered World War I at the time of the Christmas Truce.

PASSAGE V

Genius at the Last Minute

He was born in Oregon in 1954, the son of a

schoolteacher mother <u>and his father had grown up</u> in
61

a Mennonite community. <u>He never liked or excelled</u>
62

<u>in school,</u> and chose to attend a "hippie college" in
62

Washington State that had been founded only five

years earlier and didn't even give grades.

He stayed in college for five years, <u>and</u> writing
63

articles and drawing cartoons for the campus paper.

<u>After graduation,</u> he moved to Los Angeles to try
64

to become a writer, but couldn't catch a break and

wandered through a series of jobs: busing tables,

washing dishes, and even working at a sewage

61. **A.** NO CHANGE
    B. and father grew up
    C. and whose father grew up
    D. and a father who'd grown up

62. Which of the following alternatives to
    the underlined portion would NOT be
    acceptable?
    F. never liked school or excelled in it,
    G. neither liked nor excelled in school,
    H. disliked school, which he didn't excel in it,
    J. disliked and failed to excel in school,

63. **A.** NO CHANGE
    B. where
    C. in which
    D. DELETE the underlined portion.

64. **F.** NO CHANGE
    G. Although after graduation,
    H. After graduation, when
    J. After graduation, however,

treatment plant. Finally, he ended up working <u>in a</u>
65

record store, a job he was able to stand. ☐66☐

To amuse himself and make a little extra money,

he drew comic books about how miserable he was

in Los Angeles and sold photocopies of them in the

store.

The <u>comics were sarcastic</u> black-and-white
67

doodles featuring a family of odd-looking,

dysfunctional rabbits, became popular with

neighborhood artists and intellectuals, and soon he

was getting paid to draw a daily strip featuring his

odd rabbits for a local alternative newspaper. (The

paper also gave him a music column, but he lost

that after admitting <u>that he</u> just made up the names
68

of all the bands and albums he reviewed as a joke.)

65. Which of the following alternatives to the underlined portion would NOT be acceptable?
   A. at
   B. of
   C. for
   D. the register in

66. At this point, the writer is considering adding the following true statement:

The name of the store was Licorice Pizza.

Should the writer make this addition?

   F. Yes, because it helps explain why he was able to stand the job.
   G. Yes, because otherwise readers will wonder which store it was.
   H. No, because it is a minor detail that disrupts the flow of the paragraph.
   J. No, because many readers will not believe that this was really the store's name.

67. A. NO CHANGE
   B. comics, sarcastic
   C. sarcastically comic
   D. sarcastic comic's

68. Which of the following alternatives to the underlined portion would NOT be acceptable?
   F. he
   G. he had
   H. that he had
   J. because he had

The rabbit strip, called *Life in Hell*, came to the

attention of a successful <u>producer, who contacted</u>
69

the thirty-one-year-old cartoonist about the

possibility <u>to do</u> animated shorts for television. The
70

artist was thrilled, but while waiting in the lobby

of the producer's building before his big meeting,

he had a series of terrifying thoughts. What if the

television series bombed and ruined the reputation

of his beloved comic?

Or what if he had to give up the rights to the

characters, and no longer had any control over how

they were used?

<u>Crazy stuff happens to young artists all the</u>
71

<u>time.</u> So just before being called into the meeting,
71

he quickly drew another group of characters and

named them after his own family: he used the real

names of his parents and two little sisters, but

invented another for the sarcastic, academically

unmotivated male child, thinking that using his

69. **A.** NO CHANGE
    B. producer then contacted
    C. producer, and contacted
    D. producer contacted

70. **F.** NO CHANGE
    G. of doing
    H. he could do
    J. that this would do

71. Which of the following sentences makes for the best transition between the first and second parts of the paragraph?
    A. NO CHANGE
    B. At times like this, he wished he were still at college in Washington.
    C. It was probably silly for him to be worrying so much.
    D. He wanted the TV gig badly, but didn't want to risk losing *Life in Hell*.

own name would give away how little work he had
72

put into the idea. To the animator's great relief, the

producer loved the hurriedly created new characters.

Their first animated short debuted in 1987, and by

the end of 1989 they had their own half-hour show.

By now, you may have guessed that the

cartoonist's name, Matt Groening, and that the
73

family he invented off the top of his head in that

lobby is now known to the whole world as *The*

Simpsons. The cartoon in which they star has
74

become the longest-running sitcom in TV history,

as well as one of the most beloved, by viewers and

critics alike. Although it may not happen every day,
75

don't ever let anyone tell you that a work of genius
75

was never done at the last minute.

72. Which of the following alternatives to
the underlined portion would be LEAST
acceptable?
F. betray
G. evince
H. mask
J. tip the producer off to

73. A. NO CHANGE
B. name was Matt Groening
C. name, was Matt Groening
D. name, Matt Groening

74. F. NO CHANGE
G. cartoon which they star in
H. cartoon, which they star in,
J. cartoon they star in which

75. A. NO CHANGE
B. day, but don't
C. day; don't
D. day, don't people

STOP

If there is still time remaining, you may review your answers.

MATHEMATICS TEST

Time: 60 Minutes—60 Questions

Directions: Solve each problem, choose the correct answer, and then fill in the corresponding oval on your answer sheet.

Do not linger over problems that take too much time. Solve as many as you can; then return to the others in the time you have left for this test.

You are permitted to use a calculator on this test. You may use your calculator for any problems you choose, but some of the problems may best be done without using a calculator.

Note: Unless otherwise stated, all of the following should be assumed.

1. Illustrative figures are NOT necessarily drawn to scale.
2. Geometric figures lie in a plane.
3. The word *line* indicates a straight line.
4. The word *average* indicates arithmetic mean.

1. If $3x - 5 = 7$, then $3x = ?$

    A. $\dfrac{2}{3}$

    B. $\dfrac{4}{3}$

    C. 4

    D. $\dfrac{22}{3}$

    E. 12

2. What is the complement of $70°$?

    F. $10°$

    G. $20°$

    H. $30°$

    J. $80°$

    K. $110°$

3. 70 is 10% of what number?

    A. 7

    B. 63

    C. 77

    D. 700

    E. $7,000$

DO YOUR FIGURING HERE

DO YOUR FIGURING HERE

4. The sum of three consecutive integers is 99. What is the value of the greatest of the three integers?

F. 32

G. 33

H. 34

J. 35

K. 36

5. What is the area of the figure below?

A. 54 in.^{2}

B. 90 in.^{2}

C. 108 in.^{2}

D. 135 in.^{2}

E. 180 in.^{2}

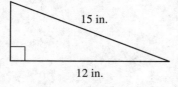

15 in.

12 in.

6. Miller earns $13.00 per hour for the first 40 hours he works each week. For each hour beyond 40 that he works in 1 week, Miller earns $19.50 per hour. Last week Miller earned $1,027.00. How many hours did Miller work last week?

F. 26

G. 30

H. 53

J. 66

K. 79

7. Which of the following inequalities is equivalent to $3 - 4(x + 7) < 19$?

A. $x > \dfrac{9}{2}$

B. $x < \dfrac{9}{2}$

C. $x < -11$

D. $x > -11$

E. $x < 11$

PRACTICE TEST 3

8. Which of the following is equivalent to
$3\sqrt{300} - 5\sqrt{75}$?

DO YOUR FIGURING HERE

F. $-2\sqrt{225}$

G. $5\sqrt{3}$

H. $15\sqrt{3}$

J. $2\sqrt{225}$

K. $15\sqrt{225}$

9. $|-2 + 3^2| - |-2 - 3^2| = ?$

A. −24

B. −4

C. 0

D. 18

E. 26

10. For triangle ABC, m$\angle A = 75°$ and
m$\angle B = 36°$. Which segment of triangle ABC
is the longest?

F. AB

G. BC

H. AC

J. AB and AC are both
the longest sides.

K. Not enough information

11. Which of the following is a factor of
$3x^2 + x - 4$?

A. $(x + 2)$

B. $(x - 2)$

C. $(3x - 4)$

D. $(x + 1)$

E. $(x - 1)$

12. Which of the following lines passes through the point (–3, 5)?

F. $y = -2x - 3$

G. $y = -4x + 5$

H. $y = -x + 2$

J. $y = 4x + 5$

K. $y = 5x + 9$

DO YOUR FIGURING HERE

13. If $f(x) = \dfrac{-x^2 + 4}{x}$, then $f(-2) = $?

A. –4

B. –1

C. 0

D. 6

E. 10

14. Which of the following lines is parallel to $y = -\dfrac{3}{4}x + 2$ in the standard (x, y) coordinate plane?

F. $y = -\dfrac{3}{4}x$

G. $y = \dfrac{4}{3}x + 2$

H. $y = -\dfrac{4}{3}x + 2$

J. $y = \dfrac{3}{4}x + 2$

K. $y = \dfrac{3}{4}x - 2$

15. An aquarium has exactly two types of fish: goldfish and angelfish. If the ratio of goldfish to angelfish is 2:5 and there are 25 angelfish in the aquarium, how many total fish are in the aquarium?

A. 7

B. 32

C. 35

D. 50

E. 125

16. Three different lines in the same plane can intersect at how many points?

    F. 1

    G. 1 or 2

    H. 1 or 3

    J. 1, 2, or 3

    K. 0, 1, 2, or 3

DO YOUR FIGURING HERE

17. If $-1 < a < 0$, $-4 < b < -3$, and $c = a - b$, then which of the following statements is true?

    A. $c < a$

    B. $c < b$

    C. $c < a + b$

    D. $c < 0$

    E. $c > 0$

18. What is the slope of the line through the points $(-2, 5)$ and $(0, 8)$?

    F. $-\dfrac{3}{2}$

    G. $-\dfrac{2}{3}$

    H. $\dfrac{7}{8}$

    J. $\dfrac{8}{7}$

    K. $\dfrac{3}{2}$

19. Rosemary and Caroline are baking cupcakes for a party. They are working from a recipe that will make 32 cupcakes. The recipe requires $2\frac{1}{2}$ cups of sugar to make 1 full batch. If they need to make 250 cupcakes for the party, which of the following amounts (to the nearest whole cup) is the LEAST amount of sugar they need to make all 250 cupcakes?

A. 5 cups

B. 10 cups

C. 15 cups

D. 20 cups

E. 25 cups

DO YOUR FIGURING HERE

20. For the following triangle, $\angle B$ is a right angle, $BC = 8$, and $AC = 17$. What is the value of $\sin(C)$?

F. $\dfrac{8}{17}$

G. $\dfrac{15}{17}$

H. $\dfrac{\sqrt{353}}{17}$

J. $\dfrac{17}{15}$

K. $\dfrac{17}{8}$

Use the following information to answer questions 21–24.

The Knight family plans to remodel their kitchen. They have a total budget of $30,000 for the project. They have sorted the budget into 6 categories. Some of the budget amounts are shown in the table below.

Expense category	Budget amount
Appliances	$3,500
Cabinets	$7,000
Flooring	$4,000
Lighting	$2,500
Labor	?
Other	?
Total budget	$30,000

21. The amount budgeted for the Appliances category is the sum of the prices of 4 appliances. What is the average price per appliance?

    A. $ 583
    B. $ 625
    C. $ 700
    D. $ 875
    E. $1,000

22. What fraction represents the ratio of the budget for Lighting compared to the budget for Flooring?

    F. $\frac{5}{7}$

    G. $\frac{5}{8}$

    H. $\frac{1}{2}$

    J. $\frac{5}{14}$

    K. $\frac{1}{12}$

23. In a circle graph illustrating the 6 budget amounts in the table, what should be the measure of the central angle of the Lighting sector?

A. 30°

B. 42°

C. 48°

D. 72°

E. 84°

24. Which of the following percentages is closest to the percent of the total budget for the Labor and Other categories combined?

F. 37%

G. 43%

H. 45%

J. 48%

K. 57%

---

25. If $5^3 \cdot 5^{-7} = \dfrac{1}{5^x}$, then $x = $?

A. −21

B. −4

C. 4

D. 7

E. 21

26. In the figure below, m∠WYZ = 28° and $\overline{YM}$ bisects ∠ZYX. Which of the following is the measure of ∠XYM?

F. 76°

G. 78°

H. 84°

J. 90°

K. 152°

27. In the figure below, $\overline{AC}$ is a diameter of the circle and m∠BAC = 35°. Find the measure of arc $\widehat{AB}$.

A. 35°

B. 60°

C. 70°

D. 90°

E. 110°

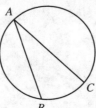

28. Which of the following is the greatest common factor of $36m^4n^3p^5$ and $24m^2n$?

F. $6m^2n$

G. $6m^4n^3p^5$

H. $12m^2n$

J. $12m^2np^5$

K. $72m^2n$

29. The perimeter of a parallelogram is 56 and the length of one side is 12 inches. If it can be determined, what are the lengths, in inches, of the other three sides?

A. 12, 12, 20

B. 12, 10, 10

C. 12, 16, 16

D. 12, 32, 32

E. Cannot be determined from the given information

Use the following information to answer questions 30–32.

In the figure below, a gas station (at Y) and radar stations (at X and Z) lie on a horizontal east-west line, with X 5,000 feet due west of Y. An airplane (at W) is shown directly above the gas station, flying due east at a constant speed of 600 feet per second and at a constant altitude of 12,000 feet. The airplane is located at a straight-line distance of 13,000 feet from the radar station at X and 20,000 feet from the radar station at Z.

DO YOUR FIGURING HERE

30. Which of the following values is closest to the distance, in feet, between the two radar stations?

   F. 12,000

   G. 16,000

   H. 18,000

   J. 20,000

   K. 21,000

31. Given that 1 mile is equal to 5,280 feet, which of the following is closest to the plane's rate of travel in miles per hour?

   A. 88

   B. 409

   C. 528

   D. 600

   E. 681

32. Let X, Y, Z, and W lie in the standard (x, y) coordinate plane such that X is at $(0, 0)$ and Y is at $(5,000, 0)$. Which of the following equations represents the line between Y and W?

   F. $x = 5,000$

   G. $x = 12,000$

   H. $x = 15,000$

   J. $y = 5,000$

   K. $y = 12,000$

33. What value of x will satisfy the following matrix equation?

$$\begin{bmatrix} 23y^2 & 13z \\ 2x-1 & -15w^3 \end{bmatrix} + \begin{bmatrix} -7 & 10 \\ -4x-2 & 13 \end{bmatrix} = \begin{bmatrix} 16 & 23 \\ 12 & -2 \end{bmatrix}$$

   A. -7.5

   B. -3.5

   C. 1

   D. 6.5

   E. 13

34. Which of the following is an expression for the area of the triangle below?

F. $2w^2 - 8w + 10$

G. $\dfrac{6w^2 - 24w + 21}{2}$

H. $6w^2 - 24w + 21$

J. $12w^2 - 48w + 42$

K. $(2w - 7)(w + 3)$

3

$2w^2 - 8w + 7$

35. If ■ is defined for all real numbers x and y by x■$y = (x + y)(x - y)$, then 1■$(2$■$2) = $?

A. 0

B. 1

C. 3

D. 4

E. 5

36. Sophie has played 6 games of soccer scoring 0, 1, 3, 2, 4, and 1 goals respectively in those games. For game 7, which of the following values will NOT yield a median of 2 goals scored?

F. 1 goal

G. 2 goals

H. 3 goals

J. 4 goals

K. 5 goals

37. What is the center of the circle with equation $(x + 7)^2 + (y - 5)^2 = 121$?

A. $(-7, -5)$

B. $(-7, 5)$

C. $(7, -5)$

D. $(7, 5)$

E. $(5, 11)$

38. Given the equation $3x - 7y = 21$, what is the equation in slope-intercept form?

DO YOUR FIGURING HERE

F. $y = -\dfrac{3}{7}x + 3$

G. $y = -\dfrac{7}{3}x + 3$

H. $y = -\dfrac{3}{7}x - 3$

J. $y = \dfrac{3}{7}x + 3$

K. $y = \dfrac{3}{7}x - 3$

39. In the graph below, line m is parallel to line n. Find the value of a.

A. $17°$
B. $22°$
C. $27°$
D. $32°$
E. $37°$

40. Dustin is in a 40-foot air traffic control tower at the local airport. He spots a plane that has just landed and using his protractor measures the angle of depression from the top of the tower to the landed plane to be $12°$. How far from the base of the control tower is the plane?

F. $\dfrac{\tan(12°)}{40}$

G. $\dfrac{40}{\tan(12°)}$

H. $\dfrac{\sin(12°)}{40}$

J. $\dfrac{40}{\sin(12°)}$

K. $\dfrac{\cos(12°)}{40}$

41. For what values of x is the function $\sqrt{x - 5}$ undefined in the real number system?

A. $x = 0$
B. $x = 5$
C. $x = -5$
D. $x < 5$
E. $x > 5$

42. In the standard (x, y) coordinate plane, what are the coordinates of point A after the graph is reflected over the line $x = 7$?

F. $(3, m)$

G. $(-3, -m)$

H. $(10, m)$

J. $(15, m)$

K. $(17, m)$

43. Given line segment AB with A $(-3, 2)$ and B $(5, 8)$, which of the following is the length of AB?

A. $\sqrt{34}$

B. $2\sqrt{10}$

C. 10

D. $9\sqrt{2}$

E. $\sqrt{170}$

44. Given similar rectangles $QUAD$ and $RECT$, the ratio of sides QU to RE is 1:4. If the area of $QUAD$ is 12, what is the area of $RECT$?

F.   0.75

G.   3

H.   12

J.   48

K.   192

45. A parking lot downtown charges x dollars for the first hour and y dollars for each hour after the first. If Daniel parks in the lot for h hours where $h > 6$, which of the following equations represents P, the amount Daniel has to pay to park in the lot?

A. $P = h(x + y)$

B. $P = x + yh$

C. $P = y + x(h - 1)$

D. $P = xh + y(h - 1)$

E. $P = x + y(h - 1)$

46. Let $y = \dfrac{2x}{3z}$. What happens to the value of z as both x and y are doubled?

F. z remains the same

G. z doubles

H. z decreases by $\dfrac{1}{2}$

J. z quadruples

K. z decreases by a factor of $\dfrac{1}{4}$

47. If $\dfrac{w^6 t^5}{m^9} > 0$, then which of the following is true?

A. $w > 0$

B. $t > 0$

C. $m > 0$

D. $wt > 0$

E. $tm > 0$

48. Which of the following is equivalent to $2 \log(x) + \dfrac{1}{2} \log(y) - 4 \log(z)$?

F. $\log(2x + \dfrac{1}{2} y - 4z)$

G. $\log(x^2 z^4 \sqrt{y})$

H. $\log\left(\dfrac{x^2 \sqrt{y}}{z^4} \right)$

J. $\log\left(\dfrac{xy}{4z} \right)$

K. $\log(2x^2 yz)$

DO YOUR FIGURING HERE

PRACTICE TEST 3

49. Given the following table, find $f(g(2))$:

x	f(x)	g(x)
1	–5	0
2	–10	3
3	–15	6
4	–20	9

A. –15
B. –10
C. 0
D. 3
E. 6

50. The number of fish, p, a small pond can sustain varies inversely with the square root of the amount of predators, q, in the pond. If a pond with 49 predators can sustain a population of 800 fish, how many fish could a pond with 100 predators sustain?

F. 560
G. 600
H. 650
J. 1,600
K. 2,000

51. Points $P(1, 1)$ and $Q(x, x^2)$ lie in the standard (x, y) coordinate plane. Which of the following is an expression for the slope between points P and Q when $x > 5$?

A. 0
B. $\dfrac{x^2 + 1}{x + 1}$
C. $x + 1$
D. $\dfrac{x + 1}{x^2 + 1}$
E. Undefined

52. Which of the following expressions is equivalent to $\dfrac{3 \cdot 3^{2x-5}}{3^{x+1}}$?

F. 3^{x-7}
G. 3^{x-5}
H. 3^{x-3}
J. 3^{x-1}
K. 1

2 △ △ △ △ △ △ △ △ **2**

53. What fraction is located exactly halfway between $\frac{3}{8}$ and $\frac{4}{5}$ on the standard number line?

   A. $\frac{15}{40}$

   B. $\frac{17}{40}$

   C. $\frac{1}{2}$

   D. $\frac{7}{13}$

   E. $\frac{47}{80}$

DO YOUR FIGURING HERE

PRACTICE TEST 3

54. Mike has taken 4 tests in algebra so far. His average after 4 tests is 85%. If he has not received a grade lower than 80% on any tests, what is the highest possible score Mike could have achieved on one test?

   F. 96%

   G. 97%

   H. 98%

   J. 99%

   K. 100%

55. Given $|x-3| > x-3$, what is the solution set for the inequality?

   A. $x > 3$

   B. $x < 3$

   C. $x > 0$

   D. $x < 0$

   E. All real numbers

PRACTICE TEST 3   253

PRACTICE TEST 3

56. For $i^2 = -1$, which of the following is equivalent to $\dfrac{i+7}{i-5} \cdot i$?

   F. -1

   G. $\dfrac{6}{13} - \dfrac{17}{13}i$

   H. $\dfrac{6}{13} + \dfrac{17}{13}i$

   J. $-\dfrac{1}{2} - \dfrac{3}{2}i$

   K. $\dfrac{1}{2} + \dfrac{3}{2}i$

DO YOUR FIGURING HERE

57. One square inch on the average pizza contains 50 calories. Alex bakes a 12" diameter pizza and cuts it into 8 equal slices. If his dad eats 3 slices and Alex only eats 2, approximately how many more calories did Alex's dad eat than he did?

   A. 100

   B. 700

   C. 1,400

   D. 2,100

   E. 2,200

58. Given $\tan(\theta) = v$, where $0° \le \theta \le 90°$, which of the following could be an expression for $\cos(\theta)$?

   F. $\dfrac{v}{\sqrt{1+v^2}}$

   G. $\dfrac{\sqrt{1+v^2}}{v}$

   H. $\dfrac{1}{\sqrt{1+v^2}}$

   J. $\sqrt{1-v^2}$

   K. $\dfrac{\sqrt{1-v^2}}{v}$

59. Lisa, Carl, Max, Jenny, and Andy go to watch a movie and all sit next to each other in the same aisle. Andy must sit at either end of the group, but everyone else can sit anywhere within the group. How many possible seating arrangements are there?

   A. 15
   B. 48
   C. 56
   D. 92
   E. 120

60. In the standard (x, y) coordinate plane, points (m, n) and $\left(m - 2, n + \dfrac{2}{g}\right)$ lie on the graph of the equation $y = \dfrac{1}{3}x - t$, where $t > 1$. What is the value of g?

   F. -3
   G. $-\dfrac{1}{4}$
   H. 1
   J. $\dfrac{7}{5}$
   K. $\dfrac{123}{5}$

DO YOUR FIGURING HERE

PRACTICE TEST 3

STOP

If there is still time remaining, you may review your answers.

READING TEST

Time: 35 Minutes—40 Questions

Directions: There are four passages in this test. Each passage is followed by several questions. After reading a passage, choose the best answer to each question and fill in the corresponding oval on your answer sheet. You may refer to the passages as often as necessary.

PASSAGE I—LITERARY NARRATIVE

This passage is adapted from the short story "A&P" by John Updike (© 1961 by John Updike).

In walks these three girls in nothing but bathing suits. I'm in the third check-out slot, with my back to the door, so I don't see them until they're over by the bread. The store's pretty
(5) empty, so there was nothing much to do except lean on the register and wait for the girls to show up again. After a while they come around out of the far aisle, around the light bulbs. Queenie puts down the jar and I take it into my fingers
(10) icy cold. Kingfish Fancy Herring Snacks in Pure Sour Cream: 49¢.

Then everybody's luck begins to run out. Lengel comes in from the lot and is about to scuttle into that door marked MANAGER behind which he
(15) hides all day when the girls touch his eye. Lengel's pretty dreary, teaches Sunday school and the rest, but he doesn't miss that much. He comes over and says, "Girls, this isn't the beach."

Queenie blushes, though maybe it's just a
(20) brush of sunburn I was noticing for the first time. "My mother asked me to pick up a jar of herring snacks." Her voice kind of startled me, the way voices do when you see the people first, coming out so flat yet kind of tony, too, the way
(25) it ticked over "pick up" and "snacks." All of a sudden I slid right down her voice into her living room. Her father and the other men were standing around in bow ties and the women were in sandals picking up herring snacks on
(30) toothpicks off a big plate and they were all holding drinks the color of water with olives and sprigs of mint in them.

"That's all right," Lengel said. "But this isn't the beach." His repeating this struck me as funny, as
(35) if it had just occurred to him. He didn't like my smiling—as I say he doesn't miss much—but he concentrates on giving the girls that sad Sunday-school-superintendent stare.

Queenie's blush is no sunburn now, and the
(40) plump one in plaid pipes up, "We just came in for the one thing."

"That makes no difference," Lengel tells her, and I could see from the way his eyes went that he hadn't noticed she was wearing a two-piece
(45) before. "We want you decently dressed when you come in here."

"We are decent," Queenie says suddenly, getting sore now that she remembers her place, a place from which the crowd that runs the A&P
(50) must look pretty crummy. Fancy Herring Snacks flashed in her very blue eyes.

"Girls, I don't want to argue with you. After this come in here with your shoulders covered. It's our policy." He turns his back. I could feel
(55) in the silence everybody getting nervous, most of all Lengel, who asks me, "Sammy, have you rung up this purchase?"

I thought and said "No." I go through the punches, 4, 9, GROC, TOT—it's more complicated
(60) than you think. I uncrease the bill and pass a half and a penny into her narrow pink palm, and nestle the herrings in a bag and hand it over, all the time thinking.

The girls, and who'd blame them, are in a hurry
(65) to get out, so I say "I quit" to Lengel quick enough for them to hear, hoping they'll stop and watch me, their unsuspected hero. They keep right on going; the door flies open and they flicker across

the lot to their car, leaving me with Lengel and
(70) a kink in his eyebrow.

"Did you say something, Sammy?"

"I said I quit."

"I thought you did."

"You didn't have to embarrass them."

(75)   "It was they who were embarrassing us. I don't think you know what you're saying," Lengel said.

"I know you don't," I said. "But I do." I pull the bow at the back of my apron and start shrugging it off my shoulders. A couple customers that had
(80) been heading for my slot begin to knock against each other, like scared pigs in a chute.

Lengel sighs and begins to look very patient and old and gray. He's been a friend of my parents for years. "Sammy, you don't want to do this to your
(85) Mom and Dad," he tells me. It's true, I don't. But it seems to me that once you begin a gesture it's fatal not to go through with it. I fold the apron, "Sammy" stitched in red on the pocket, and put it on the counter, and drop the bow tie on top of
(90) it. "You'll feel this for the rest of your life," Lengel says, and I know that's true too, but remembering how he made that pretty girl blush makes me so scrunchy inside. One advantage to this scene taking place in summer, I can follow this
(95) up with a clean exit, there's no fumbling around getting your coat and galoshes, I just saunter into the electric eye in my white shirt that my mother ironed the night before, and the door heaves itself open, and outside the sunshine is
(100) skating around on the asphalt.

I look around for my girls, but they're gone. There wasn't anybody but some young married screaming with her children about some candy they didn't get. Looking back in the big windows,
(105) I could see Lengel in my place, checking the sheep through. His face was dark gray and his back stiff, as if he'd just had an injection of iron, and my stomach kind of fell as I felt how hard the world was going to be to me hereafter.

1.   The point of view from which the passage is told is best described as that of a (an):
     A.   young man relating a significant event in his life.
     B.   young man explaining to his parents why he has quit his job.
     C.   adult describing exactly what he should have done differently at a turning point in his life.
     D.   adolescent boy imagining what his life might be like in the future.

2.   The passage contains recurring references to all of the following EXCEPT:
     F.   the narrator's family.
     G.   the other customers.
     H.   supermarket chains.
     J.   the girls' attire.

3.   The first three paragraphs (lines 1–32) establish all of the following about the narrator EXCEPT that he:
     A.   is fascinated by the girls.
     B.   is new at his job.
     C.   dislikes his manager.
     D.   feels socially inferior to Queenie.

4.   It can reasonably be inferred from the passage that the narrator aspires to be seen as:
     F.   romantic and poetic.
     G.   intellectual but rebellious.
     H.   tough but cultured.
     J.   principled and heroic.

5.   Based on the narrator's account, life in his hometown is characterized by all of the following EXCEPT:
     A.   a tendency toward conformity.
     B.   an awareness of class hierarchy.
     C.   a mistrust of organized religion.
     D.   people knowing one another's business.

6. According to the narrator, which of the following articles of his clothing is the property of the store?
   F. His shirt
   G. His coat
   H. His bow tie
   J. His galoshes

7. When the narrator refers to Queenie "getting sore now that she remembers her place" (lines 47–48), he is most likely referring to the fact that she is:
   A. much younger than Lengel and himself.
   B. backed up by her two friends.
   C. a stranger to this town.
   D. wealthier than Lengel and himself.

8. Details in the passage most strongly suggest that the narrator's decision to quit ended up seeming most admirable from the point of view of:
   F. himself.
   G. the manager.
   H. his parents.
   J. Queenie.

9. The narrator indicates that Lengel the manager is extremely:
   A. forgiving.
   B. observant.
   C. skeptical.
   D. philosophical.

10. According to the passage, the narrator's decision to quit is most strongly motivated by his desire to:
    F. impress the girls.
    G. rebel against his parents.
    H. get out of his hometown.
    J. finally stand up to Lengel.

PASSAGE II—SOCIAL SCIENCE

This passage is adapted from the essay "Into the Heart of India's Bone Trade" by Scott Carney, which appeared on NPR online in 2007.

Medical students across the world rely on anatomical models to become informed doctors. What many don't realize is that a large number of these models are stolen from graves
(5) in Calcutta, India.

For 200 years, the city has been the center of a shadowy network of bone traders who snatch up skeletons in order to sell them to universities and hospitals abroad. In colonial times, British
(10) doctors hired thieves to dig up bodies from Indian cemeteries. Despite changes in laws, a similar process is going strong today.

Throughout parts of Calcutta, many of the cemeteries have been empty for generations.
(15) "When I die, when I'm gone, my body will also be stolen," says Mohammad Jinnah Vishwas, a farmer who lives in the village of Amdanga. "Before we didn't understand where all the bones were going, now we know that they were taken
(20) by criminals."

A legal multimillion-dollar business throughout the 1970s, the export of human remains was banned by India in 1986 following rumors that traders were murdering people for their
(25) bones. The new law pushed most of the major companies out of business.

"It is kind of a sad situation because [my father] loved the business so much, and he saw it drift away from him," says Craig Kilgore, whose
(30) family founded Kilgore International, which at one point was the principal supplier of bones to the United States.

At least one organization, however, has managed to survive underground. Most prominently, a

(35) firm called Young Brothers—located conveniently between the city's biggest morgue and largest cemetery—has excelled in the black market. It has taken a bold approach—advertising its bone selection in catalogues and going to extreme (40) measures to maintain its supply, according to a former clerk who requested anonymity for fear of retaliation.

"They took the bodies from the river, from the graveyard, and from the hospital. More than (45) 5,000 dead bodies I have seen," she says.

In 2001, Javed Ahmed Khan, Calcutta's health department chief, started receiving complaints about Young Brothers. The main storefront, neighbors said, was emitting a stench so horrible (50) that it could be detected several blocks away. Neighbors also reported that they had seen bones drying on the roof and skeletons boiling in massive tubs.

A raid against the business, led by Khan, con- (55) firmed suspicions. "I went inside and saw two rooms full of human skeletons. There were huge bowls where skeletons were dipped to remove the fats and all that," Khan says.

In addition to three truckloads of bones, Khan (60) said, he found invoices for shipments headed to the United States, Europe, and Singapore. Despite the evidence, the owner of Young Brothers was released just a few days later.

"We won the case," says Vinesh Aron, the pro- (65) prietor of Young Brothers. He denied a request to be interviewed, but when asked whether skeletons were recovered from his building, he said, "Those were all export materials." This answer hits on the hollowness of the rules governing the bones (70) trade. Under the law, any bones being exported are technically "illegal"—but the question for police is often whether they are illegal enough to bother prosecuting.

That became evident again in May, when (75) police intercepted a massive cache of human remains along a well-established smuggling route. The bleached white bones from over 100 people could have fetched around $70,000 had they made it to the United States. Whether the (80) goods will ever be submitted as evidence in court is unclear.

"It depends on the seriousness that society places on it," says Rajeev Kuman, director inspector general of police in Calcutta. Kuman says he (85) doesn't have enough resources to enforce the law. The fact that it's legal to import the bones into the United States and Europe, and that the "victims" are already dead, only serves to make the situation that much murkier.

(90) Few retailers in the United States possess a steady supply of human bones. Those that do often purchase them through a chain of middlemen that spans the globe. The longer the chain, the easier it is to avoid considering the nature (95) of that primary link.

11. Which of the following assumptions would be most critical for a reader to accept in order to agree fully with the author's claims in the passage?
   A. The root of the problem lies within the attitudes of Indian law enforcement.
   B. Local superstitions are keeping the illegal Indian bone market in business.
   C. The situation in India is no different than in any other Asian nation.
   D. Matters will not improve until American bone buyers insist upon greater accountability.

12. In the context of the passage, the statement "The longer the chain, the easier it is to avoid considering the nature of that primary link" (lines 93–95) most nearly suggests that:

F. American bone buyers have become complacent because they do not have to deal directly with criminals.

G. the general public does not believe that medical skeletons are made of real human bones.

H. larger criminal enterprises are harder to stop than smaller ones.

J. the bigger the bones, the more money criminals are able to get for them.

13. It can most reasonably be inferred from the passage that regarding the Indian bone trade, the author feels:

A. anger that the American media refuse to report on the problem.

B. fear that the criminals behind the enterprise will target him for exposing them.

C. sympathy for the people living in the conditions that are perpetuating the problem.

D. skepticism of whether the problem is really as widespread as people say.

14. The main purpose of the sixth paragraph (lines 33–42) is to:

F. establish that location is the primary factor determining which criminal enterprises will be more successful than others.

G. demonstrate the extreme boldness with which some bone-trafficking organizations operate.

H. convince the reader that the word of the former clerk can be trusted.

J. confirm the reader's suspicions that Young Brothers has been involved in illegal bone trafficking.

15. The main function of the eleventh paragraph (lines 64–73) is to:

A. establish that even flagrant violators of the bone laws will not necessarily end up convicted.

B. explain that Young Brothers had not been involved in illegal activity after all.

C. shift the question of blame to local police.

D. complain that American media have difficulty penetrating the veil of silence concerning Indian bone trafficking.

16. The passage notes all of the following as major contributors to the problem of illegal bone trafficking EXCEPT the:

F. power and influence of the criminals.

G. unfeasibility of prosecution.

H. frequent unreliability of witnesses.

J. willful ignorance of the American market.

17. The passage indicates that Calcutta law enforcement would do more about illegal bone trafficking if:

A. they were permitted to use the sort of weaponry necessary to win a fight with the traffickers.

B. they were better able to trust their own officers.

C. the cemeteries from which the bones were stolen lay inside their jurisdiction.

D. the public placed enough importance on the issue for the government to properly fund prosecution.

18. The passage implies that the skeletal remains of a single human might be worth approximately:

F. $100

G. $200

H. $700

J. $70,000

19. The passage implies that all of the following people oppose illegal bone trafficking EXCEPT:

A. Craig Kilgore.

B. Vinesh Aron.

C. Javed Ahmed Khan.

D. Mohammad Jinnah Vishwas.

20. The passage implies that the "catalogues" mentioned in line 39 would most likely be sent to:

F. medical students.

G. other criminals.

H. American media outlets.

J. superstitious locals.

PASSAGE III—HUMANITIES

Passage A is adapted from Mary Shelley's introduction to the 1831 second edition of her 1819 novel *Frankenstein*. Passage B is adapted from *Frankenstein* itself.

Passage A by Mary Shelley

The Publishers of the Standard Novels, in selecting "Frankenstein" for one of their series, expressed a wish that I should furnish them with some account of the origin of the story. I shall thus
(5) give a general answer to the question so frequently asked me—How I, then a young girl, came to think of and to dilate upon so very hideous an idea?

It is not singular that, as the daughter of two persons of literary celebrity, I should very early in
(10) life have thought of writing. As a child I scribbled, and my favourite pastime was to "write stories." Still I had a dearer pleasure than this, which was the formation of castles in the air—the indulging in waking dreams, which had for their subject the
(15) formation of a succession of imaginary incidents. My dreams were at once more fantastic and agreeable than my writings. In the latter I was a close imitator—rather doing as others had done than putting down the suggestions of my own mind.

(20) What I wrote was intended for other eyes, but my dreams were all my own.

I did not make myself the heroine of my tales. Life appeared to me too commonplace as regarded myself. I could not figure that romantic
(25) woes or wonderful events would ever be my lot, but I was not confined to my own identity, and I could people the hours with creations far more interesting to me than my own sensations.

After this my life became busier, and reality
(30) stood in place of fiction. My husband was very anxious that I should prove myself worthy of my parentage and enroll myself on the page of fame. He was forever inciting me to obtain literary reputation, which even on my own part I cared
(35) for then, though since I have become infinitely indifferent to it.

I thought and pondered—vainly. I felt that blank incapability of invention which is the greatest misery of authorship. *Have you thought*
(40) *of a story?* I was asked each morning, and each morning I was forced to reply with a mortifying negative.

When I placed my head on my pillow, I did not sleep, nor could I be said to think. My imagina-
(45) tion, unbidden, possessed and guided me. I saw the pale student of unhallowed arts kneeling beside the thing he had put together. I saw the hideous phantasm of a man stretched out, and then, on the working of some powerful engine,
(50) show signs of life, and stir with an uneasy motion. His success would terrify the artist; he would rush away from his odious handiwork, horror-stricken. He would hope that, left to itself, the slight spark of life which he had communicated
(55) would fade. He sleeps; but he is awakened; the horrid thing stands at his bedside, opening his curtains, and looking on him with yellow, watery, but speculative eyes.

I opened mine in terror. Swift as light and as
(60) cheering was the idea that broke in upon me. "I have found it! What terrified me will terrify others; and I need only describe the spectre which had haunted my midnight pillow." On the morrow I announced that I had *thought of a story*.

(65)   And now, once again, I bid my hideous progeny go forth and prosper. I have an affection for
it, for it was the offspring of happy days, when
death and grief were but words, which found
no true echo in my heart.

Passage B by Mary Shelley

(70)   It was on a dreary night of November that I
beheld the accomplishment of my toils. With
an anxiety that almost amounted to agony, I
collected the instruments of life around me,
that I might infuse a spark of being into the life-
(75) less thing that lay at my feet. The rain pattered
dismally against the panes, and my candle was
nearly burnt out, when, by the glimmer of the
half-extinguished light, I saw the dull yellow
eye of the creature open; it breathed hard, and
(80) a convulsive motion agitated its limbs.

    How can I describe my emotions at this ca-
tastrophe, or how delineate the wretch whom
with such infinite pains and care I had endeav-
oured to form? His limbs were in proportion,
(85) and I had selected his features as beautiful.
Beautiful! Great God! His yellow skin scarcely
covered the work of muscles and arteries
beneath; his hair was of a lustrous black, and
flowing; his teeth of a pearly whiteness; but
(90) these luxuriances only formed a more horrid
contrast with his watery eyes, that seemed
almost of the same colour as the dun-white
sockets in which they were set, his shrivelled
complexion and straight black lips.

(95)   I had worked hard for nearly two years, for
the sole purpose of infusing life into an inani-
mate body. I had desired it with an ardour that
far exceeded moderation; but now that I had
finished, the beauty of the dream vanished, and
(100) breathless horror and disgust filled my heart.
Unable to endure the aspect of the being I had
created, I rushed out of the room and continued
a long time traversing my bed-chamber, unable
to compose my mind. I slept, but I was disturbed
(105) by the wildest dreams. I thought I saw Elizabeth,

in the bloom of health, walking in the streets of
Ingolstadt. Delighted and surprised, I embraced
her, but as I imprinted the first kiss on her lips,
her features appeared to change, and I thought
(110) that I held the corpse of my dead mother in my
arms. I started from my sleep with horror when,
by the dim and yellow light of the moon, as it
forced its way through the window shutters,
I beheld the wretch—the miserable monster
(115) whom I had created.

Questions 21–25 ask about Passage A.

21. When Shelley writes "once again, I bid my
hideous progeny go forth and prosper" (lines
65–66), she most nearly means that:
    A. she is launching the new edition of her
       most famous novel into the world, as she
       did with the first.
    B. she is prone to daydreaming about earlier
       times in her life when she was happier.
    C. she feels confident that the new edition
       will make more money than the first did,
       regardless of what the critics say.
    D. she is reluctant to publish the story but
       has no choice.

22. Passage A indicates that Shelley came to
consider her earliest attempts at writing
to be:
    F. cynical attempts at widespread
       popularity.
    G. unwilling to confront death and grief.
    H. too unrealistic to be critically respected.
    J. inorganic and insufficiently personal.

23. Shelley's claim that "since I have become infinitely indifferent to it" (lines 35–36) is meant to suggest that, over the course of the previous decade, she has:

  A. learned to write well without being emotionally affected by her subject matter.

  B. become more interested in writing nonfiction than unrealistic fiction.

  C. come to care far less about getting famous for her writing.

  D. developed a method of expertly disguising her own literary voice.

24. In the sixth and seventh paragraphs of Passage A (lines 43–64), Shelley explains the genesis of her realization that:

  F. her own psyche could in fact be the wellspring of effective literature.

  G. a tale of horror would be the last sort of book anyone expected from her.

  H. her novel would sell better if she wrote from the point of view of a male protagonist.

  J. she had already thought of the perfect story many years ago, when she was a child.

25. In Passage A, Shelley implies that, in the years since she wrote the first edition of *Frankenstein*:

  A. she has been surprised by how dramatically the public's taste in novels has changed.

  B. she has experienced profound personal tragedy in her own real life for the first time.

  C. she has been somewhat annoyed by how frequently the book's message is misinterpreted.

  D. her relationship with her parents has become less stressful and more one of mutual respect.

Questions 26–27 ask about Passage B.

26. In the second paragraph of Passage B (lines 81–94), the narrator describes his creation in a manner that:

  F. emphasizes the exhaustive degree of biological knowledge and long process of trial-and-error that went into creating him.

  G. apologizes for the creature's bizarre appearance by attempting to explain it logically and dispassionately.

  H. ironically juxtaposes the glory of the scientific knowledge involved in his creation with the grotesque form of the creature itself.

  J. emphasizes the personal jealousy he feels regarding the creature's prodigious physical strength.

27. Within Passage B, the narrator's dream in lines 105–115 functions symbolically to represent the idea that:

  A. true love gradually becomes impossible for anyone who knows too much about science.

  B. though the narrator has literally created life, he has metaphorically created death.

  C. death is a natural and inevitable part of life that should be embraced rather than feared.

  D. family is ultimately more important than either work or wisdom.

Questions 28–30 ask about both passages.

28. Both Passage A and Passage B highlight Shelley's taste for presenting:

  F. contrasting points of view via the device of frame narrative.

  G. necessary information in a roundabout fashion, in order to build suspense.

  H. the concepts of both death and genius as mere illusions.

  J. the depths of the human imagination as the source of true horror.

29. Based on Shelley's description in Passage A of her writing process, which of the following methods is likely to depict a way in which she might have gone about composing Passage B?

- **A.** Trying to analyze and then imitate other novels that have been widely regarded as terrifying
- **B.** Allowing herself to feel frightened and then writing in a way that puts the reader in her position
- **C.** Doing research into the biological mechanisms that cause fear and logically discerning how best to activate them
- **D.** Jotting down unstructured notes while half-asleep and then examining them in the morning

30. Elsewhere in the essay from which Passage A is adapted, Shelley writes:

> Invention, it must be humbly admitted, does not consist in creating out of void, but out of chaos; the materials must, in the first place, be afforded: it can give form to dark, shapeless substances, but cannot bring into being the substance itself. Invention consists in the capacity of seizing on the capabilities of the subject, and in the power of moulding and fashioning ideas suggested to it.

How do these statements apply to both Shelley's approach to storytelling as depicted in Passage A and the narration of her character Victor Frankenstein provided in Passage B?

- **F.** They suggest that Shelley considered the origins of both art and life itself to be mysterious, and the role of any "creator" to be that of a conduit for an external force.
- **G.** They amount to a cynical admission that every artistic idea is ultimately a copy of another, and that every supposedly "original" idea is actually "monstrous."
- **H.** They describe Shelley's conviction that the concept of "inspiration" is actually a lie, and that all true beauty is the result of a process that is messy and ugly.
- **J.** They suggest Shelley's viewpoint that all artistic creation is actually an act of destruction because we can only find words for what is already dead in our hearts.

PASSAGE IV—NATURAL SCIENCE

This passage is adapted from "Magnetic Attraction" by Robert L. Park, Prof. emeritus of Physics, U. of Maryland.

In the early 16th century, the power of lodestone (magnetite) to attract iron filings without touching them suggested great power. Paracelsus, the famous Swiss alchemist and physician, (5) began using powdered lodestone in salves to promote healing. William Gilbert, however, physician to Queen Elizabeth I and father of the scientific study of magnetism, pointed out that the process of grinding the lodestone into (10) powder destroyed the magnetism. Nevertheless, a century later, magnetic cures were introduced into England by Robert Fludd as a remedy for all disease. The patient was placed in the "boreal position" with the head north and the feet south (15) during the treatment.

By far the most famous of the magnetizers was Franz Mesmer (1734–1815), who carried the technique from Vienna to Paris in 1778 and soon became the rage of Parisian society.

(20) Dressed in colorful robes, he would seat patients in a circle around a vat of "magnetized water." While Mesmer waved magnetic wands over them, the patients held iron rods protruding from the vat. He would later discover that the (25) cure was just as effective if he left the magnets out and merely waved his hand. He called this "animal magnetism."

Benjamin Franklin, in Paris on a diplomatic assignment, suspected that Mesmer's patients did (30) indeed benefit from the strange ritual because it kept them away from the bloodletting and purges of other Paris physicians. Those physicians bitterly resented Mesmer, an outsider who was attracting their most affluent patients. At (35) the urging of the medical establishment, King Louis XVI appointed a royal commission to investigate his claims. This remarkable group included Franklin, then the world's greatest authority on electricity; Antoine Lavoisier, the (40) founder of modern chemistry; and Joseph Guillotine, the physician whose famous invention would one day be used to sever the head of his friend Lavoisier.

The commissioners designed a series of inge-(45) nious tests in which some subjects were deceived into thinking they were receiving Mesmer's treatment when they were not, and others received the treatment but were led to believe they had not. The results established beyond any doubt (50) that the effects were due solely to the power of suggestion. Their report, never surpassed for clarity or reason, destroyed Mesmer's reputation in France, and he returned to Vienna.

Nevertheless, magnetic therapy eventually (55) crossed the Atlantic. Its most famous practitioner in the United States was Daniel Palmer, who in 1890 opened Palmer's School of Magnetic Cure in Davenport, Iowa. Like Mesmer, Palmer soon discovered that his patients recovered just as (60) quickly if he omitted the magnets and merely "laid on hands." Thus was founded "chiropractic

therapy," and the school became Palmer's College of Chiropractic.

In recent years, an enormous amount of re-(65) search has been done on the effect of magnetic fields on the human body, driven not by magnetic therapy, but by safety considerations associated with the phenomenal growth in the use of magnetic resonance imaging (MRI) for medical (70) diagnoses and research. MRI subjects the whole body to a magnetic field about a hundred times stronger than the localized field of even the most powerful therapy magnet. Happily, no ill-effects have been found from exposure to MRI fields. (75) Indeed, there are almost no effects at all—just a few reports of faint sensory responses, such as a slight metallic taste and visual sensations of flashing lights if patients move their eyes too rapidly. The fact is that the stuff we're made of (80) just isn't very magnetic.

That's why scientists were surprised two years ago when Dr. Carlos Vallbona at the Baylor College of Medicine in Houston reported results of a double-blind trial of magnets in the treatment (85) of 50 patients suffering post-polio pain. Some of the patients were treated with commercial therapy magnets; others were treated with sham magnets. Seventy-six percent of those treated with real magnets reported a decrease in pain, (90) while only 19 percent receiving the placebo felt an improvement. The most frequent claim, which Vallbona supports, is that magnets promote the flow of blood to the treated area.

It's easy to check. An excess of blood shows (95) up as a flushing or reddening of the skin. That's why the skin turns red when you apply heat; blood is being diverted to the heated area to serve as a coolant. But you will discover that placing a magnet of any strength against your (100) skin produces no reddening at all. There is no indication that Vallbona tried this.

The argument is that blood, because it contains iron, should be attracted by the magnets. The iron in hemoglobin, however, is not ferromagnetic.

(105) The hemoglobin molecule itself is very weakly paramagnetic, but the fluid that carries the red cells, consisting mostly of water, is diamagnetic—it is weakly repelled. Indeed, small animals have even been levitated in powerful magnetic fields.

(110)   As medical scams go, magnet therapy may not seem like a big deal. Magnets generally cost less than a visit to the doctor and they certainly do no harm. But magnet therapy can be danger-ous if it leads people to forego needed medical

(115) treatment. Worse, it tends to reinforce a sort of upside-down view of how the world works, leaving people vulnerable to predatory quacks if they become seriously ill. It's like trying to find your way around San Francisco with a map of

(120) New York. That could be dangerous for someone who is really sick—or really lost.

31. One of the main ideas established by the passage is that:

A. Benjamin Franklin helped to start a feud between Franz Mesmer and other physicians.

B. English scientists did more than Swiss ones to develop the science of magnetic therapy.

C. if it hadn't been for Franz Mesmer, we wouldn't have MRI technology now.

D. the alleged benefits of magnetic therapy are dubious at best.

32. Which of the following did the most to turn public opinion against Mesmer's theories?

F. The execution of Lavoisier

G. Benjamin Franklin's writings on electricity

H. The findings of the royal commission

J. The urging of King Louis XVI

33. The main purpose of the fifth paragraph (lines 54–63) is to establish that:

A. poorly supported medical theories became popular in the United States despite the lack of evidence.

B. Mesmer's theories were in fact not sufficiently disproved after all.

C. The bodies of some people are more magnetic than those of others.

D. Daniel Palmer ended up being a more important scientist than Franz Mesmer.

34. The passage states that, on the whole, human blood is actually:

F. ferromagnetic.

G. repelled by magnetic fields.

H. predominantly composed of iron.

J. capable of levitating small animals.

35. The passage notes that the MRI:

A. was invented in 1890.

B. is used primarily to treat post-polio pain.

C. promotes the flow of blood.

D. is about 100 times stronger than a therapy magnet.

36. As it is used in line 90, the word *placebo* most nearly means:

F. phony treatment.

G. powerful magnet.

H. traditional cure.

J. psychological boost.

37. As it is used in line 117, the word *quacks* most nearly means:

A. theories.

B. treatments.

C. dishonest therapists.

D. animal-borne diseases.

38. The passage indicates that skin turns red when exposed to heat because:

    F. heat is absorbed and stored in the skin.

    G. one function of blood is cooling hot skin.

    H. hemoglobin is very weakly magnetic.

    J. humans are not very magnetic.

39. The passage most strongly emphasizes that the process of bloodletting was:

    A. an important step in the development of magnet therapy.

    B. still popular in France long after it had ceased to be popular in America.

    C. harmful enough to make magnet therapy appear beneficial.

    D. indirectly involved with the discovery of hemoglobin.

40. According to the passage, the only legitimate experiment that involved magnet therapy was conducted by:

    F. Benjamin Franklin.

    G. Daniel Palmer.

    H. William Gilbert.

    J. Carlos Vallbona.

STOP

If there is still time remaining, you may review your answers.

SCIENCE TEST

Time: 35 Minutes—40 Questions

> **Directions:** There are six passages in this test. Each passage is followed by several questions. After reading a passage, choose the best answer to each question and fill in the corresponding oval on your answer sheet. You may refer to the passages as often as necessary.
>
> You are NOT permitted to use a calculator on this test.

PASSAGE I

Tornado intensity is commonly estimated by analyzing damage to structures and then correlating it with the wind speed required to produce such destruction. This method is essential to assigning tornadoes specific values on the *Fujita Scale* (F scale) of tornado intensity (see Figure 1).

Damage f scale		Little Damage	Minor Damage	Roof Gone	Walls Collapse	Blown Down	Blown Away	
		f 0	f 1	f 2	f 3	f 4	f 5	
Windspeed F scale		17 m/s 32 F 0 50 F 1 70 F 2 92 F 3 116 F 4 142 F 5 40 mph 73 113 158 207 261 319						
To convert f scale into F scale, add the appropriate number								
Weak Outbuilding	−3	f 3	f 4	f 5	f 5	f 5	f 5	
Strong Outbuilding	−2	f 2	f 3	f 4	f 5	f 5	f 5	
Weak Framehouse	−1	f 1	f 2	f 3	f 4	f 5	f 5	
Strong Framehouse	0	F 0	F 1	F 2	F 3	F 4	F 5	
Brick Structure	+1	−	f 0	f 1	f 2	f 3	f 4	
Concrete Structure	+2	−	−	f 0	f 1	f 2	f 3	

Figure 1

A tornado is formed when the following occurs: (1) warm, moist air rises into cool, dry air; (2) when the barrier is breached, a bulge of warm, moist air expands and condenses to form a cloud; (3) as air moves upward, the resulting instability creates a spiral of air called a *mesocyclone*; (4) cold air moves downward and rain falls as the cloud becomes a *supercell*; (5) cool, moist air from rain cycles back into a cloud, forming a spinning wall-cloud; and (6) horizontal spiraling wind "tubes" are pushed upward by warm, moist air, forming a tornado. (See Figure 2.)

Figure 2

The United States has the most tornadoes of any country, and most of these tornadoes form in an area of the central United States known as "Tornado Alley." Figure 3 displays a geographical (state-by-state) breakdown of the occurrence of tornadoes in the United States in 2005.

Figure 3

PRACTICE TEST 3

1. In Figure 2, the tornado is labeled with which number?
   A. 1
   B. 3
   C. 5
   D. 6

2. A tornado with an intensity of F4 on the Fujita Scale could have winds of which of the following speeds?
   F. 70 mph
   G. 155 mph
   H. 190 mph
   J. 210 mph

3. Which of the following does NOT precede the formation of a mesocyclone?
   A. Warm air flowing upward
   B. Cool air forming a spinning wall-cloud
   C. Cloud formation
   D. Moist air condensing

4. Based on the data provided in Figure 3, which of the following states can be inferred to be part of "Tornado Alley?"
   F. Texas
   G. Florida
   H. Michigan
   J. Washington

5. If the wind speed of a tornado was unknown, but it was observed that several brick buildings in the area sustained minor damage, what value would the tornado be assigned on the F scale?
   A. F0
   B. F1
   C. F2
   D. F3

6. In the aftermath of a small-town tornado, the most severe damage observed included collapsed walls on brick buildings, and missing roofs from strong frame houses. According to the intensity scale, what is the strongest possible tornado that could have hit the town?
   F. F1
   G. F2
   H. F3
   J. F0

PASSAGE II

Acid deposition delivers acids and acidifying compounds to the Earth's surface. Once on the surface, they move through soil, vegetation, and surface waters and, in turn, set off a cascade of adverse ecological effects. Acid deposition occurs in three forms: wet deposition, which falls as rain, snow, sleet, and hail; dry deposition, which includes particles, gases, and vapor; and cloud or fog deposition, which occurs at high altitudes and in coastal areas. Acid deposition is comprised of sulfuric acid, nitric acid, and ammonium derived from sulfur dioxide (SO_2), nitrogen oxides (NO_x), and ammonia (NH_3). Sulfuric and nitric acid lower the pH of rain, snow, soil, lakes, and streams.

Table 1

Study 1

A specially designed collection bucket was used to gather rain samples. The collector opened automatically during wet weather, allowing the precipitation to fall into the collection bucket, and then closed as soon as the precipitation stopped. The sample was then taken to a laboratory, where it was weighed and its acidity was measured. Finally, the concentrations of important inorganic chemicals found in the precipitation were analyzed. The results are shown in Table 2.

Table 2

Sample	pH	Cl (mg/L)	Mg (mg/L)	Na (mg/L)	NH_3 (mg/L)
1	5.41	0.02	0.002	0.010	0.01
2	5.28	0.09	0.009	0.029	0.05
3	5.43	0.15	0.008	0.084	0.03
4	5.16	0.08	0.006	0.038	0.01
5	5.45	0.00	0.002	0.003	0.00

Study 2

Another study was done to compare the average pH of precipitation across various months. The same procedure was used as in Study 1, and the results are shown in Table 3.

Table 3

Month	Average pH	Precipitation (cm)
Jan	4.58	8.45
Feb	4.77	8.20
Mar	4.90	7.01
Apr	5.16	17.12
May	4.81	11.48
Jun	4.68	51.67
Jul	4.79	9.24
Aug	4.18	23.52
Sep	4.92	42.26
Oct	4.34	9.74
Nov	4.89	11.76
Dec	4.91	4.67

7. It is known that precipitation with a higher concentration of chlorine (Cl) does more damage to bodies of water than precipitation with a lower concentration of Cl. Based on this information, which sample tested in Study 1 would cause the most harm to rivers?
   A. Sample 1
   B. Sample 2
   C. Sample 3
   D. Sample 4

8. Based on the results of Study 2, it can be concluded that the deposition is least acidic during which season?
   F. Spring
   G. Summer
   H. Fall
   J. Winter

9. Based on the results of Study 1, which of the following can be concluded about the relationship between sodium (Na) concentration and the acidity of deposition?
   A. The lower the concentration of Na, the more basic the precipitation.
   B. The higher the concentration of Na, the more basic the precipitation.
   C. The higher the concentration of Na, the more acidic the precipitation.
   D. There is no correlation between the concentration of Na and acidity of the precipitation.

10. During which of the following months should there be the *least* concern for the health of frogs?
    F. January
    G. April
    H. August
    J. September

11. The precipitation collected in Study 1 is an example of which type of acid deposition?
    A. Wet deposition
    B. Dry deposition
    C. Cloud deposition
    D. Fog deposition

12. If the collection bucket used in Study 1 had been rinsed with sulfuric acid before collecting sample number 2, the resulting pH measurement would have been:
    F. impossible to determine.
    G. exactly 5.28.
    H. lower than 5.28.
    J. higher than 5.28.

13. Scientists in a southern area of the country discovered a "dead zone" in a nearby river that caused fish to die and float to the top of the water. However, snails, frogs, and crawfish seemed unaffected. According to the information in the tables, what could be the best explanation for this "dead zone"?
    A. The pH fell below a reading of 4 and was too acidic for the fish to survive.
    B. The pH rose above 5 and was too basic for the fish to survive.
    C. The pH fell below a reading of 6 and was too acidic for the fish to survive.
    D. The pH rose above 8 and was too basic for the fish to survive.

PASSAGE III

Blood type is a hereditary trait. The type is established by the genes inherited from the mother and father. The ABO system is widely accepted as the best blood classification system. In the ABO system, there are four types of blood: A, B, AB, and O. The combination of inherited genes is known as the *genotype* and the actual blood type is known as the *phenotype*. The genes ensure that only the blood cells of the proper blood type remain in the body.

Table 1

		Father's Blood Type			
		A	B	AB	O
Mother's Blood Type	A	A or O	A, B, AB, or O	A, B, or AB	A or O
	B	A, B, AB, or O	B or O	A, B, or AB	B or O
	AB	A, B, or AB	A, B, or AB	A, B, or AB	A, B, or AB
	O	A or O	B or O	A or B	O

The Rh (+/−) factor is inherited separately from the blood type. It is possible to have the Rh+ phenotype yet still carry the recessive gene for Rh−. The Rh+ (R) is the dominant gene and Rh− (r) is recessive. Table 2 shows the Rh phenotypes resulting from the various genotypes inherited from parents.

Table 2

Genotype	Phenotype
R R	Rh+
R r	Rh+
r r	Rh−

The surface of every red blood cell is covered with proteins. Rh factor and blood type determine the proteins and the compatibility of donated blood as shown in Table 3.

Table 3

Type	Can Donate Blood To	Can Receive Blood From
A+	A+ AB+	A+ A− O+ O−
O+	O+ A+ B+ AB+	O+ O−
B+	B+ AB+	B+ B− O+ O−
AB+	AB+	Everyone
A−	A+ A− AB+ AB−	A− O−
O−	Everyone	O−
B−	B+ B− AB+ AB−	B− O−
AB−	AB+ AB−	AB− B− O−

14. According to Table 1, parents with blood types O and B can only produce offspring with which blood types?
    F. B or O
    G. A or B
    H. A or O
    J. A

15. Parents with which blood types could produce offspring with AB+ blood?
    A. O+ and A–
    B. A– and B+
    C. AB– and AB–
    D. B+ and B+

16. A person who can donate blood to anyone could have parents with which of the following blood types?
    F. A+ and AB–
    G. AB– and AB–
    H. B– and B–
    J. AB+ and AB+

17. List all of the blood types possible for the offspring of parents of blood types A+ and O+.
    A. A+ or O+
    B. A+, A–, O–, or O+
    C. O– or O+
    D. AB+, A–, or O–

18. The genes that determine blood type are also responsible for:
    F. Rh factor.
    G. controlling the types of cells in the blood.
    H. controlling blood volume.
    J. creating proteins on white blood cells.

19. If a child suffered an injury that required a blood transfusion and was blood type AB+, what blood type(s) could the doctors safely give the child when treating his injury?
    A. Only AB+
    B. Only O–
    C. A+ or B+
    D. Any blood type

PASSAGE IV

In a study of the effects of Ritalin and Adderall on children with ADHD, subjects were given one of four possible doses of medication. Their behavior in social and academic settings was then monitored and rated. The four possible doses were placebo (P), Ritalin given once in the morning (R1), Ritalin given twice daily (R2), or Adderall given once in the morning (A1).

The results for each group were averaged. Figure 1 shows the average behavioral rating (on a scale of 0–15, with 0 meaning no undesirable behavior) at various time periods throughout the day. Figure 2 shows the percentage of children who demonstrated side effects at a moderate or severe level on at least one day.

Figure 1

Figure 2

20. Based on Figure 1, during which of the following time periods was the average behavior rating most similar for the four groups of children?

F. 8:15–9:25
G. 9:25–10:35
H. 10:35–11:45
J. 3:35–4:45

21. A scientist claimed that children given one dose of Adderall daily would exhibit fewer behavior problems than children given either one or two doses of Ritalin daily. During which of the following time periods shown in Figure 1 are the results *inconsistent* with this claim?

A. 9:25–10:35
B. 10:35–11:45
C. 2:35–3:35
D. 3:35–4:45

22. According to Figure 2, for the group given Ritalin twice daily, the percentage of children who experienced an adverse side effect was greatest for which side effect?

F. Dull
G. Headache
H. Withdrawn
J. Appetite loss

23. According to Figure 1, which dose of medication was the least successful in controlling children's behavior problems from 3:35 to 4:45?

A. P
B. R1
C. R2
D. A1

24. Suppose four groups of children were given one of the four possible medication regimens. Between 12:15 and 1:25, one group had a behavior rating of 5. Which medication regimen was most likely given to them?

F. P
G. R1
H. R2
J. A1

25. Assume that an ideal medication is one that has the fewest side effects, yet is most effective. Based on the data provided, which dose of medication is the most ideal?

A. P
B. R1
C. R2
D. A1

26. If a parent was concerned about his son losing weight while taking ADHD medication, which of the following medications would have the least effect on appetite while still keeping a behavior rating below 4 after the first two hours of taking the recommended dosage?

F. P
G. R1
H. R2
J. A1

PASSAGE V

A solution consists of a solute dissolved in a solvent. For example, in a saltwater solution, the salt is the solute and the water is the solvent. Osmosis is the movement of solvent molecules across a barrier in order to equalize solution concentrations. When a saltwater solution is placed in a u-shaped tube with a selectively permeable barrier or semipermeable membrane, the phenomenon of osmotic pressure can be observed. Osmotic pressure is the pressure required to prevent the flow of a solvent across a barrier. In Figure 1, saltwater was poured in the right half of the tube and pure water was poured in the left half of the tube. As water passes from left to right in the figure below due to osmosis, the level of solution on the right rises. Eventually, the weight of the solution due to gravity becomes sufficient to prevent the further flow of water from right to left.

Figure 1

The following experiments were carried out to study how varying the molecular weight percentage of solvents and the temperature of solutions affects osmotic pressure. Table 1 shows the molecular weight percentages of the different solvents studied and Table 2 displays the temperatures of the various solutions used.

Table 1

Solution	Solution Concentration (% weight of solute)
1	5
2	10
3	15
4	20

Table 2

Trial	Temperature (°C)
1	20
2	30
3	40
4	50

Experiment 1

A 1000 ml u-shaped tube was fitted with a semipermeable membrane and 300 ml of solution was added on the right half and 300 ml of water was added on the left half. Table 1 shows the four solutions used in four separate trials of Experiment 1. The percent weight was measured by computing the ratio of the weight of the solute (salt) to the weight of the solution after dissolution. Every 5 seconds, the height of the solution on the right side of the tube was measured and recorded. Figure 2 shows the results of Experiment 1 recorded at 20°C.

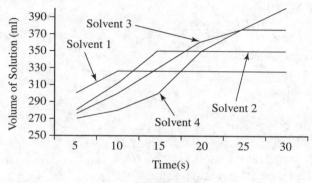

Figure 2

Experiment 2

Four more trials were performed but only the 10% solution was used. For each trial, the temperature was varied as shown in Table 2 and the results were graphed in Figure 3. In each trial, the height was measured 5 minutes after the water and solution were poured.

Figure 3

27. Based on Figure 2 and Table 2, which solution resulted in the greatest osmotic pressure after 30 seconds?
   A. Solution 1
   B. Solution 2
   C. Solution 3
   D. Solution 4

28. Based on the results of Experiment 2, what is the relationship between osmotic pressure and temperature?
   F. Osmotic pressure increases with an increase in temperature.
   G. Temperature and osmotic pressure are unrelated.
   H. Osmotic pressure decreases with an increase in temperature.
   J. Five minutes was insufficient time to allow the effects of osmotic pressure to be observed.

29. Based on Experiment 1, how does solution concentration affect osmotic pressure?
   A. Osmotic pressure increases with concentration.
   B. Osmotic pressure decreases with concentration.
   C. There is no relationship between osmotic pressure and concentration.
   D. The results were inconclusive because all solution heights were still fluctuating after 30 seconds.

30. Was Experiment 1 successful in determining the *relative* osmotic pressure of the four solutions tested?
   F. Yes. There is a clear difference in osmotic pressure between the four solutions with Solution 1 having the greatest osmotic pressure.
   G. Yes. There is a clear difference in osmotic pressure between the four solutions with Solution 4 having the greatest osmotic pressure.
   H. No. All osmotic pressures were too similar to make any determination.
   J. No. All solution heights were still fluctuating after 30 seconds.

31. *Reverse osmosis* occurs when the solvent flows from a solution of *higher* concentration to a solution of *lower* concentration. In Experiments 1 and 2, reverse osmosis can be observed by pouring more solution in the right side of the tube. Assuming the pressure required for reverse osmosis occurs at twice the osmotic pressure, approximately what pressure would a 30° solution have to reach for reverse osmosis to occur?
   A. 0.7 atm
   B. 1.2 atm
   C. 2.8 atm
   D. 3.2 atm

32. Data in Figure 2 is consistent with which of the following trials?
   F. Trial 1 and Trial 3
   G. Trial 1 only
   H. Trial 2 only
   J. Trial 2, Trial 3, and Trial 4

33. If scientists continued Experiment 1 under the same conditions, what would be the expected volume of the solution for Solvent 1 after 40 seconds?
   A. 320 ml
   B. 350 ml
   C. 370 ml
   D. 400 ml

PASSAGE VI

Students studying mirrors and reflection were given the following information:

There is a definite relationship between image characteristics and the distance an object is placed with regard to a concave mirror (see Figure 1). If an object is located beyond the center of curvature (C), its reflected image will be inverted (upside down) and smaller than the object itself. If an object is located precisely at C, the image will also be located at C; it will appear inverted and true to the object's actual size. When the object is placed between C and the focal length (F), the image will be inverted and larger than the object. When the object is located precisely at F, no image is formed whatsoever. Lastly, if an object is placed between F and the mirror, its image will appear upright and larger than the object.

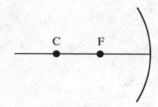

Figure 1

Given no further information, the students were asked to explain how the following magic trick is performed:

A famous Chinese magician conducts a classic magic trick utilizing a concave mirror with a focal length (F) of 1.6 m and a center of curvature (C) of 2.2 m. He is able to utilize the mirror in such a manner as to produce an image of a lightbulb at the same location and of the same size as the actual lightbulb itself.

Student 1

The lightbulb must have been placed exactly 1.6 m in front of the mirror, creating a perfect reflection. The image would thus be in the same location as the lightbulb, have the same dimensions as the lightbulb, and be an upright image.

Student 2

The lightbulb must have been placed exactly 2.2 m in front of the mirror. The image would then be in the same location and have the same dimensions as the actual lightbulb, although it would be inverted.

PRACTICE TEST 3

34. The students disagreed about which aspect of the lightbulb's image?
- **F.** Its size
- **G.** Its location
- **H.** Its orientation
- **J.** Its shape

35. The two explanations were similar to each other in that both explanations:
- **A.** assumed that the image was upright.
- **B.** assumed that the exact positioning of the lightbulb was important.
- **C.** correctly interpreted the information provided by the teacher.
- **D.** incorrectly interpreted the information provided by the teacher.

36. Placing the lightbulb in front of the mirror at which of the following distances would have resulted in an upright image?
- **F.** 1.0 m
- **G.** 1.6 m
- **H.** 2.2 m
- **J.** 2.6 m

37. Did Student 2 provide an adequate explanation of the magic trick?
- **A.** No. Student 2's explanation included an image that was upside down.
- **B.** No. If the lightbulb were placed at 2.2 m, it would not have produced an image.
- **C.** Yes. 2.2 m is the center of curvature. Placing an object at C results in an image of the same size in the same place.
- **D.** Yes. The magician specified that the image was inverted; Student 2 was the only student to account for this.

38. All of the following statements concerning concave mirror reflections are true EXCEPT:
- **F.** an object placed anywhere in front of C (closer to the mirror) will produce a reflected image that is larger than the actual object.
- **G.** an object placed anywhere in front of F (closer to the mirror) will produce an upright reflection.
- **H.** an object placed anywhere beyond F (farther from the mirror) will produce an inverted reflection.
- **J.** the only possible way to produce a reflected image equal in size to the actual object is to place the object precisely at C.

39. The teacher posed another question to the students. The students were told that the magician performed another trick in which he relocated the lightbulb so as to create the illusion that it had disappeared completely. How far in front of the mirror must the lightbulb have been placed in order to NOT produce a reflection?
- **A.** 1.3 m
- **B.** 1.6 m
- **C.** 2.0 m
- **D.** 2.2 m

40. Assume that Student 2's explanation is correct. If the magician wanted to create an image of the lightbulb that was smaller than the lightbulb itself, at which of the following distances in front of the mirror could he place the lightbulb?
- **F.** 1.6 m
- **G.** 2.0 m
- **H.** 2.2 m
- **J.** 2.5 m

If there is still time remaining, you may review your answers.

WRITING TEST

Time: 40 Minutes

Gender-Separate Education

More and more educators are supporting the notion that boys and girls should be taught separately through the end of high school. In addition to the "hormone-based" arguments that students in mixed-gender classrooms are distracted by "crushes" and/or worrying more about how they look than about learning, some psychologists believe that boys and girls have different learning styles. Additionally, many feminist scholars make the argument that girls learn better when they are not intimidated or drowned out by the typically louder and more aggressive boys. Still, many people find ideas based on the notion of "separate but equal" distasteful on general principle, since in practice it usually turns out to be the case that things that are separate sooner or later end up being unequal one way or another.

Read and carefully consider these perspectives. Each suggests a particular way of thinking about the debate on gender-separate education.

Perspective One	Perspective Two	Perspective Three
Schools should do whatever they can to ensure that students get the best educations possible. If reliable research indicates that both boys and girls learn better in single-gender classrooms, then that's all that matters.	When students grow up, the real world is never going to provide them with an ideal environment free of distractions. Teenagers will get distracted by anything, and if it isn't the opposite sex, then it will be something else. Boys and girls should get used to being around each other when they're young, rather than suddenly needing to learn to do so as adults.	The suggestion that all students will be distracted by the opposite sex marginalizes gay students, and the idea that boys learn one way and girls another ignores the reality of the students who are in the process of questioning their gender identity, adding more stress to an already stressful experience. For the students' own sake, and all of society's, we need to be making traditional notions about gender less rigid, rather than reinforcing them further.

ESSAY TASK

Write a unified, coherent essay concerning gender-separate education. In your essay, be sure to:

- clearly state your own perspective on the issue and analyze the relationship between your perspective and at least one other perspective
- develop and support your ideas with reasoning and examples
- organize your ideas clearly and logically
- communicate your ideas effectively in standard written English

Your perspective may be in full agreement with any of those given, in partial agreement, or completely different.

Planning Your Response

Your prewriting notes on this page will not be considered in your score.

Use the following space to brainstorm ideas and map out your response. You may want to think about the following as you analyze the given prompt:

Strengths and weaknesses of the three viewpoints

- What good points do they make, and what potential objections do they ignore?
- Why might they be convincing to readers, and why might their perspectives fall short?

Your previous experience, background knowledge, and personal values

- What is your viewpoint on this topic, and what are the pros and cons of this viewpoint?
- How will you craft an argument in support of your point of view?

STOP

If there is still time remaining, you may review your answers.

ANSWER KEY
Practice Test 3

English

1. D	16. G	31. B	46. J	61. D
2. F	17. B	32. J	47. D	62. H
3. C	18. F	33. D	48. F	63. D
4. J	19. A	34. H	49. B	64. F
5. B	20. J	35. A	50. G	65. B
6. H	21. C	36. G	51. A	66. H
7. D	22. J	37. D	52. H	67. B
8. J	23. C	38. G	53. C	68. J
9. A	24. G	39. C	54. J	69. A
10. H	25. A	40. H	55. C	70. G
11. B	26. H	41. A	56. F	71. D
12. F	27. D	42. H	57. B	72. H
13. A	28. F	43. A	58. F	73. B
14. H	29. B	44. H	59. D	74. F
15. C	30. G	45. A	60. H	75. A

Mathematics

1. E	13. C	25. C	37. B	49. A
2. G	14. F	26. F	38. K	50. F
3. D	15. C	27. E	39. A	51. C
4. H	16. K	28. H	40. G	52. G
5. A	17. E	29. C	41. D	53. E
6. J	18. K	30. K	42. K	54. K
7. D	19. D	31. B	43. C	55. B
8. G	20. G	32. F	44. K	56. G
9. B	21. D	33. A	45. E	57. B
10. G	22. G	34. G	46. F	58. H
11. E	23. A	35. B	47. E	59. B
12. H	24. G	36. F	48. H	60. F

ANSWER KEY
Practice Test 3

Reading

1.	A	9.	B	17.	D	25.	B
2.	H	10.	F	18.	H	26.	H
3.	B	11.	D	19.	B	27.	B
4.	J	12.	F	20.	F	28.	J
5.	C	13.	C	21.	A	29.	B
6.	H	14.	G	22.	J	30.	F
7.	D	15.	A	23.	C	31.	D
8.	F	16.	H	24.	F	32.	H

33.	A
34.	G
35.	D
36.	F
37.	C
38.	G
39.	C
40.	J

Science

1.	D	9.	D	17.	B	25.	C
2.	J	10.	G	18.	G	26.	H
3.	B	11.	A	19.	D	27.	D
4.	F	12.	H	20.	F	28.	H
5.	B	13.	A	21.	C	29.	A
6.	H	14.	F	22.	J	30.	G
7.	C	15.	B	23.	A	31.	C
8.	F	16.	H	24.	F	32.	G

33.	A
34.	H
35.	B
36.	F
37.	C
38.	F
39.	B
40.	J

HOW TO SCORE YOUR PRACTICE TEST

Step 1: Add up the number correct for each section and write that number in the blank under the Raw Score column on the Score Conversion Table. (Your goal is to get more questions correct on each subsequent practice test.)

Step 2: Using the Score Conversion Chart, find your scale score for each section and write it down. Then add up all four sections and divide by 4 to find your overall composite score. (Composite scores are rounded up at .5 or higher.)

SCORE CONVERSION TABLE

Section	Raw Score	Scaled Score
English	(out of 75)	_____ / 36
Math	(out of 60)	_____ / 36
Reading	(out of 40)	_____ / 36
Science	(out of 40)	_____ / 36
		Add and divide by 4
Overall Composite =		_____ / 36

SCORE CONVERSION CHART

Number Correct					
ACT Score*	English Section	Mathematics Section	Reading Section	Science Section	ACT Score*
36	75	60	40	40	36
35	74	59	39	39	35
34	73	58	38	38	34
33	72	57	37	—	33
32	71	56	36	37	32
31	70	54–55	35	36	31
30	69	53	34	35	30
29	67–68	51–52	33	34	29
28	65–66	49–50	32	33	28
27	64	46–48	31	31–32	27
26	62–63	44–45	30	30	26
25	60–61	41–43	29	28–29	25
24	58–59	39–40	27–28	25–27	24
23	55–57	37–38	25–26	24	23

(continued)

SCORE CONVERSION CHART (*Continued*)

ACT Score*	English Section	Mathematics Section	Reading Section	Science Section	ACT Score*
		Number Correct			
22	53–54	35–36	23–24	22–23	22
21	50–52	33–34	22	20–21	21
20	47–49	31–32	21	18–19	20
19	44–46	28–30	19–20	17	19
18	42–43	25–27	18	15–16	18
17	40–41	22–24	17	14	17
16	37–39	19–21	16	13	16
15	34–36	15–17	15	12	15
14	31–33	11–14	13–14	11	14
13	29–30	09–10	12	10	13
12	27–28	07–08	10–11	09	12
11	25–26	06	08–09	08	11
10	23–24	05	07	07	10
9	21–22	04	06	05–06	9
8	18–20	03	05	—	8
7	15–17	—	—	04	7
6	12–14	02	04	03	6
5	09–11	—	03	02	5
4	07–08	01	02	—	4
3	05–06	—	—	01	3
2	03–04	—	01	—	2
1	00–02	00	00	00	1

These scores are based on student trials rather than national norms.

SCORING YOUR ESSAY

As mentioned earlier in this text, two readers will evaluate your essay and each person will then assign it a score from 1 to 6. If, by chance, these two scorers disagree by more than 1 point, a third reader will step in and resolve the discrepancy. Performance on the essay will not affect your English, math, reading, science, or composite scores. You will receive two additional scores on your score sheet—a combined English/writing score (1–36) and a writing test subscore (1–12). Neither of these scores will affect your composite score!

The sample essay that follows reflects higher-level writing. It meets the criteria that ACT has put forth for essays that demonstrate effective writing skills.

- It takes a definite position.
- It addresses and expands on the counterargument.
- It has details that support the topic sentences and is well organized.
- It is not repetitive, and while there may be errors, they do not interfere with the competence of the essay.
- It is consistent and well balanced.
- The essay has a clear introduction and a conclusion that is not just a summary but ends with a significant thought.
- The vocabulary demonstrates good use of language and the sentence structure is varied.

ANSWER EXPLANATIONS

English

1. **(D)** In the phrase *both critics and fans have agreed*, two groups of people (*critics* and *fans*) are both doing the same thing—that is, both nouns are performing the same verb. Therefore, you don't need a comma before *and*. As for what they have agreed on, in the extended phrase *both critics and fans have agreed that no individual is due more credit than Chuck Berry*, there is also no need for a comma. The relative pronoun *that* introduces essential information (as opposed to *which*, which introduces nonessential or "extra" information). You do not need a comma in front of it (but you do in front of *which*).

2. **(F)** The phrase *singer, songwriter, and guitarist* refers to a single individual (Chuck Berry), and this is the noun phrase performing the verb in question. Choice F is the only one of the options with a singular verb (*was*). The other choices all have plural verbs. There is an added prepositional phrase trick: since *behind* is a preposition, *behind such rock classics as "Maybelline" and "Johnny B. Goode"* is a prepositional phrase that must be skipped over when determining agreement.

3. **(C)** The surrounding sentence informs us that there were multiple *inductees* into the Rock and Roll Hall of Fame in 1986, of whom Chuck Berry was one. Thus, we need the verb/preposition pairing *was among* (equivalent to "was one of" or "was part of").

4. **(J)** Since the sentence would be grammatically correct without the name *Johnnie Johnson*, the name is therefore set off with commas. The relative pronoun *who* is necessary after the comma because without it the subordinate clause would have no subject (just read the sentence without the name and you will see it sounds very wrong without *who*).

5. **(B)** The sentence is a question beginning with *Could*. You would not say *Could [blank] is?* but rather *Could [blank] be?* and so the choice with *be* is correct.

6. **(H)** *Unthinkable* means "nearly impossible to believe," and thus best emphasizes how shocking the allegations were. It is the most "extreme" of the four terms given as options.

7. **(D)** *Corroborate* means to support the validity of something. Therefore, the least acceptable choice is (D) dispute.

8. **(J)** The fact that Chuck Berry joined Johnson's band at the last minute when another member happened to get sick on the night Johnson's band was playing Berry's town was a very lucky coincidence from Berry's perspective, and emphasizes how easily his life could have gone a completely different way.

9. **(A)** The subordinating conjunction *although* is like a version of *but* that goes elsewhere in the sentence (you can see how the sentence would also work if you got rid of *although* but put a *but* after the comma). The ACT English often tries to trick you with *although* because it is a conjunction that can go at the beginning of the first of two independent clauses, instead of just at the beginning of the second. Here, it is the only one of the four choices that results in a complete correct sentence that means what you want it to mean.

10. **(H)** The noun performing the underlined verb is *hits*, and so the verb needs to be plural. *Were* is the only choice that is both plural and makes grammatical sense in context. This is a classic prepositional phrase trick: the prepositional phrase *after his 1963 release* needs to be skipped over when determining agreement.

11. **(B)** The sentence establishes that Springsteen's comment was made *years earlier*, and so *had remarked* is the only one of the choices that is grammatically correct and means what you want it to mean.

12. **(F)** Information establishing that Berry had been in trouble with the law several times and cheated other partners is absolutely relevant to a passage exploring the question of whether he also cheated Johnnie Johnson.

13. **(A)** The fact that Johnson was unaware that he was entitled to more money than he was paid for the recording sessions is information relevant to the question of why he didn't speak up at the time, which is exactly the question this paragraph is addressing.

14. **(H)** What the sentence means to say is that too much time had elapsed between the time that the songs were composed and the time of the lawsuit, and so the option beginning with *since* is the appropriate choice.

15. **(C)** The passage deals only with a specific set of allegations made against Chuck Berry, and not with any other celebrities, much less with celebrities in general. (The fact that the passage deals only with one example and not an entire category is a very common answer on ACT English final "Suppose the Author …" questions!)

16. **(G)** The first thing to notice is that this sentence has more than one underlined portion; you must always be aware when this is the case, because the answers to both questions will affect each other (though there will never be more than one correct combination of answers). Since the part of the sentence before the comma is an independent clause, the part after it must either be a dependent clause or an independent clause with a conjunction. Choice G, *endlessly*, creates a grammatically correct "afterthought clause," a dependent descriptive clause preceded by a comma.

17. **(B)** The string of verbs constitutes a list, and so you need an *and* before the last of them: *endlessly admired, analyzed, and parodied* (either a comma or no comma before the *and* that precedes the last item in a list is acceptable; the ACT English will **never** test you on this directly).

18. **(F)** This option results in two independent clauses separated by a comma + *and*, forming a correct sentence that means what you want it to mean.

19. **(A)** Replacing the underlined portion with *this was* would result in a comma splice, and so this is the choice that is NOT acceptable.

20. **(J)** Choice J informs us that Perrugia disguised himself as one of the workers and walked around the museum pretending to work, and so it is the only one of the choices that provides specific information about how Perrugia avoided detection in the museum for so long.

21. **(C)** All of the other prepositions or combinations of prepositions are appropriate in context (although some are less formal than others), but *from of* is utter nonsense, and so it is the option that is LEAST acceptable.

22. **(J)** Because the subsequent clause is an independent one, the first clause of the sentence needs to be a dependent one. *Finding* is the only option that results in a sentence that is not a comma splice and means what you want to say.

23. **(C)** Since the subsequent sentence explains why people took so long to notice that the *Mona Lisa* had been stolen, the best opening sentence is the one that introduces this idea, even if some of the others relate to the end of the previous paragraph. (With questions about introductory sentences on the ACT English, it is <u>always</u> best to read a few sentences ahead and pick the sentence that best introduces the ones after it, rather than basing your answer on the previous paragraph!)

24. **(G)** Although all of the options result in complete correct sentences, only *in private* explains why no one was alarmed by the *Mona Lisa*'s absence (they assumed it was being worked on by museum staff in another room).

25. **(A)** Since it is inconceivable that another artist could be unaware of the *Mona Lisa*'s fame and importance, *out of ignorance* makes no sense as an explanation for an artist's motivation for stealing it, and so it is the choice that is the LEAST acceptable. The other three choices are so similar that they are essentially different ways of saying the same thing. (It is <u>always</u> a good idea to look for "which of these things is not like the other" on NOT and LEAST questions!)

26. **(H)** The *masterwork was feared gone forever* is the only one of the choices that makes sense and says what you mean to say. If it sounds strange, this may be because it is a situation where *to be* may be omitted, which you might not be used to hearing. The sentence means that the masterwork was feared <u>to be</u> gone forever.

27. **(D)** Since the verb of this independent clause is *led*, what goes in the underlined part needs to be a noun phrase performing that verb. *Perrugia's motivation* is the only noun phrase that forms a concise, correct sentence.

28. **(F)** Although you may not be used to seeing the formal phrase *from whence*, you should still understand from context that the painting was stolen *from* Italy, and that the other choices make no sense.

29. **(B)** The phrase *his expectations were not entirely off-base* is a way of saying that the things he believed were partially accurate, which is a paraphrase of the phrase *Perrugia might not have been as crazy as he seems* from the question.

30. **(G)** The passage does in fact explain the background, execution, and aftermath of a famous crime and this is all the question asks for. The explanation in choice G, the second of the *Yes* options, simply restates the demands of the question.

31. **(B)** *Dubbed* is a transitive verb that means *called* or *named*. So, just as you would have to say *his enemies called him* or *his enemies named him*, you have to say *his enemies dubbed him*.

32. **(J)** Preposition usage in English is largely idiomatic. The phrase is *synonymous <u>with</u>* because that is simply what we say. It is one of those things that you just have to know from reading a lot. (Preposition-choice questions are becoming more common on the ACT English, so make sure to make an effort to start noticing such things!)

33. **(D)** Although all four choices are correct complete sentences, the other three choices are awkward and/or unnecessarily complex. *Modern historians agree* is the simplest and most succinct way to put it. (On style questions, always pick the simplest way of putting

something as long as it makes a correct sentence, unless the question is specifically asking for something more complex, such as "the most detailed description.")

34. **(H)** The sentence says that most people's ideas about Attila come from Roman writers, and that these writers were unfair to him. Choice H is basically a paraphrase or summary of this.

35. **(A)** *At the time of Attila's birth in 406* is a dependent introductory clause, and so is followed by a comma. Although the rest of the sentence is long, and contains other underlined portions that should be double-checked alongside this answer, this introductory phrase could not constitute an independent clause no matter what. (Remember, when you see that two of the other choices are a semicolon and a period, this means they cancel each other out and the right answer must be a comma!)

36. **(G)** How many *Asias* are we talking about? One. And does it possess anything? Yes (the *central seas*). How many *seas* are we talking about? More than one. And do they possess anything? No. And so we need the singular possessive *Asia's* and the plural nonpossessive *seas.* It is as simple as that.

37. **(D)** Deleting the underlined portion makes the rest of the sentence into a succinct and grammatically correct "afterthought clause" describing the aforementioned *nation*.

38. **(G)** Simply saying *class division* concisely communicates the same information, whereas the other three choices are wordy and redundant.

39. **(C)** The Vikings, how they dressed, and when they sailed to America are all irrelevant to Attila, and distract the reader from the main idea.

40. **(H)** What we need here is the past tense verb *coexisted* and the modifying adverb *peacefully*.

41. **(A)** *That* is a pronoun standing in for the idea of Rome's royal line, and so the phrase *to unite his royal line with that of Rome* is correct.

42. **(H)** *Formerly the common enemy of both the Huns and Rome* is an appositive clause containing extra information, and is here set off with dashes (setting it off with commas would also be correct, but is not an option). The sentence then picks up with *further insulting Attila*, which grammatically matches up with the part of the sentence before the appositive. (On the ACT English, dashes usually come in pairs, so when you see a dash earlier in the sentence, expect the underlined part to contain the second one!)

43. **(A)** The presence of *Although* turns the first clause into a dependent one, and so the remainder of the sentence needs to be an independent clause. And since the noun being replaced here is *tactics*, the pronoun and verb need to be plural.

44. **(H)** The question asks for *relevant and specific information*, and only choice H provides a concrete example supporting the idea of Attila's high esteem in contemporary Eastern Europe.

45. **(A)** Paragraph 1 begins by building suspense about the identity of its subject, who is still a mystery until the third sentence (which also explains who Attila is). All this indicates that Paragraph 1 is definitely supposed to come first. (If a paragraph had been in the wrong place the whole time, then something probably would have sounded "off" while

you were reading the passage; if nothing did, then the paragraphs were probably in the right order!)

46. **(J)** The subsequent clause begins with a conjunction, which means that this first clause needs to be an independent one. *It started* is the only one of the choices that accomplishes this.

47. **(D)** *First reared their ugly heads* does not make sense in context, whereas the other three choices all indicate the first time. Hence, choice D is the least acceptable.

48. **(F)** The question asks for a phrase that *emphasizes the human cost of the war* (in other words, something about how many people died). Only choice F, which explains that more people died in World War I than in any war in Western history, does this.

49. **(B)** There must be a comma between *Ypres* and *Belgium*, separating the name of the city from the name of the country. There must also be a comma after *Belgium*, since this is where the appositive phrase beginning with the word *near* ends. Since both German and English forces are performing the verb *had fought*, there should not be a comma between *German* and *and*.

50. **(G)** Merely inserting a comma between *line* and *underground* would create a comma splice, and so this is the choice that is NOT acceptable.

51. **(A)** The phrase *each other* is tricky when it comes to possession. There are two armies, but relative to each army there is only one other, and so we need the singular possessive *other's: each army could hear the sound of the other's digging*. (Because *digging* is a gerund, it takes a possessive.)

52. **(H)** Although every choice seems fine if you don't read ahead, the subsequent sentence makes reference to melodies being recognized and someone's singing being responded to. Therefore, what we need here is a sentence establishing that someone was singing, and only choice H accomplishes this. (Always read ahead a little before answering "What sentence/phrase should go here?" questions!)

53. **(C)** This results in a run-on sentence (with the second of two independent clauses beginning at the word *they*), whereas the other three choices all result in grammatically correct sentences. Hence, it is the one that is NOT acceptable.

54. **(J)** Though it refers to a group of people, the phrase *high command* itself is singular, and so takes the singular verb *was*. This is a classic prepositional phrase trick: the prepositional phrase *on both sides* must be skipped over. (Though more than one high command is involved, the phrase itself is still singular.)

55. **(C)** Logically, the word *again* would have to modify something that already took place at least once. Since the truce was the thing that already took place, *again* should follow *happen* (since the noun phrase *such things* refers to the truce and is performing the verb *happen*).

56. **(F)** What we need preceding *the generals* is a word meaning "since" or "because." Of the choices, only *as* accomplishes this.

57. **(B)** Although every choice would result in a grammatically correct sentence, only the introductory phrase *in addition* accurately describes the information that follows, whereas the other three choices do not make sense in context.

58. **(F)** If neither Nazi Germany nor the Soviet Union would have existed if it hadn't been for World War I, then this phrase explains how World War I indirectly led to both World War II and the Cold War, the major conflicts of the twentieth century.

59. **(D)** The word *understand* by itself is all that is necessary. The other choices are all either redundant or grammatically incorrect. (When three choices are several words long and the fourth choice is one word, the fourth choice is almost always correct, as long as it results in a complete sentence!)

60. **(H)** The passage does not discuss protests within the armed forces in general, but only one individual famous instance of this. (The fact that the passage only discusses one specific example, rather than a larger phenomenon in general, is a <u>very</u> common answer to "Suppose the Author …" questions on the ACT English!)

61. **(D)** The descriptive phrase *the son of* needs to extend in parallel ways to the phrases *a mother* and *a father*; both nouns need to function as objects of the preposition *of*. Only choice D accomplishes this.

62. **(H)** This incorrectly attempts to link two independent clauses with the relative pronoun *which* as though it were a conjunction. Hence, it is the choice that is NOT acceptable.

63. **(D)** Deleting the underlined portion makes the second half into a dependent descriptive clause that adds more information to the initial independent clause.

64. **(F)** The sentence (before the list that follows the colon) is two independent clauses separated by a comma and a conjunction. Only the introductory prepositional phrase *After graduation* preserves the first half of the sentence as an independent clause and refrains from adding any unnecessary elements.

65. **(B)** Preposition usage is largely idiomatic, and in certain situations more than one preposition (or phrase involving a preposition) could be correct. In this case, every choice would be acceptable besides *of*. Hence, choice B is the one that is NOT acceptable.

66. **(H)** The name of the store is not important, and so this is a minor detail that interrupts the flow of the paragraph.

67. **(B)** Reading the entire sentence reveals that the main verb is *became*, which is being performed by the noun *comics*, and that therefore everything between them should be a descriptive appositive phrase set off with commas.

68. **(J)** Either including or omitting the word *that* is acceptable, and either including or omitting the word *had* is acceptable (with varying degrees of formality). Inserting the word *because* in addition to *after admitting*, however, is grammatically incorrect, and so choice J is the option that is NOT acceptable.

69. **(A)** *Strip* is the subject of the sentence, and *came* is the main verb. The word *producer* should end the initial independent clause, followed by a comma and a dependent clause beginning with the relative pronoun *who*.

70. **(G)** Preposition usage in English is largely idiomatic. The phrase *the possibility of doing* is correct simply because it is what we say. There are some other phrases that could also be correct here, but none of the other three options are. It is one of those things that you

just have to know from reading a lot. (Preposition-choice questions are becoming more common on the ACT English, so make sure you start noticing such things!)

71. **(D)** Only this phrase both summarizes his concerns and explains his motivation for what he does next, thereby linking the two halves of the paragraph. Any of the other choices might well be true, but they are not sufficiently explanatory at this point in the passage.

72. **(H)** What we need here is a word or phrase meaning "give away" (in the sense of *reveal*, like with a secret). All the other choices mean "give away," but *mask* means "conceal," which is the opposite. Hence, it is the one that is LEAST acceptable.

73. **(B)** What is needed here is an independent clause subordinated to the relative pronoun *that*, and only *the cartoonist's name was Matt Groening* (uninterrupted by a comma) accomplishes this.

74. **(F)** The prepositional phrase *in which they star* adds important information to the noun *cartoon*, and does not need to be set off with any commas.

75. **(A)** The first clause is a dependent one beginning with *Although*, and so the part of the sentence after the comma needs to be an independent clause. (The conjunction *Although* is like a *but* that goes at the beginning of the first clause instead of the beginning of the second, and so the ACT English often tries to fool you using *although*!)

Mathematics

1. **(E)** If you add 5 to both sides, you get $3x = 12$.

2. **(G)** Complementary angles are two angles whose sum is 90°: $70° + 20° = 90°$; therefore, the complement of 70 is 20.

3. **(D)** You can set up an equation using the words of the problem to get $70 = 0.10(x)$. Solve for x by dividing both sides of the equation by 0.10 to get $x = 700$.

4. **(H)** You can find the three consecutive integers by either guessing and using your calculator, or you can set up an equation if that is what you prefer. Either way you will find the three consecutive integers whose sum is 99 are 32, 33, and 34. The greatest of these integers is 34.

5. **(A)** To find the area of a triangle, use the formula $A = \frac{1}{2}b \cdot h$. To find the height of this triangle, either use the Pythagorean Theorem, or realize this is a 9–12–15 right triangle, so the height must be 9. Now that we know the height, substitute into the area formula to get $A = \frac{1}{2}(12)(9) = 54$.

6. **(J)** $1,027 - (13 \times 40) = 507$ in overtime pay. $507 \div 19.50 = 26$ overtime hours. The hours for the week would be $40 + 26 = 66$.

7. **(D)** First subtract 3 from both sides to get $-4(x + 7) < 16$, then distribute to get $-4x - 28 < 16$. Now add 28 to both sides: $-4x < 44$. Finally, divide both sides by -4, but don't forget to switch the inequality symbol to get $x > -11$.

8. **(G)** You could solve this problem using your calculator to get a decimal approximation, then plug the answers into your calculator to get a similar decimal approximation.

For those who prefer to do it using algebra: $3\sqrt{300} - 5\sqrt{75} \rightarrow 3\sqrt{100 \cdot 3} - 5\sqrt{25 \cdot 3} \rightarrow$ $3 \cdot 10\sqrt{3} - 5 \cdot 5\sqrt{3} \rightarrow 30\sqrt{3} - 25\sqrt{3}$. Subtract to get $5\sqrt{3}$.

9. **(B)** $|-2 + 3^2| - |-2 - 3^2| = |7| - |-11| = 7 - 11 = -4$.

10. **(G)** The longest side of a triangle is always opposite the largest angle in the triangle. To find the missing angle C, use the fact that the sum of the three angles of a triangle is $180°$ to get $180 - 75 - 36 = 69°$. Since angle A is $75°$, it is the largest of the three angles and, therefore, the side opposite, BC, is the longest side.

11. **(E)** $3x^2 + x - 4$ can be factored to get $(x - 1)(3x + 4)$ making the factors $(x - 1)$ and $(3x + 4)$.

12. **(H)** Substituting $(-3, 5)$ into the equation $y = -x + 2$ gives $5 = -(-3) + 2 \rightarrow 5 = 5$. Since this is a true statement, the equation $y = -x + 2$ passes through the point.

13. **(C)** Substituting -2 for x into the equation gives $\dfrac{-(-2)^2 + 4}{-2}$. Simplifying using order of operations yields $\dfrac{-4 + 4}{-2} \rightarrow \dfrac{0}{-2} = 0$.

14. **(F)** Two lines are parallel if they have the same slope. The given equation is in slope-intercept form, $y = mx + b$, where m is the slope. In this equation, the slope is $-\dfrac{3}{4}$. The only answer that has the same slope is $y = -\dfrac{3}{4}x$.

15. **(C)** You can set up a proportion to find the number of goldfish: $\dfrac{2}{5} = \dfrac{x}{25}$. Cross multiply and solve for x to get $x = 10$, the number of goldfish. However, the question asks how many TOTAL fish, so add $10 + 25 = 35$ fish.

16. **(K)** The 3 lines could be parallel yielding no points of intersection, they could all intersect at the same point giving 1 point of intersection, or 2 lines could be parallel with the third crossing the other 2 giving 2 points of intersection, and finally the 3 lines could intersect to form a triangle making 3 points of intersection. See the diagram below.

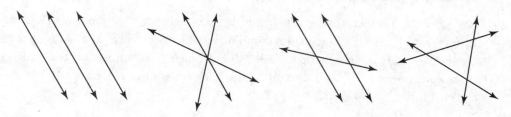

17. **(E)** Since $c = a - b$, and b is negative, its value actually gets added to a because subtracting a negative number is the same as adding a positive. When b is added to a the result will always be a positive number. Testing some numbers in the range of a and b will help lead you to the right answer.

18. **(K)** To find the slope between 2 points use the slope formula $\dfrac{y_2 - y_1}{x_2 - x_1}$ to get $\dfrac{8 - 5}{0 - (-2)}$. Simplify to get $\dfrac{3}{2}$. Always be careful and check your signs when using the slope formula; it is easy to make an integer error or a sign error.

19. **(D)** Setting up a proportion to solve for how much sugar they need gives $\dfrac{2\frac{1}{2}}{32} = \dfrac{x}{250}$. Cross multiply and solve for x to get $x \approx 19.5$, which rounds to 20.

20. **(G)** Recall that the $\sin(C) = \dfrac{\text{opposite}}{\text{hypotenuse}}$. To find the side opposite angle C, either use the Pythagorean Theorem, or memorize the special 8–15–17 right triangle. Calculating AB gives $8^2 + x^2 = 17^2 \to x = 15$. Now, using the above fact, $\sin(C) = \dfrac{15}{17}$.

21. **(D)** The average is $3,500 \div 4 = 875$.

22. **(G)** $\dfrac{2,500}{4,000}$ reduces to $\dfrac{5}{8}$.

23. **(A)** $\left(\dfrac{2,500}{30,000}\right) \times 360 = 30$.

24. **(G)** $\left(\dfrac{3,500 + 7,000 + 4,000 + 2,500}{30,000}\right) = 57\%$. This represents the known amounts. To find the portion for the Labor and Other categories take $100\% - 57\% = 43\%$.

25. **(C)** Using the rules of exponents we get $5^3 \cdot 5^{-7} = 5^{3 + (-7)} = 5^{-4}$. Recall that a negative exponent just means take the reciprocal of the base to get $5^{-4} = \dfrac{1}{5^4}$. Therefore, $x = 4$.

26. **(F)** WYX is a straight line making it 180°. Since $\angle WYZ = 28°$, the remaining angle ZYX must equal $180 - 28 = 152$. YM bisects angle ZYX, making each angle $\dfrac{152}{2} = 76°$.

27. **(E)** Recall that an angle that lies on a circle is exactly $\dfrac{1}{2}$ of its intercepted arc, making arc $BC = 2(35) = 70$. Since AC is a diameter of the circle, the total arc from A to C measures 180°. To find arc AB take $180 - 70 = 110°$.

28. **(H)** To find the greatest common factor of two numbers, first find the largest number that divides into both 24 and 36. Testing various numbers gives 12 as the GCF. To find the GCF of two like variables, always take the smallest power. The GCF of m^4 and m^2 is m^2 because it is the smaller power. Doing this for n and p as well gives the answer $12m^2n$.

29. **(C)** Since opposite sides of a parallelogram are congruent, we know there must be another 12-inch side. The two 12-inch sides combine to 24 inches. Since the total is 56 inches, the remaining two sides add up to $56 - 24 = 32$. Since the 32 represents two congruent sides, each one is $32 \div 2 = 16$. So, that means the other three sides were 12, 16, 16. We can check by adding $12 + 12 + 16 + 16 = 56$.

30. **(K)** Since $\triangle WYZ$ is a right triangle, we can use the Pythagorean Theorem to find the missing side $\overline{YZ}$. Solve $YZ^2 + 12,000^2 = 20,000^2$. $YZ = \sqrt{20,000^2 - 12,000^2} = 16,000$. Since the question asks for the distance between the two radar stations, add 5,000 and 16,000 for the answer 21,000.

31. **(B)** $\dfrac{600 \text{ feet}}{\text{seconds}} \times \dfrac{1 \text{ mile}}{5,280 \text{ feet}} \times \dfrac{60 \text{ seconds}}{1 \text{ minute}} \times \dfrac{60 \text{ minutes}}{1 \text{ hour}} = 409 \text{ miles/hour}$.

32. **(F)** The desired line is a vertical line. Vertical lines have equations of the form $x = h$ and the x-coordinates of all of the points on this line are 5,000, so $x = 5,000$ is the equation of the line.

33. **(A)** In matrix addition, you add elements in the same position to get the sum. Therefore, $(2x - 1) + (-4x - 2) = 12$. Solve the equation to get $-2x - 3 = 12 \rightarrow x = -7.5$.

34. **(G)** Use the formula $A = \frac{1}{2}b \cdot h$ to find the area of the triangle to get $A = \frac{1}{2}(2w^2 - 8w + 7)(3) = \frac{6w^2 - 24w + 21}{2}$.

35. **(B)** To evaluate $1\blacksquare(2\blacksquare2)$ begin inside the parentheses. To evaluate $2\blacksquare2$, substitute 2 into the given equation for both x and y to get $(x + y)(x - y) = (2 + 2)(2 - 2) = 0$. Therefore, the original problem becomes $1\blacksquare0$. Evaluate this expression by plugging $x = 1$ and $y = 0$ to get $(1 + 0)(1 - 0) = 1$.

36. **(F)** If she scores just 1 goal in game 7, her overall goals scored would be 0, 1, 1, 1, 2, 3, 4. The median (middle number) in that set is 1, not 2.

37. **(B)** Recall the standard form of a circle $(x - h)^2 + (y - k)^2 = r^2$, where h and k represent the center of the circle. To find the center, take the opposite of each number after the x and y. For this problem, the opposite of positive 7 and negative 5 gives a center of $(-7, 5)$.

38. **(K)** Solving for y gives $3x - 7y = 21 \rightarrow -7y = -3x + 21 \rightarrow y = \frac{3}{7}x - 3$.

39. **(A)** Using supplementary angles, parallel lines, triangles, and vertical angles you can arrive at the correct answer. See the diagram below for help.

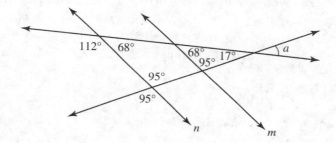

40. **(G)** To start this problem, draw and label a diagram. If the angle of depression from the control tower to the plane is 12°, then the angle of elevation from the plane to the tower is also 12°. Let x be the distance from the plane to the tower, then use $\tan(12) = \frac{40}{x}$. Solve for x to get $x \cdot \tan(12) = 40 \rightarrow x = \frac{40}{\tan(12)}$.

41. **(D)** A square root function is undefined in the real number system whenever the expression under the radical is less than zero. Set $x - 5 < 0$ and solve to get $x < 5$.

42. **(K)** The distance from $(-3, m)$ to the line $x = 7$ is $7 - (-3) = 10$ units. When reflected over the line, the point will move from its location 10 units left of $x = 7$ to its new location 10 units right of $x = 7$. The only point that is 10 units to the right of $x = 7$ is $(17, m)$.

43. **(C)** Using the distance formula $d = \sqrt{(x_2 - x_1)^2 + (y_2 - y_1)^2}$ we get

$$d = \sqrt{(5 - (-3))^2 + (8 - 2)^2} = \sqrt{64 + 36} = \sqrt{100} = 10$$

44. **(K)** If the ratio of the sides of the two rectangles is 1:4, the ratio of the areas is $(1:4)^2 = 1:16$. Set up a proportion to get $\frac{1}{16} = \frac{12}{x}$. Solve to get $x = 192$.

45. **(E)** For the first hour Daniel pays x dollars, so he pays $1(x)$ for the first hour. After the first hour, he pays y dollars for the remaining $h - 1$ hours, so he pays $y(h - 1)$. Add the expressions for the first hour and the remaining hours to get $P = x + y(h - 1)$.

46. **(F)** First, solve for z to get $3z \cdot y = 2x \rightarrow z = \frac{2x}{3y}$. Now, to find out what happens as x and y are doubled, substitute $2x$ and $2y$ in place of them to get $\frac{2(2x)}{3(2y)}$. Simplify to get $\frac{2x}{3y}$, which is the same expression as what z originally started as. You could also substitute numbers like $x = 1$, $y = 1$ into the problem, then plug in $x = 2$, $y = 2$ to see what happens to z when x and y are doubled.

47. **(E)** The only way a product and quotient of three things can be greater than zero is if all factors are positive, or if exactly two factors are negative. The only factors in the expression that can be negative are t^5 and m^9 because w^6 is always positive. This means that t and m are either both positive or both negative. Either way, the product $t \cdot m$ would be positive.

48. **(H)** Using a law of logarithms, $a \log b = \log b^a$, the expression becomes $\log(x^2) + \log(\sqrt{y}) - \log(z^4)$. Now, use the law of logarithms, $\log(a) + \log(b) = \log(a \cdot b)$, to get

$\log(x^2 \cdot \sqrt{y}) - \log(z^4)$. Finally, use the law of logarithms, $\log(a) - \log(b) = \log\left(\frac{a}{b}\right)$ to get

$\log\left(\dfrac{x^2\sqrt{y}}{z^4}\right)$.

49. **(A)** To evaluate $f(g(2))$ start inside the parentheses by finding $g(2)$. To find $g(2)$ from the table, look where $x = 2$, and read $g(x) = 3$; therefore, $g(2) = 3$. Now, evaluate $f(3)$ using the table the same way to get $f(3) = -15$.

50. **(F)** The problem states that p varies inversely with the square root of q, meaning we can set up an equation $p = \dfrac{k}{\sqrt{q}}$ where k is a constant. Using the initial criteria $q = 49$ and $p = 800$, we get $800 = \dfrac{k}{\sqrt{49}}$. Solving for k gives $800 = \dfrac{k}{7} \rightarrow k = 5{,}600$. Now that we know the constant, use it and the fact that there are 100 predators to get $p = \dfrac{5{,}600}{\sqrt{100}} = 560$.

51. **(C)** To find the slope between two points, use the slope formula $m = \dfrac{y_2 - y_1}{x_2 - x_1}$ and substitute in the points to get $\dfrac{x^2 - 1}{x - 1}$. Now, simplify the answer by factoring to get $\dfrac{(x+1)(x-1)}{x-1}$. Cancel like factors to get $x + 1$, as long as $x \neq 1$. Since the problem states "for $x > 5$," we don't have to worry about this hole.

52. **(G)** Using the laws of exponents we first get $\dfrac{3^1 \cdot 3^{2x-5}}{3^{x+1}} = \dfrac{3^{2x-4}}{3^{x+1}}$. Then, use the laws of exponents to divide and get $3^{2x-4-(x+1)} = 3^{x-5}$.

53. **(E)** A good way to find a number that is halfway between two numbers is to find the average of those two numbers. To find the average of $\dfrac{3}{8}$ and $\dfrac{4}{5}$, add them up and divide by 2. A calculator can be handy for this step, or you can do it by hand. Either way, you should get $\dfrac{47}{80}$.

54. **(K)** For Mike to achieve the highest grade on one test, we want the other 3 tests to be as low as possible. The problem states that he never scored lower than 80%, so assume he scored an 80 on each of his first 3 tests and let x be the score on his fourth test. Set up an equation to find x using the fact that his average is an 85: $\dfrac{3(80) + x}{4} = 85$. Solve for x to get $x = 100$.

55. **(B)** To solve an absolute value inequality, split the problem into two inequalities without an absolute value. The first inequality stays exactly as the problem was written but without the absolute value bars: $x - 3 > x - 3$. Solving this inequality yields $-3 > -3$, which has no solution. The other inequality we get from splitting up the absolute value is $x - 3 < -(x - 3)$. Solve this inequality to get $x < 3$.

56. **(G)** Multiplying $\dfrac{i + 7}{i - 5} \cdot \dfrac{i}{1}$ gives $\dfrac{i^2 + 7i}{i - 5}$. Recall that $i^2 = -1$; therefore, the expression becomes $\dfrac{-1 + 7i}{i - 5}$. Now, multiply the top and bottom of the fraction by $i + 5$ ($i + 5$ is the *conjugate* of the denominator) to get $\dfrac{-1 + 7i}{i - 5} \cdot \dfrac{i + 5}{i + 5} = \dfrac{-i - 5 + 7i^2 + 35i}{i^2 - 25}$. Simplify to get $\dfrac{34i - 12}{-26}$. Divide the top and bottom by 2 to get $\dfrac{-6 + 17i}{-13} \rightarrow \dfrac{6}{13} - \dfrac{17}{13}i$.

57. **(B)** First calculate the area of the pizza by using the formula $A = \pi r^2$ to get $A \approx 113.1$. If each square inch contains 50 calories, there is a total of $113.1 \cdot 50 = 5{,}655$ calories. Alex's dad eats 3 out of 8 slices, or in other words, $\dfrac{3}{8}$ of the pizza, which is $\dfrac{3}{8}(5{,}655) = 2{,}120$ calories. Alex eats two slices or $\dfrac{2}{8}(5{,}655) = 1{,}414$ calories. Subtract Alex's calories from his dad's to get $2{,}120 - 1{,}414 \approx 700$ calories.

58. **(H)** Start by drawing a right triangle with unknown angle θ as seen in the diagram below. Since $\tan(\theta) = v$, then we know the $\dfrac{\text{opposite}}{\text{adjacent}}$ from angle θ is $\dfrac{v}{1}$. Now, find the missing side using the Pythagorean Theorem to get it: $\sqrt{1^2 + v^2}$. Now, using SOH-CAH-TOA, $\cos(\theta) = \dfrac{\text{adjacent}}{\text{hypotenuse}} = \dfrac{1}{\sqrt{1 + v^2}}$.

59. **(B)** Andy only has two possible places to sit, but the other four people can sit anywhere. Starting with just the arrangements for the other 4 people, we get $4 \cdot 3 \cdot 2 \cdot 1 = 24$ possible seating arrangements for them. Then, multiply the answer by 2 for the two possible choices for Andy to get $2 \cdot 24 = 48$ total arrangements.

60. **(F)** If the two points lie on the graph of the equation, then their slope must equal $\dfrac{1}{3}$, which is the slope of the equation. Using the slope formula and setting it equal to $\dfrac{1}{3}$, we get $\dfrac{n + \dfrac{2}{g} - n}{m - 2 - m} = \dfrac{1}{3}$. Simplify the numerator and denominator to get $\dfrac{\dfrac{2}{g}}{-2} = \dfrac{1}{3}$. Keep simplifying to get $\dfrac{-1}{g} = \dfrac{1}{3}$. Solve to get $g = -3$.

Reading

1. **(A)** As is often the case on the Literary Narrative section, the broadest answer is the correct one here. The passage sounds like a young man talking, and "relating a significant event" is so open-ended that there's really no way for it to be wrong. (If nothing is wrong, then it's right!)

2. **(H)** Although the story takes place in a supermarket, specific supermarket chains are never mentioned aside from line 49, and no other chain is mentioned besides the one in which the story is set.

3. **(B)** Although it's strongly implied that Sammy is young, there's no real indication that he is new at his job. He could easily have worked there for years.

4. **(J)** Sammy mentions thinking of himself as a hero in line 67, and his decision to quit is a stand on principle (if a minor and foolish one).

5. **(C)** Although Sammy makes jokes about Lengel being a Sunday-school teacher in lines 16 and 37–38, there is no indication that the locals in general are mistrustful of organized religion.

6. **(H)** The fact that Sammy turns in his bow tie after quitting (lines 89–90) establishes that it is the store's property.

7. **(D)** The reason that *the crowd that runs the A&P must look pretty crummy* to Queenie is that she is richer than they are, as implied in lines 19–32.

8. **(F)** There is never any indication that anyone besides Sammy finds his decision to quit admirable. Even Sammy himself barely feels this way by the end.

9. **(B)** We are told twice that Lengel "doesn't miss that much" (lines 17 and 36).

10. **(F)** Sammy explicitly states in lines 65–67 that he quit solely to try and impress the girls.

11. **(D)** The final paragraph, about how "a chain of middlemen" makes it easier for buyers to avoid considering where the bones come from, places blame on the fact that the bone buyers in other nations turn a blind eye to criminal practices.

12. **(F)** The "long chain" is the chain that separates Western buyers from the criminals who actually first obtain and prepare the bones. Western buyers are able to ignore the root problem or plead ignorance because they never have to deal directly with the criminals.

13. **(C)** All of the quotations that the author selected for use emphasize the horrifying environment and the fear and powerlessness of the people. The dominant emotion of the piece is sympathy for the people caught up in all of this.

14. **(G)** The paragraph emphasizes the fact that Young Brothers acquires bones openly from every conceivable location and even goes so far as to advertise despite the fact that their business is nominally illegal. The point here is the flagrancy of the enterprise.

15. **(A)** After the quote from Aron, the rest of the paragraph is concerned with explaining that, for various reasons, the laws concerning bone trafficking do not always get enforced.

16. **(H)** The passage never mentions anything about the reliability of witnesses (indeed, it implies that very few cases ever come to trial, and so witnesses would hardly be an issue).

17. **(D)** Lines 82–89 establish that, in the eyes of police themselves, they are powerless until society decides that it cares enough about the issue to give them the resources they need to enforce the law.

18. **(H)** Lines 77–78 state that the "bones from over 100 people could have fetched around $70,000," which works out to $700 per skeleton.

19. **(B)** Vinesh Aron is the owner of Young Brothers (lines 64–65), a bone-trafficking organization, and so would not oppose bone trafficking.

20. **(F)** It is established in lines 1–3 that the buyers of the bones are medical students. Therefore, they would be the audience for the catalogues.

21. **(A)** Passage A is adapted from Mary Shelley's introduction to a later edition of her famous novel, and so "once again" (i.e., for the second time) she is offering her "progeny" (a synonym for "offspring," as she is metaphorically the "parent" of the book) to the public.

22. **(J)** The second and third paragraphs of Passage A draw explicit contrast between Shelley's early attempts at writing and her personal fantasies. She states that only her fantasies were personal, whereas her early writing consisted of mechanical attempts to copy others.

23. **(C)** The antecedent of "it" in the sentence in question is "literary reputation"—i.e., getting famous for writing.

24. **(F)** The key phrase here is "what terrified me will terrify others." Shelley's epiphany was that the dreams and fantasies she had previously kept to herself had in fact been the key to success all along.

25. **(B)** Shelley closes her introduction by stating that her novel was originally written in "happy times, when death and grief were but words"—i.e., that although she was writing about horrible things, she had not yet experienced them, but now has. (Her husband, three of their children, and several of their close friends had all died in the interim.)

26. **(H)** In the paragraph in question, Victor Frankenstein begins by alluding to his meticulous scientific process, but then describes his emotional horror at seeing the result of that process come to life.

27. **(B)** Victor Frankenstein's quest was to create life, and he has done so, but the dream about his fiancée turning into his dead mother implies and foreshadows to the reader that the eventual results will be exactly the opposite.

28. **(J)** Shelley's autobiographical introduction describes her famous novel as being the product of a dream, and Victor Frankenstein's narration establishes that his aversion to his creation is an emotional reaction, rather than being the product of anything the Creature actually does (at least, not yet …).

29. **(B)** As with Question #24, the key phrase here is "what terrified me will terrify others." Mary Shelley's grand realization was that her own personal imagination and psychology was the key to creating a work of genius.

30. **(F)** Mary Shelley (a great self-promoter, no matter how much she claimed not to care for fame) is clearly drawing an explicit comparison between her "creation" of the *Frankenstein* story and Victor Frankenstein's creation of the Monster. The "idea that broke in" in Passage A and the "spark of being" in Passage B are analogous to each other—in both cases, the creator merely harnesses a mysterious energy that originates elsewhere.

31. **(D)** The passage as a whole is concerned with the history of magnetic therapy and how there has never been any credible evidence to support it. (As is frequently the case with "main point" questions, the broadest answer is the correct one!)

32. **(H)** Lines 44–53 explain that the findings of Franklin's commission made Mesmer so unpopular that he had to flee France in disgrace.

33. **(A)** The paragraph begins with "Nevertheless" (i.e., "despite all this") and goes on to explain that the same discredited practices took hold in the United States, eventually developing into a new pseudomedical practice of dubious value.

34. **(G)** Lines 104–110 explain that human blood is actually diamagnetic, that is, repelled by magnets.

35. **(D)** Lines 70–74 state that an MRI field is about a hundred times stronger than a powerful therapy magnet. (The trick here is that 100 is written as a numeral in the answer choice, but written out as a word in the passage, so people who are scanning the passage quickly for a numeral will not see it.)

36. **(F)** A *placebo* is a fake treatment given to some patients in a medical experiment in order to rule out the psychological effect—in this case, the "sham magnets" of lines 87–88.

37. **(C)** The *predatory quacks* of line 118 are dishonest therapists. A *quack* is a doctor who believes (or pretends to believe) in false treatments.

38. **(G)** Lines 94–98 explain that skin gets red when it's heated because blood is being diverted to the area to act as a coolant.

39. **(C)** Lines 28–32 describe Benjamin Franklin correctly figuring out that magnet therapy only appeared to help because it was keeping patients away from the harmful treatments practiced by many other doctors at that time.

40. **(J)** Lines 81–93 describe an experiment conducted by Carlos Vallbona in which magnet therapy appeared to have beneficial effects, though no one knows why.

Science

1. **(D)** The tornado in Figure 2 is represented by the number 6. The paragraph above Figure 2 explains this (it is logical that the sixth and *final* step in the explanation would be the one that involves the tornado, since the paragraph is an explanation of how tornadoes are formed).

2. **(J)** The F4 box in Figure 1 (fifth box over, second one down) includes wind speeds from 207 to 261 mph.

3. **(B)** In the paragraph above Figure 2, a mesocyclone is formed in Step 3. Since a spinning wall-cloud is formed in Step 5, this would be the one that does NOT precede the formation of a mesocyclone.

4. **(F)** The paragraph above Figure 3 explains that "Tornado Alley" is in the central United States, and that the number over each state represents its number of tornadoes in 2005. Texas had 105 (higher than any of the other choices) and is in the central United States.

5. **(B)** The intersection box of the horizontal "Brick Structure" row and the vertical "Minor Damage" column says f0. The key within Figure 1 explains that the f scale (lower case) must then be *converted* into the F scale (upper case), and f0 + 1 = F1.

6. **(H)** According to the intensity scale, collapsed walls on a brick building are an F3 and missing roofs from strong frame houses occur during an F2 tornado. Therefore, the strongest tornado intensity possible is an F3.

7. **(C)** The sample with the highest concentration of chlorine in Table 2 (the table in Study 1) is Sample 3, with a concentration of 0.15 mg/L.

8. **(F)** In Table 3 (the table in Study 2), the highest grouping of numbers in the "Average pH" column occurs during the spring months: April, May, and March or June. (Remember that acidity is indicated by *low* pH, and so the *least* acidic deposition would be represented by the *highest* numbers.) Spring is still the right answer even though there are other individual high numbers in other months, and regardless of whether you count March or June as the third spring month.

9. **(D)** The order of the samples by acidity, from lowest pH to highest, is 4, 2, 1, 3, 5. The order of the samples by sodium concentration, from lowest to highest, is 5, 1, 2, 4, 3. The orders are neither the same as nor the reverse of each other, and therefore there is no correlation, neither a positive nor an inverse. (Remember that when the last choice is "no correlation" or "no relationship" or "date not included" or something weird like that, that is *probably* the answer, so test that one first!)

10. **(G)** The pH is highest in the month of April. Table 1 shows that frogs die at around a pH of 5. Clearly, the lower the pH, the greater the health risks for all animals. There is no definitive level but the question specifies *least* concerned. April is the best answer given the other three choices.

11. **(A)** The introductory paragraph above Table 1 explains that *wet deposition* refers to rain, snow, sleet, and hail. The paragraph in Study 1 explains that the samples in Study 2 were collected in the form of rain, and therefore they are examples of *wet deposition*.

12. **(H)** The introductory paragraph explains that sulfuric acid lowers the pH of rain. Since the samples in Table 2 were collected from rain, the pH of Sample 2 would necessarily be lower than its current pH of 5.28 had it been contaminated with sulfuric acid.

13. **(A)** According to Table 1, once the pH falls below 4 to a level 3 all fish will die, but frogs, crawfish, and snails can survive.

14. **(F)** As shown in Table 1, parents with blood types of O and B can only produce offspring with O or B blood as well. Whether the mother is O or B, whether the father is O or B, the results are the same.

15. **(B)** As Tables 1 and 2 make clear, to produce a child with blood type AB+, at least one parent must have a blood type with A in it (A or AB), at least one parent must have a blood type with B in it (B or AB), and at least one parent must be Rh+. The only one of the choices that has an A, a B, and a + in it is choice B.

16. **(H)** Table 3 shows that the "universal donor" is type O−. Table 1 shows that a child with type O blood could not possibly have a parent who has type AB blood (i.e., *neither* parent can be AB). When both parents have B− blood, B− or O− offspring will be produced.

17. **(B)** Parents with blood types A and O can produce either A or O offspring (Table 1). The Rh factor could be + OR − because both parents could carry the recessive gene for Rh−.

18. **(G)** In the opening paragraph, the passage clearly states, "The genes ensure that only the blood cells of the proper blood type remain in the body"—that is, they control the types of cells in the blood.

19. **(D)** According to Table 3, blood type AB+ is the universal recipient. Persons with this type can receive blood from anybody no matter what their blood type.

20. **(F)** All this question wants you to do is find the point at which the four lines in Figure 1 are the closest to one another. That would be the starting point, which represents 8:15–9:25.

21. **(C)** The text explains that lower numbers on the behavioral scale indicate better behavior, so all this question is asking you to do is find the point (out of the choices) where the line representing the Adderall kids (the one with the squares) is *not* the *lowest*. (Even if you didn't get that, choice C is still the only one of the choices where the line representing the Adderall kids is in a *different* place relative to the other four lines—when in doubt, pick the odd one out.)

22. **(J)** All this question wants you to do is find the point in Figure 2 where the line representing the double-dose Ritalin kids (the one with the triangles) is highest, which is over "appetite loss" (as it is for all the lines except the one representing the placebo kids).

23. **(A)** The text explains that lower numbers on the behavioral scale indicate better behavior, so all this question wants you to do is find the line in Figure 1 that is highest at the 3:35–4:45 mark, and it is the one representing the placebo kids (the one with the diamonds).

24. **(F)** According to the legend for Figure 1, the group with a 5 behavior rating corresponds to P—placebo.

25. **(C)** In Figure 1, the effectiveness order of the medications from most to least effective is A1, R2, R1. In Figure 2, the side-effects order of the medications from fewest to most is R1, R2, A1. The medication choice that "splits the difference" is R2.

26. **(H)** R2 medication consistently keeps the behavior rating at a 4 or lower for the duration of the day except within the first two hours, and while A1 medication does the same for the behavior rating, R2 manages the symptom of appetite loss better than A1. Therefore, the child would be less likely to lose weight while taking the prescribed medication.

27. **(D)** All this question wants you to do is find which line in Figure 2 is the highest at the 30-second mark. The lines stop before the 30-second mark, but it is still clear from extrapolation that the line representing Solvent 4 would be highest (it is continuing to rise when the other three have leveled off).

28. **(H)** Table 2 shows that Solutions 1–4 progressively increase in temperature. Figure 3 shows that osmotic pressure decreases as the number of the solution used rises. Therefore, as temperature increases, osmotic pressure decreases.

29. **(A)** Table 1 indicates that Solvents 1–4 progressively increase in terms of molecular weight percentage. Figure 2 shows that the solutions finish passing through the semipermeable membrane (i.e., the lines representing them level off) in the same order. Therefore, the lower the molecular weight percentage of a solvent, the more quickly the solution passes through a membrane.

30. **(G)** The line in Figure 2 that represents Solvent 4 has the greatest osmotic pressure.

31. **(C)** Table 2 indicates that the 30°C solution is Solution 2. In Figure 3, the height of the line above the Solution 2 hash mark is about 1.4 atm. Double this, and the answer choice that is closest is 2.8 atm.

32. **(G)** Experiment 1 indicates in the paragraph that the Figure 2 results are shown as recorded at the 20° trial, which according to Table 2 is Trial 1.

33. **(A)** The volume of Solvent 1 in the tube leveled out at 320 ml and remained there for the last 20 seconds of the experiment, so you would expect the volume to remain there through 40 seconds.

34. **(H)** Student 1 closes by specifying that the image would be upright, whereas Student 2 closes by specifying that the image would be inverted. Therefore, the students disagree about the image's orientation.

35. **(B)** The fact that both students open by specifying the distance between the object and the mirror, and then base their theories on it, shows that both know that the exact positioning of the lightbulb is important.

36. **(F)** The teacher's information specifies that an object must be between F and the mirror to appear upright, and the description of the magic trick specifies that F lies 1.6 m from the mirror. Therefore, an object 1.0 m away would produce an upright image.

37. **(C)** Student 2's explanation is perfectly accurate. The teacher's information specifies that an object at C will produce an exact but inverted image. (It is often the case on the ACT Science that remembering earlier questions in a passage can help you answer later ones!)

38. **(F)** This is not true because F is in front of C, and an object at F will produce no image at all (although an object at any point between C and the mirror *aside from F* will indeed produce a larger image).

39. **(B)** The teacher's information states that an object at F will produce no reflection, and the description of the magic trick states that F is 1.6 m away.

40. **(J)** The teacher's information states that objects placed beyond C will produce reflections smaller than the objects themselves. The description of the magic trick states that C is 2.2 m away. Therefore, an object at 2.5 m away will produce a reflection smaller than itself.

Writing Sample

Gender-Separate Education
(This essay would score in the 10–12 range)

A lot has been made recently of gender equality within education. In fact, the movement has taken on a whole new dimension over the last few years. Today, gender equality in the classroom is much more than boys and girls having equal rights; today, gender equality includes all people who identify as genders other than those listed on their birth certificates. From an early age, American children are now exposed to gender equality in all forms. This new openness places those in charge of educating children in a precarious position as they debate the age-old question of whether or not boys and girls learn better together or separated by gender. The three perspectives given on this topic each have some validity; however, none truly answer the question. Separating boys and girls during their school years is not the most effective method of creating an outstanding society through quality education. The instantaneous access to all forms of information through technology makes it clear that children should not be separated by gender in an attempt to promote better learning.

The view that students will eventually be distracted by something comes the closest to explaining how technology has made the question of gender-separate education a moot point. As perspective two points out, "the real world is never going to provide them with an ideal environment free of distractions." That "distraction" is technology and everything that goes with it. If parents want to keep their teenager away from the opposite sex in the classroom, they will need to cut off all social media, all news feeds, and all Internet access—essentially relegating their child to an education resembling what was once provided in antiquated one-room school houses. Because of technology, the world is a very small place—a place where we are all interconnected and dependent on each other for our daily interactions and information. Most teenagers learn via technology: their books are digital; their lessons are often delivered via group videos sessions; their teachers respond to them through messages and emails; and they converse with each other through emojis and text messages. A perfect example of technology making gender-separate education obsolete is the foreign language training program called Rosetta Stone. The key ingredient for success with Rosetta Stone is open dialogue with others who are native speakers of the language the learner is attempting to master. Even members of the United Nations and newly appointed foreign ambassadors use the one-to-one and group chat features of Rosetta Stone to quickly learn a new language. That's how the world works today: people learn rapidly and openly because of technology; there are no borders, no roadblocks, no discrimination or exclusion based on gender. Computers are impartial. Attempting to educate children equally through gender separation is like attempting to look at one's own face without using some type of mirror. It's simply impossible.

There are, of course, other opinions on gender-separate education. Perspective number one states that "if reliable research indicates that both boys and girls learn better in single-gender classrooms, then that's all that matters." This view has several weaknesses. Not only does it fail to provide any type of reliable research, it does not consider a host of other valid points. America is not a "separate but equal" society for a good reason. Separation based on the promise of equality always leads to one or more groups becoming marginalized. One only needs to look at the struggle of various socio-economic groups throughout America's history to see the truth: African Americans, wave after wave of immigrant groups, the entire LGBQT community, and of course women have all been marginalized because of the concept of separate but equal. Each of these groups is gaining true equality because they fight for the right to not be separate, and one fact is certain, only through inclusiveness will greatness as a society be achieved. This inclusiveness must begin in the classroom.

American society cannot afford to keep the genders separate during their most formative years, and in fact, it is impossible. Technology is the great equalizer; it provides all students access to previously unfathomable amounts of information. There is strength and power in knowledge, and to be truly knowledgeable, all students must interact with each other, regardless of gender. Technology allows all students to do this. There may be inherent differences in males and females, but those differences provide strength and knowledge for all. Educators and students know that the most effective learning happens in the spirit of cooperation between all participants regardless of gender.

ANSWER SHEET
Practice Test 4

Directions: Mark one answer only for each question. Make the mark dark. Erase completely any mark made in error. (Additional or stray marks will be counted as mistakes.)

English

1. Ⓐ Ⓑ Ⓒ Ⓓ
2. Ⓕ Ⓖ Ⓗ Ⓙ
3. Ⓐ Ⓑ Ⓒ Ⓓ
4. Ⓕ Ⓖ Ⓗ Ⓙ
5. Ⓐ Ⓑ Ⓒ Ⓓ
6. Ⓕ Ⓖ Ⓗ Ⓙ
7. Ⓐ Ⓑ Ⓒ Ⓓ
8. Ⓕ Ⓖ Ⓗ Ⓙ
9. Ⓐ Ⓑ Ⓒ Ⓓ
10. Ⓕ Ⓖ Ⓗ Ⓙ
11. Ⓐ Ⓑ Ⓒ Ⓓ
12. Ⓕ Ⓖ Ⓗ Ⓙ
13. Ⓐ Ⓑ Ⓒ Ⓓ
14. Ⓕ Ⓖ Ⓗ Ⓙ
15. Ⓐ Ⓑ Ⓒ Ⓓ

16. Ⓕ Ⓖ Ⓗ Ⓙ
17. Ⓐ Ⓑ Ⓒ Ⓓ
18. Ⓕ Ⓖ Ⓗ Ⓙ
19. Ⓐ Ⓑ Ⓒ Ⓓ
20. Ⓕ Ⓖ Ⓗ Ⓙ
21. Ⓐ Ⓑ Ⓒ Ⓓ
22. Ⓕ Ⓖ Ⓗ Ⓙ
23. Ⓐ Ⓑ Ⓒ Ⓓ
24. Ⓕ Ⓖ Ⓗ Ⓙ
25. Ⓐ Ⓑ Ⓒ Ⓓ
26. Ⓕ Ⓖ Ⓗ Ⓙ
27. Ⓐ Ⓑ Ⓒ Ⓓ
28. Ⓕ Ⓖ Ⓗ Ⓙ
29. Ⓐ Ⓑ Ⓒ Ⓓ
30. Ⓕ Ⓖ Ⓗ Ⓙ

31. Ⓐ Ⓑ Ⓒ Ⓓ
32. Ⓕ Ⓖ Ⓗ Ⓙ
33. Ⓐ Ⓑ Ⓒ Ⓓ
34. Ⓕ Ⓖ Ⓗ Ⓙ
35. Ⓐ Ⓑ Ⓒ Ⓓ
36. Ⓕ Ⓖ Ⓗ Ⓙ
37. Ⓐ Ⓑ Ⓒ Ⓓ
38. Ⓕ Ⓖ Ⓗ Ⓙ
39. Ⓐ Ⓑ Ⓒ Ⓓ
40. Ⓕ Ⓖ Ⓗ Ⓙ
41. Ⓐ Ⓑ Ⓒ Ⓓ
42. Ⓕ Ⓖ Ⓗ Ⓙ
43. Ⓐ Ⓑ Ⓒ Ⓓ
44. Ⓕ Ⓖ Ⓗ Ⓙ
45. Ⓐ Ⓑ Ⓒ Ⓓ

46. Ⓕ Ⓖ Ⓗ Ⓙ
47. Ⓐ Ⓑ Ⓒ Ⓓ
48. Ⓕ Ⓖ Ⓗ Ⓙ
49. Ⓐ Ⓑ Ⓒ Ⓓ
50. Ⓕ Ⓖ Ⓗ Ⓙ
51. Ⓐ Ⓑ Ⓒ Ⓓ
52. Ⓕ Ⓖ Ⓗ Ⓙ
53. Ⓐ Ⓑ Ⓒ Ⓓ
54. Ⓕ Ⓖ Ⓗ Ⓙ
55. Ⓐ Ⓑ Ⓒ Ⓓ
56. Ⓕ Ⓖ Ⓗ Ⓙ
57. Ⓐ Ⓑ Ⓒ Ⓓ
58. Ⓕ Ⓖ Ⓗ Ⓙ
59. Ⓐ Ⓑ Ⓒ Ⓓ
60. Ⓕ Ⓖ Ⓗ Ⓙ

61. Ⓐ Ⓑ Ⓒ Ⓓ
62. Ⓕ Ⓖ Ⓗ Ⓙ
63. Ⓐ Ⓑ Ⓒ Ⓓ
64. Ⓕ Ⓖ Ⓗ Ⓙ
65. Ⓐ Ⓑ Ⓒ Ⓓ
66. Ⓕ Ⓖ Ⓗ Ⓙ
67. Ⓐ Ⓑ Ⓒ Ⓓ
68. Ⓕ Ⓖ Ⓗ Ⓙ
69. Ⓐ Ⓑ Ⓒ Ⓓ
70. Ⓕ Ⓖ Ⓗ Ⓙ
71. Ⓐ Ⓑ Ⓒ Ⓓ
72. Ⓕ Ⓖ Ⓗ Ⓙ
73. Ⓐ Ⓑ Ⓒ Ⓓ
74. Ⓕ Ⓖ Ⓗ Ⓙ
75. Ⓐ Ⓑ Ⓒ Ⓓ

Mathematics

1. Ⓐ Ⓑ Ⓒ Ⓓ Ⓔ
2. Ⓕ Ⓖ Ⓗ Ⓙ Ⓚ
3. Ⓐ Ⓑ Ⓒ Ⓓ Ⓔ
4. Ⓕ Ⓖ Ⓗ Ⓙ Ⓚ
5. Ⓐ Ⓑ Ⓒ Ⓓ Ⓔ
6. Ⓕ Ⓖ Ⓗ Ⓙ Ⓚ
7. Ⓐ Ⓑ Ⓒ Ⓓ Ⓔ
8. Ⓕ Ⓖ Ⓗ Ⓙ Ⓚ
9. Ⓐ Ⓑ Ⓒ Ⓓ Ⓔ
10. Ⓕ Ⓖ Ⓗ Ⓙ Ⓚ
11. Ⓐ Ⓑ Ⓒ Ⓓ Ⓔ
12. Ⓕ Ⓖ Ⓗ Ⓙ Ⓚ
13. Ⓐ Ⓑ Ⓒ Ⓓ Ⓔ
14. Ⓕ Ⓖ Ⓗ Ⓙ Ⓚ
15. Ⓐ Ⓑ Ⓒ Ⓓ Ⓔ

16. Ⓕ Ⓖ Ⓗ Ⓙ Ⓚ
17. Ⓐ Ⓑ Ⓒ Ⓓ Ⓔ
18. Ⓕ Ⓖ Ⓗ Ⓙ Ⓚ
19. Ⓐ Ⓑ Ⓒ Ⓓ Ⓔ
20. Ⓕ Ⓖ Ⓗ Ⓙ Ⓚ
21. Ⓐ Ⓑ Ⓒ Ⓓ Ⓔ
22. Ⓕ Ⓖ Ⓗ Ⓙ Ⓚ
23. Ⓐ Ⓑ Ⓒ Ⓓ Ⓔ
24. Ⓕ Ⓖ Ⓗ Ⓙ Ⓚ
25. Ⓐ Ⓑ Ⓒ Ⓓ Ⓔ
26. Ⓕ Ⓖ Ⓗ Ⓙ Ⓚ
27. Ⓐ Ⓑ Ⓒ Ⓓ Ⓔ
28. Ⓕ Ⓖ Ⓗ Ⓙ Ⓚ
29. Ⓐ Ⓑ Ⓒ Ⓓ Ⓔ
30. Ⓕ Ⓖ Ⓗ Ⓙ Ⓚ

31. Ⓐ Ⓑ Ⓒ Ⓓ Ⓔ
32. Ⓕ Ⓖ Ⓗ Ⓙ Ⓚ
33. Ⓐ Ⓑ Ⓒ Ⓓ Ⓔ
34. Ⓕ Ⓖ Ⓗ Ⓙ Ⓚ
35. Ⓐ Ⓑ Ⓒ Ⓓ Ⓔ
36. Ⓕ Ⓖ Ⓗ Ⓙ Ⓚ
37. Ⓐ Ⓑ Ⓒ Ⓓ Ⓔ
38. Ⓕ Ⓖ Ⓗ Ⓙ Ⓚ
39. Ⓐ Ⓑ Ⓒ Ⓓ Ⓔ
40. Ⓕ Ⓖ Ⓗ Ⓙ Ⓚ
41. Ⓐ Ⓑ Ⓒ Ⓓ Ⓔ
42. Ⓕ Ⓖ Ⓗ Ⓙ Ⓚ
43. Ⓐ Ⓑ Ⓒ Ⓓ Ⓔ
44. Ⓕ Ⓖ Ⓗ Ⓙ Ⓚ
45. Ⓐ Ⓑ Ⓒ Ⓓ Ⓔ

46. Ⓕ Ⓖ Ⓗ Ⓙ Ⓚ
47. Ⓐ Ⓑ Ⓒ Ⓓ Ⓔ
48. Ⓕ Ⓖ Ⓗ Ⓙ Ⓚ
49. Ⓐ Ⓑ Ⓒ Ⓓ Ⓔ
50. Ⓕ Ⓖ Ⓗ Ⓙ Ⓚ
51. Ⓐ Ⓑ Ⓒ Ⓓ Ⓔ
52. Ⓕ Ⓖ Ⓗ Ⓙ Ⓚ
53. Ⓐ Ⓑ Ⓒ Ⓓ Ⓔ
54. Ⓕ Ⓖ Ⓗ Ⓙ Ⓚ
55. Ⓐ Ⓑ Ⓒ Ⓓ Ⓔ
56. Ⓕ Ⓖ Ⓗ Ⓙ Ⓚ
57. Ⓐ Ⓑ Ⓒ Ⓓ Ⓔ
58. Ⓕ Ⓖ Ⓗ Ⓙ Ⓚ
59. Ⓐ Ⓑ Ⓒ Ⓓ Ⓔ
60. Ⓕ Ⓖ Ⓗ Ⓙ Ⓚ

ANSWER SHEET
Practice Test 4

Reading

1. Ⓐ Ⓑ Ⓒ Ⓓ	9. Ⓐ Ⓑ Ⓒ Ⓓ	17. Ⓐ Ⓑ Ⓒ Ⓓ	25. Ⓐ Ⓑ Ⓒ Ⓓ	33. Ⓐ Ⓑ Ⓒ Ⓓ
2. Ⓕ Ⓖ Ⓗ Ⓙ	10. Ⓕ Ⓖ Ⓗ Ⓙ	18. Ⓕ Ⓖ Ⓗ Ⓙ	26. Ⓕ Ⓖ Ⓗ Ⓙ	34. Ⓕ Ⓖ Ⓗ Ⓙ
3. Ⓐ Ⓑ Ⓒ Ⓓ	11. Ⓐ Ⓑ Ⓒ Ⓓ	19. Ⓐ Ⓑ Ⓒ Ⓓ	27. Ⓐ Ⓑ Ⓒ Ⓓ	35. Ⓐ Ⓑ Ⓒ Ⓓ
4. Ⓕ Ⓖ Ⓗ Ⓙ	12. Ⓕ Ⓖ Ⓗ Ⓙ	20. Ⓕ Ⓖ Ⓗ Ⓙ	28. Ⓕ Ⓖ Ⓗ Ⓙ	36. Ⓕ Ⓖ Ⓗ Ⓙ
5. Ⓐ Ⓑ Ⓒ Ⓓ	13. Ⓐ Ⓑ Ⓒ Ⓓ	21. Ⓐ Ⓑ Ⓒ Ⓓ	29. Ⓐ Ⓑ Ⓒ Ⓓ	37. Ⓐ Ⓑ Ⓒ Ⓓ
6. Ⓕ Ⓖ Ⓗ Ⓙ	14. Ⓕ Ⓖ Ⓗ Ⓙ	22. Ⓕ Ⓖ Ⓗ Ⓙ	30. Ⓕ Ⓖ Ⓗ Ⓙ	38. Ⓕ Ⓖ Ⓗ Ⓙ
7. Ⓐ Ⓑ Ⓒ Ⓓ	15. Ⓐ Ⓑ Ⓒ Ⓓ	23. Ⓐ Ⓑ Ⓒ Ⓓ	31. Ⓐ Ⓑ Ⓒ Ⓓ	39. Ⓐ Ⓑ Ⓒ Ⓓ
8. Ⓕ Ⓖ Ⓗ Ⓙ	16. Ⓕ Ⓖ Ⓗ Ⓙ	24. Ⓕ Ⓖ Ⓗ Ⓙ	32. Ⓕ Ⓖ Ⓗ Ⓙ	40. Ⓕ Ⓖ Ⓗ Ⓙ

Science

1. Ⓐ Ⓑ Ⓒ Ⓓ	9. Ⓐ Ⓑ Ⓒ Ⓓ	17. Ⓐ Ⓑ Ⓒ Ⓓ	25. Ⓐ Ⓑ Ⓒ Ⓓ	33. Ⓐ Ⓑ Ⓒ Ⓓ
2. Ⓕ Ⓖ Ⓗ Ⓙ	10. Ⓕ Ⓖ Ⓗ Ⓙ	18. Ⓕ Ⓖ Ⓗ Ⓙ	26. Ⓕ Ⓖ Ⓗ Ⓙ	34. Ⓕ Ⓖ Ⓗ Ⓙ
3. Ⓐ Ⓑ Ⓒ Ⓓ	11. Ⓐ Ⓑ Ⓒ Ⓓ	19. Ⓐ Ⓑ Ⓒ Ⓓ	27. Ⓐ Ⓑ Ⓒ Ⓓ	35. Ⓐ Ⓑ Ⓒ Ⓓ
4. Ⓕ Ⓖ Ⓗ Ⓙ	12. Ⓕ Ⓖ Ⓗ Ⓙ	20. Ⓕ Ⓖ Ⓗ Ⓙ	28. Ⓕ Ⓖ Ⓗ Ⓙ	36. Ⓕ Ⓖ Ⓗ Ⓙ
5. Ⓐ Ⓑ Ⓒ Ⓓ	13. Ⓐ Ⓑ Ⓒ Ⓓ	21. Ⓐ Ⓑ Ⓒ Ⓓ	29. Ⓐ Ⓑ Ⓒ Ⓓ	37. Ⓐ Ⓑ Ⓒ Ⓓ
6. Ⓕ Ⓖ Ⓗ Ⓙ	14. Ⓕ Ⓖ Ⓗ Ⓙ	22. Ⓕ Ⓖ Ⓗ Ⓙ	30. Ⓕ Ⓖ Ⓗ Ⓙ	38. Ⓕ Ⓖ Ⓗ Ⓙ
7. Ⓐ Ⓑ Ⓒ Ⓓ	15. Ⓐ Ⓑ Ⓒ Ⓓ	23. Ⓐ Ⓑ Ⓒ Ⓓ	31. Ⓐ Ⓑ Ⓒ Ⓓ	39. Ⓐ Ⓑ Ⓒ Ⓓ
8. Ⓕ Ⓖ Ⓗ Ⓙ	16. Ⓕ Ⓖ Ⓗ Ⓙ	24. Ⓕ Ⓖ Ⓗ Ⓙ	32. Ⓕ Ⓖ Ⓗ Ⓙ	40. Ⓕ Ⓖ Ⓗ Ⓙ

ENGLISH TEST

Time: 45 Minutes—75 Questions

Directions: In the five passages that follow, certain words and phrases are underlined and numbered. In the right-hand column, you will find alternatives for the underlined part. In most cases, you are to choose the one that best expresses the idea, makes the statement appropriate for standard written English, or is worded most consistently with the style and tone of the passage as a whole. If you think the original version is best, choose "NO CHANGE." In some cases, you will find in the right-hand column a question about the underlined part. You are to choose the best answer to the question.

You will also find questions about a section of the passage, or about the passage as a whole. These questions do not refer to an underlined portion of the passage, but rather are identified by a number or numbers in a box.

For each question, choose the alternative you consider best and fill in the corresponding oval on your answer sheet. Read each passage through once before you begin to answer the questions that accompany it. For many of the questions, you must read several sentences beyond the question to determine the answer. Be sure that you have read far enough ahead each time you choose an alternative.

PASSAGE I

When Third Was Second

People often say that you're "throwing your
    1

vote away," by voting for a third-party candidate.
    1

It's true that no presidential candidate who didn't

represent one of the two major parties always win
    2

an election, but there have been a few elections in

living memory where a third-party candidate would
    3

win a few states. And although most people don't
    3

realize it, there has been one presidential election
    4

1. **A.** NO CHANGE
   B. say, that you're "throwing your vote away," by voting for
   C. say, that you're "throwing your vote away" by voting, for
   D. say that you're "throwing your vote away" by voting for

2. **F.** NO CHANGE
   G. has ever won
   H. was winning
   J. were winning

3. **A.** NO CHANGE
   B. has won
   C. have won
   D. would have won

4. **F.** NO CHANGE
   G. so there
   H. but there
   J. however, there

in American history where a third-party candidate came in second.

    <u>Born and raised on Long Island,</u> Theodore
                5

Roosevelt ascended to the presidency upon the

assassination of President William McKinley in

1901 (only 42 at the time, he remains the youngest

president ever). Despite early concerns about his

youth and <u>temperament, Roosevelt, or "Teddy"</u>
                   6

as the public affectionately nicknamed him—

soon became immensely popular, <u>steered</u> the
                      7

Republican Party in a progressive new direction

that emphasized nature conservation and

opposition to corporate power. After finishing what

had begun as McKinley's term, Roosevelt ran for

reelection in 1904, winning in the biggest landslide

since James Monroe's unopposed candidacy of 1820

<u>and becoming the first "accidental" president to</u>
                   8

<u>win an election in his own right.</u>
          8

5. Which of the following phrases best introduces the paragraph?
  A. NO CHANGE
  B. Although sickly in his youth,
  C. As the sitting vice president,
  D. One of the four presidents depicted on Mount Rushmore,

6. F. NO CHANGE
  G. temperament, Roosevelt or "Teddy,"
  H. temperament, Roosevelt—or "Teddy"
  J. temperament. Roosevelt, or "Teddy"

7. A. NO CHANGE
  B. had steered
  C. to steer
  D. steering

8. If the writer were to delete the underlined portion, the paragraph would primarily lose:
  F. an explanation of what made Teddy Roosevelt so popular.
  G. information vital to the rest of the essay.
  H. a reminder that the United States was still young in Roosevelt's day.
  J. an interesting but unnecessary piece of trivia.

Since this had never <u>occurred before, it raised</u>
9
an interesting question: the custom (though not

yet the law) was for presidents to limit themselves

to two terms, so did the term of McKinley's that

Roosevelt completed count as the first of two, or

could he run again in 1908? Roosevelt settled the

question himself by stepping aside and endorsing

<u>Secretary of War William Howard Taft</u> for the
10
Republican nomination; with the beloved Teddy's

endorsement, Taft won easily. After the election,

Roosevelt left for an extended African safari,

motivated by a desire both to pursue his lifelong

interest in nature and <u>then</u> to stay out of the
11
spotlight and let President Taft be his own man.

But when Teddy returned to find that Taft had

abandoned many of the policies he'd established

and rendered the Republican Party more

conservative, he changed his tune, announcing his

intention to run for a third—or second, depending

on your point of view—term in 1912. But the

party bosses declined to wrest the nomination

9. **A.** NO CHANGE
   B. occurred, before it raised
   C. occurred before, and it raised
   D. occurred before and raised

10. **F.** NO CHANGE
    G. Secretary of War, William Howard Taft
    H. Secretary of War William Howard Taft,
    J. Secretary of War, William Howard Taft,

11. **A.** NO CHANGE
    B. both
    C. not
    D. DELETE the underlined portion.

from the incumbent Taft and hand it to Roosevelt
                                          _____
                                              12

already had his chance in 1908, and so Teddy was
_____
   12

compelled to form his own party, which he dubbed

the Progressive Party. 13

    Lots of people are aware that Teddy Roosevelt ran

for another term on the Bull Moose ticket, but what

many don't know is that he almost won, finishing

second with a respectable 88 electoral votes. 14

    The 1912 victory went to Woodrow Wilson—who,

thanks to the divided Republicans, became only the

second Democrat to win the White House since the

Civil War—and poor Taft became the only major-

party candidate in American history ever to finish

third, winning only two states.

12. **F.** NO CHANGE
    G. Roosevelt has
    H. Roosevelt, who would have
    J. Roosevelt, who had already had

13. Given that all the following statements are
    true, which one, if added here, would most
    effectively conclude this paragraph and
    introduce the following one?
    A. Roosevelt's friend and admirer Robert
        LaFollette would later win Wisconsin in
        1924 on the Progressive ticket.
    B. But it became known by a nickname
        derived from a famous quip of Roosevelt's
        about his physical fitness: the Bull Moose
        Party.
    C. Roosevelt's rhetoric would now become
        more anticorporate than ever before.
    D. Even today, many left-wing thinkers
        prefer the term *progressive* to *liberal*.

14. At this point, the writer is considering adding
    the following true statement:

    Many people also don't realize that the
    famous incident when Roosevelt finished
    his entire speech after surviving an assas-
    sination attempt was in 1912.

    Should the writer make this addition here?

    F. Yes, because it corrects a common
        misconception.
    G. Yes, because the essay should contain as
        many facts about Roosevelt as possible.
    H. No, because the sentence does not
        explain who shot Roosevelt or why.
    J. No, because the information is
        unessential and disrupts the flow of
        the paragraph.

PRACTICE TEST 4

Question 15 asks about the preceding passage as a whole.

15. Suppose the author had intended to write a brief essay about the ways in which the major events in Teddy Roosevelt's life influenced his political beliefs. Would this essay fulfill that goal?
   A. Yes, because it explains Roosevelt's reasons both for leaving the country in 1908 and for running again in 1912.
   B. Yes, because the rift in the Republican Party is explained in sufficient detail.
   C. No, because nothing about Roosevelt's childhood is mentioned in the essay.
   D. No, because the essay does not make explicit connections between Roosevelt's personal life and his policy positions.

PASSAGE II

The Medal on Her

The Congressional Medal of Honor is the United States' highest military <u>decoration, awarded</u> for
16
gallantry above and beyond the call of duty. Its

recipients are <u>respected, which</u> a buck private
17
who wears the Medal of Honor will be saluted by

a general. The decoration is presented personally

by the president, but the requirements for winning

involve such great personal danger that nearly

half the time it is received posthumously. Since its

inception in 1862, the Medal of Honor has been

16. F. NO CHANGE
   G. decoration, and awarded
   H. decoration, it is awarded
   J. decoration. To be awarded

17. A. NO CHANGE
   B. respecting which
   C. respected, in which
   D. so respected that

awarded to 3,448 <u>people, but only</u> one of them was
                              18

a woman.

Mary Edwards <u>Walker, being born</u> on a farm in
                              19

Oswego, New York, in 1832. The youngest of five

daughters, <u>she also had one younger brother,</u> and
                              20

throughout her life would occasionally be arrested

for impersonating a man. After saving money from

working as a schoolteacher, <u>and put herself</u> through
                                        21

Syracuse Medical College, graduating in 1855 as

the only woman in her class. She and her husband

Albert opened a clinic, but <u>because</u> women doctors
                                      22

were an odd thing in those days, business was poor.

A fervent opponent of slavery, Mary offered her

services as a battlefield surgeon to the Union Army

when the Civil War broke out, but because of her

gender was only allowed to practice as a nurse.

She applied her skills at battles like First Bull Run,

18. Which of the following alternatives to
the underlined portion would NOT be
acceptable?
F. people, only
G. people; only
H. people: only
J. people. Only

19. A. NO CHANGE
B. Walker, born
C. Walker was born
D. Walker had been born

20. Given that all the choices are true, which
one provides the most specific and relevant
information?
F. NO CHANGE
G. she became accustomed to wearing male
clothing from performing farmwork,
H. Mary had a rebellious streak,
J. Mary naturally felt as if she had
something to prove,

21. A. NO CHANGE
B. putting herself
C. she put herself
D. DELETE the underlined portion.

22. Which of the following alternatives to
the underlined portion would NOT be
acceptable?
F. as
G. since
H. although
J. seeing as how

PRACTICE TEST 4

Fredericksburg, and <u>Chickamauga, occasionally</u>
                                    23

working as a surgeon when one was needed, despite

her official status. <u>It was Chickamauga that won</u>
                                      24

<u>fame for General George Thomas, known as the</u>
                              24

<u>"Rock of Chickamauga."</u> In September 1863, Mary
                    24

Walker was officially commissioned as the first

female U.S. Army surgeon. After bravely crossing

battle lines to tend to injured civilians, she was

captured by Confederate forces in April 1864,

charged with espionage, and held as a POW for four

months. After the war, she <u>recommended</u> the Medal
                                       25

of Honor by both of the famous generals William T.

Sherman and George Henry Thomas, and received it

from President Andrew Johnson in November 1865.

    Walker then <u>devoted herself to</u> the cause of
                            26

feminism, becoming an early leader in the struggle

of American <u>women for the right to vote and</u>
                               27

<u>authoring</u> two books on the subject. Sadly, she
   27

fell out of favor with other prominent feminists

over differences of opinion on strategy, and was

23. **A.** NO CHANGE
    B. Chickamauga, and occasionally
    C. Chickamauga; occasionally
    D. Chickamauga. Occasionally

24. Given that all the choices are true, which one
    would be the best transition between the first
    and last parts of the paragraph?
    F. NO CHANGE
    G. But as the war dragged on and the Army
    became more desperate, it also became
    less concerned with tradition.
    H. Thankfully, Walker was not at Antietam,
    regarded by most historians as the most
    gruesome battle of the war.
    J. At this time, it was still very much unclear
    whether the South's attempt at secession
    would succeed.

25. **A.** NO CHANGE
    B. received recommendation
    C. had recommendation to
    D. was recommended for

26. Which of the following alternatives to
    the underlined portion would be LEAST
    acceptable?
    F. threw her considerable energies into
    G. portrayed herself as supporting
    H. turned her attention to
    J. adopted

27. **A.** NO CHANGE
    B. women, for the right to vote and authoring
    C. women for the right to vote, and authoring
    D. women, for the right to vote, and
    authoring

increasingly ignored. Mary's story took an even

sadder turn in 1917, when Congress revised the

standards for the Medal of Honor, stipulating that it

could only be won for actions taken in combat. The

government ordered her to return her medal, but

Mary refused, <u>continually wore</u> it until her death in
                        28

1919. The United States finally granted women the

right to vote just one year later. <u>In accordance with</u>
                                                        29

<u>her wishes, Mary Edwards Walker was buried in a</u>
                                                29

<u>man's suit instead of a dress.</u>
                29

28. **F.** NO CHANGE
     G. continued wearing
     H. continued to wear
     J. continuing to wear

29. The writer would like to end the essay with
     a sentence that emphasizes Walker's unique
     place in U.S. military history. Given that
     all the choices are true, which one best
     accomplishes the writer's goal?
     A. NO CHANGE
     B. A 20-cent stamp was issued in Mary
             Edwards Walker's honor in 1982.
     C. The Whitman-Walker clinic in
             Washington, D.C., is named in honor of
             Mary Edwards Walker and the poet Walt
             Whitman.
     D. Mary Edwards Walker's Medal of Honor
             was officially restored by President Carter
             in 1977.

Question 30 asks about the preceding passage as a whole.

30. Suppose the writer's goal had been to write a brief essay concerning the importance of Mary Edwards Walker, with an emphasis on her military significance. Would this essay accomplish that goal?

    F. Yes, because it describes her major accomplishments, with a specific focus on the Medal of Honor.

    G. Yes, because it begins by mentioning that she is the only woman ever to receive the Medal of Honor.

    H. No, because it tells us virtually nothing about Mary Walker's family life.

    J. No, because it explicitly mentions that she never served in actual combat.

PASSAGE III

The following paragraphs may or may not be in the most logical order. Each paragraph is numbered in brackets, and question 45 will ask you to choose where Paragraph 4 should most logically be placed.

Mystery at the Roof of the World

[1]

Many trustworthy people swear, in which they
                       31

saw it with their own eyes. On the other hand, hard

physical evidence, has been notoriously difficult to
             32

come by. Does the mysterious Himalayan creature

known as the Yeti really exist? We may be closer

than ever to an answer.

31. **A.** NO CHANGE
    B. have sworn that
    C. to swear that
    D. who had sworn

32. **F.** NO CHANGE
    G. evidence; has
    H. evidence and has
    J. evidence has

PRACTICE TEST 4

[2]

After sightings, the most common pieces of Yeti

evidence are footprints. But footprints left in the
‾‾‾‾‾‾‾‾‾‾‾
33

snow or mud of such a frigid habitat are largely

unreliable, as they are distorted by repeated cycles

of freezing and thawing. 34 Some of the clearer

tracks have turned out to be hoaxes, others still
‾‾‾‾‾‾‾‾‾‾‾‾‾
35

were determined to have been made by Himalayan

Brown Bears. Still, biologists have examined several

that appear to have been made by a five-toed biped

that is neither a human nor any known species of

ape that exists.
‾‾‾‾‾‾‾‾
36

[3]

In the 1950s, it became known that a few

remote Buddhist monastery's were in possession
‾‾‾‾‾‾‾‾‾
37

33. A. NO CHANGE
B. evidence is
C. evidence was
D. evidence had

34. If the writer were to delete the preceding sentence, the paragraph would primarily lose information that:
F. explains a common obstacle to Yeti research.
G. reveals why law enforcement officials consider footprints useless.
H. suggests a possible method that Yetis developed for concealing their existence.
J. exposes how most of the Yeti hoaxes have been perpetrated.

35. A. NO CHANGE
B. hoaxes others
C. hoaxes, as others
D. hoaxes. Others

36. F. NO CHANGE
G. ever.
H. in the world.
J. DELETE the underlined portion and end the sentence with a period.

37. A. NO CHANGE
B. monasteries
C. monasterie's
D. monasteries'

PRACTICE TEST 4

of relics claimed <u>they were</u> real body parts from
38

Yeti. A supposed Yeti scalp was examined, but was

determined to have been taken from the shoulder

of an antelope. A more bizarre story is that of the

"Pangboche Hand." <u>Supposedly the</u> bones of a
39

Yeti forelimb, it was examined by adventurer Tom

Slick in 1959, but the monks would not let it be

removed for further testing. Slick covertly stole

two finger bones from the hand, replacing them

with human bones, and escaped with them into

India. From there, the bones were smuggled by the

famous actor Jimmy Stewart into London, where

testing suggested that they were fossils from a

Neanderthal. 40 In 1991, however, further testing

with more advanced equipment determined that

they were "near human," but from an unknown

creature.

[4]

The creature, most often described as a tall, hairy

biped, has for centuries been regarded with a mix

of fear and reverence by the Tibetans and Nepalese.

---

38. **F.** NO CHANGE
G. that were
H. to be
J. as literally

39. **A.** NO CHANGE
B. The
C. Supposedly, the
D. Supposedly these

40. At this point, the writer is considering adding
the following true statement:

> Obviously, Jimmy Stewart was just about
> the last person anyone could imagine
> smuggling stolen Yeti bones.

Should the writer make this addition?

F. Yes, because it is vital to know how the
bones got to London without detection.
G. Yes, because it provides the essay with
much-needed comic relief.
H. No, because it fails to explain why no one
would suspect Stewart.
J. No, because it is an unnecessary flourish
that disrupts the flow of the paragraph.

Westerners first became acquainted with him in
41

1832, a British explorer publicized the eyewitness
41

accounts of his guides. The most sensational, and
42

memorable name for the beast was coined in 1921
42

by journalist Henry Newman after interviewing the

members of an Everest expedition: "abominable

snowman." Although still used informally, this term

has fallen out of favor with serious investigators,

as the vast majority of those who lend credence to

Yeti tales believe that it is simply some unclassified

species of ape, rather than a monster or anything

supernatural.

[5]

Though the North American "Bigfoot" is
43

popularly thought to be related to the Yeti, most
43

researchers consider the Yeti's existence much
43

more likely. A 2007 investigation by an American
43

TV program obtained a hair sample that testing

revealed belonged to "an unknown primate." And

just last year, the team of Japanese adventurer

Yoshiteru Takahashi claiming to have seen a Yeti
44

in 2003, ventured into the Himalayas, determined

41. **A.** NO CHANGE
    B. in 1832 which a
    C. in 1832, when a
    D. in 1832 when, a

42. **F.** NO CHANGE
    G. sensational, and memorable name, for
    H. sensational and a memorable name for
    J. sensational—and memorable—name for

43. Given that all of the choices are true, which of the following statements would most effectively introduce the paragraph?
    A. NO CHANGE
    B. Officially, the Yeti is what's known as a "cryptid," or animal that is rumored to exist but is still undiscovered.
    C. The 2004 discovery of extinct hominid *Homo floresiensis* brought renewed interest in the Yeti and exciting new finds.
    D. Supposedly, Nazi troops on maneuvers in Asia shot a Yeti, but any records of this were lost at the end of World War II.

44. **F.** NO CHANGE
    G. Takahashi claimed
    H. Takahashi that claimed
    J. Takahashi, who claims

to capture the furry fellow on film at last. Maybe they will find nothing, or maybe one day soon your favorite show will be interrupted by a special news bulletin announcing "We bring you … the Yeti!"

PASSAGE IV

The Pirate Queen

Legends of female pirate Anne Bonny <u>are still</u>
₄₆
popular today. As piracy was a male-dominated

<u>occupation, to say the least,</u> her story has fascinated
₄₇
generations of feminists and pirate enthusiasts

alike. Everyone wants to believe that her deeds were

as fabulous as our collective imagination makes

them, but the truth is that, although we know

Bonny existed and spent some time on a pirate

ship, <u>we're not sure what became of the ship.</u>
₄₈

Question 45 asks about the preceding passage as a whole.

45. For the sake of logic and coherence, Paragraph 4 should be placed:
   A. where it is now.
   B. after Paragraph 1.
   C. after Paragraph 2.
   D. after Paragraph 5.

46. F. NO CHANGE
   G. is still
   H. to still be
   J. might still be

47. A. NO CHANGE
   B. occupation, (to say the least)
   C. occupation, to say, the least
   D. occupation—to say the least

48. The writer wishes to finish this sentence with a phrase that emphasizes the lack of information about Anne Bonny. Which of the following true statements best achieves that goal?
   F. NO CHANGE
   G. fewer people spend time thinking about her than you may imagine.
   H. accounts of her life rely heavily on speculation.
   J. the number of books that have been written about her is anyone's guess.

The famous pirate queen is said to have been

born Anne Cormac, the daughter of a successful
49

lawyer, around 1700 in Kinsale, in the south of
49

Ireland. Supposedly disowned by her family as a

teenager after stabbing another girl in the gut with

a table knife, the beautifully redhead is said then to
50

have eloped to the Bahamas with a sailor named

James Bonny, after burning down her family's estate
51

in vengeance. But aside from the fact that she arrived

in Nassau, Bahamas, as the wife of James Bonny,

none of the other information including the identity
52

of her family—can be verified, and may all just be

romantic wishful thinking done after the fact.

It is known that, while living in Nassau, she

became romantically involved with the pirate

"Calico Jack" Rackham (there are records of her

having been charged with adultery by Bonny) and

sailed off with him on his ship, the *Revenge*. Their

endeavors were successful over the next few years,
53

49. Which of the following best emphasizes the surprising nature of Anne's supposed origins?
A. NO CHANGE
B. which is a very common name in Ireland,
C. her parents' first and only girl,
D. neither a very large nor a very small baby,

50. F. NO CHANGE
G. redheaded beauty
H. redheaded, beautiful
J. beautiful and redheaded

51. A. NO CHANGE
B. familys
C. families
D. families'

52. F. NO CHANGE
G. information, including
H. information—including
J. information: including

53. The best placement for the underlined portion would be:
A. where it is now.
B. after the word *were*.
C. after the word *Revenge*.
D. after the word *ships* (and before the period).

with the *Revenge* taking several ships. We know that
<u>We know that</u>
54

<u>Anne Bonny's name appeared on lists of wanted</u>
54

<u>pirates, but how prominent she was among the</u>
54

<u>crew is disputable.</u> She apparently participated in
54

the fighting when there <u>was fighting doing</u> (less
55

often than people imagine, as most ships overtaken

by pirates surrendered immediately), but contrary

to popular belief, she never captained her own ship

or commanded her own crew.

The pirates of the *Revenge* were captured in

port by authorities in <u>1720 supposedly</u> while all
56

but Bonny and the one other female in the crew,

Mary Read, were drunk, forcing the two women to

fight alone (likely another embellishment). Every

pirate was hanged aside from Bonny and Read, who

both claimed to be pregnant and were <u>because of</u>
57

<u>this therefore</u> spared. Read subsequently died in
57

prison of a fever, but there is no reliable record of

what became of Anne Bonny. She may have been

executed after delivering her baby—if she really

was pregnant—or she may have convinced the

54. Given that all the choices are true, which one would be the best transition between the first and last parts of the paragraph?
  F. NO CHANGE
  G. In those days, the richest ships tended not to be equipped with heavy gunnery.
  H. Most pirate ships were democracies, and the captain was elected by the crew.
  J. The idea that Anne disguised herself as a man before the crew is actually a myth.

55. **A.** NO CHANGE
  B. a fight broke out
  C. was fighting to be done
  D. were any

56. **F.** NO CHANGE
  G. 1720, supposedly
  H. 1720; supposedly
  J. 1720 although supposedly,

57. **A.** NO CHANGE
  B. for this reason accordingly
  C. because of this reason
  D. therefore

law <u>was</u> a prisoner on Rackham's ship and been
58

released. <u>Another theory holds that she was secretly</u>
59
<u>ransomed by her father and lived to a ripe old</u>
59
<u>age in South Carolina.</u> We'll probably never know
59

any more about the story of Anne Bonny than we

already do, but as with King Arthur, Robin Hood,

or the many other larger-than-life figures whose

legends have little basis in fact, this will surely not

stop people from telling it.

58.
F. NO CHANGE
G. if she were
H. once she was
J. that she had been

59. If the writer were to delete the underlined sentence, the paragraph would primarily lose:
A. hard evidence that Anne Bonny spent considerable time in America.
B. additional evidence of the many varied accounts concerning Anne Bonny.
C. a suggestion that the earlier account of her family in Ireland was true.
D. an argument that people prefer happy endings to depressing ones.

Question 60 asks about the preceding passage as a whole.

60. Suppose the writer had intended to write a brief essay about women who lead lives of crime. Would this essay fulfill that goal?
F. Yes, because it establishes that Bonny definitely broke the law numerous times.
G. Yes, because Anne Bonny is a role model for female thieves the world over.
H. No, because it focuses only on Anne Bonny, and not female criminals in general.
J. No, because it strongly suggests that Bonny was merely the sidekick of a male pirate.

PASSAGE V

Most Historically Inaccurate Movie Ever?

Mel Gibson's *Braveheart* won the Academy

Award for Best Picture of 1995, took in over $200

million at the box office, and is still acclaimed

by action <u>fans to contain</u> some of the best battle
₆₁

scenes ever put on film. But how "historical" is this

historical epic? Fans are often disappointed to learn

<u>that aside from the fact that the</u> major characters
₆₂

really existed, the film is nearly entirely fiction.

Yes, there was a historical William <u>Wallace who</u>
₆₃

<u>led Scottish troops during</u> the First War of Scottish
₆₃

Independence in the late thirteenth century. But

rather than the rustic commoner depicted in

Gibson's film, he was <u>a nobleman a knight and,</u>
₆₄

<u>landowner.</u> It's documented that Wallace entered
₆₄

the war with his murder of an English sheriff in

1297, but the <u>reason for</u> this event is unknown.
₆₅

The movie follows a famous poem 66 in attributing

Wallace's anger to the murder of his wife, but there's

no evidence that this wife even existed, much less

61. **A.** NO CHANGE
 B. fans as containing
 C. fans that it contains
 D. fans, in which contains

62. **F.** NO CHANGE
 G. that aside from the fact, that the
 H. that, aside from the fact that the
 J. that aside from the fact that, the

63. **A.** NO CHANGE
 B. Wallace, who led Scottish troops, during
 C. Wallace who led Scottish troops, during
 D. Wallace, and who led Scottish troops during

64. **F.** NO CHANGE
 G. a nobleman; a knight and landowner.
 H. a nobleman—a knight, and landowner.
 J. a nobleman: a knight and landowner.

65. Which of the following alternatives to the underlined portion would NOT be acceptable?
 A. explanation for
 B. cause of
 C. impetus for
 D. story to

66. At this point, the writer is considering adding the following true parenthetical information:

   (composed 200 years later)

Should the writer make this addition?

 F. Yes, because it suggests that the account is probably inaccurate.
 G. Yes, because it suggests that the poem is probably written in modern English.
 H. No, because it neglects to mention the identity of the poet.
 J. No, because the date that a work of literature was composed never matters.

executed by the English. Older accounts claim that
67

Wallace had already been an outlaw for years after

killing five English soldiers who tried to steal his catch

after a fishing trip; still others allege that the trouble
68

started when a teenage Wallace killed an English

noble's son who bullied him at boarding school.

    Clearly, the writers chose the tales about Wallace

best suited to the hero of a blockbuster film: a

formerly peaceful farmer avenging the death of his

one true love is a more sympathetic underdog than
69

a private-school kid who psychotically overreacts to

a bit of teasing. The same impulse led the writers to

take further liberties with their depiction not only

of Wallace, but the Scots generally are presented
70

as far too primitive in relation to the English. The

facepaint Wallace wears into battle was actually

characteristic of the Picts were a tribe that lived in
71

Scotland over a thousand years earlier and battled

the Romans. By Wallace's time, the Scots were
72

fighting in chain-mail and armor, and would have
72

been visually indistinguishable from the English.

67. A. NO CHANGE
    B. was executed
    C. being executed
    D. to be executed

68. Which of the following alternatives to
    the underlined portion would NOT be
    acceptable?
    F. trip; others
    G. trip, and still others
    H. trip; while others
    J. trip, while still others

69. Which of the following alternatives to
    the underlined portion would be LEAST
    acceptable?
    A. has a
    B. works as a
    C. makes for a
    D. would be seen as a

70. F. NO CHANGE
    G. Wallace and the Scots generally are
    H. Wallace; the Scots generally, who are
    J. Wallace, but of the Scots generally, who
       are

71. A. NO CHANGE
    B. Picts, having been a
    C. Picts, and also a
    D. Picts, a

72. Which of the following alternatives to
    the underlined portion would be LEAST
    acceptable?
    F. fought
    G. had fought
    H. would have fought
    J. did their fighting

The stereotypical plaids on <u>*Braveheart*'s Scots'</u>,

73

however, are anachronistic in a different way: kilts

were not worn in battle until 400 years *later*.

The script plays fast and loose with people too:

King Edward outlived Wallace by years, Princess

Isabella was a young girl at the time and still in

France, and Andrew de Moray, who was an equally

important Scottish commander who fought beside

Wallace, is omitted entirely. But *Braveheart*'s most

troubling inaccuracy by far <u>it is</u> depiction of Robert

74

the Bruce as a coward who betrays Wallace to the

English. Not only did the historical Bruce never

<u>betray</u> Wallace, but he barely knew him, and was far

75

more instrumental in the eventual Scottish victory.

In fact, the nickname "Braveheart" itself was

historically not used for William Wallace at all, but

rather for Robert the Bruce!

73. **A.** NO CHANGE
B. *Bravehearts* Scots,
C. *Braveheart's* Scots,
D. *Bravehearts* Scots',

74. **F.** NO CHANGE
G. it is the
H. is its
J. is it's

75. **A.** NO CHANGE
B. betrayed
C. did betray
D. would have betrayed

STOP

If there is still time remaining, you may review your answers.

MATHEMATICS TEST

Time: 60 Minutes—60 Questions

> **Directions:** Solve each problem, choose the correct answer, and then fill in the corresponding oval on your answer sheet.
>
> Do not linger over problems that take too much time. Solve as many as you can; then return to the others in the time you have left for this test.
>
> You are permitted to use a calculator on this test. You may use your calculator for any problems you choose, but some of the problems may best be done without using a calculator.
>
> Note: Unless otherwise stated, all of the following should be assumed.
>
> 1. Illustrative figures are NOT necessarily drawn to scale.
> 2. Geometric figures lie in a plane.
> 3. The word *line* indicates a straight line.
> 4. The word *average* indicates arithmetic mean.

DO YOUR FIGURING HERE

1. A rectangle is four times as long as it is wide. If the width of the rectangle is 4.5 cm, what is the rectangle's area, in square centimeters?

    A. 17
    B. 18
    C. 45
    D. 72
    E. 81

2. A bubble gum machine has 120 red, blue, yellow, and green gumballs in it. If 30 are yellow, 32 are red, and 28 are green, what is the probability that the next gumball out of the machine is NOT blue?

    F. $\dfrac{1}{4}$

    G. $\dfrac{3}{4}$

    H. 25%
    J. 1:4
    K. 2:1

3. Which of the following is equivalent to
   4×10^{-5}?

   A. −2,000,000
   B. −400,000
   C. 0.00002
   D. 0.00004
   E. 0.000004

4. Which of the following is equivalent to $\sqrt{96}$?

   F. $4\sqrt{6}$
   G. $6\sqrt{4}$
   H. $8\sqrt{6}$
   J. $8\sqrt{12}$
   K. $16\sqrt{6}$

5. What is the perimeter of a square with an
   area of 49?

   A. 7
   B. 14
   C. 20
   D. 28
   E. 49

6. What is the slope of any line perpendicular
   to the line $5x - 4y = -12$ in the standard (x, y)
   coordinate plane?

   F. −4
   G. $-\dfrac{5}{4}$
   H. $-\dfrac{4}{5}$
   J. $\dfrac{4}{5}$
   K. $\dfrac{5}{4}$

7. Given △*XYZ* with the angle measures shown below, and that point *P* lies on *XZ*, what is m∠*XYZ*?

DO YOUR FIGURING HERE

A. 25°
B. 65°
C. 75°
D. 85°
E. 140°

8. What is the area of a circle with a radius of 6?

F. 8π
G. 12π
H. 16π
J. 32π
K. 36π

9. Bette's 2 pieces of bacon and 1 egg cost $2.10. Jed's 3 pieces of bacon and 2 eggs cost $3.45. How much does 1 egg cost?

A. 45 cents
B. 50 cents
C. 60 cents
D. 70 cents
E. 75 cents

10. If ∠*Y* is the vertex of isosceles △*XYZ* (shown below), what is the value of *a*?

F. 16°
G. 17°
H. 34°
J. 36°
K. 39°

11. A function f is defined by $f(x) = -3x^2 + 4x$. What is the value of $f(4)$?

   A. -40

   B. -32

   C. 32

   D. 52

   E. 136

DO YOUR FIGURING HERE

12. In the figure below, $\overline{MQ}$ intersects $\overline{PS}$ at point R, m$\angle TRS = 25°$, and $\angle QRT$ is a right angle. What is the measure of $\angle MRP$?

   F. $75°$

   G. $90°$

   H. $105°$

   J. $115°$

   K. $165°$

13. In $\triangle ABC$ below, what is $\tan\angle A$?

   A. $\dfrac{5}{13}$

   B. $\dfrac{5}{12}$

   C. $\dfrac{12}{13}$

   D. $\dfrac{12}{5}$

   E. $\dfrac{13}{5}$

14. Jenna wants to serve a large pot of soup to 25 people by 1:15 P.M. If it takes her 7 minutes to assemble the ingredients, 20 minutes to cut up the vegetables, and $2\frac{1}{2}$ hours to cook the soup on the stove, what is the latest time that Jenna could begin her meal preparation?

    F. 9:53 A.M.
    G. 9:58 A.M.
    H. 10:18 A.M.
    J. 10:21 A.M.
    K. 10:28 A.M.

15. In the standard (x, y) coordinate plane, if $\overline{AB}$ has endpoint A at $(-2, 4)$ and midpoint M at $(3, 9)$, where is endpoint B located?

    A. $(0.5, 6.5)$
    B. $(6.5, 0.5)$
    C. $(7, 1)$
    D. $(8, 14)$
    E. $(14, 8)$

16. Which of the following, if any, is equivalent to the inequality $|x| + 4 < 7$?

    F. $x < -3$ and $x > 3$
    G. $x < -3$ or $x > 3$
    H. $-3 < x < 3$
    J. $-3 > x$ and $3 < x$
    K. None of these

17. What is the sum of the interior angles of pentagon ⬠*LMNPR*?

    DO YOUR FIGURING HERE

    A. 180°
    B. 540°
    C. 600°
    D. 720°
    E. 900°

18. Which of the following values of n makes the statement $n^{1/2} = 4$ true?

    F. 16
    G. 8
    H. 4
    J. 2
    K. $\frac{1}{8}$

DO YOUR FIGURING HERE

Use the following information to answer questions 19–22.

A web site publishes nutritional information for many popular restaurant chains to promote consumer education. The 11 values listed below represent the number of fat calories in a large order of french fries from well-known fast-food restaurant chains.

228, 188, 219, 171, 258, 161, 190, 216, 188, 250, 158

19. Which of the following graphs most accurately represents the data on the number of fat calories in a large order of french fries at the 11 fast-food restaurants?

A.

D.

B.

E.

C.

20. Based on the data listed, what is the median number of fat calories in a large order of french fries at these 11 restaurants?

F. 161

G. 188

H. 190

J. 202

K. 203

21. Of the 11 fast-food restaurants, 258 is the highest number of fat calories in a large order of french fries, which represents 46% of the total number of calories. Which of the following values is closest to the total number of calories in this large order of french fries?

A. 119

B. 304

C. 377

D. 516

E. 560

22. The web site collects data from 2 additional restaurant chains and includes the new data in the list. The number of fat calories in a large order of french fries at each of the 2 additional restaurants is designated by x and y, respectively. Which of the following expressions gives the average of this larger list of values?

F. $\dfrac{2{,}039 + x + y}{12}$

G. $\dfrac{2{,}039 + x + y}{13}$

H. $\dfrac{2{,}227 + x + y}{11}$

J. $\dfrac{2{,}227 + x + y}{11 + x + y}$

K. $\dfrac{2{,}227 + x + y}{13}$

23. If a and b can be any two real numbers such that $b < -6$ and $3a - b = 21$, which of the following is a solution set for a?

A. $a \le 9$

B. $a \le 5$

C. $a < 5$

D. $a \ge 9$

E. $a \ge -5$

24. Darcy used a 12-m piece of rope to tie her dog to a tree while she mowed her front yard. The dog could only walk in a semicircle because the tree was located directly next to the house (see diagram below). Assuming 3.14 for π, how much area, in square meters, could the dog cover?

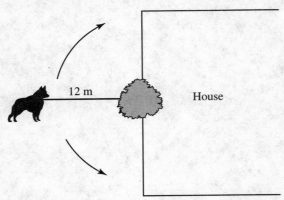

12 m   House

F. 57

G. 75

H. 113

J. 226

K. 452

25. For $3x \ne 2y$, the polynomial expression $\dfrac{24x^2 - 7xy - 6y^2}{3x - 2y}$ is equivalent to which of the following?

A. $2x - 3y$

B. $2x - 12y$

C. $3x - 2y$

D. $8x - 3y$

E. $8x + 3y$

PRACTICE TEST 4

26. Jose recently opened a new business. He projects that his profit will be $25,000 for the first year and will increase by 7% over the next 8 years. Which of the following best describes the sequence formed by his annual profits?

   F. Geometric with a common ratio of 0.07

   G. Geometric with a common ratio of 1.07

   H. Geometric with a common ratio of 1.7

   J. Arithmetic with a common difference of 25.07

   K. Arithmetic with a common difference of 25,000

27. In the figure below, M is the midpoint of $\overline{NP}$ and $\triangle LMP$ is equilateral. $\triangle LMN$ is isosceles with vertex angle M. If $\overline{NP} = 8$, what is the length of $\overline{LN}$?

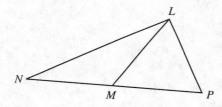

   A. 4

   B. $4\sqrt{2}$

   C. $4\sqrt{3}$

   D. 8

   E. $8\sqrt{3}$

DO YOUR FIGURING HERE

PRACTICE TEST 4

28. The equation $y = \dfrac{x+5}{x^2-9}$ is graphed in the standard (x, y) coordinate plane above. No point on the graph has which of the following x-coordinates?

F. −5

G. −3

H. −1

J. 0

K. 1

29. The formula for converting Celsius temperature to Fahrenheit temperature is $F = \dfrac{9}{5}C + 32$. If the current temperature is 122° Fahrenheit, what is the temperature in Celsius?

A. 50°

B. 59.7°

C. 65.5°

D. 162°

E. 277.2°

2 △ △ △ △ △ △ △ △ 2

30. If a ratio is selected at random from the set $\left\{\dfrac{1}{3},\dfrac{3}{5},\dfrac{3}{7},\dfrac{5}{7},\dfrac{5}{9}\right\}$, what is the probability that the ratio is greater than $\dfrac{1}{2}$?

F. $\dfrac{1}{5}$

G. $\dfrac{2}{5}$

H. $\dfrac{3}{5}$

J. $\dfrac{2}{3}$

K. $\dfrac{4}{5}$

31. Gertrude's Diner offers three different types of salads, two soups, four vegetable sides, five main dishes, and three desserts. If a customer can choose a salad **OR** a soup along with one main dish, one vegetable side, and one dessert, how many different meal combinations are possible?

A.   17
B.   19
C.   300
D.   360
E. 21,600

32. A military tank is 228 meters due north of its target. The commander's jeep is due west of the tank and 247 meters north/northwest of its target. Which of the following gives the distance, in meters, between the tank and the jeep?

F.   19
G.   95
H.   190
J.   475
K. 9,025

DO YOUR FIGURING HERE

PRACTICE TEST 4

PRACTICE TEST 4   345

33. Which of the following expresses the number of meters an athlete must travel in a 6-lap race around a circular track with a diameter of X meters?

A. $6\pi X^2$

B. $3\pi X^2$

C. $\dfrac{3}{2}\pi X^2$

D. $6\pi X$

E. $3\pi X$

DO YOUR FIGURING HERE

34. For all real numbers m and n such that the product of m and 4 is n, which of the following expressions represents the sum of m and 4 in terms of n?

F. $n + 4$

G. $4n + 4$

H. $4(n + 4)$

J. $\dfrac{n+4}{4}$

K. $\dfrac{n}{4} + 4$

35. As shown below, rectangle $KLMN$ is divided into 3 large squares (each labeled R) that measure x centimeters on a side, 12 small squares (each labeled S) that measure y centimeters on a side, and 13 rectangles (each labeled P). What is the total area, in square centimeters, of rectangle $KLMN$?

K							L
R	R	R	P	P	P	P
P	P	P	S	S	S	S
P	P	P	S	S	S	S
P	P	P	S	S	S	S
N							M

A. $3x + 4xy + 9yx + 12y$

B. $12x + 4xy + 9yx + 3y$

C. $3x^2 + 13xy + 12y^2$

D. $12x^2 + 13xy + 3y^2$

E. $3x^3 + 13xy + 12y^{12}$

36. For some real number D, the graph of the line $y = (D - 3)x + 7$ in the standard (x, y) coordinate plane passes through the point $(-5, 2)$. What is the slope of this line?

   F. −3

   G. −2

   H. 0

   J. 1

   K. 4

37. When graphed in the standard (x, y) coordinate plane, the lines $x = -6$ and $y = 2x - 4$ intersect at what point?

   A. (−16, −6)

   B. (−6, −16)

   C. (−6, 8)

   D. (−6, 16)

   E. (8, −6)

> Use the following information to answer questions 38-40.

Trapezoid $QRST$ is graphed in the standard (x, y) coordinate plane below.

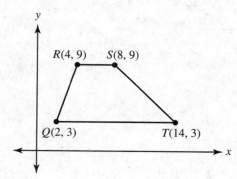

38. What is the slope of $\overline{ST}$?

   F. −3

   G. −1

   H. 0

   J. 1

   K. 3

39. When *QRST* is reflected over the *x*-axis to create *Q′R′S′T′*, what are the coordinates of *R′*?

A. (−4, 9)

B. (−4, −9)

C. (4, −9)

D. (−9, 4)

E. (9, −4)

40. What is the area of *QRST*, in square units?

F. 48

G. 54

H. 66

J. 72

K. 96

41. Given that $c \begin{bmatrix} 2 & 5 \\ 1 & 3 \end{bmatrix} = \begin{bmatrix} r & 35 \\ s & t \end{bmatrix}$ for some real number *c*, what is *r* + *t*?

A. 5

B. 7

C. $\frac{35}{2}$

D. 25

E. 35

42. In △*LMP*, shown below, $\overline{LN}$ is the perpendicular bisector of $\overline{PM}$, cos∠*LMP* = 0.4, and $\overline{PM}$ = 24 inches. How many inches long is $\overline{LM}$?

F. 9.6

G. 30

H. 40

J. 48

K. 60

43. A music instructor charges $30 per lesson, plus an additional fee for violin rental. The charge for the violin varies directly with the square root of the time the violin is used. If a lesson plus 25 minutes of violin rental costs $65, how much would it cost for a lesson plus 81 minutes of violin rental?

A. $93
B. $105
C. $111
D. $141
E. $146

DO YOUR FIGURING HERE

44. The figure below shows a small square inside of a larger square. The smaller square has sides 3 inches long, and the area of the shaded region is 16 square inches. What is the length, in inches, of one side of the larger square?

F. 4
G. $\sqrt{19}$
H. 5
J. $\sqrt{28}$
K. 25

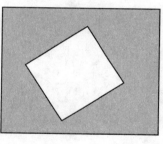

45. The quadrants of the standard (x, y) coordinate plane are labeled in the figure below. For each value of θ, let $x = \cos \theta$ and $y = \sin \theta$. Whenever $(\sin \theta)\left(\dfrac{1}{\cos \theta}\right) < 0$, the points (x, y) on the unit circle can lie in which of the following quadrants?

- **A.** III only
- **B.** IV only
- **C.** I and III only
- **D.** II and III only
- **E.** II and IV only

46. For $i^2 = -1$, $(3 - i)^2 = ?$
- **F.** 16
- **G.** $2i$
- **H.** $4i$
- **J.** $10 - 6i$
- **K.** $8 - 6i$

47. The volume of a sphere is determined by the equation $V = \dfrac{4}{3}\pi r^3$, where r is the radius of the sphere. In a given model of the solar system, all of the planets are perfect spheres. If the radius of Earth is exactly 2 times greater than the radius of Mars, how many times the volume of Mars is the volume of Earth?
- **A.** 16
- **B.** 8
- **C.** 6
- **D.** 4
- **E.** 2

48. Which of the following is equivalent to $\sqrt{16r^6}$?

F. $4r^3$

G. $4r^4$

H. $8r^3$

J. $8r^4$

K. $32r^{12}$

49. If 2 is a solution of the equation $x^2 + kx + 12 = 0$, what does k equal?

A. -12

B. -8

C. -2

D. 6

E. 8

50. In the standard (x, y) coordinate plane, the center of the circle shown below lies on the y-axis at $y = 3$. If the circle is also tangent to the x-axis, what is the equation of the circle?

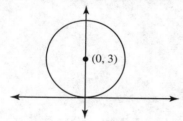

F. $x^2 + (y-3)^2 = 6$

G. $x^2 + (y-3)^2 = 9$

H. $x^2 + (y+3)^2 = 9$

J. $(x-3)^2 + y^2 = 6$

K. $(x+3)^2 + y^2 = 9$

51. Which of the following equations summarizes the data listed below?

x	−2	−1	0	1	2
y	−8	−5	−2	1	4

A. $y = -2x - 2$

B. $y = 2x - 4$

C. $y = 2x + 3$

D. $y = 3x - 2$

E. $y = 3x + 2$

52. The law of sines states that for any triangle, the ratio between the sine of an angle and the length of the side opposite that angle is the same for all of the interior angles in the triangle. In $\triangle XYZ$ shown below, $\overline{ZX} = 22$ cm, $\angle Z = 32°$, and $\angle Y = 44°$. What is the length of $\overline{ZY}$?

F. $\dfrac{22(\sin 104°)}{\sin 32°}$

G. $\dfrac{\sin 32°(\sin 104°)}{\sin 44°}$

H. $\dfrac{22(\sin 32°)}{\sin 104°}$

J. $\dfrac{22(\sin 104°)}{\sin 44°}$

K. $\dfrac{22(\sin 44°)}{\sin 104°}$

53. Which of the following is the graph of the equation $3x - 2y = 6$?

A.

B.

C.

D.

E.

54. For $\sqrt{(3)(7)} \cdot \sqrt{(m)(n)} \cdot \sqrt{(7)(5)}$ to be an integer, with m and n representing positive prime numbers, the sum of $m + n$ must equal which of the following?

F. 8
G. 10
H. 12
J. 15
K. 21

55. Cam is going into business selling umbrellas. He pays $25,000 for a building and machinery, and each umbrella costs $4.00 to manufacture. If Cam sells x umbrellas for $6.50 each, which of the following equations best represents his net profit in dollars?

A. $10.50x - 25,000$
B. $6.50x - 25,000$
C. $4.00x + 25,000$
D. $4.00x - 25,000$
E. $2.50x - 25,000$

56. In circle O shown below, chords $\overline{LN}$ and $\overline{MP}$ intersect at O. The measure of $\overparen{PN} = 100°$. Which of the following statements is NOT true?

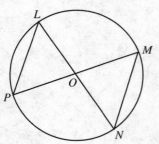

F. $m\angle PLN = 50°$
G. $m\angle POL = 80°$
H. $\angle PON \cong \angle NOM$
J. $\angle POL \cong \angle NOM$
K. $\overline{LP} \cong \overline{MN}$

57. For all real numbers m and n, when is the equation $|m - n| = |m + n|$ true?

   A. Never

   B. Always

   C. Only when $m = n$

   D. Only when $m = 0$ and $n = 0$

   E. Only when $m = 0$ or $n = 0$

58. What is the value of $\log_4 16$?

   F. 2

   G. 4

   H. 12

   J. 20

   K. 64

59. At a school fundraiser, Tanya will play a game in which she spins a spinner that is on a circle with 8 equal sections as shown in the diagram. Three of the sections are red, four are blue, and one is orange. Tanya gets 5 tokens if the spinner stops on the orange section, 3 tokens if it stops on a red section, and 1 token if it stops on a blue section. What is the expected value of x if x is the random variable that represents the number of tokens awarded on any spin?

   A. 1

   B. 2.25

   C. 3

   D. 3.25

   E. 4.25

60. When $0° < x < 90°$, which of the following is NOT equal to tan x?

F. $\dfrac{\sin x}{\cos x}$

G. $(\sin^2 x + \cos^2 x)(\tan x)$

H. $\dfrac{\sec x}{\csc x}$

J. $\dfrac{(\sin^2 x + \cos^2 x)}{\cot x}$

K. $\dfrac{\cos x}{\sin x}$

STOP

If there is still time remaining, you may review your answers.

READING TEST

Time: 35 Minutes—40 Questions

Directions: There are four passages in this test. Each passage is followed by several questions. After reading a passage, choose the best answer to each question and fill in the corresponding oval on your answer sheet. You may refer to the passages as often as necessary.

PASSAGE 1—LITERARY NARRATIVE

Title: *The Stories of Eva Luna*
Author/Editor: Isabel Allende, translated from the Spanish by Margaret Sayers Peden
ISBN: 9780689121029 / 9780684873596 / 9780743217187
Selection: pp. 9–12 of "Two Words"—as submitted.

She went by the name of Belisa Crepusculario, not because she had been baptized with that name or given it by her mother, but because
(5) she herself had searched until she found the poetry of "beauty" and "twilight" and cloaked herself in it. She made her living selling words. She journeyed through the country from the high cold mountains to the burning coasts,
(10) stopping at fairs and in markets where she set up four poles covered by a canvas awning under which she took refuge from the sun and rain to minister to her customers. She did not have to peddle her merchandise because from having
wandered far and near, everyone knew who
(15) she was. Some people waited for her from one year to the next, and when she appeared in the village with her bundle beneath her arm, they would form a line in front of her stall. Her prices were fair. For five centavos she delivered verses
(20) from memory, for seven she improved the quality of dreams, for nine she wrote love letters, for twelve she invented insults for irreconcilable enemies. She also sold stories, not fantasies but long, true stories she recited at one telling,
(25) never skipping a word.

This is how she carried news from one town to another. People paid her to add a line or two: our son was born, so-and-so died, our children got married, the crops burned in the field. Wherever
(30) she went a small crowd gathered around to listen as she began to speak. They learned about each others' doings, about distant relatives, about what was going on in the civil war. To anyone who paid her fifty centavos in trade, she gave the
(35) gift of a secret word to drive away melancholy. It was not the same word for everyone, naturally, because that would have been collective deceit. Each person received his or her own word, with the assurance that no one else would use it that
(40) way in this universe or Beyond.

Belisa Crepusculario had been born into a family so poor they did not even have names to give their children. She came into the world and grew up in an inhospitable land where some
(45) years the rains became avalanches of water that bore everything away before them and others when not a drop fell from the sky and the sun swelled to fill the horizon and the world became a desert. Until she was twelve, Belisa had no oc-
(50) cupation or virtue other than having withstood hunger and the exhaustion of centuries. During one interminable drought, it fell to her to bury four younger brothers and sisters; when she realized that her turn was next, she decided
(55) to set out across the plains in the direction of the sea, in hopes that she might trick death along the way. The land was eroded, split with deep cracks, strewn with rocks, fossils of trees and thorny bushes, and skeletons of animals
(60) bleached by the sun.

From time to time she ran into families who, like her, were heading south, following the mirage of water. Some had begun their march carrying

their belongings on their back or in small carts, but
(65) they could barely move their own bones, and after
a while they had to abandon their possessions.
They dragged themselves along painfully, their
skin turned to lizard hide and their eyes burned
by the reverberating glare. Belisa greeted them
(70) with a wave as she passed, but she did not stop,
because she had no strength to waste in acts of
compassion. Many people fell by the wayside,
but she was so stubborn that she survived to
cross through that hell and at long last reach
(75) the first trickles of water, fine, almost invisible
threads that fed spindly vegetation and farther
down widened into small streams and marshes.

Belisa Crepusculario saved her life and in
the process accidentally discovered writing. In
(80) a village near the coast, the wind blew a page of
newspaper at her feet. She picked up the brittle
yellow paper and stood a long while looking at it,
unable to determine its purpose, until curiosity
overcame her shyness. She walked over to a man
(85) who was washing his horse in the muddy pool
where she had quenched her thirst.

"What is this?" she asked.

"The sports page of the newspaper," the man
replied, concealing his surprise at her ignorance.
(90) The answer astounded the girl, but she did
not want to seem rude, so she merely inquired
about the significance of the fly tracks scattered
across the page. "Those are words, child. Here it
says that Fulgencio Barba knocked out El Negro
(95) Tizano in the third round."

That was the day Belisa Crepusculario found
out that words make their way in the world
without a master, and that anyone with a little
cleverness can appropriate them and do business
(100) with them. From that moment on, she worked at
that profession, and was never tempted by any
other. At the beginning, she offered her merchandise unaware that words can be written outside
of newspapers. When she learned otherwise,
(105) she calculated the infinite possibilities of her
trade and with her savings paid a priest twenty
pesos to teach her to read and write; with her

three remaining coins she bought a dictionary.
She poured over it from *A* to *Z* and then threw
(110) it into the sea, because it was not her intention
to defraud her customers with packaged words.

1. The main character of the passage can best
   be described as a (an):
   A. shrewd businesswoman who becomes
      wealthy through her skills.
   B. strong young woman who inadvertently
      discovers her destiny.
   C. fearless explorer who sets off in search of
      new lands and experiences.
   D. investigative journalist driven to right
      injustices.

2. The main purpose of the fourth paragraph
   (lines 61–77) is to:
   F. establish that Belisa is primarily
      concerned about herself, rather than
      others.
   G. demonstrate that Belisa is smarter
      than most of the other people from her
      hometown.
   H. acquaint the reader with the hardships
      Belisa saw others endure as she sought to
      save herself.
   J. establish that the story takes place in the
      distant past, rather than the present day.

3. The main purpose of the last paragraph (lines
   96–111) is to:
   A. establish Belisa's originality in a fanciful
      manner.
   B. contrast Belisa's approach to helping
      people with that of organized religion.
   C. imply that early in her career Belisa was
      not very sensible about money.
   D. demonstrate that Belisa has a very
      powerful memory.

4. In the passage, the exchange in lines 87–95 is most likely included to indicate that:
   F. senseless violence is celebrated in Belisa's culture.
   G. people are dismissive of Belisa because of her gender and age.
   H. Belisa does not see in the same way that normal people do.
   J. Belisa recognized the importance of words in the real world.

5. Information in the passage indicates that Belisa's dream is to provide people with something:
   A. useful and honest.
   B. valuable but ephemeral.
   C. secret and exciting.
   D. false but comforting.

6. In the context of the passage, the statement in lines 1–6 most nearly means that:
   F. the name Belisa goes by is not her real one.
   G. Belisa never knew her real mother.
   H. Belisa picked her own name based on words she liked.
   J. Belisa's name has something to do with the fact that her family was not religious.

7. The passage mentions Belisa performing all of the following tasks EXCEPT:
   A. carrying news.
   B. exposing lies.
   C. preventing sadness.
   D. reciting poetry.

8. As it is used in line 52, the word *interminable* most nearly means:
   F. very short.
   G. unexpected.
   H. illusory.
   J. very long.

9. The passage makes clear that Belisa began working with words in order to:
   A. help her people.
   B. earn an income.
   C. discover her identity.
   D. avenge her family.

10. As it is used in line 76, the word *spindly* most nearly means:
    F. dead.
    G. thorny.
    H. very thin.
    J. poisonous.

PASSAGE II—SOCIAL SCIENCE

Passage A is adapted from "Meditation XVII" by John Donne (1624). Passage B is adapted from "Ubuntu" by Kevin Hurt, from the blog *Edumacation: Lessons in Teaching and Coaching* (2010).

Passage A by John Donne

Perchance he for whom this bell tolls may be so ill, as that he knows not it tolls for him; and perchance I may think myself so much better than I am, as that they who are about me, and
(5) see my state, may have caused it to toll for me, and I know not that.

All mankind is of one author, and is one volume; when one man dies, one chapter is not torn out of the book, but translated into a
(10) better language; and every chapter must be so translated; God employs several translators; some pieces are translated by age, some by sickness, some by war, some by justice; but God's hand is in every translation, and his hand shall bind
(15) up all our scattered leaves again for that library where every book shall lie open to one another.

Who casts not up his eye to the sun when it rises? Who takes off his eye from a comet when that breaks out? Who bends not his ear to any
(20) bell which upon any occasion rings? Who can remove it from that bell which is passing a piece of himself out of this world?

No man is an island, entire of itself; every man is a piece of the continent, a part of the main. If (25) a clod be washed away by the sea, Europe is the less, as well as if a promontory were, as well as if a manor of thy friend's or of thine own were: any man's death diminishes me, because I am involved in mankind, and therefore never send (30) to know for whom the bells tolls; it tolls for thee.

Tribulation is treasure in the nature of it, but it is not current money in the use of it, except we get nearer and nearer our home, heaven, by it. Another man may be sick too, and sick to (35) death, and this affliction may lie in his bowels, as gold in a mine, and be of no use to him; but this bell, that tells me of his affliction, digs out and applies that gold to me: if by this consideration of another's danger I take mine own into (40) contemplation, and so secure myself, by making my recourse to my God, who is our only security.

Passage B by Kevin Hurt

A Zulu maxim provides perhaps the simplest definition of Ubuntu: *umuntu ngumuntu ngabantu*, which means "a person is a person through other (45) persons." It is a philosophical belief that being human means recognizing and respecting the humanity of others. As Archbishop Desmond Tutu said, "It is the essence of being human. It speaks of the fact that my humanity is caught (50) up and is inextricably bound up in yours. I am human because I belong."

A person with Ubuntu is welcoming, hospitable, warm and generous, willing to share. Such people are open and available to others, (55) willing to be vulnerable, affirming of others, do not feel threatened that others are able and good, for they have a proper self-assurance that comes from knowing that they belong in a greater whole. They know that they are dimin- (60) ished when others are humiliated, diminished when others are oppressed, diminished when others are treated as if they were less than who they are. When we truly believe in the concept of Ubuntu, we realize that when someone else (65) is degraded, then we ourselves are degraded. This leads us to a point where we are enacting justice on behalf of others.

Ubuntu does not mean that people should not enrich themselves. The question is, are you (70) going to do so in order to enable the community around you to be able to improve? Ubuntu puts our own personal gains in a larger context – the context of something greater than ourselves, some transcendent cause. Our own personal (75) gains, whether mental gains (such as education) or physical gains (such as money), inevitably benefit the greater community and make it a better place for everyone.

Respecting our humanity and the humanity (80) of others should always be the primary motive for any action. Wealth, while useful for advancing the good of the community, should never be valued above preserving the humanity of another person. For example, even something as simple (85) as an insult degrades the humanity of someone else, and given the opportunity to make money by insulting someone, we should always say no to the money, because that person's dignity is more valuable to us.

Questions 11–14 ask about Passage A.

11. The passage opens by repeatedly mentioning a bell because:
    A. a bell has been ringing in the author's town, and he is trying to figure out why.
    B. the bell represents some nameless deed about which the author feels guilty.
    C. the bell represents each human being's eventual and unknowable fate.
    D. the bell is ringing to observe the death of a specific person who was close to the author.

12. As it is used in line 31, the word *tribulation* most nearly means:
   F. affliction.
   G. nature.
   H. wealth.
   J. ringing.

13. The passage references "this bell, that tells me of his affliction" (line 37) to suggest that:
   A. people should be grateful that trouble has befallen someone else and spared them.
   B. an opportunity to show sympathy to another should be regarded as a treasure.
   C. the author is speculating whether he may be about to inherit money.
   D. in small communities, everyone is too concerned with everyone else's business.

14. The fourth paragraph (lines 23–30) mentions Europe in order to:
   F. compare it to the community of mankind.
   G. suggest that concepts of fellowship are more advanced there than in other regions.
   H. warn that it will be in trouble if the author's ideas are not taken seriously.
   J. suggest that there is less concern for morality there than in other parts of the world.

Questions 15–17 ask about Passage B.

15. The author's attitude towards the Ubuntu philosophy is partially based on the opinion that:
   A. it will help people to become educated and therefore successful in their careers.
   B. it is the best method of eliminating prejudice in the author's particular culture.
   C. it can prevent any one person from becoming wealthy to a degree that is unfair.
   D. it spiritually enriches the practitioner, as well as encouraging good to others.

16. As it is used in line 42, the word *maxim* most nearly means:
   F. translation.
   G. statute.
   H. proverb.
   J. warning.

17. The quotation from Desmond Tutu most nearly suggests that:
   A. the Zulu concept of Ubuntu is quite ancient.
   B. Ubuntu is equally applicable to all cultures.
   C. cultures that respect their ancestors are more moral than those that do not.
   D. wise people seek out the advice of others before making important decisions.

Questions 18–20 ask about both passages.

18. One of the most obvious differences between the two passages is that:
   F. Passage A explicitly ties its thesis to religion, whereas Passage B does not.
   G. Passage A uses no quotations, whereas Passage B quotes multiple famous people.
   H. Passage B does not literally discuss making money, whereas Passage A does so.
   J. One of the passages analyzes a specific part of the world, and the other the whole world.

19. Which of the following methods of support do both authors use to convey their ideas?
   A. Rhetorical questions
   B. Allusions to great literature
   C. Appraisals of the essence of humanity
   D. Long sarcastic metaphors

20. Which of the following famous expressions is most nearly in line with the central thesis of *both* passages?

   F. "To thine own self be true."

   G. "A thing of beauty is a joy forever."

   H. "Fools rush in where angels fear to tread."

   J. "He ain't heavy; he's my brother."

PASSAGE III—HUMANITIES

This passage is adapted from the article "The Trouble with Frida Kahlo" by Stephanie Mencimer, which appeared in *Washington Monthly* (© 2002 Washington Monthly).

Never has a woman with a mustache been so revered, or so marketed, as Frida Kahlo, Like a female Che Guevara, she has become a cottage industry. Feminists might celebrate Kahlo's ascent
(5) to greatness—if only her fame were related to her art. Instead, her fans are largely drawn by the story of her life, for which her paintings are often presented as simple illustration. Fridamaniacs are inspired by Kahlo's tragic tale of physical
(10) suffering—polio at six, grisly accident at 18— and fascinated with her glamorous friends and lovers. But, like a game of telephone, the more Kahlo's story has been told, the more it has been distorted, omitting uncomfortable details that
(15) show her to be a far more complex and flawed figure than the movies suggest. This elevation of the artist over the art diminishes the public understanding of Kahlo's place in history and overshadows the deeper and more disturbing
(20) truths in her work.

Until the 1970s there were almost no "great" women artists. As the feminist movement gathered steam, women sought to rectify that problem. Historically, women's limited opportunities meant
(25) there were few women artists to begin with, and even fewer whose work had been collected and could be definitively attributed to them. Once scholars did identify significant women artists, they had to demonstrate that those artists
(30) met the male standards for admission to the

canon—i.e., they had to suffer and be mostly ignored during their lifetimes. It was also helpful if the emerging female artists were beautiful and had glamorous friends.

(35) Kahlo made a perfect candidate. As if her bodily injuries weren't compelling enough, Kahlo's drama was enhanced by what she referred to as the second accident in her life: Diego Rivera, the famous Mexican muralist to whom she was mar-
(40) ried for 25 years. Rivera was a notorious woman-izer, a habit he did not abandon after marrying Kahlo. Both Kahlo and Rivers were active in the Communist Party and Mexican politics. Kahlo's paintings ofter reflect her tumultuous relation-
(45) ship with Rivera, as well as the anguish of her ever-deteriorating health. Between the time of her accident and death, Kahlo had more than 30 surgeries, and a gangrenous leg was eventu-ally amputated. She dramatized the pain in her
(50) paintings, while carefully cultivating a self-image as a "heroic sufferer."

While Kahlo's work never attracted the atten-tion her husband's did, it did win some critical acclaim. Eventually, though, her failing health
(55) left her addicted to painkillers and alcohol. She continued to paint, but the addiction destroyed the controlled, delicate brushwork that had characterized her best work. In 1954, suffering from pneumonia, Kahlo went to a Communist
(60) march. Four days later, she died in what may or may not have been a suicide.

If the focus of the art business must be on biography, that biography should at least include the artists' warts. Many of Kahlo's surgeries may
(65) have been unnecessary. She also made several suicide attempts and spent much of her adult life addicted to drugs and alcohol. More im-portantly, though, Kahlo's Communism, now treated as somehow sort of quaint, led her to
(70) embrace some unforgivable political positions. Less scandalous but worth noting is that Kahlo despised the very gringos who now champion her work, and her art reflects her obvious disdain for the United States.

(75)   Neglecting the dark side of the artist's narrative deprives the public of a full appreciation
of the art. Without knowing that by 1953 Kahlo
was so strung out that she could barely pick up
a paintbrush, how can the public possibly know
(80) why some of her late work is so bad? Which is
the really tragic part of Kahlo's story. Because
when you sweep away the sideshow, ignore the
overwrought analysis, and take a hard look at
what she painted, much of it is extraordinary.
(85) Her paintings tap into sex and violence, life and
death, in original and profound ways. So while
women might celebrate Kahlo's success, it may
be that real progress has come when a woman
can be remembered both as a great artist and
(90) as a despicable cur.

21. The author implies that Kahlo is famous
primarily because of her:
A. exceptionally liberal paintings.
B. dramatic life full of intrigue and suffering.
C. marriage to Diego Rivera.
D. being one of the first female artists.

22. Frida Kahlo's story was compared to a "game
of telephone" (line 12) because:
F. just like a message passed over the phone,
the details of her life have been told
accurately.
G. people are purposely leaving out
important pieces of her history.
H. her story has been passed on verbally
from person to person.
J. over time the story has become distorted
and parts have been omitted.

23. The author states that all of the following
contributed to the lack of great female artists
prior to 1970 EXCEPT:
A. the scarce number of female artists.
B. scholars' difficulty identifying great
female artists.
C. higher standards for admission to the
canon.
D. the small number of female artists' works
that had been collected.

24. The author's tone in this passage can best be
described as:
F. persuasive.
G. informative.
H. sarcastic.
J. humorous.

25. Based on the information presented in the
passage, the quality of Kahlo's painting began
to decline because of:
A. her injuries.
B. catching pneumonia.
C. her addiction to painkillers and alcohol.
D. her tumultuous marriage to Rivera.

26. In the context of lines 62–74, the phrase "the
artists' warts" (line 64) most nearly means:
F. Kahlo's poorer paintings.
G. the imperfections in Kahlo's appearance.
H. Kahlo's highest achievements.
J. the less pleasant parts of Kahlo's life.

27. According to the passage, all of the following
are true about Kahlo's paintings EXCEPT:
A. they reflect her complicated relationship
with Rivera.
B. they dramatized the pain from her
surgeries.
C. they were all forms of self-portraits.
D. they portray concepts in unique and
profound ways.

28. The author's purpose in writing this passage
can best be summarized as:
F. to discuss how the movies and
Fridamaniacs are distorting the story of
Kahlo's life.
G. to convince women to embrace both the
dark and light side of Kahlo's life when
choosing to celebrate her success.
H. to provide hidden details of Kahlo's life,
hoping that people will realize she is not
worthy of such high acclaim.
J. to explain why some of Kahlo's later work
is so bad.

29. What would the author probably say is the most tragic thing about Kahlo's story?
   A. That Rivera remained unfaithful even after their marriage
   B. That Kahlo died so young, and wasn't able to create more paintings
   C. The grisly accident when she was 18
   D. That people don't realize how extraordinary her work is because they are more caught up in the sordid details of her life

30. What is the "sideshow" the author refers to in line 82?
   F. The dramatic details of Kahlo's life
   G. The critical acclaim Kahlo has received
   H. The Fridamaniacs who idolize Kahlo
   J. Kahlo's addictions

PASSAGE IV—NATURAL SCIENCE

This passage is adapted from "Feces, Bite Marks Flesh Out Giant Dino-Eating Crocs" by Brian Handwekr (© 2010 National Geographic).

Rock-hard feces and oddly bitten bones are helping to flesh out one of the biggest crocs of prehistory. As long as a stretch limo, *Deinosuchus*—"terrible crocodile"—likely prowled shallow waters
(5)   and hunted dinosaurs its own size, the evidence suggests. Paleontologists announced their conclusions after analyzing pieces of 79-million-year-old fossilized dung, or coprolites, that appear to be the first known droppings from *Deinosuchus*. The
(10) discoveries offer the newest insights into the lives of the giant crocs, which roamed much of what is now the United States and northern Mexico.

Sand and shell fragments in the droppings, found within the last few years near a Georgia
(15) stream, suggest the croc preferred estuaries, where, at least in Georgia—home to a great concentration of *Deinosuchus* remains—it probably dined mostly on sea turtles. Despite the Georgia *Deinosuchus's* relatively docile prey, "we're pretty
(20) sure it was the apex predator in this region," said

Samantha Harrell of Columbus State University in Georgia, who presented her research March 17 at a Geological Society of America meeting in Baltimore.
(25) The team also found a fossilized shark tooth embedded in the outside of a coprolite. But because the tooth bears no signs of having been digested, the team suspects a shark left the tooth behind when scavenging on *Deinosuchus* drop-
(30) pings. What the researchers *didn't* find in the feces are bone or other bits of undigested animals. "That's actually good," Harrell said, "because both modern and ancient crocs have digestive juices that eat up bone, horns, teeth, and just
(35) about everything else"—so the "empty" dung supports the idea that the feces are from a croc.

Outside Georgia, *Deinosuchus* apparently took on slightly more challenging prey, according to older bite-mark evidence, which Columbus State
(40) paleontologist David R. Schwimmer presented alongside Harrell at the meeting. *Deinosuchus* tooth impressions in the bones of their prey tell the tale of titanic battles in which the 29-foot crocs took down dinosaurs their own size—
(45) including the *T. rex* relatives *Appalachiosaurus montgomeriensis* and *Albertosaurus*.

"One of the marks shows signs that the bone was healed, which means that the animal survived the bite," Schwimmer said. "That proves
(50) that at least this one specimen was obviously a predator and not scavenging." Schwimmer first noticed strange, dimpled, egg-shaped indentations in Georgia sea turtle fossils. Later he saw similar marks in dinosaur bones in Big Bend
(55) National Park in Texas and in the New Jersey State Museum. "I realized these bites were from something with really powerful jaws and lots of teeth," he said. "And it was pretty obvious that this big, blunt-toothed croc was the source.
(60) There was nothing else I've found that could create blunt bite marks like these."

Tooth marks, though, can show us only part of the picture, said Stephanie Drumheller, an expert on ancient crocodile bites. "Modern
(65) crocodilians"—crocodiles, alligators, and related

extinct forms—"are more than capable of swallowing smaller prey whole and disarticulating larger animals into bite-sized pieces," leaving little evidence behind, said Drumheller, a Ph.D. (70) candidate in geoscience at the University of Iowa. "We can infer that a giant like *Deinosuchus* would be capable of even more destructive feeding behaviors."

The bite-mark evidence that does exist, though, (75) raises a question: Why would a croc capable of taking down big, meaty dinosaurs waste its energy on turtles? In a word: location. Modern crocs, which hunt a wide range of prey, eat whatever's available in their areas. The same factor may have (80) determined whether *Deinosuchus* individuals feasted largely on turtles or dinosaurs or other prey, Drumheller said.

North America-born *Deinosuchus* also underscores that giant crocs arose at different (85) places and times, said University of Chicago paleontologist Paul Sereno, who discovered 110-million-year-old *Sarcosuchus imperator*—aka SuperCroc—in Niger. "In *Deinosuchus,* and independently in SuperCroc, we have two lineages, (90) one older than the other, that prove crocodile bodies grew to a gargantuan size—to dinosaur size," said Sereno, a National Geographic Society explorer-in-residence.

Deinosuchus, which lived just before the close (95) of the Cretaceous period, is more closely related to modern croc lineages than SuperCroc—yet still faded to extinction. What happened to these prehistoric leviathans? A fully grown giant male croc likely would have had to commandeer (100) miles of river territory to regularly find enough prey to sustain itself, Sereno explained. So space constraints likely kept population numbers low—making the giant crocs vulnerable to extinction in tough times. "It appears that every once in a (105) while the right conditions arise for giant crocs," Sereno said. "But they usually don't last."

31. The main idea of the passage is that:
   A. giant crocodiles probably still exist.
   B. ancient giant crocodiles hunted dinosaurs.
   C. dinosaurs were actually a type of crocodile.
   D. all crocodiles will eventually go extinct.

32. Which of the following phrases most accurately describes how crocodilian feeding habits are described in the passage?
   F. Destructive but mindless
   G. Uniform and predatory
   H. Voracious but cowardly
   J. Varied and opportunistic

33. The passage most strongly supports which of the following inferences about crocodilian size?
   A. Crocodilians tend to grow as large as conditions permit them to.
   B. Freshwater crocodilians are able to grow larger than saltwater ones.
   C. Crocodilians always grow large enough to ensure that they are the local apex predator.
   D. It will never again be possible for crododilians to grow as large as *Deinosuchus*.

34. Which of the following is NOT mentioned in the passage as a habitat of *Deinosuchus*?
   F. Georgia
   G. Mexico
   H. Niger
   J. Texas

PRACTICE TEST 4

35. The main purpose of the third paragraph (lines 25–36) is to:

   A. argue that ancient crocodiles preyed on sharks.

   B. argue that sharks preyed on ancient crocodiles.

   C. establish that the dung in question is crocodilian in origin.

   D. suggest that *Deinosuchus* may not always have been carnivorous.

36. According to the passage, one major similarity between *Deinosuchus* and modern crocodilians is their:

   F. teeth.

   G. diet.

   H. range.

   J. digestive processes.

37. As it is used in line 89, the word *lineages* most nearly means:

   A. habits.

   B. bloodlines.

   C. behaviors.

   D. imitators.

38. According to the passage, the best evidence that *Deinosuchus* preyed on dinosaurs was obtained from:

   F. bones.

   G. dung.

   H. teeth.

   J. eggs.

39. Based on the passage, it can reasonably be inferred that a crocodilian species whose main food source dries up will:

   A. immediately starve to extinction.

   B. begin eating something else.

   C. decrease in size.

   D. decrease its range.

40. Based on the passage, the existence of giant crocodilians can best be described as:

   F. ideal.

   G. unavoidable.

   H. destructive.

   J. anomalous.

STOP

If there is still time remaining, you may review your answers.

SCIENCE TEST

Time: 35 Minutes—40 Questions

> **Directions:** There are six passages in this test. Each passage is followed by several questions. After reading a passage, choose the best answer to each question and fill in the corresponding oval on your answer sheet. You may refer to the passages as often as necessary.
>
> You are NOT permitted to use a calculator on this test.

PASSAGE I

Friction is the force that resists movement when two surfaces are in contact and is represented by F_f. The *coefficient of friction* (COF, symbolized by μ) is a quantity used to measure the force of friction based on the normal force (F_N). There are two COFs for a given surface-to-surface contact: static COF (μ_s) and kinetic COF (μ_k). μ_s is used for objects at rest and μ_k is used for objects in motion. The normal force is an upward force, perpendicular to the surface the object is either resting on or moving on.

The basic equation for calculating the coefficient of friction is:

$$\mu = \frac{F_f}{F_N}$$

Figure 1 is a diagram of a block resting on an inclined plane. The forces shown are defined above. F_g represents the force of gravity.

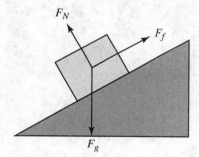

Figure 1

Scientists performed an experiment using several different materials to determine μ_s and μ_k for each pair of materials. Figures 2 and 3 show the results.

Figure 2

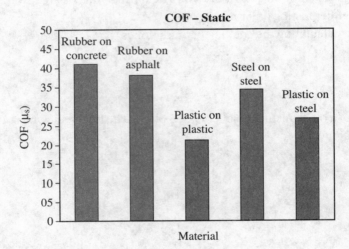

Figure 3

PRACTICE TEST 4

1. Based on the results of the experiment, which combination of materials has the largest static COF?
   A. Plastic on plastic
   B. Plastic on steel
   C. Rubber on concrete
   D. Rubber on asphalt

2. A comparison of the COFs given in Figure 2 shows that, relative to the COF for rubber on concrete, the COF for plastic on plastic is approximately:
   F. 1/100 as high.
   G. 1/2 as high.
   H. 2 times as high.
   J. 10 times as high.

3. Which of the following ranks the materials used in the experiment from lowest static COF to highest static COF?
   A. Plastic on plastic, steel on steel, plastic on steel, rubber on asphalt, rubber on concrete
   B. Rubber on concrete, rubber on asphalt, steel on steel, plastic on steel, plastic on plastic
   C. Plastic on steel, plastic on plastic, rubber on asphalt, rubber on concrete, steel on steel
   D. Plastic on plastic, plastic on steel, steel on steel, rubber on asphalt, rubber on concrete

4. A student theorized that the higher the static COF for a material, the higher the kinetic COF would be. Do the results of the experiment support this theory?
   F. Yes. The materials with the highest static COF also had the highest kinetic COF.
   G. Yes. Plastic on steel had both the highest static COF and the highest kinetic COF.
   H. No. Plastic on plastic had both the lowest static COF and the lowest kinetic COF.
   J. No. There is no relationship between static COF and kinetic COF for any of the materials.

5. According to Figures 1, 2, and 3, which block would most likely slide down the incline the fastest?
   A. A steel block on a steel incline
   B. A plastic block on a plastic incline
   C. A rubber block on a concrete incline
   D. A plastic block on a steel incline

6. If a scientist wanted to conduct an experiment to determine the static coefficient of friction for rubber on steel, what conclusions can be drawn about the results of his experiment?
   F. μ_s would equal approximately 36.
   G. μ_s would equal approximately .30.
   H. μ_s would equal approximately 23.
   J. μ_k would equal approximately .30.

PASSAGE II

The main source of the world's energy for the last century has been fossil fuels. To use fossil fuels, we must be able to locate and recover them at affordable costs, convert them to usable forms, and use them without wasting them or harming the environment.

Experiment 1

Scientists set out to determine the energy potential of various fossil fuels. They burned 1 ton of each of 5 different fuel varieties, and measured the energy produced. Table 1 shows the energy content of various fossil fuels.

Table 1

Fuel	Energy Content (Btu/Ton)
Coal	25,000,000
Crude oil	37,000,000
Gasoline	38,000,000
Natural gas	47,000,000
Peat	3,500,000

Experiment 2

Students completed an experiment to measure the heat energy obtained from natural gas, using water, a Fahrenheit thermometer, and a Bunsen burner (see Figure 1). They filled a beaker with enough water to weigh 1 pound (approximately 450 mL). They recorded the temperature of the water, then lit the Bunsen burner and stirred the water continuously. They took several measurements of the water's temperature, at 5-minute intervals. The results of the experiment are displayed in Table 2.

Figure 1

Table 2

Time (m)	Water Temperature (°F)
0	67°
5	92°
10	117°
15	142°

Each type of fossil fuel releases a different amount of energy. This energy is measured in a variety of units. Table 3 provides a conversion chart for energy units.

Table 3

1 Btu =	.252 kilocalorie .000293 kilowatt-hour
1 kilocalorie =	3.97 Btus .0012 kilowatt-hour
1 kilowatt-hour =	3,413 Btus 860 kilocalories
1 barrel of oil =	5,600,000 Btus 1,410,579 kilocalories 1,640.8 kilowatt-hours

7. According to the results of Experiment 1, which of the following ranks the different types of fossil fuels in order of energy potential, from the most Btus/ton to the least?
   A. Peat, coal, crude oil, gasoline, natural gas
   B. Natural gas, gasoline, crude oil, coal, peat
   C. Gasoline, crude oil, peat, coal, natural gas
   D. Natural gas, crude oil, peat, gasoline, coal

8. If 1 Btu is the amount of heat needed to raise the temperature of 1 pound of water 1° Fahrenheit, then how many Btus of natural gas were used during the first 5 minutes of Experiment 2?
   F. 92
   G. 67
   H. 50
   J. 25

9. The main purpose of Experiment 2 was to:
   A. determine the amount of energy natural gas creates.
   B. compare various fossil fuels to see which one produces the most energy.
   C. see how long it would take to heat water to 100°F.
   D. calculate how much water is necessary to burn 25 Btus of natural gas.

10. If Experiment 2 had been repeated using gasoline to heat the water instead of natural gas, the temperature of the water after 10 minutes would most likely have been closest to which of the following?
    F. 40°F
    G. 99°F
    H. 117°F
    J. 180°F

11. According to the data in Table 3, which unit of energy is equivalent to the most Btus?
    A. 1 kilowatt-hour
    B. 1 kilocalorie
    C. 1 barrel of oil
    D. 10,000 Btus

12. Based on the results of Experiment 2, if temperature had continued to be measured for 5 more minutes, what would the temperature of the water have most likely been at the next measurement?
    F. 85°F
    G. 142°F
    H. 167°F
    J. 200°F

13. If an experiment was set up using the same procedures as Experiment 2, but coal was used as the heat source, what would be the expected results after the beaker had been heated for ten minutes?
    A. The water temperature would be higher than 117 degrees Fahrenheit.
    B. The water temperature would be lower than 117 degrees Fahrenheit.
    C. The water temperature would be higher than 142 degrees Fahrenheit.
    D. Cannot be determined from the information given

PASSAGE III

A science class studied the pH strength of acids and bases. The terms *strong* and *weak* indicate the ability of acid and base solutions to conduct electricity. Figure 1 displays the pH scale used to rank solutions as acidic or basic, and Table 1 provides an overview of what pH levels are considered *strong* and *weak* solutions.

Figure 1

Table 1

Solution	pH
Strong acid	0–3
Weak acid	4–6
Neutral	7
Weak base	8–10
Strong base	11–14

Experiment 1

Students conducted an experiment to determine the conductivity of acid and base solutions, using a lightbulb apparatus (see Figure 2). The lightbulb circuit was incomplete. If the circuit is completed by a solution containing a large number of ions, the lightbulb will glow brightly, indicating a strong ability to conduct electricity. If the circuit is completed by a solution containing a large number of molecules and either no ions or few ions, the solution does not conduct electricity or conducts it very weakly. Students tested the conductivity of several solutions; the results are reported in Table 2.

Figure 2

Table 2

Solution	Acid or Base	Lightbulb
H_2O	Neutral	No light
HCl	Acid	Bright
$HC_2H_3O_2$	Acid	Dim
H_2SO_4	Acid	Bright
H_2CO_3	Acid	Dim
NaOH	Base	Bright
KOH	Base	Bright
NH_4OH	Base	Dim

Experiment 2

Students mixed 50 mL of each chemical with 1 liter of water and then tested the pH of the solution. Table 3 displays the pH found for each chemical.

Table 3

Chemical	pH
HCl	0.86
$HC_2H_3O_2$	2.92
H_2SO_4	1.29
H_2CO_3	3.73
NaOH	13.1
KOH	11.2
NH_4OH	9.2

14. Based on the information presented in Figure 1 and Table 1, a solution with which pH would be the strongest base?
    F. 12.5
    G. 9.7
    H. 7
    J. 0.2

15. According to the results of Experiments 1 and 2, which of the following is true?
    A. The weaker the acid or base, the brighter the lightbulb glowed.
    B. The lower the pH of the solution, the brighter the lightbulb glowed.
    C. The stronger the acid or base, the brighter the lightbulb glowed.
    D. The higher the pH of the solution, the brighter the lightbulb glowed.

16. Based on the results of Experiment 2, KOH would be classified as:
    F. a strong acid.
    G. neutral.
    H. a strong base.
    J. a weak base.

17. According to the information presented in Figure 1 and Table 3, it can be concluded that which of the following acids contains the most hydrogen?
    A. H_2CO_3
    B. H_2SO_4
    C. $HC_2H_3O_2$
    D. HCl

18. Suppose the students decided to test the conductivity of an additional solution according to the procedures outlined in Experiment 1. They tested a solution of NaOCl, and they found that the solution caused the lightbulb to glow brightly. The students would be correct in classifying the NaOCl solution as which of the following?
    F. A strong base
    G. A weak base
    H. A weak acid
    J. Cannot be determined from the given information

19. Based on Table 3, which of the following figures best represents the pH values for the 3 bases tested?

A.

B.

C.

D.

20. Suppose the students tested three unknown solutions for conductivity using the same procedure as Experiment 1. Using the results below, determine which solution would be the more ideal conductor of electricity.

Solution	pH
1	0.56
2	6.83
3	9

   F. Solution 1

   G. Solution 2

   H. Solution 3

   J. None of these

PASSAGE IV

Solid-phase microextraction (SPME) is a new technique for extracting volatile organic residue from sediment and water. The technique has several advantages (fast, simple, precise, sensitive), and requires no solvent. For this technique, a thin fused silica fiber coated with a stationary phase is exposed to a sample, either by immersion in a water or an air sample or to headspace above an aqueous or a solid sample (see Figure 1).

Figure 1: SPME device

Scientists conducted a series of experiments to determine the effectiveness of using SPME to extract white phosphorus (P_4) residues from water. All of the experiments were done using headspace immersion.

Experiment 1

To see how consistent SPME was, scientists conducted five trials using four different types of water (reagent grade, well, pond, salt marsh) at an aqueous concentration of 0.14 µg/L. Table 1 displays the results.

Table 1

Trial	White Phosphorus Mass (pg)			
	Reagent	Well	Pond	Salt Marsh
1	31.8	36.5	41.3	39.6
2	35.8	39.1	31.5	32.1
3	37.6	32.9	36.7	33.1
4	32.9	36.2	36.6	34.3
5	32.3	34.1	35.6	36.8
Mean	34.1	35.8	36.3	35.2

Experiment 2

Scientists varied the aqueous concentration and tested four different types of water using SPME, to see the effect on the mass of P_4 that could be extracted (see Figure 2).

Figure 2

Experiment 3

To see if sonication had any effect on the results of SPME, scientists ran four trials, using four identical aqueous samples, at a concentration of 0.14 µg/L. The samples were analyzed using SPME by three methods: five minutes of sonication, ten minutes of sonication, and five minutes static. Table 2 displays the results.

Table 2

Trial	White Phosphorus Mass (pg)		
	5-Min Sonic	10-Min Sonic	5-Min Static
1	30.3	32.7	29.1
2	36.8	34.5	31.5
3	36.8	35.1	30.8
4	31.2	33.6	31.0

21. According to Figure 2, as the aqueous concentration increased in the test done using salt marsh water, the white phosphorus mass:
A. decreased, and then increased.
B. increased and then decreased.
C. increased.
D. decreased.

22. Based on the results from Experiment 3, which trial resulted in the smallest amount of white phosphorus being extracted?
F. Trial 2 after 5-minutes sonication
G. Trial 3 after 5-minutes static
H. Trial 1 after 5-minutes static
J. Trial 4 after 10-minutes sonication

23. In order for the scientists to conduct these experiments, it was crucial for them to expose which part of the SPME device to the headspace above the water samples?
A. The plugger
B. The needle
C. The barrel
D. The silica fiber

24. A scientist theorized that more white phosphorus would be extracted from a sample if it were exposed to a longer period of sonication. Do the results from Experiment 3 support this theory?
F. Yes, because in every trial more white phosphorus was extracted after 10-minutes sonication than after 5-minutes sonication.
G. Yes, because in every trial more white phosphorus was extracted after 5-minutes sonication than after 5-minutes static.
H. No, because in Trials 2 and 3 more white phosphorus was extracted after 5-minutes sonication than after 10-minutes sonication.
J. No, because in all trials more white phosphorus was extracted after 5-minutes static than after 5-minutes sonication.

25. According to Table 1, the mean results demonstrate that the greatest amount of white phosphorus can be extracted from which type of water?
A. Reagent
B. Well
C. Pond
D. Salt marsh

26. Based on the results of Experiment 2, if SPME extraction was used on pond water with an aqueous concentration of 0.2 μg/L, it can be inferred that the amount of white phosphorus extracted would be closest to:
F. 45 pg.
G. 100 pg.
H. 30 pg.
J. 5 pg.

27. Assuming SPME is effective in extracting white phosphorus residue from water, a wildlife expert was utilizing the results of Experiment 1 to run further testing on water and wildlife. Based on Experiment 1, which of the following statements can the expert assume is true?
A. Of the four water sites, pond water had the highest concentration of white phosphorus mass.
B. Well water had a white phosphorus mass of 17 pg at an aqueous concentration of 0.072.
C. Of the four water sites, well water had the lowest concentration of white phosphorus mass.
D. The white phosphorus mass after 5 minutes of sonication was 36.8 pg.

PASSAGE V

The melting point of a substance is the temperature at which the solid phase transitions to the liquid phase. When a substance melts, the attractive forces holding the molecules together are reduced sufficiently to allow the molecules to flow. The stronger the intermolecular forces in solid form, the higher the melting point will be.

The boiling point of a substance is the temperature at which the vapor pressure in the liquid phase equals the atmospheric temperature of its surroundings. When a substance boils, the substance transitions from a liquid phase to a gaseous phase and the intermolecular forces are completely severed. The stronger the attractive forces between the molecules in the liquid phase, the higher the boiling point will be.

Table 1 and Figure 1 show details of some of the elements from the third row of the periodic table.

Table 1

Classification	Name	# of Protons in Nucleus	Symbol
Metal	sodium	11	Na
	magnesium	12	Mg
	aluminum	13	Al
Semiconductor	silicon	14	Si
Nonmetal	phosphorus	15	P
	sulfur	16	S
	chlorine	17	Cl

Figure 1

28. The melting point of silicon is closest to which temperature?
    F. 700 K
    G. 1200 K
    H. 1700 K
    J. 2200 K

29. Based on Table 1 and Figure 1, what can be concluded about the relationship between the number of protons in the nucleus and the attractive forces between molecules?
    A. As the number of protons increase, the intermolecular forces increase.
    B. As the number of protons increase, the intermolecular forces decrease.
    C. As the number of protons increase, the intermolecular forces are unchanged.
    D. There is no relationship between the number of protons and the intermolecular forces.

30. Based on Figure 1, what is the relationship between melting point (*MP*) and boiling point (*BP*)?
    F. There is a direct relationship between melting point and boiling point and the constant of variation is roughly 2. The equation would be $MP \approx 2 \cdot (BP)$.
    G. There is a direct relationship between melting point and boiling point and the constant of variation is roughly $\frac{1}{2}$. The equation would be $MP \approx \frac{1}{2} \cdot (BP)$.
    H. There is an inverse relationship between melting point and boiling point and the constant of variation is roughly $1.5 \cdot 10^6$. The equation would be $(BP) \approx 1.5 \cdot 10^6$.
    J. There is a direct relationship between melting point and boiling point but no constant of variation exists. When melting point increases, boiling point also increases but every element has a different numerical relationship.

31. Which element transitions from a liquid phase to a gaseous phase at 500 K?
    A. P
    B. Al
    C. Mg
    D. Na

32. Do Figure 1 and Table 1 support the conclusion that nonmetals have melting points and boiling points that are closer in temperature than the metals?
    F. Yes. Phosphorus, sulfur, and chlorine all have melting points and boiling points that are less than 500 K apart. Sodium, magnesium, and aluminum have boiling points that are 500 K or more apart.
    G. Yes. Phosphorus, sulfur, and chlorine all have melting points and boiling points that are less than 1000 K apart. Sodium, magnesium, and aluminum have boiling points that are more than 1000 K apart.
    H. No. Silicon's melting point is 1000 K less than its boiling point. Magnesium's melting point is 500 K less than its boiling point.
    J. No. There is no general relationship between melting points and boiling points and an element's classification as a metal or a nonmetal.

33. Suppose you were trying to determine the boiling point for a metal. Based on Table 1 and Figure 1, what would be the most likely temperature range for the boiling point?
    A. 1000°–1500°
    B. 0°–500°
    C. 500°–1000°
    D. 1200°–2700°

PASSAGE VI

From 1971 to 2006, there was a dramatic reduction in the number of feral honeybees in the United States, and a significant, though somewhat gradual, decline in the number of colonies maintained by beekeepers. In early 2007 the rate of attrition reached new proportions, and the term *Colony Collapse Disorder (CCD)* was coined to describe this sudden decline. CCD is said to have occurred when a bee colony abruptly disappears, with little or no build-up of dead bees in or around the colonies. The cause or causes of the syndrome are not yet well understood. Proposed causes include environmental change-related stress, malnutrition, disease, and pests.

Study 1

In an attempt to quantify the degree and extent of losses experienced in the United States, scientists tracked beekeeping operations with various numbers of colonies between September 2006 and March 2007. For the sake of this study, a colony has encountered CCD when it loses at least 90% of its population in a period of 30 days. This loss must be accompanied by little or no trace of dead bees in or around the hive. Figure 1 displays the total losses experienced by all beekeeping operations.

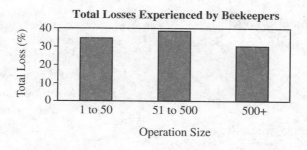

Figure 1

Study 2

Scientists studying CCD surveyed beekeepers whose hives have been affected by the disorder. The beekeepers were asked what they believe caused the CCD in their colonies. Table 1 displays the five most commonly suspected causes of CCD losses and the average percentage of loss experienced by operations of varying sizes due to each suspected cause. The scientists then surveyed beekeepers whose hives had collapsed for reasons unrelated to CCD, asking them the same question. Figure 2 compares the results from the scientists' two surveys, displaying the total loss experienced due to suspected causes of CCD and non-CCD losses, averaged for operations of all sizes.

Table 1

Cause	Size		
	1 to 50	51 to 500	500+
Starvation	40%	35%	7%
Weak in fall	16%	30%	0%
Weather	6%	15%	7%
Pests	8%	10%	43%
Queen death	12%	15%	7%

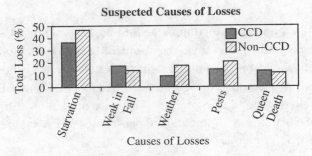

Figure 2

PRACTICE TEST 4

34. Beekeepers from operations of which size experienced the lowest total losses by percentage?

F. 1 to 50

G. 51 to 500

H. 500+

J. It cannot be determined from the data provided.

35. Based on the data in Figure 2, it can be determined that the least common suspected cause of CCD losses was:

A. starvation.

B. weak in fall.

C. weather.

D. queen death.

36. According to Study 2, for operations with between 1 and 50 colonies, what was the most common suspected cause of CCD losses?

F. Starvation

G. Weak in fall

H. Weather

J. Queen death

37. Prior to conducting the research, four scientists each proposed one of the following hypotheses. Which hypothesis is best supported by the results?

A. Environmental changes, including shifts in weather patterns, are the predominant causes of CCD-related loss.

B. An increase in pesticide-resistant pests is the main contributing factor to CCD loss at small beekeeping operations.

C. The larger a beekeeping operation, the higher the overall CCD loss will be.

D. A shortage of food sources, especially at smaller beekeeping operations, is leading to an increase in CCD loss.

38. Figure 2 indicates that, compared with the total loss for non-CCD, the total loss for CCD was higher for which of the following causes?

F. Starvation, weather, and pests

G. Weak in fall and queen death

H. Weak in fall and weather

J. Starvation and pests

39. A scientist theorized that the number of CCD losses would be higher than non-CCD losses for beekeeping operations of all sizes. Does the data support this theory?

- **A.** Yes. For all causes the total loss was higher for CCD than for non-CCD.
- **B.** Yes. Starvation was the most common cause of loss regardless of operation size.
- **C.** No. For many of the causes there were more non-CCD losses than CCD losses.
- **D.** No. Operations with 51 to 500 colonies experienced the greatest total loss.

40. Both Study 1 and Study 2 scientists gathered data directly from which of the following sources?

- **F.** Feral honeybee colonies only
- **G.** Feral honeybee colonies and non-CCD honeybee colonies
- **H.** Non-CCD honeybee colonies only
- **J.** CCD honeybee colonies and non-CCD honeybee colonies

STOP

If there is still time remaining, you may review your answers.

WRITING TEST

Time: 40 minutes

Docufiction

Though educational basic-cable channels have long bolstered ratings and filled programming gaps with light (and predictably inconclusive) documentaries about such specious fare as hauntings, aliens, and Bigfoot, this habit has recently evolved into a new form that many find troubling. "Docufictions," as they have been dubbed, do more than merely uncritically regurgitate hearsay: they present actors impersonating real scientists, presenting fabricated "evidence" made with special effects. One such program that aired on Animal Planet in 2012 alleged the real existence of mermaids, and the next year Discovery Channel aired a similar docufiction dedicated to the (utterly false) notion that the extinct giant shark Megalodon still roams the seas. The networks defend the specials as harmless fun, but many viewers were taken in—including schoolchildren, much to the displeasure of their science teachers.

Read and carefully consider these perspectives. Each suggests a particular way of thinking about the phenomenon of docufiction.

Perspective One	Perspective Two	Perspective Three
The proper response to the controversy over docufictions is the same one we should give about any programming controversy: If you don't like something on television, change the channel. Problem solved.	Harmless entertainment is one thing, but supposed "learning" channels are betraying the public's trust by paying actors to impersonate scientists and argue things that are demonstrably untrue. If you want to make a sci-fi movie, go right ahead, but don't trick people into thinking it's real.	The problem isn't docufictions itself—it's that we live in a society ruled by the profit motive. Since educational channels don't receive government funding like they do in other countries, they have no choice but to try and make money by scoring big ratings. So what do you expect to happen?

ESSAY TASK

Write a unified, coherent essay concerning docufiction. In your essay, be sure to:

- clearly state your own perspective on the issue and analyze the relationship between your perspective and at least one other perspective
- develop and support your ideas with reasoning and examples
- organize your ideas clearly and logically
- communicate your ideas effectively in standard written English

Your perspective may be in full agreement with any of those given, in partial agreement, or completely different.

PRACTICE TEST 4

Planning Your Response

Your prewriting notes on this page will not be considered in your score.

Use the following space to brainstorm ideas and map out your response. You may want to think about the following as you analyze the given prompt:

Strengths and weaknesses of the three viewpoints

- What good points do they make, and what potential objections do they ignore?
- Why might they be convincing to readers, and why might their perspectives fall short?

Your previous experience, background knowledge, and personal values

- What is your viewpoint on this topic, and what are the pros and cons of this viewpoint?
- How will you craft an argument in support of your point of view?

If there is still time remaining, you may review your answers.

ANSWER KEY
Practice Test 4

English

1. **D**	16. **F**	31. **B**	46. **F**	61. **B**
2. **G**	17. **D**	32. **J**	47. **A**	62. **H**
3. **B**	18. **F**	33. **A**	48. **H**	63. **A**
4. **F**	19. **C**	34. **F**	49. **A**	64. **J**
5. **C**	20. **G**	35. **D**	50. **G**	65. **D**
6. **H**	21. **C**	36. **J**	51. **A**	66. **F**
7. **D**	22. **H**	37. **B**	52. **H**	67. **B**
8. **G**	23. **A**	38. **H**	53. **D**	68. **H**
9. **A**	24. **G**	39. **A**	54. **F**	69. **A**
10. **F**	25. **D**	40. **J**	55. **C**	70. **J**
11. **D**	26. **G**	41. **C**	56. **G**	71. **D**
12. **J**	27. **A**	42. **J**	57. **D**	72. **G**
13. **B**	28. **J**	43. **C**	58. **J**	73. **C**
14. **J**	29. **D**	44. **J**	59. **B**	74. **H**
15. **D**	30. **F**	45. **B**	60. **H**	75. **A**

Mathematics

1. **E**	13. **D**	25. **E**	37. **B**	49. **B**
2. **G**	14. **H**	26. **G**	38. **G**	50. **G**
3. **D**	15. **D**	27. **C**	39. **C**	51. **D**
4. **F**	16. **H**	28. **G**	40. **F**	52. **J**
5. **D**	17. **B**	29. **A**	41. **E**	53. **B**
6. **H**	18. **F**	30. **H**	42. **G**	54. **F**
7. **C**	19. **D**	31. **C**	43. **A**	55. **E**
8. **K**	20. **H**	32. **G**	44. **H**	56. **H**
9. **C**	21. **E**	33. **D**	45. **E**	57. **E**
10. **G**	22. **K**	34. **K**	46. **K**	58. **F**
11. **B**	23. **C**	35. **C**	47. **B**	59. **B**
12. **J**	24. **J**	36. **J**	48. **F**	60. **K**

ANSWER KEY
Practice Test 4

Reading

1.	**B**	9.	**B**	17.	**B**	25.	**C**	33.	**A**
2.	**H**	10.	**H**	18.	**F**	26.	**J**	34.	**H**
3.	**A**	11.	**C**	19.	**C**	27.	**C**	35.	**C**
4.	**J**	12.	**F**	20.	**J**	28.	**G**	36.	**J**
5.	**A**	13.	**B**	21.	**B**	29.	**D**	37.	**B**
6.	**H**	14.	**F**	22.	**J**	30.	**F**	38.	**F**
7.	**B**	15.	**D**	23.	**C**	31.	**B**	39.	**B**
8.	**J**	16.	**H**	24.	**F**	32.	**J**	40.	**J**

Science

1.	**C**	9.	**A**	17.	**D**	25.	**C**	33.	**D**
2.	**G**	10.	**G**	18.	**J**	26.	**G**	34.	**H**
3.	**D**	11.	**C**	19.	**B**	27.	**A**	35.	**C**
4.	**F**	12.	**H**	20.	**F**	28.	**H**	36.	**F**
5.	**B**	13.	**B**	21.	**C**	29.	**D**	37.	**D**
6.	**F**	14.	**F**	22.	**H**	30.	**J**	38.	**G**
7.	**B**	15.	**C**	23.	**D**	31.	**A**	39.	**C**
8.	**J**	16.	**H**	24.	**H**	32.	**F**	40.	**J**

HOW TO SCORE YOUR PRACTICE TEST

Step 1: Add up the number correct for each section and write that number in the blank under the Raw Score column on the Score Conversion Table. (Your goal is to get more questions correct on each subsequent practice test.)

Step 2: Using the Score Conversion Chart, find your scale score for each section and write it down. Then add up all four sections and divide by 4 to find your overall composite score. (Composite scores are rounded up at .5 or higher.)

SCORE CONVERSION TABLE

Section	Raw Score	Scaled Score
English	(out of 75)	_____ / 36
Math	(out of 60)	_____ / 36
Reading	(out of 40)	_____ / 36
Science	(out of 40)	_____ / 36
		Add and divide by 4
Overall Composite =		_____ / 36

SCORE CONVERSION CHART

	Number Correct				
ACT Score*	English Section	Mathematics Section	Reading Section	Science Section	ACT Score*
36	75	60	40	40	36
35	74	59	39	39	35
34	73	58	38	38	34
33	72	57	37	—	33
32	71	56	36	37	32
31	70	54–55	35	36	31
30	69	53	34	35	30
29	67–68	51–52	33	34	29
28	65–66	49–50	32	33	28
27	64	46–48	31	31–32	27
26	62–63	44–45	30	30	26
25	60–61	41–43	29	28–29	25
24	58–59	39–40	27–28	25–27	24
23	55–57	37–38	25–26	24	23

(continued)

SCORE CONVERSION CHART (*Continued*)

ACT Score*	English Section	Mathematics Section	Reading Section	Science Section	ACT Score*
		Number Correct			
22	53–54	35–36	23–24	22–23	22
21	50–52	33–34	22	20–21	21
20	47–49	31–32	21	18–19	20
19	44–46	28–30	19–20	17	19
18	42–43	25–27	18	15–16	18
17	40–41	22–24	17	14	17
16	37–39	19–21	16	13	16
15	34–36	15–17	15	12	15
14	31–33	11–14	13–14	11	14
13	29–30	09–10	12	10	13
12	27–28	07–08	10–11	09	12
11	25–26	06	08–09	08	11
10	23–24	05	07	07	10
9	21–22	04	06	05–06	9
8	18–20	03	05	—	8
7	15–17	—	—	04	7
6	12–14	02	04	03	6
5	09–11	—	03	02	5
4	07–08	01	02	—	4
3	05–06	—	—	01	3
2	03–04	—	01	—	2
1	00–02	00	00	00	1

These scores are based on student trials rather than national norms.

SCORING YOUR ESSAY

As mentioned earlier in this text, two readers will evaluate your essay and each person will then assign it a score from 1 to 6. If, by chance, these two scorers disagree by more than 1 point, a third reader will step in and resolve the discrepancy. Performance on the essay will not affect your English, math, reading, science, or composite scores. You will receive two additional scores on your score sheet—a combined English/writing score (1–36) and a writing test subscore (1–12). Neither of these scores will affect your composite score!

The sample essay that follows reflects higher-level writing. It meets the criteria that ACT has put forth for essays that demonstrate effective writing skills.

- It takes a definite position.
- It addresses and expands on the counterargument.
- It has details that support the topic sentences and is well organized.
- It is not repetitive, and while there may be errors, they do not interfere with the competence of the essay.
- It is consistent and well balanced.
- The essay has a clear introduction and a conclusion that is not just a summary but ends with a significant thought.
- The vocabulary demonstrates good use of language and the sentence structure is varied.

ANSWER EXPLANATIONS

English

1. **(D)** Neither an essential "that" clause nor a prepositional phrase needs to be preceded by a comma, so the choice with no commas is correct here.

2. **(G)** Since the sentence concerns a *present* state of something *not having been done*, a negative version of the present perfect tense (i.e., transforming *candidate has won* into *no candidate has ever won*) is necessary. Even if you weren't aware of the factoid being discussed, this is still the only answer choice that results in a comprehensible and grammatically correct sentence.

3. **(B)** The singular present perfect form *has won* is appropriate here. (The regular past tense would also work, but is not one of the choices.)

4. **(F)** The first clause of the sentence is rendered dependent by the presence of *although*, and so the second clause must be independent; no conjunction is necessary. (The fact that the first clause also has *And* at the beginning is immaterial—the addition of *and* before *although* is merely a stylistic flourish here, and it's *although* that makes the difference.)

5. **(C)** All of the pieces of information concerning Teddy Roosevelt are both true and interesting, but the fact that he was vice president under McKinley is the one that is relevant to his ascending to the presidency in 1901.

6. **(H)** The clause about Roosevelt's nickname (from *or* to *him*) is set off from the rest of the sentence with a pair of dashes. (A pair of commas would also be correct, but is not one of the choices—and besides, a pair of dashes is preferable because the sentence is long, complex, and already contains a lot of other commas.)

7. **(D)** This choice correctly presents a dependent "afterthought" clause separated from the preceding independent clause by a comma. Since it concerns Roosevelt's ongoing actions at the time, the participial form of the initial verb (*steering*) is necessary.

8. **(G)** As the subsequent paragraph makes clear, the fact that an "accidental" president had never gone on to win an election before raised an important question about how to interpret the Constitution.

9. **(A)** This choice correctly presents an independent clause preceded by an introductory dependent clause, with the two separated by a comma.

10. **(F)** No commas are necessary, since the proper name *William Howard Taft* cannot be removed from the sentence (although it could if the definite article *the* preceded *Secretary of War*—the sentence would lack information, but it would be grammatically correct).

11. **(D)** Due to the presence of *both* and the rule of parallel phrasing, no word is necessary before the second infinitive ("*a desire both to pursue and to stay ....*").

12. **(J)** The sentence concerns an event that was in the past relative to another point in the past, so the past perfect form is necessary: *Roosevelt had had his chance.* (Don't be confused by the fact that *had* is both the past tense of *have* and the "helper" verb form used to indicate the singular past perfect.)

13. **(B)** The information that "Bull Moose Party" is an alternate name for the Progressive Party is necessary in order to comprehend the subsequent paragraph.

14. **(J)** The paragraph is more about the election of 1912 itself, and so this fact disrupts the flow, interesting though it may be.

15. **(D)** The passage is more about Teddy Roosevelt's political career than his personal life, and it never addresses his reasons for adopting the positions he did.

16. **(F)** This choice correctly presents an independent clause followed by a dependent "afterthought" clause, with the two clauses separated by a comma.

17. **(D)** An essential *that* clause is correctly used here to indicate a matter of degree: "its recipients are *so* respected *that* ...."

18. **(F)** This is a comma splice. All of the other choices are grammatically correct. (Remember, on "NOT acceptable" questions, the comma is frequently the odd one out!)

19. **(C)** This choice results in a complete, correct sentence that means what you want it to mean—a single independent clause in the past tense.

20. **(G)** Since it explains why Walker often wore male clothing, this is the only one of the choices that results in the rest of the sentence making sense.

21. **(C)** This is the only choice that results in an independent clause existing anywhere in the sentence.

22. **(H)** *Although* would mean "despite the fact that," rather than "due to the fact that," which is what you want to mean here (and what all the other choices mean).

23. **(A)** This choice correctly presents an independent clause followed by a dependent "afterthought" clause, with the two clauses separated by a comma (if the situation looks more complicated than that, it is due to the fact that the independent clause ends with items in a list, which are also separated by commas).

24. **(G)** In the previous part of the paragraph, Walker is officially only a nurse, because she is not allowed to be a doctor; in the subsequent part of the paragraph, she is made a doctor. This sentence needs to explain why the army changed its mind.

25. **(D)** We know that Walker ends up receiving the Medal of Honor, and the subsequent prepositional phrase begins with *by*—all this indicates that what we want to say here is that *Walker <u>was recommended for</u> the Medal of Honor <u>by</u> the generals* (i.e., the generals are doing the recommending, but the verb is assigned to Walker via the passive voice).

26. **(G)** Saying that Walker *portrayed herself as supporting* feminism would imply that she acted like she supported it more than actually supporting it.

27. **(A)** No comma is necessary before the prepositional phrase or before the conjunction, as the conjunction does not introduce an independent clause or a complement.

28. **(J)** This choice correctly presents an independent clause followed by a dependent participial "afterthought" clause, with the two separated by a comma.

29. **(D)** Without the Medal of Honor, Walker no longer has a unique place in U.S. military history, and so the information that her medal was restored by President Carter is essential here.

30. **(F)** It is true that most of Walker's major accomplishments are covered by the passage, with a central focus on her receiving of the Medal of Honor—and this is basically just a paraphrase of exactly what the question asks for.

31. **(B)** The sentence correctly consists of an independent clause in the present perfect tense (*people have sworn*) augmented with an essential *that* clause. The present perfect is preferable because the sentence concerns the *current* state of something *already having been* done.

32. **(J)** There is no reason to insert anything between the subject phrase (*physical evidence*) and main verb (*has been*).

33. **(A)** This is the "prepositional phrase trick." The noun is the plural *pieces*, so the verb must be the plural *are*. The words *of Yeti evidence* constitute a prepositional phrase that must be "jumped."

34. **(F)** The fact that the climate tends to distort footprints is relevant because it constitutes an obstacle to Yeti research—that is, it is impossible to conclude anything from the prints.

35. **(D)** This choice correctly separates two independent clauses into two separate sentences.

36. **(J)** The sentence already clearly means what you want to say; all of the proposed additions are redundant.

37. **(B)** The sentence indicates more than one monastery, and they do not possess anything, so what we need here is the plural nonpossessive *monasteries*. (The question tries to trick you with the fact that the sentence says the monasteries are *in possession* of relics, but grammatically speaking the word *monasteries* does not possess any other noun.)

38. **(H)** Here, the passive voice is necessary because the identity of the people doing the claiming is unknown/irrelevant. The noun *relics* is modified by the passive verb form *claimed* + the infinitive *to be* + the adjective *real*. The monasteries had relics that were *claimed to be real* (by some people).

39. **(A)** This choice correctly presents an independent clause preceded by a dependent modifying clause, with the two separated by a comma.

40. **(J)** Although the idea of Jimmy Stewart assisting in international fake-Yeti-hand-based intrigue is certainly bizarre, the idea is already clearly bizarre enough without adding this sentence. Besides, the point is about the hand, not Stewart himself.

41. **(C)** A "linking word" of some kind is necessary between the two clauses, and since 1832 is a time, the relative adverb *when* (added to the beginning of the second clause, after the comma) is the appropriate choice.

42. **(J)** The phrase *and memorable* is set off with a pair of dashes for the sake of emphasis. (It would also be correct to have no punctuation around it at all, but that is not one of the choices.)

43. **(C)** This paragraph concerns very recent attempts to find the Yeti, and so it is best introduced with a factoid about recent biological discoveries.

44. **(J)** The clause *the team of Japanese adventurer Yoshiteru Takahashi ... ventured into the Himalayas* is interrupted by the "lift-out" clause *who claims to have seen a Yeti in 2003*, which offers extra information about Takahashi and is set off with a pair of commas.

45. **(B)** Paragraph 4 explains what the Yeti is, and so should come before everything except Paragraph 1 (which obviously comes first, as it begins by building suspense before the subject is identified).

46. **(F)** This is the prepositional phrase trick again. The subject of the sentence is the plural *legends*, which agrees with the plural verb *are*, and the prepositional phrase *of female pirate Anne Bonny* must be "jumped." The rest of the paragraph makes clear that this sentence means to say that these legends *are* definitely popular, rather than that they *might* be.

47. **(A)** "To say the least" is an inessential clause, which should be set off with commas.

48. **(H)** The fact that accounts of her life rely on *speculation* (educated guessing) is the only one of the choices that emphasizes the lack of information we have about Bonny, as the question requests.

49. **(A)** The fact that she was born to a fairly wealthy family is the only piece of information offered that would be surprising about someone who became a pirate.

50. **(G)** We need a subject noun here (to agree with the main verb *is*), and this choice gives us the noun *beauty*, modified by the adjective *redheaded*.

51. **(A)** There is one *family*, and it possesses the *estate*, so what we need here is the singular-possessive form *family's*.

52. **(H)** As the dash after *family* indicates, the phrase *including the identity of her family* is a "lift-out" clause containing extra information that should be set off with a pair of dashes (a pair of commas or parentheses would also work, but these are not choices).

53. **(D)** Although it is still possible to figure out what the sentence means no matter where this prepositional phrase appears, the most logical place for it is after *ships*, since this placement results in specific information about what exact actions were performed in what exact period of time: they took *several ships over the next few years*.

54. **(F)** The subsequent portion of the paragraph concerns Anne's exact rank and station among the crew (she fought, but was never in charge). Only this sentence sets up the question that is subsequently examined.

55. **(C)** Although it is the longest of the choices, only this one is grammatically correct. Anne participated in the fighting *when there was fighting to be done*. The end of the phrase describes a hypothetical imperative situation: *there was fighting* (that needed) *to be done*.

56. **(G)** This choice correctly presents an independent clause followed by a dependent clause containing additional information. Because the dependent clause begins with *supposedly*, it is preceded by a comma (it would not be if it just began with *while*).

57. **(D)** All that is needed is *therefore* (i.e., for this reason). All of the other choices are either redundant or prohibitively awkward.

58. **(J)** *Anne* (noun) *convinced* (verb) the *law* (direct object) *that she had been* a prisoner on Rackham's ship. The past perfect tense (*she had been*) is used because the idea takes place in the past relative to another moment in the past. All of the other choices are either grammatically incorrect or do not mean what you want them to mean.

59. **(B)** All this sentence does is provide yet another example of a legend about Anne Bonny that may or may not be true. (Don't be confused by the presence of the word *evidence*—the sentence is not evidence that the legend is true, but merely evidence that there are a lot of legends.)

60. **(H)** Anne Bonny is the only female criminal discussed in the passage, and so this would hardly constitute an essay about female criminals in general.

61. **(B)** The convention in a situation like this is to follow the verb with *as* and the participial form of the next verb: the film is *acclaimed as containing* good action scenes. This may sound hard, but think for a bit and you'll remember that you see this construction all the time (e.g., the source was *quoted as saying*). In situations like this, you have to trust in your instincts about what sounds right, even if you don't know why.

62. **(H)** The words from *aside* to *existed* constitute a "lift-out" clause containing extra information, and so this phrase is set off with a pair of commas. The rest of the sentence forms a single independent clause around it. (This question is tricky because it involves commas near *that*, but remember, the rule is that you don't need a comma <u>before</u> a *that* clause—you need a comma <u>after</u> *that* here because a "lift-out" clause *happens to follow* the word *that*.)

63. **(A)** The *who* clause here is an *essential* or *limiting* one, and so no commas are necessary. (In other words, it is the type of clause where you would use *that* instead of *which* if you were talking about an object, but since you are talking about a person here, you use *who*, but still with no comma.)

64. **(J)** Here, a colon is correctly used to divide an initial independent clause from a subsequent phrase that "emanates from" it. (The colon is an incredibly versatile punctuation mark, so the best rule is often that "It's the choice with the colon when the other three are wrong.")

65. **(D)** What we need here is a phrase synonymous with *reason for*, *explanation for*, and so on. The story uses an incorrect preposition.

66. **(F)** The fact that the first reference to Wallace's alleged murdered wife is in a poem composed 200 years later is highly relevant, as it strongly suggests that the story is made up (and the question of which stuff in *Braveheart* is made up is the point of the passage).

67. **(B)** We need the passive voice here: the wife *was executed* by the English. Although the passive voice is not usually preferred, it is necessitated here by the structure of the sentence, since we need the noun to extend to both verb phrases: there's no evidence that the wife *existed* (active voice) or *was executed* (passive voice).

68. **(H)** A semicolon here would separate two independent clauses, and so this choice is grammatically incorrect. The others are all fine.

69. **(A)** The character *is* an underdog (i.e., the David figure in a David-and-Goliath story); the character does not *have* an underdog (that would make the character and the underdog two different entities). The other choices are all fine.

70. **(J)** The phrase *not only* earlier in the sentence indicates that we need a *not only, but also* construction here. Only choice J is constructed in this manner (the word *also* does not appear, but it is implied).

71. **(D)** This choice correctly presents an independent clause followed by an explanatory "afterthought" clause, with the two separated by a comma.

72. **(G)** Saying *had fought* (past perfect tense) here would imply that by Wallace's time the Scots *had fought in the past* in armor (but didn't necessarily still do so), when what you mean to say was that they fought in armor *at* that time.

73. **(C)** The *Scots* do not possess anything in this sentence, but the film *Braveheart* grammatically possesses the Scots (i.e., they are the Scots *of* the movie *Braveheart*). So, *Braveheart* needs to be possessive, but *Scots* does not.

74. **(H)** We need the third-person singular form of the verb *to be* and the possessive pronoun *its* (the one without the apostrophe): The film's most troubling inaccuracy *is its* depiction of Robert the Bruce.

75. **(A)** Although the sentence is in the past tense, and the subsequent verb *knew* is also in the past tense, the *not only did* construction means that we need the infinitive *betray*. The verb *did* is in the past tense, and *betray* is attached to it. You would say *He never betrayed*, but *Not only did he never betray, but he ....*

Mathematics

1. **(E)** The width is given as 4.5 cm and the length is given as four times the width, which is $4 \cdot 4.5 = 18$ cm. Using the area of a rectangle formula $A = L \cdot W$, we get $A = 4.5 \cdot 18 = 81$.

2. **(G)** Probability is calculated as the number of successful outcomes divided by the total possible outcomes. The number of gumballs that are NOT blue is 30 yellow + 32 red + 28 green = 90 gumballs. The formula becomes P(NOT blue) $= \dfrac{90}{120}$. Simplify the fraction to get $\dfrac{3}{4}$.

3. **(D)** 4×10^{-5} is scientific notation for 0.00004. Most calculators can perform scientific notation using the exponent key.

4. **(F)** $\sqrt{96} = \sqrt{16} \cdot \sqrt{6} = 4\sqrt{6}$.

5. **(D)** The formula for the area of a square is $A = s^2$. Plugging in 49 for the area yields $49 = s^2$. Taking the square root gives $s = 7$. The question asks for the perimeter of the square. To find the perimeter, use the formula $P = 4 \cdot s$. Plugging in 7 for s gives $P = 4 \cdot 7 = 28$.

6. **(H)** The slope of a line can be found using the formula $y = mx + b$, where m is the slope of the line and b is the y-intercept. To find the slope of $5x - 4y = -12$, first solve for y. This yields $y = \dfrac{5}{4}x + 3$, so the slope of the line is $\dfrac{5}{4}$. The slope of a perpendicular line can be found by taking the opposite reciprocal. The opposite reciprocal of $\dfrac{5}{4}$ is $-\dfrac{4}{5}$.

7. **(C)** The measure of $\angle XZY$ is supplementary to the measure of $\angle YZP$, which was given as 115. Calculating $\angle XZY$ yields $180 - 115 = 65$. The sum of the measures of the three angles of a triangle is 180, so to find $\angle XYZ$ take $180 - (40 + 65) = 180 - 105 = 75$.

8. **(K)** The area of a circle can be calculated by the formula $A = \pi r^2$. Plugging 6 in for the radius gives $A = \pi(6)^2 = 36\pi$.

9. **(C)** We can use the problem to set up two equations. Let $B =$ the cost of a strip of bacon and $E =$ the cost of one egg. The first sentence yields the equation $2B + E = \$2.10$. The second sentence yields the equation $3B + 2E = \$3.45$. Solving the first equation for E yields $E = 2.10 - 2B$. Substituting $2.10 - 2B$ into the second equation for E yields $3B + 2(2.10 - 2B) = 3.45$. Solving this equation for B gives $B = \$0.75$. However, the question asks for the price of an egg, so plugging 0.75 into the first equation for B and solving for E gives $E = 0.60$ or 60 cents.

10. **(G)** $\triangle XYZ$ is an isosceles triangle with vertex Y meaning angles X and Z are congruent; therefore, angle Z has measure $2a$ as well. The sum of the 3 angles of a triangle is 180. Use this to set up the equation $112 + 2a + 2a = 180$. Solving for a gives $112 + 4a = 180 \rightarrow 4a = 68 \rightarrow a = 17$.

11. **(B)** $f(4) = -3(4)^2 + 4(4) = -48 + 16 = -32$.

12. **(J)** $\angle MRP$ is vertical to $\angle QRS$. Angle QRS is composed of 2 smaller angles, SRT and TRQ. $\angle SRT = 25°$ and $\angle TRQ = 90°$, making $\angle QRS = 25 + 90 = 115°$. Vertical angles are congruent, so $\angle MRP$ is equal to $\angle QRS$; therefore, $\angle MRP = 115°$.

13. **(D)** Recall SOH-CAH-TOA from trigonometry, $\tan A = \dfrac{\text{opposite}}{\text{adjacent}}$. The side opposite angle A measures 24 cm and the adjacent side measures 10 cm. Dividing 24 by 10 and simplifying gives $\dfrac{24}{10} = \dfrac{12}{5}$. So, $\tan A = \dfrac{12}{5}$.

14. **(H)** Jenna needs 2 hours 30 minutes to cook the soup, 7 minutes to assemble the ingredients, and 20 minutes to cut the vegetables. Adding these times together gives 2 hours 57 minutes. If she wants the meal ready at 1:15 P.M., she needs to start it 2 hours and 57 minutes before 1:15 P.M., which is 10:18 A.M. Checking your work gives 10:18 + 2 hours = 12:18 + 57 minutes = 1:15 P.M.

15. **(D)** The midpoint formula is $M = \left(\dfrac{x_1 + x_2}{2}, \dfrac{y_1 + y_2}{2} \right)$. One endpoint and the midpoint were given in the problem. Using (x, y) for endpoint B, $(-2, 4)$ for endpoint A, and $(3, 9)$ for midpoint M, we get the equation $(3, 9) = \left(\dfrac{-2 + x}{2}, \dfrac{4 + y}{2} \right)$. Solving for x and y, we get the equations $\dfrac{-2 + x}{2} = 3$ and $\dfrac{4 + y}{2} = 9$. Finish solving each equation to get $x = 8$ and $y = 14$; therefore, the answer is $(8, 14)$.

16. **(H)** To solve an absolute value inequality, you must first isolate the absolute value. Subtracting 4 from both sides makes the inequality $|x| < 3$. This is equivalent to the compound sentence "$x < 3$ and $x > -3$". This is equivalent to $-3 < x < 3$, so choice H is the correct answer.

17. **(B)** To find the sum of the interior angles of a polygon use the formula $(n-2) \cdot 180$, where n represents the number of sides of the polygon. A pentagon has 5 sides, so the formula becomes $(5-2) \cdot 180 = (3) \cdot 180 = 540°$.

18. **(F)** $n^{1/2}$ means the square root of n, so the equation becomes $\sqrt{n} = 4$. To solve a square root equation, square both sides of the equal sign to get $n = 16$. Another good way to solve this problem is by plugging the answers in for n and using your calculator. If you plug 16 in for n, you get $16^{1/2} = 4$.

19. **(D)** Once the numbers are written in order from least to greatest, there are 6 in the 150–199 interval, 3 in the 200–249 interval, and 2 in the 250–299 interval.

20. **(H)** To find the median of a set of data, you must write the numbers in order and find the middle number.

21. **(E)** To find the total calories, 258 should be divided by 46% (or 0.46).

22. **(K)** To find the average, we need to add all of the original numbers (sum of 2,227) along with the additional two numbers (x and y) and divide by how many numbers there are, which is now 13 because the list started with 11 numbers and added two more.

23. **(C)** The problem states that $b < -6$ and $3a - b = 21$. Solving for b in the second equation, $b = 3a - 21$. Next, substitute $3a - 21$ in for b in the original inequality yielding $3a - 21 < -6$. Solve for a, $a < 5$.

24. **(J)** The path the dog can walk forms a semicircle of radius 12 blocked on the right side by the house. To find the area of a semicircle, use the formula $A = \frac{1}{2}\pi r^2$. Plugging 12 in for the radius and 3.14 for pi, we get $A = \frac{1}{2}(3.14)(12)^2 = \frac{1}{2}(3.14)(144) = 226.08$, which would round to about 226 meters.

25. **(E)** If you factor the numerator it becomes $\dfrac{(3x - 2y)(8x + 3y)}{(3x - 2y)}$. Canceling the like factors in the numerator and denominator, the fraction becomes $\dfrac{\cancel{(3x - 2y)}(8x + 3y)}{\cancel{(3x - 2y)}} = 8x + 3y$.

26. **(G)** Jose's profit the first year will be $25,000, and next year's profit can be found by taking $25,000 + 0.07(25,000) = \$26,750$. A geometric sequence is a sequence with a common ratio. The ratio of the profit for the second year to the first year is $26{,}750/25{,}000 = 1.07$. Therefore, choices F and H are both incorrect. Because the difference between the second year's profit and the first year's is $26{,}750 - 25{,}000 = 1{,}750$, neither answer choice J nor K is correct.

27. **(C)** After labeling the given information, $NM = MP = PL = ML = 4$. Since $\triangle LMP$ is equilateral, angles LMP and LPM equal 60°. Because $\angle LMP = 60°$, $\angle LMN = 180 - 60 = 120°$. Since $\triangle LMN$ is isosceles, angles LNM and MLN each equal $\dfrac{180 - 120}{2} = \dfrac{60}{2} = 30°$. Finally, since $\angle LNM = 30$ and $\angle LPM = 60$, $\triangle LNP$ is a 30°–60°–90° triangle with a hypotenuse of 8 and one leg of 4. Using 30°–60°–90° ratios, side $LN = 4 \cdot \sqrt{3} = 4\sqrt{3}$.

28. **(G)** The denominator would be $-32 - 9 = 9 - 9 = 0$ and division by 0 is undefined. Inspection of the graph also reveals vertical asymptotes at $x = -3$ and $x = 3$.

29. **(A)** Plugging 122° in for F in the given formula gives $122 = \frac{9}{5}C + 32$. Subtracting 32 from both sides yields $90 = \frac{9}{5}C \rightarrow C = 50°$.

30. **(H)** To calculate probability, use the formula $P = \dfrac{\text{number of successful outcomes}}{\text{number of total outcomes}}$. The fractions greater than $\frac{1}{2}$ are $\frac{3}{5}, \frac{5}{7}$, and $\frac{5}{9}$ so the number of successful outcomes is 3. The total number of outcomes is 5 because there are 5 fractions. Therefore, the probability is 3 out of 5 or $\frac{3}{5}$.

31. **(C)** To calculate the total number of possible outcomes, multiply all of the choices together. This problem has one kicker in it: the word *or* implies when the customer first chooses a salad OR a soup, he or she has a total of $3 + 2 = 5$ choices for his or her first course. The customer then chooses a main dish (5 choices), a vegetable (4 choices), and a dessert (3 choices). Multiply all these choices together to get $5 \cdot 5 \cdot 4 \cdot 3 = 300$ total choices for his or her meal.

32. **(G)** Labeling the given information in the correct places gives the hypotenuse of the right triangle to be 247 and one of the legs to be 228. Use the Pythagorean Theorem to find the missing leg of a right triangle. Setting up the formula we get $a^2 + b^2 = c^2 \rightarrow x^2 + 228^2 = 247^2 \rightarrow x^2 + 51,984 = 61,009 \rightarrow x^2 = 9,025$. Taking the square root of both sides gives $x = 95$.

33. **(D)** To calculate the distance a person would have to run around a circular track, use the formula $C = \pi d$. Using a diameter of X, one lap around the track would be $C = \pi d \rightarrow C = \pi X$. The problem asks how far the athlete would run in a 6-lap race. If each lap is πX meters, 6 laps would be $6 \cdot \pi X = 6\pi X$.

34. **(K)** Using the first sentence to set up an equation and solving for m, we get $m \cdot 4 = n \rightarrow 4m = n \rightarrow m = \dfrac{n}{4}$. We want to express the sum of m and 4 in terms of n. The sum of m and 4 is written as $m + 4$. Substituting $\dfrac{n}{4}$ in for m gives $\dfrac{n}{4} + 4$.

35. **(C)** We are given 3 squares labeled R with side length x. To find the area of a square use the formula $A = s^2$. Plugging x in for s we get $A = x^2$. Since there are 3 squares labeled R, their total area would be $3x^2$. Using similar logic we get 12 squares labeled S that have a total area of $12y^2$, and 13 rectangles each labeled P have a total area of $13xy$. Adding all these areas together we get $3x^2 + 13xy + 12y^2$.

36. **(J)** If the line $y = (D-3)x + 7$ passes through the point $(-5, 2)$, we can plug $x = -5$ into the equation and $y = 2$, then solve for D. Plugging in these values and solving for D, we get $2 = (D-3)(-5) + 7 \rightarrow -5 = (D-3)(-5) \rightarrow 1 = (D-3) \rightarrow D = 4$. Now, the question asks for the slope of the line that is the coefficient of x. In this case, the coefficient of x is $(D-3)$. Plugging in 4 for D we get the slope to equal $4 - 3 = 1$.

37. **(B)** The first equation states $x = -6$; plugging -6 into the second equation for x gives $y = 2(-6) - 4 \rightarrow y = -12 - 4 \rightarrow y = -16$. Therefore, the point of intersection is $(-6, -16)$.

38. **(G)** Slope is defined as the change in y divided by the change in x, or $m = \dfrac{y_2 - y_1}{x_2 - x_1}$. For the slope of $\overline{ST}$, we would have $m = \dfrac{3-9}{14-8} = \dfrac{-6}{6} = -1$.

39. **(C)** When a point (x, y) is reflected over the x-axis, its image is $(x, -y)$, so $(4, 9)$ would become $(4, -9)$.

40. **(F)** The area of a trapezoid is $A = \frac{1}{2}h(b_1 + b_2)$. The distance between the y-coordinates 3 and 9 is the height of the trapezoid, which is 6. The bases are found by calculating the distances between the x-coordinates of the points: from 2 to 14 is 12 and from 4 to 8 is 4. So, $A = \frac{1}{2} \times 6 \times (12 + 4) = 3 \times (16) = 48$.

41. **(E)** We know that $c \times 2 = r$ and $c \times 3 = t$. We also know that $c \times 5 = 35$, so $c = 7$. So, $c \times 2$ becomes $7 \times 2 = 14 = r$ and $c \times 3$ becomes $7 \times 3 = 21 = t$ and $r + t = 14 + 21 = 35$.

42. **(G)** $\cos M = 0.4 = \dfrac{2}{5}$. Recalling SOH-CAH-TOA, cosine is the ratio of the adjacent side to the hypotenuse of a right triangle. Since $PM = 24$ and LN is the perpendicular bisector of PM, $NM = 12$. Labeling LM as x, we can set up a proportion, $\dfrac{\text{adjacent}}{\text{hypotenuse}} = \dfrac{\text{adjacent}}{\text{hypotenuse}} \rightarrow \dfrac{2}{5} = \dfrac{12}{x}$. Cross multiplying and solving for x gives $2x = 5(12) \rightarrow 2x = 60 \rightarrow x = 30$.

43. **(A)** From the given information we can set up the formula $C = 30 + k\sqrt{t}$, where $C = 30 + k\sqrt{t}$ represents how much the violinist charges, k is the constant of variation, and t is the time the violin is rented. Plugging in 25 minutes for time and \$65 for C, we can solve for k to get $65 = 30 + k\sqrt{25} \rightarrow 35 = k\sqrt{25} \rightarrow 35 = 5k \rightarrow k = 7$. Now that we know the constant of variation, plug 81 minutes in for t and solve for C to find the cost of renting the violin for 81 minutes. $C = 30 + 7\sqrt{81} \rightarrow C = 30 + 7(9) \rightarrow C = 30 + 63 \rightarrow C = 93$.

44. **(H)** The area of the shaded region can be found by subtracting the area of the smaller square from the area of the larger square. Labeling the sides of the larger square x and using the area of a square formula $A = s^2$, we get $A_{\text{shaded region}} = A_{\text{large square}} - A_{\text{small square}} \rightarrow 16 = x^2 - 3^2 \rightarrow 16 = x^2 - 9 \rightarrow 25 = x^2$. Taking the square root of both sides gives $x = 5$.

45. **(E)** Substituting $x = \cos\theta$ and $y = \sin\theta$ into the inequality $(\sin\theta)\left(\dfrac{1}{\cos\theta}\right) < 0$ gives $(y)\left(\dfrac{1}{x}\right) < 0$. The problem is asking when the product of y and $\left(\dfrac{1}{x}\right)$ is negative. The only way the product of 2 factors can be negative is if exactly 1 of them is negative. The quadrants where x and y have opposite signs are quadrants II and IV.

46. **(K)** $(3 - i)^2 = (3 - i)(3 - i) = 9 - 3i - 3i + i^2 = 9 - 6i + i^2$. Recalling $i^2 = -1$, the problem becomes $9 - 6i + (-1) = 8 - 6i$. A helpful tip is that TI-83 and TI-84 graphing calculators have an i button above the decimal point. Plugging $(3 - i)^2$ into your calculator will also give you $8 - 6i$.

47. **(B)** $(2r)^3 = 8r^3$ and everything else in the formula stays the same, so the volume is 8 times the original volume.

48. **(F)** $\sqrt[2]{16r^6} = \sqrt[2]{16} \cdot \sqrt[2]{r^6} = 4 \cdot r^3 = 4r^3$.

49. **(B)** If 2 is a solution for x, we can plug 2 into the equation for x and solve for k. This gives $(2)^2 + k(2) + 12 = 0$. Solving for k gives $4 + 2k + 12 = 0 \rightarrow 2k = -16 \rightarrow k = -8$.

50. **(G)** The standard form of a circle is $(x - h)^2 + (y - k)^2 = r^2$ where (h, k) is the center of the circle and r is the radius. The center of this circle is $(0, 3)$ and the radius is 3. Plugging these numbers in for h, k, and r, respectively, gives $(x - 0)^2 + (y - 3)^2 = 3^2$. Simplifying the equation gives $x^2 + (y - 3)^2 = 9$.

51. **(D)** To find the equation of a line we calculate the slope and the y-intercept. The slope can be found by finding the change in y divided by the change in x. The slope of the line through the first two data points is $m = \dfrac{y_2 - y_1}{x_2 - x_1} = \dfrac{-5 - (-8)}{-1 - (-2)} = \dfrac{3}{1} = 3$. The y-intercept is the value of y when $x = 0$. The third data point is $(0, -2)$; therefore, -2 is the y-intercept. Plugging what we found into the formula $y = mx + b$, we get $y = 3x - 2$.

52. **(J)** The sum of the angles of a triangle equals $180°$. Using this, angle $X = 180 - 32 - 44 = 104°$. Using the law of sines, we get $\dfrac{x}{\sin X} = \dfrac{y}{\sin Y} \rightarrow \dfrac{x}{(\sin 104°)} = \dfrac{22}{(\sin 44°)}$. Cross multiplying and solving for x gives $x \cdot (\sin 44°) = 22 \cdot (\sin 104°) \rightarrow x = \dfrac{22(\sin 104°)}{\sin 44°}$.

53. **(B)** In order to graph the equation $3x - 2y = 6$, it is often easier to write it in $y = mx + b$ form. Solving for y in the equation gives $-2y = -3x + 6 \rightarrow y = \frac{3}{2}x - 3$, so the slope of the equation is $\frac{3}{2}$ and the y-intercept is -3. The only graphs that have a y-intercept of -3 are choices B and E. The slope of the line in choice E is $\frac{2}{3}$ and the slope of the line in choice B is $\frac{3}{2}$ making choice B correct.

54. **(F)** For $\sqrt{(3)(7)} \cdot \sqrt{(m)(n)} \cdot \sqrt{(7)(5)}$ to simplify to an integer, each factor under the radical must have a pair. So far, there are two 7's, one 3, one 5, an m, and an n. For 3 and 5 to each have a pair, m and n must be 3 and 5, respectively. Checking to make sure we have the correct m and n we get $\sqrt{(3)(7)} \cdot \sqrt{(3)(5)} \cdot \sqrt{(7)(5)} = \sqrt{(3)(7)(3)(5)(7)(5)} = \sqrt{11{,}025} = 105$, which is an integer; therefore, m and n equal 3 and 5, respectively. Now, answering the question asked gives $m + n = 3 + 5 = 8$.

55. **(E)** To calculate profit we use the formula profit equals revenue minus cost, or $P = R - C$. To calculate revenue, Cam makes \$6.50 per umbrella or $R = 6.5x$, where x represents the number of umbrellas sold. To calculate cost, Cam has to pay a one-time cost of \$25,000 for the building and machinery along with \$4.00 per umbrella, making his total cost $C = 25{,}000 + 4x$. Plugging these into the formula $P = R - C$, we get $P = 6.5x - (25{,}000 + 4x) = 2.50x - 25{,}000$.

56. **(H)** The question asks which statement is NOT true. $\angle PON = \overset{\frown}{PN} = 100°$. $\overline{PM}$ is a diameter, so $\overset{\frown}{PM} = 180°$. Therefore, $\overset{\frown}{MN} = 180 - 100 = 80°$. If $\overset{\frown}{MN} = 80°$, then $\angle NOM = 80°$. Since $\angle PON = 100°$, $\angle PON \neq \angle NOM$.

57. **(E)** The best way to solve this problem is to plug in clever numbers for m and n to eliminate wrong answers. Starting with $m = 1$ and $n = 1$, the equation becomes $|1 - 1| = |1 + 1|$ $\rightarrow 0 = 2$, which is a false statement. This eliminates choices B and C. Now, plug in $m = 0$ and $n = 0$ and the equation becomes $|0 - 0| = |0 + 0| \rightarrow 0 = 0$, which is a true statement, eliminating choice A. Finally, plug in $m = 0$ and $n = 1$ to get $|0 - 1| = |0 + 1| \rightarrow |-1| = |1| \rightarrow$ $1 = 1$, which is a true statement. This eliminates choice D, leaving choice E as the correct answer.

58. **(F)** Using the change of base formula $\log_a b = \frac{\log b}{\log a}$ the expression becomes $\log_4 16 = \frac{\log 16}{\log 4}$. Now, plug $\frac{\log 16}{\log 4}$ into a calculator to get 2.

59. **(B)** The expected value is found by multiplying the probability of each outcome by the corresponding reward. The probabilities are blue $\frac{4}{8}$, red $\frac{3}{8}$, and orange $\frac{1}{8}$. Therefore, the expected value is $\frac{4}{8}(1) + \frac{3}{8}(3) + \frac{1}{8}(5) = \frac{18}{8} \rightarrow \frac{18}{8} = 2\frac{2}{8} \rightarrow 2.25$.

60. **(K)** $\tan x = \frac{\sin x}{\cos x}$, which is not equivalent to $\frac{\cos x}{\sin x}$.

Reading

1. **(B)** The *strong young woman* part is definitely true, and the *inadvertently discovers her destiny* part is so broad that it can't really be wrong. There is nothing in it to make it wrong, and therefore it is right.

2. **(H)** The entire paragraph definitely details *hardships* that Belisa *saw*, and since there is no way that this general answer can be wrong, there is no need to gamble on any of the more specific ones.

3. **(A)** As is so often the case on the Literary Narrative passage, the right answer is the most broad one. The passage definitely establishes Belisa's *originality*, and it is definitely written in a *fanciful* (which means "surreal" and "stylized") manner, and since that is basically all that choice A says, it can't be wrong. (Some of the other choices seem like they might be close to true, but choice A contains the aspects of them that are true!)

4. **(J)** A newspaper with a sports section that contains an article about a boxing match is the most "real-world" thing that appears in the passage. Belisa recognizes that she can use words to advance her position in the real world.

5. **(A)** We know that Belisa's services are *useful* because the first two paragraphs establish that she was in great demand and that people were excited and grateful to purchase her words. We know that it was a goal of Belisa's to be *honest* because line 37 mentions her wanting to avoid *deceit* and line 111 mentions her not wanting to *defraud* people. (When questions on the ACT Reading present choices of paired adjectives, the right answer is <u>almost always</u> one with *and* between them, rather than *but*!)

6. **(H)** The phrase *she herself had searched* implies that Belisa had named herself based on words she liked. (And it helps to know that words beginning with *bel-* indicate "beauty" in the Romance languages, and how *crepuscular* means "active at twilight!")

7. **(B)** Although Belisa is strongly opposed to dishonesty in her own personal business, the passage never says anything about her exposing the lies of others. She does all of the options EXCEPT this one.

8. **(J)** *Interminable* means "very long" or "endless" (think of how a *term* is "a set period of time," and *terminate* means "to end something").

9. **(B)** Lines 96–100 clearly state that Belisa's primary goal was to *make a living* (she knew she had to, somehow). Some of the other choices were eventually effects of her work, but not her primary motivation at first.

10. **(H)** *Spindly* means "very thin," and in context here <u>frail</u> is by far the closest.

11. **(C)** The first and fourth paragraphs establish that the bell (like "Europe" and other things) is a metaphor. The references to God and the future in the second and final paragraphs establish that the concern is fate or unknowable future troubles.

12. **(F)** *Tribulation* means *troubles* (as in "trials and tribulations"). The word *affliction*, which appears several times subsequently in the paragraph, is clearly being used to signify the same idea.

13. **(B)** Ironically, *gold* serves as a metaphor for another person's troubles (rather than something good, as you'd expect). What's good about these troubles is that they remind someone else (the author) that we are all connected, and so are *gold* in that sense.

14. **(F)** The idea in this metaphor is that any one person's death diminishes the human race, just as the loss of land would make a continent smaller.

15. **(D)** As is often the case on the ACT Reading, this broad and positive answer contains nothing that is falsified by the text.

16. **(H)** *Maxim* and *proverb* are rough synonyms, both indicating a phrase that espouses a "philosophical belief," a phrase that appears shortly thereafter.

17. **(B)** Tutu thinks Ubuntu is "the essence of being human"; then obviously that must imply that it is applicable to all human cultures.

18. **(F)** Passage A makes mention of God several times, and Passage B never explicitly does so.

19. **(C)** Both passages are attempts to characterize what it truly means to be human (*appraisals* means *characterizations*).

20. **(J)** As can be intuited even if you've never heard it, the expression "He ain't heavy; he's my brother" indicates that it is no burden to care for others—exactly the point of both passages.

21. **(B)** The main focus of the passage is on Kahlo's life, and the closing sentence of the first paragraph makes reference to the *elevation of the artist over the art* (lines 16–17). (The first and last sentences of the first and last paragraphs are <u>always</u> good places to look when answering "main idea" questions!)

22. **(J)** The author's point in comparing Kahlo's story to a *game of telephone* is that it has been changed in the telling to suit the priorities and biases of the tellers. Choice J is the nearest paraphrase of this idea.

23. **(C)** Lines 30–31 establish that the standards applied to women for admission to the canon were the same as those used for men. All the answer choices identify phenomena that contributed to the lack of great female artists prior to 1970 EXCEPT this one.

24. **(F)** The author is presenting and supporting an argument; the point of the passage is to *persuade* people that it is short-sighted to selectively edit Kahlo's biography and to focus more on that biography than on her work. The last sentence of the first paragraph and the first and last sentences of the last paragraph all present assertions that the author is trying to support.

25. **(C)** Lines 55–58 establish that the quality of Kahlo's work severely declined due to her abuse of alcohol and painkillers.

26. **(J)** *Warts* in line 64 is a metaphor for *the less pleasant parts of Kahlo's life.* The expression "warts and all" means to describe someone fully, including their negative qualities. The

sentence avowedly concerns *biography*, and the rest of the paragraph concentrates on Kahlo's personal flaws.

27. **(C)** The passage never says anything about *any* of Kahlo's paintings being self-portraits, and certainly does not imply that *all* of them were. All of the answer choices are true EXCEPT this one.

28. **(G)** The purpose of the passage is to convince Kahlo enthusiasts—specifically feminist women—to acknowledge a more complete picture of the artist's life. The last sentence of the first paragraph, the first sentence of the last paragraph, and the last sentence of the last paragraph are all paraphrases of this exhortation.

29. **(D)** The first paragraph, and especially its last sentence, establish that the author thinks people are paying far too much attention to Kahlo's life and not enough to her work. In the last paragraph, line 81 explicitly states that *the really tragic part of Kahlo's story* is how much her biography overshadows her work. The other three answer choices are all biographical details, and focusing on them is exactly what the author says people should *not* do. (As with many places on the ACT, "which of these things is not like the others" is a good strategy here!)

30. **(F)** If the author thinks it should be *swept away*, then we know that the *sideshow* must refer to all the things the author wants people to pay *less* attention to: the dramatic details of Kahlo's life.

31. **(B)** The second sentence of the passage establishes that it concerns the discovery of fossils from crocodiles so large that they preyed on dinosaurs. (You can also get a clue from looking above the passage at the title, which includes the phrase *Dino-Eating Crocs!*)

32. **(J)** Lines 76–78 state that crocodiles *hunt a wide range of prey* and *eat whatever's available in their areas*. Therefore, their eating habits are *varied* and *opportunistic*. (When questions on the ACT Reading present choices of paired adjectives, the right answer is almost always one with *and* between them, rather than *but*!)

33. **(A)** Line 104 suggests that crocodiles can grow to enormous sizes when *the right conditions arise*, and lines 83–84 establish that disparate lineages of giant crocs have arisen in different places and times. This all logically adds up to the idea that *crocodilians tend to grow as large as conditions permit them to*.

34. **(H)** Line 87 states that SuperCroc, and not *Deinosuchus*, lived in Niger.

35. **(C)** Paragraph 3 (lines 24–35) mainly discusses the fact that no undigested material was present in the fossilized dung, and that, since crocodiles' digestive systems digest everything, this suggests a crocodilian source.

36. **(J)** Lines 32–34 state that *both modern and ancient crocs* have digestive systems that eat up everything.

37. **(B)** *Lineages* means "bloodlines" (i.e., "ancestry"). It is the word from the choices that makes the most sense when plugged into the sentence.

38. **(F)** Lines 41–43 and 55–60 explain that *Deinosuchus* bite marks were found in fossilized dinosaur bones.

39. **(B)** Lines 77–78 state that crocs *eat whatever's available in their areas,* suggesting that a crocodilian whose main food source dries up will simply eat something else. The fact that the answer to question 32 was choice J should have given you a clue here. (It is often the case on the ACT Reading that getting one right answer can help you figure out one or more others!)

40. **(J)** Lines 100–105 explain that the conditions necessary for the existence of giant crocs occur very rarely. Thus, the existence of giant crocs is *anomalous,* which means "not typical."

Science

1. **(C)** Look in Figure 3, which represents Static COF and the bar representing "Rubber on concrete" is the highest—that's all you have to do here! The only slightly tricky thing is that in Figure 2 (the graph for Kinetic COF) the bars for "Rubber on concrete" and "Rubber on asphalt" appear to be nearly equal, so someone who looks in the wrong place first might waste a few seconds being confused. (When you see something that appears to make no sense, always immediately double-check the labels to make sure you're looking at the right graph!)

2. **(G)** Look at the numbers on the vertical axis in Figure 2 and you'll see that the "Rubber on concrete" bar is at about 0.7 and the "Plastic on plastic" bar is at about 0.3. That's roughly (though not exactly) half as high. (But even without the numbers, you can easily just eyeball it—look at how far off the other answer choices are!)

3. **(D)** All this question wants you to do is look at Figure 3 (Static COF) and put the bars in order from lowest to highest. The order in choice D is correct.

4. **(F)** Even though the bars for "Rubber on concrete" and "Rubber on asphalt" in Figure 2 look roughly even, the "Rubber on concrete" bar is actually slightly higher, and so the height order of the bars in both graphs is indeed the same. (And even if you couldn't perceive that it is slightly higher, look how wrong the other choices are!)

5. **(B)** All this question is asking is which bar is the lowest (in both graphs). The bars represent friction, and less friction equals more speed. The "Plastic on plastic" bar is lowest in both graphs.

6. **(F)** You would expect the static COF for rubber on steel to be higher than the static COF for steel on steel but lower than steel rubber on asphalt since steel, according to Figure 2, requires less static COF than rubber. If rubber on concrete and asphalt are about 38 and 42, respectively, rubber on steel should be slightly below that number. Even though you can't find an exact amount on a bar graph, there are no other answer choices that come any closer to the static COF for rubber on concrete and asphalt.

7. **(B)** All this question wants you to do is look in Table 1 and put those substances in highest to lowest order going by the numbers next to them.

8. **(J)** The water was 67°F when they started and 92°F after 5 minutes, so it went up by 25°F, meaning that 25 Btus were used (the text above Table 2 establishes that one pound of water was used).

9. **(A)** The first sentence of the paragraph in Experiment 2 clearly says that the students are measuring the amount of energy natural gas creates.

10. **(G)** Exact math is not necessary on this question, just guesstimating. Experiment 2 tells us that natural gas will heat one pound of water to 117°F after 10 minutes, and Experiment 1 tells us that the Btu/ton produced by gasoline is about 4/5 of the Btu/ton produced by natural gas. So, you know that the answer is going to be around 4/5 of 117°F (less, but not too much less). The only choice that works is 99°F (it's less, but more than half).

11. **(C)** Table 3 says that a barrel of oil equals 5,600,000 Btus. That's way more than any of the other choices.

12. **(H)** The temperature in Table 2 is going up by 25°F every 5 minutes, and $142 + 25 = 167$.

13. **(B)** Coal has an energy content of 25 million BTU/ton while natural gas has an energy content much higher at 47 million BTU/ton. Therefore, one would expect that the water heated by coal would have a lower temperature after ten minutes than water heated by natural gas. Natural gas had a water temperature of 117 degrees after ten minutes, so the water temperature in the new experiment should be under 117 degrees.

14. **(F)** As Figure 1 and Table 1 indicate (and as you may already have known from school), low pH means acid and high pH means base, so a solution with a pH of 12.5 would be the strongest base.

15. **(C)** We look at Table 2 to see which substances made the bulb glow brightest, and then look at Table 3 to see the pH levels of those substances. You will notice that both strong acids and strong bases make the bulb glow brightest (in other words, the farther the pH is from 7 in either direction, the better a conductor the substance is).

16. **(H)** Table 3 says that KOH has a pH of 11.2, and Table 2 says that it made the bulb glow brightly, meaning that it is a strong base.

17. **(D)** Figure 1 says that stronger acids have more hydrogen, and Table 3 says that HCl has a pH of 0.86, making it a stronger acid than the other choices, and meaning it therefore has more hydrogen.

18. **(J)** A substance that makes the bulb glow brightly could be either a strong acid or a strong base, so the answer can't be determined from the information in the passage. (If you happen to know that NaCOl is the chemical formula for bleach, which is a strong base, you should ignore that knowledge, since the question is asking about what you can tell from the passage!)

19. **(B)** All you have to do here is plot the pH values listed in Table 3 for these substances as a bar graph. Table 3 says that the pH values for NaOH, KOH, and NH_4OH are 13.1, 11.2, and 9.2, respectively, so the graph in choice B is correct.

20. **(F)** The experiments found that solutions that are very basic (closest to 14 on pH scale) and very acidic (closest to 0 on the pH scale) conduct the most electricity. Solution 1 is very basic at 0.56, compared to 6.83, so it is the best conductor of electricity.

21. **(C)** That is the relationship shown in Figure 2. The key shows that salt marsh water is represented by the line with the x markers. The *x*-axis represents the aqueous concentration. The line with x markers clearly increases steadily, showing a direct relationship between the aqueous concentration and the white phosphorus mass: as the concentration increases, so does the mass.

22. **(H)** This is correct because of the data presented in Table 2. Look for the smallest number in the table. It is 29.1, in the first row and the last column. Look at the column and row headings to determine the answer is Trial 1 after 5-minutes static.

23. **(D)** This is correct because of the information presented in the opening passage. The third sentence explains the SPME technique and states, "a thin fused silica fiber ... is exposed to a sample ...."

24. **(H)** This is correct because of the data presented in Table 2. In order for the scientist's theory to be supported by the data, the numbers in the third column, titled 10-Min Sonic, would need to be larger than the numbers in the second column, titled 5-Min Sonic. However, that is not the case. The numbers in the second column are larger than those in the third column for Trials 2 and 3, meaning that more white phosphorus was extracted after 5-minutes sonication for those two trials only.

25. **(C)** Choice C is correct because of the data presented in Table 1. The last row in the table displays the mean mass of white phosphorus extracted from each type of water. The largest number in this row is 36.3, in the column with the heading Pond.

26. **(G)** This is correct because of the data presented in Figure 2. The x-axis represents the aqueous concentration, but the graph only includes concentrations up to 0.14 g/L. To infer the amount of white phosphorus that would be extracted at a concentration of 0.2 g/L, the line that represents pond water needs to be traced farther to the right along the x-axis. The key shows that the line with the triangle marker represents pond water. Following this line to the right demonstrates that the white phosphorus mass would continue to increase as the aqueous concentration increases. Since the line increases at a steep slope, and 0.2 g/L is much larger than 0.14 µg/L, we can infer that the answer would be much larger than 45, making 100 pg the only reasonable answer.

27. **(A)** Table 1 shows the largest mean for white phosphorus mass in pond water at a measurement of 36.3 pg.

28. **(H)** This is a simple "Go Up, Hit Line, Go Over" question. In Figure 1, go up from silicon, hit the melting-point line (the broken one—and also the one on the bottom, since obviously substances melt at a lower temperature than the one at which they boil), and go over from there to the vertical axis, which reads about halfway between 1500 K and 2000 K below 1000 K. Of the choices, only 1700 K is a logical answer.

29. **(D)** The proton numbers of the elements in Table 1 get progressively greater, whereas the lines for melting point and boiling point in Table 2 go up and then back down. Remember, the passage states that both melting point and boiling point trend higher as intermolecular forces increase. Since there is no relationship with melting point and/or boiling point, there can be no relationship with the intermolecular forces.

30. **(J)** The two lines in Figure 1 basically each go up and down when the other does, but not exactly—that is, the lines are not always parallel and therefore there is no constant that can relate the two quantities.

31. **(A)** "Transitions from a liquid phase to a gaseous phase" means boiling point. According to the solid line in Figure 1, the element that boils at 500 K is phosphorus.

32. **(F)** The lines in Figure 1 are closer together above the elements that Table 1 names as nonmetals than they are above the elements identified as metals, so the conclusion is correct.

33. **(D)** Table 1 includes metals of sodium, magnesium, and aluminum which, when displayed in Figure 2, show a temperature range for the boiling point between approximately 1,200 and 2,700 degrees.

34. **(H)** The bar representing 500+ size operations is the lowest in Figure 1, which represents total losses by percentage.

35. **(C)** The bar representing CCD losses (the dark one) due to weather is the lowest bar in Figure 2, which plots the data for suspected causes of losses.

36. **(F)** The bar representing CCD losses (the dark one) due to starvation is the highest bar in Figure 2, which plots the data for suspected causes of losses.

37. **(D)** In Table 1 (which plots only CCD losses) the largest loss percentages are due to starvation in the smaller operations.

38. **(G)** All this question wants you to do is identify the suspected causes in Figure 2 that have CCD bars (the dark ones) higher than non-CCD bars (the light ones). The two that do are weak in fall and queen death.

39. **(C)** For three of the suspected causes in Figure 2—starvation, weather, and pests—the non-CCD bars are higher than the CCD bars. It would help you here to remember the answer to question 38. (It is often the case on the ACT Science that remembering answers to earlier questions on a passage can help you on later ones!)

40. **(J)** The scientists surveyed beekeepers to study CCD. The results of both Studies 1 and 2 show numbers related to CCD. Obviously, the beekeepers also had some colonies that did not experience CCD.

WRITING SAMPLE

Docufiction

Critics cannot contain their outrage at the latest blow to unsuspecting viewers' trust in the firm boundary between tried-and-true reality and pie-in-the-sky fantasy. The object of their scorn? A "new" cinematographic hybrid: the docufiction. These people object to the "trickery" involved in bolstering the "real" (the fact that giant prehistoric sharks probably once swam our seas) with fictitious elements (fake "scientists" who produce fake "evidence" to "prove" their supposedly outlandish claims). While this apparently unorthodox melding of genres is easily dismissed as nothing more than networks' self-serving strategy to boost ratings, docufiction is neither simply "harmless" nor sinister. In fact, this latest programming controversy provides an ideal opportunity for a thoughtful assessment about knowledge, belief, and the extent to which we consumers of advertising, news, and entertainment can distinguish among them, especially in a world of information overload where the lines between "fake" and "real" are becoming increasingly blurred.

As with most programming, the perils or potential of docufiction happen to reside in the eye of the beholder. If teachers, students, or home viewers are "tricked" into believing that the prehistoric Megalodon still swims our seas, are their fears different from those who saw Jaws for the first time and thereafter believed that facsimiles of such a shark lay in wait for them along U.S. beaches? The gullible and uninformed will always be taken in by what they see on their screens, but adults bear the responsibility to help students contextualize/assess the possibility that mermaids or centaurs or werewolves roam the planet. My Biology teacher might use the giant shark film as a way of piquing our interest in the ways in which animal life has evolved (or not) over the millennia. After all, common turtles, crocodiles, and iguanas look like they hark from a much earlier era. Docufiction, at the very least, in daring us to imagine scientists reporting on mermaids, reminds us to what extent we take for granted our awe-inspiring natural world.

Those who rail against docufiction as a genre would also do well to consider that the melding of fact with fiction is neither a new nor a necessarily harmful phenomenon. On the contrary, such blending, though momentarily disconcerting, opens up new opportunities for discussion and debate. Considered by some the original docufiction, Orson Welles' adaptation of H.G. Wells' The War of the Worlds, with its fake reporting on a Martian invasion of the U.S., was initially considered dangerous, given the susceptibility of the general public at the time. Today, we simply cannot get the aliens out of our heads, and UFO sightings, whether real or imagined, continue to haunt us. Speaking of yet another controversy over inappropriate depictions of "reality," what diehard Oprah fan and book lover could forget her shock upon learning that the unforgettable opening scene of James Frey's memoir is largely a product of the author's imagination? Her disenchantment with the writer/genre had more to do with her own preconceived notions about truth-telling than any failure on the author's part. The debate raged for months after Frey's revelation, opening up endless conversations regarding the very nature of the genre. For a more contemporary example of the uncertain mixing of fact and fiction, we need look no farther than the recent uproar regarding "fake news" and its effects on a public that some would argue has become much more vigilant since the 2016 presidential election. Controversial, cheesy, occasionally dishonest – call it what you will – docufiction makes us think.

Within an educational setting, most docufiction seems to do nothing more or less than provide opportunities for students to examine how art and "real life" come together to produce both the plausible and the highly unlikely. As long as younger audiences are adequately briefed on the many ways in which the form plays around with reality, there is no reason to deprive them of this opportunity to let their imaginations run wild. If used responsibly, docufiction's supposed trickery ironically explores the means and motives behind various genres, quite possibly transforming students like me into more cautious and discerning consumers.

ANSWER SHEET
Practice Test 5

Directions: Mark one answer only for each question. Make the mark dark. Erase completely any mark made in error. (Additional or stray marks will be counted as mistakes.)

English

1. Ⓐ Ⓑ Ⓒ Ⓓ
2. Ⓕ Ⓖ Ⓗ Ⓙ
3. Ⓐ Ⓑ Ⓒ Ⓓ
4. Ⓕ Ⓖ Ⓗ Ⓙ
5. Ⓐ Ⓑ Ⓒ Ⓓ
6. Ⓕ Ⓖ Ⓗ Ⓙ
7. Ⓐ Ⓑ Ⓒ Ⓓ
8. Ⓕ Ⓖ Ⓗ Ⓙ
9. Ⓐ Ⓑ Ⓒ Ⓓ
10. Ⓕ Ⓖ Ⓗ Ⓙ
11. Ⓐ Ⓑ Ⓒ Ⓓ
12. Ⓕ Ⓖ Ⓗ Ⓙ
13. Ⓐ Ⓑ Ⓒ Ⓓ
14. Ⓕ Ⓖ Ⓗ Ⓙ
15. Ⓐ Ⓑ Ⓒ Ⓓ

16. Ⓕ Ⓖ Ⓗ Ⓙ
17. Ⓐ Ⓑ Ⓒ Ⓓ
18. Ⓕ Ⓖ Ⓗ Ⓙ
19. Ⓐ Ⓑ Ⓒ Ⓓ
20. Ⓕ Ⓖ Ⓗ Ⓙ
21. Ⓐ Ⓑ Ⓒ Ⓓ
22. Ⓕ Ⓖ Ⓗ Ⓙ
23. Ⓐ Ⓑ Ⓒ Ⓓ
24. Ⓕ Ⓖ Ⓗ Ⓙ
25. Ⓐ Ⓑ Ⓒ Ⓓ
26. Ⓕ Ⓖ Ⓗ Ⓙ
27. Ⓐ Ⓑ Ⓒ Ⓓ
28. Ⓕ Ⓖ Ⓗ Ⓙ
29. Ⓐ Ⓑ Ⓒ Ⓓ
30. Ⓕ Ⓖ Ⓗ Ⓙ

31. Ⓐ Ⓑ Ⓒ Ⓓ
32. Ⓕ Ⓖ Ⓗ Ⓙ
33. Ⓐ Ⓑ Ⓒ Ⓓ
34. Ⓕ Ⓖ Ⓗ Ⓙ
35. Ⓐ Ⓑ Ⓒ Ⓓ
36. Ⓕ Ⓖ Ⓗ Ⓙ
37. Ⓐ Ⓑ Ⓒ Ⓓ
38. Ⓕ Ⓖ Ⓗ Ⓙ
39. Ⓐ Ⓑ Ⓒ Ⓓ
40. Ⓕ Ⓖ Ⓗ Ⓙ
41. Ⓐ Ⓑ Ⓒ Ⓓ
42. Ⓕ Ⓖ Ⓗ Ⓙ
43. Ⓐ Ⓑ Ⓒ Ⓓ
44. Ⓕ Ⓖ Ⓗ Ⓙ
45. Ⓐ Ⓑ Ⓒ Ⓓ

46. Ⓕ Ⓖ Ⓗ Ⓙ
47. Ⓐ Ⓑ Ⓒ Ⓓ
48. Ⓕ Ⓖ Ⓗ Ⓙ
49. Ⓐ Ⓑ Ⓒ Ⓓ
50. Ⓕ Ⓖ Ⓗ Ⓙ
51. Ⓐ Ⓑ Ⓒ Ⓓ
52. Ⓕ Ⓖ Ⓗ Ⓙ
53. Ⓐ Ⓑ Ⓒ Ⓓ
54. Ⓕ Ⓖ Ⓗ Ⓙ
55. Ⓐ Ⓑ Ⓒ Ⓓ
56. Ⓕ Ⓖ Ⓗ Ⓙ
57. Ⓐ Ⓑ Ⓒ Ⓓ
58. Ⓕ Ⓖ Ⓗ Ⓙ
59. Ⓐ Ⓑ Ⓒ Ⓓ
60. Ⓕ Ⓖ Ⓗ Ⓙ

61. Ⓐ Ⓑ Ⓒ Ⓓ
62. Ⓕ Ⓖ Ⓗ Ⓙ
63. Ⓐ Ⓑ Ⓒ Ⓓ
64. Ⓕ Ⓖ Ⓗ Ⓙ
65. Ⓐ Ⓑ Ⓒ Ⓓ
66. Ⓕ Ⓖ Ⓗ Ⓙ
67. Ⓐ Ⓑ Ⓒ Ⓓ
68. Ⓕ Ⓖ Ⓗ Ⓙ
69. Ⓐ Ⓑ Ⓒ Ⓓ
70. Ⓕ Ⓖ Ⓗ Ⓙ
71. Ⓐ Ⓑ Ⓒ Ⓓ
72. Ⓕ Ⓖ Ⓗ Ⓙ
73. Ⓐ Ⓑ Ⓒ Ⓓ
74. Ⓕ Ⓖ Ⓗ Ⓙ
75. Ⓐ Ⓑ Ⓒ Ⓓ

Mathematics

1. Ⓐ Ⓑ Ⓒ Ⓓ Ⓔ
2. Ⓕ Ⓖ Ⓗ Ⓙ Ⓚ
3. Ⓐ Ⓑ Ⓒ Ⓓ Ⓔ
4. Ⓕ Ⓖ Ⓗ Ⓙ Ⓚ
5. Ⓐ Ⓑ Ⓒ Ⓓ Ⓔ
6. Ⓕ Ⓖ Ⓗ Ⓙ Ⓚ
7. Ⓐ Ⓑ Ⓒ Ⓓ Ⓔ
8. Ⓕ Ⓖ Ⓗ Ⓙ Ⓚ
9. Ⓐ Ⓑ Ⓒ Ⓓ Ⓔ
10. Ⓕ Ⓖ Ⓗ Ⓙ Ⓚ
11. Ⓐ Ⓑ Ⓒ Ⓓ Ⓔ
12. Ⓕ Ⓖ Ⓗ Ⓙ Ⓚ
13. Ⓐ Ⓑ Ⓒ Ⓓ Ⓔ
14. Ⓕ Ⓖ Ⓗ Ⓙ Ⓚ
15. Ⓐ Ⓑ Ⓒ Ⓓ Ⓔ

16. Ⓕ Ⓖ Ⓗ Ⓙ Ⓚ
17. Ⓐ Ⓑ Ⓒ Ⓓ Ⓔ
18. Ⓕ Ⓖ Ⓗ Ⓙ Ⓚ
19. Ⓐ Ⓑ Ⓒ Ⓓ Ⓔ
20. Ⓕ Ⓖ Ⓗ Ⓙ Ⓚ
21. Ⓐ Ⓑ Ⓒ Ⓓ Ⓔ
22. Ⓕ Ⓖ Ⓗ Ⓙ Ⓚ
23. Ⓐ Ⓑ Ⓒ Ⓓ Ⓔ
24. Ⓕ Ⓖ Ⓗ Ⓙ Ⓚ
25. Ⓐ Ⓑ Ⓒ Ⓓ Ⓔ
26. Ⓕ Ⓖ Ⓗ Ⓙ Ⓚ
27. Ⓐ Ⓑ Ⓒ Ⓓ Ⓔ
28. Ⓕ Ⓖ Ⓗ Ⓙ Ⓚ
29. Ⓐ Ⓑ Ⓒ Ⓓ Ⓔ
30. Ⓕ Ⓖ Ⓗ Ⓙ Ⓚ

31. Ⓐ Ⓑ Ⓒ Ⓓ Ⓔ
32. Ⓕ Ⓖ Ⓗ Ⓙ Ⓚ
33. Ⓐ Ⓑ Ⓒ Ⓓ Ⓔ
34. Ⓕ Ⓖ Ⓗ Ⓙ Ⓚ
35. Ⓐ Ⓑ Ⓒ Ⓓ Ⓔ
36. Ⓕ Ⓖ Ⓗ Ⓙ Ⓚ
37. Ⓐ Ⓑ Ⓒ Ⓓ Ⓔ
38. Ⓕ Ⓖ Ⓗ Ⓙ Ⓚ
39. Ⓐ Ⓑ Ⓒ Ⓓ Ⓔ
40. Ⓕ Ⓖ Ⓗ Ⓙ Ⓚ
41. Ⓐ Ⓑ Ⓒ Ⓓ Ⓔ
42. Ⓕ Ⓖ Ⓗ Ⓙ Ⓚ
43. Ⓐ Ⓑ Ⓒ Ⓓ Ⓔ
44. Ⓕ Ⓖ Ⓗ Ⓙ Ⓚ
45. Ⓐ Ⓑ Ⓒ Ⓓ Ⓔ

46. Ⓕ Ⓖ Ⓗ Ⓙ Ⓚ
47. Ⓐ Ⓑ Ⓒ Ⓓ Ⓔ
48. Ⓕ Ⓖ Ⓗ Ⓙ Ⓚ
49. Ⓐ Ⓑ Ⓒ Ⓓ Ⓔ
50. Ⓕ Ⓖ Ⓗ Ⓙ Ⓚ
51. Ⓐ Ⓑ Ⓒ Ⓓ Ⓔ
52. Ⓕ Ⓖ Ⓗ Ⓙ Ⓚ
53. Ⓐ Ⓑ Ⓒ Ⓓ Ⓔ
54. Ⓕ Ⓖ Ⓗ Ⓙ Ⓚ
55. Ⓐ Ⓑ Ⓒ Ⓓ Ⓔ
56. Ⓕ Ⓖ Ⓗ Ⓙ Ⓚ
57. Ⓐ Ⓑ Ⓒ Ⓓ Ⓔ
58. Ⓕ Ⓖ Ⓗ Ⓙ Ⓚ
59. Ⓐ Ⓑ Ⓒ Ⓓ Ⓔ
60. Ⓕ Ⓖ Ⓗ Ⓙ Ⓚ

ANSWER SHEET
Practice Test 5

Reading

1. Ⓐ Ⓑ Ⓒ Ⓓ	9. Ⓐ Ⓑ Ⓒ Ⓓ	17. Ⓐ Ⓑ Ⓒ Ⓓ	25. Ⓐ Ⓑ Ⓒ Ⓓ	33. Ⓐ Ⓑ Ⓒ Ⓓ
2. Ⓕ Ⓖ Ⓗ Ⓙ	10. Ⓕ Ⓖ Ⓗ Ⓙ	18. Ⓕ Ⓖ Ⓗ Ⓙ	26. Ⓕ Ⓖ Ⓗ Ⓙ	34. Ⓕ Ⓖ Ⓗ Ⓙ
3. Ⓐ Ⓑ Ⓒ Ⓓ	11. Ⓐ Ⓑ Ⓒ Ⓓ	19. Ⓐ Ⓑ Ⓒ Ⓓ	27. Ⓐ Ⓑ Ⓒ Ⓓ	35. Ⓐ Ⓑ Ⓒ Ⓓ
4. Ⓕ Ⓖ Ⓗ Ⓙ	12. Ⓕ Ⓖ Ⓗ Ⓙ	20. Ⓕ Ⓖ Ⓗ Ⓙ	28. Ⓕ Ⓖ Ⓗ Ⓙ	36. Ⓕ Ⓖ Ⓗ Ⓙ
5. Ⓐ Ⓑ Ⓒ Ⓓ	13. Ⓐ Ⓑ Ⓒ Ⓓ	21. Ⓐ Ⓑ Ⓒ Ⓓ	29. Ⓐ Ⓑ Ⓒ Ⓓ	37. Ⓐ Ⓑ Ⓒ Ⓓ
6. Ⓕ Ⓖ Ⓗ Ⓙ	14. Ⓕ Ⓖ Ⓗ Ⓙ	22. Ⓕ Ⓖ Ⓗ Ⓙ	30. Ⓕ Ⓖ Ⓗ Ⓙ	38. Ⓕ Ⓖ Ⓗ Ⓙ
7. Ⓐ Ⓑ Ⓒ Ⓓ	15. Ⓐ Ⓑ Ⓒ Ⓓ	23. Ⓐ Ⓑ Ⓒ Ⓓ	31. Ⓐ Ⓑ Ⓒ Ⓓ	39. Ⓐ Ⓑ Ⓒ Ⓓ
8. Ⓕ Ⓖ Ⓗ Ⓙ	16. Ⓕ Ⓖ Ⓗ Ⓙ	24. Ⓕ Ⓖ Ⓗ Ⓙ	32. Ⓕ Ⓖ Ⓗ Ⓙ	40. Ⓕ Ⓖ Ⓗ Ⓙ

Science

1. Ⓐ Ⓑ Ⓒ Ⓓ	9. Ⓐ Ⓑ Ⓒ Ⓓ	17. Ⓐ Ⓑ Ⓒ Ⓓ	25. Ⓐ Ⓑ Ⓒ Ⓓ	33. Ⓐ Ⓑ Ⓒ Ⓓ
2. Ⓕ Ⓖ Ⓗ Ⓙ	10. Ⓕ Ⓖ Ⓗ Ⓙ	18. Ⓕ Ⓖ Ⓗ Ⓙ	26. Ⓕ Ⓖ Ⓗ Ⓙ	34. Ⓕ Ⓖ Ⓗ Ⓙ
3. Ⓐ Ⓑ Ⓒ Ⓓ	11. Ⓐ Ⓑ Ⓒ Ⓓ	19. Ⓐ Ⓑ Ⓒ Ⓓ	27. Ⓐ Ⓑ Ⓒ Ⓓ	35. Ⓐ Ⓑ Ⓒ Ⓓ
4. Ⓕ Ⓖ Ⓗ Ⓙ	12. Ⓕ Ⓖ Ⓗ Ⓙ	20. Ⓕ Ⓖ Ⓗ Ⓙ	28. Ⓕ Ⓖ Ⓗ Ⓙ	36. Ⓕ Ⓖ Ⓗ Ⓙ
5. Ⓐ Ⓑ Ⓒ Ⓓ	13. Ⓐ Ⓑ Ⓒ Ⓓ	21. Ⓐ Ⓑ Ⓒ Ⓓ	29. Ⓐ Ⓑ Ⓒ Ⓓ	37. Ⓐ Ⓑ Ⓒ Ⓓ
6. Ⓕ Ⓖ Ⓗ Ⓙ	14. Ⓕ Ⓖ Ⓗ Ⓙ	22. Ⓕ Ⓖ Ⓗ Ⓙ	30. Ⓕ Ⓖ Ⓗ Ⓙ	38. Ⓕ Ⓖ Ⓗ Ⓙ
7. Ⓐ Ⓑ Ⓒ Ⓓ	15. Ⓐ Ⓑ Ⓒ Ⓓ	23. Ⓐ Ⓑ Ⓒ Ⓓ	31. Ⓐ Ⓑ Ⓒ Ⓓ	39. Ⓐ Ⓑ Ⓒ Ⓓ
8. Ⓕ Ⓖ Ⓗ Ⓙ	16. Ⓕ Ⓖ Ⓗ Ⓙ	24. Ⓕ Ⓖ Ⓗ Ⓙ	32. Ⓕ Ⓖ Ⓗ Ⓙ	40. Ⓕ Ⓖ Ⓗ Ⓙ

ENGLISH TEST

Time: 45 Minutes—75 Questions

Directions: In the five passages that follow, certain words and phrases are underlined and numbered. In the right-hand column, you will find alternatives for each underlined part. In most cases, you are to choose the one that best expresses the idea, makes the statement appropriate for standard written English, or is worded most consistently with the style and tone of the passage as a whole. If you think the original version is best, choose "NO CHANGE." In some cases, you will find in the right-hand column a question about the underlined part. You are to choose the best answer to the question.

You will also find questions about a section of the passage, or about the passage as a whole. These questions do not refer to an underlined portion of the passage, but rather are identified by a number or numbers in a box.

For each question, choose the alternative you consider best and fill in the corresponding oval on your answer sheet. Read each passage through once before you begin to answer the questions that accompany it. For many of the questions, you must read several sentences beyond the question to determine the answer. Be sure that you have read far enough ahead each time you choose an alternative.

PASSAGE 1

A Never-Ending Battle

Not many people know it, but the character was originally a villain. Intending it as an allegory for the growing Nazi menace in Europe, in 1933 two teenage, Jewish-American science-fiction fans— Jerry Siegel and Joe Shuster—concocted a story for a pulp magazine about an evil figure with strange mind-control powers bent on world domination. No one took much notice.

As the political situation in Europe and the Great Depression in America both worsened, and after Siegel's father died during a robbery of his

1. **A.** NO CHANGE
   B. two, teenage Jewish-American, science-fiction
   C. two teenage, Jewish-American, science-fiction,
   D. two teenage Jewish-American science-fiction

2. **F.** NO CHANGE
   G. powers being bent
   H. powers, which bent
   J. powers were bent

New York City clothing <u>store; the</u> two boys became
3

disenchanted with writing about a villain. They

decided that what the world needed were uplifting

stories about a hero who used his abilities to

protect <u>societies'</u> downtrodden and defenseless,
4

rather than <u>by exploiting</u> them.
5

<u>Over the next few years they revamped their creation</u>
6
<u>along these lines altering his appearance</u> and attributes
6
but retaining the original name: Superman.

An instant success from his first appearance in 1938,

<u>when</u> Superman gave rise to the concept of the
7

superhero, which quickly became the dominant

genre of the comic-book medium. Today, everyone

knows that a superhero is someone with special

powers and a flashy costume involving <u>shorts over</u>
8
<u>tights, a cape and a logo</u>, on the chest. But few stop
8
to consider the complex and moving psychological

3. **A.** NO CHANGE
   B. store, the
   C. store. The
   D. store, therefore the

4. **F.** NO CHANGE
   G. societys
   H. society's
   J. societies

5. **A.** NO CHANGE
   B. from exploiting
   C. was exploiting
   D. to exploit

6. **F.** NO CHANGE
   G. Over the next few years, they revamped
   their creation along these lines, altering
   his appearance
   H. Over the next few years they revamped
   their creation along these lines, altering
   his appearance,
   J. Over the next few years, they revamped
   their creation, along these lines altering
   his appearance

7. **A.** NO CHANGE
   B. however
   C. after which
   D. DELETE the underlined portion.

8. **F.** NO CHANGE
   G. shorts, over tights, a cape and a logo
   H. shorts over tights, a cape, and a logo
   J. shorts over tights a cape and a logo

underpinnings of this cultural phenomenon. ☐9

Although he became a powerful symbol of "the

American way," Superman is, like Siegel and

Shuster's parents, an immigrant: the last survivor
                    10

of his doomed home planet of Krypton. In addition
10

to his refugee status, some of Superman's other

distinguishing characteristics also reflect his
                                              11

creators heritage. His Kryptonian name, Kal-El, is
  11

similar to the Hebrew for "voice of God," and there

has even been speculation that the famous "S"

insignia on Superman's chest is a subtle portrayal
                                              12

by the yellow badges that Jews were forced to wear
12

in Nazi Germany.

   The "Man of Steel" himself is invulnerable,

but the story of his creation involves a great deal

of suffering: a boy's mourning for his father, a

people fleeing murderous oppression, and the

9. If the writer were to delete the preceding sentence, the passage would primarily lose:
   A. a logical transition into the following sentence.
   B. details supporting the claim that the story of the creation of Superman is a moving one.
   C. insight into why so few people stop to consider the ideas concerned.
   D. an explanation of the psychological underpinnings of the creation of superheroes.

10. F. NO CHANGE
    G. parents an immigrant, the last survivor of
    H. parents, an immigrant, the last survivor: of
    J. parents, an immigrant—the last survivor—of

11. A. NO CHANGE
    B. his creators'
    C. Superman's creators
    D. Supermans creators'

12. F. NO CHANGE
    G. reference to
    H. definition of
    J. symbol within

struggle of immigrant groups <u>became</u> "more
13

American than the Americans." Now and for all

time, Superman symbolizes humanity's hope that

the great power possessed by <u>some will use</u> for
14

the benefit of all. 15

13. A. NO CHANGE
B. have became
C. to become
D. had become

14. F. NO CHANGE
G. some use
H. some have used
J. some will be used

Question 15 asks about the preceding passage as a whole.

---

15. Suppose the author had intended to write an essay about the ways in which popular entertainment has been inspired by tragedy. Would this essay fulfill that goal?
A. Yes, because it explains how suffering, on both personal and grand scales, led inevitably to the popularity of superhero comics.
B. Yes, because Superman has appeared in a wide variety of media besides comic books.
C. No, because the essay deals primarily with one specific character.
D. No, because superhero comics are a niche medium that is only popular with a select audience.

PASSAGE II

Splat, You're Out

I'm not sure whose idea it was, but around

the end of ninth grade, a bunch of guys from my

<u>class, myself included: started</u> playing paintball.
16

16. F. NO CHANGE
G. class, myself included started
H. class—myself included—started
J. class. Myself included, started

If your not familiar, its that game where two
   17
teams run around shooting at each other with

gas-powered guns that fire little pellets of

brightly colored paint: get hit with a pellet, and
                        18
you're out.
   18

[1] The first thing I learned about paintball is that

it's quite an investment. [2] A decent gun at the time

costs about seventy-five dollars, but that wasn't the
 19
end of it. [3] Pads aren't necessary, because getting

shot in the arm or leg doesn't hurt much, but you'd

be a fool to play without a facemask, throatguard,

and another piece of athletic equipment specific to

male players.

[4] You'll be sufficiently sick, after your first day
                                20
too, to shell out for a suit of camouflage after—
                      20
the odds are—getting spotted a mile away and
              20
immediately peppered. [5] And of course, paintball
      20
means regular bike rides to the sporting-goods

store to buy more ammunition and get your gas

17. **A.** NO CHANGE
    B. you're not familiar, it's
    C. your not familiar, it's
    D. you're not familiar, its

18. Which of the following alternatives to
    the underlined portion would NOT be
    acceptable?
    F. getting hit with a pellet means you're out.
    G. when a player is hit, they're out.
    H. a direct hit means that a player is out.
    J. you're out once you get hit, but only until
    the next game.

19. **A.** NO CHANGE
    B. having cost
    C. costing
    D. cost

20. **F.** NO CHANGE
    G. The odds are, to shell out for a suit of
    camouflage, you'll be sufficiently sick
    after your first day of getting spotted,
    a mile away too, and immediately
    peppered.
    H. To shell out for a suit of camouflage
    after your first day, the odds are you'll be
    sufficiently sick of getting spotted a mile
    away and immediately peppered too.
    J. After your first day, the odds are you'll be
    sufficiently sick of getting spotted a mile
    away and immediately peppered to shell
    out for a suit of camouflage too.

canister refilled. [6] A bunch of protective gear is

required too. 21

Nowadays, there are official paintball ranges you
$\underline{}$
22

can pay to play on, but we just played in the woods
$\underline{}$
22

behind Bobby's house. It was the only location
$\underline{}$
22

where we could be sure not to hit any homes, cars,

or innocent bystanders, that surely would have
$\underline{}$
23

brought our paintball days to an abrupt end. We

cleared brush to make paths, and dug pits and

erected walls to make two opposing forts. This was

more yardwork than we would have done even if

our parents had paid us, but no hardship was going

to stand between the thrill of sneaking up on a
$\underline{}$
24

friend and shooting him in the butt with exploding

pellets of neon goo.

21. For the sake of logic and coherence, Sentence 6 should be placed:
   A. where it is now.
   B. before Sentence 4.
   C. after Sentence 1.
   D. after Sentence 2.

22. Which of the following choices best introduces the paragraph?
   F. NO CHANGE
   G. There weren't any official paintball ranges near us (at least, not that we knew of).
   H. There were a few different guys in our crew whose houses had back woods big enough to play in.
   J. What we needed now was a safe place to play.

23. A. NO CHANGE
   B. bystanders
   C. bystanders, whom
   D. bystanders; any such occurrence

24. F. NO CHANGE
   G. our thrill
   H. us and the thrill
   J. ourselves, and the thrill

Now and then, the memories of my heroism that

summer still <u>bring</u> a smile to my face. There was the
25

time I discovered a secret trail up a hillside full of

pricker-bushes and picked off three guys without

<u>their having</u> any idea where I was. Then there was
26

the time I snuck a giant sheet of clear plexiglass into

Bobby's woods, put it up between two trees, and

tauntingly danced safely behind it while opponents

wasted their ammo. <u>Sure, it was cheating, but it was</u>
27

<u>also hilarious.</u>
27

    [1] I guess, one by one, everyone got a girlfriend

and stopped coming out to the games. [2] After a

year or two, he probably did the same. [3] I ended

up selling my gun and all my gear to a kid a couple

of grades younger. [4] I <u>didn't exactly remember</u> why
28

we stopped playing. [5] And I'd like to believe that,

even now, that same equipment is still being used

by some ninth grader <u>he is</u> discovering the joy of
29

squeezing the trigger on a paintball gun and hearing

25. A. NO CHANGE
     B. brings
     C. brought
     D. have brought

26. F. NO CHANGE
     G. having
     H. him having
     J. DELETE the underlined portion.

27. The author is considering deleting the underlined sentence. Should the author make this deletion?
     A. Yes, because such specific information about the rules of paintball is unnecessary in this brief essay.
     B. Yes, because it contradicts information presented elsewhere in the essay.
     C. No, because it is a humorous way of establishing that the author and his friends did not take the game too seriously.
     D. No, because it is important for the reader to know that the author is someone who once cheated at paintball.

28. F. NO CHANGE
     G. don't exactly remember
     H. hadn't exactly remembered
     J. wouldn't remember exactly

29. A. NO CHANGE
     B. just
     C. and
     D. whose

his shot followed by a loud pop and a swear word

from his friend echoing through the woods. 30

PASSAGE III

The following paragraphs may or may not be in the most logical order. Each paragraph is numbered in brackets, and question 45 will ask you to choose where paragraph 3 should most logically be placed.

On the Borderline of History

[1]

The now-familiar story of King Arthur, complete
                                           31
with Merlin the wizard, and the magic sword
                                           31
Excalibur first appeared in a fanciful history of
                31
England composed in the 12th century by a monk

named Geoffrey of Monmouth. Since today we

know that there are no such things as wizards or

magic swords, and discount this version of events,
         32
but there are earlier works that mention Arthur as

well. His first appearance in a surviving text is in

the *Historia Brittonum*, composed by a Welsh monk

around the year 830. Since Arthur's famous victory's
                                        33
are all supposed to have taken place over three

hundred years prior, the fact that no source in all

30. The most logical order for the sentences in the final paragraph would be:
   F. NO CHANGE
   G. 4, 3, 5, 1, 2.
   H. 4, 1, 3, 2, 5.
   J. 3, 5, 4, 2, 1.

31. A. NO CHANGE
   B. story, of King Arthur complete with Merlin the wizard and the magic sword Excalibur first appeared
   C. story of King Arthur, complete with Merlin the wizard and the magic sword Excalibur, first appeared
   D. story of King Arthur complete with Merlin the wizard and the magic sword Excalibur first appeared

32. F. NO CHANGE
   G. swords discounted
   H. swords, we had discounted
   J. swords, we must discount

33. A. NO CHANGE
   B. Arthur's famous victories
   C. Arthurs famous victories'
   D. Arthur's famous victories'

those intervening years <u>mentions</u> him is suspicious.
34
On the other hand, this was not a terribly literate

age, and of the few histories that were <u>composed</u>
35

<u>we know, of which</u> many have been simply lost.
35

[2]

Most of the battles and people mentioned in the

Historia can be historically verified, which seems

to support the historicity of Arthur. 36 And yet, the

earlier texts that corroborate the accounts of the

battles make no mention of him. <u>Therefore,</u> the
37
Historia does not even call Arthur a king at all, but

only a "war leader" who <u>succeeding commands</u>
38
the Britons in several battles against the invading

Saxons. This would seem an account sufficiently

humble at least to persuade us that *someone* named

34. **F.** NO CHANGE
G. mention
H. have mentioned
J. were mentioning

35. **A.** NO CHANGE
B. composed, but
C. composed, we know that
D. composed. Unfortunately,

36. The author is considering adding the following sentence at the point indicated:
Vortigern, for example, was widely written about prior to the 9th century.

Should the author make this addition?

F. Yes, because without it the essay would contain no proof that the author has actually read any earlier texts.
G. No, because it is information that most people already possess.
H. Yes, because otherwise readers might assume that the author knows only about Arthur and no other famous kings.
J. No, because it is a minor fact that interrupts the flow of the paragraph.

37. **A.** NO CHANGE
B. Although,
C. Meanwhile,
D. Curiously,

38. **F.** NO CHANGE
G. successfully commanded
H. successful command
J. succeed commanding

"Arthur" was involved in British history at this time,

if not for the fact that the deeds attributed

to him are so obviously exaggerated, such as the
                                        39

claim that he killed 960 men single-handedly at the
                                        39

Battle of Badon.
        39

[3]

Most of us can't even remember being young
   40

enough not to have heard of him. His name is

inseparable from all our romantic ideas about

knights and chivalry. A majority of people think

of him as an actual historical figure. But did King

Arthur really exist? It's possible, but there is less

evidence to support this claim than most realize.
                              41

[4]

Every such early reference to Arthur seeming
                                        42

strongly like an insertion of popular legend into
42

an otherwise historical text. The two most reliable

accounts of first-millennium England are the
                                        43

Anglo-Saxon Chronicle and Bede's *Ecclesiastical*

39. The author is considering deleting the
    underlined portion and ending the sentence
    after the word *exaggerated*. Should the author
    make this deletion?
    A. Yes, because there is no point in including
       a claim that we know can't possibly be true.
    B. Yes, because the essay fails to explain the
       significance of the Battle of Badon.
    C. No, because it provides support for the
       claim that Arthur's deeds are clearly
       unrealistic.
    D. No, because it establishes that even battles
       this long ago had high casualty rates.

40. Which of the following alternatives to
    the underlined portion would NOT be
    acceptable?
    F. Many of them
    G. You probably
    H. The odds are that anyone you might ask
    J. Even today, people

41. A. NO CHANGE
    B. claim then you might think
    C. claim then there used to be
    D. claim, and than most realize

42. F. NO CHANGE
    G. seems strongly to be
    H. seemed strong until
    J. seems strong, but

43. A. NO CHANGE
    B. England, the
    C. England except for the
    D. England—the

History—make no mention of Arthur, though they

do include accounts of the battles with which

he was allegedly involved. Countless scholars

have labored for year's hope of proving Arthur's
                  44

existence, only to meet with the frustration that

caused archaeologist Nowell Myres to remark that

"no figure on the borderline of history and mythology

has wasted more of the historian's time." 45

44. **F.** NO CHANGE
G. years hoped
H. years in the hopes
J. years and hoping

Question 45 asks about the preceding passage as a whole.

45. For the sake of logic and coherence, Paragraph 3 should be placed:
A. where it is now.
B. before Paragraph 1.
C. after Paragraph 1.
D. after Paragraph 4.

PASSAGE IV

A Van Full of Nerds

They say boys won't dance unless their lives
                                   46

depend on it, but in my case all it took was for this
   46

girl I had a major crush on to start a ballroom dance

club near the end of our sophomore year in college,
                                              47

where we'd been for almost two years. Since I'd
                  47

been hearing for years about how impossible it is

to get boys to dance, I hypothesized that no guys
              48

would show up except total nerds who couldn't find

46. Which of the following alternatives to the underlined portion would NOT be acceptable?
F. until pigs fly,
G. like the deserts miss the rain,
H. for all the tea in China,
J. even if you pay them,

47. **A.** NO CHANGE
B. college, which was almost halfway over.
C. college, which we had just gotten used to.
D. college.

48. **F.** NO CHANGE
G. dance, and
H. dance, so
J. dance. I

any other way to interact with girls. <u>Afterwards,</u>
49

this category included me as well, but I figured that

maybe out of all the nerds I'd be the coolest one.

    <u>I made sure to wear comfortable shoes to the</u>
50

<u>first meeting.</u> So did lots of cool kids, and lots of
50

people in between. Pretty much half the school

showed up, actually. I wasn't the only one who

had a crush on Emily, so I guess lots of other guys

had the same idea. And as for the girls, well, they

never need an excuse to dance. Guys and girls

switched partners every few minutes <u>until the</u>
51

<u>instructor finally started to lead us</u> through the
51

basics of several dances that I'd heard of, but knew

nothing about, like the foxtrot, rhumba, and cha-

cha. Emily was way up at the front of the banquet

hall somewhere, <u>but the place was so packed that I</u>
52

<u>would've needed a stepladder and binoculars to see</u>
52

<u>her.</u> For some reason, I bothered attending the next
52

few meetings, and I noticed an odd <u>insight:</u> there
53

were fewer popular kids there each time.

49. **A.** NO CHANGE
    B. Allegorically,
    C. Apparently,
    D. Although

50. Which of the following sentences best introduces the paragraph?
    F. NO CHANGE
    G. Sure enough, lots of nerds showed up to the first meeting.
    H. The first meeting was held in a banquet hall on the north end of campus.
    J. I had so much going on that week that I nearly spaced on attending the first meeting.

51. **A.** NO CHANGE
    B. when an instructor appeared and guided us
    C. as the instructor the club had hired led us
    D. and, meanwhile, the instructor put us

52. Given that all the choices are true, which one best expresses the author's feelings of distance from Emily?
    F. NO CHANGE
    G. in that vintage maroon dress that flared out whenever she spun around.
    H. with that friend of hers who always pulled her away whenever I tried to talk to her.
    J. probably dancing with that jerk who always wore soccer shorts, even in the winter.

53. **A.** NO CHANGE
    B. portrayal
    C. aspect
    D. phenomenon

The funny thing about popular <u>kids are</u> terrified
54
of doing anything that isn't popular. So when they

noticed that there were also nerds at the meetings,

they figured "Better safe than sorry" and stopped

coming. Since I wasn't cool enough to have a

reputation to worry about, I stuck things <u>out, and</u>
55
<u>after</u> a few weeks I was practically the most popular
55
guy there (or at least, the least unpopular).

My plan to get closer to Emily would have

worked perfectly if not for two <u>things, like the</u> fact
56
that sophomore year ended and I had to wait out

the summer, and the fact that Emily had decided

to take her junior year abroad and wasn't there

anymore in the fall. But this disappointing turn of

events <u>weren't my only problems:</u> by this time, the
57
club was ready to start attending ballroom dance

competitions, and somehow, I was one of the best

dancers and felt too guilty to quit!

For the rest of college, I spent one weekend a

month driving to some stupid dance competition

in a van full of nerds. If you're about to enter college

yourself, heed my advice: never join a club for a

54. **F.** NO CHANGE
G. kids is
H. kids, who are
J. kids is that they're

55. Which of the following alternatives to the underlined portion would NOT be acceptable?
A. out, after
B. out; after
C. out: after
D. out. After

56. **F.** NO CHANGE
G. things, and the
H. things: the
J. things. Like the

57. **A.** NO CHANGE
B. was suddenly the least of my problems:
C. were surpassed by a bigger problem:
D. is my only problem:

girl, or at least make sure that she first isn't about to
                                      58

disappear to France for a year.

Anyway, at least now, when my friend got
                                  59

married, I'm the only guy at the wedding who
  59

knows how to dance.

And I also know a lot of knock-knock jokes about
                                              60

math!
60

58. The best placement in the sentence for the underlined portion would be:
- **F.** where it is now.
- **G.** after the word *sure.*
- **H.** after the word *disappear.*
- **J.** after the word *France.*

59. **A.** NO CHANGE
- **B.** our friends got married, I was
- **C.** my friends were married, I was
- **D.** a friend gets married, I'm

60. The author is considering deleting this sentence and ending the essay with the previous one. Should the author make this deletion?
- **F.** Yes, because the sentence is sarcastic, and so far the essay has been utterly free of sarcasm.
- **G.** Yes, because it is unrelated to dance, and the essay is primarily a sociological one about ballroom dancing's recent resurgence in popularity.
- **H.** No, because it provides humorous insight into the author's experience of having to hang out with nerds.
- **J.** No, because the sentence is useless without specific examples of these jokes.

PASSAGE V

The Greatest

[1]

In Louisville Kentucky, in 1954 12-year-old
                    61

Cassius Clay's bike was stolen. Devastated, he
                                          62

vowed to beat up the thief if he ever found him, and
  62

61. **A.** NO CHANGE
- **B.** Louisville Kentucky, in 1954, 12-year-old
- **C.** Louisville, Kentucky in 1954, 12-year-old
- **D.** Louisville, Kentucky, in 1954, 12-year-old

62. **F.** NO CHANGE
- **G.** Devastation vows
- **H.** Devastatedly vowing
- **J.** Devastated, and he vowed

someone suggested that Cassius <u>had taken</u> boxing
63

lessons before making such boasts.

[2]

[1] It would not be the last time he would prove

everyone wrong, but even <u>bigger, greater struggles</u>
64

lay ahead.

[2] <u>After winning a gold medal at the 1960 Olympics</u>
65

<u>he turned pro, and stunned the sporting world,</u>
65

<u>by defeating Sonny Liston for the heavyweight</u>
65

<u>championship.</u> [3] He turned out to be a very gifted
65

boxer, and decided to stick with the sport, working

his way up through the amateur ranks.

[4] Liston had been heavily favored, and Cassius's

<u>brashness; prior to the fight he'd</u> called himself "too
66

fast" and "too pretty" to lose—had made people

think he was in for a rude awakening. 67

[3]

After the victory, Clay announced that he had

converted to Islam, and changed his name to the

63. **A.** NO CHANGE
    B. took
    C. would take
    D. had better take

64. **F.** NO CHANGE
    G. bigger struggles
    H. greater, more challenging struggles
    J. more challenges to overcome

65. **A.** NO CHANGE
    B. After winning a gold medal, at the 1960 Olympics he turned pro and stunned the sporting world, by defeating Sonny Liston for the heavyweight championship.
    C. After winning a gold medal at the 1960 Olympics, he turned pro and stunned the sporting world by defeating Sonny Liston, for the heavyweight championship.
    D. After winning a gold medal at the 1960 Olympics, he turned pro and stunned the sporting world by defeating Sonny Liston for the heavyweight championship.

66. **F.** NO CHANGE
    G. brashness prior to the fight, and
    H. brashness prior to the fight—he'd
    J. brashness: prior to the fight he'd

67. The most logical order for the sentences in Paragraph 2 would be:
    A. NO CHANGE
    B. 1, 3, 2, 4.
    C. 3, 2, 4, 1.
    D. 3, 1, 4, 2.

one by which we know him today: Muhammad
68

Ali. In addition to defeating one challenger after

another, Ali became active in the Black civil rights

movement, which upset many conservative boxing
69

fans. In 1966, the U.S. government tried to draft Ali

into service in the Vietnam War. Unsurprisingly, on
70

religious grounds, he refused to go, and was stripped

of his title and imprisoned.

[4]

Released in 1970, another shot at the
71

championship was soon in the works for Ali,
71

against the undefeated George Foreman. Foreman

seemed invincible, and fans feared that Ali might be

seriously hurt or even killed. Ali spent the beginning

of the fight on the ropes, and seemed to be losing

badly, but then his strategy became clear: after
72

Foreman exhausted him, Ali sprang to life, knocking
72

out the younger fighter in the eighth round.

68. F. NO CHANGE
    G. one, which we know
    H. one in which we know
    J. one that we know of him

69. Which of the following alternatives to
    the underlined portion would be LEAST
    acceptable?
    A. movement; this upset
    B. movement, this choice upset
    C. movement, thereby upsetting
    D. movement, a decision that upset

70. F. NO CHANGE
    G. Therefore, on
    H. Although on
    J. On

71. A. NO CHANGE
    B. the championship would be Ali's again if
       he managed to win his bout
    C. the boxing commission eventually
       granted Ali a chance to regain the
       championship: a match
    D. Ali worked his way up to another shot at
       the championship,

72. F. NO CHANGE
    G. exhausted,
    H. when Foreman had exhausted himself,
    J. quickly, before Foreman was exhausted,

[5]

Ali retired in 1981, and was eventually diagnosed

with Parkinson's disease, but the sporting world
                        73

he'd once shocked now revered him. He lit the
        73

Olympic flame before an adoring crowd in 1996,

and *Sports Illustrated* magazine later named him

"Sportsman of the Century," for his combination
                        74

of skill, bravery and magnetism. Ali himself still
        74

prefers the familiar title he correctly predicted he

would hold: "The Greatest of All Time." 75

73. **A.** NO CHANGE
    B. finally shocking the sporting world into revering him.
    C. both shocking and revering the sporting world.
    D. which the sporting world first shocked, but then revered.

74. **F.** NO CHANGE
    G. Century" for his combination of skill, bravery, and magnetism.
    H. Century" for his combination, of skill, bravery and magnetism.
    J. Century" for his combination of skill bravery and magnetism.

Question 75 asks about the preceding passage as a whole.

75. Suppose the author had intended to write an essay for boxing fans about what made Muhammad Ali such a successful boxer. Did this essay achieve that goal?
    A. Yes, because it makes very clear that Ali is widely considered the greatest boxer of all time.
    B. No, because it is more an essay for a general audience about Ali's cultural importance.
    C. Yes, because the essay describes the strategy Ali used to win one very famous fight.
    D. No, because the essay's style is much too flowery and verbose to appeal to boxing fans.

STOP

If there is still time remaining, check your answers to this section.

MATHEMATICS TEST

Time: 60 Minutes—60 Questions

> **Directions:** Solve each problem, choose the correct answer, and then fill in the corresponding oval on your answer sheet.
>
> Do not linger over problems that take too much time. Solve as many as you can; then return to the others in the time you have left for this test.
>
> You are permitted to use a calculator on this test. You may use your calculator for any problems you choose, but some of the problems may best be done without using a calculator.
>
> Note: Unless otherwise stated, all of the following should be assumed.
>
> 1. Illustrative figures are NOT necessarily drawn to scale.
> 2. Geometric figures lie in a plane.
> 3. The word *line* indicates a straight line.
> 4. The word *average* indicates arithmetic mean.

DO YOUR FIGURING HERE

1. If $\dfrac{5x}{3} + 6 = 4$, then $x = ?$

    A. 6
    B. $\dfrac{6}{5}$
    C. 0
    D. $\dfrac{-6}{5}$
    E. −4

2. Carol worked one summer and earned money that she spent on new clothes. After spending 65% of her money, Carol had $875 left. How much money did Carol earn for the summer?

    F. $1,625
    G. $2,500
    H. $3,375
    J. $4,125
    K. $7,375

3. What vector is the result of adding the vectors $\langle 5, -3 \rangle$, $\langle -2, 4 \rangle$, and $\langle 1, -6 \rangle$?

   A. $\langle -3, 1 \rangle$

   B. $\langle 4, -5 \rangle$

   C. $\langle 8, 13 \rangle$

   D. $\langle -1, -2 \rangle$

   E. $\langle -10, 72 \rangle$

DO YOUR FIGURING HERE

4. $(x^4)^{15}$ is equivalent to:

   F. $60x$

   G. $15x^4$

   H. $15x^{11}$

   J. x^{19}

   K. x^{60}

5. Doris and Clyde volunteered to help paint their friend's apartment. Doris used $1\frac{3}{4}$ gallons of paint and Clyde used $2\frac{1}{2}$ gallons. If 5 gallons of paint were purchased, how many gallons were left?

   A. $\frac{3}{4}$

   B. $1\frac{3}{4}$

   C. $3\frac{1}{4}$

   D. $4\frac{1}{4}$

   E. $4\frac{1}{2}$

6. The expression $(3p + 4)(5p - 6)$ is equivalent to:

   F. $8p^2 - 24$

   G. $8p^2 + 2p - 24$

   H. $15p^2 - 24$

   J. $15p^2 - 4p - 24$

   K. $15p^2 + 2p - 24$

7. What is a possible equation for a line that is parallel to $4x - 3y = 6$?

A. $y = -\dfrac{4}{3}x + 2$

B. $y = \dfrac{3}{4}x - 2$

C. $y = -4x + 6$

D. $y = \dfrac{4}{3}x + 2$

E. $y = -\dfrac{3}{4}x - 2$

8. In an isosceles triangle, the measure of each of the base angles is one-third the measure of the vertex angle. What is the measure, in degrees, of each of the base angles?

F. $36°$

G. $60°$

H. $72°$

J. $108°$

K. $216°$

9. Which of the following augmented matrices represents the system of linear equations below?

$$5x + 3y = 24$$
$$x - 2y = 12$$

A. $\begin{bmatrix} 5 & 3 & | & -24 \\ 1 & -2 & | & -12 \end{bmatrix}$

B. $\begin{bmatrix} 5 & 3 & | & 24 \\ 1 & -2 & | & 12 \end{bmatrix}$

C. $\begin{bmatrix} 5 & 3 & | & 24 \\ 0 & -2 & | & 12 \end{bmatrix}$

D. $\begin{bmatrix} 5 & 3 & | & 24 \\ 1 & 2 & | & 12 \end{bmatrix}$

E. $\begin{bmatrix} 5 & 1 & | & 24 \\ 3 & -2 & | & 12 \end{bmatrix}$

DO YOUR FIGURING HERE

PRACTICE TEST 5

10. The lengths of the corresponding sides of 2 similar right triangles are in the ratio of 3:4. If the hypotenuse of the larger triangle is 6 inches long, how many inches long is the hypotenuse of the smaller triangle?

   F. 3.5

   G. 4

   H. 4.5

   J. 8

   K. 18

DO YOUR FIGURING HERE

11. To the nearest foot, what is the length of a diagonal of the top of a rectangular platform that is 14 feet wide and 15 feet long?

   A. 16

   B. 19

   C. 21

   D. 22

   E. 29

12. Which real number satisfies $(3^x)(9) = 27^2$?

   F. 1

   G. 3

   H. 4

   J. 4.5

   K. 8

13. A rectangular room that is 3 feet longer than it is wide has an area of 54 square feet. How many feet long is the room?

   A. 6

   B. 9

   C. 15

   D. 18

   E. 27

14. The perimeter of a parallelogram is 36 inches, and one side measures 6 inches. What are the lengths, in inches, of the other 3 sides?

F. 6, 6, 18
G. 6, 9, 9
H. 6, 12, 12
J. 6, 15, 15
K. Cannot be determined from the given information

DO YOUR FIGURING HERE

15. The average of 5 numbers is 7. If each of the numbers is decreased by 4, what is the average of the 5 new numbers?

A. 0.0
B. 1.0
C. 2.0
D. 3.0
E. 7.0

16. Julie works in a clothing store and gets a base salary of $48.00 plus a fixed amount for each item she sells per day. Yesterday she earned $68.00 because she sold 4 items. If Julie sells 3 more items today than yesterday, what will she earn for the day?

F. $51.00
G. $55.00
H. $63.00
J. $78.00
K. $83.00

17. If $\frac{6}{x} \geq \frac{1}{4}$, what is the largest possible value for x?

A. $\frac{2}{3}$
B. $\frac{3}{2}$
C. 10
D. 24
E. 36

18. Starting at midnight, how many degrees has the hour hand of a clock moved when it gets to 8:00 A.M.?

F. 80°

G. 100°

H. 120°

J. 240°

K. 270°

DO YOUR FIGURING HERE

19. An airplane has r rows of seats with $(s + d)$ seats in each row. Which of the following is an expression for the number of seats in the entire airplane?

A. $(r \cdot s) + d$

B. $(r \cdot s) + (r \cdot d)$

C. $s + (r \cdot d)$

D. $r \cdot s \cdot d$

E. $r + s + d$

20. If $f(x) = 7x^2 - 4x - 10$, then $f(-3) = ?$

F. 85

G. 65

H. 41

J. −1

K. −61

21. Which nonnegative value of x makes the expression $\dfrac{1}{16 - x^2}$ undefined?

A. 256

B. 32

C. 16

D. 8

E. 4

22. A punch recipe calls for 3 parts fruit juice to 2 parts soda. In order to make 20 quarts of punch, how many quarts of fruit juice should be used?

F. 12

G. 9

H. 8

J. 6

K. 4

23. A line contains the points E, F, G, and H. Point F is between points E and G. Point H is between points G and F. Which of the following inequalities must be true about the lengths of these segments?

A. $FG < EF$

B. $GH < FG$

C. $FH < GH$

D. $GH < EF$

E. $FH < EF$

24. One endpoint of a diameter of a circle with center $(3, -4)$ has coordinates $(5, -3)$ in the standard (x, y) plane. What are the coordinates of the other endpoint of that diameter?

F. $(1, -5)$

G. $(1, 2)$

H. $(-1, 5)$

J. $(3 + \sqrt{5}, -3 + \sqrt{5})$

K. $(3 - \sqrt{5}, -3 - \sqrt{5})$

DO YOUR FIGURING HERE

25. Which of the following expressions represents the product xy, if $x = 4a^3$ and $y = -3a^5 + b$?

A. $a^3 + b$

B. $a^5 + b$

C. $-12a^8 + 4a^3b$

D. $-12a^{15} + 4a^3b$

E. $-243a^{15} + 4a^3b$

26. Ann is wrapping a gift for her friend's shower. She wants to cut ribbon so that she can place it on the gift as shown in the picture below. What is the minimum length of the ribbon, in centimeters, that Ann would need to cut in order to wrap the box, assuming no overlap?

F. 52

G. 104

H. 120

J. 128

K. 3,072

Use the following information to answer
questions 27–29.

A rectangular region of grass is 60 feet long by
26 feet wide and has an area of 1,560 square
feet. A landscaper installed a 4-foot wide paver
walkway along all 4 sides of the region of grass,
as shown below. The outer edge of the paver
border is 68 feet long and 34 feet wide.

27. The landscaper plans to re-seed the region of
grass. If one bag of seed covers a 125 square
foot region, what is the minimum number of
bags of seed the landscaper needs to buy?
A. 12
B. 13
C. 15
D. 18
E. 19

28. If the landscaper wanted to install a fence
around the outer edge of the paver walkway,
how many feet of fencing would be needed?
F. 204
G. 200
H. 188
J. 180
K. 172

29. A gravel bocce ball court is going to be added along one of longest sides of the paver walkway and will be equal in length to that side. The top of the bocce court will be a rectangle with a width of 10 feet. The gravel will be 6 inches $\left(\frac{1}{6}\ yard\right)$ thick. How many cubic *yards* of gravel will be needed for the bocce court?

DO YOUR FIGURING HERE

A. $12\frac{16}{27}$

B. $75\frac{5}{9}$

C. $226\frac{2}{3}$

D. $1,360$

E. $4,080$

---

30. For all nonzero x and y, $\dfrac{(9x^{-2}y^2)(-8x^2y^3)}{(4x^2y^4)} = ?$

F. $\dfrac{-9x^6y}{4}$

G. $\dfrac{x^2y^2}{18}$

H. $-18x^{-2}$

J. $-18x^{-2}y$

K. $-18x^2y^2$

31. What is the area in centimeters of the polygon below?

A. 30
B. 32.5
C. 35
D. 42
E. 46.5

32. A boat is anchored in a small lake with a rope that is 34 feet long. A wind blows the boat until the rope is taut and the water is 16 feet deep. Measuring across the bottom of the lake, how many feet has the boat moved from the anchor?

F. 30
G. 50
H. 60
J. 80
K. 120

DO YOUR FIGURING HERE

33. If a and b are real numbers and $\sqrt{3\left(\dfrac{a^2}{b}\right)} = 1$,

then what must be true of the value of b?

A. b must be positive.

B. b must be negative.

C. b must equal $\dfrac{1}{3}$.

D. b must equal 3.

E. b may have any value.

34. In the figure below, ℓ_1 is parallel to ℓ_2, and ℓ_3 is parallel to ℓ_4. What is the value of $\angle b$?

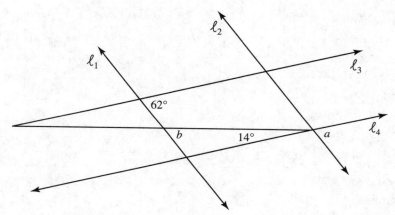

F. 44

G. 46

H. 48

J. 62

K. 132

DO YOUR FIGURING HERE

Use the following information to answer questions 35–37.

Square *WXYZ*, shown below, has side length 3 feet. The square is divided into 9 nonoverlapping congruent squares. Point *A* is the center of *WXYZ*.

35. The perimeter of 1 of the 9 congruent squares is how many feet?
   A. 1
   B. 3
   C. 4
   D. 9
   E. 12

36. Point *P* starts on *Z* and is rotated clockwise (℃) about A a total of 540°. After the rotation, *Z* is at the same location as which of the following points?
   F. *A*
   G. *W*
   H. *X*
   J. *Y*
   K. *Z*

37. Suppose *WXYZ* is in the standard (x, y) coordinate plane such that $\overline{YZ}$ is on the *x*-axis, the midpoint of $\overline{YZ}$ is at the origin, *X* has positive coordinates, and 1 coordinate unit is equal to 1 foot. What are the coordinates of *W*?
   A. (0, 3)
   B. (−1.5, 3)
   C. (−1.5, 1.5)
   D. (−1.5, 0)
   E. (−3, 3)

38. If $0° \leq x \leq 90°$ and $\cos x = \dfrac{8}{17}$ then $\tan x = ?$

    F. $\dfrac{8}{15}$

    G. $\dfrac{15}{17}$

    H. $\dfrac{17}{15}$

    J. $\dfrac{15}{8}$

    K. $\dfrac{17}{8}$

DO YOUR FIGURING HERE

39. In the figure, AD is a diameter of the circle with center O and $AO = 5$. What is the measure of arc BCD?

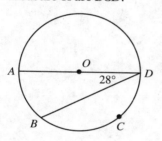

    A. 56°
    B. 116°
    C. 120°
    D. 124°
    E. 128°

40. If $\sin \theta = \dfrac{1}{2}$ and $\cos \theta = \dfrac{\sqrt{3}}{2}$ then $\csc \theta = ?$

    F. 2

    G. $\sqrt{3}$

    H. $\dfrac{2\sqrt{3}}{3}$

    J. $\dfrac{2}{3}$

    K. $\dfrac{\sqrt{3}}{3}$

PRACTICE TEST 5

41. Triangle *PQR* is equilateral. Find the sum of $a + b + c + d$.

DO YOUR FIGURING HERE

   A. 180°
   B. 210°
   C. 240°
   D. 270°
   E. 300°

42. If $\oplus$ is defined for all positive numbers a and b by $a \oplus b = \dfrac{ab}{a+b}$, then $8 \oplus 2 = ?$

   F. $\dfrac{1}{2}$
   G. $\dfrac{2}{3}$
   H. $\dfrac{8}{9}$
   J. 1
   K. $\dfrac{8}{5}$

43. The measures of the lengths of the 3 sides of a triangle are prime numbers. If 2 of the sides are 5 and 23, how many different lengths are possible for the third side?

   A. 1
   B. 2
   C. 9
   D. More than 18 but less than 29
   E. An infinite number

44. If a wheel on a stationary bike is 26 inches in diameter and Mike pedals to make the wheel revolve 50 times, what would be the total distance that the wheel would travel if it weren't stationary?

F. 169π

G.   1,300

H. 676π

J. $1,300\pi$

K. $2,600\pi$

45. What is the equivalent of $(3i + 4)^2$?

A. $12i^2$

B. $9i^2 + 16$

C. $3i^2 + 24i + 16$

D. $7 + 24i$

E. $13 + 24i$

46. Maureen wants to put an exercise wheel in her hamster's cage. The height of the cage is 22 inches, but there must be a 1-inch space above and below the wheel to allow for the wheel frame. What is the radius of the largest wheel that Maureen can place in the cage?

F.   5

G. $2\sqrt{5}$

H.   10

J.   11

K.   20

47. If $\dfrac{n!}{(n-1)!} = 5$, then $(n-2)! = ?$

A.   6

B.   20

C.   30

D.   60

E.   120

DO YOUR FIGURING HERE

PRACTICE TEST 5

PRACTICE TEST 5

DO YOUR FIGURING HERE

48. At a local restaurant a customer can order a lunch special with the following choices: a salad OR 2 kinds of soup and a sandwich with 4 types of meat, 2 types of bread, and 3 types of cheese. How many different combinations could be made for the lunch special?

F. 11

G. 12

H. 48

J. 72

K. 96

49. What is the distance, in coordinate units, between the points $S(-\sqrt{2}, 7)$ and $T(-3\sqrt{2}, 9)$ in the standard (x, y) coordinate plane?

A. 2

B. 3

C. $2\sqrt{3}$

D. $4\sqrt{2}$

E. 6

50. Which of the following expressions is equivalent to $\dfrac{a}{b}$ if all integers a, b, and c are positive?

F. $\dfrac{a \cdot c}{b \cdot c}$

G. $\dfrac{b \cdot a}{a \cdot b}$

H. $\dfrac{a \cdot a}{b \cdot b}$

J. $\dfrac{a + c}{b + c}$

K. $\dfrac{a - c}{b - c}$

51. The sum of twice a smaller number and three times a larger number is 49. The larger of the two numbers exceeds four times the smaller number by 7. If x is the smaller number, which equation below determines the correct value of x?

   A. $2(4x + 7) + 3x = 49$

   B. $2(4x - 7) + 3x = 49$

   C. $(12x + 7) + 2x = 49$

   D. $3(4x + 7) + 2x = 49$

   E. $3(4x - 7) + 2x = 49$

52. If $x = 3t - 7$ and $y = 4 - t$, which of the following expresses y in terms of x?

   F. $y = 5 - x$

   G. $y = \dfrac{5 - x}{3}$

   H. $y = 4 - x$

   J. $y = 11 - 3x$

   K. $y = \dfrac{19 - x}{3}$

53. In polar coordinates, the graph of $r = \sec \theta$ is:

   A. a circle with a radius of $\dfrac{1}{2}$.

   B. a circle with a radius of 1.

   C. a line through the pole with a slope equal to 1.

   D. a horizontal line.

   E. a vertical line.

DO YOUR FIGURING HERE

PRACTICE TEST 5

54. How much larger, in degrees, is the measure of one angle in a regular 8-sided polygon than the measure of one angle in a regular 6-sided polygon?

F. 15°

G. 27°

H. 108°

J. 120°

K. 135°

55. In the circle shown below, radius $\overline{PR}$ is 18 inches long, chord $\overline{QT}$ is 12 inches long, and $\overline{PR}$ is perpendicular to $\overline{QT}$ at S. How many inches long is $\overline{PS}$?

A. $12\sqrt{3}$

B. $12\sqrt{2}$

C. 18

D. 12

E. $6\sqrt{2}$

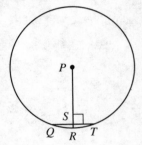

56. Which of the following data sets has the greatest standard deviation?

F. 10, 10, 10, 100, 100, 100

G. 10, 20, 30, 40, 50, 60

H. 20, 60, 60, 100, 100, 120

J. 50, 50, 50, 50, 50, 50

K. 50, 60, 70, 80, 90, 100

57. What is the period of the function $f(x) = 3\sec(2x)$?

A. $\dfrac{1}{3}$

B. 3

C. π

D. 2π

E. 4π

58. If $90° < x < 180°$, which of the following equals sin x, if tan $x = -\dfrac{24}{7}$?

DO YOUR FIGURING HERE

F. $\dfrac{-24}{25}$

G. $\dfrac{-7}{25}$

H. $\dfrac{7}{25}$

J. $\dfrac{7}{24}$

K. $\dfrac{24}{25}$

59. Which of the following is the factored form of the expression $12x^2 - x - 6$?

A. $(3x + 2)(4x - 3)$

B. $(3x - 2)(4x + 3)$

C. $(4x + 2)(3x - 3)$

D. $(6x + 1)(2x - 6)$

E. $(x - 2)(12x + 3)$

60. Harry has a bag containing jelly beans: 7 pink, 8 blue, and 9 orange. How many additional pink beans must be added to the 24 jelly beans already in the bag so that the probability of randomly drawing a pink jelly bean is $\dfrac{1}{2}$?

F. 1

G. 5

H. 7

J. 9

K. 10

STOP

If there is still time remaining, check your answers to this section.

READING TEST

Time: 35 Minutes—40 Questions

Directions: There are four passages in this test. Each passage is followed by several questions. After reading a passage, choose the best answer to each question and fill in the corresponding oval on your answer sheet. You may refer to the passages as often as necessary.

PASSAGE I—LITERARY NARRATIVE

Passage A is adapted from *Leaves of Grass* by Walt Whitman, written in 1855. Passage B is adapted from *The Negro Artist and the Racial Mountain* by Langston Hughes, written in 1926. Mr. Hughes, a black man, is credited as the founder of the Harlem Renaissance. He is considered to be one of the greatest and most prolific writers ever. His use of the words Negro and Colored are not meant to offend but to illustrate in modern society the historical changes in acceptable language.

Passage A by Walt Whitman

The Americans of all nations at any time upon the earth have probably the fullest poetical nature. The United States themselves are essentially the greatest poem. Here at last is something in the doings of
(5) man that corresponds with the broadcast doings of the day and night. Here is not merely a nation, but a teeming nation of nations. Here is action untied from strings, necessarily blind to particulars and details, magnificently moving in vast masses. Here
(10) is the hospitality which forever indicates heroes.

The genius of the United States is not best or most in its executives or legislatures, nor in its ambassadors or authors or colleges or churches or parlors, nor even in its newspapers or inventors,
(15) but always most in the common people. Their deathless attachment to freedom—their aversion to anything indecorous or soft or mean—their self-esteem and wonderful sympathy—the air they have of persons who never knew how it felt
(20) to stand in the presence of superiors—these too are unrhymed poetry. It awaits the gigantic and generous treatment worthy of it.

The American poets are to enclose old and new, for America is the race of races. Of them a bard
(25) is to be commensurate with a people. His spirit responds to his country's spirit—the expression of the American poet is to be transcendant and new. It is to be indirect and not direct or descriptive or epic. Its quality goes through these to much
(30) more. Here comes one among the well-beloved stonecutters and plans with decision and science and sees the solid and beautiful forms of the future where there are now no solid forms.

Of all nations the United States most needs
(35) poets and will doubtless have the greatest. Their Presidents shall not be their common referee so much as their poets shall. Of all mankind the great poet is the equable man. He is the arbiter of the diverse and he is the key. He is the equal-
(40) izer of his age and land. Obedience does not master him; he masters it. The power to destroy or remould is freely used by him, but never the power of attack. What is past is past. If he does not expose superior models and prove himself
(45) by every step he takes, he is not what is wanted.

Dismiss whatever insults your own soul, and your very flesh shall be a great poem. A heroic person walks at his ease through and out of that custom or precedent or authority that suits him not. Of
(50) the traits of the brotherhood of writers, nothing is finer than silent defiance advancing from new free forms. The cleanest expression is that which finds no sphere worthy of itself and makes one.

Passage B by Langston Hughes

One of the most promising of the young Negro
(55) poets said to me once, "I want to be a poet—not a

Negro poet," meaning, I believe, "I want to write like a white poet." I was sorry the young man said that, for no great poet has ever been afraid of being himself. And I doubted then that, with
(60) his desire to run away spiritually from his race, this boy would ever be a great poet. But this is the mountain standing in the way of any true Negro art in America—this urge toward whiteness, the desire to pour racial individuality into the mold
(65) of American standardization, and to be as little Negro and as much American as possible.

This young poet's home is, I believe, a fairly typical home of the colored middle class. One sees immediately how difficult it would be for
(70) an artist born in such a home to interest himself in interpreting the beauty of his own people. He is never taught to see that beauty. He is taught rather not to see it, or if he does, to be ashamed of it when it is not according to Caucasian
(75) patterns. For racial culture the home of a self-styled "high-class" Negro has nothing better to offer. Instead there will perhaps be more aping of things white than in a less cultured or less wealthy home. A very high mountain indeed
(80) for the would-be racial artist to climb in order to discover himself and his people.

But then there are the low-down folks, the so-called common element, and they are the majority—may the Lord be praised! They live
(85) on Seventh Street in Washington, or State Street in Chicago, and they do not particularly care whether they are like white folks or anybody else. Their religion soars to a shout. These common people are not afraid of spirituals, as for a
(90) long time their more intellectual brethren were, and jazz is their child. They furnish a wealth of colorful, distinctive material for any artist because they still hold their own individuality in the face of American standardizations. And
(95) perhaps these common people will give to the world its truly great Negro artist, the one who is not afraid to be himself.

An artist must be free to choose what he does, certainly, but he must also never be afraid to do

(100) what he might choose. We younger Negro artists who create now intend to express our individual dark-skinned selves without fear or shame. If white people are pleased, we are glad. If they are not, it doesn't matter. We know we are beautiful.
(105) And ugly too. If colored people are pleased, we are glad. If they are not, their displeasure doesn't matter either. We build our temples for tomorrow, strong as we know how, and we stand on top of the mountain, free within ourselves.

Questions 1–3 ask about Passage A.

---

1. Based on the assessment he offers in the third paragraph (lines 24–35), the author of Passage A seems to believe that American poets will have a unique relationship to:
   A. new concepts of race.
   B. revealed truth.
   C. science and technology.
   D. previously rare literary genres.

2. Which of the following statements could accurately be said to capture a sense in which Passage A, taken as a whole, is paradoxical?
   F. It is patriotic because it praises the United States as a symbol, yet it is also deeply skeptical of the structure of its government.
   G. It is populist because it praises the common man as a collective, yet it also exalts the lone individual who rejects and surpasses them.
   H. It flatters the American people for their "aversion" to anything "mean," but it later expresses admiration for the American poet's comfortability with physical violence.
   J. It unambiguously asserts that America will make its poets the greatest in the world, but it closes with a bittersweet implication that these poets are destined to leave America.

3. Based on the characterizations he offers in the passage, it can reasonably be inferred that the author of Passage A believes American poets will be great largely because:

A. so many different and interesting languages are spoken in America.

B. the figure of the American president is not enshrouded with mysticism like that of a European king.

C. American poets will know when to remain silent.

D. the American people themselves are inherently poetic.

Questions 4–7 ask about Passage B.

---

4. The author of Passage B uses all of the following metaphorically except

F. spirituals (line 93).

G. mountain (line 66).

H. wealth (line 95).

J. temples (line 111).

5. The author of Passage B obliquely believes that young Negro poets cannot succeed if they do not do the following:

A. Embrace the middle class and aspire to be a member of it

B. Spend time trying to make Negro art conform to white standards

C. Express their race proudly and without fear

D. Ignore spirituals because they are too standardized

6. As it is used in line 98, the word *standardizations* most nearly means:

F. uncomfortable silences.

G. invisible attacks.

H. hypocritical laws.

J. stifling expectations.

7. Over the course of the passage as a whole, the author of Passage B argues that, somewhat ironically, African-American poets of his generation needed to:

A. abandon the home in order to build a temple.

B. forget how to sing in order to learn how to shout.

C. first learn to see themselves as members bound to a group in order to eventually see themselves as unconstrained individuals.

D. first stop caring about whether other African-Americans liked their work in order to be able to stop caring about whether white people liked it.

Questions 8–10 ask about both passages.

---

8. The author of Passage B would presumably object most strongly to the fact that the rhetoric of Passage A:

F. repeatedly implies that no other nation, including the nations of the distant past, has ever been as essentially poetic as the United States.

G. characterizes Americans as a unified whole distinct from peoples of other nations without acknowledging disparate levels of privilege within America.

H. implies that American poets are both obliged and willing to abandon traditional verse forms such as the epic.

J. asserts that it is specifically the American poet alone who is to be the "arbiter of the diverse," rather than this task falling equally to all types of American artists.

9. Of the following phrases from Passage A, which is most nearly synonymous with the depiction in Passage B of the artist who is "not afraid to be himself?" (lines 100–101)

   A. "aversion to anything indecorous" (lines 17–18)

   B. "to be indirect and not direct" (lines 29–30)

   C. "their common referee" (line 38)

   D. "expose superior models" (line 46)

10. Of all the paragraphs in Passage A, which is the only one with which the author of Passage B would presumably agree *in its entirety*?

   F. Paragraph 2 (lines 12–23)

   G. Paragraph 3 (lines 24–35)

   H. Paragraph 4 (lines 36–48)

   J. Paragraph 5 (lines 49–57)

PASSAGE II—SOCIAL SCIENCE

This passage is adapted from the essay "The Trouble with Bright Girls" by Heidi Grant Halvorson (© 2011 by Heidi Grant Halvorson).

Successful women know only too well that in any male-dominated profession, we often find ourselves at a disadvantage. We are rou-tinely underestimated, underutilized and even
(5) underpaid. Studies show that women need to perform at extraordinarily high levels just to appear moderately competent compared to our male coworkers.

But in my experience, smart and talented
(10) women rarely realize that one of the toughest hurdles they'll have to overcome lies within. Compared with our male colleagues, we judge our own abilities not only more harshly but fundamentally differently. Understanding why
(15) we do it is the first step to righting a terrible wrong. And to do that, we need to take a step back in time.

Chances are good that if you are a successful professional today, you were a pretty bright fifth
(20) grade girl. Psychologist Carol Dweck conducted a series of studies in the 1980s looking at how bright girls and boys in the fifth grade handled new, difficult and confusing material.

She found that bright girls, when given some-
(25) thing to learn that was particularly foreign or complex, were quick to give up; the higher the girls' IQ, the more likely they were to throw in the towel. In fact, the straight-A girls showed the most helpless responses. Bright boys, on
(30) the other hand, saw the difficult material as a challenge, and found it energizing. They were more likely to redouble their efforts than give up.

Why does this happen? What makes smart girls less confident when they should be the
(35) most confident kids in the room? At the 5th-grade level, girls routinely outperform boys in every subject, including math and science. So there were no differences between these boys and girls in ability, nor in past history of suc-
(40) cess. The only difference was how bright boys and girls interpreted difficulty—what it meant to them when material seemed hard to learn. Bright girls were much quicker to doubt their ability, to lose confidence and to become less
(45) effective learners as a result.

Researchers have uncovered the reason for this difference in how difficulty is interpreted: more often than not, bright girls believe that their abilities are innate and unchangeable,
(50) while bright boys believe that they can develop ability through effort and practice.

How do girls and boys develop these different views? Most likely, it has to do with the kinds of feedback we get from parents and teachers as
(55) children. Girls, who develop self-control earlier and are better able to follow instructions, are often praised for their "goodness." When we do well in school, we are told that we are "so smart," "so clever," or "such a good student." This

(60) kind of praise implies that traits like smartness, cleverness and goodness are qualities you either have or you don't.

Boys, on the other hand, are a handful. Just trying to get boys to sit still and pay attention is (65) a real challenge for any parent or teacher. As a result, boys are given feedback that emphasizes effort (e.g., "If you would just pay attention you could learn this," "If you would just try a little harder you could get it right"). The result: when (70) learning something new is difficult, girls take it as a sign that they aren't "good" and "smart," and boys take it as a sign to try harder.

We continue to carry these beliefs, often unconsciously, around with us throughout our lives. (75) And because bright girls are particularly likely to see their abilities as innate and unchangeable, they grow up to be women who are far too hard on themselves—women who will prematurely conclude that they don't have what it takes to (80) succeed in a particular arena, and give up way too soon.

Even if every external disadvantage is removed—every inequality of opportunity, every chauvinistic stereotype, all the challenges we face (85) balancing work and family—we would still have to deal with the fact that through our mistaken beliefs about our abilities, we may be our own worst enemy.

How often have you found yourself avoiding (90) challenges and playing it safe, sticking to goals you knew would be easy for you to reach? Are there things you decided long ago that you could never be good at? Skills you believed you would never possess? If the list is a long one, you were (95) probably one of the bright girls—and your belief that you are stuck being exactly as you are has done more to determine the course of your life than you probably ever imagined.

No matter the ability—whether it's intel-(100) ligence, creativity, self-control, charm or athleticism—studies show them to be profoundly malleable. When it comes to mastering any skill, your experience, effort and persistence matter a lot. So if you were a bright girl, it's time to

(105) toss out your mistaken belief about how ability works, embrace the fact that you can always improve and reclaim the confidence that you lost so long ago.

11. The main idea of the passage is that:
   A. educational methodology in our society is biased against girls, especially bright ones.
   B. paradoxically, bright girls grow up to be far less confident in themselves than they should be.
   C. because they mature faster, girls are better at following directions than boys are.
   D. contrary to popular belief, there are actually no differences in how girls and boys learn.

12. The passage's tone is best described as:
   F. bitter.
   G. lighthearted.
   H. sardonic.
   J. analytical.

13. One of the main ideas of the seventh paragraph (lines 52–62) is that:
   A. adults unintentionally contribute to the low confidence of bright girls.
   B. bright boys at the elementary school level do not receive sufficient praise from adults.
   C. most adults mistakenly believe that girls develop self-control earlier than boys.
   D. adults should make more of an effort to praise all students, rather than just the bright ones.

14. According to the passage, which of the following factors does NOT contribute to eventual confidence problems in bright girls?
    F. Their knowledge of the fact that adult women, even bright ones, are often underpaid
    G. The fact that young girls tend to be better behaved than young boys are
    H. A valuable approach to challenges that adults unintentionally instill only in boys
    J. Bright girls believe their abilities are innate and are almost impossible to change

15. The passage best supports which of the following as a possible solution to the confidence problems of bright adult women?
    A. Removing inequalities of opportunity and chauvinistic stereotypes
    B. Encouraging women to reexamine their own views about the nature of ability
    C. Refraining from informing children of their IQs until they are much older
    D. Teaching boys to develop self-control earlier

16. As it is used in lines 101–102, the phrase *profoundly malleable* most nearly means:
    F. philosophically accurate.
    G. significantly different.
    H. extremely changeable.
    J. inspirationally beneficial.

17. In the context of the passage, the statement in lines 9–11 most nearly means that:
    A. the author believes that her experiences have made her uniquely qualified to address this subject matter.
    B. smart women are harmed by the fact that they were not encouraged to participate in sports as young girls.
    C. professional women often don't devote enough time to maintaining their emotional health.
    D. many women don't realize that their own beliefs may be holding them back as much as the sexism of others.

18. The passage best supports which of the following claims about Carol Dweck's study?
    F. It uncovered a problem in learning development unique to the smartest girls.
    G. It found that IQ is a more accurate predictor of scholastic success in boys than in girls.
    H. The methodology used to conduct the study was a great innovation for the time.
    J. More recent research has uncovered possible flaws in its conclusions.

19. The passage mentions all of the following as differences between girls and boys EXCEPT:
    A. how fast they mature.
    B. how easy they are to control.
    C. which subjects they tend to excel at.
    D. the ways that adults talk to them.

20. According to the passage, success in overcoming challenges of all kinds is:
    F. determined very early in life.
    G. largely the result of self-image.
    H. completely unrelated to gender.
    J. completely unrelated to IQ.

PASSAGE III—HUMANITIES

This passage is adapted from the essay "Song-writers and Scientists Both Hope to Peer Over God's Shoulder, If Only for a Moment" by John Roderick (© 2011 by John Roderick).

It's a popular adage that you should never decide to become a musician for the money. This is absolutely sane advice, as the vast majority of musicians don't make enough money to live on
(5) comfortably, and there is no retirement plan. The people who give this advice usually follow it by saying "You should only play music if you love it."

This is also good advice, but what does it mean? Everybody loves music. Do they mean
(10) that you should only play music if you love it like a psychopath and have no other interests? I mean, what good is music? It toys with emotions

in a manner that, if a friend acted the same way, you would hate their guts. And far from bringing
(15) people together, most music is listened to now in solitude on headphones at the gym, or wherever. So why is it still so powerful? What does it do?

There are plenty of things about the universe that we know to be true. Energy equals mass
(20) times the speed of light squared. The speed of light in a vacuum is 186,000 miles per second. The quadratic formula is X equals negative B plus or minus the square root of B squared minus four times A times C, all divided by two times A. This
(25) is science, and it makes up the indisputable body of known fact that enables us to build computer networks, suspension bridges, predator drones, and mechanical bulls.

But outside this illuminated circle of un-
(30) derstanding are vast dark places where other truths about the universe still live in shadow. What is gravity, exactly? Is there really such a thing as dark matter or dark energy, and if so, does it speak in a low, menacing voice? Do trees
(35) communicate telepathically with one another? Physicists and mathematicians working at the forefront of human discovery are leaning into these shadows and trying to expand the circle of light. Imagine how their hearts must soar when
(40) they develop a theory and see it proved, thrilled to be the first sentient creature to divine this aspect of the mechanics of the universe.

Musicians can feel the same exact thing. Some people might scoff at the comparison between
(45) some kid wearing white Ray-Bans and singing about how "love" is like "a flower" and a super-genius physicist peering into the darkness at the beginning of time, but both occupations are capable, in their greatest moments, of getting a
(50) brief glimpse over God's shoulder.

When John Lennon wrote "Imagine," he was standing at the center of 10,000 years of science, religion, music, and myth. That song is his Theory of Relativity, describing the universe of emotion
(55) and belief as surely as Einstein did time and space. Mathematicians roll their eyes, protesting

that the touchy-feely realm of emotion cannot be compared to the certainty of math, but emotion cannot be inconsistent with math. Emotion is just
(60) another aspect of the universe about which some small portion of our understanding is illuminated while the vast majority waits in shadow.

Both music and science are keys and codes which describe and unlock connections, pat-
(65) terns, and truths that were formerly felt but never drawn. In the right hands, both science and song allow recipients to experience personally the revelation, the excitement of the moment of discovery, in their own minds.

(70) Just as scientists build on the discoveries of those who've come before, so do songwriters. There's no chord change on Nirvana's *Nevermind* that hadn't been discovered and used hundreds of times before. But Nirvana combined this
(75) ribonucleic acid of rock to create music that reverberated with millions across languages and cultures instantaneously. It may still be difficult for us to determine exactly what universal truths are contained in "Smells Like Teen Spirit," but
(80) the results of the experiment are unequivocal.

It's impossible to consider this prospect without traipsing over into what sounds like hippie balderdash, but the principles of fractal geometry and of melody and rhythm converge
(85) somewhere out on the horizon, somewhere much closer to the Grand Unified Theory than we're able to connect at present. After all, music is math at its heart. But music transcends basic math just as string theory does. How can you
(90) mathematically account for Aretha Franklin's voice? How can you plot on a graph the effect of her voice on various listeners?

It's no mistake to consider music one of the sciences. Whatever your creed, the idea of glimps-
(95) ing some small aspect of the universal clockwork is irresistible. Theoretical physics attempts to describe multiple universes and scales of large and small that we may never fully comprehend. Likewise, every day musicians deliver new infor-
(100) mation about the very real, tangible, formative

realm of thinking and feeling. Our appreciation of music is the closest to practical philosophy most of us will experience.

21. The main purpose of the passage is to:
   A. suggest that people who only pay attention to trivial things like pop music should try to learn about more important things like science.
   B. argue that the mission of artists has more in common with the mission of the hard sciences than most realize.
   C. analyze the ways in which both science and art have emerged from and been inspired by various religious traditions.
   D. declare a personal belief that science and religion are not as incompatible as many seem to think, and that art reveals this.

22. The passage describes popular music as being all of the following EXCEPT:
   F. usually completely original.
   G. currently impossible to analyze mathematically.
   H. occasionally silly at first glance.
   J. a synthesis of emotional traditions.

23. Based on the passage, how should the assertion that artists and scientists are capable of "getting a brief glimpse over God's shoulder" (lines 49–50) be read?
   A. Literally; both professions can reveal truths that a deity intended to remain mysterious.
   B. Literally; both professions occasionally arrive at sound arguments for the existence of a deity.
   C. Metaphorically; both professions are methods of arriving at answers about human existence.
   D. Ironically; both scientists and artists tend to be less religious than the average person.

24. The passage most strongly implies that John Lennon viewed "Imagine" as:
   F. more a work of science than a work of art.
   G. a mission statement of personal philosophy.
   H. the intersection of artistic and religious history.
   J. a rebuke to skeptical mathematicians.

25. It can reasonably be inferred that the author believes Nirvana's "Smells Like Teen Spirit" is:
   A. a work that is inarguably important, though it is impossible to say exactly why.
   B. secretly a tribute to John Lennon's "Imagine."
   C. a song that is unique in being accessible to listeners who do not understand English.
   D. a piece of derivative songwriting that gets more attention than it probably deserves.

26. Through his comparison of music to a friend, the author reveals his belief that music:
   F. is always there for us when we need it most.
   G. cannot always be trusted to challenge us.
   H. influences our beliefs in gentle ways.
   J. is, in a sense, designed to be manipulative.

27. According to the passage, which of the following is part of an "indisputable body of known fact"?
   A. The theory of relativity
   B. The existence of dark matter
   C. The formula used to calculate energy
   D. The ribonucleic acid of rock

28. The statement in lines 86–92 most nearly means that:

    F. one should be aware that referring to music as a science will sound silly to most people.

    G. some other cultures understand the relationship between music and science much better than we.

    H. geometry might end up being more accurate if we would allow it to be influenced by music.

    J. in some way that we cannot comprehend, music and math are ultimately the same thing.

29. In the passage, the significance of mechanical bulls is that they are:

    A. proof that scientific knowledge can be used to create fun and "cool" things.

    B. the result of science, but associated with people who like a certain style of music.

    C. far less important than things like computers, bridges, and military aircraft.

    D. an example of something that would not work if our ideas about science were inaccurate.

30. As it is used in line 80, the word *unequivocal* most nearly means:

    F. absolutely clear.

    G. surprising to most people.

    H. not yet possible to see.

    J. difficult to express in words.

PASSAGE IV—NATURAL SCIENCE

This passage is adapted from the article "Could Jupiter Moon Harbor Fish-Sized Life?" by Victoria Jaggerd (© 2009 by *National Geographic*).

Below its icy crust Jupiter's moon Europa is believed to host a global ocean a hundred miles deep, with no land at the surface. And the extraterrestrial ocean is currently being fed more (5) than a hundred times more oxygen than previous models had suggested, according to provocative new research. That amount of oxygen would be enough to support more than just microscopic life-forms: at least three million tons of fishlike (10) creatures could theoretically live and breathe on Europa, said study author Richard Greenberg of the University of Arizona. "There's nothing saying there is life there now," said Greenberg. "But we do know there are the physical condi- (15) tions to support it."

Based on what we know about the Jovian moon, parts of Europa's seafloor should greatly resemble the environments around Earth's deep-ocean hydrothermal vents, said (20) deep-sea molecular ecologist Timothy Shank. "I'd be shocked if no life existed on Europa," said Shank, of the Woods Hole Oceanographic Institution. Despite the promising new estimates, it's too early to do more than speculate (25) about how Europan life might have evolved. A closer look—perhaps by a NASA orbiter now in development—will be needed to tell exactly how chemicals are distributed on Europa and how the moon's geologic history might have (30) contributed to life's chances.

It wasn't until Galileo, the NASA spacecraft, reached the Jupiter system in 1995 that scientists were able to study the moon in detail. What the Galileo probe found was so exciting that NASA (35) deliberately crashed the spacecraft into Jupiter in 2003 to prevent the craft from contaminating one of its own discoveries: the salty, subsurface ocean on Europa. Although the probe didn't see the ocean directly, scientists are pretty sure (40) it's there, based on the age, composition, and structure of the moon's icy surface.

Europa, like the other planets and moons in our solar system, is more than four billion years old.

But a relative lack of impact craters implies that the
(45) icy crust is just 50 million years old. "It's an entirely
different surface now than it was at the time the
dinosaurs went extinct on Earth," Greenberg said.
Europa's smooth surface is marred only by dark,
crisscrossing ridges that suggest the icy shell is
(50) being stretched and compressed by tidal forces.

"We're used to thinking of tides on Earth as
something seen on the shore," Greenberg explained. But on a larger scale, gravity from the
sun and moon constantly squishes and stretches
(55) Earth. Europa, which is about as big as our moon,
also gets tidally stretched, not by the sun but by
the gravity of massive Jupiter. The friction from
all this tidal stretching probably heats Europa
enough to maintain liquid water, Greenberg said.

(60) The warmer ocean material may be oozing
up through cracks in the ice and freezing on
the surface at the same rate that older ice sinks
and melts into the liquid interior. This cycle of
"repaving" would explain the young look of the
(65) surface ice—and would open the door for oxygen at the surface to permeate the subsurface
ocean. Oxygen is created when charged particles
from Jupiter's magnetic field hit the ice. Given
his estimates for the moon's rate of repaving,
(70) Greenberg thinks it would have taken one to
two billion years for the first surface oxygen to
reach the ocean below.

A few million years after the ice-repaving
process had started, oxygen levels in Europan
(75) seas reached their current levels—which exceed
levels in Earth's oceans—Greenberg speculates.
This timeframe actually improves the chances
that life as we know it took root on Europa. For
starters, the most primitive life-forms need an
(80) absence of oxygen to form, Greenberg said.
"Oxygen tends to cause other molecules to
come apart," he said, so genetic material such
as DNA can't freely assemble with oxygen present. "You need the delay so genetic material and
(85) structures can take shape," he said. "And then
when oxygen arrives, organisms will at least
have a fighting chance." Greenberg's generous

estimate of oxygen in Europa's ocean—and the
resulting speculation that fishlike creatures may
(90) exist there—depends on the surface repaving to
have happened at a relatively stable rate, in this
case, a complete renewal every 50 million years.

But planetary scientist Robert Pappalardo said
the process may have been more intermittent,
(95) and therefore the oxygen level—and chance
for fishlike life—lower. "Maybe 50 million years
ago it was churning away, and now it's slowed
down," said Pappalardo. Europa is gravitationally
locked with its neighboring moon Io, which may
(100) be pushing and pulling on Europa in extreme
cycles, resulting in periods of high and low tidal
friction. If tidal activity on Europa comes in fits
and starts, that would change the rates at which
heat and nutrients from the rocky mantle be-
(105) come available, he said. "Say there are microbes
down there," Pappalardo added. "What would
it mean for their evolution if every hundred
thousand years there was much more heat and
chemicals? It might lead to much more hardy
(110) organisms"—but not necessarily complex life.

31. Based on the passage as a whole, the main
factor that makes some scientists suspect
Europan life is the:
A. high oxygen levels of its ocean.
B. unusual warmth of its ocean.
C. fact that NASA kept the Galileo probe
from contaminating its ocean.
D. fact that its tidal activity comes in fits
and starts.

32. In terms of the passage as a whole, the third
paragraph (lines 31–41) mainly serves to:
F. provide evidence that, contrary to popular
belief, NASA still does important work.
G. explain why the possibility of an ocean on
Europa is so exciting.
H. demonstrate the level of control that
NASA has over its exploratory craft.
J. emphasize both the importance and
recentness of the discovery of Europa's ocean.

33. The passage suggests that compared to other bodies in our solar system, Europa has:
  A. been the focus of much more scientific attention.
  B. a unique system of tidal activity.
  C. much more resilient microbes.
  D. a surface formed much more recently.

34. Lines 80–87 primarily serve to illustrate the point that, to have resulted in advanced life, oxygen levels in Europa's ocean would need to:
  F. exceed levels in Earth's oceans.
  G. have slowed in the last 50 million years.
  H. have risen gradually.
  J. have been consistently high all along.

35. It can reasonably be inferred from the passage that which of the following bodies has the LEAST gravitational effect on Europa?
  A. The sun
  B. The Earth
  C. Jupiter
  D. Io

36. Which of the following is NOT mentioned in the passage as being something about which scientists are not yet sure?
  F. Whether life of any kind exists on Europa
  G. Whether Europa is gravitationally locked with Io
  H. Whether Europa is warm enough for liquid water
  J. Whether Europa's ocean even exists

37. As it is used in line 91, the word *stable* most nearly means:
  A. regular.
  B. sturdy.
  C. average.
  D. safe.

38. The main purpose of the final paragraph (lines 93–110) is to:
  F. represent the viewpoint that any life on Europa is impossible.
  G. explain the process by which microbes evolve into larger life forms.
  H. explore the possibility that evolution on Europa works differently from how it does on Earth.
  J. suggest that advanced life on Europa may be unlikely.

39. As it is used in lines 102–103, the expression *in fits and starts* most nearly means:
  A. unpredictably.
  B. effectively.
  C. intermittently.
  D. dangerously.

40. It can most reasonably be inferred from the passage that tidal activity on any celestial body is due to:
  F. the moon.
  G. surface repaving.
  H. the influence of other celestial bodies.
  J. oxygen-rich liquid water.

If there is still time remaining, check your answers to this section.

SCIENCE TEST

Time: 35 Minutes—40 Questions

> **Directions:** There are six passages in this test. Each passage is followed by several questions. After reading a passage, choose the best answer to each question and fill in the corresponding oval on your answer sheet. You may refer to the passages as often as necessary.
>
> You are NOT permitted to use a calculator on this test.

PASSAGE I

Radium-226 (^{226}Ra) activity is often elevated in bodies of water that have been augmented with groundwater. Samples were collected over a two-year period in order to study ^{226}Ra activity in Florida Marsh and Cypress wetlands. Figure 1 shows the average ^{226}Ra activity from surface sediment samples collected in 2002 and 2004. Cores were taken from shallow sediment (0 to 4 cm) in the wetlands and analyzed for ^{226}Ra activity. The activity, in disintegration per minute per gram (dpm/g), found in the Marsh and Cypress wetlands is displayed in Figures 2 and 3.

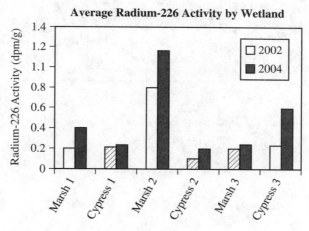

Figure 1

PRACTICE TEST 5

Figure 2

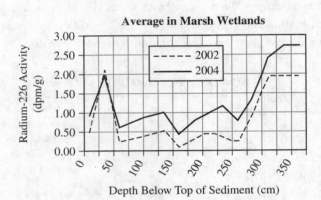

Figure 3

1. According to Figure 2, the average radium-226 activity in Cypress wetlands in 2004 at a depth of 200 cm was closest to which of the following?
   A. 0.30 dpm/g
   B. 0.70 dpm/g
   C. 1.00 dpm/g
   D. 2.50 dpm/g

2. Based on the information in Figure 3, if the average radium-226 activity had been measured in Marsh wetlands at the depth of 400 cm in 2002, it most likely would have been closest to which of the following?
   F. 2.75 dpm/g
   G. 2.50 dpm/g
   H. 2.00 dpm/g
   J. 1.80 dpm/g

3. Which of the following is the most likely explanation for the difference in the average ^{226}Ra activity between 2002 and 2004?
   A. In 2004 the wetlands were augmented with groundwater, which caused an increase in ^{226}Ra activity.
   B. In 2002 the wetlands were augmented with groundwater, and in 2004, they were not. This resulted in more ^{226}Ra activity in 2004.
   C. The amount of groundwater the wetlands were augmented with was higher in 2002 than in 2004.
   D. In 2004 there was more rainfall than in 2002, which created a decrease in ^{226}Ra activity.

4. If the data in Figures 2 and 3 are typical of Cypress and Marsh wetlands, one would most likely make which of the following conclusions about the ^{226}Ra activity in a wetland?
   F. ^{226}Ra activity is highest in wetlands in the top 50 cm of the sediment layer.
   G. ^{226}Ra activity gets higher as the sediment gets deeper.
   H. ^{226}Ra activity is highest in wetlands at around 325 cm below the top of the sediment.
   J. Each year, the ^{226}Ra activity in wetlands will become less.

5. According to Figures 2 and 3, the ^{226}Ra activity increased between the depths of 200 and 250 cm for which wetlands?
   A. Cypress wetlands in 2002
   B. Cypress wetlands in 2004
   C. Marsh wetlands in 2002
   D. Marsh wetlands in 2004

6. Suppose an environmentalist was doing research on the effects of ^{226}Ra on the wetlands in 2002. Assuming the element is detrimental to the environment, which wetland would be least affected by ^{226}Ra?
   F. Cypress 1
   G. Cypress 2
   H. Marsh 1
   J. Marsh 3

PASSAGE II

The balanced chemical equation for the dissociation of acetic acid in water is shown below:

$$CH_3COOH(aq) \leftrightarrows CH_3COO^-(aq) + H^+(aq)$$

The reaction can proceed in either direction in order to maintain a constant value for the acid dissociation constant. Acetic acid is an acid because it contributes H^+ ions to the solution. The acid dissociation constant for the above reaction can be expressed as follows:

$$K_a = \frac{[H^+(aq)][CH_3COO^-(aq)]}{[CH_3COOH(aq)]}$$

$$K_a = 1.82 \cdot 10^{-5} \text{ at } 25$$

The expression [A] represents *the concentration of substance A in moles/liter*. One mole is $6.02 \cdot 10^{23}$ molecules.

Experiment 1

NaOH is a strong base because it dissociates readily in water and contributes OH^- ions to the water. A 1 M solution of NaOH, a strong base, is slowly added to a 100 ml, 2 M (M represents *molarity*, a measure of concentration in $\frac{moles}{liter}$) solution of acetic acid. The NaOH solution contributes OH^- ions to the mixture. An ion is a charged atom or molecule. The OH^- ions from the NaOH combine with the H^+ ions from the acetic acid to form water as shown below:

$$H^+(aq) + OH^-(aq) \rightarrow H_2O(l)$$

Various measurements were taken and the results are shown in Table 1 and graphed in Figure 1.
Note: pH = $-\log[H^+]$

Table 1

NaOH added (ml)	$[CH_3COO(aq)]$ (moles/liter)	$[H^+(aq)]$ (moles/liter)	$[CH_3COOH(aq)]$ (moles/liter)	pH	$K_a (\cdot 10^{-5})$
0	$6.0 \cdot 10^{-3}$	$6.0 \cdot 10^{-3}$	2	2.2	1.8
100	.45	$1.9 \cdot 10^{-5}$	.51	4.7	1.7
200	.68	$6.0 \cdot 10^{-10}$	$2.0 \cdot 10^{-5}$	9.3	2.0
300	.69	$5.0 \cdot 10^{-14}$	$2 \cdot 10^{-10}$	13.4	1.7
400	.69	$2.5 \cdot 10^{-14}$	$9 \cdot 10^{-10}$	13.5	1.9

ml of NaOH added

Figure 1

7. Using Table 1 and Figure 1, how much NaOH was added in order to increase the pH to 9.3?
   A. 0 ml
   B. 100 ml
   C. 200 ml
   D. 300 ml

8. If only 50 ml of NaOH had been added, what approximate value would the pH have been?
   F. 1.5
   G. 3.5
   H. 5.5
   J. 7.5

9. Using all the information in the passage, why did the concentration of $CH_3COOH(aq)$ continue to decrease while the concentration of $CH_3COO^-(aq)$ remained nearly unchanged?
   A. Looking at the K_a, $[CH_3COOH(aq)]$ is in the denominator and $[CH_3COO^-(aq)]$ is in the numerator. The system counteracts the decrease in $[H^+(aq)]$ by dissociating more molecules of CH_3COOH.
   B. Looking at the K_a, $[CH_3COOH(aq)]$ is in the denominator and $[CH_3COO^-(aq)]$ is in the numerator. The system counteracts the increase in $[H^+(aq)]$ by synthesizing more molecules of CH_3COOH.
   C. The NaOH produces Na^+ ions that must be combining with the CH_3COOH molecules in such a way that the concentration continues to decrease.
   D. Clearly, the data must be inaccurate. Looking at the balanced equation, for every molecule of acetic acid that dissociates, one CH_3COO^- ion must form and the $[CH_3COO^-(aq)]$ should have continued to increase.

10. What would be the effect on the results if 100 ml of 1 M acetic acid was used instead of 100 ml of 2 M?

   F. The decreased concentration of acetic acid will decrease acidity and increase the initial pH.

   G. The decreased concentration of acetic acid will decrease acidity and decrease the initial pH.

   H. The increased concentration of acetic acid will increase acidity and increase the initial pH.

   J. The increased concentration of acetic acid will increase acidity and decrease the initial pH.

11. How could you lower the pH back to 2.2?

   A. Adding enough NaOH will eventually lower the pH because the cycle will repeat.

   B. Adding enough water will dilute the base and lower the pH.

   C. Evaporating some of the water will increase the concentration of H^+ ions sufficiently to lower the pH.

   D. Adding a sufficient amount of acetic acid will add H^+ ions and lower the pH.

12. What is true about the relationship between $[H^+(aq)]$ and pH?

   F. There is an inverse relationship; as $[H^+(aq)]$ decreases, the pH increases.

   G. There is a direct relationship; as $[H^+(aq)]$ decreases, the pH decreases.

   H. The relationship is complex. Because the concentrations are so small, the pH jumps after 200 ml of NaOH is added because small quantities of H^+ ions increase the pH greatly, whereas large quantities of H^+ ions have little effect.

   J. There is no relationship between $[H^+(aq)]$ and pH.

13. How many milliliters of NaOH should be added to a 100 ml 2 molarity solution of acetic acid to obtain an acid dissociation constant (K_a) of 1.9×10^{-5}?

   A. 100 ml

   B. 200 ml

   C. 300 ml

   D. 400 ml

PASSAGE III

Air permeability is defined as the ability of soil to transmit air through interconnected air-filled pores under an imposed air pressure gradient. Air permeability is a function of volumetric water content, porosity, pore size distribution, and pore geometry. Scientists used a soil corer air permeameter (SCAP) to digitally measure the *flow rates* of air through desert soil under low-pressure gradients. The SCAP measured air permeability both in situ, with the instrument inserted in the soil and ex situ, after the soil corer had been removed from the soil. Figures 1 and 2 display the results of field testing conducted at two of the four sites in Arizona, over the course of three months. The porosity of the soil at each site is displayed in Figure 3. Figure 4 shows the relationship between the air pressure used and the flow rate of the air for each site.

Figure 1

Figure 2

Site Porosity

Figure 3

Pressure vs. Flowrate

Figure 4

14. According to Figure 2, the air permeability measured ex situ in October was closest to which of the following?
   F. 5 μm²
   G. 15 μm²
   H. 20 μm²
   J. 30 μm²

15. Based on Figure 4, if the air permeability had been tested at Site 1 using 800 Pa, the flow rate would most likely have been closest to which of the following?
   A. 0.5 m³/s
   B. 0.6 m³/s
   C. 0.4 m³/s
   D. 0.3 m³/s

16. Which of the following is the most likely explanation for the difference in air permeability at Site 1 versus Site 2?
   F. The overall air permeability is higher at Site 1 due to the lower porosity of the soil.
   G. The overall air permeability is higher at Site 2 due to the higher porosity of the soil.
   H. The overall air permeability at Site 2 is higher because less pressure was used when testing the soil.
   J. The overall air permeability at Site 2 is higher because more pressure was used when testing the soil.

17. If the data in Figures 1 and 2 is typical of air permeability measurements, one would most likely make which of the following conclusions about air permeability in situ versus ex situ?

A. The permeability will always be higher ex situ than in situ.

B. The permeability will always be lower ex situ than in situ.

C. Water permeability is higher than air permeability in situ and ex situ.

D. At high pressures, air permeability is greater in situ than ex situ.

18. According to Figure 1, which of the following statements is most accurate regarding permeability during the month of November?

F. Permeability was lower than in previous months.

G. Permeability was highest for air measured while the SCAP was still inserted in the ground.

H. Permeability was highest for air measured after the SCAP had removed a core from the soil.

J. Permeability was highest for water.

19. According to the information in the figures, one of the four sites has a higher porosity than the others. A farmer wants to plant a crop on the site with the highest porosity. Which location would fit the farmer's needs best?

A. Site 1

B. Site 2

C. Site 3

D. Site 4

PASSAGE IV

Scientists studying sucrose examined oranges and lemons to determine how the two fruits form and synthesize sucrose. Studies were conducted both on extractions from the fruits and on small, intact fruits.

Study 1

Mature lemon and orange fruits were obtained and then juiced by hand. Formation of fructose was determined using two portions of the fruits: the juice, and the particulate sediment. The results are shown in Table 1.

Table 1—Formation of Sucrose by Fructose Reaction

Preparation	Sucrose Synthesized (μmoles)
Oranges	
Juice	0.12
Particulate sediment	0.9
Lemons	
Juice	0.4
Particulate sediment	0.17

Study 2

Scientists found lemons of varying ages from the same fruit grove. Each piece of fruit was cut into sections, and various tissue samples were isolated for testing. The three tissue types tested were the *flavedo* (colored, outer layer of the peel), the *albedo* (white peel layer), and the *vesicle* (fleshy part of the fruit). The results of the formation of sucrose in lemons are shown in Figure 1.

Figure 1

Study 3

Whole fruits (each weighing approximately 5 g) were tested and then cut into sections to measure sucrose activity in the various tissues. Figure 2 displays the results.

Figure 2

20. Based on Figure 1, which type of lemon tissue forms the most sucrose?

    F. The albedo tissue in a large lemon

    G. The albedo tissue in a small lemon

    H. The flavedo tissue in a large lemon

    J. The vesicles in a small lemon

21. According to the results of Study 2, as fruit size increased, the sucrose found in the vesicles:

    A. increased only.

    B. increased, then decreased.

    C. decreased only.

    D. decreased, then increased.

22. Based on the results of Study 3, the largest difference in sucrose activity was found in:

    F. oranges between the flavedo tissue and the albedo tissue.

    G. oranges between the albedo tissue and the vesicle tissue.

    H. lemons between the flavedo tissue and the vesicle tissue.

    J. lemons between the flavedo tissue and the albedo tissue.

23. Based on the results of Study 1, which of the following is most accurate about the formation of sucrose?

    A. Orange juice is more effective at forming sucrose than lemon juice.

    B. Orange juice is less effective at forming sucrose than lemon juice.

    C. Lemon juice and orange juice are equally effective at forming sucrose.

    D. Lemon juice forms less sucrose than lemon particulate sediment.

24. Assume Study 2 was repeated using oranges instead of lemons. Based on the information presented in Figures 1 and 2, and assuming that the fruits used in Study 3 were 30 mm in diameter, which of the following would most likely be the sucrose formation (as a percent of total activity) in the albedo tissue of the oranges?

    F. 0

    G. 3

    H. 9

    J. 20

25. Based on the results of Study 2, which statement most accurately summarizes the formation of sucrose in lemons?

    A. The fleshy part of the lemon formed the majority of the sucrose.

    B. The colored outer layer of the peel does not form any sucrose.

    C. The part of the lemon that forms the most sucrose is dependent on the size of the lemon.

    D. More sucrose is formed in the white peel layer of a lemon than anywhere else.

26. If scientists wanted to study the sucrose in a lemon with a 55 mm diameter, which of the following outcomes would most likely represent the formation of sucrose?

    F. 6% Vesicles, 1% Flavedo, and 12% Albedo activity

    G. 2% Vesicles, 3% Flavedo, and 8% Albedo activity

    H. 2% Vesicles, 0% Flavedo, and 10% Albedo activity

    J. 0% Vesicles, 1% Flavedo, and 10% Albedo activity

PASSAGE V

Since carbon is essential to life on Earth, understanding the global carbon cycle can provide valuable information. Through the process of photosynthesis, plants on land or algae living in water convert carbon dioxide into organic products. Through the process of respiration, organisms convert these organic compounds into energy and release carbon dioxide. Figure 1 displays the global carbon cycle.

Global Carbon Cycle

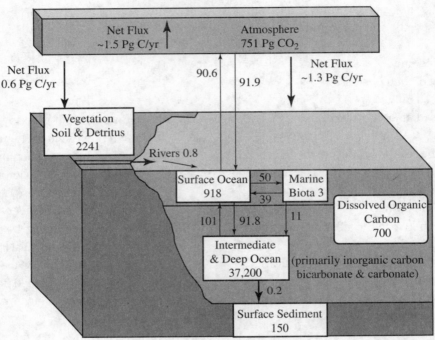

Figure 1

A significant amount of carbon is released through the burning of fossil fuels. Some of this carbon is stored in the atmosphere, while a significant portion is stored in ocean waters and sediments. Carbon in the ocean is described as dissolved inorganic carbon, particulate inorganic carbon, particulate organic carbon (POC), and dissolved organic carbon (DOC). Particulates are defined as those larger than 0.2 micrometers, whereas dissolved matter is that smaller than 0.2 micrometers (see Figure 2).

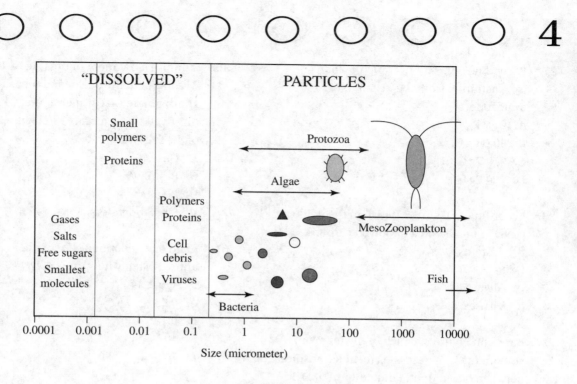

Figure 2

Chromophoric dissolved organic matter (CDOM) is the colored portion of DOC. It is colored because it intensely absorbs violet and blue light. Figure 3 displays DOC and CDOM absorption in the tropical North Atlantic Ocean.

Figure 3

27. Based on Figure 1, how much carbon is transmitted from the ocean to the atmosphere?
   A. 91.9 Pg C/yr
   B. 90.6 Pg C/yr
   C. 918 Pg C/yr
   D. 700 Pg C/yr

28. According to Figure 2, which of the following is NOT considered a dissolved carbon?
   F. Proteins
   G. Salts
   H. Algae
   J. Viruses

29. Based on Figure 3, which of the following statements best describes the relationship between ocean depth and amount of DOC?
   A. As the ocean depth increased, the amount of DOC remained fairly constant, then decreased steadily, then began to increase again.
   B. As the ocean depth increased, the amount of DOC steadily decreased.
   C. As the ocean depth increased, the amount of DOC remained fairly constant, then decreased steadily, then became fairly constant again.
   D. As the ocean depth increased, the amount of DOC steadily increased.

30. Suppose a fragment of organic carbon was found in the ocean and measured approximately 0.01 micrometers. It would mostly likely be featured in Figure 2 by which of the following?
   F. Gases
   G. Protozoa
   H. Bacteria
   J. Small polymers

31. At an ocean depth of 100 m, there is approximately how much CDOM, according to Figure 3?
   A. 0.25
   B. 0.12
   C. 40
   D. 70

32. Which of the following fragments, if found in the ocean, would be described as dissolved inorganic carbon?
   F. Bacteria
   G. Protozoa
   H. Viruses
   J. Polymers

33. In a sampling taken from the ocean, scientists uncovered many carbons measuring 120 micrometers. What classification would they give these carbons?
   A. Dissolved protein
   B. Protozoa particle
   C. Algae particle
   D. Dissolved cell debris

PASSAGE VI

Three substances have been shown to inhibit respiration in various organisms: hydrocyanic acid, hydrogen sulfide, and carbon monoxide. An experiment was conducted to determine the effect that each of these substances has on the respiration of the green alga *Chlorella*. Figure 1 shows the results.

Figure 1

Researcher 1 argued that glucose would have a contradictory effect on the alga, so that if the *Chlorella* were suspended in a solution containing 1 percent glucose, there would be less of an effect on respiration. Figure 2 displays the results of the experiment.

Figure 2

Researcher 2 hypothesized that light may play an active part in respiration of *Chlorella*, so an experiment was done to measure the effect of successive periods of light and darkness on the respiration of cells suspended in carbon monoxide and in nitrogen. The results are shown in Figure 3.

Figure 3

34. The theories of the two researchers are similar in that both researchers believe that:
   F. glucose will increase the respiration of *Chlorella*.
   G. HCN and H_2S have no effect on the respiration of *Chlorella*.
   H. an additional factor will have an effect on the respiration of *Chlorella*.
   J. CO and N also affect the respiration of *Chlorella*.

35. According to Figure 1, *Chlorella* would typically consume about how much oxygen after half an hour?
   A. 10 mm^3
   B. 18 mm^3
   C. 22 mm^3
   D. 35 mm^3

36. If Researcher 1 was correct about the effect of glucose on the respiration of *Chlorella*, then based on the information in Figure 2, Researcher 1 would most likely predict that *Chlorella* suspended in a solution containing 2 percent glucose and HCN would consume how much oxygen after 20 minutes?
   F. 15 mm^3
   G. 25 mm^3
   H. 30 mm^3
   J. 40 mm^3

37. Does the data in Figure 3 support Researcher 2's hypothesis?
   A. Yes. It shows that light is necessary for the respiration of *Chlorella*.
   B. Yes. It shows that equal respiration occurs in the darkness and in light.
   C. No. More respiration of *Chlorella* occurred in the darkness.
   D. No. Varying the amount of light did not yield significantly different rates of respiration.

38. Suppose a third researcher studied the effect of glucose and CO on the respiration of *Chlorella*, using the same conditions and methods as Researcher 1. After 20 minutes the results showed that the sample suspended in CO had consumed 50 mm^3 of oxygen, while the sample suspended in a mixture of CO and glucose had consumed 60 mm^3 of oxygen. How would this experiment most likely affect the researchers' viewpoints?

   F. It would weaken Researcher 2's viewpoint only.

   G. It would weaken Researcher 1's viewpoint only.

   H. It would strengthen both researchers' viewpoints.

   J. It would have no effect on either researcher's viewpoint.

39. According to Figure 2, which substance had the LEAST effect on respiration of *Chlorella* after 30 minutes?

   A. HCN

   B. H$_2$S

   C. Glucose + HCN

   D. Glucose + H$_2$S

40. According to Researcher 2, experiment findings indicate the following is FALSE regarding the relationship between *Chlorella* cells suspended in carbon monoxide and *Chlorella* cells suspended in nitrogen EXCEPT:

   F. *Chlorella* cells suspended in carbon monoxide consume more oxygen.

   G. *Chlorella* cells suspended in nitrogen consume less oxygen.

   H. *Chlorella* cells suspended in carbon monoxide and nitrogen consume the same amount of oxygen.

   J. *Chlorella* cells suspended in nitrogen consume more oxygen.

STOP

If there is still time remaining, check your answers to this section.

WRITING TEST

Time: 40 minutes

Schools Policing Social Media

The last several years have seen a sharp rise in incidents of college students, or even professors, being disciplined by their institution for comments made on Facebook or other social media. As a consequence of making allegedly "offensive" comments, students have been compelled to undergo sensitivity training or even suspended, and some professors have been forced to delete online comments and make public apologies under threat of dismissal. While some cases have involved hateful or even threatening speech, sometimes students and faculty have been punished for "offenses" that amount to nothing more than expressing a political opinion with which the majority of their peers disagree.

Read and carefully consider these perspectives. Each suggests a particular way of thinking about the idea of schools policing social media.

Perspective One	Perspective Two	Perspective Three
Although a social media site is not a classroom or school property, students and faculty speaking online in their real identities still represent the school, which has a right to protect its reputation. People are still free to voice whatever opinion they like, as long as they don't use their real names.	When only certain opinions are permitted to be voiced, people learn less. This is true in the classroom, and so there's no reason it should stop being true outside of the classroom. The notion that "majority rule" within a peer group should determine the truth at an institution of learning is absurd.	Students go to school to learn, and being held accountable for what they say online is a part of that process. Professors, however, are trained and intelligent professionals, and the standard of academic freedom must be upheld. Professors should be given considerably more leeway than students are to express themselves online.

ESSAY TASK

Write a unified, coherent essay about schools' right, or lack thereof, to police students and faculty on social media, and the pros and cons of their doing so. In your essay, be sure to:

- clearly state your own perspective on the issue and analyze the relationship between your perspective and at least one other perspective
- develop and support your ideas with reasoning and examples
- organize your ideas clearly and logically
- communicate your ideas effectively in standard written English

Your perspective may be in full agreement with any of those given, in partial agreement, or completely different.

Planning Your Response

Your prewriting notes on this page will not be considered in your score.

Use the following space to brainstorm ideas and map out your response. You may want to think about the following as you analyze the given prompt:

Strengths and weaknesses of the three viewpoints

- What good points do they make, and what potential objections do they ignore?
- Why might they be convincing to readers, and why might their perspectives fall short?

Your previous experience, background knowledge, and personal values

- What is your viewpoint on this topic, and what are the pros and cons of this viewpoint?
- How will you craft an argument in support of your point of view?

_____

_____

_____

_____

_____

_____

_____

_____

_____

_____

_____

_____

_____

_____

If there is still time remaining, you may review your answers.

ANSWER KEY
Practice Test 5

English

1. D	16. H	31. C	46. G	61. C
2. F	17. B	32. J	47. D	62. F
3. B	18. G	33. B	48. F	63. D
4. H	19. D	34. F	49. C	64. G
5. D	20. J	35. C	50. G	65. D
6. G	21. D	36. J	51. C	66. H
7. D	22. F	37. D	52. F	67. C
8. H	23. D	38. G	53. D	68. F
9. A	24. H	39. C	54. J	69. B
10. F	25. A	40. F	55. A	70. J
11. B	26. F	41. A	56. H	71. D
12. G	27. C	42. G	57. B	72. H
13. C	28. G	43. D	58. G	73. A
14. J	29. B	44. H	59. D	74. G
15. C	30. H	45. B	60. H	75. B

Mathematics

1. D	13. B	25. C	37. B	49. C
2. G	14. H	26. H	38. J	50. F
3. B	15. D	27. B	39. D	51. D
4. K	16. K	28. F	40. F	52. G
5. A	17. D	29. A	41. E	53. E
6. K	18. J	30. J	42. K	54. F
7. D	19. B	31. E	43. B	55. B
8. F	20. G	32. F	44. J	56. F
9. B	21. E	33. A	45. D	57. C
10. H	22. F	34. H	46. H	58. K
11. C	23. B	35. C	47. A	59. A
12. H	24. F	36. H	48. J	60. K

ANSWER KEY
Practice Test 5

Reading

1.	**B**	9.	**D**	17.	**D**	25.	**A**	33.	**D**
2.	**G**	10.	**J**	18.	**F**	26.	**J**	34.	**H**
3.	**D**	11.	**B**	19.	**C**	27.	**C**	35.	**B**
4.	**F**	12.	**J**	20.	**G**	28.	**J**	36.	**G**
5.	**C**	13.	**A**	21.	**B**	29.	**D**	37.	**A**
6.	**J**	14.	**F**	22.	**F**	30.	**F**	38.	**J**
7.	**C**	15.	**B**	23.	**C**	31.	**A**	39.	**C**
8.	**G**	16.	**H**	24.	**G**	32.	**J**	40.	**H**

Science

1.	**B**	9.	**A**	17.	**A**	25.	**D**	33.	**B**
2.	**H**	10.	**F**	18.	**J**	26.	**H**	34.	**H**
3.	**A**	11.	**D**	19.	**B**	27.	**B**	35.	**B**
4.	**H**	12.	**F**	20.	**G**	28.	**H**	36.	**F**
5.	**D**	13.	**D**	21.	**B**	29.	**C**	37.	**D**
6.	**G**	14.	**J**	22.	**H**	30.	**J**	38.	**G**
7.	**C**	15.	**A**	23.	**B**	31.	**B**	39.	**B**
8.	**G**	16.	**G**	24.	**H**	32.	**G**	40.	**J**

HOW TO SCORE YOUR PRACTICE TEST

Step 1: Add up the number correct for each section and write that number in the blank under the Raw Score column on the Score Conversion Table. (Your goal is to get more questions correct on each subsequent practice test.)

Step 2: Using the Score Conversion Chart, find your scale score for each section and write it down. Then add up all four sections and divide by 4 to find your overall composite score. (Composite scores are rounded up at .5 or higher.)

SCORE CONVERSION TABLE

Section	Raw Score	Scaled Score
English	(out of 75)	____ / 36
Math	(out of 60)	____ / 36
Reading	(out of 40)	____ / 36
Science	(out of 40)	____ / 36
		Add and divide by 4
Overall Composite =		____ / 36

SCORE CONVERSION CHART

		Number Correct			
ACT Score*	English Section	Mathematics Section	Reading Section	Science Section	ACT Score*
36	75	60	40	40	36
35	74	59	39	39	35
34	73	58	38	38	34
33	72	57	37	—	33
32	71	56	36	37	32
31	70	54–55	35	36	31
30	69	53	34	35	30
29	67–68	51–52	33	34	29
28	65–66	49–50	32	33	28
27	64	46–48	31	31–32	27
26	62–63	44–45	30	30	26
25	60–61	41–43	29	28–29	25
24	58–59	39–40	27–28	25–27	24
23	55–57	37–38	25–26	24	23

(continued)

SCORE CONVERSION CHART (*Continued*)

ACT Score*	English Section	Mathematics Section	Reading Section	Science Section	ACT Score*
22	53–54	35–36	23–24	22–23	22
21	50–52	33–34	22	20–21	21
20	47–49	31–32	21	18–19	20
19	44–46	28–30	19–20	17	19
18	42–43	25–27	18	15–16	18
17	40–41	22–24	17	14	17
16	37–39	19–21	16	13	16
15	34–36	15–17	15	12	15
14	31–33	11–14	13–14	11	14
13	29–30	09–10	12	10	13
12	27–28	07–08	10–11	09	12
11	25–26	06	08–09	08	11
10	23–24	05	07	07	10
9	21–22	04	06	05–06	9
8	18–20	03	05	—	8
7	15–17	—	—	04	7
6	12–14	02	04	03	6
5	09–11	—	03	02	5
4	07–08	01	02	—	4
3	05–06	—	—	01	3
2	03–04	—	01	—	2
1	00–02	00	00	00	1

These scores are based on student trials rather than national norms.

SCORING YOUR ESSAY

As mentioned earlier in this text, two readers will evaluate your essay and each person will then assign it a score from 1 to 6. If, by chance, these two scorers disagree by more than 1 point, a third reader will step in and resolve the discrepancy. Performance on the essay will not affect your English, math, reading, science, or composite scores. You will receive two additional scores on your score sheet—a combined English/writing score (1–36) and a writing test subscore (1–12). Neither of these scores will affect your composite score!

The sample essay that follows reflects higher-level writing. It meets the criteria that ACT has put forth for essays that demonstrate effective writing skills.

- It takes a definite position.
- It addresses and expands on the counterargument.
- It has details that support the topic sentences and is well organized.
- It is not repetitive, and while there may be errors, they do not interfere with the competence of the essay.
- It is consistent and well balanced.
- The essay has a clear introduction and a conclusion that is not just a summary but ends with a significant thought.
- The vocabulary demonstrates good use of language and the sentence structure is varied.

ANSWER EXPLANATIONS

English

1. **(D)** Even though there are a bunch of adjectives here, the right answer is the one with no commas, because the adjectives are not the kind you would separate with commas. Don't panic! It's not that hard, and in fact you already knew this. If you wrote "The three young French girls," would you use commas anywhere in there? No, right? This is because the adjectives concern *number*, *age*, and *nationality/ethnicity*. This makes them feel like they are part of the noun idea, and so even though they are adjectives, we don't use commas the same way we would if we were writing "The nice, funny, pretty girls." The other tricky part here is "science-fiction fans," because you have to realize that that entire phrase is the noun idea, not just "fans." I know this sounds complicated, but I bet you still *felt like* the answer with no commas was right, and if you missed this one it was probably because you second-guessed your instincts.

2. **(F)** The noun controlling the verb *bent* is *figure*, not *powers*. There is an implied "who is" there: "an evil figure with strange mind-control powers *who* is bent on world domination." If you are unfamiliar with the expression "bent on," it means something like "obsessed with" or "determined to achieve."

3. **(B)** Only what comes after the punctuation mark is an independent clause, and the two clauses before it are dependent ones beginning with *as* and *after*, so you need a comma. It is a huge clue that two of the other choices are a semicolon and a period: if one of those is right, the other one is too, so when you see that, odds are they cancel each other out and the answer is the one with the comma.

4. **(H)** How many societies are we talking about? One. And does it possess something here? Yes (the downtrodden and defenseless). This means we need the singular possessive: *society's*. It is just that simple. (Okay, maybe it seems tricky because when you say *society* you are talking about a bunch of people, so it may feel plural, but the bottom line is that *society* is still a singular word!)

5. **(D)** The relevant rule here is parallel phrasing. Earlier in the sentence we see "who used his abilities to protect," and then right before the underlined part we see "rather than." So, the verb in the underlined part needs to be in the infinitive tense, just like "to protect," giving us "to exploit." *To protect rather than to exploit.*

6. **(G)** "They revamped their creation along these lines" is the core independent clause of the sentence. What comes before it is an introductory dependent clause followed by a comma, and what comes after it is an afterthought clause preceded by a comma.

7. **(D)** You've got three clauses here, so at least one of them has to be an independent clause. The first and third clauses aren't, so the middle one has to be, which means you have to get rid of *when*. This question is an excellent example of why you always have to read the entire sentence.

8. **(H)** The idea here is commas separating items in a list, but the items are all more than one word long. All you need to do is group the words correctly and put the commas in the appropriate places: *shorts over tights* is one idea, *a cape* is one idea, and *a logo on the chest* is one idea, so the commas separate those things. Be aware that whether you have a

comma before the *and* that precedes the last item in a list does not matter (either way is correct). A question on the ACT will never ask you about that (some choices here have a comma before the *and* while others do not, but the wrong choices are all wrong for other reasons).

9. **(A)** As with many style questions, this is a case of "the simplest explanation is probably the correct one." Is the sentence a logical transition into the following paragraph? Yes, because the next paragraph begins to discuss the psychological underpinnings of the creation of Superman. If choice A can't be wrong, then it must be right. The subsequent choices are tempting because they sound more complex, but this is only a trick that the test plays on us: something that sounds harder isn't necessarily right, even though the pressure of the test can make us feel this way.

10. **(F)** The comma after *parents* completes the appositive clause that was begun before the underlined part, and then the colon after *immigrant* properly introduces an explanatory clause. The phrase "like Siegel and Shuster's parents" is extra information that has been dropped into the middle of the independent clause "Superman is an immigrant," and so it must be set off with commas.

11. **(B)** How many creators are we talking about? Two. And do they possess something here? Yes (their heritage). This means we need the plural possessive. It is just that simple. The question also *appears to be* asking you to choose between *his* and *Superman's*, but this part doesn't matter: either is correct as long as *Superman's* is possessive.

12. **(G)** A *reference* is a word or idea that calls up the memory of another idea, and the preposition used with *reference* would be *to*.

13. **(C)** The full verb phrase is *struggle to become*, and this is interrupted by the prepositional phrase of *immigrant groups* to signal whose struggle it was.

14. **(J)** *Power* is the noun here, and *will be used* is the verb. *Possessed by some* is extra information concerning the power. To determine agreement, all you need to do is ignore the words *possessed by some* and see what sounds right or makes sense: "The power will be used for the benefit of all."

15. **(C)** The essay deals only with how the creation of Superman was inspired by tragedy, and does not discuss even one other example of popular entertainment, much less popular entertainment in general. The Yes/No questions that often end ACT English passages frequently use variations of this same trick, so watch out for it.

16. **(H)** The clause is "a bunch of guys from my class started playing paintball," and the additional information "myself included" is inserted into that clause. It needs to be set off with two of the same punctuation mark, and choice H, with two commas, is the only choice that does so.

17. **(B)** We need the word *you're* (the contraction for "you are") and the word *it's* (the contraction for "it is"), and choice B is the one that has both. *Your* and *its* are both possessive pronouns, and would be wrong here. (It can be hard to remember this, because apostrophes usually indicate possession, but not with pronouns.) Whenever you're not sure in a situation like this, just substitute *you are* or *it is* for the word and see whether it makes sense.

18. **(G)** This answer uses *they're* ("they are"), which is plural, to replace the antecedent *a player*, which is singular. Even though we often use *they* as a gender-neutral singular pronoun when speaking, remember that it is technically grammatically wrong, and therefore wrong on the test! The other trick here is that choice G is the shortest alternative, and we are used to longer choices being wrong due to awkwardness or inefficiency. But whether a choice is grammatically right or wrong is always more important!

19. **(D)** The sentence is in the past tense, and so we need the past-tense form *cost*. This is a tricky one because, although the story takes place in the past, some of the phrases near this sentence state ongoing truths, and so are in the present tense, like "it's quite an investment" or "Pads aren't necessary." The clues are that this sentence contains the phrase *at the time* before the underlined part and the word *wasn't* after it, both of which clearly indicate past tense. Correct answers to verb-tense questions on the ACT usually involve simpler tenses, as opposed to more complex ones.

20. **(J)** This answer contains a single, comprehensible independent clause, preceded by the introductory dependent clause "after your first day." All of the other choices involve chopping up and rearranging this sentence into nonsensical variations on it. With questions like this one, which involve rearranging an entire long sentence, look for the "smoothest" answer, or the one that sounds the most like everyday speech (it is frequently the last choice, but not always).

21. **(D)** Since the sentence "A bunch of protective gear is required too" introduces the topic of protective gear, it should come <u>before</u> the parts that talk about such equipment. But the sentence ends with the word *too*, which indicates that it comes <u>after</u> some other requirement was stated.

22. **(F)** Although all the choices concern finding a place to play, the beginning of the following sentence implies that a specific location ("It was the only…") has already been chosen. Only choice F settles on a specific location.

23. **(D)** This is the only grammatically correct choice, as it creates two independent clauses and separates them appropriately with a semicolon. It may sound wordy, but the other three choices are grammatically wrong.

24. **(H)** Since the underlined part is preceded by *stand between*, you know you need <u>two</u> things. The test tries to trick you with the *and* that occurs later in the sentence, but that is just part of the prepositional phrase (*of* and everything after it) that adds more information about the nature of *the thrill*. Choice H has two things and uses the correct *us* with no comma.

25. **(A)** The sentence is in the present tense (it talks about the *memories* of the past, not the past itself), and the noun performing the verb here is *memories*, which is plural, and so you need *bring*. This is the prepositional phrase trick: the words *of my heroism that summer* are extra information that can be taken out, so you have to jump over them. Someone who doesn't notice this could be fooled by the word *heroism* or the word *summer*, which are both singular.

26. **(F)** We need the plural possessive here. *Their having* might sound weird, but since *having* is a gerund, it takes a possessive pronoun. In speech, you would probably be more likely to say "without *them* having any idea," but this is a test.

27. **(C)** When a sentence should be deleted, it is usually obvious. The underlined sentence is funny, consistent with the author's voice and the mood of the essay, and relevant to the action at this point. There is no reason to get rid of it.

28. **(G)** The author here is speaking in the present tense about the past. He *currently* does not remember why they stopped playing.

29. **(B)** This is the only choice that creates a correct sentence that means what you want it to say.

30. **(H)** This is the sentence order that establishes a clear narrative in which each sentence makes sense after the one before it. The biggest clues are that sentence 5 seems like it should be last, sentence 4 seems like it should be first, and sentence 2 should come right after sentence 3. Only choice H satisfies all these requirements.

31. **(C)** The core independent clause is "The now-familiar story of King Arthur first appeared in a fanciful history," and this clause is being interrupted with the extra information "complete with Merlin the wizard and the magic sword Excalibur," so the extra information must be set off with commas. The test is trying to trick you by using an appositive clause that contains the word *and*, which makes you want to put a comma before it, but don't be fooled! The *story* is *complete* with both of those things (the *wizard* and the *sword*), so no comma is necessary.

32. **(J)** This is the only choice that makes the middle clause into an independent one in the present tense.

33. **(B)** How many Arthurs are we talking about? One. And does he possess something? Yes ("famous victories"). How many victories are we talking about? More than one. And do they possess anything? No. So, we need the singular possessive *Arthur's* and the plural nonpossessive *victories*. It is just that simple.

34. **(F)** The noun performing the verb is *source*, which is singular, and so we need the form *mentions*. This is the prepositional phrase trick: you have to jump over the extra information "in all those intervening years" (even though *years*, which is plural, comes right before the verb, it is not the relevant noun). The tense changes are just a red herring to confuse you; the only issue here is singular versus plural, so don't even worry about what tenses the wrong answers are in.

35. **(C)** This sentence is two independent clauses joined by a comma and conjunction, and so everything after the central *and* must constitute an independent clause. Choice C is the only choice that accomplishes this.

36. **(J)** The aside about Vortigern is unnecessary. The preceding assertion is not disputable to a point where other examples need to be listed, and the selection of Vortigern out of all the historical figures mentioned in the *Historia Brittonum* is irrelevant and distracting.

37. **(D)** The sentence contains information that is surprising and suspicious, and so *Curiously* would be the proper introductory word.

38. **(G)** This answer contains the past-tense verb *commanded* and modifies it with the adverb *successfully*.

39. **(C)** The example of the impossible deeds attributed to Arthur at Badon provides needed support for the preceding claim that the *Historia Brittonum's* claims are *obviously exaggerated*.

40. **(F)** The underlined phrase needs to convey some idea of "the average person" or "people in general." *Many of them* implies some specific group of people, which doesn't work here, so choice F is the one that would NOT be acceptable.

41. **(A)** Since the issue is comparison, we need *than* (with an *a*), and choice A is the only one that has *than* and forms a complete correct sentence.

42. **(G)** This is the only one of the choices that forms a complete correct sentence.

43. **(D)** The sentence contains an explanatory appositive clause set off with a pair of dashes, and only choice D inserts a dash between *England* and *the* to match the one between *History* and *make*.

44. **(H)** This is the only choice that correctly finishes the initial independent clause ("Countless scholars have labored for years") with the nonpossessive plural *years* and goes on to correctly augment it with a prepositional phrase ("in the hopes of proving Arthur's existence").

45. **(B)** Paragraph 3 is clearly supposed to be the first paragraph of the essay, as it opens by being suspenseful about the subject's identity, and closes by posing the direct question *Did King Arthur really exist?* which we would expect to come at the beginning.

46. **(G)** The acceptable choices are all designed to indicate that boys will only dance under extreme circumstances, if at all. Choice G, *like the deserts miss the rain*, is a completely unrelated simile describing loneliness, and hence it is NOT acceptable.

47. **(D)** All of the other choices contain information that is either redundant or unnecessary. There is no reason not to simply end the sentence at the word *college*. (When the last choice is just a single word and all the other choices feature that word plus more information, the choice with just the single word is almost always correct!)

48. **(F)** The inclusion of the word *Since* at the beginning of the sentence makes the first clause a dependent one, and so the second clause must be an independent one that is a part of the same sentence. This is a common trick, and usually involves the words *since* and *although*.

49. **(C)** The introductory word *Apparently* indicates that the narrator has realized that the joke he made in the previous sentence applies to him too.

50. **(G)** The two subsequent sentences are about how many people, and what kinds of people, attended the first meeting, and so the paragraph is best introduced by a sentence that also concerns this. The sentence immediately following clearly refers to the content of choice G.

51. **(C)** The sentence is meant to communicate that the dancers switched partners at the same time that they were being guided by the instructor, and only choice C does so in a grammatically correct and sensible way.

52. **(F)** Although all four choices are eloquent and vivid ideas appropriate to the essay and consistent with the authorial voice, the question specifically asks for the one that best

expresses the narrator's *feelings of distance* from Emily, and choice F is the only one about distance. (Even when it seems obvious what you are supposed to do, <u>always</u> read the little directions above a style question, as they frequently give very big hints.)

53. **(D)** What is needed here is a word meaning something like "development" or "series of events," and *phenomenon* is by far the closest of the four choices.

54. **(J)** The noun performing the verb in the underlined part is *thing*, not *kids*, which is part of the prepositional phrase *about popular kids*. (It is the prepositional phrase trick once again.) Choice J is the only one that results in a complete correct sentence.

55. **(A)** This would result in a comma splice, and thus is the only choice that is NOT acceptable. Every other option would form one or two complete sentences. (When you see that options like a semicolon, a colon, or a period and a new sentence form <u>two or more</u> of the other choices, you know that the one with the comma and no conjunction is wrong!)

56. **(H)** Though it frequently does, a colon doesn't have to precede an independent clause. It can also precede things like a list, a quotation, or an explanation. In this case, an independent clause referencing *two things* ends with a colon, which is then correctly followed by a list of what the two things were.

57. **(B)** This is the prepositional phrase trick again. The noun performing the verb here is *turn*, not *events*, and so we need a singular verb. Choice B is the only option that has a singular verb and means what you want it to mean.

58. **(G)** The order implied in the advice the sentence is trying to give is that you should make sure <u>before</u> joining a club that the girl you like isn't going to subsequently go to France. Only choice G, which places *first* after the verb phrase *make sure*, achieves this.

59. **(D)** The sentence is supposed to imply an ongoing condition, and so should be in the present tense. Choice D is the only option that creates a correct sentence in the present tense.

60. **(H)** Although deleting the underlined sentence and ending the essay with the previous one might also be acceptable, you have to look at the explanations. Choice H states that the underlined sentence *provides humorous insight into the author's experience of having to hang out with nerds,* which is true, and the other three choices say things that are not true. Even if you think the essay works better with the other ending, none of the choices gives a valid reason for deleting this one.

61. **(C)** Commas are required to separate the name of the city from the name of the state and to separate the introductory dependent clause from the main independent clause, and so commas go after *Louisville* and after *1954*, and nowhere else.

62. **(F)** This is the only option that results in a complete correct sentence that means what you want it to mean. (Since the second half of the sentence, starting at *someone*, is an independent clause preceded by a comma and conjunction, you know the entire sentence before that comma needs to be an independent clause too!)

63. **(D)** The person means that Cassius should take boxing lessons (in the immediate future) if he plans to beat someone up (at a later point in the future). Even though *had* is the

past tense of *have*, the idiomatic construction *had better* is used to give advice about the future. (*You'd better* is a contraction of *You had better*.)

64. **(G)** The brief and to-the-point *bigger struggles* is the only one of the four choices that is not redundant.

65. **(D)** This includes the necessary comma after the introductory dependent clause, and does not include any unnecessary additional commas.

66. **(H)** The phrase *he'd called himself "too fast" and "too pretty" to lose* is an appositive clause that interrupts the main independent clause. The dash between *lose* and *had* shows that the clause is set off with dashes, and so the correct answer is the one that places a complementary dash between *fight* and *he'd*.

67. **(C)** Turning out to be gifted and deciding to stick with boxing would obviously come before the Olympics, which would come before turning pro and winning the heavyweight championship, which would come before an explanation of why this was so surprising, which would come before foreshadowing of the next paragraph. So, the correct sentence order is 3, 2, 4, 1.

68. **(F)** *The one by which we know him* is a more proper way of saying *the one we know him by*.

69. **(B)** This choice contains a comma splice. There are two sentences connected by just a comma, which is incorrect.

70. **(J)** There is no real need to begin the sentence with an introductory word, and in any case all of the options that include introductory words are clearly wrong. (When three options begin with an introductory or a transition word and one does not, the one that does not is almost always correct!)

71. **(D)** Since the sentence begins with the dependent descriptive clause *Released in 1970* followed by a comma, the noun idea after the comma has to be the person or thing that was released in 1970, or it results in a misplaced modifier. Muhammad Ali was the person released in 1970 here, and choice D is the only one that begins with *Ali*.

72. **(H)** The sentence needs to mean that it was Foreman who was exhausted, and that Ali sprang to life after this. Only choice H successfully communicates both.

73. **(A)** The sentence means to say that the sporting world was shocked by Ali in the past, but reveres him now.

74. **(G)** Commas are unnecessary before the prepositional phrases beginning with *for* and *of*, but commas are necessary to separate the items in the list: *skill, bravery, and magnetism*. (Whether or not there is a comma before the final *and* when separating items in a list is immaterial; either way is acceptable, and no question will ever come down to this rule.)

75. **(B)** The essay is not a technical one for boxing fans about what made Ali successful as a boxer; it is an essay for a general audience about Ali's cultural importance. It contains very little analysis of what went on in the ring, and discusses many things that went on outside the ring. (On questions like this, the choices that imply the passage is aimed at any type of audience other than *a general audience* are almost always wrong!)

Mathematics

1. **(D)** Solving the equation for x gives $\frac{5x}{3} + 6 - 6 = 4 - 6 \rightarrow \frac{5x}{3} = -2 \rightarrow \frac{3}{5} \cdot \frac{5x}{3} = \frac{3}{5} \cdot \frac{-2}{1} \rightarrow$ $x = \frac{-6}{5}$.

2. **(G)** If Carol spent 65% of her money, she had $100\% - 65\% = 35\%$ remaining. Setting up a proportion using 35% remaining and $875 remaining gives $\frac{35}{100} = \frac{875}{x}$. Cross multiplying and solving for x gives $35x = 87{,}500 \rightarrow x = \$2{,}500$.

3. **(B)** To add vectors, corresponding elements should be added. That is, the first elements of the vectors should be added to each other and the second elements of the vectors should be added to each other. $5 + (-2) + 1 = 4$ and $(-3) + 4 + (-6) = (-5)$.

4. **(K)** The power rule for exponents is $(x^a)^b = x^{a \cdot b}$. Applying this rule, the expression becomes $(x^4)^{15} = x^{4 \cdot 15} = x^{60}$.

5. **(A)** Together Doris and Clyde used $1\frac{3}{4} + 2\frac{1}{2} = 4\frac{1}{4}$ gallons of paint. To find the amount of paint remaining, subtract this answer from the total amount of paint to get $5 - 4\frac{1}{4} = \frac{3}{4}$ gallon left.

6. **(K)** Distributing (FOIL) the given expression gives $(3p + 4)(5p - 6) = 15p^2 - 18p + 20p - 24$. Combine like terms to get $15p^2 + 2p - 24$.

7. **(D)** Getting the equation in slope-intercept form by solving for y gives $4x - 3y = 6 \rightarrow -3y = -4x + 6 \rightarrow y = \frac{4}{3}x - 2$. The slope of the line is $\frac{4}{3}$, and recall for two lines to be parallel they must have the same slope. The only answer choice with a slope of $\frac{4}{3}$ is D.

8. **(F)** Let x equal the vertex angle, then each of the base angles would be $\frac{1}{3}x$. The sum of the three angles of a triangle equals $180°$, so set up the equation: $x + \frac{1}{3}x + \frac{1}{3}x = 180$. Solve for x to get $\frac{5}{3}x = 180 \rightarrow x = 108$. Since the vertex equals $108°$, each base angle equals $\frac{1}{3}(108) = 36°$.

9. **(B)** An augmented matrix has the coefficient of the variables and the solutions in the same positions as they appear in the system, when written in standard form.

10. **(H)** Setting up a ratio for the corresponding parts of the triangles gives $\frac{3}{4} = \frac{x}{6}$. Cross multiply and solve for x to get $18 = 4x \rightarrow x = 4.5$.

11. **(C)** The diagonal of a rectangle divides the rectangle into two right triangles with legs formed by the length and width of the rectangle. Setting up the Pythagorean Theorem to find the hypotenuse we get $a^2 + b^2 = c^2 \rightarrow 14^2 + 15^2 = c^2 \rightarrow 421 = c^2$. Taking the square root, we get $c = \sqrt{421} \approx 20.5$. The closest given answer is 21.

12. **(H)** Solving the equation gives $3^x \cdot 9 = 729 \rightarrow 3^x = 81$. Since $3^4 = 81$, $x = 4$. Another way you could solve this problem is using your calculator and plugging the answers in for x until you find one that makes the left side of the equation equal the right.

13. **(B)** Setting up expressions from the given information we get $x =$ width and $x + 3 =$ length. Use the area formula of a rectangle: $A = L \cdot W$ to set up the equation $54 = (x + 3)(x)$. Distribute and put in standard form to get $54 = x^2 + 3x \rightarrow x^2 + 3x - 54 = 0$. Factor to get $(x + 9)(x - 6) = 0$; therefore, $x = -9$ and $x = 6$. Since the width of a rectangle cannot be negative, the only answer left is $x = 6$. The question asks for the length of the rectangle, which is $6 + 3 = 9$.

14. **(H)** Opposite sides of a parallelogram are congruent. Since one side measures 6, the opposite side also measures 6, leaving $36 - 6 - 6 = 24$ inches for the remaining two sides. Dividing by 2, we get each of the remaining two sides to equal 12 inches. Therefore, the other three sides have measures: 6, 12, 12.

15. **(D)** If each of the five numbers was decreased by 4, the average would also be decreased by 4, making it $7 - 4 = 3$.

16. **(K)** Setting up an equation for Julie's overall salary we get *salary* = *base salary* + *amount for sales* $\rightarrow S = 48 + (k)(i)$, where S is her salary, k is the amount she makes per sale, and i is the number of items she sells. Substituting the values from the problem, the equation becomes $68 = 48 + (k)(4)$. Solving for k gives $k = 5$. If Julie sells 3 more items today than yesterday, that is a total of $3 + 4 = 7$ items. Using the formula again we get $S = 48 + (5)(7) = \$83$.

17. **(D)** Sometimes the easiest way to solve a problem is to plug in answers. Substitute in answers to find the largest number that will make a true statement. Trying 24, we get $\frac{6}{24} \geq \frac{1}{4}$, which simplifies to $\frac{1}{4} \geq \frac{1}{4}$, which is a true statement. Therefore, 24 is the correct answer.

18. **(J)** There are 12 hours on a clock; set up a proportion to get $\dfrac{\text{hours}}{\text{total hours}} = \dfrac{\text{degrees}}{\text{total degrees}}$
$\rightarrow \dfrac{8}{12} = \dfrac{x}{360}$. Cross multiply and solve for x to get $2880 = 12x \rightarrow x = 240°$.

19. **(B)** To find the total number of seats on the airplane we multiply the number of rows by the number of seats in each row to get $r \cdot (s + d)$. Since this answer is not one of the choices, distribute to get $(r \cdot s) + (r \cdot d)$.

20. **(G)** $f(-3) = 7(-3)^2 - 4(-3) - 10 = 63 + 12 - 10 = 65$.

21. **(E)** A rational expression is undefined when the denominator equals zero. To find the value that makes the denominator equal zero, set the denominator equal to zero and solve the equation: $16 - x^2 = 0 \rightarrow x^2 = 16 \rightarrow x = 4$.

22. **(F)** Mixing 3 quarts juice to 2 quarts soda would make 5 quarts punch. According to the problem we need 20 quarts of punch, which is $5 \cdot 4$. Multiplying each of the other dimensions by 4 we get $3 \cdot 4 = 12$ quarts juice and $2 \cdot 4 = 8$ quarts soda. We are asked how much juice we need: 12 quarts.

23. **(B)** Point H is between F and G, meaning $GH < FG$. Choice B is correct.

24. **(F)** The midpoint formula is $midpoint = \left(\dfrac{x_1 + x_2}{2}, \dfrac{y_1 + y_2}{2}\right)$. Remember, the center of the circle is the midpoint of any diameter of the circle. Substituting $(3, -4)$ for the midpoint, $(5, -3)$ for (x_1, y_1), and (x, y) for (x_2, y_2) we get $(3, -4) = \left(\dfrac{5 + x}{2}, \dfrac{-3 + y}{2}\right)$. Solve for x to get $3 = \dfrac{5 + x}{2} \rightarrow 6 = 5 + x \rightarrow x = 1$. Solving for y the same way gives $-4 = \dfrac{-3 + y}{2} \rightarrow -8 = -3 + y \rightarrow y = -5$. Therefore, the other endpoint lies at $(1, -5)$.

25. **(C)** $xy = (4a^3)(-3a^5 + b)$. Distribute and use the laws of exponents to get $4a^3 \cdot (-3a^5) + 4a^3 \cdot b = -12a^8 + 4a^3b$.

26. **(H)** To find the length of ribbon, add the length of ribbon needed for each side of the box. The top needs $32 + 12 = 44$ cm. All 4 sides each need 8 cm for a total of $8 \cdot 4 = 32$ cm. The bottom needs $32 + 12 = 44$ cm. Add the top, bottom, and all 4 sides together to get $44 + 32 + 44 = 120$ cm.

27. **(B)** When 1,560 is divided by 125, the result is 12.48. Since more than 12 bags are needed, 13 bags would be the minimum number of bags to complete the job.

28. **(F)** To go around the outer edge, you would need $68 + 34 + 68 + 34 = 204$.

29. **(A)** This situation requires volume, which is $l \times w \times h$. Here, that would be $68 \times 10 \times 6$. Since 1 yard is equal to 3 feet, those units are incorrect (feet, feet, inches), so it should be $\dfrac{68}{3} \times \dfrac{10}{3} \times \dfrac{1}{6} = \dfrac{340}{27} = 12\dfrac{16}{27}$.

30. **(J)** Starting with the multiplication rule of exponents the expression becomes $\dfrac{-72x^0y^5}{4x^2y^4}$. Now, use the division rule of exponents to get $-18x^{-2}y$.

31. **(E)** We draw two strategic lines to divide the shape into two rectangles and a trapezoid. The area of the small rectangle is $A = L \cdot W = 1 \cdot 6 = 6$. The area of the larger rectangle is $A = L \cdot W = 9 \cdot 3 = 27$. The area of the trapezoid is $A = \dfrac{1}{2}h(b_1 + b_2) = \dfrac{1}{2}(3)(3 + 6)$. Simplify to get $(1.5)(9) = 13.5$. Add all the areas together to get $6 + 27 + 13.5 = 46.5$.

32. **(F)** Making a sketch from the information gives the following right triangle. Find the missing side using the Pythagorean Theorem to get $x^2 + 16^2 = 34^2 \rightarrow x^2 = 900 \rightarrow x = 30$.

33. **(A)** You cannot evaluate the square root of a negative expression. Since a^2 is always positive, b must also be positive; otherwise, the quotient $\dfrac{a^2}{b}$ would be negative.

34. **(H)** Same-side interior angles are supplementary making the third angle in the triangle with b and 14, $180 - 62 = 118°$. Now we have the measure of two angles of a triangle; find the third angle, b: $180 - (118 + 14) = 48°$.

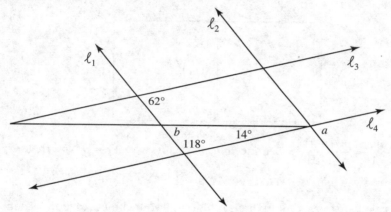

35. **(C)** The 9 congruent squares have sides of length 1 foot. Since a square has 4 sides, the perimeter is $4 \times 1 = 4$.

36. **(H)** A rotation of 540° is the same as a full rotation (360°) plus an additional rotation of 180°, which is 1½ rotations, which lands at X.

37. **(B)** If the midpoint of $\overline{YZ}$ is at the origin, we need to move half the width of $WXYZ$ to the left and up the full height of $WXYZ$ to get to W. That means we would need to move 1.5 units left, or –1.5 and up 3, which would be (–1.5, 3).

38. **(J)** Recall $\cos x = \dfrac{\text{adjacent}}{\text{hypotenus}}$ and $\tan x = \dfrac{\text{opposite}}{\text{adjacent}}$. Find the opposite side using the Pythagorean Theorem: $8^2 + x^2 = 17^2 \rightarrow x = 15$. Therefore, $\tan x = \dfrac{\text{opposite}}{\text{adjacent}} = \dfrac{15}{8}$.

39. **(D)** $\overline{AD}$ is a diameter of the circle meaning $\overset{\frown}{ABD} = 180°$. Since angle ADB is 28°, arc $AB = 2 \cdot 28 = 56°$. Finally, $\overset{\frown}{BCD} = 180 - 56 = 124°$.

40. **(F)** $\csc \theta = \dfrac{1}{\sin \theta} = \dfrac{1}{\frac{1}{2}} = \dfrac{2}{1} = 2$.

41. **(E)** b and c form a linear pair; therefore, $b + c = 180$. Since $\triangle PQR$ is an equilateral, a and d each measure 60°. The sum of $a + b + c + d = 60 + (180) + 60 = 300°$.

42. **(K)** $8 \oplus 2 = \dfrac{8 \cdot 2}{8 + 2} = \dfrac{16}{10} = \dfrac{8}{5}$.

43. **(B)** Using the triangle inequality, we know the length of the third side of the triangle is between $23 - 5 = 18$ and $23 + 5 = 28$. Between 18 and 28 there are exactly two prime numbers, 19 and 23. Therefore, the answer is 2.

44. **(J)** To find the total distance traveled after 50 revolutions we find the circumference of the wheel and multiply that answer by 50. Calculating, we get $C = \pi d = 26\pi$. Multiplying by 50 we get $26\pi \cdot 50 = 1{,}300\pi$.

45. **(D)** $(3i + 4)^2 = (3i + 4)(3i + 4) = 9i^2 + 12i + 12i + 16$. Recalling $i^2 = -1$ we get $9(-1) + 24i + 16 = 7 + 24i$.

46. **(H)** From the diagram we can tell the diameter of the wheel is 20 inches. If the diameter is 20 inches, the radius is $\dfrac{1}{2}(20) = 10$ inches.

47. **(A)** $\dfrac{n!}{(n-1)!} = \dfrac{n \cdot (n-1)!}{(n-1)!} = 5$. Canceling like factors we get $n = 5$. Now that we know n, plug it into the given expression to get $(5-2)! = 3! = 3 \cdot 2 \cdot 1 = 6$.

48. **(J)** To calculate total combinations multiply all your choices together. There is one hitch in this problem: your first decision is either 1 salad OR 2 different soups, which is a total of 3 options for your first choice. Multiplying this number with your choices for meat (4), bread (2), and cheese (3), we get $3 \cdot 4 \cdot 2 \cdot 3 = 72$.

49. **(C)** The distance formula is $d = \sqrt{(x_2 - x_1)^2 + (y_2 - y_1)^2}$. Substitute the given points to get $d = \sqrt{(-3\sqrt{2} - (-\sqrt{2}))^2 + (9 - 7)^2} = \sqrt{(-2\sqrt{2})^2 + (2)^2}$. Continue simplifying to get $d = \sqrt{(4 \cdot 2) + 4} = \sqrt{12}$. Simplify the square root to get $d = \sqrt{4} \cdot \sqrt{3} = 2\sqrt{3}$.

50. **(F)** You can simplify a fraction by canceling like factors. In choice F, cancel the c in both the numerator and denominator to get $\dfrac{a \cdot c}{b \cdot c} = \dfrac{a}{b}$.

51. **(D)** Using x as the smaller number and y as the larger number you can write two equations from the given information: $2x + 3y = 49$ and $y = 4x + 7$. Substituting the second equation into the first one we get $2x + 3(4x + 7) = 49$, which is equivalent to choice D.

52. **(G)** To express y in terms of x, first solve the x equation for t to get $x = 3t - 7 \rightarrow$ $t = \dfrac{x+7}{3}$. Substitute into the second equation to get $y = 4 - \left(\dfrac{x+7}{3}\right)$. Simplify to get $y = \dfrac{12}{3} - \dfrac{x+7}{3} = \dfrac{5-x}{3}$.

53. **(E)** The relationship between the Cartesian coordinate system and polar coordinates is $x = r\cos\theta$ and $y = r\sin\theta$. Since $\sec\theta = \dfrac{1}{\cos\theta} \rightarrow r = \dfrac{1}{\cos\theta} \rightarrow r\cos\theta = 1 \rightarrow x = 1$, which is a vertical line.

54. **(F)** To find the sum of the interior angles of a convex polygon, you can use the formula $\dfrac{(n-2)180}{n}$. If you don't remember that formula, you could divide each polygon into triangles drawn from the same vertex and multiply the number of triangles by 180° to find the sum of the angles. This way the octagon would be 6 triangles: $6 \cdot 180 = 1080$ and the hexagon would be 4 triangles: $4 \cdot 180 = 720$. Each of these numbers needs to be divided by the number of angles to find the measure of one angle: $\dfrac{180}{8} = 135$ and $\dfrac{720}{6} = 120$. Subtracting these leaves $135 - 120 = 15$.

55. **(B)** Since the radius is perpendicular to the chord, it bisects the chord, creating a right triangle with hypotenuse $\overline{PT}$ with length 18 (since it is also a radius) and leg $\overline{ST}$ with length 6. Using the Pythagorean Theorem $a^2 + b^2 = c^2$, we get $a^2 + 6^2 = 18^2$; $a^2 = 18^2 - 6^2$; $a^2 = 288$; $a = \sqrt{288} = \sqrt{144} \cdot \sqrt{2} = 12\sqrt{2}$.

56. **(F)** Standard deviation represents the average spread of a data set. Since the numbers in data set A are either all very small or all very large, set A is the most spread out and will have the largest standard deviation.

57. **(C)** The period of $f(x) = a \cdot \sec(bx)$ is $\dfrac{2\pi}{b}$. Here, $\dfrac{2\pi}{b} = \dfrac{2\pi}{2} = \pi$.

58. **(K)** $\tan x = \dfrac{\text{opposite}}{\text{adjacent}}$. Find the hypotenuse using the Pythagorean Theorem to get $(-24)^2 + (7)^2 = \text{hypotenuse}^2 \rightarrow \text{hypotenuse} = 25$. Now that we know the hypotenuse, recall $\sin x = \dfrac{\text{opposite}}{\text{hypotenuse}} = \dfrac{24}{25}$. Because $90° < x < 180°$, the angle is in the second quadrant and the sine must be positive.

59. **(A)** Checking each of the solutions using FOIL gives $(3x + 2)(4x - 3) = 12x^2 - 9x + 8x - 6$ $= 12x^2 - x - 6$.

60. **(K)** To calculate probability we use the formula $\dfrac{\text{number of successful outcomes}}{\text{total number of outcomes}}$. Since we are adding pink jelly beans, both the number of successful outcomes and total outcomes are increased by x. Therefore, the formula becomes $P = \dfrac{7+x}{24+x}$. Substitute 0.5 in for P, the probability, and solve for x to get $0.5 = \dfrac{7+x}{24+x} \rightarrow 12 + 0.5x = 7 + x \rightarrow 5 = 0.5x \rightarrow x = 10$.

So, we must add 10 pink jelly beans to get a probability of $\dfrac{1}{2}$.

1. **(B)** In saying that the American poet will be "commensurate with [the] people," and that "his spirit responds to his country's spirit," as well as with phrases like "transcendent" and "indirect," and in speaking of a quality in the poetry that "goes through these to much more," Whitman is painting a picture of the American poet just magically knowing what to say as the result of some spiritual bond with the people and the land—this is what is meant by the expression "revealed knowledge," knowledge gained because some "spirit" or other spoke to you, as opposed to being gained through, say, scientific experiment.

2. **(G)** Indeed, Whitman's rhapsodizing here is oddly both communal and individualist—proclaiming, for example, "his spirit responds to his country's spirit" in line 27, but also "A heroic person walks at his ease through and out of that custom or precedent or authority that suits him not" in lines 50–53.

3. **(D)** The very first sentence of the passage says this fairly directly.

4. **(F)** The author uses the word "spirituals" to refer to the spirituals the Negro sang.

5. **(C)** Hughes strongly emphasizes in the last paragraph the Negro artists must be proud of who they are.

6. **(J)** You might have noticed that, in addition to the usage in line 98, Hughes also used the term *standardizations* in the same sense in line 69. In both places, he is referring to American society's idea that whiteness and white culture are the norm, or standard—a notion that doesn't leave people of color much room to negotiate. Hence, it means "stifling expectations."

7. **(C)** In the first three paragraphs, Hughes discusses the importance for a developing African-American artist of perceiving, and gaining a sense of his place in, the wider African-American culture and its history, rather than allowing this to be erased by the supposed "norm" of white culture. But then, in the final paragraph, this hypothetical, emblematic young African-American artist is on a solitary quest as an individual, one that might even necessitate disregarding the opinions of the African-American culture he had previously needed to work so hard to perceive.

8. **(G)** By far, the most glaring irony in Whitman's piece when it is placed alongside Hughes's like this is the fact that Whitman speaks only of "Americans" as a "race," and describes all of them as dedicated to the principles of equality and diversity—a legitimately painful oversight given the massive racially based inequality under the law of Whitman's day (Whitman *himself* was fiercely unprejudiced, but the same could not be said for the wider society of his time, and so he is guilty of embarrassing levels of wishful thinking here).

9. **(D)** In the very same sentence, Whitman speaks of the artist "proving himself." To "expose superior models," in this context, is to correct or reject the imperfect artistic forms of the past and create new ones to serve the future. Hughes speaks *specifically* of African-American artists in particular doing so, but it is still the same idea.

10. **(J)** If we imagine that it is an African-American poet "dismissing" and "defying" the prejudice and stereotypes that "suit him not," then every last sentence in Whitman's closing paragraph could just as easily have been written by Hughes—Whitman is talking about American poets broadly, and Hughes about African-American poets specifically, but aside from this difference in specificity, the advice is exactly the same.

11. **(B)** The main idea is not always explicitly stated in the first paragraph. Here, it is slowly developed over the course of the first five paragraphs, before being explicitly stated in lines 43–45. Going by the last paragraph—the other place to look on "main idea" questions—would have been a good idea here: lines 104–108 make it very clear that the main idea concerns bright girls losing confidence.

12. **(J)** When you saw this question, you were probably thinking that there isn't really a tone at all, and that the passage is just presenting facts and theories without any emotion. Well, exactly—that should have been a clue that the passage is *analytical* in nature.

13. **(A)** The first sentence of the seventh paragraph asks a question, and the second answers it: *it has to do with the kinds of feedback we get from parents and teachers* (lines 53–54). The rest of the paragraph gives examples to support that assertion and explains what the problem with those comments is.

14. **(F)** Although the idea that adult women are underpaid may seem like a key idea here because it is mentioned in the first paragraph, it is actually unrelated to the *causes* of the issue being discussed. There is no indication in the passage that young girls are even aware that adult women are underpaid. The other three choices, however, are all closely related to one another and presented as possible causes of the problem.

15. **(B)** The final paragraph—specifically the final sentence of the final paragraph—posits that the solution is for bright women to reexamine their beliefs about ability.

16. **(H)** The subsequent sentence emphasizes *skill, experience, effort,* and *persistence* (lines 102–103), so it should have been clear that *profoundly malleable* means "extremely changeable."

17. **(D)** The sentence in question asserts that one of women's biggest obstacles *lies within*—that is, within their own beliefs about themselves.

18. **(F)** Lines 24–32 explicitly state that Carol Dweck's study uncovered an odd confidence problem unique to bright girls. (The fact that *Carol Dweck* is the antecedent of *she* is established by the previous sentence.)

19. **(C)** Lines 35–37 state that, at the elementary school level, girls outperform boys at *every* subject, and so which subjects girls and boys excel at is not presented as a *difference* between them in the passage.

20. **(G)** The final paragraph explains that success can be achieved with persistence, and that persistence is the result of believing in yourself.

21. **(B)** The author is arguing a similarity between music and science. This is first established in line 43 (in relation to the previous paragraph), and explicitly stated as the thesis in lines 63–66.

22. **(F)** In lines 72–74, the author establishes his position that popular music can be brilliant despite being largely derivative of previous popular music.

23. **(C)** The previous phrase, concerning a super-genius physicist, and the subsequent paragraph, about the emotional power of John Lennon's "Imagine," involve people unlocking truths about the universe and human experience in it. There is nothing literal about a deity or supernatural being in this area (or anywhere in the passage), and so it is clear that "God" here is a metaphor.

24. **(G)** The sixth paragraph—particularly in lines 53–56, which compare Lennon's "Imagine" to Einstein's theory of relativity—figures the song as Lennon's personal masterpiece of ethical and emotional philosophy.

25. **(A)** In lines 74–80, the author says that even though we cannot scientifically describe why "Smells Like Teen Spirit" was so important, we cannot deny that for some reason it was ("the results of the experiment are unequivocal").

26. **(J)** In lines 11–13, the author states that music *toys with emotions in a manner that, if a friend acted the same way, you would hate their guts*—that is, that music is designed to be emotionally manipulative.

27. **(C)** The phrase *indisputable body of known fact* is used in lines 25–28 to describe those aspects of science that are solidly mathematically verifiable. One example he gives (lines 19–23) is the formula used to calculate energy. The tricky part is that the formula is written out in words instead of symbols or numerals, and so it might not immediately jump out at someone who is scanning the passage for symbols and numerals (watch out for that trick—the ACT Reading uses it often!).

28. **(J)** When the author says that the principles of geometry and music converge somewhere out on the horizon, he means that somehow the "rules" of music must be governed by basic math in some way that we have not yet figured out. (The grand unified theory is a still hypothetical idea about a concept or realization that will unite all the sciences into one.)

29. **(D)** The author isn't judging mechanical bulls (line 28) or the people who ride them. He just names them as one example in a list of things that we have been able to build as a result of mastering certain aspects of science. (It is worth noting that all of the other choices are "bigger" than this one—this answer can be right by itself, but the others can't be true without this one *also* being true.)

30. **(F)** The previous sentence establishes that "Smells Like Teen Spirit" was a phenomenally successful song. The author says here that, although we don't know from a scientific standpoint what it is that makes a song successful, we know for a fact that successful songs *are* successful. This fact is *inarguable*, or *unequivocal*, or *absolutely clear*.

31. **(A)** Lines 7–12 explicitly state that it is the oxygen levels of Europa's ocean that would theoretically make advanced life possible.

32. **(J)** The fact that Europa's ocean was only discovered in the last decade or so, and that NASA was excited enough by this to destroy a valuable spacecraft, is the point of the paragraph—this is a *recent* and *exciting* discovery (this helps establish why the reader should care).

33. **(D)** Lines 44–47 state that Europa's icy crust is startlingly new.

34. **(H)** *You need the delay*, Greenberg says, because the building blocks of life can't form in the presence of too much oxygen, but subsequent advanced life wouldn't survive without it. Oxygen levels would need to have risen gradually.

35. **(B)** There's no reason why a small, faraway planet would exert gravitational influence on the moon of a much larger planet.

36. **(G)** Lines 98–99 state it as a fact that Europa and Io are gravitationally locked.

37. **(A)** If a *stable* rate involves *a complete renewal every 50 million years*, then in this context *stable* must mean "regular."

38. **(J)** In the final paragraph, Pappalardo offers some scenarios under which advanced life might not exist on Europa after all. He doesn't prove that it *definitely* doesn't, but establishes that it *may* be *unlikely*.

39. **(C)** If the process of surface repaving happened in *extreme cycles*, resulting in *high and low periods of activity*, then it's clear that *fits and starts* means "intermittently" (see the use of *intermittent* in line 94).

40. **(H)** The explanation of tidal activity in lines 51–59 makes it clear that tides on a body with water are affected by other celestial bodies in the vicinity.

Science

1. **(B)** This question is a classic "Go Up, Hit Line, Go Over." Go to Figure 2 (being careful to notice that the labels are <u>below</u> the figures, so you don't accidentally look at Figure 3), find 200 cm on the *x*-axis (the horizontal line), look up to the solid line representing 2004, and see how high up it is on the *y*-axis (the vertical line) at that point. It is a little less than halfway between 0.50 and 1.00, making 0.70 the closest answer by far.

2. **(H)** This is a simple "extrapolation" question, meaning that you have to guess about a value not pictured on the graph based on the way that the data are trending. Though the dotted line in Figure 3 representing 2002 stops at 350 cm, around 315 cm it appears to level off at 2.00 dpm/g, meaning that if the line were to continue, the radium-226 activity at 400 cm below the top of the sediment would almost certainly be 2.00 dpm/g.

3. **(A)** The first sentence of the introductory paragraph states that "^{226}Ra activity is often elevated in bodies of water that have been augmented with groundwater." We know that there was more ^{226}Ra activity in 2004 than in 2002, so, therefore, the wetlands were probably augmented with groundwater in 2004.

4. **(H)** A question that begins "If the data are typical …" is simply asking you to identify which one of the choices is true of all the given figures. In this case, it is true that both Figure 2 and Figure 3 show ^{226}Ra activity peaking somewhere around 325 cm below the top of the sediment in both 2002 and 2004. (Though ^{226}Ra activity does not peak at <u>exactly</u> 325 cm below the top of the sediment in all four lines, choice H is still clearly much better than the other three.)

5. **(D)** The question is simply asking: in which of the four lines contained in Figures 2 and 3 were ^{226}Ra levels higher at 250 cm below the top of the sediment than they were at 200 cm below the top of the sediment? This is only the case with the solid line (representing 2004) in Figure 3 (representing marshes), and so the answer is "Marsh wetlands in 2004."

6. **(G)** Figure 1 (the year 2002) is represented by a light gray bar and the lowest bar is for Cypress 2, measuring approximately 0.1 dpm/g. Therefore, with the lowest amount, Cypress 2 should show the least effects.

7. **(C)** The row in Table 1 that corresponds to a pH of 9.3 corresponds to 200 ml NaOH.

8. **(G)** A 3.5 pH intersects the graph at about 50 ml. You could also use the table to see that 3.5 falls between 2.2 and 4.7. Clearly, a 3.5 pH would result from somewhere between 0 and 100 ml of NaOH added.

9. **(A)** The reasoning is correct. The OH^- ions from NaOH will combine with OH^+ ions to form water. The trend in the table is lower and lower concentrations of OH^+ and CH_3COOH and higher concentrations of CH_3COO^-. The only way to counteract the decrease in H^+ ions and keep the K_a a constant is to reduce the denominator or increase the numerator. Since the two quantities are interrelated, $[CH_3COOH(aq)]$ decreases while $[CH_3COO^-(aq)]$ increases. It only appears that $[CH_3COO^-(aq)]$ is unchanged because the orders of magnitudes of the two quantities are drastically different after 200 ml NaOH have been added. The increase in $[CH_3COO^-(aq)]$ is not noticeable.

10. **(F)** The figure and the table support this choice. A lower initial concentration of acetic acid will lower the concentration of H^+ ions, which lowers acidity. The lower $[H^+(aq)]$ would correspond to higher pH based on all the data.

11. **(D)** The presence of acetic acid and H^+ is what made the pH 2.2 in the first place. As the $[H^+(aq)]$ decreased, the pH increased.

12. **(F)** As the $[H^+(aq)]$ decreases going down the table, the pH increases consistently.

13. **(D)** According to Experiment 1 and Table 1, to reach an acid dissociation constant (K_a) of 1.9×10^{-5} you must add 400 ml of NaOH as indicated in the first column of the table. Carefully read the first square in the last column that explains that all K_a readings must be multiplied by 10^{-5}.

14. **(J)** This is a simple "Go Up, Hit Line, Go Over." Starting from October in the x-axis (horizontal) of Figure 2, the line representing ex situ permeability (the one with squares on it) is roughly as high as 30 on the y-axis (vertical).

15. **(A)** This is an "extrapolation" question, meaning that you have to guess about a value not pictured on the graph based on the way the data are trending. The Site 1 line (squares) in Figure 4 appears to rise roughly 0.1 m^3/s for every 100 Pa of pressure, and at that rate would have been at around 0.5 m^3/s by 800 Pa.

16. **(G)** This question just asks you to compare the data in the figures and paragraph and then pick the answer that presents true statements as indicated by that data. Figure 3 indicates that soil porosity is highest at Site 2, as choice G suggests, and Figure 4 indicates that flow rate is highest at Site 2, another indicator that choice G is a good bet.

17. **(A)** This is an "If the data are typical …" question, asking you to select which of the choices is true based on what has been observed. In both Figure 1 and Figure 2, air permeability is higher ex situ than it is in situ. (This is to be expected, since the paragraph explains that *in situ* means that the instrument is buried in the dirt, and *ex situ* means that it is not!)

18. **(J)** In Figure 1, permeability was highest for water during all the months, including November.

19. **(B)** Using the Figure 2 bar graph it is obvious that Site 2 has the highest porosity at 0.51 cm^3, while sites 1, 3, and 4 have lower porosities at 0.48, 0.47, and 0.44 cm^3, respectively.

20. **(G)** Although no official distinction between a "small" lemon and a "large" lemon is given, the lemons on the left-hand side of the x-axis (horizontal) in Figure 1 are smaller than those on the right-hand side, and the highest peak (representing greater sucrose formation) of any line occurs in the albedo tissue line (dark circles) on the left-hand side.

21. **(B)** The line representing sucrose production in the vesicles goes up between the diameters of 20 and 30 mm, and then down between 30 and 50 mm: in other words, the sucrose production increases and then decreases.

22. **(H)** The question is simply asking you to look at Figure 2 and compare the length of the bars to determine which of the four answer choices represents the greatest difference in bar height. Of the four answer choices, the greatest difference is between flavedo tissue and vesicle tissue in lemons.

23. **(B)** In Table 1, the number representing sucrose formed from orange juice (0.12) is lower than the number representing sucrose formed from lemon juice (0.4).

24. **(H)** By comparing the appropriate bars in Figure 2, we see that sucrose production in albedo tissue of oranges is roughly half that of albedo tissue in lemons. Since Figure 1 indicates that sucrose production in the albedo tissue of a 30-mm lemon is around 17, we can intuit that sucrose production in an orange of the same size would be roughly half that, and 9 is the only one of the choices that is anywhere close to half of 17.

25. **(D)** The paragraph at the beginning of Study 2 explains that *albedo* is just the name for the "white peel layer" of a fruit, and according to Figure 2 it is indeed true that more sucrose is formed in the albedo tissue of a lemon than in any other part.

26. **(H)** Using Figure 1 you can project the percent of sucrose in the tissues of a 55-mm lemon. Vesicles tissue is 2% at 50 mm, so you project 1% at 55 mm. Flavedo tissue is 0% at 50 mm, so you project 0% at 55 mm, and Albedo tissue is 11% at 50 mm, so you project 10% at 55 mm.

27. **(B)** The arrows in Figure 1 show how much carbon is transmitted in the global carbon cycle. There is an arrow at the top of the figure, in the center, which illustrates carbon being transmitted from the ocean to the atmosphere, and the number next to the arrow is 90.6.

28. **(H)** This is correct because of the data presented in Figure 2. The right side of the figure is labeled Particles, and the left side of the figure is labeled Dissolved, with the line dividing them at 0.2 micrometers. Algae is the only type of carbon listed that is on the right side of the figure, making it the only type of carbon that is NOT a dissolved carbon.

29. **(C)** This is correct because of the information presented in Figure 3. The *y*-axis represents ocean depth and the *x*-axis on the top of the figure represents DOC. The key identifies the line with circular markers as the one for DOC. Trace the line representing DOC down to determine what happens as the depth increases. It goes straight down for a while, remaining constant, then it moves to the left, decreasing the amount of DOC. Then it becomes fairly consistent again.

30. **(J)** This is correct because of the information presented in Figure 2. The line at the bottom of the figure represents the size of the carbon fragments. The third dash from the left is labeled 0.01. Trace your finger up from that dash to find that two types of dissolved carbon are listed: small polymers and proteins, making choice D the correct answer.

31. **(B)** This is correct because of the data presented in Figure 3. The *y*-axis represents ocean depth. The key shows that the line with the square markers represents CDOM. The *x*-axis on the bottom of the figure represents CDOM. Find the dash on the *y*-axis labeled 100 and trace your finger over to the line with the square markers. Then, trace your finger down to the *x*-axis to find that 0.12 is the best answer.

32. **(G)** Figure 2 displays which types of carbon fragments are considered dissolved and which are particles. Organic matter is living, whereas inorganic matter is not. Polymers are not living, so they are inorganic carbon, and they are displayed on the left side of Figure 2, under the heading Dissolved.

33. **(B)** The paragraph above Figure 2 tells you that if a carbon is bigger than 0.2 millimeters, it is considered a particle. Since you are looking for a 120-mm particle in Figure 2, you can follow the graph straight up and see that the carbon would be called a protozoa.

34. **(H)** The second paragraph begins by stating that Researcher 1 expected glucose to have an effect on alga respiration, and the third paragraph begins by stating that Researcher 2 expected light to have an effect.

35. **(B)** For this question it is necessary either to know or to intuit that *control* is the term for the version of a scientific experiment in which nothing has been altered, and that is run so that the experimenters can have something to compare the results of the experiments in which something has been altered. Other than that, it is a standard "Go Up, Hit Line, Go Over" question. The solid line in Figure 1 representing the control (*Chlorella* to which nothing has been added) is at around 18 mm^3 on the *y*-axis (vertical) after 30 minutes.

36. **(F)** Researcher 1 predicted in the paragraph that the addition of glucose would inhibit respiration even further, and Figure 1 shows that the lines representing HCN and H$_2$S plus glucose are indeed lower than the lines representing HCN and H$_2$S alone (so Researcher 1 was right). The question asks what effect a solution with 2 percent glucose would have, and since the paragraph established that the previous solutions contained 1 percent glucose, that is twice as much. Twice as much glucose should drop the lines down to roughly half their current levels. The dotted line representing glucose + HCN is currently at around 28 mm^3 after 20 minutes, and so 15 mm^3 would be around half as much (although it is not exactly half as much, 15 mm^3 is the only one of the choices that is substantially lower at all).

37. **(D)** Neither of the lines representing *Chlorella* respiration altered direction as a response to the presence or absence of light, and this did not support Researcher 2's hypothesis.

38. **(G)** Researcher 1 hypothesized that the addition of glucose would result in the *Chlorella* consuming less oxygen, and so an experiment in which the addition of glucose causes *Chlorella* to consume more would weaken his viewpoint.

39. **(B)** The substance that had the least effect would be whatever substance is represented by the line that is closest to the solid control line. After 30 minutes, the line that is closest to the control line is the dotted line with circles on it, which represents H_2S.

40. **(J)** In Figure 3, the solid line representing nitrogen is higher than the dotted line representing carbon monoxide. Therefore, it is true that *Chlorella* cells suspended in nitrogen consume more oxygen than cells suspended in carbon monoxide (in other words, all of the choices are false except for that one).

WRITING SAMPLE

Schools Policing Social Media

What you say on the Internet can hurt you. This a hard lesson learned by ten teens who, shortly before their characters were called into question, believed their exclusive invitations to Harvard's 2017 incoming freshman class would stick. Dreams dashed by Internet indiscretions, the ten will now have to consider other schools. Was Harvard right to consider private "conversations" in their admissions process, and should the school hold the ten accountable for what they posted online? True enough, companies make hire-and-fire decisions like these on a daily basis. In any case, attempting to police students' social media posts seems to be a difficult, hit-or-miss proposition whose few "successes" happen to make headlines. A more proactive than punitive approach—educating young people about how to tactfully represent their selves online—seems the more effective and lasting alternative, one that just might allow more ambitious students to take advantage of well-deserved educational and career-related opportunities, all without compromising their reputations.

Any serious discussion of the pros and cons (and even the viability) of policing the Internet involves questioning its appropriate reach and rules. In "Tinker," a precedent-setting 1969 Supreme Court case that we happened to study in my U.S. History class this year, students were suspended from school for wearing black armbands in protest of the Vietnam War. Decades before the advent of the Internet, a judge ultimately ruled in favor of the students, neither punishing or prohibiting their speech because he deemed that it did not significantly interfere with the work and discipline of the school. Harvard College, which accepts a meager 5 percent of applicants, rescinded admissions offers to the ten otherwise highly qualified students, its change of heart based on offensive memes exchanged, not on school-owned property or devices, but in private group chat messages on Facebook—images that mocked sexual assault, the Holocaust, and violence against children. Like other schools, Harvard provided ample warning: accepted students' offers can be withdrawn in the event that their behavior calls into question their "honesty," "maturity," or "moral character." One could argue that, unlike in the "Tinker," case, admitting the students in question would, indeed, have interfered with the work of the school, if the work of the school was to actively promote integrity among its members.

First Amendment champions characterize Harvard's decision as just another example of colleges' unwillingness to stand up for free speech and, furthermore, ridicule the idea of monitoring the Internet, given the trivial nature of most rants. Not surprisingly, the National Coalition Against Censorship website is chock-full of outlandish real-life examples of "policing" run amok: a student suspended for posting criticism of his school's football team, another high schooler suspended for posting an anti-bullying video for a school assignment (because a parent who reported the post was unaware that the video scenario was fabricated). Equally ridiculous to some are instances of censorship based on unpopular views: a college admissions officer's public apology for saying, "All lives matter," a Wisconsin judge's vote to suspend a Marquette professor for voicing his views on marriage, and, in a more extreme case, an Evergreen State professor teaching off campus for his own safety when his "take" on the school's programming became known. The apparently simple proposition of policing takes on a new level of complexity as university presidents side with naïve, emotionally wrought students over experienced professors with stellar reputations.

If the purpose of a high school, and, to an even greater extent, a university, is to provide a forum for the free exchange of competing ideas so as to avoid the tyranny of "majority rule," then presidents, principals, administrators, teachers, and students should band together to preserve this essential freedom, primarily with a focus on preparedness rather than policing. My sister attends SDSU, where students receive media safety training during their very first orientation. Armed with guidelines for communicating effectively within an online environment,

she is better able to voice her views while also protecting her own reputation. Why not provide such training in middle schools and/or high schools? While there is no guarantee that educating the public in this way will substantially reduce the instances of online offenses, I believe that awareness campaigns will be at least as effective as efforts to curtail offensive language and images after they have been sent into cyberspace.

Had the smart, talented, but careless (or character-less?) ten been educated on the social and legal consequences of their social media presences, they may have walked Harvard Yard this fall. Perhaps the answer to the free/harmful speech conundrum lies in the mutual agreement of vigilant, educated community members, a social contract by which individuals vow to adhere to certain rules of Internet etiquette. Agreeing to exemplify the good online as in real life, students could more often harness the power of numbers, peer pressure in the best sense of the word, to police themselves.

ANSWER SHEET
Practice Test 6

English

1. Ⓐ Ⓑ Ⓒ Ⓓ
2. Ⓕ Ⓖ Ⓗ Ⓙ
3. Ⓐ Ⓑ Ⓒ Ⓓ
4. Ⓕ Ⓖ Ⓗ Ⓙ
5. Ⓐ Ⓑ Ⓒ Ⓓ
6. Ⓕ Ⓖ Ⓗ Ⓙ
7. Ⓐ Ⓑ Ⓒ Ⓓ
8. Ⓕ Ⓖ Ⓗ Ⓙ
9. Ⓐ Ⓑ Ⓒ Ⓓ
10. Ⓕ Ⓖ Ⓗ Ⓙ
11. Ⓐ Ⓑ Ⓒ Ⓓ
12. Ⓕ Ⓖ Ⓗ Ⓙ
13. Ⓐ Ⓑ Ⓒ Ⓓ
14. Ⓕ Ⓖ Ⓗ Ⓙ
15. Ⓐ Ⓑ Ⓒ Ⓓ

16. Ⓕ Ⓖ Ⓗ Ⓙ
17. Ⓐ Ⓑ Ⓒ Ⓓ
18. Ⓕ Ⓖ Ⓗ Ⓙ
19. Ⓐ Ⓑ Ⓒ Ⓓ
20. Ⓕ Ⓖ Ⓗ Ⓙ
21. Ⓐ Ⓑ Ⓒ Ⓓ
22. Ⓕ Ⓖ Ⓗ Ⓙ
23. Ⓐ Ⓑ Ⓒ Ⓓ
24. Ⓕ Ⓖ Ⓗ Ⓙ
25. Ⓐ Ⓑ Ⓒ Ⓓ
26. Ⓕ Ⓖ Ⓗ Ⓙ
27. Ⓐ Ⓑ Ⓒ Ⓓ
28. Ⓕ Ⓖ Ⓗ Ⓙ
29. Ⓐ Ⓑ Ⓒ Ⓓ
30. Ⓕ Ⓖ Ⓗ Ⓙ

31. Ⓐ Ⓑ Ⓒ Ⓓ
32. Ⓕ Ⓖ Ⓗ Ⓙ
33. Ⓐ Ⓑ Ⓒ Ⓓ
34. Ⓕ Ⓖ Ⓗ Ⓙ
35. Ⓐ Ⓑ Ⓒ Ⓓ
36. Ⓕ Ⓖ Ⓗ Ⓙ
37. Ⓐ Ⓑ Ⓒ Ⓓ
38. Ⓕ Ⓖ Ⓗ Ⓙ
39. Ⓐ Ⓑ Ⓒ Ⓓ
40. Ⓕ Ⓖ Ⓗ Ⓙ
41. Ⓐ Ⓑ Ⓒ Ⓓ
42. Ⓕ Ⓖ Ⓗ Ⓙ
43. Ⓐ Ⓑ Ⓒ Ⓓ
44. Ⓕ Ⓖ Ⓗ Ⓙ
45. Ⓐ Ⓑ Ⓒ Ⓓ

46. Ⓕ Ⓖ Ⓗ Ⓙ
47. Ⓐ Ⓑ Ⓒ Ⓓ
48. Ⓕ Ⓖ Ⓗ Ⓙ
49. Ⓐ Ⓑ Ⓒ Ⓓ
50. Ⓕ Ⓖ Ⓗ Ⓙ
51. Ⓐ Ⓑ Ⓒ Ⓓ
52. Ⓕ Ⓖ Ⓗ Ⓙ
53. Ⓐ Ⓑ Ⓒ Ⓓ
54. Ⓕ Ⓖ Ⓗ Ⓙ
55. Ⓐ Ⓑ Ⓒ Ⓓ
56. Ⓕ Ⓖ Ⓗ Ⓙ
57. Ⓐ Ⓑ Ⓒ Ⓓ
58. Ⓕ Ⓖ Ⓗ Ⓙ
59. Ⓕ Ⓖ Ⓗ Ⓙ
60. Ⓕ Ⓖ Ⓗ Ⓙ

61. Ⓐ Ⓑ Ⓒ Ⓓ
62. Ⓕ Ⓖ Ⓗ Ⓙ
63. Ⓐ Ⓑ Ⓒ Ⓓ
64. Ⓕ Ⓖ Ⓗ Ⓙ
65. Ⓐ Ⓑ Ⓒ Ⓓ
66. Ⓕ Ⓖ Ⓗ Ⓙ
67. Ⓐ Ⓑ Ⓒ Ⓓ
68. Ⓕ Ⓖ Ⓗ Ⓙ
69. Ⓐ Ⓑ Ⓒ Ⓓ
70. Ⓕ Ⓖ Ⓗ Ⓙ
71. Ⓐ Ⓑ Ⓒ Ⓓ
72. Ⓕ Ⓖ Ⓗ Ⓙ
73. Ⓐ Ⓑ Ⓒ Ⓓ
74. Ⓕ Ⓖ Ⓗ Ⓙ
75. Ⓐ Ⓑ Ⓒ Ⓓ

Mathematics

1. Ⓐ Ⓑ Ⓒ Ⓓ Ⓔ
2. Ⓕ Ⓖ Ⓗ Ⓙ Ⓚ
3. Ⓐ Ⓑ Ⓒ Ⓓ Ⓔ
4. Ⓕ Ⓖ Ⓗ Ⓙ Ⓚ
5. Ⓐ Ⓑ Ⓒ Ⓓ Ⓔ
6. Ⓕ Ⓖ Ⓗ Ⓙ Ⓚ
7. Ⓐ Ⓑ Ⓒ Ⓓ Ⓔ
8. Ⓕ Ⓖ Ⓗ Ⓙ Ⓚ
9. Ⓐ Ⓑ Ⓒ Ⓓ Ⓔ
10. Ⓕ Ⓖ Ⓗ Ⓙ Ⓚ
11. Ⓐ Ⓑ Ⓒ Ⓓ Ⓔ
12. Ⓕ Ⓖ Ⓗ Ⓙ Ⓚ
13. Ⓐ Ⓑ Ⓒ Ⓓ Ⓔ
14. Ⓕ Ⓖ Ⓗ Ⓙ Ⓚ
15. Ⓐ Ⓑ Ⓒ Ⓓ Ⓔ

16. Ⓕ Ⓖ Ⓗ Ⓙ Ⓚ
17. Ⓐ Ⓑ Ⓒ Ⓓ Ⓔ
18. Ⓕ Ⓖ Ⓗ Ⓙ Ⓚ
19. Ⓐ Ⓑ Ⓒ Ⓓ Ⓔ
20. Ⓕ Ⓖ Ⓗ Ⓙ Ⓚ
21. Ⓐ Ⓑ Ⓒ Ⓓ Ⓔ
22. Ⓕ Ⓖ Ⓗ Ⓙ Ⓚ
23. Ⓐ Ⓑ Ⓒ Ⓓ Ⓔ
24. Ⓕ Ⓖ Ⓗ Ⓙ Ⓚ
25. Ⓐ Ⓑ Ⓒ Ⓓ Ⓔ
26. Ⓕ Ⓖ Ⓗ Ⓙ Ⓚ
27. Ⓐ Ⓑ Ⓒ Ⓓ Ⓔ
28. Ⓕ Ⓖ Ⓗ Ⓙ Ⓚ
29. Ⓐ Ⓑ Ⓒ Ⓓ Ⓔ
30. Ⓕ Ⓖ Ⓗ Ⓙ Ⓚ

31. Ⓐ Ⓑ Ⓒ Ⓓ Ⓔ
32. Ⓕ Ⓖ Ⓗ Ⓙ Ⓚ
33. Ⓐ Ⓑ Ⓒ Ⓓ Ⓔ
34. Ⓕ Ⓖ Ⓗ Ⓙ Ⓚ
35. Ⓐ Ⓑ Ⓒ Ⓓ Ⓔ
36. Ⓕ Ⓖ Ⓗ Ⓙ Ⓚ
37. Ⓐ Ⓑ Ⓒ Ⓓ Ⓔ
38. Ⓕ Ⓖ Ⓗ Ⓙ Ⓚ
39. Ⓐ Ⓑ Ⓒ Ⓓ Ⓔ
40. Ⓕ Ⓖ Ⓗ Ⓙ Ⓚ
41. Ⓐ Ⓑ Ⓒ Ⓓ Ⓔ
42. Ⓕ Ⓖ Ⓗ Ⓙ Ⓚ
43. Ⓐ Ⓑ Ⓒ Ⓓ Ⓔ
44. Ⓕ Ⓖ Ⓗ Ⓙ Ⓚ
45. Ⓐ Ⓑ Ⓒ Ⓓ Ⓔ

46. Ⓕ Ⓖ Ⓗ Ⓙ Ⓚ
47. Ⓐ Ⓑ Ⓒ Ⓓ Ⓔ
48. Ⓕ Ⓖ Ⓗ Ⓙ Ⓚ
49. Ⓐ Ⓑ Ⓒ Ⓓ Ⓔ
50. Ⓕ Ⓖ Ⓗ Ⓙ Ⓚ
51. Ⓐ Ⓑ Ⓒ Ⓓ Ⓔ
52. Ⓕ Ⓖ Ⓗ Ⓙ Ⓚ
53. Ⓐ Ⓑ Ⓒ Ⓓ Ⓔ
54. Ⓕ Ⓖ Ⓗ Ⓙ Ⓚ
55. Ⓐ Ⓑ Ⓒ Ⓓ Ⓔ
56. Ⓕ Ⓖ Ⓗ Ⓙ Ⓚ
57. Ⓐ Ⓑ Ⓒ Ⓓ Ⓔ
58. Ⓕ Ⓖ Ⓗ Ⓙ Ⓚ
59. Ⓐ Ⓑ Ⓒ Ⓓ Ⓔ
60. Ⓕ Ⓖ Ⓗ Ⓙ Ⓚ

ANSWER SHEET
Practice Test 6

Reading

1. Ⓐ Ⓑ Ⓒ Ⓓ
2. Ⓕ Ⓖ Ⓗ Ⓙ
3. Ⓐ Ⓑ Ⓒ Ⓓ
4. Ⓕ Ⓖ Ⓗ Ⓙ
5. Ⓐ Ⓑ Ⓒ Ⓓ
6. Ⓕ Ⓖ Ⓗ Ⓙ
7. Ⓐ Ⓑ Ⓒ Ⓓ
8. Ⓕ Ⓖ Ⓗ Ⓙ

9. Ⓐ Ⓑ Ⓒ Ⓓ
10. Ⓕ Ⓖ Ⓗ Ⓙ
11. Ⓐ Ⓑ Ⓒ Ⓓ
12. Ⓕ Ⓖ Ⓗ Ⓙ
13. Ⓐ Ⓑ Ⓒ Ⓓ
14. Ⓕ Ⓖ Ⓗ Ⓙ
15. Ⓐ Ⓑ Ⓒ Ⓓ
16. Ⓕ Ⓖ Ⓗ Ⓙ

17. Ⓐ Ⓑ Ⓒ Ⓓ
18. Ⓕ Ⓖ Ⓗ Ⓙ
19. Ⓐ Ⓑ Ⓒ Ⓓ
20. Ⓕ Ⓖ Ⓗ Ⓙ
21. Ⓐ Ⓑ Ⓒ Ⓓ
22. Ⓕ Ⓖ Ⓗ Ⓙ
23. Ⓐ Ⓑ Ⓒ Ⓓ
24. Ⓕ Ⓖ Ⓗ Ⓙ

25. Ⓐ Ⓑ Ⓒ Ⓓ
26. Ⓕ Ⓖ Ⓗ Ⓙ
27. Ⓐ Ⓑ Ⓒ Ⓓ
28. Ⓕ Ⓖ Ⓗ Ⓙ
29. Ⓐ Ⓑ Ⓒ Ⓓ
30. Ⓕ Ⓖ Ⓗ Ⓙ
31. Ⓐ Ⓑ Ⓒ Ⓓ
32. Ⓕ Ⓖ Ⓗ Ⓙ

33. Ⓐ Ⓑ Ⓒ Ⓓ
34. Ⓕ Ⓖ Ⓗ Ⓙ
35. Ⓐ Ⓑ Ⓒ Ⓓ
36. Ⓕ Ⓖ Ⓗ Ⓙ
37. Ⓐ Ⓑ Ⓒ Ⓓ
38. Ⓕ Ⓖ Ⓗ Ⓙ
39. Ⓐ Ⓑ Ⓒ Ⓓ
40. Ⓕ Ⓖ Ⓗ Ⓙ

Science

1. Ⓐ Ⓑ Ⓒ Ⓓ
2. Ⓕ Ⓖ Ⓗ Ⓙ
3. Ⓐ Ⓑ Ⓒ Ⓓ
4. Ⓕ Ⓖ Ⓗ Ⓙ
5. Ⓐ Ⓑ Ⓒ Ⓓ
6. Ⓕ Ⓖ Ⓗ Ⓙ
7. Ⓐ Ⓑ Ⓒ Ⓓ
8. Ⓕ Ⓖ Ⓗ Ⓙ

9. Ⓐ Ⓑ Ⓒ Ⓓ
10. Ⓕ Ⓖ Ⓗ Ⓙ
11. Ⓐ Ⓑ Ⓒ Ⓓ
12. Ⓕ Ⓖ Ⓗ Ⓙ
13. Ⓐ Ⓑ Ⓒ Ⓓ
14. Ⓕ Ⓖ Ⓗ Ⓙ
15. Ⓐ Ⓑ Ⓒ Ⓓ
16. Ⓕ Ⓖ Ⓗ Ⓙ

17. Ⓐ Ⓑ Ⓒ Ⓓ
18. Ⓕ Ⓖ Ⓗ Ⓙ
19. Ⓐ Ⓑ Ⓒ Ⓓ
20. Ⓕ Ⓖ Ⓗ Ⓙ
21. Ⓐ Ⓑ Ⓒ Ⓓ
22. Ⓕ Ⓖ Ⓗ Ⓙ
23. Ⓐ Ⓑ Ⓒ Ⓓ
24. Ⓕ Ⓖ Ⓗ Ⓙ

25. Ⓐ Ⓑ Ⓒ Ⓓ
26. Ⓕ Ⓖ Ⓗ Ⓙ
27. Ⓐ Ⓑ Ⓒ Ⓓ
28. Ⓕ Ⓖ Ⓗ Ⓙ
29. Ⓐ Ⓑ Ⓒ Ⓓ
30. Ⓕ Ⓖ Ⓗ Ⓙ
31. Ⓐ Ⓑ Ⓒ Ⓓ
32. Ⓕ Ⓖ Ⓗ Ⓙ

33. Ⓐ Ⓑ Ⓒ Ⓓ
34. Ⓕ Ⓖ Ⓗ Ⓙ
35. Ⓐ Ⓑ Ⓒ Ⓓ
36. Ⓕ Ⓖ Ⓗ Ⓙ
37. Ⓐ Ⓑ Ⓒ Ⓓ
38. Ⓕ Ⓖ Ⓗ Ⓙ
39. Ⓐ Ⓑ Ⓒ Ⓓ
40. Ⓕ Ⓖ Ⓗ Ⓙ

ENGLISH TEST

Time: 45 Minutes—75 Questions

> **Directions:** In the five passages that follow, certain words and phrases are underlined and numbered. In the right-hand column, you will find alternatives for the underlined part. In most cases, you are to choose the one that best expresses the idea, makes the statement appropriate for standard written English, or is worded most consistently with the style and tone of the passage as a whole. If you think the original version is best, choose "NO CHANGE." In some cases, you will find in the right-hand column a question about the underlined part. You are to choose the best answer to the question.
>
> You will also find questions about a section of the passage, or about the passage as a whole. These questions do not refer to an underlined portion of the passage, but rather are identified by a number or numbers in a box.
>
> For each question, choose the alternative you consider best and fill in the corresponding oval on your answer sheet. Read each passage through once before you begin to answer the questions that accompany it. For many of the questions, you must read several sentences beyond the question to determine the answer. Be sure that you have read far enough ahead each time you choose an alternative.

PASSAGE I

How Romantic!

When you hear the word *romantic,* you probably

think to "chick flick" movies and Valentine's Day,
$\overline{1}$

but the time in history known as the Romantic

Period was a lot more exciting than that. In

Europe in the late eighteenth and early nineteenth

centuries, communities of writers, painters, and

musicians begins feeling stifled by the rationality
$\overline{2}$

and orderliness of the Age of Enlightenment,

and started producing work that emphasized

uncontrollable emotion and the dark side of

Nature.

1. **A.** NO CHANGE
   B. in
   C. of
   D. like

2. **F.** NO CHANGE
   G. feeling
   H. has felt
   J. had begun to feel

Most people think of classical music as

"relaxing," but the stirring urgently with
                                    3

compositions of Romantic musicians like
          3

Beethoven and Wagner are anything but, and

would come to influence rock and roll music over a

century later. In the visual arts, painters like Henry

Fuseli and Eugène Delacroix created disturbing,

chaotic works emphasizing struggle, fear, and

loneliness that inspired today's horror and "goth"
              4

imagery.

But the movement is most closely associated
    5

with literature, and indeed Romanticism radically

changed people's ideas not only of the function

of literature, but also of what writers themselves

would be like. Previously, most famous writers
    6

had been educated aristocrats who wrote complex

works about human society, but the reflective

nature poems of William Wordsworth and the short,

sad life of the brilliant, struggling commoner John

3. **A.** NO CHANGE
   B. stirring, urgent compositions
   C. compositions stirring in their urgency
   D. urgent compositions that stirred

4. **F.** NO CHANGE
   G. loneliness inspired
   H. loneliness, in which inspired
   J. loneliness; inspired

5. Which of the following alternatives to
   the underlined portion would NOT be
   acceptable?
   A. However,
   B. Meanwhile,
   C. Still,
   D. Today,

6. **F.** NO CHANGE
   G. would have been
   H. to be
   J. are

Keats have much more in common with how we think of poetry and poets today. [7]

Perhaps Romanticism's most influential innovation was the "Byronic hero," named for the central figures in the works of rebellious English poet Lord Byron.

<u>He defined</u> a supremely gifted individual troubled by
8
a dark past, torn between good and evil, and plagued by tragic love affairs, the figure of the Byronic hero is everywhere in pop culture even today, <u>from *Star Wars'*
9
Anakin Skywalker, to *X-Men*'s Wolverine, to *Twilight*'s
9
brooding vampire Edward Cullen.</u>
9

The Romantic Movement <u>was largely
10
unconcerned with</u> science. Researchers turned
10
their attention away from the microscope and

7. If the writer were to delete the phrase "brilliant, struggling commoner" in the preceding sentence and replace it with "masterful sonneteer," the paragraph would primarily lose:
   A. a link between Keats and the idea of the struggling artist of today.
   B. support for the idea that Keats was actually more talented than Wordsworth.
   C. an explanation of what made the work of Keats so original and groundbreaking.
   D. proof that "John Keats" was Keats's real name, rather than a pseudonym he used when writing.

8. F. NO CHANGE
   G. Having defined
   H. Defined as
   J. Defining

9. If the writer were to delete the underlined portion (ending the sentence with a period after *today*), the paragraph would primarily lose:
   A. an explanation of why Byronic heroes are so appealing.
   B. proof of the fact that Byronic heroes are more suited to film than to literature.
   C. support for the assertion that all Byronic heroes are male.
   D. some examples of current fictional Byronic heroes.

10. F. NO CHANGE
    G. took a long time to penetrate the realm of
    H. tried to warn humanity about
    J. even had an influence on

toward the dynamic forces of electricity and

magnetism. [A] The fascination with nature

inspired the new science of biology. [B] And the

emphasis on mystery and human behavior led to

the beginnings of what would eventually become

psychology. [C] <u>Since</u> most artistic movements
11

fade into history, <u>becoming</u> of interest mainly
12

to academics, the ideals and aesthetics of

Romanticism have remained popular and continue

to influence mainstream culture to this day,

whether people know it or not. [D] <u>The writers of</u>
13

<u>the Romantic Period are studied more frequently in</u>
13

<u>college courses than any others, with the exception</u>
13

<u>of Shakespeare.</u> 14
13

11. **A.** NO CHANGE
    B. While
    C. Because
    D. However,

12. **F.** NO CHANGE
    G. became
    H. and became
    J. to have become

13. Given that all the choices are true, which one best serves to conclude the passage with an emphasis on how Romanticism has widely affected popular culture?
    A. NO CHANGE
    B. In the 1970s, bands like Rush and Led Zeppelin made frequent reference to "Kubla Khan," a poem by Samuel Taylor Coleridge.
    C. If it hadn't been for a certain few artists who lived 200 years ago, then today we probably wouldn't have rock music, horror movies, or superheroes.
    D. Most people aren't aware of this, but James Dean's middle name was "Byron!"

14. If the writer were to divide this paragraph into two, the most logical place to begin the new paragraph would be at point:
    F. A.
    G. B.
    H. C.
    J. D.

Question 15 asks about the preceding passage as a whole.

15. Suppose the writer's goal had been to write a brief essay about the ways in which pop culture is greatly influenced by high culture. Would this essay accomplish that goal?
   A. Yes, because it contains many examples of mass entertainment derived from principles in great art.
   B. Yes, because it establishes that Romanticism has been more influential than other artistic movements.
   C. No, because it contains no examples of Romanticism's influence on pop culture.
   D. No, because it concerns only Romanticism, and also describes its influence on things besides pop culture.

PASSAGE II

My Favorite Place

Whenever someone asks me what my favorite

place on earth is, I have trouble to decide between
16

two candidates: the American Museum of Natural

History and the Bronx Zoo. Of course, there are a

lot of obvious similarities between the two—they

are both in New York City, and they both appeal to

people who are interested in animals—but there

are a lot of important differences too, at least to me

there are.
17

16. F. NO CHANGE
   G. and decide
   H. about deciding
   J. deciding

17. A. NO CHANGE
   B. they are different.
   C. it would seem.
   D. DELETE the underlined portion and end the sentence with a period.

PRACTICE TEST 6

Obviously, the zoo is outdoors, and the animals

in it are alive, which is nice for them. Being at
                   18
the zoo *feels* different: it's hot, there are bees and

screaming kids everywhere, and the smell of the

city mixes with the smells of animals and snack

food. It's just so full of life and exciting. Even as a

kid, that place was way more exciting than going to
     19
a rollercoaster park or sporting event. To this day,

nothing fills me with joy and energy quite like a day

at the zoo.

The museum, on the other hand, makes me feel
                                               20
more like what I imagine other people must feel
                     20
like in church. It's just so dark and cool and quiet,
   20

and its high ceilings and long echoes always fill me
   21

with a feeling of deep reverence, though I'm not
                       22
exactly sure toward what. Unlike the zoo, which is

always changing, the museum is basically the same

18. Which choice most logically supports the
   first part of this sentence?
   F. NO CHANGE
   G. but those aren't the differences I'm talking
      about.
   H. and most of them are mammals, like you
      and me.
   J. which is a relief, since so many are
      endangered species.

19. A. NO CHANGE
    B. the zoo was
    C. I found it
    D. would you believe it was

20. Given that all the choices are true, which
    one provides material most relevant to what
    follows in this paragraph?
    F. NO CHANGE
    G. The museum, on the other hand, makes
       me just as happy and just as hungry.
    H. People don't realize it, but the museum
       hasn't always been in its present location.
    J. I can't possibly express how the museum
       makes me feel, so I'm not even going to
       try.

21. A. NO CHANGE
    B. with its
    C. although its
    D. because its

22. Which of the following alternatives to
    the underlined portion would be LEAST
    acceptable?
    F. respect
    G. veneration
    H. awe
    J. grandeur

every time you go. The same animals have been
23

frozen in the same positions in their clear tombs
23

since my grandfather was little, and even when the

scientific information on the plaques beside them

gets outdated, the staff sometimes doesn't bother

to change it. And of course, every trip ends with the

dinosaurs on the top floor, their fossilized bones

older than anything you're ever likely to see.

I can remember going from each other to both places
24

often as a child, but even those trips were different. I

would go to the zoo in the summer on a car trip, along

with my whole family, but the museum was a special

wintertime thing between my father and me, and the

23. Which of the following alternatives to the underlined portion would NOT be acceptable?

A. animals have frozen
B. mounted animals have been
C. animals have been there
D. mounted animals have been frozen

24. The best placement for the underlined portion would be:

F. where it is now.
G. after the word *places*.
H. after the word *trips*.
J. after the word *different*.

two of us would take the train, which was exciting in
                              25

itself—rather than drive. 26

   I've lived all over the country, but I've tried to

visit both places at least once every year for my

whole life. I'm a little scared that the museum will

change in the future from the way I remember

it being, and even more scared that some of my

favorite friends' from the zoo, like tigers and rhinos,
               27

will go extinct during my lifetime. But I never fail to
                                        28

notice how fascinated all the kids always are at
  28

25. A. NO CHANGE
     B. train
     C. train—which
     D. train. This

26. At this point, the writer is considering adding
     the following true statement: "I've never
     understood why, but trains are the only form
     of transportation I don't get sick on."

     Should the writer make this addition here?

     F. Yes, because it provides a further link
         between his love for the museum and his
         love of trains.
     G. Yes, because it provides information that
         will become necessary later.
     H. No, because it would distract readers
         from the main focus of this paragraph.
     J. No, because the writer never discusses
         getting sick on any of the various other
         forms of transportation.

27. A. NO CHANGE
     B. friends
     C. friend's
     D. friends's

28. Which choice most effectively expresses
     the writer's great reverence for the zoo and
     museum?
     F. NO CHANGE
     G. I almost can't believe
     H. I always tell my friends about
     J. I'm also reassured and inspired by

both places; it reminds me that, at least when we're

young, we all love animals and learning. 29

PASSAGE III

The Other Golf

[1]

All my life, I've been terrible at sports. I couldn't

hit a baseball to save my life, or sink a basketball

either, and I don't even want to talk about football. I

used to think I'd never be able to experience the joy

that more athletically gifted people derive from a

sunny Sunday spent out on their field of choice. 30

All that changed when I went to college and learned

about disc golf, and now I finally have an answer

29. Which of the following sentences, if added here, would most effectively express one of the main ideas of the essay?

A. Although the zoo and museum are both fun, the real reason I love them is that they give me hope, as I look at the children's faces.

B. It's funny, but I am annoyed by kids pretty much everywhere else.

C. When I was a kid, the zoo had elephant rides, but nowadays they only have camel rides.

D. People always have trouble choosing between the zoo and the museum. I wonder why.

30. The author is thinking about deleting the previous sentence. Should it be deleted or kept?

F. Kept, because it supports the theme of the opening paragraph with memorable imagery.

G. Kept, because it is the only place that the author mentions being bad at traditional sports.

H. Deleted, because it contradicts information presented elsewhere in the opening paragraph.

J. Deleted, because not all sports are played outdoors.

when someone asks me what one of my favorite

sports are.
      ‾‾
      31

[2]

Affectionately known as a "non-sport"—that is,

a sport for people who don't like sports: disc golf is
                                    ‾‾‾‾‾‾
                                     32

very similar to regular golf, but instead of hitting

balls with a club, players throw weighted flying

discs at basketlike targets. [A] Just like in traditional

"ball golf," you start from a tee, and the object is

to get your disc in the hole in the fewest number

of shots. Disc-golf courses are similar to those

of traditional golf in that course's normally have
                                  ‾‾‾‾‾‾‾‾
                                    33

18 holes, some of which are harder than others,
                                         ‾‾‾‾‾‾
                                          34

all with unique combinations of traditional golf
‾‾‾‾‾‾‾
  34

obstacles like trees, bushes, and ponds.[B]

[3]

Disc golf is sometimes mistakenly referred to as
                                     ‾‾‾‾‾‾‾‾‾‾‾
                                          35

"Frisbee golf," but the discs used are actually very

different from Frisbees: they're weighted and have

tapered edges, and so can be thrown much farther

31. A. NO CHANGE
B. is
C. were
D. have been

32. F. NO CHANGE
G. sports,
H. sports;
J. sports—

33. A. NO CHANGE
B. courses'
C. courses's
D. courses

34. Which of the following alternatives to the underlined portion would NOT be acceptable?
F. others, and all have
G. others; all have
H. others; all with
J. others, and all of which have

35. A. NO CHANGE
B. referred, to as
C. referred to, as
D. referred to as,

with much greater accuracy. 36 There are even

different kinds of discs, designed for different types

of shots: drivers for distance, putters to land safely

in the basket, and "trick" discs that curve to get

around obstacles.[C]

[4]

Despite the game's "non-sport" reputation,

because it takes skill and practice to get good at
37

throwing a disc accurately. The people, who play in
38

professional disc-golf tournaments, have obviously
38

spent a lot of time getting good enough making
39

those amazing shots.[D]

Currently, the #1 ranked disc golfer in the world
40

is David Feldberg. Most people who play disc golf
40

are so laid-back that the game is more about being

36. At this point, the author is thinking of adding the following true statement: *True Frisbees were invented much earlier, in 1957.*

Should the writer make this addition here?

F. Yes, because it emphasizes the degree to which times have changed since the days of Frisbees.
G. Yes, because the information is crucial to an understanding of the evolution of disc golf.
H. No, because the sentence does not explain what qualifies as a "true" Frisbee.
J. No, because it is of little relevance to this paragraph and stalls its development.

37. A. NO CHANGE
B. although
C. therefore
D. DELETE the underlined portion.

38. F. NO CHANGE
G. people who play in professional disc-golf tournaments
H. people, who play in professional disc-golf tournaments
J. people who play in professional disc-golf tournaments,

39. A. NO CHANGE
B. they made
C. to make
D. at making

40. Which choice provides the most logical and effective transition to the rest of this paragraph?
F. NO CHANGE
G. There are videos on YouTube of people making the craziest shots you've ever seen!
H. But it doesn't take much time at all to become good enough to have fun with your friends.
J. The biggest teams tournament is held every year in Austin, Texas.

pleasantly surprised <u>in that</u> you make a good shot
41

than embarrassed when you make a bad one.

[5]

Although such a claim is hard to prove, disc golf

is commonly referred to as the fastest-growing

sport in the world. <u>It wasn't invented until the</u>
42

<u>1970s, but there are now over 3,000 courses in the</u>
42

<u>United States.</u> Most of them are located in public
42

parks and are free to play on. The discs can be

found at almost any sporting-goods store, and a

quick Internet search will <u>inform</u> you about courses
43

in your area. So if <u>there's</u> someone who thought
44

you'd never be good at sports, what are you waiting

for?

41. **A.** NO CHANGE
    B. when
    C. before
    D. whereas

42. Given that all the choices are true, which one
    provides the best support for the statement
    in the preceding sentence?
    F. NO CHANGE
    G. Before disc golf got so popular, people used
    to say the same thing about kickboxing.
    H. Designing a disc-golf course doesn't
    exactly take a rocket scientist.
    J. There was even an episode of *Seinfeld*
    where George plays disc golf.

43. Which of the following alternatives to the
    underlined portion would be LEAST acceptable?
    A. persuade
    B. acquaint
    C. teach
    D. enlighten

44. **F.** NO CHANGE
    G. your
    H. one is
    J. you're

Question 45 asks about the preceding passage as
a whole.

45. The writer is considering adding the
    following sentence to the essay: A disc stuck
    in a tree more than 2 meters off the ground is
    a one stroke penalty.

    If the writer were to add this sentence, it
    would most logically be placed at

    A. point A in Paragraph 2.
    B. point B in Paragraph 2.
    C. point C in Paragraph 3.
    D. point D in Paragraph 4.

PASSAGE IV

The Best Party

Here in the United States, <u>we're politically</u>
                                        46
comedians can sometimes seem to understand

things better than <u>politician's</u> do, people often
                            47
jokingly suggest that comedians should run for

office. But just this year, the small European island

nation of Iceland went even further: it actually

elected a stand-up comedian the mayor of its

capital city of Reykjavik, and the political party he

founded as a prank now controls more than a third

of the seats on the City Council.

Comedian and film <u>actor Jon Gnarr</u> was already
                            48

well known to Icelanders. In 2008, after <u>the collapse</u>
                                                49
devastated Iceland's economy, he started a web

site for a fictitious political party that he called

the "Best Party" and began writing blogs satirizing

the nation's policies. When the web site became

unexpectedly popular, Gnarr began <u>at actually</u>
                                        50
<u>staffing</u> the Best Party, mostly with people from
 50
the punk and alternative music scenes he has long

46.
F. NO CHANGE
G. were political
H. we're political
J. where political

47.
A. NO CHANGE
B. politicians'
C. our politicians
D. some politicians'

48.
F. NO CHANGE
G. actor, Jon Gnarr
H. actor Jon Gnarr,
J. actor, Jon Gnarr,

49.
A. NO CHANGE
B. a severe banking collapse
C. a banking collapse that severely affected the financial sector
D. it

50.
F. NO CHANGE
G. by actually staffing
H. to actually staff
J. by which to staff

PRACTICE TEST 6

been close to (Gnarr's wife is best friends with

Iceland's most famous musician, the eccentric
                                51

singer Björk).

    Gnarr's 2010 campaign for mayor of Reykjavik—

which is only one city, but over a third of Iceland's
                                52

population—was hardly a serious one. His

campaign promises included free towels, more

polar bears at the zoo, and a Disneyland at the

airport. Still, the humorous platform highlighted
                                          53

serious issues: polar bears have recently been

showing up in Iceland, where they did not live

before, because of global warming. 54

    [1] Though Gnarr did not expect to win, he

has high hopes for his time in office. [2] Constant

political shake-ups have ejected Reykjavik's last

several mayors from office sooner than expected,

and he hopes to be the first of the twenty-first

century to serve out a full four-year term. [3] Gnarr

says his surprise political career has given him

"the greatest sense of contentment" of anything

51. A. NO CHANGE
B. musician; the
C. musician being
D. musician is

52. F. NO CHANGE
G. home
H. it is a third
J. home to over a third

53. Which of the following alternatives to the underlined portion would NOT be acceptable?
A. recommended
B. mirrored
C. called attention to
D. called to mind

54. The writer is considering deleting the phrase "where they did not live before, because of global warming" from the preceding sentence (and ending it with a period after "Iceland").

Should this phrase be kept or deleted?

F. Kept, because it proves that global warming will affect everyone.
G. Kept, because it explains why the presence of polar bears is a "serious issue."
H. Deleted, because there are some people who don't believe in global warming.
J. Deleted, because the majority of people like polar bears and would love to have more of them around.

he's ever worked on in his career. [4] This would
                        55

be an impressive feat for someone who dropped

out of school at age 16 and identifies himself as an

anarchist, but the comedian has apparently gotten

serious. 56

57 It is the world's oldest parliamentary

democracy, having had an elected legislature since

930 A.D. In 1117, it became the first European

country to outlaw the slave trade. And in 2009, the

people of Iceland elected Johanna Sigurthardottir

as prime minister, making her the world's first

openly gay head of state. So is they're election of
                              58
a comedian mayor and his satirical party a sign of

things to come? Only time will tell.

55. **A.** NO CHANGE
      B. the whole time.
      C. so far in his life.
      D. DELETE the underlined portion and end
           the sentence with a period.

56. For the sake of the logic and coherence of this
      paragraph, Sentence 4 should be placed:
      F. where it is now.
      G. before Sentence 1.
      H. after Sentence 1.
      J. after Sentence 2.

57. Given that all of the following statements are
      true, which one, if added here, would most
      clearly and effectively introduce the main
      subject of this paragraph?
      A. Genetically speaking, Iceland has the
           peculiar distinction of being home to the
           highest percentage of green-eyed people
           of any nation.
      B. All Icelandic schoolchildren learn to read
           the *Old Icelandic Sagas* in the original,
           which would be like if all American kids
           could understand *Beowulf*!
      C. Though it may not be a country you hear
           about much, Iceland has often been
           ahead of the curve in political matters.
      D. Though Iceland and Greenland are right
           next to each other, Iceland counts as part
           of Europe, whereas Greenland counts as
           part of North America.

58. **F.** NO CHANGE
      G. their
      H. there
      J. his or her

Question 59 asks about the preceding passage as a whole.

59. Suppose the writer's goal had been to write a brief essay focusing on the unique political history of Iceland. Would this essay accomplish that goal?

   A. Yes, because it provides information about several key figures in Iceland's government.

   B. Yes, because it mentions several of the important political events in Icelandic history.

   C. No, because it primarily concerns Jon Gnarr and the 2010 Reykjavik mayoral election.

   D. No, because it only mentions Iceland, so readers have no basis for deciding whether its politics are unique.

PASSAGE V

The End of Trivia?

Ever since the 1960s, when trivia was popularized as a pastime by the invention of collegiate Quizbowl and the premiere of the beloved quiz show *Jeopardy!,* bars and restaurants all over the country has attracted patrons with
                                               60

quiz nights, during which patrons form teams
                     61
with friends or strangers and compete for prizes of food, beverages, or even cash. Of course, the environment is much less formally than on a game
                     62

60. **F.** NO CHANGE
   G. attracted
   H. had attracted
   J. have been attracting

61. **A.** NO CHANGE
   B. nights that
   C. nights; where
   D. nights, and these

62. **F.** NO CHANGE
   G. less formal
   H. less formality
   J. fewer formalities

show: instead of using buzzers, players sit with their

teams and write down answers to the questions a

bar employee asks over a microphone, then turn in

their sheets to be scored at the end of the night. But

now that nearly everyone carries a phone or some

other portable device with Internet access, trivia
63

cheating has become nearly impossible to control.

   Ironically, trivia questions involve information
   64

that is obscure but interesting, such as "Who is the

only president to have also served as chief justice of

the Supreme Court?" (the answer is William Howard

Taft) or "What was the first animated film to receive

an Academy Award nomination for Best Picture?"

(the answer is *Beauty and the Beast*). In a pub-quiz

setting, and talking the possible answers over with
65

your friends is half the fun. When people first began

carrying cell phones, players sometimes called friends

during games, but even then, you still could of had
66

a friend who knew the answer, because it wasn't
67

that much of a problem.

63. **A.** NO CHANGE
    B. access; trivia
    C. access, and trivia
    D. access. Therefore, trivia

64. **F.** NO CHANGE
    G. Predictably,
    H. Lamentably,
    J. Traditionally,

65. **A.** NO CHANGE
    B. setting, talking
    C. sitting to talk
    D. sit, and talk

66. **F.** NO CHANGE
    G. would have had
    H. had to have
    J. can had

67. **A.** NO CHANGE
    B. so
    C. since
    D. DELETE the underlined portion.

But phones with Internet access are a different

story: if cheating on those <u>continues to not be</u>
                             68
<u>looked out for</u> by the pub's staff, then every team
  68
will know the answer to every question! But

stopping this is very hard indeed: someone typing

into a tiny phone under the table is tough to spot in

a big bar, and if a player sneaks into the bathroom

to cheat with a <u>phone, then stopping</u> him or her is
                    69
impossible!

    Some quiz nights have chosen to trust in the honor

system, <u>with moderators simply not caring whether</u>
                          70
<u>people cheat or not.</u> Other venues have tried to de-
  70
velop "cheat-proof" questions, like playing very short

clips from pop songs or projecting celebrity yearbook

pictures onto a screen and asking players to <u>identify</u>
                                             71
<u>them all by name.</u> But trivia purists often balk at such
  71

<u>practices,</u> identifying yearbook pictures or drum fills,
  72
they argue, is not true trivia. True trivia concerns bits

68. **F.** NO CHANGE
    G. doesn't get itself regulated
    H. wouldn't be put an end to
    J. is not adequately policed

69. **A.** NO CHANGE
    B. phone then stopping
    C. phone, than stopping
    D. phone than stopping

70. Given that all the choices are true, which
one most effectively concludes the sentence
by offering specific examples of what the
sentence begins by discussing?
    F. NO CHANGE
    G. stationing staff at every table as observers.
    H. begging patrons not to use their phones
and encouraging teams to turn in
cheaters.
    J. deliberately holding events in buildings
where phones don't get reception.

71. **A.** NO CHANGE
    B. identify them.
    C. identify the ones.
    D. identify.

72. **F.** NO CHANGE
    G. practices;
    H. practices; therefore,
    J. practices, when they are

of information … but every bit of information can be

looked up on a portable device! [73]

73. The writer is considering deleting the portion of the preceding sentence that follows the ellipses (and replacing the ellipses with a period). If the writer were to make this deletion, the paragraph would primarily lose:

   A. unnecessary information that constitutes a digression from the main idea of the passage.

   B. an identification of a problem that the writer has just realized and mentions nowhere else.

   C. an explanation of how modern devices affect trivia.

   D. an argument that trivia buffs should purchase gadgets with Internet access.

In a few years, phones will probably be able to
                   74
identify songs and pictures too, but even this is not
                   74
the biggest threat to the great sport of pub quiz.
                74
The biggest threat is that future generations raised

74. Given that all of the choices are true, which one makes for the most effective transition into this paragraph from the preceding one?

   F. NO CHANGE

   G. Sometimes patrons who aren't even playing yell out the answers, but this is not the biggest threat to pub quizzes.

   H. Cell phones are also hazardous when people talk on them while driving, but this is not the biggest threat they pose.

   J. The biggest threat to pub quizzes is something I am going to tell you about right now.

on technology in the first place that can instantly
                75
summon up any factoid at the push of a button will

have no motivation to memorize them, and hence

no interest in trivia!

75. The best placement for the underlined portion would be:

   A. where it is now.

   B. after the word *generations*.

   C. after the word *factoid*.

   D. after the word *trivia* (and before the exclamation point).

If there is still time remaining, you may review your answers.

MATHEMATICS TEST

Time: 60 Minutes—60 Questions

Directions: Solve each problem, choose the correct answer, and then fill in the corresponding oval on your answer sheet.

Do not linger over problems that take too much time. Solve as many as you can; then return to the others in the time you have left for this test.

You are permitted to use a calculator on this test. You may use your calculator for any problems you choose, but some of the problems may best be done without using a calculator.

Note: Unless otherwise stated, all of the following should be assumed.

1. Illustrative figures are NOT necessarily drawn to scale.
2. Geometric figures lie in a plane.
3. The word *line* indicates a straight line.
4. The word *average* indicates arithmetic mean.

1. Last week Kylie spent the following amounts of time doing homework. Sunday: $1\frac{3}{4}$ hours, Monday: $1\frac{1}{2}$ hours, Tuesday: 3 hours, Wednesday: $2\frac{1}{3}$ hours, Thursday: $1\frac{1}{2}$ hours. What was the median number of hours Kylie spent doing homework last week?

   A. 3
   B. $2\frac{1}{3}$
   C. $2\frac{1}{60}$
   D. $1\frac{3}{4}$
   E. $1\frac{1}{2}$

2. What is $(-2x^5)^4$ equivalent to?

   F. $-16x^9$
   G. $-2x^9$
   H. $-2x^{20}$
   J. $2x^{20}$
   K. $16x^{20}$

DO YOUR FIGURING HERE

3. Parveen has earned the following scores on four 100-point tests this grading period: 85, 83, 91, and 94. What score must Parveen earn on the fifth and last 100-point test of the grading period to earn an average grade of exactly 90 for the 5 tests?

A. 85
B. 87
C. 89
D. 97
E. 99

DO YOUR FIGURING HERE

4. If $x = -3$ and $y = 2$, then $2x^2 - 5xy + y^2 = ?$

F. -44
G. 16
H. 27
J. 52
K. 70

5. What is the solution set for the inequality $2x - 3 < 5x + 6$?

A. $x < -3$
B. $x = -3$
C. $x > -3$
D. $x < 4$
E. $x > 5$

6. In regular hexagon $ABCDEF$, $CD = 12$ cm. What is the length of $\overline{BE}$ in cm?

F. 12
G. $12 + 2\sqrt{b}$
H. $12 + 4\sqrt{2}$
J. 24
K. 72

7. If 18% of a given number is 63, then what is 45% of the given number?

A. 126
B. 157.5
C. 189
D. 220.5
E. 350

DO YOUR FIGURING HERE

8. What is $(x^3 - 4x^2 + 5) - (3x^3 + 6x^2 - 9)$
   equivalent to?

   F. $-2x^3 - 10x^2 + 14$

   G. $4x^3 + 2x^2 - 4$

   H. $-2x^6 - 10x^4 + 14$

   J. $-2x^3 + 2x^2 - 4$

   K. $-2x^3 - 10x^2 - 4$

9. In the diagram, B, C, and D are collinear. The
   measures of $\angle A$ and $\angle ABC$ are 56° and 69°,
   respectively. The measure of $\angle ACD = ?$

   A. 55°

   B. 111°

   C. 115°

   D. 121°

   E. 125°

10. What is the expression $(5x - 4y)(3x + y)$
    equivalent to?

    F. $15x^2 - 17xy - 4y^2$

    G. $15x^2 - 7xy + 4y^2$

    H. $15x^2 - 7xy - 4y^2$

    J. $15x + 7xy - 4y$

    K. $8x^2 - 7xy - 4y^2$

11. What value of x makes the equation
    $8x - 2(x - 5) = 2x - 20$ true?

    A. $-7\frac{1}{2}$

    B. $-2\frac{1}{2}$

    C. $-1\frac{1}{4}$

    D. 1

    E. $1\frac{2}{3}$

PRACTICE TEST 6

12. Which of the following matrices is equal

to $5\begin{bmatrix} -4 & 0 \\ -2 & 10 \end{bmatrix}$?

F. $\begin{bmatrix} -\dfrac{4}{5} & 0 \\ -\dfrac{2}{5} & 2 \end{bmatrix}$

G. $\begin{bmatrix} -20 & 0 \\ -10 & 50 \end{bmatrix}$

H. $\begin{bmatrix} 1 & 5 \\ 3 & 15 \end{bmatrix}$

J. $\begin{bmatrix} -20 & 30 \end{bmatrix}$

K. $\begin{bmatrix} -30 \\ 50 \end{bmatrix}$

13. The figure shows quadrilateral *ABCD* with angles measured as marked. What is the measure of ∡ *C*?

A. 120°
B. 115°
C. 105°
D. 100°
E. 80°

14. A tank currently holds 5,000 gallons of water. Each gallon of water weighs about 8 pounds. About how many pounds does the water in the tank weigh?

F. 625
G. 4,000
H. 4,992
J. 5,008
K. 40,000

15. A 3-pound bag of oranges costs $1.99 at Yong's Grocery. A 3-pound bag of the same type of oranges costs $2.17 at Pat's Pantry. How much cheaper, per pound, are the Yong's Grocery oranges than Pat's Pantry oranges?

A. $0.02
B. $0.04
C. $0.06
D. $0.18
E. $1.00

16. Graeme is going to replace his kitchen floor that is 12 feet by 16 feet. He will use tiles that are 8 inches by 8 inches. How many tiles will Graeme need?

F.   3
G. 24
H. 36
J. 360
K. 432

> Use the following information to answer questions 17–19.

Lucy conducted a survey of 10th-grade students from her school to determine which subject is the students' favorite. Each student who responded to the survey selected 1 subject as their favorite. The circle graph below shows the number of students who selected each subject. A total of 60 students responded to the survey.

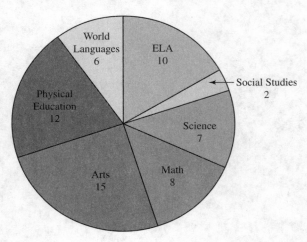

DO YOUR FIGURING HERE

17. To the nearest 0.1%, what percent of the students who responded to the survey selected Science?

   A. 3.3%
   B. 10.0%
   C. 11.7%
   D. 13.3%
   E. 16.7%

18. In this survey, what is the ratio of the number of students who selected Physical Education to the number of students who selected Math?

   F. 2:3
   G. 3:2
   H. 3:4
   J. 4:1
   K. 5:3

19. In the circle graph, what is the angle measure of the sector that represents the number of students who responded to the survey who selected World Languages?

   A. 6°
   B. 10°
   C. 12°
   D. 36°
   E. 42°

20. Five patients arrived at a doctor's office about the same time. The nurse decided to call them in to see the doctor in random order. In how many different orders can these 5 patients be called?

   F.   4
   G.   5
   H.   25
   J.   120
   K. 3,125

21. What is the y-intercept of the line in the standard (x, y) coordinate plane that goes through the points $(-3, 2)$ and $(3, 6)$?

A. 0
B. 2
C. 4
D. 6
E. 8

22. In the diagram, $\overleftrightarrow{AB}$ is parallel to $\overleftrightarrow{CD}$. The measure of $\angle PCD = 37°$ and the measure of $\angle BPD$ is $40°$. What is the measure of $\angle CPD$?

F. 100°
G. 103°
H. 106°
J. 140°
K. CANNOT be determined

23. What is the slope of the line $2x - 3y + 7 = 0$?

A. $-\dfrac{7}{3}$
B. $-\dfrac{2}{3}$
C. $\dfrac{2}{3}$
D. $\dfrac{3}{2}$
E. 2

24. In △PQR, shown, what is the cos ∡R?

F. $\dfrac{12}{20}$

G. $\dfrac{12}{16}$

H. $\dfrac{16}{20}$

J. $\dfrac{16}{12}$

K. $\dfrac{\sqrt{656}}{20}$

25. If $x \neq -2$ or 3, what is $\dfrac{x^2 + x - 12}{x^2 - x - 6}$ equivalent to?

A. -2

B. 2

C. $\dfrac{x-4}{x-2}$

D. $\dfrac{x+4}{x+2}$

E. 0

26. In a certain year, Lincoln Middle School had an enrollment of exactly 1,000 students. The following year, the enrollment increased by 5%. In the third year, the enrollment decreased by 2% of what the enrollment was in the second year. What was the enrollment for the third year?

F. 1,030

G. 1,029

H. 990

J. 980

K. 971

27. Zinc, tin, and copper are used in the ratio of 2:3:4, respectively, in making a certain type of engine. If each engine weighs 63 ounces, how many ounces of tin are in each engine?

A. 7

B. 9

C. 14

D. 21

E. 28

28. Driving home from school, Joan spotted her brother Andrew and picked him up after he'd walked $\frac{1}{2}$ of the way home. A while later they saw younger brother Bill and picked him up after he'd walked $\frac{2}{3}$ of the way home from the same school. If they live $4\frac{1}{2}$ miles from school, how many miles farther than Andrew had Bill walked?

    F. $\frac{3}{8}$

    G. $\frac{1}{2}$

    H. $\frac{2}{3}$

    J. $\frac{3}{4}$

    K. $1\frac{1}{2}$

29. What positive value of k would make the lines below parallel in the (x, y) coordinate plane?
    $kx + 2y = 6$
    $32x + ky = 18$

    A. 0
    B. 3
    C. 6
    D. 8
    E. 12

30. In the standard (x, y) coordinate plane, what is the distance between the points $(-2, 1)$ and $(4, -7)$?

    F. $\sqrt{28}$
    G. $\sqrt{40}$
    H. $\sqrt{68}$
    J. 10
    K. 14

31. What is the value of $\log_3 \sqrt{27}$?

  A. $\frac{1}{2}$

  B. $\frac{2}{3}$

  C. $\frac{3}{2}$

  D. 1

  E. 3

DO YOUR FIGURING HERE

32. What are the solutions of the polynomial equation $2x^2 - 5x = 12$?

  F. −4 or 1.5

  G. −4 or −3

  H. −1.5 or 4

  J. 1.5 or 4

  K. 4 or 6

33. For what positive values of x is it true that $x^2 < 2x < x + 4$?

  A. No positive values

  B. Only positive values < 2

  C. Only positive values between 2 and 4

  D. Only positive values > 4

  E. All positive values

34. In the figure all angles are right angles and each dimension given is in inches. What is the perimeter of the figure in inches?

  F. 21

  G. 35

  H. 36

  J. 54

  K. 72

35. Which of the following graphs represents the solution set of the inequality $|x| > 2$ on the real number line?

  A.
  B.

  C.
  D.

  E.

36. In a game, 100 marbles numbered 0–99 are placed into a box. A player draws 1 marble at random from the box. Without replacing the first marble, the player draws a second marble at random. If both marbles drawn have the same tens digit (that is, both are numbered 0–9 or 10–19 or 20–29, etc.), the player is a winner. If the first marble drawn is numbered 56, what is the probability that Terry will be a winner on the next draw?

F. $\dfrac{1}{8}$

G. $\dfrac{1}{9}$

H. $\dfrac{1}{10}$

J. $\dfrac{1}{11}$

K. $\dfrac{1}{99}$

37. In the diagram $\overline{AE}$ intersects $\overline{BD}$ at C and $\overline{AB}$ is parallel to $\overline{DE}$. Which of the following statements must be true?

A. ∡A is congruent to ∡D.

B. $\triangle ACB$ is congruent to $\triangle ECD$.

C. $\overline{AC}$ is congruent to $\overline{EC}$.

D. $\triangle ACB$ is similar to $\triangle ECD$.

E. ∡ACB is congruent to ∡CED.

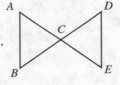

38. At the same time that a 6-foot man has a 4-foot shadow, a flag pole has a 14-foot shadow. What is the height of the flag pole, in feet?

F. $9\dfrac{1}{3}$

G. 12

H. 16

J. 21

K. 28

39. The formula for surface area of a right circular cylinder is $A = 2\pi r(r + h)$, where A is surface area, r = radius of the cylinder, and h is the height of the cylinder. Then, $h = ?$

A. $A - 2\pi r - r$

B. $\dfrac{A - 2\pi r}{r}$

C. $\dfrac{A}{2\pi r} - r$

D. $\dfrac{A}{2\pi r} + r$

E. $\dfrac{A}{2\pi r^2}$

DO YOUR FIGURING HERE

40. The width of a rectangle is 27 feet and the length is 36 feet. What is the length of a diagonal of the rectangle in feet?

F. 63

G. 54

H. 45

J. 42

K. 36

41. The vertices of a parallelogram in the coordinate plane are (3, 3), (7, 3), (8, 8), and (4, 8). What is the area of this parallelogram?

A. 10

B. $2\sqrt{26}$

C. 16

D. 20

E. $4\sqrt{26}$

42. The point (–1, 1) is the midpoint of the line segment in the standard (x, y) coordinate plane joining the point (1, 6) and the point (a, b). Which of the following is (a, b)?

F. (–2, 3)

G. (–3, –4)

H. (0, 3.5)

J. (3, 11)

K. (2, 5)

43. The first term of the geometric sequence below is 27. What is the twelfth term?

27, 9, 3, …

A. $\dfrac{1}{3^7}$

B. $\dfrac{1}{3^8}$

C. $\dfrac{1}{3^{10}}$

D. $\dfrac{1}{3^{11}}$

E. $\dfrac{1}{3^{12}}$

44. In $\triangle ABC$, $AB = AC = 14$. Which of these values could NOT be the length of the third side, $\overline{BC}$?

F. 5
G. 7
H. 14
J. 16
K. 28

45. If $4^{3x+1} = 8^{x+2}$, then $x = $?

A. $\dfrac{1}{2}$

B. $\dfrac{3}{4}$

C. $\dfrac{4}{3}$

D. 3

E. None of these

46. If $f(x) = x^2$ and $g(x) = 2x - 1$, then $f(g(x)) = ?$

    F. $4x^2 - 4x + 1$

    G. $4x^2 + 1$

    H. $2x^2 - 1$

    J. $x^2 - 1$

    K. $4x^2 + 4x + 1$

47. In the diagram B, D, and C are collinear. $m\angle B = 30°$ and $m\angle C = 45°$. $\overline{AD}$ is perpendicular to $\overline{BC}$ and $\overline{AD} = 6$. What is the perimeter of $\triangle ABC$ to the nearest tenth? (Note: Figure not drawn to scale.)

    A. 29.9

    B. 30

    C. 32.5

    D. 34.4

    E. 36.9

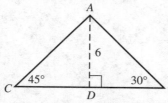

48. Quadrilateral $ABCD$ is a trapezoid with $\overline{AB}$ parallel to $\overline{CD}$, $\overline{AE}$ and $\overline{BF}$ are perpendicular to $\overline{CD}$. $AB = 6$, $CD = 12$, and $AE = 4$. What is the sum of the areas of $\triangle AED$ and $\triangle BFC$?

    F. 12

    G. 24

    H. 36

    J. 48

    K. 120

49. $(2 - 3i)^2 = ?$ [Note: $i = \sqrt{-1}$.]

    A. -5

    B. 13

    C. $-5 - 6i$

    D. $-5 - 12i$

    E. $-5 + 12i$

Use the following information to answer questions 50–52.

In the figure below, a large circle with center C has a diameter $\overline{XZ}$ that is 80 inches long. Point Y lies on the large circle such that the measure of $\angle XZY$ is 60°. $\overline{XC}$ is a diameter of the small circle.

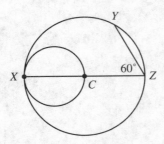

50. What is the area, in square inches, of the small circle?

F. 40π

G. 80π

H. 320π

J. $1,600\pi$

K. $6,400\pi$

51. The figure is placed in the standard (x, y) coordinate plane so that X has coordinates $(-40, 0)$ and Z has coordinates $(40, 0)$. What is the x-coordinate of Y?

A. 0

B. 20

C. 40

D. 60

E. 80

52. What is the length, in inches, of arc XZ?

F. 40π

G. 40

H. 80π

J. 80

K. 160π

53. If $(x + 2)$ is a factor of $3x^2 - 13x + k$, what is the value of k?

A. -38

B. -14

C. -2

D. 14

E. 38

54. If the radius of a sphere is tripled, the volume of the resulting sphere is how many times the volume of the original sphere?

[The volume of a sphere $= \dfrac{4\pi r^3}{3}$.]

F. 1

G. 3

H. 9

J. 27

K. 81

55. If $f(x) = x^2 - 2x + 4$, then $f(t + 2) = ?$

A. $t^2 - 2t + 4$

B. $t^2 - 2t$

C. $t^2 + 2t + 8$

D. $t^2 + 6t + 12$

E. $t^2 + 2t + 4$

56. If $x = 4y + 2$, what is $y + 6$ in terms of x?

F. $x + 4$

G. $x + 6$

H. $\dfrac{x + 22}{4}$

J. $\dfrac{x + 2}{4} + 6$

K. $\dfrac{x - 4}{2} + 6$

57. If $\sin \theta = \dfrac{5}{7}$, $\dfrac{\pi}{2} < \theta < \pi$, then $\cos \theta = ?$

A. $-\dfrac{7}{2\sqrt{6}}$

B. $-\dfrac{2\sqrt{6}}{5}$

C. $-\dfrac{2\sqrt{6}}{7}$

D. $\dfrac{2\sqrt{6}}{7}$

E. $\dfrac{2\sqrt{6}}{5}$

58. The measures of $\angle A$ and $\angle B$ are 35° and 44°, respectively. The length of $\overline{AB}$ is 12 miles. Which of the following expressions, if any, gives the approximate distance, in miles, of side $\overline{AC}$?

[Note: The law of sines states that the ratio between the length of the side opposite an angle and the sine of that angle is the same for all interior angles in the same triangle.]

F. The distance cannot be approximated without more information.

G. $\sqrt{35^2 + 44^2}$

H. $\dfrac{12 \cos 44°}{\cos 101°}$

J. $\dfrac{12 \sin 101°}{\sin 44°}$

K. $\dfrac{12 \sin 44°}{\sin 101°}$

59. For how many different integers b (consider positive integers, negative integers, and zero) does $x^2 + bx + 20$ factor into linear factors with integer coefficients?

A. 1
B. 2
C. 3
D. 4
E. 6

DO YOUR FIGURING HERE

60. M and N are prime numbers. If $\sqrt{21(M)(N)(5)(7)}$ is a rational number, then $(M)(N) = ?$

F. 8
G. 15
H. 21
J. 35
K. 735

If there is still time remaining, you may review your answers.

READING TEST

Time: 35 Minutes—40 Questions

Directions: There are four passages in this test. Each passage is followed by several questions. After reading a passage, choose the best answer to each question and fill in the corresponding oval on your answer sheet. You may refer to the passages as often as necessary.

PASSAGE I—LITERARY NARRATIVE

Passage A is adapted from "Tradition and the Individual Talent" by T.S. Eliot. Passage B is adapted from the Preface to *Lyrical Ballads* by William Wordsworth.

Passage A by T.S. Eliot

In English writing we seldom speak of tradition. At most, we employ the adjective in saying that the poetry of So-and-so is "traditional," or even "too traditional." Seldom does the word appear
(5) except in a phrase of censure. When we praise a poet, we insist upon those aspects of his work in which he least resembles anyone else. But if we approach a poet without this prejudice, we shall often find that not only the best, but the
(10) most individual parts of his work may be those in which the dead poets, his ancestors, assert their immortality most vigorously.

If the only form of tradition consisted in blind adherence to the ways of the generation before
(15) us, "tradition" should positively be discouraged. Novelty is better than repetition. Tradition is a matter of much wider significance. It cannot be inherited, and if you want it you must obtain it by great labour. It involves the historical sense,
(20) and the historical sense involves a perception not only of the pastness of the past, but of its presence. The historical sense compels a man to write with a feeling that the whole of literature has a simultaneous existence and composes
(25) a simultaneous order. This historical sense, a sense of the timeless and of the temporal together, is what makes a writer traditional. And it is at the same time what makes a writer most

acutely conscious of his place in time, of his
(30) contemporaneity.

No poet, no artist of any art, has meaning alone. His significance is the appreciation of his relation to the dead poets and artists. You cannot value him alone; you must set him, for contrast and
(35) comparison, among the dead. What happens when a new work of art is created is something that happens simultaneously to all the works of art which preceded it. The existing monuments form an ideal order among themselves, which is
(40) modified by the introduction of the new work of art among them. The existing order is complete before the new work arrives; for order to persist after the supervention of novelty, the *whole* existing order must be, if ever so slightly, altered.
(45) And the poet who is aware of this will be aware of great difficulties and responsibilities.

Passage B by William Wordsworth

The first volume of these poems was published as an experiment, to ascertain how far, by fitting to metrical arrangement a selection of the real
(50) language of men in a state of vivid sensation, that sort and quantity of pleasure may be imparted that a poet may rationally endeavor to impart.

Several of my friends advised me to prefix a defense of the theory upon which the poems were
(55) written. I was unwilling to undertake the task, knowing that I might be suspected of the foolish hope of reasoning the reader into approbation. Yet there would be something like impropriety in abruptly obtruding upon the public, without a few words
(60) of introduction, poems so different from those upon which approbation is at present bestowed.

By the act of writing in verse an author makes a formal engagement: he not only apprises the reader that certain classes of ideas and expres-
(65) sions will be found in his book, but that others will be carefully excluded. It will undoubtedly appear to many persons that I have not fulfilled the terms. I hope therefore the reader will not censure me for attempting to explain, so that I
(70) may be protected from one of the most dishonorable accusations which can be brought against an author—namely, that of an indolence which prevents him from endeavoring to ascertain his duty.

(75) The principal object in these poems was to choose incidents from common life, and to describe them in a selection of language really used by men. Humble and rustic life was generally chosen, because in that condition the essential
(80) passions of the heart find a better soil in which they can attain their maturity. Being less under the influence of social vanity, these men convey their feelings in simple and unelaborated expressions. Such language is far more philosophical
(85) than that which is substituted for it by poets who think they are conferring honor upon their art by separating themselves from the sympathies of men in order to furnish food for appetites of their own creation.

Questions 1–3 ask about Passage A.

1. According to Passage A, in the opinion of the author of the passage, most English writers are too:
   A. secretive about tradition.
   B. obsessed with originality.
   C. prejudiced concerning immortality.
   D. adherent to discouragement.

2. Which of the following characterizations of art that was created in the past is best supported by Passage A?
   F. Contemporary art is meaningless without it.
   G. Its values were ideal because they were orderly.
   H. It is extremely difficult, as well as irresponsible, for anyone to alter it.
   J. It takes more work to understand because historical knowledge is required.

3. Based on the approach to writing he advocates in the second paragraph (lines 13–30), the author of Passage A presumably sees himself as someone who:
   A. could never produce work that is "too traditional."
   B. has discerned that all significant works of art ultimately have the same meaning.
   C. views the present in the most accurate way possible.
   D. understands why all literature should be written in the same way.

Questions 4–7 ask about Passage B.

4. The "formal engagement" referred to in line 63 of Passage B most nearly refers to the author's sense that most people expect poets to:
   F. employ diction and grammar appropriate to ceremonial occasions.
   G. reach an agreement with one another regarding their duty before publishing.
   H. educate readers concerning notable events.
   J. avoid using unworthy forms of expression.

5. In the context of Passage B, when the passage's author refers to "appetites of their own creation" (lines 88–89), he is accusing some other poets of:
   A. false bravado.
   B. malicious slandering.
   C. indolent wickedness.
   D. elitist tastemaking.

6. In taking his friends' suggestion as described in the second paragraph (lines 53–61), the author of Passage B is conscious of attempting to balance:
   F. his private obsession with theory with his carefree and spontaneous public image.
   G. his wish to obscure his literary influences with his obligation to honor his poetic heroes.
   H. a risk of appearing pompous with a reluctance to take his audience for granted.
   J. his untutored logical-reasoning skills with his unshakeable moral principles.

7. As it is used in lines 57 and 61, the word *approbation* most nearly means:
   A. approval.
   B. boredom.
   C. bemusement.
   D. dread.

Questions 8–10 ask about both passages.

8. It can reasonably be inferred from the passages that, regarding their responsibility to poetry as a whole, both passage authors would agree that new poets should:
   F. honorably decide which traditions to discourage.
   G. innovate out of a respect for its history.
   H. allow its readers to explain what their duty is.
   J. consider its debts to history and philosophy.

9. The passages most strongly indicate that, in terms of their opinions about their peers, both passage authors were:
   A. appreciative of those who mastered form and order.
   B. surprised by those who became most celebrated.
   C. dismayed by those who refused to explain their work.
   D. annoyed by those who cherished novelty too much.

10. Which of the following statements best compares the concluding sentences of the passages?
   F. Both passages end with the authors warning poets about what not to do.
   G. Both passages end with the authors making veiled criticisms of themselves.
   H. The author of Passage A compliments responsible poets, whereas the author of Passage B criticizes irresponsible ones.
   J. The author of Passage A emphasizes the difficulty of writing traditional poetry, whereas the author of Passage B emphasizes the honesty of writing nontraditional poetry.

PASSAGE II—SOCIAL SCIENCE

This passage is adapted from "Music Piracy," which appeared on UKEssays.com., February 2009.

In the future, the only way musicians will make money is by playing live. New federal legislation says universities must agree to provide not just deterrents but also "alternatives" to peer-to-peer
(5) piracy, such as paying monthly subscription fees to the music industry for their students, on penalty of losing all financial aid.

When record companies appeared, the services they provided were necessary in order for people
(10) to listen to recorded music. Making and selling records was a major undertaking. At that time, making recorded music available to the masses

required significant capital and investments, which in turn required a legal structure that
(15) would provide stable profits and return on the required investment. The music industry used to provide people with tools that were essential to listen to recorded music. The difference between that time and our day is that record companies
(20) now charge people for permission to use tools they already have that the record companies did not provide—that in fact people paid someone else for—yet the legal structure that developed during the time when those services were useful
(25) remains. The legal structure says if you don't pay, you are breaking the law.

In our day, there is no need of publishers, distributors, and in most cases manufacturers. Modern technology allows people to burn CDs
(30) at home or publish their own records using the internet, distributing the material across the web digitally.

The problem of piracy has been rising for the past ten years, and the numbers of "pirates" is
(35) growing day by day. The reason is simple: user-friendly peer-to-peer software takes only a couple of minutes to set up and another minute to become familiar with all the features. In another ten minutes it is possible to find your favorite
(40) artist and download your favorite album. It's so convenient that it is becoming only a question of conscience whether to become a pirate.

It is becoming more and more difficult for the music industry to ignore the basic economics,
(45) technological progress, and the outdated legal structures of the industry such as unenforceable property rights (because it is impossible to sue everyone) and "zero" production costs (peer-to-peer and file sharing systems became way too
(50) popular). Music companies are still trying to charge for their music, but it's becoming more and more clear that as long as there is a free alternative (peer-to peer and other file sharing systems), the price of music and other media
(55) will have to fall.

Some artists have already started to accept the situation, and instead of fighting the "problems" have started to look for opportunities. Marginal production costs are zero, and with
(60) software applications, it doesn't cost anything to produce another digital copy that would be as good as the original; as soon as the first copy exists, anyone can create additional copies. Unless effective technical, legal or other artificial
(65) barriers to production can be created, simple economic theory dictates that zero marginal cost plus competition (the possibility that the consumer will create and spread another copy) results in a zero price, unless government creates
(70) artificial barriers to a free market.

In October 2007, Radiohead announced that their new album *In Rainbows* would be available to download free of charge. But the networks and file-sharing systems had grown even easier to use
(75) than what Radiohead was offering. Radiohead's only requirement was for downloaders to set up an account on their website, but according to the statistics, that turned out to be not "cheap" enough.

(80) A new era is coming—the era of free music. Recorded music will become one of the marketing tools to get people to pay for live concerts, which will put emphasis on performance quality, resulting in cultural socialization and stronger
(85) musical communites. In countries like Brazil, people have already started to use the situation as an opportunity, doing huge amounts of remixes, resulting in new styles and music cultures like Techno Brega.

(90) Record labels are going down, struggling to make profits from CD sales, and it appears that digital music selling is more reliable for revenue. Copyright and intellectual-property law have to be updated, and the CD-sales model has to
(95) be reinvented as the CD-promotional model in order to regain the value of a physical product with the emphasis now on live performances.

11. The passage's author most strongly implies that over time, record companies:
   A. reported increased profits as production costs increasingly approached zero.
   B. have taken positive steps to build stronger musical communities.
   C. have broken the law by trying to sue everybody.
   D. began feeling as if they had the right to charge people for the services of others.

12. According to the passage, the "new era" mentioned in line 80 will partly be characterized by:
   F. increased governmental regulation of the record industry.
   G. recorded music being used mainly to promote concerts.
   H. increased popularity in the United States of foreign musical styles such as Techno Brega.
   J. reinvention of the CD-sales model so that CD sales will become more profitable than ever.

13. As portrayed in the passage, so-called music "piracy" has been:
   A. increased by the public's mastery of difficult computer software.
   B. decreased by successful updating of intellectual-property laws.
   C. increased by the user-friendliness of downloading sites and programs.
   D. decreased by the record industry's appeals to conscience.

14. In the statement in lines 59–70, the author most strongly stresses:
   F. his opinion that more government intervention in the matter is necessary.
   G. the economic realities of where the record business is headed.
   H. the suspicion that most consumers are distributing free music to their friends.
   J. his distrust of the free market as it applies to the music business of today.

15. According to the passage, the reaction of record companies to the realities of the digital age has been to:
   A. stubbornly demand unchanged profits in exchange for fewer provided services.
   B. put more advertising money into the promotion of live performances.
   C. start depicting themselves as an arm of the federal government.
   D. look for opportunities in the "problems" and reform their business model.

16. The passage most strongly suggests that the author sees the modern music-consuming public as behaving:
   F. dishonorably.
   G. aggressively.
   H. logically.
   J. unimaginatively.

17. In lines 2–7, the author depicts an example of what he feels is:
   A. young music pirates beginning to see themselves as a unified group with common interests.
   B. record companies using their connections to influence legislation in illegal ways.
   C. a commonsense move that will become normal in the near future.
   D. the government passing responsibility for music piracy onto an institution not directly related to it.

18. The passage's author characterizes peer-to-peer filesharing technology as:
   F. something that should be approached with caution, as it is still in its infancy.
   G. something that will ultimately lead to increased creativity on the part of musicians.
   H. something that the record companies should have more direct control over.
   J. the most significant artistic development of the twenty-first century so far.

19. For the author, lines 90–97 mainly serve to support his earlier point that:

A. the CD will soon be a thing of the past.

B. most CDs will soon have data on them other than music.

C. CDs will continue to exist, but serve a different purpose.

D. CDs will soon only be manufactured by the consumers themselves.

20. Another cultural analyst discussing the controversy over peer-to-peer filesharing has this to say:

We have to ask whether allowing or prohibiting filesharing would promote the greatest amount of happiness for the greatest amount of people. Thus, we have to examine how many people are affected by the prohibition or permission of filesharing.

How does this account compare to that of the passage's author?

F. Both agree that the record companies have been foolish to ignore the way things are headed.

G. Both agree that the actions taken by music consumers have been predictable, if not necessarily morally correct.

H. The second author feels that filesharing is a matter of individual conscience, whereas the author of the passage feels it should be up to the law to decide.

J. The second author attempts to apply universal moral truths to the issue, whereas the author of the passage is more of a pragmatic realist.

PASSAGE III—HUMANITIES

This passage is adapted from the essay "Why TV Lost" by Paul Graham (© 2009 Paul Graham).

Moore's Law is a principle of computer hardware engineering stating that the number of transistors on an integrated circuit will double every two years.

(5) About twenty years ago people noticed computers and TV were on a collision course and started to speculate about what they'd produce when they converged. We now know the answer: computers. It's clear now that even by using the (10) word "convergence" we were giving TV too much credit. This won't be convergence so much as replacement. People may still watch things they call "TV shows," but they'll watch them mostly on computers.

(15) What decided the contest for computers? Four forces, three of which one could have predicted, and one that would have been harder to. One predictable cause of victory is that the Internet is an open platform. Anyone can build (20) whatever they want on it, and the market picks the winners. So innovation happens at hacker speeds instead of big-company speeds. The second is Moore's Law, which has worked its usual magic on Internet bandwidth. The third (25) reason computers won is piracy. Users prefer it not just because it's free, but because it's more convenient. BitTorrent and YouTube have already trained a new generation of viewers that the place to watch shows is on a computer screen.

(30) The somewhat more surprising force was one specific type of innovation: social applications. The average teenage kid has a pretty much infinite capacity for talking to their friends. But they can't physically be with them all the time. (35) When I was in high school the solution was the telephone. Now it's social networks, multiplayer games, and various messaging applications. The way you reach them all is through a computer, which means every teenage kid wants a computer (40) with an Internet connection, has an incentive to figure out how to use it, and spends countless hours in front of it.

After decades of running an IV drip right into their audience, people in the entertainment (45) business had understandably come to think of them as rather passive. They thought they'd be able to dictate the way shows reached audiences. But they underestimated the force of their desire to connect with one another. Facebook killed

(50) TV. That is wildly oversimplified, of course, but probably as close to the truth as you can get in three words.

The TV networks already seem, grudgingly, to see where things are going, and have responded (55) by putting their stuff, grudgingly, online. But they're still dragging their heels. They still seem to wish people would watch shows on TV instead, just as newspapers that put their stories online still seem to wish people would wait till the next (60) morning and read them printed on paper. They should both just face the fact that the Internet is the primary medium.

They'd be in a better position if they'd done that earlier. When a new medium arises that's (65) powerful enough to make incumbents nervous, then it's probably powerful enough to win, and the best thing they can do is jump in immediately. Whether they like it or not, big changes are coming, because the Internet dissolves the two (70) cornerstones of broadcast media: synchronicity and locality. On the Internet, you don't have to send everyone the same signal, and you don't have to send it to them from a local source. People will watch what they want when they want it, (75) and group themselves according to whatever shared interest they feel most strongly. Maybe their strongest shared interest will be their physical location, but I'm guessing not—which means local TV is probably dead. It was an arti- (80) fact of limitations imposed by old technology. If someone were creating an Internet-based TV company from scratch now, they might have some plan for shows aimed at specific regions, but it wouldn't be a top priority.

(85) TV networks will fight these trends, because they don't have sufficient flexibility to adapt to them. They're hemmed in by local affiliates in much the same way car companies are hemmed in by dealers and unions. Inevitably, the people (90) running the networks will take the easy route and try to keep the old model running for a couple more years, just as the record labels have done.

The networks used to be gatekeepers. They distributed your work, and sold advertising on (95) it. Now the people who produce a show can distribute it themselves. The main value networks supply now is ad sales, which will tend to put them in the position of service providers rather than publishers.

(100) Shows will change even more. On the Internet there's no reason to keep their current format, or even the fact that they have a single format. Indeed, the more interesting sort of convergence that's coming is between shows and games. But (105) on the question of what sort of entertainment gets distributed on the Internet in 20 years, I wouldn't dare to make any predictions, except that things will change a lot. We'll get whatever the most imaginative people can cook up.

(110) That's why the Internet won.

21. The passage's author most strongly implies that over time, TV's hold over its audience grew:
   A. stronger, because people group themselves according to shared interests.
   B. weaker, due to the effects of Moore's Law on the content of Web programming.
   C. stronger, because TV shows are always changing to better reflect the times.
   D. weaker, because of limitations in the medium of TV and formats of TV shows.

22. According to the passage, which of the following is NOT an obvious predictable force that led to the supremacy of computers?
   F. Facebook
   G. The magic of Internet bandwidth
   H. Free pirated content
   J. The Internet's status as an open platform

23. As portrayed in the passage, the computer industry has benefited from the fact that teenagers are:

A. energetic and social.

B. adaptable but lazy.

C. friendly but shy.

D. trendy and easily amused.

24. In the statement in lines 73–78, the author most strongly stresses the:

F. idea that people should take more of an interest in their physical location.

G. fact that national news covers more important issues than local news.

H. fact that TV's self-image is based on the technological limitations of the past.

J. threat of local stations being outcompeted or bought up by national networks.

25. According to the passage, the reaction of TV networks to the Internet phenomenon has been to:

A. try to dissolve the cornerstones of the Internet.

B. rush to put all their content on the Internet, just as newspapers put their stories online.

C. put some of what they produce on the Web, but resist the change in spirit.

D. become hemmed in by local affiliates, in an effort to develop sufficient flexibility.

26. The passage most strongly suggests that the author sees traditional media outlets like TV and newspapers as exhibiting:

F. determined originality.

G. resentful stubbornness.

H. open hostility.

J. petulant solicitousness.

27. Lines 89–92 most nearly mean that the networks:

A. will try their best to converge with the record labels.

B. will wait for Web-based business models to make innovations and then buy them out.

C. are fighting among themselves about what their next step should be.

D. will squeeze as much life as possible out of their current business practices.

28. The passage's author characterizes the younger generation as being:

F. prohibitively ignorant of the rich histories of TV and newspapers.

G. soundly conditioned to the idea of computers meeting all their entertainment needs.

H. easily amused by culturally destructive habits like social networking.

J. unintentionally subversive of international commerce in the twenty-first century.

29. For the author, lines 79–84 mainly serve to support his earlier point that:

A. Internet writers still have fewer plans for shows than TV writers do.

B. Internet companies have done better market research than TV networks have.

C. programming aimed at specific regions is not what people really want.

D. Internet creators are true artists who have priorities other than making money.

30. Another cultural analyst discussing the relationship between TV and the Internet had this to say:

> The era of appointment-to-view TV is coming to an end. It will continue to exist for the simple reason that some things—like, say, a World Cup final—are best covered using a few-to-many technology. But it will lose its dominant position in the ecosystem.

How does this account compare to that of the passage's author?

F. Both agree that sooner or later the Internet will completely replace TV.

G. Both agree that the battle between TV and the Internet will go on forever.

H. This account suggests that TV's dominance will continue, whereas the passage does not.

J. This account concedes that TV is better suited to some things, whereas the passage does not.

PASSAGE IV—NATURAL SCIENCE

This passage is adapted from "The Creepy Scientific Explanation Behind Ghost Sightings" by Jack Mendoza, which appeared on cracked.com (October, 2010).

There is simply no evidence that dead people wander aimlessly around old houses, and no known scientific principle that would make it possible, but a lot of people have seen ghosts.
(5) There are certain spots and buildings where separate, unrelated witnesses have reported ghosts, without having talked to each other or being aware of the area being "haunted."

It appears that science has stumbled across
(10) the reason for it. It has nothing to do with the supernatural, but the answer is almost as weird. While working in his robotics laboratory, Vladimir Gavreau noticed that one of his assistants was bleeding from the ears. Puzzled, Gavreau started

(15) researching the phenomenon, and soon realized that a vibrating pipe of the right length and girth can cause a number of unpleasant effects ranging from mild irritation to serious pain.

What he had discovered was infrasound. It's
(20) noise at a low enough frequency that you don't consciously hear it, but your ears still sense it. The process of receiving sensory input without your conscious mind understanding where it's coming from wreaks havoc with your emotions.
(25) Specifically, researchers found that sounds between 7 and 19 Hz could induce fear, dread or panic.

As an experiment, acoustic scientists sneaked in low-frequency sounds at a live concert. Most of the concertgoers had no idea what was going
(30) on. At the end of the experiment, 22 percent of the people involved reported feelings of unexplainable dread, chills and depression when infrasound was blasted into the crowd.

Why would it have this effect? It may be evo-
(35) lution. It doesn't take a mad-scientist device to create infrasound: nature creates this type of low-frequency vibration all the time. Volcanos, earthquakes, strong ocean waves and even winds hitting the hillside in just the right spot can cre-
(40) ate infrasound. Even animals can create it. The frequency of a tiger's roar is around 18 Hz. All the things that create the sound are huge, powerful and dangerous. Evolution might have taught us that this sound means bad news.

(45) So now we have a phenomenon that occurs in nature, is invisible, is imperceptible on a conscious level, but can spontaneously make you feel irrational fear, even if you're sitting in an empty room. We've just described one of the first
(50) and primary signs of a "haunting"—unexplained feelings of fear or dread. But what about actual *sightings* of ghosts? For that we need to go to a researcher named Vic Tandy. In the engineering building where Tandy worked, cleaning staff as
(55) well as fellow researchers complained of feeling dread, depression and a strange feeling that someone was watching them. Every so often, the staff would see dark figures out of the corners

of their eyes. After one particularly strange ex-
(60) perience when a gray shape sat next to his desk
for several minutes, Tandy was determined to
figure out what was going on. After eliminating
gas poisoning and rogue equipment, he realized
that the ghostly apparitions seemed to almost
(65) always occur in a certain section of the lab. He
also realized that if he put a metal sheet in a vice,
it would spontaneously vibrate uncontrollably
for no apparent reason.

Poltergeist? No, just infrasound. A silent exhaust
(70) fan was sending out low-frequency vibrations
that bounced back and forth on the lab's walls
until they formed a powerful wave at 18.9 Hz,
right at the top of the panic range. According to
a NASA study, it was powerful enough to reso-
(75) nate with the average human eyeball, causing
"smeared" vision, a phenomenon where the
eye vibrates just enough to register something
static—say, the frame of your glasses or a speck
of dust—as large, moving shapes. Once the fan
(80) was removed, the strange apparitions and feelings of fear disappeared.

Convinced that he had stumbled onto something, Tandy went on to test this explanation
for ghostly apparitions in the cellar of a nearby
(85) "haunted" abbey. According to the locals, as soon
as someone would step into the cellar they would
freeze up, see strange gray ghosts and have to
leave because of nausea. Vic discovered that the
shape of the cellar and the hallway leading to
(90) it, as well as nearby factories, all contributed to
making the haunted cellar a perfect resonating
chamber. The vibrations created were exactly
18.9 Hz and were most powerful at the threshold
of the cellar, where most people became sick
(95) and terrified.

So if you're ever troubled by strange noises in
the middle of the night or you experience feelings of dread in your basement or attic or even
if someone in your family sees a ghost .... Well,
(100) call the repair guy, because it might be caused
by a malfunctioning ventilation fan.

31. The primary purpose of the passage is to:
   A. suggest that the vast majority of ghost
      sightings have in fact been elaborate
      hoaxes.
   B. explain why legends about supernatural
      experiences have gotten more numerous
      as technology advanced.
   C. suggest that the myths associated with
      ghosts and hauntings are caused by an
      explainable phenomenon.
   D. gently satirize the types of people who
      claim to have seen ghosts or believe in
      hauntings.

32. The main function of the fifth paragraph
   (lines 34–44) in relation to the passage as a
   whole is to:
   F. explain that most people who reported
      supernatural experiences were probably
      actually hearing animals.
   G. suggest that virtually anyone could
      successfully fake a haunting without a lot
      of elaborate equipment.
   H. argue in favor of belief in evolution over
      belief in supernatural things like ghosts.
   J. explain why humans would have evolved
      the responses that cause them to imagine
      ghosts.

33. The author uses the story of the concert
   experiment (lines 27–33) primarily to
   demonstrate that:
   A. the feelings normally reported in
      conjunction with a "haunting" are
      replicable even in people who are not
      expecting to feel them.
   B. the percentage of people who respond
      to infrasound goes down when they are
      exposed to it in large groups.
   C. many reported supernatural experiences
      are probably the result of elaborate pranks.
   D. the scientists who developed the
      infrasound theory of hauntings were
      irresponsible, and therefore further study
      is needed.

34. The scientific theories described in the passage would appear to explain all of the phenomena traditionally associated with ghosts and haunting EXCEPT:
    F. sudden feelings of unease or panic.
    G. information supposedly communicated by ghosts.
    H. personal injury supposedly inflicted by ghosts.
    J. distinct, moving visual apparitions.

35. According to the author, it's entirely possible that most of the people in history who reported seeing ghosts were actually:
    A. making an honest mistake.
    B. unusually superstitious, even for their time.
    C. inventing stories to explain their inexplicable emotions.
    D. knowledgeable about science.

36. According to the passage, Tandy discovered that the cause of ghost apparitions was the result of a (an):
    F. animal's roar at 14 Hz.
    G. powerful wind vibrating at 7 Hz.
    H. ventilation fan vibrating at 12 Hz.
    J. silent exhaust fan vibrating at 18 Hz.

37. As it is used in line 24, *havoc* most nearly means:
    A. depression.
    B. chaos.
    C. misunderstanding.
    D. surprise.

38. In the context of the passage, the phrase "bad news" most nearly represents something:
    F. liable to cause depression and sadness.
    G. incomprehensible to the human mind.
    H. real and potentially dangerous.
    J. imaginary and potentially frightening.

39. The passage indicates that Vladimir Gavreau was initially motivated by a desire to:
    A. discover infrasound.
    B. find a scientific explanation for ghost sightings.
    C. investigate a specific physical ailment.
    D. make his work with robotics more efficient.

40. Suppose a group of researchers wanted to construct a "haunted house." They would most likely need to make use of:
    F. a device sending out vibrations at a certain frequency.
    G. live animals.
    H. rooms of a precise, predetermined shape.
    J. both F and H.

If there is still time remaining, you may review your answers.

SCIENCE TEST

Time: 35 Minutes—40 Questions

> **Directions:** There are six passages in this test. Each passage is followed by several questions. After reading a passage, choose the best answer to each question and fill in the corresponding oval on your answer sheet. You may refer to the passages as often as necessary.
>
> You are NOT permitted to use a calculator on this test.

PASSAGE I

A *catalyst* is a substance that speeds up a reaction, but is chemically unchanged at the end of the reaction. Catalysts can be divided into two main types—*heterogeneous* and *homogeneous*. In a heterogeneous reaction, the catalyst is in a different phase (such as solid, liquid, or gas) from the reactants. In a homogeneous reaction, the catalyst is in the same phase as the reactants. Most examples of heterogeneous catalysis go through the same stages (see Table 1).

Table 1

Stage	Description
1	One or more of the reactants are absorbed onto the surface of the catalyst.
2	There is some sort of interaction between the surface of the catalyst and the reactant molecules, which makes them more reactive.
3	The reaction happens.
4	The product molecules are desorbed, meaning that the product molecules break away.

Students did experiments to convert propanol to propene using alumina beads, and then to convert propene to propanol using a palladium catalyst.

Experiment 1

Two glass syringes were connected to an alumina-bead catalyst tube (see Figure 1). The 1 mL syringe was filled with 1 mL of propanol. Next, the apparatus was held above a burner's flame and the alumina-bead catalyst tube was gently heated while the liquid propanol was slowly introduced into the catalyst tube. The liquid flowed through the tube until it hit the hot region. Then it vaporized, reacted with the catalyst, and exited the catalyst tube as gaseous propene into the 60-mL receiver syringe. The procedure was repeated with various amounts of propanol and alumina beads and the amount of gaseous propene collected was recorded (see Table 2).

Figure 1

Table 2

Trial	Volume of Propanol (mL)	Volume of Alumina Beads (g)	Volume of Propene (mL)
1	1	1.75	58
2	1	1	49
3	0.5	1.75	28
4	0.75	1.75	45

Experiment 2

A reactant syringe was filled with equal volumes of hydrogen and propene. The reactant syringe and receiver syringe were connected to the catalyst tube filled with solid palladium as shown in Figure 2. Then the hydrogen-propene mixture was slowly passed over the catalyst, the reaction occurred, and the propane was collected in the receiver syringe. The procedure was repeated several times, varying the amount of time the reactant was passed over the catalyst. The results are shown in Table 3.

Figure 2

Table 3

Trial	Volume of Hydrogen (mL)	Volume of Propene (mL)	Time Reactant Passed Over Catalyst(s)	Volume of Propane in Receiver Syringe (mL)
1	30	30	60	56
2	30	30	45	52
3	30	30	30	49
4	30	30	15	0

1. In Experiment 2, as the amount of time the reactant was passed over the catalyst decreased, the volume of propane created:
   A. increased only.
   B. decreased only.
   C. increased and then remained constant.
   D. decreased and then remained constant.

2. Which is the most likely explanation for why 0 mL of propane was produced in Trial 4 of Experiment 2?
   F. There was not enough volume of hydrogen and propene to create a reaction.
   G. Fifteen seconds was too long a time for the reactant to pass over the catalyst.
   H. There was not enough volume of palladium in the catalyst tube to create a reaction and produce propane.
   J. The reactant was not allowed enough time to interact with the catalyst; therefore, no reaction occurred and no propane was produced.

3. What type of catalyst was used in Experiment 1?
   A. It cannot be determined from the information given.
   B. A liquid catalyst
   C. A heterogeneous catalyst
   D. A homogeneous catalyst

4. In Experiment 2, the hydrogen-propene mixture turns into propane at what stage of the catalysis?
   F. Stage 1
   G. Stage 2
   H. Stage 3
   J. Stage 4

5. Based on the data in Table 2, which two trials illustrate the effect that varying the volume of the catalyst has on the volume of propene produced?
   A. Trials 1 and 2
   B. Trials 1 and 3
   C. Trials 3 and 4
   D. Trials 2 and 4

6. Which of the following best describes what occurred to the plunger of the 60-mL syringe during Experiment 1? When propanol was injected into the catalyst tube, the distance between the end of the plunger and the syringe tip:
   F. decreased slowly over 30 seconds.
   G. increased immediately, and then decreased as the reaction occurred.
   H. remained in place until the reaction occurred, and then decreased.
   J. remained in place until the reaction occurred, and then increased.

7. In Experiment 2, what is the best explanation as to why the volume of hydrogen and propene remained the same throughout all four trials?
   A. Only a certain amount of propane and hydrogen could fit in the syringe.
   B. When conducting this experiment, propene and hydrogen acted as control variables.
   C. When conducting this experiment, the scientists used the propane and hydrogen as the catalyst.
   D. In higher amounts, the propane and hydrogen would convert to vapor and stop the chemical reaction.

PRACTICE TEST 6

PASSAGE II

Table 1 lists two genes found in *Sesamum indicum* (sesame), the possible alleles of each gene, and the possible genotypes for each gene.

Table 1

Gene	Alleles	Genotypes
P	P, p	PP, Pp, pp
L	L, l	LL, Ll, ll

Table 2 lists various sesame genotypes and the phenotype associated with each genotype. Each gene affects only one of the phenotype traits listed.

Table 2

Genotype	Phenotype	
	Pod Number	Leaf Texture
PPLL	1	normal
PpLL	1	normal
ppLL	3	normal
ppLl	3	normal
PpLl	1	normal
PPLl	1	normal
PPll	1	wrinkled
Ppll	1	wrinkled
ppll	3	wrinkled

Table 3 lists four sesame plant crosses, the genotypes of the parents, and the percent of offspring that had each phenotype for the traits listed in Table 2. In each cross, each parent donated one allele to each offspring at each gene.

Table 3

	Genotype of:		Offspring Phenotype	
Cross	Female parent	Male parent	Pod number	Leaf texture
1	PpLL	ppll	50% 1 pod	50% normal
2	PpLl	Ppll	75% 1 pod	50% wrinkled
3	ppLl	ppLl	100% 3 pods	75% normal
4	PPLL	PPLL	100% 1 pod	100% normal

8. Based on Table 2, which of the 2 genes affects leaf texture?
    F. P
    G. L
    H. Neither
    J. Both

9. Based on Table 2, a sesame plant with 2 recessive alleles for each of the 2 genes will have which of the following phenotypes?
    A. 1 pod and normal leaves
    B. 3 pods and normal leaves
    C. 3 pods and wrinkled leaves
    D. 1 pod and wrinkled leaves

10. Based on the information provided, all of the offspring of Cross 3 had 3 pods because each received:
    F. allele p from its female parent and allele p from its male parent.
    G. allele L from its female parent and allele l from its male parent.
    H. allele l from its female parent and allele L from its male parent.
    J. allele P from its female parent and allele P from its male parent.

11. In Cross 3, what percent of the offspring had genotype pp?
    A. 0%
    B. 25%
    C. 50%
    D. 100%

12. Based on the information provided, a sesame plant with 3 pods and normal leaves could have which of the following genotypes?
    F. PPll
    G. PPLL
    H. ppll
    J. ppLl

13. A farmer wants to grow a sesame plant with 1 pod and wrinkled leaves. Which sesame plant cross in Table 3 has the greatest chance of producing this offspring?
    A. Cross 1
    B. Cross 2
    C. Cross 3
    D. Cross 4

PRACTICE TEST 6

PASSAGE III

Ecological *indicators* are used to assess the condition of the environment, to provide early warning signals of changes in the environment, or to diagnose the cause of environmental problems. Some important criteria for selecting an indicator include:

1. The indicator should provide an accurate picture of what it is supposed to indicate, such as "ecosystem health."
2. The indicator should respond quickly to environmental changes.
3. The indicator should be easy to monitor.
4. The responses of the indicator in one or a few locations should indicate the state of the ecosystem in a larger area.

It has been suggested that seabirds are useful indicators. Two researchers discuss the effectiveness of using seabirds as indicators.

Researcher 1

Seabirds are valuable indicators because they are top predators in their ecosystem. Seabird populations and reproduction rates are regulated by prey abundance, and will therefore reflect environmentally induced changes in prey availability. The effects of reductions in prey resources, such as declining numbers of seabirds, are usually very rapid, due to the short food chain, which is another advantage.

A few species of small fishes are important species of the ecosystem, having a major effect on the ecosystem as a whole. Seabirds that eat mainly these key fish are good indicators of the ecosystem in general.

Additional demographic parameters that can easily be monitored in seabirds are population size, duration of foraging trips, and changes in body mass and offspring growth rate, all of which are useful environmental monitors.

Overall, seabirds are a cost-effective, useful, and meaningful indicator of environmental changes in ocean ecosystems.

Researcher 2

There are several reasons why seabirds may not be suitable as indicators of the impacts of environmental changes. First of all, not all marine ecosystems follow a top-down food chain. Some marine food webs are dynamic and can alternate between bottom-up and top-down. In addition, change in seabird numbers due to food scarcity usually has a lag of several months or even years. Because of this seabirds are not suitable as indicators of the food supply in all ecosystems.

In general, the effect of environmental change on seabird populations may take many years to become apparent. Its effect is complex and involves many physical and biological processes. This is a severe drawback to using seabirds as indicators. Another drawback is the handling effect. It is not fully understood what effect handling seabirds has on them. There is some evidence that bands placed on penguins to track them can reduce both breeding success and survival rates. With seabirds that are tagged and handled, it is difficult to be sure that observed effects are actually due to changes in the environment and not other factors.

The effect of environmental changes on seabirds is complex and it is not clear what the best way to monitor seabirds is. Therefore, seabirds are not a good choice for indicators.

PRACTICE TEST 6

14. Based on Researcher 1's discussion, demographic factors that can be easily monitored in seabirds include all of the following EXCEPT:
   F. population size.
   G. changes in offspring growth rate.
   H. mortality rates.
   J. length of foraging trips.

15. Sardines are plentiful in Chiriqui Bay, and their presence affects the entire ecosystem of the bay. Kingfisher birds eat mostly sardines and because their numbers are declining, scientists are concerned about the environmental health of Chiriqui Bay. Is this concern consistent with the viewpoint of Researcher 1?
   A. No, because Researcher 1 states that changes in the food chain are not adequate indicators of the environmental health of a body of water.
   B. No, because Researcher 1 states that only changes in body mass and offspring growth rate are valuable indicators of environmental changes.
   C. Yes, because Researcher 1 states that the effect of environmental changes on seabirds will be slow due to the short food chain in a marine ecosystem.
   D. Yes, because Researcher 1 states that seabirds that consume key fish in an ecosystem are valuable indicators of the ecosystem in general.

16. Which researcher believes that handling seabirds may affect the validity of the results gathered by monitoring them?
   F. Researcher 1, because that researcher states that changes in prey resources are very quick, and therefore results gathered will be valid.
   G. Researcher 1, because that researcher states that overall, seabirds are a useful indicator of environmental changes.
   H. Researcher 2, because that researcher states that placing bands on penguins has been shown to reduce their survival rates.
   J. Researcher 2, because that researcher states that it is clear that handling seabirds will always reduce their breeding rates.

17. A study found that within two months of an oil spill in a bay, there was a drastic reduction in the number of small forage fish found in the water, and that the number of seabirds in the area was drastically reduced as well. Which researcher would most likely use this study to support his or her viewpoint?
   A. Researcher 1, because it would demonstrate how quickly environmental changes impact prey resources and seabird behavior.
   B. Researcher 1, because it would demonstrate how important seabirds are for the overall ecosystem.
   C. Researcher 2, because it would demonstrate how quickly environmental changes impact prey resources and seabird behavior.
   D. Researcher 2, because it would demonstrate how important seabirds are for the overall ecosystem.

PRACTICE TEST 6

18. Based on Researcher 2's discussion, seabirds would not be effective indicators because they do not meet which criteria of a good indicator?

  F. Point 1 only
  G. Points 1 and 2 only
  H. Points 1, 2, and 3 only
  J. Points 2 and 3 only

19. Which of the following graphs is most consistent with Researcher 1's view on the relationship between prey abundance and seabird population?

  A.

  B.

  C.

  D.

20. Researcher 2 cites all of the following as reasons why seabirds may not be suitable as indicators EXCEPT:

  F. the impact of food scarcity on seabird numbers may not be apparent for several months or years.
  G. it is not known how handling seabirds might impact them.
  H. it is expensive to use seabirds as indicators.
  J. it is uncertain how to best monitor seabirds.

PASSAGE IV

Scientists used gas chromatography to analyze benzene concentrations in fuel vapors. The results of the analysis are displayed in Table 1.

Samples from four different brands of fuel were collected, with each brand offering both leaded and unleaded versions of fuel. A portion of each sample was analyzed for benzene concentration in the liquid, while the rest of the sample was placed in a vial and prepared for vapor analysis. Each vial was put into an oven, heated, and the gas chromatograph detected the concentrations of benzene in the vapor. Figure 1 displays the oven temperature during the experiment.

Figure 1

Table 1

Brand	Liquid (mg/l)	Vapor (mg/l)
A (leaded)	191	431
A (unleaded)	198	334
B (leaded)	176	447
B (unleaded)	271	414
C (leaded)	245	500
C (unleaded)	222	488
D (leaded)	197	513
D (unleaded)	264	350

A *gasohol* is a fuel blended with certain alcohols such as ethanol or methanol. Two of the fuels tested in this experiment (brands C and D) were gasohols. Figure 2 shows the average concentrations of benzene found in the liquid and vapor form of the leaded and unleaded fuels tested. Figure 3 compares the average concentrations of benzene found in gasohols and regular unleaded fuels.

Figure 2

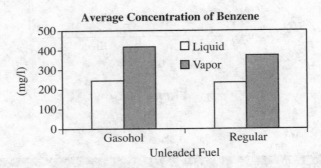

Figure 3

PRACTICE TEST 6

21. According to Figure 2, the average concentration of benzene found in the liquid form of leaded fuel was approximately:
    A. 200 mg/l.
    B. 240 mg/l.
    C. 480 mg/l.
    D. 400 mg/l.

22. Based on Figure 2, which type of fuel tested was found to contain the highest average concentration of benzene?
    F. Liquid unleaded
    G. Liquid leaded
    H. Vapor leaded
    J. Vapor unleaded

23. Suppose that during the experiment the samples of fuel had been kept in the oven for 20 minutes. Based on Figure 1, the temperature in the oven after 20 minutes would most likely have been:
    A. less than 100°C.
    B. between 100°C and 150°C.
    C. between 150°C and 200°C.
    D. greater than 200°C.

24. A scientist claimed that, in liquid form, a leaded fuel would emit more benzene than an unleaded fuel. Does the data in Table 1 support this claim?
    F. Yes. For all fuel brands tested, the benzene levels were higher in the leaded fuel than in the unleaded fuel.
    G. Yes. For all fuels tested, the amount of benzene found in the vapor form was higher than that found in the liquid form.
    H. No. The amount of benzene found in the leaded fuel was only higher than the amount found in the unleaded fuel for one brand tested.
    J. No. Only nongasohols emit more benzene in the leaded version of the fuel.

25. According to Figure 3, how did vaporizing the gasohol fuels affect the average concentration of benzene found in the fuel? In the gasohol fuels, the average concentration of benzene found in the liquid form of the gas was about:
    A. two times the average concentration found in the vapor form.
    B. one-half the average concentration found in the vapor form.
    C. one-quarter the average concentration found in the vapor form.
    D. the same as the average concentration found in the vapor form.

26. If scientists wish to recommend to car manufacturers a fuel that puts off the lowest amount of benzene in vapor form, which brand fuel would they recommend?
    F. B (leaded)
    G. D (leaded)
    H. C (leaded)
    J. A (unleaded)

PRACTICE TEST 6

PASSAGE V

Students conducted experiments to determine what factors affect the *period* of a *pendulum*. A pendulum is a swinging weight, or bob, attached to a string (see Figure 1). When released from an angle, a pendulum will move back and forth. One complete back-and-forth movement is called a *period*.

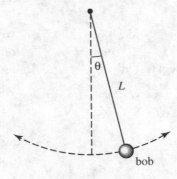

θ

L

bob

Figure 1

Three variables may affect the period of a pendulum: swing amplitude, measured as the angle at which the bob is released; the length of the string; and the mass of the bob. Students created pendulums by attaching a string to the ceiling and then tying a bob onto the other end of the string. They conducted three experiments. In each experiment all variables except the one tested were kept constant.

Experiment 1

In this experiment students varied the mass of the bob. Bobs of 20 g, 100 g, and 200 g were tested for three trials each. The string length was 1 m and the amplitude was 45 degrees. The results are shown in Table 1.

Table 1

Mass (g)	Trial 1 (s)	Trial 2 (s)	Trial 3 (s)	Average Period (s)
20	1.72	1.81	1.84	1.79
100	1.78	1.82	1.88	1.83
200	1.9	1.85	1.91	1.89

Experiment 2

The second variable tested was amplitude. Bobs were dropped from 15-, 45-, and 75-degree angles for three trials each. The string length was 1 m and the bobs used were 100 g. Figure 2 displays the average results.

PRACTICE TEST 6

Figure 2

Experiment 3

Next the students tested the effect of varying the string length. Strings of 1 m, 0.6 m, and 0.3 m were tested in three trials each; 100 g bobs were used and the amplitude was 45 degrees. The results are displayed in Table 2 and Figure 3.

Table 2

Length (m)	Trial 1 (s)	Trial 2 (s)	Trial 3 (s)	Average Period (s)
1	1.85	1.84	1.84	1.84
0.6	1.44	1.44	1.47	1.45
0.3	0.97	1.06	1.06	1.03

Figure 3

PRACTICE TEST 6

27. Based on the results of Experiment 1, the average period for a bob of 100 g was:
   A. 1.79 s.
   B. 1.83 s.
   C. 1.89 s.
   D. 1.91 s.

28. If an additional trial had been conducted in Experiment 3 with the length of the string being 0.8 m, the average period would most likely have been:
   F. between 1.03 and 1.45.
   G. between 1.45 and 1.84.
   H. less than 1.45.
   J. greater than 1.84.

29. For each trial in Experiment 1, as the mass of the bob increased, the time of the period:
   A. stayed the same.
   B. increased.
   C. decreased.
   D. increased and then decreased.

30. Based on the information presented in Figure 2, which of the following pendulums would have the longest average period? Assume that the string length and bob weight are equal.

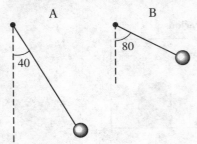

   F. Pendulum A
   G. Pendulum B
   H. The average period would be about the same.
   J. It is impossible to determine from the information given.

31. In Experiment 3, Trial 2, how long did it take the pendulum with the string length of 0.6 m to complete one back-and-forth movement?
   A. 1.06 s
   B. 1.44 s
   C. 1.47 s
   D. 1.84 s

32. Which of the following variables was NOT tested during the experiments conducted by the students?
   F. Mass of the bob
   G. Length of string
   H. Size of bob
   J. Swing amplitude

33. In Experiment 3, 100 g bobs were used and the amplitude was 45 degrees for all trials conducted. What is the best explanation for why the students didn't vary the mass and amplitude in each experiment?
   A. The experiment was designed to test the effects of varying string length, so the mass and amplitude were the control variables in the experiment.
   B. The pendulum did not allow for a string longer than 1 meter.
   C. There was no way to vary the amplitude when the string length was smaller than 1 meter.
   D. The experiment was designed to test the effects of amplitude and mass, so those variables could not be changed in the experiment.

PRACTICE TEST 6

PASSAGE VI

Scientists conducted a series of experiments to determine the effect of changes in temperature on the intertidal rocky shore crab, *Petrolisthes granulosus* (*P. granulosus*). Several fitness-related traits, such as body size and reproductive capacity in *P. granulosus* individuals from three sites were compared after the crabs were exposed to various temperatures. In addition, metabolic rate experiments were conducted to determine the energetic cost associated with crab exposure to high temperatures.

Table 1 displays the temperatures (°C) used in the experiments. Thermal category TC1 refers to the maximum temperature registered at each site, while TC2 refers to the average of maximum temperatures recorded every day. The Control thermal category is defined as the average temperature experienced by the crabs during the acclimation period.

Table 1

Thermal Category	Site		
	Iquique	Coquimbo	Concepcion
TC1	26	22	19
TC2	22	20	17
Control	16	16	16

Figure 1 displays the average size (cephalothorax length) of *P. granulosus* in the 3 populations, while Figure 2 displays the average egg volume in the 3 populations.

Average Size

Figure 1

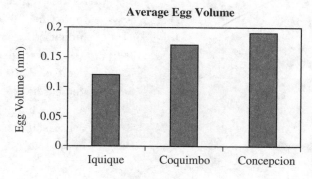

Average Egg Volume

Figure 2

Figure 3 shows the average standard metabolic rates (SMR) of male crabs from the 3 populations exposed to 3 thermal categories.

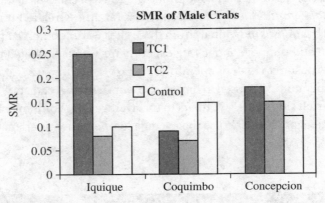

Figure 3

34. According to Table 1, crabs from which site were exposed to the highest temperatures during the experiments?
   F. Iquique
   G. Coquimbo
   H. Concepcion
   J. Crabs at all of the locations were exposed to the same maximum temperatures.

35. Based on the information in Figure 2, the average eggs of crabs from the Coquimbo site were found to be closest to which size?
   A. 0.1 mm
   B. 0.17 mm
   C. 0.2 mm
   D. 0.25 mm

36. According to Figure 3, adult male crabs from which category were found to have the highest average standard metabolic rates?
   F. TC1 from Concepcion
   G. Control from Coquimbo
   H. TC1 from Iquique
   J. TC2 from Concepcion

37. Based on the information provided, which of the following best describes the effect that average maximum temperature has on the average size of the crabs?
   A. As the average maximum temperature increased, the average size of the crabs stayed the same.
   B. As the average maximum temperature increased, the average size of the crabs increased.
   C. As the average maximum temperature decreased, the average size of the crabs decreased.
   D. As the average maximum temperature decreased, the average size of the crabs increased.

38. Suppose the scientists had measured the average egg volume of crabs in the control groups. Based on the information in Table 1 and Figure 2, the average egg volume of crabs at the Concepcion site would have been closest to:

F. 0.05 mm.

G. 0.1 mm.

H. 0.2 mm.

J. 0.3 mm.

39. The scientists started this experiment with the theory that crabs exposed to higher temperatures would develop higher standard metabolic rates. Do the results of the experiment support this theory?

A. Yes. The crabs at Iquique in the thermal category TC2 were exposed to the highest temperatures and were found to have the highest SMR.

B. Yes. At all locations the crabs from thermal category TC1 were found to have the highest SMR.

C. No. At all locations the crabs from thermal category TC1 were found to have the lowest SMR.

D No. The results were mixed. At two locations the crabs from thermal category TC1 were found to have the highest SMR, but at one location the crabs from the control group had the highest SMR.

40. According to Table 1 and Figure 3, what is the highest standard metabolic rate for the average maximum temperature registered at each site daily?

F. 0.075

G. 0.15

H. 0.25

J. 0.18

STOP

If there is still time remaining, you may review your answers.

PRACTICE TEST 6

WRITING TEST

Time: 40 Minutes

Video-Game Scholarships

Recently, some U.S. colleges have begun offering scholarships to students based on their skill at video games. But the phenomenon doesn't simply amount to a reward for a talent that was traditionally considered "pointless": the schools have video-gaming teams that compete against those of other colleges, and so the process functions like that of any other college sport. However, in addition to requiring a considerable widening of the definition of "sport," there is another key difference: established college sports like football and basketball generate revenue for schools in the forms of ticket sales and merchandising. Video-game teams, at least so far, do not.

Read and carefully consider these perspectives. Each suggests a particular way of thinking about the prospect of video-game scholarships.

Perspective One	Perspective Two	Perspective Three
Video-games aren't merely "being counted as" a sport—they *are* a sport. True, they aren't physically strenuous, instead relying more on concentration and hand-eye coordination, but the same is true of golf and archery, and nobody claims those don't count as real sports.	The point of college sports isn't just to reward students for whatever they happen to be good at, or to compete against other schools in any old thing just for the sake of competing. It's to celebrate physical prowess alongside intellectual prowess. Real sports achieve this, and video games don't.	The point of school is to learn, not to play games. Traditional college sports were tolerated because they generated revenue and provided a gateway to education for less intellectually gifted students. But unlike football, video-gaming is often a distraction for the brightest kids, the ones whom society most needs to be concentrating on their studies.

ESSAY TASK

Write a unified, coherent essay about video-game scholarships. In your essay, be sure to:

- clearly state your own perspective on the issue and analyze the relationship between your perspective and at least one other perspective
- develop and support your ideas with reasoning and examples
- organize your ideas clearly and logically
- communicate your ideas effectively in standard written English

   Your perspective may be in full agreement with any of those given, in partial agreement, or completely different.

Planning Your Response

Your prewriting notes on this page will not be considered in your score.

Use the following space to brainstorm ideas and map out your response. You may want to think about the following as you analyze the given prompt:

Strengths and weaknesses of the three viewpoints

- What good points do they make, and what potential objections do they ignore?
- Why might they be convincing to readers, and why might their perspectives fall short?

Your previous experience, background knowledge, and personal values

- What is your viewpoint on this topic, and what are the pros and cons of this viewpoint?
- How will you craft an argument in support of your point of view?

If there is still time remaining, you may review your answers.

ANSWER KEY
Practice Test 6

English

1. **C**	16. **J**	31. **B**	46. **J**	61. **A**
2. **J**	17. **D**	32. **J**	47. **C**	62. **G**
3. **B**	18. **G**	33. **D**	48. **F**	63. **A**
4. **F**	19. **C**	34. **H**	49. **B**	64. **J**
5. **B**	20. **F**	35. **A**	50. **H**	65. **B**
6. **J**	21. **A**	36. **J**	51. **A**	66. **H**
7. **A**	22. **J**	37. **D**	52. **J**	67. **B**
8. **H**	23. **A**	38. **G**	53. **A**	68. **J**
9. **D**	24. **J**	39. **C**	54. **G**	69. **A**
10. **J**	25. **C**	40. **H**	55. **D**	70. **H**
11. **B**	26. **H**	41. **B**	56. **J**	71. **B**
12. **F**	27. **B**	42. **F**	57. **C**	72. **G**
13. **C**	28. **J**	43. **A**	58. **G**	73. **C**
14. **H**	29. **A**	44. **J**	59. **C**	74. **F**
15. **D**	30. **F**	45. **A**	60. **J**	75. **D**

Mathematics

1. **D**	13. **A**	25. **D**	37. **D**	49. **D**
2. **K**	14. **K**	26. **G**	38. **J**	50. **J**
3. **D**	15. **C**	27. **D**	39. **C**	51. **B**
4. **J**	16. **K**	28. **J**	40. **H**	52. **F**
5. **C**	17. **C**	29. **D**	41. **D**	53. **A**
6. **J**	18. **G**	30. **J**	42. **G**	54. **J**
7. **B**	19. **D**	31. **C**	43. **B**	55. **E**
8. **F**	20. **J**	32. **H**	44. **K**	56. **H**
9. **E**	21. **C**	33. **B**	45. **C**	57. **C**
10. **H**	22. **G**	34. **H**	46. **F**	58. **K**
11. **A**	23. **C**	35. **C**	47. **E**	59. **E**
12. **G**	24. **F**	36. **J**	48. **F**	60. **G**

ANSWER KEY
Practice Test 6

Reading

1.	**B**	9.	**D**	17.	**D**	25.	**C**	33.	**A**
2.	**F**	10.	**H**	18.	**G**	26.	**G**	34.	**G**
3.	**C**	11.	**D**	19.	**C**	27.	**D**	35.	**A**
4.	**J**	12.	**G**	20.	**J**	28.	**G**	36.	**J**
5.	**D**	13.	**C**	21.	**D**	29.	**C**	37.	**B**
6.	**H**	14.	**G**	22.	**F**	30.	**J**	38.	**H**
7.	**A**	15.	**A**	23.	**A**	31.	**C**	39.	**C**
8.	**G**	16.	**H**	24.	**H**	32.	**J**	40.	**J**

Science

1.	**B**	9.	**C**	17.	**A**	25.	**B**	33.	**A**
2.	**J**	10.	**F**	18.	**H**	26.	**J**	34.	**F**
3.	**C**	11.	**D**	19.	**A**	27.	**B**	35.	**B**
4.	**H**	12.	**J**	20.	**H**	28.	**G**	36.	**H**
5.	**A**	13.	**G**	21.	**A**	29.	**B**	37.	**D**
6.	**J**	14.	**H**	22.	**H**	30.	**H**	38.	**H**
7.	**B**	15.	**D**	23.	**D**	31.	**B**	39.	**D**
8.	**G**	16.	**H**	24.	**H**	32.	**H**	40.	**G**

HOW TO SCORE YOUR PRACTICE TEST

Step 1: Add up the number correct for each section and write that number in the blank under the Raw Score column on the Score Conversion Table. (Your goal is to get more questions correct on each subsequent practice test.)

Step 2: Using the Score Conversion Chart, find your scale score for each section and write it down. Then add up all four sections and divide by 4 to find your overall composite score. (Composite scores are rounded up at .5 or higher.)

SCORE CONVERSION TABLE

Section	Raw Score	Scaled Score
English	(out of 75)	____ / 36
Math	(out of 60)	____ / 36
Reading	(out of 40)	____ / 36
Science	(out of 40)	____ / 36
		Add and divide by 4
Overall Composite =		____ / 36

SCORE CONVERSION CHART

	Number Correct				
ACT Score*	English Section	Mathematics Section	Reading Section	Science Section	ACT Score*
36	75	60	40	40	36
35	74	59	39	39	35
34	73	58	38	38	34
33	72	57	37	—	33
32	71	56	36	37	32
31	70	54–55	35	36	31
30	69	53	34	35	30
29	67–68	51–52	33	34	29
28	65–66	49–50	32	33	28
27	64	46–48	31	31–32	27
26	62–63	44–45	30	30	26
25	60–61	41–43	29	28–29	25
24	58–59	39–40	27–28	25–27	24
23	55–57	37–38	25–26	24	23

(continued)

SCORE CONVERSION CHART (*Continued*)

	Number Correct				
ACT Score*	English Section	Mathematics Section	Reading Section	Science Section	ACT Score*
22	53–54	35–36	23–24	22–23	22
21	50–52	33–34	22	20–21	21
20	47–49	31–32	21	18–19	20
19	44–46	28–30	19–20	17	19
18	42–43	25–27	18	15–16	18
17	40–41	22–24	17	14	17
16	37–39	19–21	16	13	16
15	34–36	15–17	15	12	15
14	31–33	11–14	13–14	11	14
13	29–30	09–10	12	10	13
12	27–28	07–08	10–11	09	12
11	25–26	06	08–09	08	11
10	23–24	05	07	07	10
9	21–22	04	06	05–06	9
8	18–20	03	05	—	8
7	15–17	—	—	04	7
6	12–14	02	04	03	6
5	09–11	—	03	02	5
4	07–08	01	02	—	4
3	05–06	—	—	01	3
2	03–04	—	01	—	2
1	00–02	00	00	00	1

*These scores are based on student trials rather than national norms.

SCORING YOUR ESSAY

As mentioned earlier in this text, two readers will evaluate your essay and each person will then assign it a score from 1 to 6. If, by chance, these two scorers disagree by more than 1 point, a third reader will step in and resolve the discrepancy. Performance on the essay will not affect your English, math, reading, science, or composite scores. You will receive two additional scores on your score sheet—a combined English/writing score (1–36) and a writing test subscore (1–12). Neither of these scores will affect your composite score!

The sample essay that follows reflects higher-level writing. It meets the criteria that ACT has put forth for essays that demonstrate effective writing skills.

- It takes a definite position.
- It addresses and expands on the counterargument.
- It has details that support the topic sentences and is well organized.
- It is not repetitive, and while there may be errors, they do not interfere with the competence of the essay.
- It is consistent and well balanced.
- The essay has a clear introduction and a conclusion that is not just a summary but ends with a significant thought.
- The vocabulary demonstrates good use of language and the sentence structure is varied.

ANSWER EXPLANATIONS
English

1. **(C)** Preposition usage in English is largely idiomatic. The phrase is *think of* because that is simply what we say (*think about* would also be correct, but is not one of the choices). It is one of those things that you just have to know from reading a lot. (Preposition-choice questions are becoming more common on the ACT English, so you should make an effort to start.)

2. **(J)** The subject of the sentence is the plural *communities*, and the communities in question lived over 200 years ago, and so the main verb phrase is *had begun to feel*, the past perfect form of *begin* followed by the infinitive form of *feel*. This verb form may seem complicated, but it is the only one of the choices that is both plural and in any kind of past tense, so it is obviously correct even if you don't understand the past perfect.

3. **(B)** The prepositional phrase *of Romantic musicians* that follows signifies possession, which indicates that we need a noun phrase here. The correct answer is *stirring, urgent compositions*—a noun preceded by two adjectives.

4. **(F)** The main idea that the artists *created works that inspired* is interrupted by the descriptive phrase *emphasizing struggle, fear, and loneliness*, which is placed after *works* (the noun it describes). Although the underlined words may not look correct, they are in the context of the sentence as a whole. (The ACT English will often place underlines at the most confusing possible place in a sentence!)

5. **(B)** What is needed here is a transition phrase indicating that *despite* everything that was just said about music and painting, Romanticism's most famous legacy is literature. All of the choices communicate this in one way or another EXCEPT for *Meanwhile*, which means "at the same time, but elsewhere," and so is nonsense in context.

6. **(J)** The sentence means to imply an ongoing condition, and so the correct phrase is *what writers themselves are like*—in other words, what is true of all writers as a general rule.

7. **(A)** The information communicated in the phrase *brilliant, struggling commoner* is that Keats was born poor and had to pull himself up using only his talent, rather than any advantages of birth. This links him with the stereotype of the "starving artist."

8. **(H)** This sentence opens with a long dependent descriptive phrase, and the main independent clause begins with the words *the figure*. The dependent clause is about the defining characteristics of the Byronic hero, and so opens with the phrase *defined as*.

9. **(D)** The three popular fictional characters mentioned in the underlined portion are specific examples of modern Byronic heroes, and so if the underlined portion were deleted, the sentence would lose examples.

10. **(J)** It is necessary to read ahead in order to answer this question correctly. The sentences following the one with the underlined portion describe the effects that Romanticism had on the sciences, and so *The Romantic movement even had an influence on science* is the correct choice.

11. **(B)** The sentence means to set up a contrast: most artistic movements fade into history, but Romanticism is still famous. The way to do this is to start the first clause with *While* (effectively a synonym for *although*).

12. **(F)** The extra descriptive phrase modifying *most artistic movements* correctly begins with *becoming*.

13. **(C)** The sentence that mentions rock music, horror movies, and superheroes best demonstrates how *wide* Romanticism's influence has been, because it touches upon three different popular genres.

14. **(H)** This long paragraph discusses Romanticism's influence on science in the first part, and the general popular legacy of Romanticism in the second part. The most logical place to divide it would be at point C—after the part about science, but before the part about its legacy.

15. **(D)** The influence of "high culture" in general is not the issue here, but only the influence of Romanticism specifically. Furthermore, not all of the passage is about influence on popular culture—some of it concerns influence on science, or on subsequent genres of art.

16. **(J)** The participial form *deciding* is what we need here: I *have trouble deciding* between …. There is no rule to be memorized on this one—this is simply the answer that would sound right to someone who is familiar with English prose.

17. **(D)** In order for the portion of the sentence after the second dash to end with an acceptable "afterthought" phrase rather than an unacceptable comma error, the part after the final comma must not constitute an independent clause. All of the other choices would add a subject and verb to the final phrase, and so we must DELETE the underlined portion.

18. **(G)** The first part of this sentence, taking its cue from the end of the previous paragraph, is introducing some of the *important differences*. The only answer that makes this clear is choice G.

19. **(C)** Since the introductory modifying phrase *Even as a kid* refers to the author, a noun referring to the author—in this case, the pronoun *I*—must immediately follow the comma in order to avoid creating a misplaced modifier.

20. **(F)** This paragraph goes on to describe the ways that the museum feels different from the zoo. The transition phrase *on the other hand* signals this, and the comparison of the museum with a church is supported by the description in the subsequent sentence.

21. **(A)** The conjunction *and* introduces the second independent clause connecting two ideas.

22. **(J)** Respect, veneration, and awe are all synonyms for reverence. Grandeur is not a synonym, so it is the least acceptable.

23. **(A)** No matter which verb you pick, the idea is that the animals have been acted upon by humans, rather than having performed the action themselves. Therefore, the "odd one out" is *animals have frozen* (because the animals did not freeze in those positions themselves), which does NOT successfully communicate this idea, and in fact contradicts it.

24. **(J)** The phrase *from each other* modifies *different*; the trips were *different from each other*.

25. **(C)** The presence of the dash later in the sentence indicates that the *which* clause should be set off with a pair of dashes. There is no reason why *rather than drive* would be set off with a single dash.

26. **(H)** Neither the passage in general nor this paragraph in particular is about trains. An additional sentence about trains (rather than about the zoo, museum, or the author's memories of his family) would constitute a distracting tangent.

27. **(B)** All we need here is the plural form *friends*. Nothing is possessed by the friends, and so no apostrophe is necessary anywhere.

28. **(J)** The author saying that he is *reassured and inspired* most effectively captures his *reverence* (spiritually profound respect) for the museum.

29. **(A)** In the preceding sentence (among other places in the essay as a whole), the author is using the kids' fascination at the zoo and museum as evidence that the human race is essentially good. In other words, seeing this gives him hope.

30. **(F)** Although the sentence is not strictly necessary in order for the reader to know what is going on, it is an eloquent characterization of the author's problem that is both emotionally affecting and highly relevant to the subject of the passage. The passage would suffer if it were deleted.

31. **(B)** This is the infamous prepositional phrase trick. The noun that governs the verb is the singular *one*, not the plural *sports*. The word *sports* is part of the prepositional phrase *of my favorite sports*, which must be "jumped" so that the main noun and verb of the clause agree. The tense differences between the choices are a red herring—the only issue is singular versus plural.

32. **(J)** The dash that appears earlier in the sentence is a clue that we are dealing with a "lift-out" clause (explaining what "*non-sport*" means) set off with a pair of dashes. A single independent clause exists around it.

33. **(D)** What we need here is just the regular plural form *courses*. No possession is going on, and so no apostrophe is necessary. (Although the sentence says that the courses *have* 18 holes, which is a possessive idea, grammatically speaking the noun *courses* does not possess "18 holes"; the verb *have* does—watch out for this trick!)

34. **(H)** The part of the sentence after the semicolon does not constitute an independent clause. All of the other choices are grammatically correct, but NOT this one.

35. **(A)** No comma is necessary anywhere in this region of the sentence. It is a single independent clause with normal word order.

36. **(J)** The history of Frisbees would be an irrelevant distraction at this point, since the sport being discussed is not even played with Frisbees. All that is necessary is to point out that disc-golf discs are not Frisbees and move on.

37. **(D)** This is the only choice that results in a complete correct sentence that makes sense. It presents a dependent clause followed by a comma and an independent clause.

38. **(G)** This part of the sentence involves a limiting (or "essential") clause followed by a verb being performed by the people in that clause. No comma is necessary at any point. Although limiting and nonlimiting clauses about animals or things can be distinguished by the use of *that* (with no comma) versus *which* (with a comma), when the clause is about people you use *who* in either case, with the only difference being the absence or presence of a comma.

39. **(C)** The infinitive form is necessary here. The players are *good enough to make* the shots.

40. **(H)** The sentence that goes here needs to transition between talking about world-class players (like in the sentence before it) and talking about amateurs who play for fun (like in the sentence after it). Only choice H does so—the other three are all still about the pros.

41. **(B)** Due to the rule of parallel phrasing, we need a double *when* here: the game is more about being surprised *when* you make a good shot than embarrassed *when* you make a bad one.

42. **(F)** Of the choices, only this sentence provides actual statistics to indicate how popular disc golf has gotten in a specific amount of time.

43. **(A)** Three of the choices mean the same as inform: persuade does not. An Internet search will not persuade you about courses in your area.

44. **(J)** As the rest of the sentence indicates, the reader is being addressed: if *you're someone who thought you'd never be good at sports, what are you waiting for?*

45. **(A)** The proceeding sentence discusses obstacles like trees. Therefore, the appropriate placement would be after point B in paragraph 2.

46. **(J)** The *United States* is a place, so we need the relative pronoun *where*, and *comedians* is a noun, so it needs to be modified with the adjective *political*.

47. **(C)** What we need here is the plural form *politicians*. Nothing is being possessed, and so no apostrophe is necessary. The addition of *our* makes no difference one way or the other.

48. **(F)** The nouns being used as adjectives here, *comedian* and *film actor*, do not specify Gnarr's identity by themselves (there are lots of comedians and film actors). Because of this, the name "Jon Gnarr" could not be lifted out of the sentence, and so it is not set off with commas.

49. **(B)** The phrase *a severe banking collapse* is the only one of the choices that is neither ambiguous nor redundant.

50. **(H)** A past tense verb followed by another in the infinitive form is needed here: Gnarr *began to staff* the party. The addition of *actually* makes no difference one way or the other (it breaks a very old-fashioned rule about not "splitting" infinitives, but the other choices are all wrong for much more important reasons).

51. **(A)** This choice correctly presents an "afterthought" clause specifying Björk's identity preceded by a comma.

52. **(J)** The city of Reykjavik is *home to over a third* of Iceland's population (i.e., over one-third of Icelanders live there).

53. **(A)** What's needed here is a term indicating that Gnarr's platform reminded people about serious issues even though it was funny. All of the other choices accomplish this, but NOT *recommended*. Gnarr's platform did not *recommend* issues to people.

54. **(G)** Without this additional information, readers would not know that there are not normally polar bears in Iceland, or why their presence there now is a bad sign.

55. **(D)** The sentence is complete and clear if it ends with a period after the word *on*. All of the other choices are redundant.

56. **(J)** Since the sentence begins *This would be an impressive feat*, it logically needs to come after a reference to something that would be an impressive feat. Sentence 2 closes by mentioning that Gnarr has a chance to become the first mayor of Reykjavik this century to serve a full term—this is the only prospective "impressive feat" mentioned in the paragraph, so the sentence should be inserted after sentence 2.

57. **(C)** The paragraph goes on to discuss a few politically progressive landmarks in Icelandic history, and this sentence is the only one of the choices that introduces this theme ("ahead of the curve in political matters").

58. **(G)** What we need here is the possessive pronoun *their*. The people of Iceland elected a comedian mayor—it was *their* election of a comedian mayor.

59. **(C)** Although it contains some tidbits about Icelandic history, the passage as a whole is overwhelmingly concerned with Jon Gnarr and the 2010 Reykjavik mayoral election.

60. **(J)** This is the infamous prepositional phrase trick with an added element of verb-tense trickiness. The noun phrase that governs the underlined verb is *bars and restaurants*—not *country*, which is part of the prepositional phrase *all over the country* (though *all* itself is not a preposition, *all over* is an expression that functions as a preposition, with a definition similar to *throughout*). So, the verb must be plural. And since the verb must also express an ongoing action, the present perfect continuous form *have been attracting* is necessary (even if you don't understand that tense, you should still be able to eliminate the other choices).

61. **(A)** This choice presents a comprehensible sentence that correctly consists of an independent clause followed by a comma and a dependent *which* clause.

62. **(G)** The choice in which an adverb modifies an adjective, *less formal*, is grammatically correct and makes sense in context.

63. **(A)** This choice correctly presents a dependent clause followed by a comma and an independent clause. It is worth noting that all three of the wrong answers are wrong for the same reason—they involve a semicolon, a comma + conjunction, and a period, all of which must separate two independent clauses. The comma is the "odd one out."

64. **(J)** Only *Traditionally*, which expresses the idea that trivia questions have worked a certain way for a long time, makes sense in context.

65. **(B)** This choice correctly consists of a dependent introductory clause followed by a comma and an independent clause.

66. **(H)** To get the answer from a friend, you *had to have* a friend who knew the answer. If you cut away "extra" words to get down to the core idea, the right answer just clearly sounds right.

67. **(B)** This clause states that people phoning friends wasn't that much of a problem, and the previous clause explains why. Therefore, the conjunction *so* is correct. *You still had to have a friend who knew, so* (i.e., "and for this reason") *it wasn't that much of a problem.*

68. **(J)** This is the only one of the choices that is not horribly awkward. If cheating *is not adequately policed*, the game will be ruined.

69. **(A)** We need the adverb *then*, which refers to chronological order. In an *if … then* construction, the *if* clause and the *then* clause are separated with a comma.

70. **(H)** The *honor system* means that authorities are trusting people to police themselves. Only choice H describes such a situation.

71. **(B)** This is the only one of the choices that is neither redundant nor insufficiently specific.

72. **(G)** This choice correctly separates two independent clauses with a semicolon.

73. **(C)** The second part of the sentence is also necessary in order for the problem to be clear: trivia concerns knowledge, and all knowledge can now be looked up on cell phones.

74. **(F)** This choice provides a smooth transition from the previous subject (phone cheating) into the new problem that the author brings up at the end.

75. **(D)** What the sentence means to express is the possibility that, in the future, the issue of people cheating at trivia will be moot, because no one will even be interested in it *in the first place*—that is, this problem will *precede* the other one.

Mathematics

1. **(D)** The median is the middle number when arranged in order from least to greatest: $1\frac{1}{2}$, $1\frac{1}{2}$, $1\frac{3}{4}$, $2\frac{1}{3}$, 3.

2. **(K)** $(-2x^5)^4 = (-2)^4 x^{20} = 16x^{20}$.

3. **(D)** $\frac{85 + 83 + 91 + 94 + x}{5} = 90 \rightarrow \frac{353 + x}{5} = 90 \rightarrow 353 + x = 450 \rightarrow x = 97$.

4. **(J)** $2(-3)^2 - 5(-3)(2) + (2)^2 = 2(9) + 30 + 4 = 18 + 30 + 4 = 52$.

5. **(C)** $2x - 3 < 5x + 6 \rightarrow -3x < 9 \rightarrow x > -3$. Remember you need to change the inequality sign when dividing by a negative number.

6. **(J)** $\overline{BE}$ is twice the length of $\overline{CD}$ since the 6 triangles are equilateral.

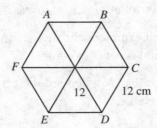

7. **(B)** This type of problem works well with proportions $\frac{18}{63} = \frac{45}{x} \rightarrow 18x = 2{,}835 \rightarrow x = 157.5$.

8. **(F)** You need to distribute the "negative": $x^3 - 4x^2 + 5 - 3x^3 - 6x^2 + 9 = -2x^3 - 10x^2 + 14$.

9. **(E)** $\angle ACD$ is an exterior angle of $\triangle ABC$. Its measure equals the sum of the 2 remote interior angles: $56 + 69 = 125$ or $180 - 55 = 125$.

10. **(H)** The FOIL method applies to this equation: $(5x - 4y)(3x + y) = 15x^2 + 5xy - 12xy - 4y^2 = 15x^2 - 7xy - 4y^2$.

11. **(A)** $8x - 2(x - 5) = 2x - 20$; $8x - 2x + 10 = 2x - 20 \rightarrow 4x = -30 \rightarrow -7\frac{1}{2}$.

12. **(G)** The constant on the outside of the matrix needs to be multiplied by each element on the inside of the matrix.

13. **(A)** The sum of the angles of a quadrilateral is $(4 - 2)180 = 360$. Therefore, $93 + 75 + 72 + x = 360$; $240 + x = 360$; $x = 120$.

14. **(K)** Each gallon of water weighs 8 pounds, so 5,000 gallons = $5{,}000(8) = 40{,}000$ pounds.

15. **(C)** To find the price per pound, divide the price for 3 pounds by 3. To find how much cheaper, we subtract these values, $\frac{\$2.17}{3} - \frac{\$1.99}{3} = \$0.06$. Alternately, it costs $0.18 more (2.17 − 1.99) for 3 pounds: $\frac{\$0.18}{3} = \$0.06$.

16. **(K)** In this problem there are different units of measure. It is imperative to have the same units. It is easier to change feet into inches since 1 foot = 12 inches. 12 feet = $12(12) = 144$ inches, 16 feet = $12(16) = 192$ inches. To cover the floor indicates area. Area of room = $144(192) = 27{,}648$ square inches. Area of tile = $8(8) = 64$ square inches. $27{,}648 \div 64 = 432$.

17. **(C)** 7 out of the 60 students selected Science and $7 \div 60 = 0.11\overline{6} = 11.7\%$.

18. **(G)** The ratio of Physical Education to Math responses is 12:8. Both of these numbers are divisible by 4, so the ratio reduces to 3:2.

19. **(D)** 6 of the 60 students selected World Languages, which represents 10% of the students. 10% of the 360° in a circle is 36°.

20. **(J)** This is a case in which order is important. Therefore, it is a "permutations" problem. The answer is found by finding the number of permutations of 5 things taken 5 at a time. Symbolically it is $_5P_5$. You can do this on your calculator. It equals 120. You can also solve this by making 5 spaces such as $\underline{(5)}\ \underline{(4)}\ \underline{(3)}\ \underline{(2)}\ \underline{(1)}$. The first space can be filled in 5 ways, the second in 4 ways, and so on. Then, you multiply $5 \times 4 \times 3 \times 2 \times 1 = 120$.

21. **(C)** Once you graph the 2 points and draw a line, 4 is the only possible choice. Mathematically, find the slope $\frac{6 - 2}{3 - (-3)} = \frac{4}{6} = \frac{2}{3}$. Then, from $y = mx + b$, $6 = \frac{2}{3}(3) + b \rightarrow 6 = 2 + b$. So, $b = 4$. $y = \frac{2}{3}x + 4$. The y-intercept is 4.

22. **(G)** Since $\overrightarrow{AB}$ is parallel to $\overrightarrow{CD}$, the measure of $\angle APC = 37°$, by alternate interior angles. Then, $37 + 40 + y = 180$. So, the measure of $\angle CPD = 103°$. This could also be done by seeing that the measure of $\angle PDC = 40°$ by alternate interior angles. Then, the sum of the angles of a triangle is $180°$.

23. **(C)** If we transform $2x - 3y + 7 = 0$ into $y = mx + b$ form, the slope will be the coefficient of x. You get $-3y = -2x - 7$ by subtraction. Then, divide each term by (-3) to get $y = \frac{2}{3}x + \frac{7}{3}$. The slope is $\frac{2}{3}$.

24. **(F)** You need to use the Pythagorean Theorem: $(QR)^2 + 16^2 = 20°$; $(QR)^2 + 256 = 400$; $(QR)^2 = 144$; $QR = 12$. Then, by using SOH-CAH-TOA, $\cos = \frac{adj}{hyp}$. Thus, $\cos\angle R = \frac{12}{20}$. Also, 12, 16, 20 is a Pythagorean triple (3, 4, 5).

25. **(D)** This factors both polynomials: $\frac{(x+4)(x-3)}{(x+2)(x-3)}$. After factoring we can cancel common factors. So, the $(x-3)$ factor that is in top and bottom can be reduced, leaving us with $\frac{x+4}{x+2}$.

26. **(G)** 5% of 1,000 is 50: $[0.05(1,000)]$. So, the second-year enrollment was $1,000 + 50 = 1,050$. For the third year it decreased by 2% of the second-year enrollment: 2% of $1,050 = 21$; $1,050 - 21 = 1,029$.

27. **(D)** If we rewrite 2:3:4 as $2x: 3x: 4x$, then $2x + 3x + 4x = 63 \rightarrow 9x = 63 \rightarrow x = 7$. Tin is the $3x$. Therefore, tin $= 3(7) = 21$. The ratio then is 14:21:28.

28. **(J)** Andrew walked $\frac{1}{2}$ of $4\frac{1}{2} = 2\frac{1}{4}$ miles. Bill walked $\frac{2}{3}$ of $4\frac{1}{4} = 3$ miles. $3 - 2\frac{1}{4} = \frac{3}{4}$.

29. **(D)** For the lines to be parallel, the ratio of the x-coefficients has to equal the ratio of the y-coefficients, while the ratio of the constant terms must be different. If the ratio of the constant terms is not different, the two equations would represent the same line. Therefore, $\frac{k}{32} = \frac{2}{k} \rightarrow k^2 = 64 \rightarrow k = 8$ and $\frac{2}{k} \neq \frac{6}{18}$.

30. **(J)** Using the distance formula $\sqrt{(x_2 - x_1)^2 + (y_2 - y_1)^2}$, we get $\sqrt{(4 - -2)^2 + (-7 - 1)^2} = \sqrt{6^2 + (-8)^2} = \sqrt{36 + 64} = \sqrt{100} = 10$.

31. **(C)** The question is equivalent to $3^? = \sqrt{27}$. Since $3^3 = 27$ and $\sqrt{27} = 27^{1/2}$, we have $3^? = \sqrt{27} = 27^{1/2} = \left(3^3\right)^{1/2} = 3^{3/2}$.

32. **(H)** This is a quadratic equation. The first thing to do is get 1 side of the equation equal to zero: $2x^2 - 5x - 12 = 0$. This factors to $(x - 4)(2x + 3) = 0$. Set each factor equal to zero: $x - 4 = 0 \rightarrow x = 4$ and $2x + 3 = 0 \rightarrow x = -1.5$. You could also use the quadratic formula

$$x = \frac{-b \pm \sqrt{b^2 - 4ac}}{2a}, a = 2, b = -5, \text{ and } c = -12; x = \frac{5 \pm \sqrt{(-5)^2 - 4(2)(-12)}}{2(2)} = \frac{5 \pm \sqrt{121}}{4} = \frac{5 \pm 11}{4}.$$

It would be easier if you had a program that would solve a quadratic equation on your calculator.

33. **(B)** You need to use the first part of the inequality and you have $x^2 < 2x$. Since x is positive we divide by x and get $x < 2$. The second half of the compound inequality yields $2x < x + 4 \rightarrow x < 4$. Because this compound inequality represents an AND, the intersection of the two solutions is used and the final answer is $x < 2$.

34. **(H)** We can calculate the length of all but two of the segments. Call these two segments x and y. By adding the horizontal segments, we get $3 + x + y = 12 \rightarrow x + y = 9$. Now the perimeter equals $6 + 3 + 3 + x + 1 + y + 2 + 12$. This yields $27 + (x + y) = 27 + 9 = 36$. The same answer would be obtained by making a rectangle and adding the perimeter of it. Note: it is not possible to get values for x and y, but we can find their sum.

35. **(C)** The inequality $|x| > 2$ is equivalent to the compound inequality $x > 2$ OR $x < -2$. The correct answer is easily obtained by choosing numbers.

36. **(J)** After the first marble is drawn, there are 99 marbles left in the box. A winning marble must have a 5 in the tens digit. Originally, there were 10 marbles in the 50's but after the first was drawn, only 9 are left. Probability is $\dfrac{\text{successes}}{\text{outcomes}} = \dfrac{9}{99} = \dfrac{1}{11}$.

37. **(D)** Two triangles are similar if 2 corresponding angles are congruent (Angle Angle Similarity). In this case, $\angle A$ must be congruent to $\angle E$, and $\angle B$ must be congruent to $\angle D$, by alternate interior angles. By vertical angles $\angle ACB$ is congruent to $\angle ECD$. Therefore, $\triangle ACB$ must be similar to $\triangle ECD$.

38. **(J)** These are similar triangles and the following proportion is true: $\dfrac{6}{x} = \dfrac{4}{14} \rightarrow 4x = 84 \rightarrow x = 21$ ft.

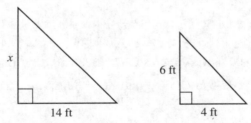

39. **(C)** Since we are multiplying by $2\pi r$ in $A = 2\pi r(r + h)$, we should divide by $2\pi r$ to solve. We get $\dfrac{A}{2\pi r} = \dfrac{2\pi r(r + h)}{2\pi r} \rightarrow \dfrac{A}{2\pi r} = r + h$. Then, subtract r from both sides and get $\dfrac{A}{2\pi r} - r = h$.

40. **(H)** For a problem involving a rectangle, make a sketch. The rectangle has 4 right angles. When we draw the diagonal we make a right triangle in which we know 2 sides. The Pythagorean Theorem applies: $a^2 + b^2 = c^2$, so $27^2 + 36^2 = c^2 \rightarrow 729 + 1{,}296 = c^2 \rightarrow c^2 = 2{,}025$; $c = \sqrt{2{,}025} = 45$. Also, 27, 36, 45 is a Pythagorean triple (3, 4, 5).

41. **(D)** When given coordinates of points, we graph them. The segment joining (3, 3) and (7, 3) is horizontal, so its length is $7 - 3 = 4$. The height of the parallelogram is the distance between the 2 horizontal segments. That distance is 5. It is the distance from 3 to 8 on the y-axis. Area of a parallelogram $= bh$; $A = 4(5) = 20$.

42. **(G)** We use the midpoint formula to get this equation: $\left(\dfrac{a+1}{2}, \dfrac{b+6}{2}\right) = (-1, 1)$. Thus, $\dfrac{a+1}{2} = -1$ and $\dfrac{b+6}{2} = 1 \rightarrow a + 1 = -2$ and $b + 6 = 2 \rightarrow a = -3$ and $b = -4$. Graph the points in the (x, y) plane. By your knowledge of what a midpoint is, you should see that the other endpoint has to be in quadrant III; $(-3, -4)$ is the only choice that is in quadrant III.

43. **(B)** We could get the correct answer by noticing that we get successive terms by dividing by 3. Writing out 12 terms, $27, 9, 3, 1, \dfrac{1}{3}, \dfrac{1}{3^2}, \dfrac{1}{3^3}, \dfrac{1}{3^4}, \dfrac{1}{3^5}, \dfrac{1}{3^6}, \dfrac{1}{3^7}, \dfrac{1}{3^8}$, the twelfth term is $\dfrac{1}{3^8}$. Using the formula for the nth term of a geometric sequence: $a_n = a_1 r^{n-1} \rightarrow a_{12} = 27(3)^{(12-1)}$ $\rightarrow a_{12} = \dfrac{3^3}{3^{11}} = \dfrac{1}{3^8}$.

44. **(K)** The triangle inequality states that the sum of any two sides of a triangle must be greater than the third side. Since $14 + 14 = 28$, the third side has to be less than 28.

45. **(C)** Both 4 and 8 are powers of 2 ($4 = 2^2$ and $8 = 2^3$, respectively); therefore, we can write both expressions as 2 to a power: $4^{3x+1} = (2^2)^{(3x+1)} = 2^{6x+2}$ and $8^{x+2} = (2^3)^{x+2} = 2^{3x+6}$. The equation can then be written as $2^{6x+2} = 2^{3x+6}$. Since the base (2) is the same, the exponents must be equal: $6x + 2 = 3x + 6$: $3x = 4$: $x = \dfrac{4}{3}$.

46. **(F)** $f(g(x))$ is equivalent to $f(2x-1)$, which is equivalent to $(2x-1)^2$. This is a FOIL problem: $(2x-1)(2x-1) = 4x^2 - 2x - 2x + 1 = 4x^2 - 4x + 1$.

47. **(E)** In the diagram, there is a 30°–60°–90° triangle and a 45°–45°–90° triangle. The ratio of sides in the 30°–60°–90° is $x:x\sqrt{3}:2x$, so $BD = 6\sqrt{3}$ and $AB = 12$. The ratio of sides in the 45°–45°–90° is $x:x:x\sqrt{2}$, so $CD = 6$ and $AC = 6\sqrt{2}$. The perimeter is $6 + 6\sqrt{3} + 12 + 6\sqrt{2} \approx 36.9$.

48. **(F)** Subtracting the area of the rectangle $ABFE$ from the area of the trapezoid $ABCD$ gives the sum of the areas of $\triangle AED$ and $\triangle BFC$. Area of a trapezoid: $\dfrac{h(b_1 + b_2)}{2} = \dfrac{4(6+12)}{2} = \dfrac{72}{2} = 36$. The area of a rectangle: $bh = 6(4) = 24$. Subtracting the areas: $36 - 24 = 12$.

49. **(D)** The easiest way to do this problem is to use your calculator to do $(2 - 3i)^2 = -5 - 12i$. Alternatively, do $(2 - 3i)(2 - 3i)$, which is FOIL: $4 - 6i - 6i + 9i^2 = 4 - 12i + 9(-1) = -5 - 12i$. Remember, $i^2 = -1$.

50. **(J)** The area of a circle is πr^2. Here we were given the diameter of 80 inches, so the radius is 40 inches. $\pi 40^2 = 1,600\pi$.

51. **(B)** Given the coordinates of X and Z, we can deduce that C is located at the origin. Since CZ and CY are both radii, they are equal. Since we have the 60°, we have an equilateral triangle and C will be directly above the midpoint of $\overline{CZ}$. Since Z has an x-coordinate of 40, Y will have an x-coordinate of 20. A 30–60–90 triangle can also be used to solve this problem.

52. **(F)** The desired arc is a semicircle because $\overline{XZ}$ was defined as a diameter. The length of the arc is equal to half of the circumference, or $\frac{1}{2}\pi d = \frac{1}{2}\pi 80 = 40\pi$.

53. **(A)** If $(x + 2)$ is a factor, then substituting -2 for x in $3x^2 - 13x + k$ must yield zero: $3(-2)^2 - 13(-2) + k = 0$; $3(4) + 26 + k = 0$: $k = -38$.

54. **(J)** Tripling the radius means the new radius is $3r$ and the new volume would be $\frac{4\pi}{3}(3r)^3 = \frac{4\pi}{3}(27r^3) = 27\left(\frac{4\pi r^3}{3}\right) = 27$ times the volume of the original sphere.

55. **(E)** If $f(x) = x^2 - 2x + 4$, then $f(t + 2) = (t + 2)^2 - 2(t + 2) + 4$ by substitution. This expression must be expanded and simplified: $(t + 2)^2 - 2(t + 2) + 4 = t^2 + 4t + 4 - 2t - 4 + 4$, which simplifies to $t^2 + 2t + 4$.

56. **(H)** If $x = 4y + 2$, then $4y = x - 2$ and $y = \frac{x - 2}{4}$, so $y + 6 = \frac{x - 2}{4} + 6$. Find a common denominator and this becomes $\frac{x - 2}{4} + \frac{24}{4} = \frac{x + 22}{4}$.

57. **(C)** Since $\frac{\pi}{2} < \theta < \pi$, θ is in quadrant II. If we make a reference triangle in quadrant II, we get this triangle by using $\sin\theta = \frac{5}{7}$ and SOH-CAH-TOA. By the Pythagorean Theorem $a^2 + 5^2 = 7^2$, $a^2 = 24$, $a = \pm 2\sqrt{6}$. The x-coordinate is negative in quadrant II: $a = \pm 2\sqrt{6}$. Then, $\cos\theta = -\frac{2\sqrt{6}}{7}$.

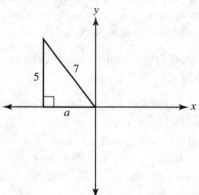

58. **(K)** The third angle of the triangle is $180 - (35 + 44) = 101°$. Then by the law of sines: $\frac{12}{\sin 101°} = \frac{AC}{\sin 44°}$. At this point, we could eliminate choices F, G, H, and J comparing each to our equation. However, we can easily solve for AC by multiplying both sides of our equation by $\sin 44°$. The result is $AC = \frac{12 \sin 44°}{\sin 101°}$.

59. **(E)** Listing all the possible factors of 20, we would be able to write linear factors of the form $(x+\ )(x+\ )$ or $(x-\ )(x-\ )$ since the coefficient of x^2 is 1. We could factor 20 as $(1)(20)$, $(2)(10)$, $(4, 5)$, $(-1)(-20)$, $(-2, 10)$, and $(-4, -5)$. Then the possible linear factors are

$(x + 1)(x + 20) = x^2 + 21x + 20$
$(x + 2)(x + 10) = x^2 + 12x + 20$
$(x + 4)(x + 5) = x^2 + 9x + 20$
$(x - 1)(x - 20) = x^2 - 21x + 20$
$(x - 2)(x - 10) = x^2 - 12x + 20$
$(x - 4)(x - 5) = x^2 - 9x + 20.$

So, b could be any of these numbers $\{21, 12, 9, -21, -12, -9\}$. There are 6 possibilities. Thus, the only possible choice is E. All of the other choices do not consider all possibilities.

60. **(G)** There are 2 important conditions. They are that M and N are prime numbers and that $\sqrt{21(M)(N)(5)(7)}$ is a rational number. If we factor 21 as $(3)(7)$, we get $\sqrt{(3)(7)(M)(N)(5)(7)} = 7\sqrt{(3)(M)(N)(5)}$. Since $\sqrt{(3)(M)(N)(5)}$ must be rational, $(3)(M)(N)(5)$ has to be a perfect square. We are dealing with prime numbers. Therefore, $(M)(N) = 15$. The prime factorization of 15 is $3(5)$, which means M and N must be 3 and 5, in any order.

Reading

1. **(B)** Eliot spends most of his opening paragraph explaining how his contemporaries exclusively use "traditional" (an antonym of "original") as an insult, and he then closes it by suggesting that this viewpoint is misguided.

2. **(F)** The first *three* sentences of Paragraph 3 (lines 31–35) are *all* paraphrases of this answer choice.

3. **(C)** Eliot spends most of Paragraph 2 (specifically, lines 20–29) describing the opinions and feelings that will inevitably be present in a writer who has developed the "historical sense." As he appears to understand this historical sense so well, Eliot presumably believes that he possesses it himself—and as he closes the paragraph by stating (in lines 25–30) that the historical sense also provides superior insight into the present day, he must believe that he possesses this as well.

4. **(J)** The rest of the sentence (after the colon) more or less directly states this: Wordsworth both understands and agrees with the notion that anyone who buys a book of poetry has the right to expect that the poems will utilize superior/noble/uplifting forms of expression and deliberately avoid utilizing "low" forms of it (at least, it was so in Wordsworth's day).

5. **(D)** In lines 75–84, Wordsworth explains how (in his opinion) the rustic men lead a "natural" existence, and so their speech is simple and direct, unlike certain poets who snobbishly separate themselves from both nature and their fellow man (i.e., they are *elitists*) and, as a result, produce work that responds to literary trends and fads (i.e., *tastemaking*) instead of addressing the "real world."

6. **(H)** Wordsworth did not wish to appear so *pompous* (self-important) as to attempt "reasoning the reader into approbation" (i.e., arguing with people until they liked his new poems), but he acknowledges that there might be some "impropriety" in expecting readers to go along with such a radical new poetic style without any explanation (i.e., he did not want to assume that his readers would still like his poems no matter what, or "take them for granted").

7. **(A)** *Approbation* is an exact synonym for *approval*, and even if you didn't already know this, it is the only one of the four choices that makes sense when you plug it into the contexts of lines 57 and 61. Why would any writer *want to* reason a reader into boredom, bemusement (confusion), or dread?

8. **(G)** Eliot admits in lines 16–19 that new poets do have to do something differently from their predecessors or there's no point to new poetry, but warns that they must be different in the "right" way—out of the "historical sense"—in lines 20–30. For his part, Wordsworth explains in lines 62–74 that he hopes nobody will think he developed his new style out of disrespect for what people have traditionally expected from poetry.

9. **(D)** Eliot explains that he thinks such people are misguided in lines 7–16, and Wordsworth does so in lines 65–84.

10. **(H)** The "poet who is aware" in line 45 is indeed a good one in Eliot's opinion, and the "poets who think they are conferring honor upon their art by separating themselves" in lines 85–87 are indeed bad ones in Wordsworth's opinion. As this answer choice asserts nothing else, there's no way for it to be wrong. The other answer choices either rely on objective misreadings or make conjectures unsupported by the passages.

11. **(D)** The author explains in paragraph 2 that most music is now obtained by consumers using software that was developed and sold by businesses external to the record companies, and yet the record companies still feel entitled to the same "cut" that they got back when they did all the work.

12. **(G)** The author sees the "CD-promotional model" mentioned in the last paragraph as the basis of a new system whereby music itself would be free, and record companies would make money from concerts.

13. **(C)** The author explains in paragraph 4 that peer-to-peer software is now so easy to use that there are no longer any technical obstacles to music piracy.

14. **(G)** In these lines, the author describes an economic reality: technological advances have led to a state where people can get music without paying for it unless the government stops them somehow.

15. **(A)** The opening paragraphs explain the ways in which the music industry has changed, and assert that record companies still expect to make just as much money even though they do less work.

16. **(H)** The author repeatedly asserts that consumers who download music for free are a natural consequence of the new technology, and so he sees these consumers as behaving *logically*.

17. **(D)** The first paragraph depicts the government "passing the buck," as it were, trying to make schools culpable for music piracy just because lots of music pirates go to school, even though music piracy is not the school's fault.

18. **(G)** In the closing paragraphs, the author details a few ways that musicians and remixers have gotten more creative as a result of the situation.

19. **(C)** The author closes by predicting that CDs will continue to exist, but for a different purpose: they will become free promotions for concerts, rather than a source of revenue.

20. **(J)** The second author examines filesharing as a moral issue in the light of older moral philosophy (in this case, Utilitarianism), while the author of the passage simply seems to think that you can't stop progress, so there is no use in philosophizing about it.

21. **(D)** The passage as a whole is about the Internet outcompeting TV (the title is "Why TV Lost," after all), so you know it's going to be one of the choices that begins with "weaker." Of those choices, only the assertion about TV's limitations is consistent with the passage. (Right answer + true statement.)

22. **(F)** Lines 15–42 allude to three predictable forces, and one that would have been "harder to" predict. The three predictable forces are outlined in the rest of paragraph 2. Paragraphs 3 and 4 then discuss the "somewhat more surprising" (line 30) force: *social applications* (for example, Facebook).

23. **(A)** Lines 32–34 address how important to teenagers socializing is, and lines 37–42 explain that this fact gives them the energy and motivation to learn a lot about computers very quickly. Therefore, the relevant traits are that teens are *energetic* and *social*.

24. **(H)** This section of the passage discusses how TV technology forces stations to tailor content to local concerns, and how this puts TV at a disadvantage compared with the Internet, where geographical location doesn't matter. The sentence immediately following in lines 76–79 is basically a paraphrase of the correct answer.

25. **(C)** Lines 53–60 explain that TV networks "grudgingly" put some shows online, but wish they didn't have to.

26. **(G)** Paragraphs 5, 6, and 7 (lines 53–92) discuss the attitudes of "old media" toward the changes brought by the Internet. They are portrayed as angrily resisting the new business models. Therefore, *resentful stubbornness* is correct.

27. **(D)** "Keep the old model running" is an automotive metaphor about patching up an old machine rather than caving in and buying a new one; choice D is basically a paraphrase of the sentence indicated.

28. **(G)** Lines 27–29 state that the younger generation is used to everything they're interested in being available on computers. It is worth noting that the other three answer choices are all *critical* of young people, whereas the passage and the right answer are not (young people expect to be criticized by adults, and so the wrong answers are playing on the expectations of the test takers).

29. **(C)** The last sentence of paragraph 6 echoes the main point it has been making: that the only reason TV shows are aimed at local audiences is because TV itself relies on broadcasting a limited signal from a local source, not because it was ever what people wanted.

30. **(J)** Whereas the passage suggests that the Internet will soon completely replace TV, which will essentially have no reason to exist anymore, the author of this excerpt points out that TV is better suited to some specific situations (like a live sporting event).

31. **(C)** The passage argues that virtually all of the phenomena traditionally associated with ghosts and hauntings are scientifically explainable.

32. **(J)** This paragraph explains why humans would have evolved a fear reponse to certain vibrations (because those vibrations are usually made by dangerous things).

33. **(A)** The concert experiment proves that humans will exhibit fear responses to infrasound even when they are not expecting to be scared (as someone who knowingly enters a reputedly haunted house might).

34. **(G)** The passage never addresses accounts of people who supposedly received information from ghosts.

35. **(A)** The passage implies that many of the people who have reported seeing ghosts were probably confused by infrasound and making an honest mistake.

36. **(J)** The passage in lines 69–73 explains that the cause of the sound was made by a silent exhaust fan.

37. **(B)** *Havoc* most nearly means "*chaos.*" To "wreak havoc" on something is to throw it into chaos or extreme disarray.

38. **(H)** When the passage says that evolution taught us that these sounds represent "bad news," it means that they are frequently made by things that pose real dangers, like wild animals or storms.

39. **(C)** Gavreau's initial motivation was to figure out why his assistant's ear was suddenly bleeding. He didn't know at first that he was going to discover infrasound or that this would explain hauntings.

40. **(J)** For a good haunted house, you would need both vibrations in the infrasound "panic range" and a properly shaped room for them to bounce around in. It doesn't matter what is making the vibrations, as long as they are in the right range.

Science

1. **(B)** The fourth column in Table 3 lists the amount of time the reactant was passed over the catalyst. The fifth column lists the amount of propane collected for each trial. As the numbers in the fourth column get smaller, the numbers in the fifth column get smaller also.

2. **(J)** As stated in the first paragraph of text, a catalyst is a substance that speeds up a reaction. Since no propane was collected in Trial 4, we can assume the hydrogen and propene did not have enough time to interact with the catalyst and no reaction occurred.

3. **(C)** Paragraph 1 of the text states that a heterogeneous catalyst is when the catalyst is in a different phase from the reactants. In the description of Experiment 1, it is stated that the catalyst is made up of alumina beads and that the propanol is in a vapor phase when it reacts with the catalyst. Vapor and solid are two different phases, so it is a heterogeneous catalyst.

4. **(H)** Table 1 clearly states that Stage 3 is when the reaction occurs. The description of Experiment 2 states that the reaction occurs after the hydrogen-propene mixture passed over the catalyst, and then the propane was collected. Table 1 describes the four stages of catalysis.

5. **(A)** The volume of propanol was the same for each trial, whereas the volume of alumina beads was different. Look at Table 2. We know from reading the description of Experiment 1 that the catalyst is the alumina beads. The third column in Table 2 lists the volume of the catalyst used for each trial. The amounts would have to be different, while the volume of propanol used as reactant would have to be the same, to test the effect that varying the amount of catalyst has on the outcome.

6. **(J)** There was no reason for the plunger to move until the propene entered the syringe.

7. **(B)** The experiment was designed to evaluate the results after varying times. All other variables except time had to remain constant to ensure the results were due to the time elapsed and nothing else.

8. **(G)** When there are two recessive L alleles in the genotype, the leaf texture is wrinkled, so it can be determined that the L gene affects leaf texture.

9. **(C)** The last row in Table 2 lists the phenotypes for this genotype.

10. **(F)** The genotype would contain two recessive P alleles. Table 3 contains the data for the four different crosses performed. It can be determined from Table 2 that if a plant has 3 pods, the genotype is made up of two recessive P alleles.

11. **(D)** It can be determined from Table 2 that the genotype pp results in 3 pods. Table 3 shows that 100% of the offspring for Cross 3 had 3 pods, so 100% of the offspring must have the genotype pp.

12. **(J)** Table 2 displays all the possible genotypes and the associated phenotypes. There are only two rows where the phenotypes are 3 pods and normal leaves, and the associated genotypes listed are ppLL and ppLl. All other answers can be eliminated.

13. **(G)** According to Table 3, Cross 2 has 75% chance of 1 pod and 50% chance of wrinkled leaves. While Cross 2 also has 50% chance of wrinkled leaves or normal leaves, it only has a 50% chance of 1 pod, which is less than Cross 2.

14. **(H)** Look at the section under the heading Researcher 1. The third paragraph lists the demographic parameters that can be monitored in seabirds. Mortality rates are not listed.

15. **(D)** Look at the section under the heading Researcher 1. The second paragraph makes this point.

16. **(H)** Look at the section under the heading Researcher 2. The second paragraph addresses this issue and mentions that placing bands on penguins has been shown to reduce both breeding success and survival rates.

17. **(A)** Look at the section under the heading Researcher 1. The last sentence of paragraph 1 supports this answer.

18. **(H)** The first paragraph of the passage discusses indicators, and there is a 4-point list of important criteria for an effective indicator. Researcher 2's views state that seabirds do not fit the first three criteria and do not address the fourth item in the list. Look at the section under the heading Researcher 2 to understand how his or her views are related to each point. Point 1—the last sentence of paragraph 1 explains why seabirds don't meet this criterion. Point 2—the first sentence of paragraph 2 explains why seabirds don't meet this criterion. Point 3—the first sentence of paragraph 3 explains why seabirds don't meet this criterion.

19. **(A)** When the amount of prey is low, so is the number of seabirds. Look at the section under the heading Researcher 1. The last sentence of paragraph 1 makes it clear that as there is less prey available, the seabird population will decline. This is a direct relationship and the graph to reflect that will be a diagonal line.

20. **(H)** Researcher 2 doesn't mention the cost associated with using seabirds as indicators. The last paragraph of Researcher 1's point of view states that "seabirds are…cost-effective."

21. **(A)** Look at Figure 2. The first set of columns is for liquid fuel, as the label shows. The white column represents leaded fuel, as the legend states. Follow the top of the white column over to the left, and you will see that it is at about the 200 mark on the y-axis.

22. **(H)** Look at Figure 2. The highest column represents the type of fuel found to have the highest average concentration of benzene. The third column is the highest. Looking down we see that it is labeled as a vapor, and the legend tells us that the white columns represent leaded fuel, so we can determine the highest average concentration of benzene was found in leaded vapor fuel.

23. **(D)** Look at Figure 1. Follow the line on the graph. After 5 minutes, the line steadily climbs up as time passes. It can be deduced that after 20 minutes the line would have continued to climb, meaning that the temperature would have continued to increase. Choice D is the only answer that reflects this outcome.

24. **(H)** Brand C is the only brand that had a higher concentration of benzene in the leaded fuel. Look at the data in Table 1. The second column lists the concentration of benzene found in the liquid form of the fuels. Compare the amounts found in each brand for leaded versus unleaded. Brand C is the only brand that had a higher concentration of benzene in the leaded fuel.

25. **(B)** Look at Figure 3. The first set of columns represents the gasohol fuels, according to the x-axis labels. The legend tells us that the white column represents the liquid form of the fuel, and the gray column represents the vapor form of the fuel. By looking at the relative heights of the columns, it can be determined that the white column is about half the size of the gray column.

26. **(J)** According to the vapor column in Table 1, the A (unleaded) brand of fuel has the lowest amount of benzene at 334 mg/l.

27. **(B)** Look at Table 1. The second row displays the data for the bob with a mass of 100 g. The last column displays the average period. Follow the second row over to the last column to find the number 1.83.

28. **(G)** Look at Table 2. The longer the length of the string, the longer the average period; 1 m was the longest length of string tested, and the average period was 1.84 s. We can deduce that if the string was 0.8 m, then the average period would be less than 1.84 s and greater than 1.45 m.

29. **(B)** Look at Table 1. The first column shows the mass of the bob tested. As the column for each trial shows, as well as the average period, the larger the mass of the bob, the longer the period.

30. **(H)** Figure 2 displays the effect that changing the amplitude of the pendulum has on the average period. Each column in the figure is roughly the same size, meaning that regardless of the amplitude, the average period is about the same. We can deduce that pendulums A and B would have about the same average period.

31. **(B)** Look at Table 2. The third column displays the results for Trial 2. Look at the second row down that displays the results for the string with a length of 0.6 m. The table shows 1.44 s as the period recorded.

32. **(H)** Based on the information in the text preceding the explanation of the experiments, and the descriptions of the experiments and results displayed, it can be determined that the mass of the bob, the length of the string, and the swing amplitude were all varied.

33. **(A)** The paragraph in Experiment 3 states that "the students tested the effect of varying the string length"; therefore, the string length was the only variable that could be changed in each trial. Keeping the mass and amplitude constant ensured that all results were caused by the string length and nothing else.

34. **(F)** Look at Table 1 and find the largest number, which is 26. Follow the column up to find that the location is Iquique.

35. **(B)** Look at the middle column in Figure 2, which is labeled Coquimbo. Trace your finger to the left from the top of the bar to find that the average egg size is between 0.15 and 0.2 mm.

36. **(H)** Look at Figure 3. Find the tallest bar, which represents the average SMR. The bar on the left is the tallest and it is a solid black bar. The legend tells you this represents the TC1 thermal category. Now look down to find the label on the x-axis, which is Iquique.

37. **(D)** *Several things must be consulted to answer this question.* Table 1 contains the temperatures that the crabs were exposed to at each location. The text in paragraph 2 defines TC2 as the average maximum temperature, so you know you need to pay attention to the numbers in that row of the table. In addition, Figure 1 must be consulted because it contains information about the size of the crabs. Table 1 shows that crabs at Iquique were exposed to the highest average temperatures at 22, then Coquimbo at 20, and Concepcion at 17. Figure 1 shows that the average size of the crabs was smallest at Iquique, slightly larger at Coquimbo, and then largest at Concepcion.

38. **(H)** The information in Table 1 and Figure 2 needs to be analyzed to answer this question. Table 1 shows that the temperatures were highest at Iquique, then Coquimbo, and lowest at Concepcion. The control temperature was only 1° lower than the average maximum temperature at Concepcion. Using this information, and looking at Figure 2, it can be determined that at lower temperatures, the egg volume is greater. So, if scientists had measured the egg volume of crabs in the control groups, they would have most likely found larger sizes than at any of the sites measured.

39. **(D)** Look at the information in Table 1 and Figure 3 to answer this question. For both Iquique and Concepcion the black column in Figure 3 is the highest, but for Coquimbo the white column is the highest. So, there is no clear relationship between temperature exposure and SMR.

40. **(G)** TC2 refers to the average of the maximum temperatures recorded daily, so when looking at Figure 3 the gray bar represents TC2. The highest gray bar representing the highest standard metabolic rate is at the Concepcion site measuring 0.15.

Writing Sample

Video-game scholarships

I've never quite understood the appeal of video games. My twelve-year-old brother holes himself up in his room without food or drink for hours at a time, playing virtual baseball, basketball, and football. After several hours of nonstop screen action, his opponents often hit "quit" if they happen to be losing so that the results won't diminish their "perfect" records. Admittedly, I'd prefer reading a book to playing some seemingly pointless, time-wasting game. Reading rather than gaming, I'd be more likely to pick up higher level vocabulary, hone my critical thinking skills, and prepare for college. Thus my surprise when I discovered that Robert Morris University in my hometown of Chicago would be the first U.S. institution of higher learning to offer scholarships to gamers. I was baffled. How could such a trivial pursuit suddenly be sanctioned by respected schools whose focus should be on academics? After further research, however, I unearthed universities' perfectly sensible ulterior motives. Considered by critics as an annoying distraction from the more serious enterprise of learning, video-gaming, an increasingly popular spectator "sport," translates into big money, with scholarships playing an integral role in schools' strategies to lure top math and engineering students to their programs.

Sport or not, video-gaming has an unhealthy reputation to overcome before players will be fully embraced by the public in the same way that student-athletes are worshipped for representing their schools.

Chess, considered a skill rather than a sport, has true scholarship potential because smart people play it. Up until just recently, gaming and higher education did not seem to share much in common, due in part to the public's biases against the former. Golf and archery conjure up films like The Legend of Bagger Vance with its profound lessons about winning, losing, perseverance, and sportsmanship applicable to sport as well as life. Gaming gets no such general veneration: in a memorable, irreverent "South Park" episode, Cartman and friends compete in marathon "World of Warcraft" sessions, developing physical ailments including carpal tunnel and facial acne as their obsession leaves them deprived of food and sleep. Gaming, unlike golf, appears anti-social and hardly relevant to the outside world, teaching you little if anything about real life, let alone valuable career-related skills. Within such a set of preconceived notions, scholarships make little sense.

A closer look at available scholarships, however, sheds light on the motives and potential pluses of rewarding those who excel. True, detractors argue that "the point of school is to learn, not to play games" and base their claims on a rather narrow view of what it means to be a student. Video-gaming, unlike popular, revenue-generating sports, they argue, steals the "brightest" kids away from academics, rendering them unable to do well at both school work and other activities. One online list of monetary awards and requirements tells a different story: Adobe and Microsoft scholarships include minimum G.P.A.'s and stipulate that applicants demonstrate much more than hours spent on a couch. "History of high academic performance" and "interest in artificial intelligence development" are just two of the more formidable stipulations. And there are scholarships for women and minority students, one specifically reserved for the African American kid who develops a video game dealing with social issues. Not yet a significant money-maker like college football or basketball, gaming has the potential to generate significant revenue as well, a trend illustrated by the willingness of spectators to pay $50 each to watch a "League of Legends" competition which recently sold out Madison Square Garden two nights in a row. NBA owners invest in gaming teams, and well-known sponsors are beginning to see the money-making potential of gaming.

To dismiss all video gamers as pale, anti-social, bleary-eyed Cartmans and to ridicule scholarships as concessions to idle play over academics is to miss the significance of an important trend. I may not get the appeal of video gaming and the devotion to this new "sport" or skill or potential revenue generator, but I understand universities' eagerness as they vie for the brightest STEM stars who also happen to be the best gamers. Detractors should not let negative stereotypes influence their arguments against an increasingly popular and lucrative choice that, though seemingly distracting, more often than not lays the groundwork for highly respected and rewarded careers in computer science and engineering.